The
RANGERS
Football Companion

A Factual History, 1946–1986

Rangers Chief Executive David Holmes (left) and Chairman John Paton are pictured with Graeme Souness after his appointment as player-manager.

The RANGERS *Football Companion*

DAVID DOCHERTY

FOREWORD
WILLIE WADDELL

PUBLISHED BY JOHN DONALD PUBLISHERS LTD
IN ASSOCIATION WITH
RANGERS FOOTBALL CLUB

For Betty, Rab and Archie

ISBN 0 85976 172 X

The Publishers would like to thank
D. C. Thomson & Co. Ltd., Dundee,
for kindly supplying many of the
illustrations used in this book; also
Sportapics Ltd. of Glasgow

Phototypeset by Quorn Selective Repro Ltd., Loughborough.
Printed in Great Britain by Bell & Bain Ltd., Glasgow.

Foreword

It was 50 years ago almost to the day that our paths first crossed – Glasgow Rangers and Willie Waddell. What a glorious half century it has been – for Waddell. Player, Manager, General Manager, Director, Vice-Chairman and now Honorary Director.

Memories are made of this. Of the ecstasy of glorious victories in a blue jersey, of League Championships won, of Glasgow Cups and Charity Cups. Yes, and Alliance (Reserves) League titles. Even five-a-side tournaments in the close season when they were popular with the sporting public.

But it was not all glory. There were days of utter despondancy and defeat when you didn't feel like going out the front door to face the world, 99 per cent of which we thought was populated with disgruntled Rangers fans. Defeat to us was a national disaster. A feeling of gloom pervaded the Dressing Room until we had the next victory to compensate. But fortunately there were not many 'lows'.

It had all begun for me in 1936 when I was hustled out of a Lanark Grammar School classroom to be told by my father, who by the way was a fair left-back with Forth Wanderers in his day, that I was 'Going to Glasgow to play for Rangers'.

I must have passed that exam for a short time later I was invited to Ibrox to be offered terms to sign by Manager Mr. William Struth.

'£2.00 per week my boy and I can promise you that if you accept and sign for Rangers you will never regret it. You will have the opportunity of a wonderful career. If you can get any more than that elsewhere you are welcome to take it.' Though I had been offered £6.00 per week by Portsmouth a few days earlier, I accepted the Rangers' terms and the interview which had lasted five minutes was concluded.

Mr. Struth was a wise man.

As I look back I owe a debt to this publication for the in-depth detail during ten of the glory years, of team selections, of results, of goal-scorers, of the magical attendances of the decade 1946–47 to 1955–56.

These were pulsating, throbbing years. On January 1st 1947, this book recalls, 85,000 fans filled Ibrox to capacity, a record crowd for a Club game in Britain at that time.

But it is not only Rangers/Celtic clashes that pulled in the crowds. Ten years later St. Mirren and Rangers pulled 43,000 out at Love Street, Paisley.

But without doubt it is the players I played beside that make the most memorable memories – men like Willie Thornton, Willie Woodburn, Torry Gillick, Sammy Cox, George Young and Ian McColl.

Rangers in these days were not just a Team, they were a family. All played with pride for the jersey. Multi-talented they were too. From the resolute defensive qualities of Woodburn and Shaw, the craft of Gillick and the goal-scoring talents of Thornton, most with his head. We used to kid him that if he could have scored with his feet at the same rate as he did with his head he would have created a world scoring record.

Facts and figures paint pictures and make personalities. *The Rangers Football Companion* formulates the details. Sketch your own pictures. I wish this book every success.

Willie Waddell

Acknowledgements

I would like to thank the following organisations and people who have helped in the production of this book: the *Glasgow Herald* and the *Daily Record* and *Sunday Mail* for permission to quote extracts from contemporary newspaper reports; the D.C. Thomson Organisation and particularly Ian Bruce of the *Sunday Post* in Glasgow for kind permission to reproduce the many illustrations of theirs in the book; and Harry Davidson of the *Daily Record*, Duncan Hart and my family for their support and encouragement.

David Docherty

Rangers' new goalkeeper Chris Woods is pictured at Ibrox with Walter Smith (left), assistant manager; David Holmes, Chief Executive; Fred Fletcher (right), Director.

Contents

A fine action study of Terry Butcher, Rangers' new captain.

Introduction

Rangers Football Club was founded in the summer of 1873. Now well over a hundred years later they have long been established as one of the world's most famous club sides.

The club was formed by a group of young men, mostly natives of Gareloch, who were attracted by the new craze that was sweeping the country and having played the game for a team known as Argyle decided to form their own club. The leading lights behind the new club bore the surname of McNeil. There were seven brothers in all – but only three of them, William, Moses and Peter, were to figure prominently in the early years of development. It was Moses McNeil who was to propose the name of the new club – the Rangers Association Football Club. The motion was agreed unanimously and their very first colours were royal blue jerseys, white knickers and blue and white stockings.

New clubs in the early days did not have their troubles to seek and the 'light blues' were no exception. Their first ground – the Fleshers Haugh on Glasgow Green – was too popular by far; youngsters had to be paid to occupy the pitch all morning to reserve it for the afternoon game. This state of affairs was not to the liking of the ambitious founders. Soon they were on the move – first to Burnbank on the North side of the river, then to Kinning Park in 1876. Eleven short years later they were on the move again, and the first Ibrox Park was opened on 20th August 1887. The mighty Preston North End were the first visitors. It was the finest Stadium in Scotland at the time but it soon proved inadequate because of the growing popularity of football and the ever increasing following of the club. In 1890 the club moved to its present site which today can fairly claim to be one of the finest Stadiums in the World.

It is only right in any book about Rangers to honour the players who overcame the early setbacks and disappointments so successfully to launch what has become an institution in Scotland. The following players took part in the very first Scottish Cup tie against Oxford in October 1874: James Yuill; Peter McNeil (captain), Tom Vallance; William McBeth, William McNeil, Moses McNeil; David Gibb, Peter Campbell, John Campbell, George Phillips and James Watson.

Over the years Rangers have contributed many players to the Scottish International team: Jock Drummond, Alan Morton, Davie Meiklejohn, Bob McPhail, Willie Woodburn, 'Tiger' Shaw, George Young, Willie Waddell, Willie Thornton, Eric Caldow, Jim Baxter, Willie Henderson, John Greig and Davie Cooper plus others too numerous to mention. Even back in 1876 the club was answering the call of international service when Moses McNeil turned out for his country against Wales in Glasgow. Rangers players have also represented Ireland, Denmark, Iceland, Sweden, Canada, Australia and more recently even England!

The first ever trophy the club won was the Glasgow Charity Cup in 1879 when they beat Vale of Leven in the Final. In Season 1886–87 they entered the English Cup and reached the Semi-Final before losing 3-1 to eventual winners Aston Villa at Crewe.

Rangers won their first League Championship in 1891, sharing the title with Dumbarton. Both clubs finished with 29 points from their 18 matches. A deciding match between the teams ended 2-2 and they were declared joint Champions (the only time ever the Championship has been shared). Their first Scottish Cup success came in 1894, beating Celtic (founded 1887) 3-1 in the Final. The team was: Haddow; N. Smith, Drummond; Marshall, A. McCreadie, Mitchell; Steel, H. McCreadie, Gray, McPherson and Barker. The goalscorers were Hugh McCreadie, Barker and McPherson.

In season 1896–97 they won three trophies – The Scottish Cup, The Glasgow Cup and The Glasgow Charity Cup and in season 1898–99 they smashed all records by winning the League Championship without dropping a single point. Amazingly from 12th February 1899 to the end of the century Rangers did not lose one single League game (Playing 35, Winning 31 and Drawing 4 – they also scored 145 goals with the loss of only 39).

The new century opened with the retention of the League Championship – only one of the 18 matches was lost. It was won again in 1901 and 1902. On April 15th, 1902 a catastrophe hit the Club when during the Scotland v. England International a portion of the west terracing gave way under the surge of the crowd and 25 people were killed and 517 injured.

Rangers turned themselves into a limited company on May 27th, 1899. At that time William Wilton was the Manager and Secretary. He had been with the club for several years and had played for one of the minor elevens. But it was as an administrator that he made his mark and is best remembered. When the Scottish League was formed in 1890 he became the club's first delegate. He became the Scottish League's first treasurer. He was responsible for the scheme that covered the stand at the first Ibrox Park, against the advice of the many sceptics. He introduced the Club handbook that was an annual institution for many years. It was a tragedy when he drowned in an accident at Gourock Bay on Sunday 2nd May 1920.

Trainer Bill Struth, a former professional sprinter, was appointed as his successor. In his first season in charge only 1 of the 42 matches was lost and the Championship was won by a 10-point margin. This was a magnificent achievement by the man whose reputation as a strict disciplinarian beame legendary. Remarkably, Rangers were to win the Championship a further 13 times between 1923 and 1939. The Scottish Cup which had not been won since 1903 was eventually won in 1928 – Celtic being beaten 4-0 in a memorable Final. The Rangers team that day was: T. Hamilton; Gray, R. Hamilton; Buchanan, Meiklejohn, Craig; Archibald, Cunningham, Fleming, McPhail and Morton. The goals were scored by Meiklejohn (from the penalty spot), McPhail and Archibald (2). The Cup was won a further five times before the outbreak of the Second

World War – 1930, 1932, 1934, 1935 and 1936. Bob McPhail who had won a Cup winners medal with Airdrie in 1924 appeared in all 6 Final winning teams. The Club won everything played for in both 1929–30 and 1933–34. Below is Bill Struth's full record as Manager from 1920 until he stood down in 1954 but still remained as a Director of the Club:

18 League Championships: 1921, 1923, 1924, 1925, 1927, 1928, 1929, 1930, 1931, 1933, 1934, 1935, 1937, 1939, 1947, 1949, 1950, 1953.

10 Scottish Cups: 1928, 1930, 1932, 1934, 1935, 1936, 1948, 1949, 1950 and 1953.

2 Scottish League Cups: 1947 and 1949.

In addition the Glasgow Cup was won 18 times and the Glasgow Charity Cup on 20 occasions. They won 6 League and Cup 'Doubles' and the 'Treble' in Season 1948–49. The Victory Cup (to celebrate the end of hostilities in the Second World War) came to Ibrox in 1946 and the Southern League Cup was won 4 times.

Rangers played Hibs in the Final of the Victory Cup at Hampden Park, defeating the Easter Road side by 3 goals to 1. Rangers team that day was: Brown; Cox, Shaw; Watkins, Young, Symon; Waddell, Gillick, Thornton, Duncanson and Caskie. Duncanson scored two of the goals and Gillick the other.

Still to come were the many thrilling duels of the late forties and early fifties, often attended by vast crowds – 143,570 watched the pair at Hampden in March, 1948. In many of the matches Rangers 'Iron Curtain' defence was bolstered by the forward talents of Willie Waddell and Willie Thornton against Hibs' talented free-scoring attack, the legendary 'Famous Five'.

Of foreign sides to visit Ibrox, one of the most famous was the Russian side, Moscow Dynamo. They were on a goodwill tour of Britain at the end of the War and were undefeated when the match took place in November 1945. The match had captured the imagination of the Glasgow public and Ibrox was packed to capacity when the teams took the field. The Russians soon proved their class and built up a 2-goal lead. Roared on from the terraces, Rangers fought back and equalised with goals from Jimmy Smith and George Young who converted a penalty. Willie Waddell had the misfortune to miss an earlier penalty award. The Russians used substitutes freely and at one point in the match Torry Gillick had to point out to the referee that Moscow Dynamo had 12 players on the pitch! The home side in this famous match was: Dawson; Gray, Shaw; Watkins, Young, Symon; Waddell, Gillick, Smith (Duncanson), Williamson and Johnstone.

The record attendance at Ibrox was 118,567 for the league match against Celtic on January 2nd, 1939. Rangers' first floodlighting system was officially opened on December 8th, 1953 when 68,000, then a record for a floodlit match in Britain, watched Arsenal win 2-1.

The *Rangers Football Companion* starts after the Second World War, with season 1946–47, and continues season by season to 1985–86. Each competitive match in the major competitions is fully covered giving both teams, the score, the scorers and times of goals and attendance. Occasionally, after consulting various sources it has not been possible to track down information. When this happens the letters na have been inserted = not available. Some of the more important and interesting matches carry a short match summary which has been collated using contemporary newspaper reports. It is hoped memories will stir and forgotten heroes will be remembered as you turn the pages and that friendly disagreement in pub or club can be easily resolved.

Rangers' new signing Colin West is pictured with Ally McCoist at Ibrox. They were formerly team mates at Sunderland.

Season 1946-47

Rangers won this first Post-War League Championship, their 25th Title, by 2 points from Hibernian, despite dropping 3 of the 4 League points to the Edinburgh side. They scored 76 goals during the campaign, running up big scores at home to Third Lanark and away at Falkirk and doomed Hamilton. The defence conceded only 26 goals in the 30 matches, by far the best record in the Division. Thornton finished top scorer with 19 goals.

They had an early exit from the Scottish Cup, losing to Hibs, to late goals from Ormond and Cuthbertson, in a Second Round Replay at Easter Road, but they landed the newly inaugurated League Cup in great style, reserving their best performances for the Semi-Final and Final itself. They won their Section without the loss of a point, and overcame plucky Dundee United, from Division B, after 2 tough Quarter-Final matches. Hibs were beaten by 3 goals to 1 in the Semi-Final, in front of a crowd of 125,154; their 3rd goal, a spectacular angular drive by Waddell just before half-time, effectively killing off the Edinburgh side. Eventual Scottish Cup Winners, Aberdeen, were beaten by 4 clear goals, courtesy of Gillick, Williamson and Duncanson (2) in the Hampden Final where Rutherford replaced the injured Waddell on the right wing.

Willie Thornton scored 27 goals in all competitive club matches followed by Jimmy Duncanson on 24. Famous Rangers Dougie Gray and Jimmy Smith were given free transfers at the end of the season.

> League: Champions
> League Cup: Winners
> Scottish Cup: Second Round

SCOTTISH LEAGUE DIVISION A

August 6th: Charlie Johnstone was transferred to Queen of the South. John Galloway was transferred to Chelsea for £4,000.

August 10th:
MOTHERWELL (1) 2   RANGERS (2) 4
Brown (12, 79)   Thornton (11),
     Duncanson 2 (14, 72),
     Waddell (71)

MOTHERWELL: Johnston; Kilmarnock, Shaw; McLeod, Paton, Russell; Henderson, Redpath, Brown, Bremner, Barclay

RANGERS: Brown; Cox, Shaw; Watkins, Young, Symon; Waddell, Gillick, Thornton, Duncanson, Caskie

Attendance: 30,000

August 14th:
RANGERS (1) 1   HIBERNIAN (1) 2
Young (1 pen)   Aitkenhead (30),
     Weir (77)

RANGERS: Brown; David Gray, Shaw; Watkins, Young, Cox; Waddell, Gillick, Thornton, Duncanson, Caskie

HIBERNIAN: Kerr; Howie, Shaw; Kean, Aird, McCabe; Smith, Cuthbertson, Weir, Buchanan, Aitkenhead

Attendance: 50,000. Goalkeeper Kerr of Hibs was given an ovation by the crowd at the end.

August 17th:
RANGERS (1) 3   KILMARNOCK (2) 2
Cox (23), Gillick (55),   Devlin (7), Welsh (27)
Waddell (62)

RANGERS: Brown; Gray, Shaw; Watkins, Young, Cox; Waddell, Gillick, Thornton, Duncanson, Caskie

KILMARNOCK: Downie; Hood, Landsborough; Turnbull, McLure, Davie; Gavin, Devlin, Walsh, McDonald, McAvoy

Attendance: 25,000

August 21st:
FALKIRK   (0) 0   RANGERS   (3) 5
                           Thornton 3 (1, 53, 55),
                           Duncanson (8),
                           Waddell (36)

FALKIRK: Dawson; Whyte, McPhee; McCreary, Ogilvie, Gallacher; Henderson, Rice, Brooks, McLennan, Fitzsimmons

RANGERS: Brown; Gray, Shaw; Cox, Young, Symon; Waddell, Gillick, Thornton, Duncanson, Caskie

August 24th: Shaw, Waddell and Thornton represented Scotland against England in a match in aid of the Bolton Disaster victims. Thornton scored twice in a 2-2 draw.

August 28th:
RANGERS   (4) 8   THIRD LANARK   (1) 1
   Thornton 3 (29, 36, 42),   Mitchell (23)
   Caskie 3 (41, 57, 65),
   Duncanson 2 (78, 79)

RANGERS: Brown; Gray, Shaw; Cox, Young, Symon; Duncanson, Gillick, Thornton, Williamson, Caskie

THIRD LANARK: Petrie; Carabine, Kelly; Bolt, Barclay, Mooney; McCulloch, Ayton, Venters, Henderson, Mitchell

Attendance: 22,000

August 31st:
RANGERS   (1) 2   QUEENS PARK   (0) 0
   Duncanson 2 (35, 52)

RANGERS: Brown; Gray, Shaw; Cox, Young, Symon; Waddell, Gillick, Arnison, Duncanson, Caskie

QUEENS PARK: R. Simpson; J. McColl, W. Johnstone; D. Letham, J. Whigham, I. Harnett; J. Jordan, J. McAulay, R. Stirling, A. Aitken, J. Irvine

Attendance: 20,000

September 4th:
ABERDEEN   (1) 1   RANGERS   (0) 0
   Taylor (40)

ABERDEEN: Johnstone; Cowie, McKenna; Dunlop, Waddell, Taylor; McCall, Hamilton, Harris, Baird, Williams

RANGERS: Brown; Gray, Shaw; Cox, Young, Symon; Watkins, Gillick, Arnison, Duncanson, Caskie

Attendance: 25,000

September 7th:
CELTIC   (1) 2   RANGERS   (2) 3
   Kiernan (29),   Duncanson 2 (10, 30),
   Bogan (58)   Parlane (58)

CELTIC: Miller; McDonald, Milne; McMillan, Corbett, McAuley; Bogan, Kiernan, Cantwell, W. Gallacher, Hazlett

RANGERS: Brown; Gray, Shaw; Cox, Young, Symon; Stead, Gillick, Parlane, Duncanson, Caskie

Playing with something like the fighting spirit of their teams of the past, Celtic came near to achieving their first home win of the season. They had 3 penalty claims turned down and seemed particularly unlucky not to be awarded one late in the game when Young's arm stopped Bogan's cross shot. In Kiernan, the home side had the cleverest individual player on the field – in the first half especially he had Symon running round in circles and labouring in his rear. Rangers were overwhelmingly superior in the art of making the telling pass.

September 14th:
RANGERS   (2) 4   ST MIRREN   (0) 0
   Gillick (4),
   Duncanson 3 (22, 62, 67)

RANGERS: Brown; Gray, Shaw; Cox, Young, Symon; Stead, Gillick, Arnison, Duncanson, Caskie

ST MIRREN: Newlands; Telfer, Lindsay; Smith, Drinkwater, Scott; Crowe, Stenhouse, Aikman, McLaren, Milne

Young missed a penalty
Attendance: 15,000

September 30th:
PARTICK THISTLE   (3) 3 RANGERS   (2) 2
   Chisholm (17), McKennan (30), Gillick (24),
   Parker (41 pen)   Duncanson (32)

PARTICK THISTLE: Steadward; McGowan, Curran; Husband, Parker, Brown; Glover, McKennan, Sharp, Chisholm, Smith

RANGERS: Brown; Gray, Shaw; Cox, Woodburn, Symon; Waddell, Gillick, Thornton, Duncanson, Caskie
Attendance: 36,000

October 19th: Waddell and Thornton were in the Scotland team beaten 3-1 by Wales. Waddell scored Scotland's goal from the penalty spot.

November 2nd:
RANGERS   (1) 2   MORTON   (1) 1
   Thornton (10), Cox (70)   Cupples (26)

RANGERS: Brown; Young, Shaw; McColl, Woodburn, Rae; Waddell, Cox, Thornton, Williamson, McNee

MORTON: McFeat; Maley, Fyfe; Campbell, Aird, Whyte; McGowan, Cupples, Gibson, Jones, McInnes

Attendance: 40,000

League positions

	P	W	D	L	F	A	Pts
1 Hibernian	11	8	0	3	30	10	16
2 RANGERS	11	8	0	3	34	14	16
3 Aberdeen	11	6	3	2	21	13	15
4 Clyde	10	6	2	2	23	13	14
5 Partick Thistle	11	6	2	3	25	17	14

November 9th:
HAMILTON   RANGERS   (4) 6
   ACADEMICALS   (0) 0   Thornton 3 (15, 33,
                                   85), McNee (10),
                                   Gillick (17),
                                   Duncanson (57)

HAMILTON: Jenkins; McGurk, Johnstone; Stewart,
Rothera, Lindsay; McGuigan, Daly, Devlin, Gillan,
Devine

RANGERS: Brown; Cox, Shaw; McColl, Young, Rae;
Waddell, Gillick, Thornton, Duncanson, McNee

Attendance: 15,000

November 16th:
CLYDE   (1) 2   RANGERS   (1) 4
   Dixon (37 pen),   McNee (36), McColl
   Galletly (89)   (46), Duncanson (56),
                                   Thornton (87)

CLYDE: Sweeney; Duffy, Galbraith; Campbell,
McCormack, Long; Galletly, Riley, Johnston, Dixon,
Keith

RANGERS: Brown; Young, Shaw; McColl,
Woodburn, Rae; Waddell, Gillick, Thornton,
Duncanson, McNee

Attendance: 27,000

November 23rd:
RANGERS   (1) 2   QUEEN OF THE
   Thornton (10),   SOUTH   (0) 1
   Gillick (53)   Armstrong (46)

RANGERS: Brown; Rae, Shaw; McColl, Young,
Symon; Rutherford, Gillick, Thornton, Duncanson,
McNee

QUEEN OF THE SOUTH: Henderson; Savage,
Haxton; Fitzsimmons, Denmark, Collier; Oakes,
Cumming, Armstrong, Dempsey, Johnstone

Attendance: 10,000

**November 27th: Brown, Young, Thornton and
Duncanson were in the Scotland team which drew
0-0 with Ireland at Hampden Park.**

**November 29th: Former Ranger Sandy Archibald,
manager of Dunfermline, died.**

November 30th:
HEARTS   (0) 0   RANGERS   (2) 3
                                   Duncanson (9),
                                   McNee (37),
                                   Thornton (84)

HEARTS: Brown; McSpadyen, McKenzie; Cox,
Baxter, Miller; Sloan, Conn, Kelly, McCrae, Walker

RANGERS: Brown; Young, Lindsay; McColl,
Woodburn, Rae; Waddell, Gillick, Thornton,
Duncanson, McNee

Attendance: 45,000

December 7th:
RANGERS   (1) 2   MOTHERWELL   (1) 1
   Thornton (29),   Bremner (47)
   Young (80 pen)

RANGERS: Brown; Young, Shaw; McColl,
Woodburn, Rae; Waddell, Gillick, Thornton,
Duncanson, McNee

MOTHERWELL: Johnstone; Kilmarnock, Shaw;
McLeod, Paton, Redpath; Humphries, Watson, Brown,
Bremner, Barclay

Attendance: 35,000

December 14th:
HIBERNIAN   (0) 1   RANGERS   (1) 1
   Ormond (85)   Duncanson (43)

HIBERNIAN: Kerr; Howie, Shaw; Finnigan, Aird,
Kean; Smith, Peat, Weir, Turnbull, Ormond

RANGERS: Brown; Young, Shaw; McColl,
Woodburn, Rae; Waddell, Gillick, Thornton,
Duncanson, McNee

Attendance: 41,378

The final whistle must have been welcome to Rangers as
their defence had almost reached breaking point. Had
Hibs scored earlier than they did in the 2nd half –
Ormond's equalising goal came only 5 minutes from the
end – Rangers may not have held out.

December 21st:
RANGERS   (1) 2   FALKIRK   (1) 1
   Duncanson (20),   Bain (30),
   Gillick (81)

RANGERS: Brown; Young, Shaw; McColl,
Woodburn, Rae; Waddell, Gillick, Thornton,
Duncanson, Caskie

FALKIRK: Dawson; Whyte, McPhee; Rice,
Henderson, Sinclair; Fiddes, Bain, Inglis, Campbell,
Allison

Attendance: 15,000

League positions

	P	W	D	L	F	A	Pts
1 RANGERS	18	14	1	3	54	20	29
2 Aberdeen	18	11	4	3	36	20	26
3 Hibernian	18	11	3	4	35	21	25
4 Hearts	18	9	5	4	31	27	23
5 Partick Thistle	18	10	2	6	44	31	22

December 28th:

THIRD LANARK   (0) 1   RANGERS   (0) 1
  Mitchell (90)   Gillick (49)

THIRD LANARK: Fraser; Balunas, Kelly; Bolt, Palmer, Mooney; Bogan, Mason, McCulloch, Ayton, Mitchell

RANGERS: Brown; Young, Shaw; McColl, Woodburn, Rae; Waddell, Gillick, Thornton, Duncanson, Stead

Attendance: 35,000

January 1st:

RANGERS   (0) 1   CELTIC   (1) 1
  Gillick (60)   Hazlett (10)

RANGERS: Brown; Young, Shaw; McColl, Woodburn, Rae; Waddell, Gillick, Thornton, Duncanson, McNeee

CELTIC: Miller; Hogg, Mallan; Lynch, McMillan, Milne; Evans, McAloon, Airlie, Gallacher, Hazlett

Attendance: 85,000

A record crowd for a club game in Britain this season witnessed a game of punishing pace and he-man exchanges. Of the 50 free-kicks awarded in the match, Celtic conceded no fewer than 34 of them. The visitors opened the scoring – a terrific 30-yard free-kick by Lynch was on its way to the net when Brown turned the ball out but young Hazlett was following up and scored. From the start of the 2nd half Rangers took the initiative and after 15 minutes Waddell tricked Mallan and crossed to the far post where Duncanson headed the ball back for Gillick to prod into the net. Late in the game a Gallacher cross came back off the face of the bar and was scrambled clear by Shaw.

January 2nd:

KILMARNOCK   (0) 0   RANGERS   (2) 2
                                    Gillick 2 (n.a., 16)

KILMARNOCK: Downie; Hood, Turnbull; Devlin, Thyne, Davie; Stevenson, Reid, Walsh, Collins, Drury

RANGERS: Brown; Young, Shaw; McColl, Woodburn, Rae; Waddell, Gillick, Thornton, Duncanson, McNee

January 4th:

ST MIRREN   (1) 1   RANGERS   (0) 0
  Wilson (36)

ST MIRREN: Newlands; Telfer, Drinkwater; Stenhouse, Lindsay, Cunningham; Smith, Telford, Wilson, Deakin, McLaren

RANGERS: Brown; Young, Shaw; McColl, Woodburn, Rae; Waddell, Gillick, Thornton, Duncanson, McNee

Attendance: 18,00

January 11th:

RANGERS   (4) 4   PARTICK THISTLE   (0) 0
  Waddell (2),
  Thornton (14),
  Young (18 pen),
  Gillick (34)

RANGERS: Brown; Young, Shaw; McColl, Woodburn, Rae; Rutherford, Gillick, Thornton, Parlane, Waddell

PARTICK THISTLE: Steadward; McGowan, Curran; Hewitt, Husband, Brown; Campbell, O'Donnell, Mathie, Sharp, Chisholm

Brown saved a penalty from Sharp
Attendance: 18,000

January 18th:

RANGERS   (1) 1   ABERDEEN   (0) 0
  Waddell (12)

RANGERS: Brown; Young, Shaw; McColl, Woodburn, Rae; Rutherford, Gillick, Thornton, Parlane, Waddell

ABERDEEN: Johnstone; Cooper, McKenna; McLaughlin, Dunlop, Taylor; A. Kiddie, Hamilton, Harris, Williams, McCall

Attendance: 60,000

February 1st:

QUEENS PARK   0   RANGERS   0

QUEENS PARK: R. Simpson; J. McColl, R. Mitchell; D. Letham, J. Whigham, I. Harnett; L. Hodge, H. Millar, A. Aitken, W. McPhail, C. Liddell

RANGERS: Brown; Young, Shaw; McColl, Woodburn, Rae; Waddell, Gillick, Arnison, Thornton, Duncanson

Attendance: 40,000

February 8th:

QUEEN OF THE   RANGERS   (1) 2
  SOUTH (0) 0   Young (34 pen),
                                    Arnison (59)

QUEEN OF THE SOUTH: Wilson; Savage, James; Gilmour, Fitzsimmons, Collier; Cumming, Armstrong, Houliston, Law, Baker

RANGERS: Brown; Young, Shaw; McColl, Woodburn, Rae; Waddell, Gillick, Arnison, Thornton, Duncanson

Attendance: 11,000

February 15th:

MORTON   (0) 0   RANGERS   (1) 1
                                    Thornton (18)

MORTON: McFeat; Westwater, Fyfe; Maley, Aird, Whyte; Cupples, Divers, Henderson, McGarritty, McInnes

RANGERS: Brown; Young, Shaw; McColl, Woodburn, Rae; Waddell, Gillick, Arnison, Thornton, Duncanson

Attendance: 18,000

League Positions

	P	W	D	L	F	A	Pts
1 RANGERS	27	19	4	4	66	23	42
2 Hibernian	25	14	6	5	59	31	34
3 Partick Thistle	25	15	2	8	65	44	32
4 Hearts	26	13	6	7	43	39	32
5 Aberdeen	24	13	5	6	44	32	31

March 29th:
RANGERS (3) 5 CLYDE (0) 0
  Williamson 4 (2, 25, 44, 78),
  Rutherford (62)

RANGERS: Brown; Young, Shaw; Watkins, Woodburn, Rae; Rutherford, Gillick, Williamson, Thornton, Duncanson

CLYDE: Sweeney; Duffy, Galbraith; Campbell, McCormack, Long; Galletly, Hepburn, Gourlay, Dixon, Cameron

Attendance: 15,000

April 7th:
RANGERS (0) 1 HEARTS (1) 2
  Thornton (86) McFarlane (42),
    Dewar (57)

RANGERS: Brown; Young, Shaw; McColl, Woodburn, Rae; Duncanson, Williamson, Arnison, Thornton, Caskie

HEARTS: Brown; McLure, MacKenzie; Laing, Pithie, Neilson; McFarlane, Conn, Kelly, Urquhart, Dewar

Attendance: 12,000

April 12th: Young, Shaw and Woodburn were in the Scotland team which drew 1-1 with England at Wembley.

April 12th:
RANGERS (3) 4 HAMILTON
  Williamson 2 (4, 35), ACADEMICALS (1) 1
  Parlane (20), McVinish (6)
  Duncanson (67)

RANGERS: Brown; Cox, Lindsay; Watkins, McColl, Symon; Rutherford, Parlane, Williamson, Duncanson, Caskie

HAMILTON: Campbell; McGurk, Devine; Stewart, Daly, Lindsay; Ogilvie, Gillan, Smith, Fitzsimmons, McVinish

Attendance: 8,000

Scottish League Divison A

	P	W	D	L	F	A	Pts
1 RANGERS	30	21	4	5	76	26	46
2 Hibernian	30	19	6	5	69	33	44
3 Aberdeen	30	16	7	7	58	41	39
4 Hearts	30	16	6	8	52	43	38
5 Partick Thistle	30	16	3	11	74	59	35
6 Morton	30	12	10	8	58	45	34
7 Celtic	30	13	6	11	53	55	32
8 Motherwell	30	12	5	13	58	54	29
9 Third Lanark	30	11	6	13	56	64	28
10 Clyde	30	9	9	12	55	65	27
11 Falkirk	30	8	10	12	62	61	26
12 Queen of South	30	9	8	13	44	69	26
13 Queens Park	30	8	6	16	47	60	22
14 St Mirren	30	9	4	17	47	65	22
15 Kilmarnock	30	6	9	15	44	66	21
16 Hamilton	30	2	7	21	38	85	11

May 1st: Dougie Gray and Jimmy Smith were given free transfers.

May 4th: Scot Symon was appointed manager of East Fife.

May 18th: Scotland were beaten 2-1 by Belgium in Brussels. Young, Shaw and Woodburn were in the team.

May 24th: Scotland beat Luxembourg 6-0. Young, Shaw and Woodburn were in the team.

LEAGUE CUP

September 21st:
RANGERS (2) 4 ST MIRREN (0) 0
  Cox (30), Stead (42),
  Arnison 2 (75, 79)

RANGERS: Brown; Gray, Shaw; Cox, Young, Symon; Stead, Gillick, Arnison, Duncanson, Caskie

ST MIRREN: Rennie; Smith, Lindsay; Stenhouse, Drinkwater, Scott; Telfer, Crowe, Milne, Deakin, McLaren

Attendance: 15,000

September 28th:
QUEENS PARK (1) 2 RANGERS (1) 4
  Liddell (34) Duncanson 2 (24, 76),
  Aitken (51) Gillick (52),
    Thornton (74)

QUEENS PARK: G. Hamilton; J. Mitchell, W. Johnstone; D. Letham, J. Whigham, I. Harnett; A. Aitken, A. McAulay, C. Liddell, H. Millar, I. Irvine

RANGERS: Brown; Gray, Shaw; Cox, Woodburn, Symon; Waddell, Gillick, Thornton, Duncanson, Caskie

Attendance: 30,000

October 5th:
RANGERS (0) 3   MORTON (0) 0
  Duncanson (52), Caskie (78),
  Thornton (85)

RANGERS: Brown; Gray, Shaw; Watkins, Young,
Cox; Waddell, Gillick, Thornton, Duncanson, Caskie

MORTON: McFeat; Westwater, Fyfe; Aird, Kelly,
Whyte; Henderson, McKillop, Newall, Divers, McInnes

Attendance: 50,000

October 12th:
ST MIRREN (0) 0   RANGERS (2) 4
                          Gillick 2 (6, 22),
                          Thornton 2 (58, 78)

ST. MIRREN: Rennie; Telfer, Lindsay; Henderson,
Drinkwater, Cunningham; Hunter, Crowe, Milne,
Deakin, Telford

RANGERS: Brown; Young, Shaw; McColl,
Woodburn, Watkins; Waddell, Gillick, Thornton,
Duncanson, Caskie

Attendance: 20,000

October 19th:
RANGERS (0) 1   QUEENS PARK (0) 0
  Arnison (56)

RANGERS: Brown; Young, Shaw; McColl,
Woodburn, Rae; Rutherford, Cox, Arnison, Williamson,
Caskie

QUEENS PARK: G. Hamilton; J. Mitchell, W.
Johnstone; I. Harnett, J. Whigham, Dr A. Cross; A.
McAulay, J. B. Dall, A. Aitken, D. Letham, H. Millar

Attendance: 20,000

October 26th:
MORTON (0) 0   RANGERS (1) 2
                          Young (30 pen),
                          Thornton (70)

MORTON: McFeat; Kelly, Fyfe; Maley, Aird,
Whyte; Cupples, Divers, McKillop, Garth, McInnes

RANGERS: John Shaw; Young, Jock Shaw; McColl,
Woodburn, Rae; Waddell, Cox, Thornton, Williamson,
Caskie

Attendance: 18,000

League Cup Section Table

	P	W	D	L	F	A	Pts
RANGERS	6	6	0	0	18	2	12
Morton	6	4	0	2	17	9	8
St Mirren	6	1	1	4	7	19	3
Queens Park	6	0	1	5	5	17	1

March 1st: Quarter-Final First Leg
RANGERS (1) 2   DUNDEE UNITED (0) 1
  Waddell (12),   Lister (61 pen)
  Caskie (66)

RANGERS: Brown; Young, Shaw; McColl,
Woodburn, Rae; Waddell, Gillick, Thornton,
Duncanson, Caskie

DUNDEE UNITED: Muir; Simpson, Berry; Ross,
Miller, Rae; Pacione, Grant, Crothers, Lister, Mackay

Attendance: 40,000

March 5th: Quarter-Final Second Leg
DUNDEE UNITED (0) 1   RANGERS (1) 1
  Lister (61)   Duncanson (6)

DUNDEE UNITED: Muir; Simpson, Berry; Ross,
Miller, Rae; Pacione, Grant, Crothers, Lister, Mackay

RANGERS: Brown; Young, Shaw; McColl,
Woodburn, Rae; Waddell, Gillick, Thornton,
Duncanson, Caskie

Attendance: 18,000

(Rangers won 3-2 on aggregate)

March 22nd: Semi-Final   At Hampden Park
HIBERNIAN (0) 1   RANGERS (3) 3
  Cuthbertson (78)   Gillick (19),
                           Thornton (32),
                           Waddell (43)

HIBERNIAN: Kerr; Govan, Shaw; Howie, Aird,
Kean; Smith, Finnigan, Cuthbertson, Turnbull,
Buchanan

RANGERS: Brown; Young, Shaw; McColl,
Woodburn, Rae; Waddell, Gillick, Williamson,
Thornton, Duncanson

Attendance: 125,154

Rangers were never in danger of losing despite the fact that
for almost the entire 2nd half they were virtually a man
short, Waddell having pulled a muscle.

April 5th: Final
RANGERS (3) 4   ABERDEEN (0) 0
  Gillick (25)
  Williamson (33)
  Duncanson 2 (41, 57)

RANGERS: Brown; Young, Shaw; McColl,
Woodburn, Rae; Rutherford, Gillick, Williamson,
Thornton, Duncanson

ABERDEEN: Johnstone; Cooper, McKenna;
McLaughlin, Dunlop, Taylor; Harris, Hamilton,
Williams, Baird, McCall

Attendance: 82,684

Having won the toss, the Aberdeen captain gave Rangers
the benefit of the sweeping wind and set himself and his
colleagues the task of battling against it and the sheets of
rain that fell during the first half. Despite this, Aberdeen
had 3 clear scoring chances before Rangers took the lead in
the 25th minute. McLaughlin failed to trap a goal-kick
from Johnstone and Thornton sent Duncanson away. The

winger crossed and Gillick, practically on the goal-line, headed home. In 33 minutes Gillick's pass let Rutherford cross and Williamson bustled the ball over the line. 4 minutes from the interval Duncanson dribbled past Cooper and Johnstone for Rangers' 3rd goal. Duncanson added a 4th goal 12 minutes after the restart. Rutherford proved an excellent substitute for the injured Waddell.

SCOTTISH CUP

January 26th: First Round
RANGERS   (2) 2   CLYDE   (0) 1
   Duncanson (4),   Johnston (82)
   Thornton (42)

RANGERS: Brown; Young, Shaw; McColl, Woodburn, Rae; Duncanson, Gillick, Parlane, Thornton, Waddell

CLYDE: Sweeney; Duffy, Galbraith; Campbell, McCormack, Long; Hepburn, Gourlay, Johnston, McGill, Dixon

Attendance: 74,606

February 22nd: Second Round
RANGERS   0   HIBERNIAN   0

RANGERS: Brown; Young, Shaw; McColl, Woodburn, Rae; Waddell, Gillick, Arnison, Thornton, Duncanson

HIBERNIAN: Kerr; Govan, Shaw; Howie, Aird, Kean; Smith, Finnigan, Cuthbertson, Turnbull, Ormond

Attendance: 95,000

March 8th: Second Round Replay
HIBERNIAN   (0) 2   RANGERS   (0) 0
   Smith (85)
   Cuthbertson (87)

HIBERNIAN: Kerr; Govan, Shaw; Howie, Aird, Kean; Smith, Finnigan, Cuthbertson, Turnbull, Ormond

RANGERS: Brown; Young, Shaw; McColl, Woodburn, Watkins; Waddell, Parlane, Thornton, Duncanson, Caskie

Attendance: 48,816

APPEARANCES

	League	League Cup	Scottish Cup	Glasgow Cup	Charity Cup	Friendlies
Brown	30	9	3	2	2	2
Cox	13	5	-	2	1	-
Shaw	28	10	3	2	2	2
Watkins	6	2	1	-	-	-
Young	28	9	3	2	1	-
Symon	10	2	-	2	-	-
Waddell	22	7	3	-	-	2
Gillick	27	8	2	2	2	2
Thornton	25	8	3	-	2	2
Duncanson	27	8	3	2	2	1
Caskie	13	8	1	1	2	1+1 sub
David Gray	9	3	-	2	-	-
Williamson	5	4	-	1	2	1
Arnison	7	2	1	2	-	1
Stead	3	1	-	2	-	-
Parlane	4	-	2	-	-	-
Woodburn	18	8	3	-	2	2
McColl	19	7	3	-	2	2
Rae	19	6	2	-	2	2
McNee	10	-	-	-	-	-
Rutherford	5	2	-	-	-	-
Lindsay	2	-	-	-	-	-
John Shaw	-	1	-	-	-	-

GOALSCORERS

League: Thornton 19, Duncanson 17, Gillick 12, Williamson 6, Waddell 5, Young 4 (pens), Caskie 3, McNee 3, Cox 2, Parlane 2, Arnison 1, McColl 1, Rutherford 1.

League Cup: Duncanson 6, Thornton 6, Gillick 5, Arnison 3, Caskie 2, Waddell 2, Young 1 (pen), Williamson 1, Cox 1, Stead 1.

Scottish Cup: Duncanson 1, Thornton 1.

Glasgow Cup: Arnison 3, Gillick 1.

Charity Cup: Williamson 3, Gillick 1, Caskie 1

Friendlies: Arnison 1, Caskie 1, Gillick 1, Thornton 1.

Jerry Dawson, the legendary Rangers' goalkeeper.

George Young with some of the many mementoes and Scottish caps he earned in his career.

Season 1947–48

Rangers surrendered the League Title to Hibernian by a 2-point margin. They had led by 2 points and had 2 games in hand at Christmas, but a disastrous home run with defeats by Queen of the South, relegation-bound Queens Park and Hearts cost them the Championship. They scored 64 League goals with Thornton and Duncanson contributing 28 between them, but that figure was well short of Hibs' total. Brown, Cox and Thornton were ever-presents but injury restricted Waddell to only 12 League appearances.

They did gain revenge over Hibs in the Scottish Cup, knocking them out in the Semi-Final by a Thornton goal in front of a record 143,570 crowd. Hibs apart, they had some tough ties along the way, in particular away against Stranraer and at home against League Cup Winners, East Fife. Morton proved to be stuffy opposition in the Final which went to extra time and then a replay. Findlay, a close season signing from Albion Rovers, was brought in for his first Scottish Cup appearance in the first game of the Final, but it was his replacement in the replay, Williamson, also playing in his first Scottish Cup-tie of the season, who scored the only goal, 5 minutes from the end of extra time, which took the Cup back to Ibrox for the first time in 12 years.

Rangers were knocked out of the League Cup by Falkirk at the Semi-Final stage, Aikman scoring the only goal of the game 2 minutes from the end.

Benfica were trounced 3-0 in a prestigious friendly match in Portugal.

League: Runners-up
League Cup: Semi-Finalists
Scottish Cup: Winners

SCOTTISH LEAGUE DIVISION A

August 7th: Joe Craven was appointed assistant to trainer Bob McDonald at Ibrox.

August 13th:
RANGERS (1) 5   THIRD LANARK (2) 2
  Williamson (40),   McCulloch (18),
  Thornton 3 (n.a.)   Reid (44)
  Gillick (78)

RANGERS: Brown; Cox, Shaw; McColl, Woodburn, Rae; Waddell, Gillick, Williamson, Thornton, Duncanson

THIRD LANARK: Fraser; Balunas, Kelly; Baillie, Palmer, Mooney; McCulloch, Mason, Reid, Ayton, Mitchell

August 27th:
PARTICK THISTLE (0) 0 RANGERS (1) 1
                           Thornton (21)

PARTICK THISTLE: Ledgerwood; McGowan, Curran; Hewitt, Husband, Candlin; Glover, Brown, Mathie, Sharp, McInnes

RANGERS: Brown; Cox, Shaw; McColl, Woodburn, Rae; Waddell, Gillick, Williamson, Thornton, Duncanson

Attendance: 35,000

September 20th:
RANGERS (1) 2   CELTIC (0) 0
  Williamson (16),
  Findlay (77)

RANGERS: Brown; Young, Shaw; McColl, Woodburn, Cox; Waddell, Findlay, Williamson, Thornton, Duncanson

CELTIC: Miller; Ferguson, Milne; R. Quinn, Corbett, McAuley; Bogan, McAloon, Gallacher, Evans, Kapier

Attendance: 50,000

13

Waddell had something of a field day against Milne and it was only splendid goalkeeping by Miller and a magnificent display by Corbett, who was as often at right or left-back as he was at centre-half, that prevented a rout.

October 4th: Young, Shaw, Woodburn and Thornton were all in the Scotland team beaten 2-0 by Ireland. Shaw captained the side.

October 18th:
RANGERS   (1) 2   HIBERNIAN   (1) 1
  Paton (44), Williamson (46)   Combe (15)

RANGERS: Brown; Young, Shaw; McColl, Woodburn, Cox; Rutherford, Paton, Williamson, Thornton, Duncanson

HIBERNIAN: Brown; Govan, Shaw; Buchanan, Aird, Kean; Smith, Combe, Reilly, Turnbull, Ormond

October 20th: Jimmy Smith was appointed as trainer in succession to Bob 'Whitey' McDonald.

October 25th:
ST MIRREN   (1) 2   RANGERS   (1) 1
  Jack 2 (31, 77)   Thornton (25)

ST MIRREN: Newlands; Smith, Lindsay; W. Reid, Telfer, Martin; Burrell, Stenhouse, Jack, Deakin, Lesz

RANGERS: Brown; Cox, Shaw; McColl, Woodburn, Rae; Rutherford, Paton, Williamson, Thornton, Duncanson

Attendance: 24,000

League Positions

	P	W	D	L	F	A	Pts
1 Partick	8	7	0	1	24	8	14
2 Motherwell	8	7	0	1	23	11	14
3 Hibernian	8	5	1	2	20	9	11
4 Dundee	8	5	0	3	17	11	10
5 RANGERS	5	4	0	1	11	5	8

November 1st:
RANGERS   (1) 3   AIRDRIE   (0) 0
  Thornton (23), Shaw (56 pen),
  Marshall (77)

RANGERS: Brown; Cox, Shaw; McColl, Woodburn, Rae; Rutherford, Findlay, Thornton, Marshall, Duncanson

AIRDRIE: Downie; Peters, Cunningham; McKenzie, Kelly, Duncan; McCulloch, Stevenson, Flavell, Picken, Clapperton

Attendance: 15,000

November 8th:
QUEEN OF THE
  SOUTH   (0) 0   RANGERS   (2) 3
                         Findlay 2 (14, 76),
                         Marshall (30)

QUEEN OF THE SOUTH: Henderson; Fulton, James; Scott, Aird, Sharp; Nutley, Brown, Houliston, Jenkins, Johnstone

RANGERS: Brown; Cox, Shaw; McColl, Woodburn, Rae; Waddell, Findlay, Thornton, Marshall, Duncanson

Attendance: 21,000 (a record)

November 12th: Willie Woodburn captained the Scotland team beaten 2-1 by Wales at Hampden Park.

November 15th:
CLYDE   (0) 1   RANGERS   (0) 2
  Johnston (60)   Thornton (61),
                         Marshall (76)

CLYDE: Sweeney; Gibson, Deans; Campbell, McCormack, Long; Galletly, Hepburn, Johnston, McPhail, Fitzsimmons

RANGERS: Brown; Cox, Shaw; McColl, Woodburn, Rae; Rutherford, Findlay, Thornton, Marshall, Duncanson

Attendance: 23,000

November 22nd:
RANGERS   (1) 1   MORTON   (1) 1
  Duncanson (20)   Liddell (34)

RANGERS: Brown; Cox, Shaw; McColl, Woodburn, Rae; Gillick, Findlay, Thornton, Marshall, Duncanson

MORTON: Stephenson; Mitchell, Fyfe; Campbell, Millar, Whyte; Henderson, Orr, Liddell, Divers, Gillies

Attendance: 25,000

November 29th:
QUEENS PARK   (1) 1   RANGERS   (3) 4
  Farquhar (35)   Gillick 2 (34, 37),
                            Parlane (43),
                            Duncanson (85)

QUEENS PARK: R. Simpson; G. Dow, W. Johnstone; D. McBain, D. Letham, J. Hardie; T. Alexander, A. Millar, J. Farquhar, A. Aitken, H. G. Millar

RANGERS: Brown; Cox, Shaw; McColl, Woodburn, Rae; Rutherford, Gillick, Parlane, Thornton, Duncanson

Attendance: 28,000

December 6th:
HEARTS   (0) 1   RANGERS   (1) 2
  Sloan (80)   Duncanson (32),
                         Rutherford (47)

HEARTS: Brown; Mathieson, McKenzie; Cox, Parker, Laing; Sloan, Urquhart, Kelly, Dixon, Williams

RANGERS: Brown; Cox, Shaw; McColl, Woodburn, Rae; Rutherford, Gillick, Thornton, Duncanson, Caskie

Attendance: 40,000

December 13th:
RANGERS (2) 4   ABERDEEN (0) 0
Rutherford (20),
Gillick 2 (29, 48),
Thornton (86)

RANGERS: Brown; Cox, Shaw; McColl, Woodburn, Rae; Rutherford, Gillick, Thornton, Duncanson, Caskie

ABERDEEN: Johnstone; Cowie, McKenna; Waddell, Dunlop, Taylor; Millar, Hamilton, Williams, Harris, McCall

Attendance: 25,000

December 18th: Willie Dougal joined Preston North End.

December 20th:
THIRD LANARK (0) 0   RANGERS (0) 1
                       Gillick (65)

THIRD LANARK: Petrie; Balunas, Kelly; Young, Barclay, Mooney; Bogan, Mason, McCulloch, Baillie, McGeachie

RANGERS: Brown; Cox, Shaw; McColl, Woodburn, Rae; Rutherford, Gillick, Thornton, Duncanson, Caskie

Attendance: 20,000

December 25th:
DUNDEE (1) 1   RANGERS (2) 3
Ewen (13)   Duncanson 3 (16, 21, 77)

DUNDEE: Steadward; Follon, Ancell; Cowie, Boyd, Smith; Gray, Ewen, Pattillo, Gallacher, Hill

RANGERS: Brown; Cox, Shaw; McColl, Young, Rae; Rutherford, Gillick, Thornton, Duncanson, Caskie

Attendance: 25,000

December 27th:
RANGERS (2) 2   PARTICK THISTLE (1) 1
Rutherford (15),   Wright (17)
Gillick (40)

RANGERS: Brown; Cox, Shaw; McColl, Woodburn, Rae; Rutherford, Gillick, Thornton, Duncanson, Caskie

PARTICK THISTLE: Henderson; McGowan, Husband; Brown, Forsyth, Candlin; Wright, Chisholm, Mathie, Sharp, Walker

Attendance: 20,000

League Positions

	P	W	D	L	F	A	Pts
1 RANGERS	15	13	1	1	36	11	27
2 Hibernian	17	11	3	3	50	15	25
3 Partick Thistle	17	10	2	5	40	25	22
4 Motherwell	16	9	1	6	30	23	19
5 Dundee	17	8	2	7	37	31	18

January 2nd:
CELTIC (0) 0   RANGERS (3) 4
                      McColl (9),
                      Thornton (26),
                      Rutherford (38),
                      Duncanson (79)

CELTIC: Miller; Mallan, Milne; McPhail, Corbett, McAuley; Bogan, McDonald, Walsh, Evans, Paton

RANGERS: Brown; Cox, Shaw; McColl, Young, Rae; Rutherford, Gillick, Thornton, Duncanson, Caskie

Attendance: 60,000

Rangers meandered back to the top of A Division. In 9 minutes Cox's free-kick, awarded for a foul by Milne on Rutherford, was only partially cleared and McColl's shot from the edge of the penalty area went in low off the post with Miller blinded by the ruck of players in front of him. A cracking first-time shot by Thornton taken on the half-turn in 26 minutes, after Rutherford's corner-kick, ended the match as a contest.

January 3rd:
RANGERS (1) 2   DUNDEE (0) 1
Thornton 2 (28, n.a.) Juliussen (50)

RANGERS: Brown; Cox, Shaw; McColl, Young, Rae; Rutherford, Gillick, Thornton, Duncanson, Caskie

DUNDEE: Lynch; Irvine, Ancell; Gallacher, Gray, Boyd; Gunn, Pattillo, Juliussen, Smith, Hill

Attendance: 35,000

January 8th: Jimmy Parlane signed for Airdrie.

January 10th:
FALKIRK (0) 1   RANGERS (2) 5
Inglis (78)   Gillick 2 (30, 42),
                       Duncanson 2 (46, 57),
                       Waddell (85)

FALKIRK: J. Dawson; Whyte, McPhee; Bolt, Fiddes, Whitelaw; Inglis, Aikman, Aitken, J. Henderson, K. Dawson

RANGERS: Brown; Young, Shaw; McColl, Woodburn, Cox; Waddell, Gillick, Thornton, Duncanson, Caskie

Attendance: 20,000

January 14th: Cox, Young, Rutherford, Gillick and Duncanson were all in the Scottish League team which beat the Irish League 3-0 at Parkhead. Duncanson scored one of the goals.

January 17th:
RANGERS (0) 2   MOTHERWELL (0) 0
Thornton (72),
Young (75)

RANGERS: Brown; Young, Shaw; McColl, Woodburn, Cox; Waddell, Gillick, Thornton, Duncanson, Caskie

MOTHERWELL: Johnstone; Kilmarnock, Sinclair; McCleod, Paton, Redpath; McRoberts, Watson, Humphries, Bremner, Barclay

Attendance: 35,000

January 31st:
HIBERNIAN   (0) 1   RANGERS (0) 0
  Cuthbertson (90)

HIBERNIAN: Kerr; Govan, Shaw; Finnigan, Howie, Buchanan; Smith, Combe, Linwood, Cuthbertson, Ormond

RANGERS: Brown; Young, Shaw; McColl, Woodburn, Cox; Waddell, Gillick, Thornton, Duncanson, Caskie

Attendance: 52,750 (a record)

Though it was not until the last minute that Cuthbertson scored, Waddell came close to equalising in the dying seconds. Gillick, a key man, had suffered a family bereavement and the decision to field the player proved, not surprisingly, to be a mistake.

February 14th:
RANGERS   (2) 3   ST MIRREN   (1) 2
  Thornton 3 (34, 35, 75)   Milne (45),
                             Burrell (70)

RANGERS: Brown; Young, Shaw; McColl, Woodburn, Cox; Rutherford, Gillick, Thornton, Duncanson, Waddell

ST MIRREN: Kirk; Smith, Lindsay; Drinkwater, Telfer, Martin; Burrell, Crowe, Milne, Deakin, Lesz

Attendance: 20,000

February 28th:
RANGERS   (1) 2   QUEEN OF THE
  Gillick (17),   SOUTH   (1) 3
  Thornton (78)   Hamilton (21),
                           Stephen (52),
                           Houliston (83)

RANGERS: Brown; Young, Shaw; McColl, Woodburn, Cox; Rae, Gillick, Thornton, Duncanson, Caskie

QUEEN OF THE SOUTH: Henderson; Fitzsimmons, James; Laurie, Aird, Hamilton; Stephen, Jenkins, Houliston, Law, Hope

Attendance: 34,000

League positions

	P	W	D	L	F	A	Pts
1 Hibernian	24	17	4	3	69	20	38
2 RANGERS	22	18	1	3	54	19	37
3 Partick Thistle	25	13	3	9	48	35	29
4 Dundee	24	12	3	9	52	37	27
5 Motherwell	22	12	1	9	40	31	25

March 13th:
MORTON   (0) 0   RANGERS   (1) 1
                          Thornton (40)

MORTON: Cowan; Mitchell, Whigham; Campbell, Millar, Whyte; Hepburn, Murphy, Cupples, Orr, Liddell

RANGERS: Brown; Cox, Shaw; McColl, Young, Rae; Waddell, Gillick, Thornton, Duncanson, Rutherford

Attendance: 18,000

March 20th:
RANGERS   (1) 1   QUEENS PARK   (0) 2
  Rutherford (37)   Aitken (79),
                           Burgess (89½)

RANGERS: Brown; Cox, Shaw; McColl, Young, Rae; Waddell, Gillick, Thornton, Duncanson, Rutherford

QUEENS PARK: J. Curran; J. McColl, A. Carmichael; D. McBain, J. Ross, D. Letham: G. Cunningham, J. Farquhar, W. Burgess, A. Aitken, T. Alexander

Attendance: 37,000

March 29th:
RANGERS   (1) 1   FALKIRK   (1) 1
  Duncanson (44)   Aikman (25)

RANGERS: Brown; Young, Shaw; Cox, Woodburn, Rae; Waddell, Gillick, Thornton, Duncanson, Rutherford

FALKIRK: Dawson; Whyte, McPhee; Whitelaw, R. Henderson, Telfer; J. Henderson, Aikman, Inglis, Fiddes, Allison

April 3rd:
ABERDEEN   (0) 1   RANGERS   (0) 1
  Kelly (57)   Duncanson (69)

ABERDEEN: Johnstone; McLaughlin, McKenna; Waddell, Roy, Taylor; A. Kiddie, Harris, Kelly, Baird, Pearson

RANGERS: Brown; Young, Shaw; McColl, Woodburn, Cox; Waddell, Gillick, Thornton, Duncanson, Rutherford

April 10th: Young and Thornton played for Scotland against England at Hampden Park. Young captained the side which lost 2-0. Waddell was selected but had to withdraw through injury.

April 24th:
MOTHERWELL   (0) 1   RANGERS   (1) 1
Humphries (58)   Duncanson (43)

MOTHERWELL: Johnstone; Sinclair, Shaw; McLeod, Paton, Russell; Waters, Bremner, Humphries, Anderson, Barclay

RANGERS: Brown; Cox, Lindsay; Little, McColl, Watkins; Rutherford, Paton, Williamson, Thornton, Duncanson

Attendance: 25,000

April 26th:
RANGERS   (2) 2   CLYDE   (0) 1
McPherson (19), Cox (24)   Ackerman

RANGERS: Brown; Lindsay, Shaw; McColl, Johnston, Watkins; Rutherford, Paton, McPherson, Thornton, Cox

CLYDE: Grant; Gibson, Deans; McCormick, Milligan, Campbell; Davis, Carson, Ackerman, Galletly, McPhail

May 1st:
AIRDRIE   (0) 1   RANGERS   (1) 2
Kelly (81 pen)   Findlay 2 (45, 75)

AIRDRIE: Downie; Hadden, Cunningham; Stevenson, Kelly, Duncan; W. Brown, Parlane, Orr, Picken, H. Watson

RANGERS: Brown; Young, Shaw; McColl, Woodburn, Cox; Rutherford, Findlay, Williamson, Thornton, Duncanson

Attendance: 18,000

May 3rd:
RANGERS   (0) 1   HEARTS   (1) 2
Findlay (53)   Laing (6),
                           Hamilton (75)

RANGERS: Brown; Cox, Lindsay; McColl, Woodburn, Watkins; Rutherford, Findlay, Gillick, Thornton, Duncanson

HEARTS: Brown; Mathieson, McKenzie; Laing, Rodger, Dougan; Sloan, Hamilton, Flavell, Dixon, Williams

Attendance: n.a.

Brown saved a penalty from Dixon

Scottish League Division A

	P	W	D	L	F	A	Pts
1 Hibernian	30	22	4	4	86	27	48
2 RANGERS	30	21	4	5	64	28	46
3 Partick Thistle	30	16	4	10	61	42	36
4 Dundee	30	15	3	12	67	51	33
5 St Mirren	30	13	5	12	54	58	31
6 Clyde	30	12	7	11	52	57	31
7 Falkirk	30	10	10	10	55	48	30
8 Motherwell	30	13	3	14	45	47	29
9 Hearts	30	10	8	12	37	42	28
10 Aberdeen	30	10	7	13	45	45	27
11 Third Lanark	30	10	6	14	56	73	26
12 Celtic	30	10	5	15	41	56	25
13 Queen of South	30	10	5	15	49	74	25
14 Morton	30	9	6	15	47	43	24
15 Airdrie	30	7	7	16	39	78	21
16 Queens Park	30	9	2	19	45	75	20

May 17th: Young was in the Scotland team beaten 2-1 by Switzerland in Berne.

May 23rd: Young, Cox and Rutherford were in the Scotland team beaten 3-0 by France in Paris.

May 30th: Rangers announced that they would listen to offers for Torry Gillick after the player had stated that playing for them, after his considerable period in the game, was a shade too exacting. The player later changed his mind and re-signed for the club.

LEAGUE CUP

August 9th:
RANGERS   (0) 2   CELTIC   (0) 0
Williamson 2 (61, 71)

RANGERS: Brown; Cox, Shaw; McColl, Woodburn, Rae; Waddell, Gillick, Williamson, Thornton, Duncanson

CELTIC: Miller; Hogg, Mallan; McPhail, Corbett, McAuley; F. Quinn, McAloon, Kiernan, Sirrell, Paton

Attendance: 80,000

Never before had so big a crowd watched a game on the opening day of the season in Britain. Both Rangers' goals, within 10 minutes of each other in the second half, were made by Duncanson and finished off by Williamson. Apart from a 20-yard drive from Sirrell that bounced from the post with Brown helpless, Celtic's forwards never looked like scoring.

August 16th:
THIRD LANARK   (1) 1   RANGERS   (2) 3
McCulloch (45)   Williamson 2 (17, 41),
                          Duncanson (63)

THIRD LANARK: Fraser; Middleton, Kelly; Baillie, Palmer, Mooney; McCulloch, Mason, Reid, Ayton, Mitchell

RANGERS: Brown; Cox, Shaw; McColl, Woodburn, Rae; Waddell, Gillick, Williamson, Thornton, Duncanson

Attendance: 25,000

August 23rd:

RANGERS   (1) 3   DUNDEE   (0) 0
  Williamson (23),
  Gillick (62),
  Thornton (81)

RANGERS: Brown; Cox, Shaw; McColl, Woodburn, Rae; Waddell, Gillick, Williamson, Thornton, Duncanson

DUNDEE: Brown; Follon, Lynch; Pattillo, Gray, Boyd; Gunn, Ewen, Turnbull, Juliussen, Hill

Attendance: 25,000

August 30th:

CELTIC   (0) 2   RANGERS   (0) 0
  Gallacher (52), Paton (58)

CELTIC: Miller; Hogg, Mallan; McPhail, Corbett, McAuley; Bogan, R. Quinn, Gallacher, Evans, Paton

RANGERS: Brown; Cox; Shaw; Watkins, Woodburn, Rae; Waddell, Gillick, Williamson, Thornton, Duncanson

Attendance: 50,000

Rangers' cloak of invincibility was torn to shreds by Celtic. The keystone of Celtic's victory was the excellent play of their half-back line. The zest and cleverness of McPhail and McAuley made Rangers look ordinary.

September 6th:

RANGERS   (1) 3   THIRD LANARK   (0) 0
  Gillick (27),
  Findlay 2 (47, 56)

RANGERS: Brown; Young, Shaw; McColl, Woodburn, Cox; Waddell, Gillick, Thornton, Findlay, Duncanson

THIRD LANARK: Fraser; Young, Kelly; McMillan, Palmer, Mooney; Staroscik, Mason, McCulloch, Ayton, Mitchell

Attendance: 20,000

September 13th:

DUNDEE   (1) 1   RANGERS   (0) 1
  Gallacher (23)   Paton (53)

DUNDEE: Lynch; Follon, Ancell; Cowie, Boyd, Smith; Pattillo, Ewen, Turnbull, Gallacher, Juliussen

RANGERS: Brown; Young, Shaw; McColl, Woodburn, Cox; Waddell, Paton, Thornton, Findlay, Duncanson

Attendance: 39,000 (a record)

League Cup Section Table

	P	W	D	L	F	A	Pts
RANGERS	6	4	1	1	12	4	9
Dundee	6	2	2	2	12	13	6
Celtic	6	2	1	3	9	11	5
Third Lanark	6	2	0	4	12	17	4

September 27th: Quarter-Final   At Ibrox

RANGERS   (1) 2   STENHOUSEMUIR   (0) 0
  Findlay (2),
  Thornton (67)

RANGERS: Brown; Young, Shaw; McColl, Woodburn, Cox; Waddell, Gillick, Thornton, Findlay, Duncanson

STENHOUSEMUIR: Allan; Jack, Allison; Anderson, Syme, Miller; Thomson, Bow, McFarlane, Dick, Napier

Attendance: 25,000

October 12th: Semi-Final   At Hampden Park

FALKIRK   (0) 1   RANGERS   (0) 0
  Aikman (88)

FALKIRK: J. Dawson; Whyte, McPhee; Bolt, R. Henderson, Whitelaw; Fiddes, Fleck, Aikman, J. Henderson, K. Dawson

RANGERS: Brown; Young, Shaw; McColl, Woodburn, Cox; Rutherford, Gillick, Thornton, Findlay, Duncanson

Attendance: 44,500

Rangers' defence made few mistakes against Falkirk but one, Woodburn's, when his hesitancy in clearing allowed Aikman in to score, cost his team a place in the Final, and this when all thoughts were on extra time. Rangers' forwards made 10 times as many errors as the men behind them, and the responsibility for the defeat was theirs. For all Rangers' failings, full credit was due to centre-half Henderson, who blotted out Thornton.

SCOTTISH CUP

January 24th: First Round

STRANRAER   (0) 0   RANGERS   (0) 1
                             Thornton (70)

STRANRAER: Park; Kirkland, Dyer; Cox, Milliken, Haxton; Cormack, Jeffrey, Logan, Jones, McGuffie

RANGERS: Brown; Young, Shaw; McColl, Woodburn, Cox; Waddell, Gillick, Thornton, Duncanson, Caskie

Attendance: 6,000

February 7th: Second Round

RANGERS   (2) 4   LEITH
  Thornton (35), Waddell (42),   ATHLETIC   (0) 0
  Cox (55), Rutherford (88)

RANGERS: Brown; Young, Shaw; McColl, Woodburn, Cox; Rutherford, Gillick, Thornton, Duncanson, Waddell

LEITH ATHLETIC: Goram; Paterson, Peat; Skinner, Gilchrist, McCall; Johnstone, Robertson, McLean, Love, Landles

Attendance: 17,000

February 21st: Third Round
RANGERS (2) 3   PARTICK THISTLE (0) 0
   Young (15 pen),
   Duncanson (43),
   McGowan o.g. (68)
RANGERS: Brown; Young, Shaw; McColl, Woodburn, Cox; Rutherford, Gillick, Thornton, Duncanson, Caskie

PARTICK THISTLE: Henderson; McGowan, Husband; Candlin, Forsyth, Hewitt; Wright, Brown, O'Donnell, Sharp, Walker

Attendance: 65,000

March 6th: Fourth Round
RANGERS (1) 1   EAST FIFE (0) 0
   Duncanson (44)
RANGERS: Brown; Cox, Shaw; McColl, Young, Rae; Rutherford, Gillick, Thornton, Duncanson, Caskie

EAST FIFE: Niven; Laird, Stewart; Philp, Finlay, Aitken; Adams, D. Davidson, Morris, J. Davidson, Duncan

Attendance: 90,000

March 27th: Semi-Final
HIBERNIAN (0) 0   RANGERS (1) 1
                     Thornton (30)
HIBERNIAN: Farm; Govan, Shaw; Kean, Howie, Buchanan; Smith, Combe, Linwood, Cuthbertson, Turnbull

RANGERS: Brown; Young, Shaw; McColl, Woodburn, Cox; Waddell, Gillick, Thornton, Duncanson, Rutherford

Attendance: 143,570 (a record)

Rangers' tactics of concentrating on defence after they had been given the present of a goal in 30 minutes were in the end successful. Hibs held the initiative for over two-thirds of the match yet failed to pierce Rangers' defence. Brown was outstanding for Rangers with one world-class save from Smith in the second half. Cox was Rangers' outstanding outfield player.

April 17th: Final   At Hampden Park
RANGERS (1) 1   MORTON (1) 1
   Gillick (12)   Whyte (2)
                After Extra Time
RANGERS: Brown; Young, Shaw; McColl, Woodburn, Cox; Rutherford, Gillick, Thornton, Findlay, Duncanson

MORTON: Cowan; Mitchell, Whigham; Campbell, Millar, Whyte; Hepburn, Murphy, Cupples, Orr, Liddell

Attendance: 131,975
Referee: J. M. Martin (Blairgowrie)

Whyte's 35-yard free-kick in only the 2nd minute, aided by the wind, left Brown stranded. After 12 minutes Millar allowed Thornton to beat him to a lob from Cox and head the ball to Gillick, who scored the equaliser. Midway through the 2nd half an attempted back-pass eluded Cowan but he grasped it just as it reached the goal-line and as the Rangers' forwards were throwing their hands up in ecstasy. McColl and Cox were not in the same class as Whyte and Campbell, and Liddell was the cleverest forward on the field despite the fact that he was marked by an outstanding player.

April 21st: Final Replay
RANGERS (0) 1   MORTON (0) 0
   Williamson (115)
                After Extra Time
RANGERS: Brown; Young, Shaw; McColl, Woodburn, Cox; Rutherford, Thornton, Williamson, Duncanson, Gillick

MORTON: Cowan; Mitchell, Whigham; Campbell, Millar, Whyte; Hepburn, Murphy, Cupples, Orr, Liddell

Attendance: 129,176 (a record for a midweek match)
Referee: J. M. Martin (Blairgowrie)

There were just over 4 minutes left for play in a hard-fought Final when Cox drove a long low pass over to the left touchline. Rutherford, far out on his beat, collected the pass and crossed with his left foot. Williamson, rushing in at full tilt, met the ball with his forehead and the header was in the net before Cowan could move.

APPEARANCES

	League	League Cup	Scottish Cup	Glasgow Cup	Charity Cup	Friendlies
Brown	30	8	7	4	2	1
Cox	30	8	7	4	2	1
Shaw	28	8	7	4	2	1
McColl	29	7	7	4	2	1
Woodburn	23	8	6	4	2	1
Rae	19	4	1	1	-	-
Young	15	4	7	3	2	1
Waddell	12	7	3	3	-	1
Gillick	21	7	7	3	-	1
Williamson	7	4	1	1	2	-
Thornton	30	8	7	4	2	1
Duncanson	29	8	7	4	2	1
Findlay	7	4	1	3	2	-
Rutherford	21	1	6	1	2	-
Paton	4	1	-	1	-	-
Marshall	4	-	-	-	-	-
Caskie	11	-	3	-	-	1
Lindsay	3	-	-	-	-	-
Little	1	-	-	-	-	-
Watkins	3	1	-	-	-	-
Johnston	1	-	-	-	-	-
Parlane	1	-	-	-	-	-
McPherson	1	-	-	-	-	-

GOALSCORERS

League: Thornton 16, Duncanson 12, Gillick 9, Findlay 6, Rutherford 5, Williamson 4, Marshall 3, Waddell 2, Paton 1, Shaw 1 (pen), Parlane 1, McColl 1, Young 1, McPherson 1, Cox 1

League Cup: Williamson 5, Findlay 3, Thornton 2, Gillick 2, Paton 1, Duncanson 1

Scottish Cup: Thornton 3, Duncanson 2, Waddell 1, Cox 1, Rutherford 1, Young 1 (pen), Own Goals 1

Glasgow Cup: Thornton 4, Findlay 2, Cox 1, Duncanson 1, Rutherford 1, Gillick 1

Charity Cup: Findlay 3, Williamson 1, Duncanson 1

Friendlies: Duncanson 2, Thornton 1

'Tiger' Khomich, Moscow Dynamo's goalkeeper, prepares to dive at the feet of Willie Waddell. The match at Ibrox was Rangers first big post-war friendly.

Season 1948–49

Rangers had a clean sweep of all the domestic honours. The League Championship returned to Ibrox in the most dramatic fashion. Dundee needed to win their last match of the season, against Falkirk at Brockville, to clinch the title but lost 4-1. Rangers beat bottom club Albion Rovers by the same score and so took the title by one point. Hibs were the only team to take both points away from Ibrox but that defeat was avenged at Easter Road. Celtic were beaten 4-0 in the Ne'erday game at Ibrox. Throughout the season the defensive 6 missed only 7 out of the 180 appearances. Thornton scored 23 goals and Duncanson and Paton were next best with 10 and 9 goals respectively.

The Scottish Cup was retained. The Final itself against Clyde will be remembered for penalties – those which were awarded and those which were not. Williamson, as in the previous year, played in the Final only of the competition, this time to the exclusion of Paton, and scored one of the 4 goals. Rangers used only 12 players throughout the competition.

The League Cup was also won. Hibs, Celtic and Clyde were overcome in the Section. A Thornton goal eliminated St Mirren. 4 goals were scored against Dundee in the opening 25 minutes of a sensational Semi-Final and Gillick and Paton scored the goals which won the Cup in the Final against B Division Raith Rovers.

League: Champions
League Cup: Winners
Scottish Cup: Winners

SCOTTISH LEAGUE DIVISION A

August 14th:

MOTHERWELL (0) 1   RANGERS (1) 1
   Mathie (78)   Thornton (5)

MOTHERWELL: Johnston; Kilmarnock, Shaw; McLeod, Paton, Redpath; Humphries, Watson, Mathie, Bremner, Barclay

RANGERS: Brown; Young, Shaw; McColl, Woodburn, Cox; Waddell, Findlay, Thornton, Duncanson, Caskie

Woodburn was ordered off

Attendance: 35,000

August 16th: Billy Arnison was transferred to Luton Town for £7,000.

August 18th:

RANGERS (1) 4   FALKIRK (2) 3
   Thornton (11),   Young 2 o.g.'s (36, n.a.)
   Findlay (69),   Aikman (51)
   Gillick 2 (77, 87)

RANGERS: Brown; Young, Shaw; McColl, Woodburn, Cox; Rutherford, Gillick, Thornton, Findlay, Duncanson

FALKIRK: Dawson; Whyte, McPhee; Burnett, R. Henderson, Whitelaw; Fiddes, Fleck, Aikman, J. Henderson, Allison

Attendance: 40,000

August 21st:

CELTIC (0) 0   RANGERS (1) 1
                         Findlay (6)

CELTIC: Miller; Milne, Mallan; Evans, Boden, McAuley; Docherty, McPhail, Weir, Tully, Paton

RANGERS: Brown; Young, Shaw; McColl, Woodburn, Cox; Rutherford, Gillick, Thornton, Findlay, Duncanson

Mallan missed a penalty

Attendance: 50,000

In only 6 minutes an apologetic effort of a shot by Findlay from fully 30 yards seemed to be dropping outside Miller's right-hand post when the goalkeeper casually attempted to pull it in with his right arm. The ball, however, spun inward off his arm and into the net.

August 28th:

RANGERS (1) 1	DUNDEE (1) 1
Findlay (4)	Stott (41)

RANGERS: Brown; Young, Lindsay; McColl, Woodburn, Cox; Frame, Gillick, Thornton, Findlay, Duncanson

DUNDEE: Lynch; Follon, Ancell; Gallacher, Gray, Boyd; Gunn, Pattillo, Stott, Ewen, Andrews

Attendance: 55,000. Young missed a penalty

September 1st:

PARTICK THISTLE (0) 1	RANGERS (1) 1
Sharp (80)	Thornton (11)

PARTICK THISTLE: Henderson; McGowan, Curran; Davidson, Forsyth, Brown; McKenzie, McCallum, Kinnell, Sharp, O'Donnell

RANGERS: Brown; Young, Lindsay; McColl, Woodburn, Rae; Rutherford, Gillick, Thornton, Findlay, Duncanson

September 4th:

RANGERS (2) 2	THIRD LANARK (1) 1
Williamson (21),	Mitchell (14)
Duncanson (40)	

RANGERS: Brown; Young, Lindsay; McColl, Woodburn, Marshall; Waddell, Gillick, Williamson, Thornton, Duncanson

THIRD LANARK: Petrie; Balunas, Kelly; Orr, Barclay, Harrower; McCulloch, Reid, Stirling, Mason, Mitchell

Attendance: 30,000

September 21st: Charlie Watkins left Ibrox for Luton Town.

October 23rd:

HEARTS (1) 2	RANGERS (0) 0
Wardhaugh (42), Conn (57)	

HEARTS: Brown; Parker, McKenzie; Cox, Dougan, Laing; Sloan, Conn, Bauld, Wardhaugh, Williams

RANGERS: Brown; Cox, Shaw; McColl, Woodburn, Rae; Rutherford, Thornton, Williamson, Findlay, Duncanson

Attendance: 40,000

League Positions

	P	W	D	L	F	A	Pts
1 Hibernian	8	5	2	1	27	16	12
2 St Mirren	7	5	1	1	13	8	11
3 East Fife	7	5	0	2	17	10	10
4 Falkirk	8	4	1	3	23	14	9
5 RANGERS	7	3	3	1	10	9	9

October 23rd: Young and Waddell were in the Scotland team which beat Wales 3-1 in Cardiff. Waddell scored 2 goals.

November 6th:

RANGERS (1) 2	HIBERNIAN (4) 4
Thornton (42), Gillick (82)	Smith 2 (10, 43),
	Cuthbertson (20),
	Turnbull (33)

RANGERS: Brown; Lindsay, Shaw; McColl, Woodburn, Cox; Gillick, Thornton, Williamson, Duncanson, Rutherford

HIBERNIAN: Kerr; Govan, Cairns; Finnigan, Aird, Kean; Smith, Turnbull, Cuthbertson, Combe, Reilly

Attendance: 50,000

November 13th:

ST MIRREN (0) 0	RANGERS (1) 2
	Gillick (30 secs),
	Waddell (82)

ST MIRREN: Kirk; Lapsley, Martin; Drinkwater, Telfer, W. Reid; Burrell, Stewart, Milne, Davie, Lesz

RANGERS: Brown; Young, Shaw; McColl, Woodburn, Cox; Waddell, Gillick, Thornton, Duncanson, Rutherford

Attendance: 40,000

November 17th: Brown, Young and Waddell were in the Scotland team which beat Ireland 3-2 at Hampden Park.

November 27th:

EAST FIFE (1) 1	RANGERS (0) 2
Duncan (40)	Thornton (56),
	Duncanson (81)

EAST FIFE: Clark; Laird, Stewart; Philp, Finlay, Aitken; Adams, Fleming, Morris, Brown, Duncan

RANGERS: Brown; Young, Shaw; McColl, Woodburn, Cox; Rutherford, Findlay, Thornton, Paton, Duncanson

Attendance: 20,737

December 4th:

CLYDE (1) 1	RANGERS (3) 3
Wright (25)	Thornton 2 (9, 19),
	Paton (18)

CLYDE: Gullan; Gibson, Garwood; Dunn, Campbell, Daly; Davies, Garth, Ackerman, Wright, Bootland

RANGERS: Brown; Young, Shaw; McColl, Woodburn, Cox; Rutherford, Findlay, Thornton, Paton, Duncanson

Attendance: 22,000

December 11th:
RANGERS (3) 4   MORTON (1) 1
  Findlay (20),   Farquhar (10),
  Rutherford (25),
  Thornton 2 (35, 61)

RANGERS: Brown; Young, Shaw; McColl, Woodburn, Cox; Rutherford, Findlay, Thornton, Paton, Duncanson

MORTON: Clark; Mitchell, Westwater; Campbell, Batton, Whyte; Stevenson, Farquhar, Mochan, McGarritty, Liddell

Attendance: 25,000

December 18th:
QUEEN OF THE   RANGERS (0) 2
  SOUTH (0) 0   Thornton (57),
                                  Rutherford (65)

QUEEN OF THE SOUTH: Henderson; McColl, James; McBain, Aird, Hamilton; McCulloch, Brown, Houliston, Jenkins, Johnstone

RANGERS: Brown; Young, Shaw; McColl, Woodburn, Cox; Waddell, Findlay, Thornton, Paton, Rutherford

Attendance: 20,200

League Positions

	P	W	D	L	F	A	Pts
1 Hibernian	15	8	4	3	40	30	20
2 RANGERS	13	8	3	2	25	16	19
3 Dundee	12	7	3	2	25	14	17
4 St Mirren	14	7	3	4	23	18	17
5 Falkirk	14	6	4	4	40	30	16

December 25th:
FALKIRK (1) 2   RANGERS (1) 2
  Anderson (7), Aikman (87)   Paton (17),
                                      Waddell (71)

FALKIRK: J. Dawson; Whyte, McPhee; Fiddes, Henderson, Telfer; Inglis, Anderson, Aikman, Allison, McLaughlin

RANGERS: Brown; Young, Shaw; McColl, Woodburn, Cox; Waddell, Findlay, Thornton, Paton, Rutherford

Attendance: 20,000

January 1st:
RANGERS (3) 4   CELTIC (0) 0
  Thornton (3)
  Duncanson 3 (26, 43, 88)

RANGERS: Brown; Young, Shaw; McColl, Woodburn, Cox; Waddell, Paton, Thornton, Duncanson, Rutherford

CELTIC: Miller; Milne, Mallan; Evans, Boden, McAuley; Weir, Johnston, Gallacher, Tully, Paton

Attendance: 85,000

Rangers played football of the highest quality in difficult conditions. The left-wing of Duncanson and Rutherford was a tremendous success. The outside-left gave Milne, the Celtic right-back, a roasting. McColl took full revenge on Tully for the latter's joy day at his expense earlier in the season.

January 3rd:
DUNDEE (2) 3   RANGERS (1) 1
  Ewen (11), Stott 2 (24, 82)   Marshall (10)

DUNDEE: Lynch; Follon, Irvine; Gallacher, Cowie, Boyd; Gunn, Pattillo, Stott, Ewen, Hill

RANGERS: Brown; Young, Shaw; McColl, Woodburn, Cox; Waddell, Paton, Thornton, Marshall, Rutherford

Attendance: 39,000

Dundee displayed a blend of skill and courage on a pitch resembling a skating rink. Against the run of play Marshall scrambled the ball in at the far post in 10 minutes. 30 seconds later Ewen equalised with a full-blooded 30-yard drive. In 24 minutes Dundee took a lead they never relinquished, an innocuous-looking shot from Stott going in off Brown's right-hand post as the 'keeper stood transfixed. Dundee repelled a Rangers onslaught which lasted nearly 30 minutes and they broke away 8 minutes from time to make the match secure – Stott heading home a beautifully placed cross from Hill. Waddell and Paton were scarcely in the game and Duncanson was sorely missed.

January 8th:
RANGERS (1) 2   MOTHERWELL (0) 0
  Paton (43), Thornton (69)

RANGERS: Brown; Young, Shaw; McColl, Woodburn, Cox; Waddell, Paton, Thornton, Marshall, Rutherford

MOTHERWELL: Johnstone; Kilmarnock, Shaw; Russell, Paton, Redpath; McColl, Humphries, Mathie, Bremner, Aitkenhead

Attendance: 55,000

January 15th:
THIRD LANARK (1) 2   RANGERS (1) 1
  McCulloch (21),   Thornton (40)
  Henderson (85)

THIRD LANARK: Fraser; Balunas, Harrower; Orr, Barclay, Mooney; Henderson, Mason, McCulloch, Staroscik, Mitchell

RANGERS: Brown; Young, Shaw; McColl, Woodburn, Cox; Waddell, Gillick, Thornton, Paton, Rutherford

Attendance: 35,000

January 29th:
RANGERS   (1) 2   PARTICK THISTLE   (0) 2
  Thornton (14),   Sharp (62), O'Donnell (65)
  Cox (76)

RANGERS: Brown; Young, Shaw; McColl, Woodburn, Cox; Waddell, Paton, Thornton, Duncanson, Rutherford

PARTICK THISTLE: Ledgerwood; McGowan, Gibb; Thomson, Forsyth, Hewitt; McKenzie, Wright, O'Donnell, Sharp, Walker

Attendance: 55,000

February 12th:
ABERDEEN   (0) 0   RANGERS   (1) 2
                           Thornton (45 secs),
                           Paton (72)

ABERDEEN: Curran; Ancell, McKenna; Anderson, Thomson, Harris; Rice, Williams, Emery, Smith, Hather

RANGERS: Brown; Young, Shaw; McColl, Woodburn, Cox; Waddell, Paton, Thornton, Duncanson, Rutherford

Attendance: 40,000

February 19th:
HIBERNIAN   (0) 0   RANGERS   (0) 1
                           Paton (67)

HIBERNIAN: Kerr; Govan, Cairns; Finnigan, Kean, Buchanan; Smith, Combe, Plumb, Turnbull, Ormond

RANGERS: Brown; Young, Shaw; McColl, Woodburn, Cox; Waddell, Paton, Thornton, Duncanson, Rutherford

Attendance: 49,000

February 26th:
RANGERS   (0) 2   ST MIRREN   (0) 1
  Thornton (72),   Guthrie (89)
  Duncanson (92)

RANGERS: Brown; Young, Shaw; McColl, Woodburn, Cox; Waddell, Paton, Thornton, Duncanson, Rutherford

ST MIRREN: Kirk; Lapsley, Martin; Drinkwater, Telfer, W. Reid; Burrell, Guthrie, Milne, Deakin, Lesz

Attendance: 25,000

League Positions

	P	W	D	L	F	A	Pts
1 Hibernian	23	17	4	2	64	24	38
2 RANGERS	22	17	3	2	45	20	37
3 Hearts	24	16	2	6	64	29	34
4 Dundee	23	11	7	5	41	26	29
5 Celtic	24	11	6	7	40	42	28

March 19th:
RANGERS   (1) 4   CLYDE   (1) 1
  Paton 2 (7, 57),   Garth (26)
  Thornton (53),
  Duncanson (67)

RANGERS: Brown; Young, Shaw; McColl, Woodburn, Cox; Rutherford, Paton, Thornton, Duncanson, Walmsley

CLYDE: Gullan; Gibson, Mennie; Campbell, McCormack, Long; Galletly, Davies, Linwood, Wright, Garth

Attendance: 50,000

April 2nd:
RANGERS   (0) 3   QUEEN OF THE
  Thornton 2 (56, 80),   SOUTH   (0) 0
  Duncanson (88)

RANGERS: Brown; Young, Shaw; McColl, Woodburn, Cox; Waddell, Paton, Thornton, Duncanson, Rutherford

QUEEN OF THE SOUTH: Henderson; McColl, James; McBain, Aird, Sharp; McCulloch, J. Brown, Houliston, Jenkins, Johnstone

Attendance: 28,000

April 5th:
RANGERS   (0) 2   HEARTS   (1) 1
  Cox (62), Paton (70)   Conn (20)

RANGERS: Brown; Young, Shaw; McColl, Woodburn, Cox; Waddell, Paton, Thornton, Duncanson, Rutherford

HEARTS: Brown; Mathieson, McKenzie; Cox, Dougan, Laing; MacFarlane, Conn, Bauld, Wardhaugh, Flavell

Attendance: 45,000

April 9th: Scotland beat England 3-1 at Wembley. Young captained the team which also included Cox, Woodburn and Waddell.

April 13th:
RANGERS   (2) 3   EAST FIFE   (0) 1
  Paton (18),   Davidson (71)
  Young 2 pens (34, 73)

RANGERS: Brown; Young, Shaw; McColl, Woodburn, Cox; Waddell, Paton, Thornton, Duncanson, Rutherford

EAST FIFE: Niven; Laird, Stewart; Philp, Finlay, Brown; Black, Fleming, Morris, Davidson, Duncan

Attendance: 35,000

April 16th:
RANGERS   (0) 1   ABERDEEN   (1) 1
  Duncanson (61)   Hather (17)

RANGERS: Brown; Young, Shaw; McColl, Woodburn, Cox; Waddell, Paton, Thornton, Duncanson, Rutherford

ABERDEEN: Curran; Ancell, McKenna; Stenhouse, Roy, Waddell; Pearson, Williams, Emery, Harris, Hather

Attendance: 40,000

April 19th:
RANGERS   (1) 3   ALBION
  Williamson (3),   ROVERS   (1) 1
  Waddell (65),   McKinnon (42)
  Young (75 pen)

RANGERS: Brown; Young, Shaw; McColl, Woodburn, Cox; Waddell, Paton, Williamson, Duncanson, Rutherford

ALBION ROVERS: Henderson; Muir, Kerr; Martin, English, Hunter; McKinnon, Dickson, Wallace, Devlin, J. Smith

Attendance: 16,000

April 25th:
MORTON   (0) 0   RANGERS   (1) 1
                          Thornton (13)

MORTON: Cowan; Mitchell, Westwater; Orr, Whigham, Whyte; Farquhar, Divers, Mochan, McGarritty, Liddell

RANGERS: Brown; Young, Shaw; McColl, Woodburn, Cox; Waddell, Findlay, Thornton, Williamsom, Rutherford

Attendance: 40,000

April 27th: Young, Cox, Woodburn, Waddell and Thornton were in the Scotland team which beat France 2-0 at Hampden Park.

April 30th:
ALBION ROVERS   (0) 1   RANGERS   (2) 4
  Wallace (52)   Thornton 3 (20, 60,
                            80), Duncanson (26)

ALBION ROVERS: McGregor; Muir, Kerr; Martin, English, Hunter; McKinnon, Craig, Wallace, Devlin, J. Smith

RANGERS: Brown; Young, Shaw; McColl, Woodburn, Cox; Waddell, Duncanson, Thornton, Williamson, Rutherford

Attendance: 15,000

Scottish League Division A

	P	W	D	L	F	A	Pts
1 RANGERS	30	20	6	4	63	32	46
2 Dundee	30	20	5	5	71	48	45
3 Hibernian	30	17	5	8	75	52	39
4 East Fife	30	16	3	11	64	46	35
5 Falkirk	30	12	8	10	70	54	32
6 Celtic	30	12	7	11	48	40	31
7 Third Lanark	30	13	5	12	56	52	31
8 Hearts	30	12	6	12	64	54	30
9 St Mirren	30	13	4	13	51	47	30
10 Queen of South	30	11	8	11	47	53	30
11 Partick Thistle	30	9	9	12	50	63	27
12 Motherwell	30	10	5	15	44	49	25
13 Aberdeen	30	7	11	12	39	48	25
14 Clyde	30	9	6	15	50	67	24
15 Morton	30	7	8	15	39	51	22
16 Albion Rovers	30	3	2	25	30	105	8

LEAGUE CUP

September 11th:
RANGERS   (1) 1   CLYDE   (1) 1
  Findlay (16)   Wright (19)

RANGERS: Brown; Young, Shaw; McColl, Woodburn, Cox; Waddell, Gillick, Thornton, Findlay, Duncanson

CLYDE: Gullan; Gibson, Deans; Dunn, McCormack, Campbell; Davies, Wright, Johnston, McPhail, Ackerman

Attendance: 45,000

September 18th:
HIBERNIAN 0   RANGERS 0

HIBERNIAN: Kerr; Howie, Shaw; Buchanan, Aird, Kean; Smith, Combe, Linwood, Turnbull, Reilly

RANGERS: Brown; Lindsay, Shaw; McColl, Young, Cox; Waddell, Gillick, Thornton, Findlay, Caskie

Attendance: 47,000

September 25th:
CELTIC   (2) 3   RANGERS   (1) 1
  J. Gallacher (39),   Findlay (10)
  W. Gallacher (44),
  Weir (70)

CELTIC: Miller; Milne, Mallan; Evans, Boden, McAuley; Weir, W. Gallacher, J. Gallacher, Tully, Paton

RANGERS: Brown; Lindsay, Shaw; McColl, Young, Cox; Waddell, Findlay, Thornton, Duncanson, Gillick

Attendance: 65,000

October 2nd:
CLYDE (1) 1   RANGERS (2) 3
  Davies (44)   Waddell 3 (2 pen, 17,
                            88 pen)

CLYDE: Gullan; Gibson, Deans; Dunn, McCormack, Campbell; Davies, Wright, Ackerman, Fitzsimmons, Galletly

RANGERS: Brown; Young, Shaw; Cox, Woodburn, Rae; Waddell, Thornton, Williamson, Marshall, Duncanson

Attendance: 27,000

October 9th:
RANGERS (0) 1   HIBERNIAN (0) 0
  Thornton (68)

RANGERS: Brown; Young, Shaw; Cox, Woodburn, Rae; Waddell, Thornton, Williamson, Marshall, Duncanson

HIBERNIAN: Kerr; Howie, Shaw; Buchanan, Aird, Kean; Smith, Combe, Linwood, Cuthbertson, Reilly

Attendance: 76,466

October 16th:
RANGERS (1) 2   CELTIC (0) 1
  Williamson (39),   McPhail (49 pen)
  Waddell (72)

RANGERS: Brown; Young, Shaw; Cox, Woodburn, Rae; Waddell, Thornton, Williamson, Marshall, Duncanson

CELTIC: Miller; Milne, Mallan; Evans, Boden, McAuley; Weir, McPhail, J. Gallacher, Tully, Paton

Attendance: 105,000

The crowd of 105,000 was the biggest of the season in Britain. Many spectators were not admitted as the gates were closed 10 minutes after the start. Rangers' opening goal in 39 minutes was extremely fortuitous. Williamson's back was to the Celtic goal when 20 yards out he lunged in to block Boden's clearance and fortunately the ball struck his boot, rose in the air, and sailed over Miller's head. Celtic's goal, 4 minutes after half-time, was the cause of much complaint as Rangers appealed to the referee that Woodburn's tackle on Gallacher was fair. McPhail scored from the spot. Celtic questioned the validity of Waddell's score 17 minutes from the end but his anticipation of Thornton's pass was timed to perfection.

League Cup Section Table

	P	W	D	L	F	A	Pts
RANGERS	6	3	2	1	8	6	8
Hibernian	6	3	1	2	12	5	7
Celtic	6	3	0	3	12	13	6
Clyde	6	1	1	4	9	17	3

October 30th: Quarter-Final   At Ibrox
RANGERS (1) 1   ST MIRREN (0) 0
  Thornton (17)

RANGERS: Brown; Young, Shaw; McColl, Woodburn, Cox; Waddell, Thornton, Williamson, Duncanson, Rutherford

ST MIRREN: Kirk; Lapsley, Drinkwater; W. Reid, Telfer, Martin; Burrell, Crowe, Milne, Davie, Lesz

Attendance: 45,000

November 20th: Semi-Final   At Hampden Park
RANGERS (4) 4   DUNDEE (0) 1
  Rutherford (2),   Smith (85 pen)
  McColl (5),
  Duncanson (7), Thornton (25)

RANGERS: Brown; Young, Shaw; McColl, Woodburn, Cox; Waddell, Findlay, Thornton, Duncanson, Rutherford

DUNDEE: Brown; Follon, Ancell; Cowie, Gray, Boyd; Gunn, Gallacher, Pattillo, Smith, McKay

Attendance: 50,996

Dundee lost a goal in 2 minutes and their centre-half at the same time because of injury. They lost 3 more goals, 2 of them before Gray returned, with only 25 minutes gone. Rutherford, McColl, Duncanson and Thornton in 2, 5, 7 and 25 minutes scored for Rangers. In a 20-minute spell in the 2nd half Brown had to pull off brilliant saves from Boyd, Smith and Gray and McKay's shot rebounded from the crossbar before Smith converted a late penalty.

March 12th: Final   At Hampden Park
RANGERS (0) 2   RAITH ROVERS (0) 0
  Gillick (46), Paton (59)

RANGERS: Brown; Young, Shaw; McColl, Woodburn, Cox; Gillick, Paton, Thornton, Duncanson, Rutherford

RAITH ROVERS: Westland; McLure, McNaught; Young, Colville, Leigh; Maule, Collins, Penman, Brady, Joyner

Attendance: 57,450. *Referee*: W. G. Livingstone (Glasgow)

In the 7th minute Brown had to stretch to flick a brilliant Joyner header over the bar and 5 minutes later he palmed a searing 20-yarder from Penman round the post. The only real thrill for Rangers' supporters came in the 33rd minute when Thornton rose, bird-like, to head high over Colville, whipped round him and fired in a shot from 20 yards at rocket pace that brought out a magnificent save from Westland. 4 minutes before half-time Penman had a goal disallowed for offside. After less than a minute of the 2nd half B Division Rovers were a goal behind when Thornton swerved past McNaught, steadied until Gillick had taken over the centre-forward position, and then lobbed the ball right on to the running Gillick's head for a sparkling goal. 13 minutes later Paton cracked home a 14-yarder from a Thornton back header.

SCOTTISH CUP

January 22nd: First Round
RANGERS (4) 6   ELGIN CITY (0) 1
  Thornton 2 (9, 78),   Logie (47)
  Cox (35), Duncanson 2 (40, 42),
  Rutherford (85)

RANGERS: Brown; Young, Shaw; McColl, Woodburn, Cox; Waddell, Paton, Thornton, Duncanson, Rutherford

ELGIN CITY: Munro; Mrowonski, McLaughlin; Mathers, Wyllie, McAulay; Fearn, Stewart, Armstrong, Davies, Logie

Attendance: 29,000

February 5th: Second Round
MOTHERWELL (0) 0   RANGERS (0) 3
                      Young (51 pen),
                      Paton (71),
                      Thornton (74)

MOTHERWELL: John tone; Kilmarnock, Shaw; Russell, Paton, Redpath; Goodall, Watson, Mathie, McCall, Aitkenhead

RANGERS: Brown; Young, Shaw; McColl, Woodburn, Cox; Waddell, Paton, Thornton, Duncanson, Rutherford

Attendance: 31,000

March 5th: Fourth Round
RANGERS (3) 4   PARTICK THISTLE (0) 0
  Duncanson (14)
  Thornton 2 (20, 44),
  Paton (71)

RANGERS: Brown; Young, Shaw; McColl, Woodburn, Cox; Waddell, Paton, Thornton, Duncanson, Rutherford

PARTICK THISTLE: Ledgerwood; McGowan, Gibb; Davidson, Forsyth, Hewitt; McKenzie, McCallum, O'Donnell, McCreadie, Walker

Attendance: 65,000

March 26th: Semi-Final   At Hampden Park
RANGERS (2) 3   EAST FIFE (0) 0
  Thornton 3 (5½, 33, 46)

RANGERS: Brown; Young, Shaw; McColl, Woodburn, Cox; Waddell, Paton, Thornton, Duncanson, Rutherford

EAST FIFE: Niven; Laird, Stewart; Philp, Finlay, Aitken; Black, Fleming, Morris, Brown, Duncan

Attendance: 104,958

East Fife had no answer to the tactics of Waddell and Thornton. Thornton scored all 3 goals from practically the same position. In 5½ minutes he took up position near the far post as Waddell prepared to centre, and though Duncanson glanced the cross when it came, Thornton was not closely marked when he made his brilliant header. In 33 minutes East Fife lost a 2nd goal in almost identical fashion – Paton this time having made the cross. A minute after half-time Thornton again got his forehead to Waddell's cross and again there was no one there to jump with him. Yet for all East Fife's slackness in marking, these were extraordinarily good goals. Late in the game Thornton thundered a shot from 18 yards against the crossbar.

April 23rd: Final   At Hampden Park
RANGERS (2) 4   CLYDE (0) 1
  Young 2 pens (40, 54)   Galletly (48)
  Williamson (43),
  Duncanson (84)

RANGERS: Brown; Young, Shaw; McColl, Woodburn, Cox; Waddell, Duncanson, Thornton, Williamson, Rutherford

CLYDE: Gullan; Gibson, Mennie; Campbell, Milligan, Long; Davies, Wright, Linwood, Galletly, Bootland

Attendance: 120,162

This Cup Final will be remembered for penalties – those that were awarded and those that were not. Midway through the first half a flagrant offence by McColl in holding Galletly, when the inside-forward was about to shoot, was ignored by the referee. Rangers, without touching their best form at any stage in the match, always looked like the side more likely to score. Thornton was mastered by the immature Milligan whose 2 mistakes in conceding the penalty kicks went a long way to costing his side the match. Sandwiched between Young's penalties, Waddell swung over a cross and Williamson catapulted through the air to crash a header home. Waddell was the best forward of the ten.

'Tiger' Shaw, a great captain for Rangers in the immediate post-war period.

APPEARANCES

	League	League Cup	Scottish Cup	Glasgow Cup	Charity Cup
Brown	30	9	5	2	1
Young	28	9	5	2	1
Shaw	27	9	5	1	1
McColl	30	6	5	1	1
Woodburn	30	7	5	2	1
Cox	28	9	5	2	1
Waddell	20	8	5	1	1
Findlay	12	4	-	1	-
Thornton	29	9	5	2	1
Duncanson	24	8	5	2	1
Caskie	1	1	-	1	-
Rutherford	27	3	5	1	1
Gillick	8	4	-	-	-
Lindsay	4	2	-	1	-
Frame	1	-	-	-	-
Rae	2	3	-	-	-
Marshall	2	3	1	-	-
Williamson	6	4	1	1	1
Paton	19	1	4	-	-
Walmsley	1	-	-	-	-
Little	-	-	-	1	-

GOALSCORERS

League: Thornton 23, Duncanson 10, Paton 9, Findlay 4, Gillick 4, Waddell 3, Young 3 (all pens), Williamson 2, Rutherford 2, Cox 2, Marshall 1

League Cup: Waddell 4 (2 pens), Thornton 3, Findlay 2, Williamson 1, Rutherford 1, McColl 1, Duncanson 1, Gillick 1, Paton 1

Scottish Cup: Thornton 8, Duncanson 4, Young 3 (all pens), Paton 2, Cox 1, Rutherford 1, Williamson 1

Glasgow Cup: Thornton 2, Findlay 1

Willie Thornton, Rangers centre-forward, meets Monty before the 1948 Scotland v England match at Hampden Park.

Season 1949–50

The League title was again won, this time by a point from Hibernian. A crowd of 101,000 watched the penultimate League match between the clubs at Ibrox which ended goalless, and the Championship was clinched in the last match against Third Lanark at Cathkin Park. Rangers led 2-0 after 20 minutes but Thirds fought back to level, their outside-right Henderson missed a penalty, but Rangers held on for the crucial point in a nailbiting finish. The only other League match lost was away to Motherwell almost 5 months previously.

Brown, Young, Cox and McColl played in all the matches. Shaw and Woodburn missed only one. 13 forwards were used during the season and Thornton and Williamson finished joint top scorer with 11 goals.

The Scottish Cup was won for the 3rd successive season. Raith Rovers were overcome in the Quarter-Final after two replays, relegation-bound Queen of the South after a replayed Semi-Final, and East Fife were beaten in the Final, thanks mainly to a vintage performance by Thornton. Williamson played in every round of the Cup except the Final. This victory was sweet revenge for the League Cup Semi-Final defeat in extra time at the hands of the Fife team. Cowdenbeath created a major shock in the Quarter-Final of the competition by winning at Ibrox. However, a goal from Cox in extra time in the second leg saw Rangers through.

League: Champions
League Cup: Semi-Finalists
Scottish Cup: Winners

SCOTTISH LEAGUE DIVISION A

September 10th:
RANGERS (2) 2   PARTICK THISTLE (0) 0
    Waddell (22), Findlay (41)

RANGERS: Brown; Young, Shaw; McColl, Woodburn, Cox; Waddell, Findlay, Williamson, Duncanson, Hubbard

PARTICK THISTLE: Ledgerwood; McGowan, Gibb; Davidson, Forsyth, Hewitt; McKenzie, Howitt, Kinnell, Sharp, Walker

Attendance: 60,000

September 24th:
RANGERS (2) 4   CELTIC (0) 0
    Rutherford (6),
    Findlay (43),
    Waddell (85 pen), Williamson (88)

RANGERS: Brown; Young, Shaw; McColl, Woodburn, Rae; Waddell, Findlay, Williamson, Cox, Rutherford

CELTIC: Miller; McGuire, Milne; Evans, Boden, Baillie; Collins, McPhail, Haughney, Taylor, Rennett

Attendance: 64,000

The absence in Rangers' team of Thornton and Duncanson, and of McAuley and Tully from Celtic, reduced the skill element.

October 1st: Scotland beat Ireland 8-2 in Belfast. Young, Cox, Woodburn and Waddell were in the side. Waddell scored two goals, one from the penalty spot.

October 15th:
FALKIRK (0) 0   RANGERS (1) 2
                            Williamson (6),
                            Rutherford (74)

29

FALKIRK: Nicol; Whyte, McPhee; Kinloch, Henderson, Whitelaw; Brown, Fiddes, Inglis, Reid, McCue

RANGERS: Brown; Young, Shaw; McColl, Woodburn, Cox; Rutherford, Findlay, Williamson, Paton, Hubbard

Attendance: 20,000

October 19th: Young, Woodburn and Waddell were in the Scottish League team which beat the League of Ireland 1-0 in Dublin.

October 22nd:
RANGERS   (1) 1   HEARTS   (0) 0
  Findlay (2)

RANGERS: Brown; Young, Shaw; McColl, Woodburn, Cox; Rutherford, Findlay, Thornton, Williamson, Duncanson

HEARTS: Brown; Parker, McKenzie; Cox, Dougan, Laing; Sloan, Conn, Bauld, Wardhaugh, Flavell

Attendance: 50,000

October 29th:
ABERDEEN   (0) 1   RANGERS   (2) 3
  Hamilton (81)   McKenna o.g. (12),
                            Thornton (44),
                            Rutherford (60)

ABERDEEN: Curran; Emery; McKenna; Anderson, Waddell, Harris; Rice, Hamilton, Kelly, Yorston, Hather

RANGERS: Brown; Young, Shaw; McColl, Woodburn, Cox; Gillick, Findlay, Thornton, Williamson, Rutherford

Attendance: 38,000

League Positions

	P	W	D	L	F	A	Pts
1 St Mirren	8	4	3	1	21	13	11
2 RANGERS	5	5	0	0	12	1	10
3 Dundee	7	4	2	1	18	10	10
4 Celtic	8	4	2	2	15	16	10
5 Hibernian	6	4	1	1	16	7	9

November 5th:
HIBERNIAN   (0) 1   RANGERS   (0) 0
  Turnbull (57)

HIBERNIAN: Younger; Govan, Cairns; Combe, Paterson, Buchanan; Smith, Johnstone, Reilly, Turnbull, Ormond

RANGERS: Brown; Young, Shaw; McColl, Woodburn, Cox; Rutherford, Findlay, Thornton, Williamson, Rae

Attendance: 51,500

Rangers lost their 100% record. With a makeshift attack including half-back Rae on the left-wing they often looked dangerous in the first half. 12 minutes after the interval Reilly received the ball 12 yards out and to the right of the right-hand post. He dodged Woodburn and cut the ball inward to Turnbull who hooked the ball home as Brown hit the grass in a desperate dive. After this, only sheer determination and traditional fighting spirit brought the by now insipid Ibrox attack to some kind of life.

November 12th:
RANGERS   (0) 1   ST MIRREN   (0) 0
  Johnson (85)

RANGERS: Brown; Young, Shaw; McColl, Woodburn, Cox; Gillick, Findlay, Thornton, Johnson, Rutherford

ST MIRREN: Miller; Lapsley, Martin; Drinkwater, Telfer, Reid; Burrell, Blyth, Crowe, Davie, Milne

Attendance: 45,000

November 19th:
RAITH ROVERS   (0) 1   RANGERS   (1) 3
  Maule (87)   Williamson 2 (41, 90),
                           Thornton (72)

RAITH ROVERS: McGregor; Farrell, McNaught; Till, Woodcock, Colville; Smith, Maule, Penman, McLaughlin, Joyner

RANGERS: Brown; Young, Shaw; McColl, Woodburn, Cox; Rutherford, Thornton, Williamson, Johnson, Paton

Attendance: 24,800

November 26th:
RANGERS   (1) 2   STIRLING ALBION   (1) 1
  Thornton (27),   Dick (26)
  Williamson (61)

RANGERS: Brown; Young, Shaw; McColl, Woodburn, Cox; Rutherford, Thornton, Williamson, Johnson, Duncanson

STIRLING ALB: Gerhard; Muir, McKeown; Bain, Whiteford, Wilson; Dick, Keith, Jones, Martin, Kinnear

Attendance: 45,000

December 5th:
RANGERS   (2) 5   CLYDE   (3) 4
  Johnson (10),   Linwood 2 (8, 37),
  Thornton 2 (34, 56),   Deakin 2 (21, 62)
  Cox 2 (75, 80)

RANGERS: Brown; Young, Shaw; Rae, Woodburn, Cox; McCulloch, McColl, Thornton, Johnson, Rutherford

CLYDE: Hewkins; Gibson, S. Dunn; Campbell, Milligan, Long; Ackerman, Galletly, Linwood, Deakin, Barclay

Attendance: 25,000

December 10th:
MOTHERWELL (3) 4   RANGERS (0) 0
  Kelly 2 (27, 42),
  McCall (32), Watson (64)

MOTHERWELL: Hamilton; Kilmarnock, Higgins; McLeod, Paton, Redpath; McCall, Watson, Kelly, Bremner, Aitkenhead

RANGERS: Brown; Young, Shaw; Rae, Woodburn, Cox; McCulloch, McColl, Thornton, Johnson, Rutherford

Attendance: 28,000

December 17th:
RANGERS (0) 1   QUEEN OF THE
  Thornton (67)   SOUTH (0) 0

RANGERS: Brown; Young, Shaw; McColl, Woodburn, Cox; McCulloch, Duncanson, Thornton, Johnson, Rutherford

QUEEN OF THE SOUTH: Henderson; W. Brown, Sharp; McBain, Waldie, Hamilton; Wootton, McKinnon, J. Brown, Neilson, Johnstone

Attendance: 15,000

December 24th:
PARTICK THISTLE (0) 1 RANGERS (1) 3
  Sharp (46)   Johnson 2 (17, 64),
         Thornton (73)

PARTICK THISTLE: Ledgerwood; McGowan, Gibb; Davidson, Kinnell, Hewitt; Brown, Howitt, Stott, Sharp, Walker

RANGERS: Brown; Young, Shaw; McColl, Woodburn, Cox; Rutherford, Findlay, Thornton, Johnson, Duncanson

Attendance: 35,000

League Positions

	P	W	D	L	F	A	Pts
1 Hibernian	14	12	1	1	40	14	25
2 RANGERS	13	11	0	2	27	13	22
3 Hearts	15	10	1	4	43	18	21
4 Dundee	15	8	4	3	30	17	20
5 Celtic	16	8	4	4	28	26	20

December 31st:
RANGERS (1) 2   DUNDEE (2) 2
  Thornton (16),   Toner (23),
  Findlay (57)   Stewart (31)

RANGERS: Brown; Young, Shaw; McColl, Woodburn, Cox; McCulloch, Findlay, Thornton, Johnson, Duncanson

DUNDEE: Lynch; Mathie, Ancell; Cowie, Pattillo, Boyd; Gunn, Toner, Stewart, Gerrie, Hill

Attendance: 35,000

January 2nd:
CELTIC (1) 1   RANGERS (0) 1
  Weir (36)   McCulloch (82)

CELTIC: Bonnar; Boden, Mallan; Evans, McGrory, Baillie; Collins, Haughney, Weir, Taylor, Tully

RANGERS: Brown; Young, Shaw; McColl, Woodburn, Cox; McCulloch, Findlay, Thornton, Johnson, Marshall

Attendance: 65,000

8 minutes from time Mallan astonishingly lost his balance, completely missed the ball and McCulloch, far and away Rangers' best forward, accepted the Ne'erday gift and equalised. The forward honours could easily be apportioned – to McCulloch for his quick acceleration and accurate crossing, to Weir for his enthusiastic leadership of the Celtic attack, and to Tully for many titbits of ball manipulation. Celtic's goal in 36 minutes was the result of a defensive mistake by Woodburn who should have intercepted Taylor's through pass to Weir.

January 3rd:
RANGERS (0) 3   THIRD LANARK (0) 1
  Johnson (60),   Orr (48)
  Thornton 2 (n.a.)

RANGERS: Brown; Young, Shaw; McColl, Woodburn, Cox; McCulloch, Thornton, Williamson, Johnson, McIntyre

THIRD LANARK: McKellar; Balunas, Crawford; Mooney, Barclay, Christie; Henderson, Mason, Harrower, Orr, Dalziel

Attendance: 30,000

January 7th:
EAST FIFE (0) 0   RANGERS (1) 2
         Williamson (22),
         Rutherford (72)

EAST FIFE: Niven; Laird, Stewart; Philp, Finlay, Aitken; Gardiner, Bonthrone, Morris, J. Brown, Duncan

RANGERS: Brown; Young, Shaw; McColl, Woodburn, Cox; McCulloch, Findlay, Williamson, Johnson, Rutherford

Attendance: 18,674

January 14th:
RANGERS (2) 3   FALKIRK (0) 0
  Young (12 pen),
  Rutherford (20),
  Williamson (47)

RANGERS: Brown; Young, Shaw; McColl, Woodburn, Cox; McCulloch, Findlay, Williamson, Johnson, Rutherford

FALKIRK: Carrie; Whyte, McPhee; J. Gallacher, Fiddes, McCabe; Inglis, Wright, Plumb, W. Gallacher, McCue

Attendance: 35,000

January 21st:

HEARTS (0) 0	RANGERS (1) 1
	Findlay (43)

HEARTS: Brown; Parker, McKenzie; Cox, Dougan, Laing; Sloan, Conn, Bauld, Wardhaugh, Flavell

RANGERS: Brown; Young, Shaw; McColl, Woodburn, Cox; McCulloch, Findlay, Williamson, Johnson, Duncanson

Attendance: 47,000

February 4th:

RANGERS (2) 2	ABERDEEN (1) 2
Young 2 pens (34, 45)	Hamilton (5),
	Yorston (74)

RANGERS: Brown; Young, Shaw; McColl, Woodburn, Cox; McCulloch, Findlay, Williamson, Johnson, Paton

ABERDEEN: Watson; Emery, McKenna; Anderson, McKenzie, Harris; Stenhouse, Yorston, Hamilton, Baird, Pearson

Emery missed a penalty

Attendance: 50,000

February 18th:

ST MIRREN (1) 1	RANGERS (1) 2
Lapsley (26 pen)	Rutherford (33),
	Waddell (76)

ST MIRREN: Kirk; Lapsley, Martin; Reid, Drinkwater, Johnston; Burrell, Blyth, Milne, Davie, Lesz

RANGERS: Brown; Young, Lindsay; McColl, Woodburn, Cox; Waddell, Paton, Williamson, Johnson, Rutherford

Attendance: 40,000

February 25th:

RANGERS (1) 2	RAITH ROVERS (0) 0
Williamson (12),	
Waddell (64)	

RANGERS: Brown; Young, Shaw; McColl, Woodburn, Cox; Waddell, Paton, Williamson, Johnson, Rutherford

RAITH ROVERS: Johnstone; McSpadyen, McNaught; Till, Colville, Leigh; Young, Maule, McLaughlin, Collins, Penman

Attendance: 35,000

League Positions

	P	W	D	L	F	A	Pts
1 Hibernian	22	16	2	4	58	21	34
2 Dundee	24	14	5	5	39	20	33
3 Aberdeen	25	14	4	7	55	41	32
4 Hearts	23	12	4	7	53	32	28
5 RANGERS	22	11	4	7	44	28	26

March 4th:

STIRLING ALBION (0) 0	RANGERS (1) 2
	Williamson (2),
	Paton (85)

STIRLING ALBION: Little; Muir, McKeown; Bain, Rodgers, Guy; Walker, Martin, Inglis, Dick, Henderson

RANGERS: Brown; Young, Shaw; McColl, Woodburn, Cox; Waddell, Paton, Williamson, Johnson, Duncanson

Attendance: 25,000

March 18th:

RANGERS (0) 2	MOTHERWELL (0) 0
Findlay (48),	
Rutherford (63)	

RANGERS: Brown; Young, Shaw; McColl, Woodburn, Cox; Rutherford, Findlay, Williamson, Johnson, McIntyre

MOTHERWELL: Hamilton; Kilmarnock, Shaw; McLeod, Paton, Telford; Watters, Watson, Kelly, Bremner, Aitkenhead

Attendance: 38,000

March 25th:

QUEEN OF THE SOUTH (0) 1	RANGERS (2) 2
Johnstone (75 pen)	Thornton (9),
	Williamson (25)

QUEEN OF THE SOUTH: Henderson; Sharp, James; McBain, Waldie, Hamilton; Wootton, J. Brown, Houliston, McAvoy, Johnstone

RANGERS: Brown; Young, Shaw; McColl, Woodburn, Cox; Rutherford, Findlay, Thornton, Williamson, Duncanson

Attendance: 18,000

April 8th:

RANGERS (1) 2	EAST FIFE (1) 2
Cox (13), Findlay (74)	Morris (14),
	Bonthrone (80)

RANGERS: Brown; Lindsay, Shaw; McColl, Young, Cox; Waddell, Findlay, Thornton, Johnson, Rutherford

EAST FIFE: Niven; Laird, Stewart; Philp, Finlay, Brown; Black, Fleming, Morris, Bonthrone, Duncan

Attendance: 35,000

April 10th:
CLYDE   (1) 1   RANGERS   (1) 2
   Barclay (11)   Rae (10), Cox (80)
CLYDE: Hewkins; Lindsay, S. Dunn; J. Dunn,
Milligan, Haddock; Galletly, Ackerman, Linwood,
Davies, Barclay

RANGERS: Brown; Young, Shaw; McColl,
Woodburn, Cox; Waddell, Findlay, Thornton,
Duncanson, Rae

Attendance: 25,000

April 15th: Scotland were beaten 1-0 by England at Hampden Park. Young, Cox, McColl, Woodburn and Waddell were in the team.

April 17th:
DUNDEE   (0) 0   RANGERS   (0) 1
                                    Duncanson (60)
DUNDEE: Brown; Follon, Cowan; Gallacher, Boyd,
Rattray; Gunn, Pattillo, Gerrie, Ewen, Hill

RANGERS: Brown; Young, Shaw; McColl,
Woodburn, Cox; Rutherford, Findlay, Thornton,
Duncanson, Rae

Attendance: 32,000

April 26th: Young and Cox were in the Scotland team which beat Switzerland 3-1 at Hampden Park.

April 29th:
RANGERS   0   HIBERNIAN   0

RANGERS: Brown; Young, Shaw; McColl,
Woodburn, Cox; Rutherford, Findlay, Thornton,
Duncanson, Rae

HIBERNIAN: Younger; Govan, Cairns; Howie,
Paterson, Combe; Smith, Johnstone, Reilly, Turnbull,
Ormond

Attendance: 101,000

The defenders took the glory in this match. The elegant Johnny Paterson was a master tactician in defence and emerged as the dominant figure afield. Govan and Cairns were heroic and Willie Woodburn, with head and foot, repeatedly threw back the surging men in green and white by his judicious timing and anticipation.

May 1st:
THIRD LANARK   (1) 2   RANGERS   (2) 2
   Mason (37),   Williamson (15),
   Cuthbertson (47)   Paton (20)
THIRD LANARK: Goram; Balunas, Harrower; Orr,
Christie, Mooney; Henderson, Mason, Cuthbertson,
Dick, Staroscik

RANGERS: Brown; Young, Shaw; McColl,
Woodburn, Cox; Rutherford, Paton, Thornton,
Williamson, Johnson

Henderson of Thirds missed a penalty with the score 1-2.

Attendance: 32,800

Scottish League Division A

	P	W	D	L	F	A	Pts
1 RANGERS	30	22	6	2	58	26	50
2 Hibernian	30	22	5	3	86	34	49
3 Hearts	30	20	3	7	86	40	43
4 East Fife	30	15	7	8	58	43	37
5 Celtic	30	14	7	9	51	50	35
6 Dundee	30	12	7	11	49	46	31
7 Partick Thistle	30	13	3	14	55	45	29
8 Aberdeen	30	11	4	15	48	56	26
9 Raith Rovers	30	9	8	13	45	54	26
10 Motherwell	30	10	5	15	53	58	25
11 St Mirren	30	8	9	13	42	49	25
12 Third Lanark	30	11	3	16	44	62	25
13 Clyde	30	10	4	16	56	73	24
14 Falkirk	30	7	10	13	48	72	24
15 Queen of South	30	5	6	19	31	63	16
16 Stirling Albion	30	6	3	21	38	77	15

May 16th: Young, Cox, Woodburn, McColl and Waddell were named in the Scotland party to tour North America.

May 25th: Scotland drew 2-2 away to Portugal. Young, Cox and Woodburn were in the team.

May 27th: Scotland beat France 1-0 in Paris. Young, Cox, McColl and Woodburn were in the team.

LEAGUE CUP

August 13th:
CELTIC   (2) 3   RANGERS   (1) 2
   McPhail 2 (22, 30),   Waddell (12 pen),
   Haughney (70)   Thornton (65)
CELTIC: Miller; McGuire, Baillie; Evans, Boden,
McAuley; Collins, McPhail, Johnston, Tully, Haughney

RANGERS: Brown; Young, Shaw; McColl,
Woodburn, Cox; Waddell, Findlay, Thornton,
Duncanson, Rutherford

Attendance: 70,000

This was McAuley's match. He sold more dummies to Findlay than are usually bought in an entire season, and he prompted and spurred Tully, a collaborator in Rangers' defeat. Both Collins and Haughney made their first appearance in senior football.

August 17th:
RANGERS   (1) 5   ST MIRREN   (0) 1
   Waddell 2 (37 pen, 52),   Lesz (60)
   Rutherford (47),
   Findlay (63), Thornton (80)

RANGERS: Brown; Young, Shaw; McColl, Woodburn, Cox; Waddell, Findlay, Thornton, Duncanson, Rutherford

ST MIRREN: Miller; Lapsley, Martin; Drinkwater, Telfer, Reid; Burrell, Stewart, Milne, Deakin, Lesz

August 20th:

RANGERS (2) 4	ABERDEEN (2) 2
Findlay 2 (10, 61),	Harris (3), Emery (44)
Duncanson 2 (23, 60)	

RANGERS: Brown; Young, Shaw; McColl, Woodburn, Cox; Waddell, Findlay, Thornton, Duncanson, Rutherford

ABERDEEN: Curran; Emery, McKenna; Anderson, McKenzie, Waddell; Rice, Yorston, Kelly, Harris, Pearson

Attendance: 48,000

August 27th:

RANGERS (1) 2	CELTIC (0) 0
Findlay (40), Waddell (82)	

RANGERS: Brown; Young, Shaw; Cox, Woodburn, Rae; Waddell, Findlay, Thornton, Duncanson, Rutherford

CELTIC: Miller; Mallan, Baillie; Evans, Boden, McAuley; Collins, McPhail, Johnston, Tully, Haughney

Attendance: 95,000. Young missed a penalty

In 40 minutes Findlay scored for Rangers. 10 minutes after half-time Rangers were awarded a penalty-kick after Waddell had been tackled by Boden but Young hit the crossbar from the spot. Waddell, leading Rangers' attack in place of Thornton – who had broken a bone in his foot after a tackle by Boden – gave Miller no chance with a left-foot grounder in the 82nd minute after Boden had misheaded a clearance by Cox.

August 30th:

ST MIRREN (0) 1	RANGERS (0) 1
Lesz (84)	Duncanson (51)

ST MIRREN: Miller; Lapsley, Martin; Crowe, Telfer, Reid; Burrell, Stewart, Milne, Deakin, Lesz

RANGERS: Brown; Young, Shaw; McColl, Woodburn, Cox; Waddell, Findlay, Williamson, Duncanson, Rutherford

Attendance: 40,000

September 3rd:

ABERDEEN (0) 1	RANGERS (0) 1
Emery (55)	Findlay (75)

ABERDEEN: Curran; Emery, McKenna; Anderson, Roy, Harris; Kiddie, Yorston, Kelly, Smith, Pearson

RANGERS: Brown; Young, Shaw; McColl, Woodburn, Cox; Waddell, Findlay, Williamson, Gillick, Duncanson

League Cup Section Table

	P	W	D	L	F	A	Pts
RANGERS	6	3	2	1	15	8	8
Celtic	6	3	0	3	13	13	6
Aberdeen	6	2	1	3	12	14	5
St Mirren	6	2	1	3	7	12	5

September 17th: Quarter-Final First Leg

RANGERS (1) 2	COWDENBEATH (1) 3
Williamson (23),	Dick (31),
Marshall (57)	Armstrong 2 (46, 67)

RANGERS: Brown; Young, Shaw; McColl, Woodburn, Cox; Waddell, Findlay, Williamson, Marshall, Rutherford

COWDENBEATH: Moodie; Hamilton, Cameron; Menzies, Holland, Durie; McGurn, Mackie, Armstrong, Reid, Dick

Attendance: 46,670

September 21st: Quarter-Final Second Leg

COWDENBEATH (1) 1	RANGERS (2) 3
Menzies (6)	Cox 2 (48, 102),
	Rutherford (89½)
After Extra Time	

COWDENBEATH: Moodie; Hamilton, Cameron; Menzies, Holland, Durie; McGurn, Mackie, Armstrong, Reid, Dick

RANGERS: Brown; Young, Shaw; McColl, Woodburn, Rae; Waddell, Findlay, Williamson, Cox, Rutherford

Attendance: 25,586 (a record)

(Rangers won 5-4 on aggregate)

October 8th: Semi-Final   At Hampden Park

EAST FIFE (1) 2	RANGERS (0) 1
Brown (19), Fleming (111)	Marshall (84)

EAST FIFE: McGarritty; Laird, Stewart; Philp, Finlay, Aitken; Black, Fleming, Morris, Brown, Duncan

RANGERS: Brown; Young, Shaw; McColl, Woodburn, Cox; Waddell, Findlay, Williamson, Marshall, Rutherford

Attendance: 74,000

East Fife beat Rangers for the first time in their history, and while every member of the team played a distinguished part it was the magnificent display of Stewart against Waddell which settled the issue. In the first 30 minutes of the match East Fife almost ran Rangers off their feet. In the second half Rangers were the fitter side, physically at least, and deserved the equalising goal scored by Marshall in 84 minutes. It was East Fife who mustered the vitality in extra time.

SCOTTISH CUP

January 28th: First Round

MOTHERWELL (0) 2   RANGERS (3) 4
Aitkenhead (80 pen),   Williamson (8),
Kelly (84)   Paton (29),
    McCulloch (32),
    Findlay (65)

MOTHERWELL: Hamilton; Kilmarnock, Higgins; McLeod, Paton, Redpath; McCall, Watson, Kelly, Bremner, Aitkenhead

RANGERS: Brown; Young, Shaw; McColl, Woodburn, Cox; McCulloch, Findlay, Williamson, Johnson, Paton

Attendance: 32,000

February 11th: Second Round

RANGERS (3) 8   COWDENBEATH (0) 0
McCulloch 2 (24, 73),
Williamson 2 (38, 63), Paton (40),
Johnson 2 (54, 67), Rutherford (86)

RANGERS: Brown; Young, Lindsay; McColl, Woodburn, Cox; McCulloch, Paton, Williamson, Johnson, Rutherford

COWDENBEATH: Moodie; Hamilton, Cameron; Menzies, Holland, Durie; McGurn, Ramsay, Armstrong, Dempsey, Dick

Attendance: 24,000

March 11th: Fourth Round

RANGERS (1) 1   RAITH ROVERS (0) 1
Findlay (30)   Penman (66)

RANGERS: Brown; Young, Shaw; McColl, Woodburn, Cox; Waddell, Thornton, Williamson, Findlay, Paton

RAITH ROVERS: Johnstone; McSpadyen, Young; Till, Colville, Leigh; Maule, Crawford, Penman, McLaughlin, Stirling

Attendance: 43,000

March 15th: Fourth Round Replay

RAITH ROVERS (0) 1   RANGERS (1) 1
McLaughlin (73)   Williamson (27)
After Extra Time

RAITH ROVERS: Johnstone; McSpadyen, McLure; Till, Colville, Young; Maule, Crawford, Penman, McLaughlin, Urquhart

RANGERS: Brown; Young, Shaw; McColl, Woodburn, Cox; Waddell, Findlay, Thornton, Williamson, Duncanson

Attendance: 28,500 (a record)

March 27th: Fourth Round Second Replay

RANGERS (2) 2   RAITH ROVERS (0) 0
Findlay (25), Cox (34)

RANGERS: Brown; Young, Shaw; McColl, Woodburn, Cox; Rutherford, Findlay, Thornton, Williamson, Rae

RAITH ROVERS: Johnstone; McSpadyen, McLure; Till, Colville, Young; Maule, McLaughlin, Collins, Urquhart, Penman

Attendance: 63,000

April 1st: Semi-Final   At Hampden Park

QUEEN OF THE   RANGERS (0) 1
SOUTH (1) 1   Rutherford (59)
J. Brown (43)

QUEEN OF THE SOUTH: Henderson; Sharp, James; McBain, Waldie, Hamilton; Wootton, Patterson, Houliston, J. Brown, Johnstone

RANGERS: Brown; Young, Shaw; McColl, Woodburn, Cox; Waddell, Findlay, Thornton, Williamson, Rutherford

Attendance: 52,924

Although Queens were doomed to relegation, there was no apparent difference in class though Rangers fielded 7 full internationalists. Queens matched them in every department and thoroughly earned their draw.

April 5th: Semi-Final Replay   At Hampden Park

RANGERS (0) 3   QUEEN OF THE
Williamson (47),   SOUTH (0) 0
Young (72 pen), Findlay (76)

RANGERS: Brown; Young, Shaw; McColl, Woodburn, Cox; Rutherford, Thornton, Williamson, Findlay, Rae

QUEEN OF THE SOUTH: Henderson; Sharp, James; McBain, Waldie, Hamilton; Wootton, Patterson, Houliston, J. Brown, Johnstone

Attendance: 58,975

In the 72nd minute with the score 1-0 for Rangers, Rae in the inside-left position was tackled by McBain inside the penalty area. Queen of the South's captain emerged with the ball as Rae fell. Suddenly the referee awarded a penalty kick. Young came up and scored and the match as a contest was over. 4 minutes later Findlay scored an easy 3rd.

April 22nd: Final   At Hampden Park

RANGERS (1) 3   EAST FIFE (0) 0
Findlay (30 secs),
Thornton 2 (63, 65)

RANGERS: Brown; Young, Shaw; McColl, Woodburn, Cox; Rutherford, Findlay, Thornton, Duncanson, Rae

EAST FIFE: Easson; Laird, Stewart; Philp, Finlay, Aitken; Black, Fleming, Morris, Brown, Duncan

Attendance: 120,015 *Referee*: J. A. Mowat (Burnside)

Thornton, the Ibrox leader, gave a glorious display. Findlay dived flat to head the first goal in only 30 seconds. Shortly after Duncanson had almost decapitated Laird with a thunderbolt, Thornton hit the Fifers with 2 great goals inside 2 minutes. Rutherford tore past Stewart and lifted a high searching ball into the middle. Thornton raced towards the right corner flag, became airborne and glided a beautiful header into the far side of the net. Then Rutherford again trailed the ball upfield, Findlay darted ahead and Rutherford poked the ball towards him near the bye-line. A flick into the middle and there was Thornton beating Finlay to the jump to make it 3.

APPEARANCES

	League	League Cup	Scottish Cup	Glasgow Cup	Charity Cup	Friendlies
Brown	30	9	8	2	3	3
Young	30	9	8	–	3	3
Shaw	29	9	7	2	2	2
McColl	30	9	8	–	3	3
Woodburn	29	9	8	2	3	3
Cox	30	9	8	1	3	3
Waddell	7	9	3	–	3	–
Findlay	20	9	7	–	2	3
Williamson	19	5	7	–	3	–
Duncanson	12	6	2	2	1	2
Hubbard	2	–	–	2	–	1
Rae	7	1	3	–	1	–
Rutherford	22	8	5	1	3	–

	League	League Cup	Scottish Cup	Glasgow Cup	Charity Cup	Friendlies
Paton	7	–	3	1	1	3
Thornton	19	4	6	2	–	3
Gillick	2	1	–	1	2	2
Johnson	20	–	2	–	–	–
McCulloch	10	–	2	–	–	–
Marshall	1	2	–	1	–	–
McIntyre	2	–	–	–	–	–
Lindsay	2	–	1	2	–	1
Little	–	–	–	2	–	–
Forbes	–	–	–	–	–	1

GOALSCORERS

League: Thornton 11, Williamson 11, Finlay 7, Rutherford 7, Johnson 5, Cox 4, Waddell 4 (1 pen), Young 3 (all pens), Paton 2, McCulloch 1, Rae 1, Duncanson 1, Own Goals 1

League Cup: Findlay 5, Waddell 4 (1 pen), Duncanson 3, Cox 2, Marshall 2, Thornton 2, Rutherford 2, Williamson 1

Scottish Cup: Williamson 5, Findlay 5, McCulloch 3, Paton 2, Johnson 2, Rutherford 2, Thornton 2, Young 1 (pen), Cox 1

Glasgow Cup: Gillick 2, Williamson 1, Findlay 1, Rutherford 1, Waddell 1(pen)

Charity Cup: Thornton 4 (1 pen), Duncanson 1, Gillick 1

Friendlies: Findlay 3, Thornton 1

Scottish Cup success for Rangers in 1950. Jock, 'Tiger' Shaw chaired by his happy team mates.

Season 1950–51

This was a season of great disappointment for Rangers. They finished 2nd in the Championship but were a massive 10 points behind Hibernian, and lost almost as many League matches as in the previous 3 seasons combined. Their League form was highly inconsistent, especially away from home – Aberdeen and Partick Thistle were the only teams to win at Ibrox in the competition. Brown and Young were the only ever-presents. Billy Simpson was signed from Linfield for £11,500 and he contributed 11 of the 64 goals scored to finish joint top scorer with Thornton.

Rangers were knocked out of the Scottish Cup by Hibernian, in the Second Round, in front of their own fans. A crowd of 102,342 watched the match.

They failed to qualify from their League Cup Section, suffering home and away defeats to eventual winners Aberdeen. Thornton scored 7 goals in the 6 matches.

League: Runner-up
League Cup: Failed to Qualify
Scottish Cup: Second Round

SCOTTISH LEAGUE DIVISION A

September 9th:
EAST FIFE (0) 0   RANGERS (2) 3
            Thornton(13),
            Findlay (44),
            Waddell (n.a.)

EAST FIFE: Niven; Proudfoot, Stewart; Philip, Weir, Addison; Gardiner, Fleming, Morris, Bonthrone, Duncan
RANGERS: Brown; Young, Shaw; McColl, Woodburn, Cox; Waddell, Findlay, Thornton, Paton, Rutherford
Attendance: 20,000

September 16th:
RANGERS 0   DUNDEE 0

RANGERS: Brown; Young, Shaw; McColl, Woodburn, Rae; Rutherford, Findlay, Thornton, Paton, Duncanson
DUNDEE: Brown; Follon, Cowan; Gallacher, Cowie, Boyd; Gunn, Toner, Williams, Gerrie, Andrews
Young missed a penalty
Attendance: 35,000

September 23rd:
CELTIC (0) 3   RANGERS (0) 2
   D. Weir (60),   Rae (61),
   McPhail (80 pen),   Thornton (74)
   Peacock (85)

CELTIC: Brown; Follon, Milne; Evans, Mallan, Baillie; Collins, D. Weir, McPhail, Peacock, Tully
RANGERS: Brown; Young, Lindsay; McColl, Woodburn, Cox; Rutherford, Findlay, Thornton, Johnson, Rae
Attendance: 53,789

September 30th:
RANGERS (2) 4   AIRDRIE (0) 1
   Thornton 2 (4,62)   McMillan (60)
   Bobby Simpson 2 (9,77)

RANGERS: Brown; Young, Lindsay; McColl, Woodburn, Cox; Waddell, Bobby Simpson, Thornton, Paton, Rutherford
AIRDRIE: Fraser; Cosh, Elliot; Docherty, Kelly, Shankland; Quinn, Welsh, Orr, Picken, McMillan
Attendance: 20,000

October 7th:
PARTICK THISTLE (0) 2   RANGERS (1) 1
   O'Donnell (59),   Thornton (35)
   Walker (69)

PARTICK THISTLE: Ledgerwood; McGowan, Gibb; Davidson, Kinnell, Hewitt; McKenzie, McCallum, O'Donnell, Sharp, Walker
RANGERS: Brown; Young, Lindsay; McColl, Woodburn, Cox; Waddell, Bobby Simpson, Thornton, Paton, Rutherford
Attendance: 33,000

October 14th:

RANGERS (0) 2　　　　　　THIRD LANARK (1) 1
　Cox (69),　　　　　　　　McCall (32)
　Rutherford (75)

RANGERS: Brown; Young, Lindsay; McColl, Woodburn, Cox; Waddell, Paton, Thornton, Johnson, Rutherford

THIRD LANARK: Simpson; Balunas, Harrower; Orr, Samuel, Mooney; Staroscik, Mason, Muir, Dick, McCall

Attendance: 35,000

October 19th: Billy Simpson signed from Linfield for £11,500.

October 21st: Scotland beat Wales 3–1 in Cardiff. Young, McColl and Woodburn were in the side.

October 28th:

RANGERS (0) 1　　　　　　ABERDEEN (1) 2
　Thornton (47)　　　　　　Boyd (12),
　　　　　　　　　　　　　Yorston (84)

RANGERS: Brown; Young, Shaw; McColl, Woodburn, Rae; Waddell, Paton, Billy Simpson, Thornton, Rutherford

ABERDEEN: Martin; Emery, Shaw; Anderson, Young, Glen; Boyd, Yorston, Hamilton, Baird, Hather

Attendance: 45,000

	P	W	D	L	F	A	Pts
1 Dundee	8	5	2	1	12	6	12
2 Hearts	8	5	1	2	17	10	11
3 Morton	8	5	1	2	19	13	11
4 Aberdeen	7	5	0	2	18	14	10
5 Raith Rovers	8	4	1	3	17	15	9
8 RANGERS	7	3	1	3	13	9	7

November 1st: Scotland beat Ireland 6–1 at Hampden Park. Young, McColl and Woodburn were in the team.

November 4th:

RANGERS (1) 1　　　　　　HIBERNIAN (0) 1
　Paterson o.g. (8)　　　　Reilly (51)

RANGERS: Brown; Young, Shaw; McColl, Woodburn, Rae; Waddell, Paton, Williamson, Thornton, Rutherford

HIBERNIAN: Younger; Govan, Ogilvie; Buchanan, Paterson, Combe; Smith, Johnstone, Reilly, Thornton, Ormond

Attendance: 80,000

In 8 minutes Paton's misdirected forward lob to Waddell went straight to Paterson on the 18-yard line. He looked as if he was about to wheel round and clear when suddenly he changed his mind and passed back to his goal.

Unfortunately for him, Younger had run out anticipating a short one and this was not only a long one but one destined for the far corner of the net. In the 19th minute Younger brought off a marvellous save from a Waddell thunderbolt free-kick from 25 yards. 6 minutes after the interval Hibs got a deserved equaliser. Combe slung the ball fiercely into the goal. Reilly beat the defence in the jump and headed the ball into the far corner. 2 minutes later Ormond blazed a 30-yarder that cannoned off the crossbar.

November 8th: Joe Johnson was transferred to Falkirk.

November 11th:

ST MIRREN (0) 0　　　　　RANGERS (0) 2
　　　　　　　　　　　　　Paton (61),
　　　　　　　　　　　　　Thornton (68)

ST MIRREN: Miller; Lapsley, Drinkwater; Reid, Telfer, Johnstone; Burrell, Neilson, Stewart, Davie, Lesz

RANGERS: Brown; Lindsay, Shaw; McColl, Young, Rae; Waddell, Paton, Williamson, Thornton, Rutherford

Attendance: 18,000

November 18th:

RANGERS (2) 4　　　　　　RAITH ROVERS (1) 1
　Williamson 2 (8, 48),　　Young (34)
　Paton (35),
　Young (86 pen)

RANGERS: Brown; Young, Shaw; McColl, Woodburn, Rae; Waddell, Paton, Williamson. Thornton, Rutherford

RAITH ROVERS: Johnstone; McLure, McNaught; McLaughlin, Colville, Leigh; Stockdale, Maule, Young, Collins, Brander

Attendance: 18,000

November 2nd: Willie Gardiner was signed from Bo'ness United and Ian McIntyre joined Airdrie on temporary transfer.

November 25th:

FALKIRK (1) 1　　　　　　RANGERS (0) 1
　J. Gallacher (22)　　　　Thornton (53)

FALKIRK: Barrie; Fiddes, McPhee; W. Gallacher, Henderson, Whitelaw; Morrison, Johnson, J. Gallacher, Wright, Brown

RANGERS: Brown; Young, Shaw; McColl, Woodburn, Rae; Waddell, Paton, Williamson, Thornton, Rutherford

Attendance: 20,000

December 2nd:

CLYDE (2) 2　　　　　　　RANGERS (0) 1
　Linwood (21), Carr (32)　Williamson (67)

CLYDE: Miller; Lindsay, Mennie; Campbell, Somerville, Long; Buchanan, McPhail, Linwood, Carr, Barclay

RANGERS: Brown; Young, Shaw; McColl, Woodburn, Rae; Waddell, Paton, Williamson, Thornton, Rutherford

Attendance: 22,000

December 9th:
RANGERS (1) 2   MORTON (0) 0
  Paton 2 (3, 76)

RANGERS: Brown; Young, Shaw; Little, Woodburn, Rae; Waddell, Paton, Simpson, Thornton, Hubbard

MORTON: Cowan; Mitchell, Whigham; Boyd, Thom, Whyte; Alexander, Gourlay, Mochan, McGarritty, McVinish

Attendance: 35,000

December 13th: Scotland were beaten 1–0 by Austria at Hampden Park. Young and Woodburn were in the team.

December 24th:
RANGERS (2) 5   EAST FIFE (0) 0
  Rae (14),
  Simpson 3 (18, 69, 89),
  Hubbard (78)

RANGERS: Brown; Young, Shaw; McColl, Woodburn, Rae; Waddell, Paton, Simpson, Thornton, Hubbard

EAST FIFE: Easson; Weir, Proudfoot; Philip, Finlay, McLennan; Black, Fleming, Morris, Bonthrone, Duncan

Attendance: 20,000

December 30th:
DUNDEE (1) 2   RANGERS (0) 0
  Gunn (30), Ewen (49)

DUNDEE: Lynch: Follon, Cowan; Irvine, Cowie, Boyd; Gunn, Ewen, Williams, Steel, Christie

RANGERS: Brown; Young, Shaw; McColl, Woodburn, Cox; Waddell, Paton, Simpson, Thornton, Rae

Attendance: 37,000

League Positions

	P	W	D	L	F	A	Pts
1 Dundee	17	10	4	3	27	12	24
2 Aberdeen	16	10	2	4	37	23	22
3 Hibernian	13	10	1	2	36	10	21
4 Celtic	15	8	4	3	33	20	20
5 Hearts	17	8	4	5	34	28	20
7 RANGERS	15	7	3	5	29	16	17

January 1st:
RANGERS (1) 1   CELTIC (0) 0
  Waddell (24)

RANGERS: Brown; Young, Shaw; McColl, Woodburn, Cox; Waddell, Findlay, Simpson, Thornton, Paton

CELTIC: Bonnar; Fallon, Milne; Evans, Mallan, Baillie; Weir, Collins, McPhail, Peacock, Tully

Attendance: 55,000

It was not a game to remember. The conditions were appalling with the centre of the field dotted with puddles of water and the wings hard and greasy. Waddell scored the only goal of the game in the 24th minute.

January 6th:
RANGERS (0) 1   PARTICK THISTLE (1) 3
  Waddell (43)   Crawford (16),
                      Stott (47),
                      McKenzie (88)

RANGERS: Brown; Lindsay, Shaw; Dunlop, Young, Cox; Waddell, Findlay, Simpson, Thornton, Rae

PARTICK THISTLE: Ledgerwood; Brown, Gibb; Thomson, Forsyth, Davidson; McKenzie, Crawford, Stott, Sharp, McCreadie

Attendance: 40,000

January 20th:
RANGERS (1) 2   HEARTS (0) 1
  Thornton (24),   Wardhaugh (48)
  Simpson (69)

RANGERS: Brown; Young, Shaw; Cox, Woodburn, Rae; Waddell, Dunlop, Simpson, Thornton, Hubbard

HEARTS: Watters; Parker, McKenzie; Cox, Dougan, Laing; Sloan, Conn, Bauld, Wardhaugh, Cumming

Attendance: 50,000

February 3rd:
ABERDEEN (1) 2   RANGERS (2) 4
  Pearson (18),   Paton (3),
  Yorston (53)   Thornton 2 (23, 83),
                       Simpson (62)

ABERDEEN: Watson; Emery, Shaw; Anderson, Young, Harris; Delaney, Yorston, Hamilton, Baird, Pearson

RANGERS: Brown; Young, Shaw; Cox, Woodburn, Rae; Waddell, Findlay, Simpson, Thornton, Paton

Attendance: 42,000

February 17th:
RANGERS (0) 1   ST MIRREN (0) 1
  Simpson (53)   Lapsley (81 pen)

RANGERS: Brown; Young, Shaw; Cox, Woodburn, Rae; Waddell, Findlay, Simpson, Thornton, Paton

ST MIRREN: Kirk; Lapsley, Cunningham; Neilson, Telfer, Johnstone; Keirnan, Duncanson, Rennie, W. Reid, Lesz

Attendance: 20,000

February 24th:
RAITH ROVERS   (1) 3   RANGERS   (1) 1
  Penman (22),   Waddell (34)
  Brander (47),
  Colville (85 pen)

RAITH ROVERS: Johnstone; McLure, McNaught; McLaughlin, Colville, Leigh; Maule, Young, Penman, Murray, Brander

RANGERS: Brown; Young, Cox; McColl, Woodburn, Rae; Waddell, Paton, Williamson, Simpson, Rutherford

Attendance: 25,000

League Positions
	P	W	D	L	F	A	Pts
1 Hibernian	21	16	2	3	57	19	34
2 Dundee	23	14	4	5	37	18	32
3 Aberdeen	24	14	4	6	54	39	32
4 Hearts	22	11	4	7	45	32	26
5 RANGERS	21	10	4	7	39	26	24

March 3rd:
RANGERS   (3) 5   FALKIRK   (0) 2
  Simpson (4),   Whitelaw (55),
  Findlay 3 (9, 25, 59),   Wright (66)
  Marshall (86)

RANGERS: Brown; Young, Cox; McColl, Woodburn, Rae; Waddell, Findlay, Simpson, Marshall, Paton

FALKIRK: Scott; Fiddes, McPhee; Young, Henderson, J. Gallacher; Plumb, Wright, Ralston, Johnson, Whitelaw

Attendance: 20,000

March 7th: Billy Simpson scored Ireland's goal in a 2-1 home defeat by Wales.

March 9th: John Prentice signed from Hearts for £7,000.

March 10th:
RANGERS   (1) 4   CLYDE   (0) 0
  McColl (12), Waddell (56),
  Findlay (69),
  Sommerville o.g. (76)

RANGERS: Brown; Young, Cox; McColl, Woodburn, Rae; Waddell, Findlay, Simpson, Marshall, Beckett

CLYDE: Miller; Galloway, Mennie; Murphy, Sommerville, Long; Davies, Campbell, Linwood, Ring, Barclay

Attendance: 15,000

March 17th:
MORTON   (0) 0   RANGERS   (2) 2
                              Marshall (15),
                              Findlay (43)

MORTON: Cowan; J. Mitchell, McCluskey; G. Mitchell, Whigham, Whyte; Aird, Cupples, Mochan, McGarritty, Alexander

RANGERS: Brown; Young, Cox; McColl, Woodburn, Rae; Waddell, Findlay, Simpson, Marshall, Thornton

Attendance: 22,000

March 24th:
RANGERS   (1) 3   MOTHERWELL   (0) 0
  Findlay (43),
  Hubbard (73),
  Simpson (82)

RANGERS: Brown; Young, Cox; McColl, Woodburn, Rae; Waddell, Findlay, Simpson, Marshall, Hubbard

MOTHERWELL: Johnston; Kilmarnock, Shaw; McLeod, Paton, Redpath; Watters, Forrest, Kelly, Watson, J. Johnstone

Attendance: 30,000

March 31st:
AIRDRIE   (1) 2   RANGERS   (0) 1
  Woodburn o.g. (2),   Waddell (73)
  McGurn (46)

AIRDRIE: Fraser; T. Brown, Elliot; Cairns, Kelly, Shankland; W. Brown, Docherty, McGurn, Welsh, Elliot

RANGERS: Brown; Young, Cox; McColl, Woodburn, Rae; Waddell, Findlay, Simpson, Prentice, Hubbard

Attendance: 20,000

April 7th:
MOTHERWELL   (2) 2   RANGERS   (0) 3
  Forrest (4),   Rutherford (55),
  Humphries (15)   Woodburn (60),
                                 Findlay (85)

MOTHERWELL: Johnston; Kilmarnock, Higgins; McLeod, Paton, Redpath; Humphries, Forrest, Kelly, Watson, J. Johnstone

RANGERS: Brown; Young, Cox; McColl, Woodburn, Rae; Waddell, Findlay, Simpson, Rutherford, Hubbard

Attendance: 15,000

April 14th: Scotland beat England 3-2 at Wembley. Young, Cox, Woodburn and Waddell were in the team.

April 21st:
HEARTS　(0) 0　　　　　RANGERS　(1) 1
　　　　　　　　　　　　　　Findlay (25)

HEARTS:　Brown; Parker, McKenzie; Whitehead, Dougan, Laing; Urquhart, Conn, Bauld, Wardhaugh, Cumming

RANGERS:　Brown; Young, Shaw; McColl, Woodburn, Rae; Waddell, Findlay, Simpson, Rutherford, Hubbard

Attendance: 30,000

April 25th:
THIRD LANARK　(1) 1　RANGERS　(5) 5
　Goodall (22)　　　　　Simpson 4 (10, 16, 30, 35),
　　　　　　　　　　　　Rutherford (n.a.)

THIRD LANARK:　McFarlane; Balunas, Harrower; Adam, Samuel, Aitken; Henderson, Dick, Goodall, Mason, Bradley

RANGERS:　Brown; Young, Shaw; McColl, Woodburn, Rae; Waddell, Findlay, Simpson, Rutherford, Hubbard

April 28th:
HIBERNIAN　(2) 4　　　　RANGERS　(0) 1
　Johnstone (21),　　　　Woodburn (89)
　Reilly (44½),
　Smith 2 (74, 77)

HIBERNIAN:　Younger; Howie, Cairns; Gallacher, Paterson, Buchanan; Smith, Johnstone, Reilly, Turnbull, Combe

RANGERS:　Brown; Young, Cox; McColl, Woodburn, Rae; Waddell, Findlay, Simpson, Rutherford, Marshall

Attendance: 36,000

Hibs were so superior they played most of the game at half-pace and scored almost at will. Never can Rangers have been so outplayed. Never so humiliated.

Scottish League Division A

	P	W	D	L	F	A	Pts
1 Hibernian	30	22	4	4	78	26	48
2 RANGERS	30	17	4	9	64	37	38
3 Dundee	30	15	8	7	47	30	38
4 Hearts	30	16	5	9	72	45	37
5 Aberdeen	30	15	5	10	61	50	35
6 Partick Thistle	30	13	7	10	57	48	33
7 Celtic	30	12	5	13	48	46	29
8 Raith Rovers	30	13	2	15	52	52	28
9 Motherwell	30	11	6	13	58	65	28
10 East Fife	30	10	8	12	48	66	28
11 St Mirren	30	9	7	14	35	51	25
12 Morton	30	10	4	16	47	59	24
13 Third Lanark	30	11	2	17	40	51	24
14 Airdrie	30	10	4	16	52	67	24
15 Clyde	30	8	7	15	37	57	23
16 Falkirk	30	7	4	19	35	81	18

May 12th: Scotland beat Denmark 3-1 at Hampden Park. Young, Cox, Woodburn and Waddell were in the team.

May 16th: Scotland beat France 1-0 at Hampden Park. Young, Cox, Woodburn and Waddell were in the team.

May 20th: Scotland beat Belgium 5-0 in Brussels. Young, Cox, McColl, Woodburn and Waddell were in the side. Waddell scored one of the goals.

May 27th: Scotland were beaten 4-0 by Austria in Vienna. Young, Cox, Woodburn and Waddell were in the team.

LEAGUE CUP

August 12th:
MORTON　(0) 1　　　　　RANGERS　(2) 2
　Mochan (89)　　　　　Rutherford (7),
　　　　　　　　　　　　Findlay (32)

MORTON:　Cowan; J. Mitchell, Westwater; G. Mitchell, Whigham, Hunter; Farquhar, Orr, Mochan, Garth, Alexander

RANGERS:　Brown; Lindsay, Shaw; McColl, Woodburn, Cox; Waddell, Findlay, Thornton, Paton, Rutherford

Attendance: 18,500

August 16th:
RANGERS　(1) 1　　　　　ABERDEEN　(0) 2
　Findlay (11)　　　　　Hamilton 2 (86), (n.a.)

Attendance: 19,500

RANGERS:　Brown; Young, Shaw; McColl, Woodburn, Cox; Waddell, Findlay, Thornton, Paton, Rutherford

ABERDEEN:　Martin; Emery, D. Shaw; Anderson, Young, Harris; Boyd, Yorston, Hamilton, Baird, Hather

Attendance: 40,000

August 19th:
RANGERS　(2) 4　　　　　CLYDE　(0) 0
　Thornton 3 (15, 26, 82),
　J. Dunn o.g. (63)

RANGERS:　Brown; Young, Shaw; McColl, Woodburn, Cox; Waddell, Findlay, Thornton, Paton, Rutherford

CLYDE:　Miller; Mennie, S. Dunn; J. Dunn, Campbell, Haddock; Galletly, Davies, Linwood, McPhail, Barclay

Attendance: 45,000

August 26th:

RANGERS (3) 6	MORTON (0) 1
Findlay 2 (29, 64),	McGarritty (88)
Thornton 2 (36, 74),	
Paton 2 (41, 79)	

RANGERS: Brown; Young, Shaw; McColl, Woodburn, Cox; Waddell, Findlay, Thornton, Paton, Rutherford

MORTON: Cowan; Westwater, Whigham; Orr, Batten, Whyte; Alexander, McGarritty, Cupples, Garth, McKay

Attendance: 35,000

August 30th:

ABERDEEN (0) 2	RANGERS (0) 0
Hather (55), Baird (61)	

ABERDEEN: Martin; Emery, Shaw; Anderson, Young, Harris; Boyd, Yorston, Hamilton, Baird, Hather

RANGERS: Brown; Lindsay, Shaw; McColl, Young, Cox; Waddell, Findlay, Thornton, Paton, Rutherford

Attendance: 40,000

September 2nd:

CLYDE (1) 1	RANGERS (3) 5
McPhail (3)	Thornton 2 (15, 50),
	Findlay 2 (28, 44),
	Paton (71)

CLYDE: Allan; Lindsay, Mennie; Haddock, Campbell, Long; Ring, Galletly, Linwood, McPhail, Barclay

RANGERS: Brown; Young, Shaw; McColl, Woodburn, Cox; Waddell, Findlay, Thornton, Paton, Rutherford

Attendance: 31,000

League Cup Section Table

	P	W	D	L	F	A	Pts
Aberdeen	6	5	0	1	17	9	10
RANGERS	6	4	0	2	18	7	8
Clyde	6	1	2	3	15	21	4
Morton	6	0	2	4	10	23	2

SCOTTISH CUP

January 27th: First Round

RANGERS (1) 2	QUEEN OF THE
Simpson (21), Waddell (75)	SOUTH (0) 0

RANGERS: Brown; Young, Shaw; Cox, Woodburn, Rae; Waddell, Findlay, Simpson, Thornton, Rutherford

QUEEN OF THE SOUTH: Henderson; Dick, James; Waldie, Aird, McKnight; J. Brown, Patterson, C. Brown, McKeown, Johnstone

Attendance: 40,000

February 10th: Second Round

RANGERS (1) 2	HIBERNIAN (1) 3
Simpson 2 (4, 47)	Smith (40),
	Turnbull (75),
	Johnstone (80)

RANGERS: Brown; Young, Shaw; McColl, Woodburn, Cox; Waddell, Thornton, Simpson, Rae, Paton

HIBERNIAN: Younger; Govan, Ogilvie; Buchanan, Paterson, Gallacher; Smith, Johnstone, Reilly, Turnbull, Ormond

Attendance: 102,342

APPEARANCES

	League	League Cup	Scottish Cup	Glasgow Cup	Charity Cup	Friendlies
Brown	30	6	2	2	2	1
Young	30	5	2	2	3	1
Shaw	18	6	2	1	3	-
McColl	25	6	1	2	3	1
Woodburn	28	5	2	2	3	1
Cox	19	6	2	1	3	1
Waddell	28	6	2	-	3	-
Findlay	16	6	1	2	3	1
Thornton	21	6	2	2	3	1
Paton	19	6	1	1	-	1
Rutherford	17	6	1	2	1	1
Rae	25	-	2	1	-	-
Duncanson	1	-	-	-	-	-
Lindsay	6	2	-	1	-	1
Johnson	2	-	-	1	-	-
Simpson (Billy)	19	-	2	-	1	-
Simpson (Bobby)	2	-	-	-	-	-
Williamson	6	-	-	1	-	-
Little	1	-	-	-	-	-
Hubbard	8	-	-	-	1	-
Dunlop	2	-	-	-	-	-
Marshall	5	-	-	-	2	-
Beckett	1	-	-	-	1	-
Prentice	1	-	-	-	-	-
Wright	-	-	-	-	-	1
McCulloch	-	-	1	-	-	-

GOALSCORERS

League: Billy Simpson 11, Thornton 11, Findlay 9, Waddell 6, Paton 5, Williamson 3, Rutherford 3, Own Goals 3, Hubbard 2, Woodburn 2, Marshall 2, Rae 2, Bobby Simpson 2, Cox 1, Young 1 (pen), McColl 1

League Cup: Thornton 7, Findlay 6, Paton 3, Rutherford 1, Own Goal 1
Scottish Cup: Simpson 3, Waddell 1
Glasgow Cup: Paton 1, Cox 1, Johnson 1
Charity Cup: Findlay 3, Waddell 1, Thornton 1
Friendlies: Findlay 1, Rutherford 1

The Rangers squad that won the first ever Scottish League Cup when the tournament was launched in season 1946–47. Back row: Sammy Cox, George Young, Ian McColl, Bobby Brown, Willie Woodburn, Charlie Watkins, Willie Rae. Front row: Willie Waddell, Tony Gillick, Jock Shaw, Billy Williamson, Willie Thornton, Jimmy Duncanson. Inset are Jimmy Caskie and Eddie Rutherford.

Season 1951–52

For the 2nd successive season Rangers finished 2nd to Hibernian in the Championship. They lost the same number of matches as the Champions but drew 9 of the 30 matches, more than any other team in the Division. 5 points were dropped in the final 4 League matches. Dundee proved to be a particular bogey team throughout the season. Thornton was top scorer with 17 goals in his 28 appearances.

The Scottish Cup run ended at Motherwell in a Fourth Round Replay. Aitkenhead scored the winner from the penalty spot and Motherwell went on to win the trophy, beating Dundee by 4 clear goals in the Final.

The League Cup Section was won with the loss of only one match. Dunfermline were beaten over 2 legs in the Quarter-Final, Celtic were convincingly beaten in the Hampden Semi-Final but Rangers lost to Dundee in the Final, a last-minute goal from skipper Alf Boyd taking the trophy back to Dens Park.

> League: Runners-up
> League Cup: Finalists
> Scottish Cup: Fourth Round

SCOTTISH LEAGUE DIVISION A

July 3rd: Johnny Little joined Rangers from Queens Park. Adam Little joined Morton on a free transfer.

September 8th:
RANGERS (3) 4   PARTICK THISTLE (0) 1
  Findlay 3 (5, 15, 21),   Walker (78)
  Rutherford (77)

RANGERS: Brown; Young, Little; McColl, Woodburn, Cox; Waddell, Findlay, Simpson, Thornton, Rutherford

PARTICK THISTLE: Ledgerwood; McGowan, Gibb; Davidson, Forsyth, Mathers; McKenzie, Crawford, Walker, Sharp, McCreadie

Attendance: 60,000

September 14th: Jimmy Forbes was transferred to Dumbarton.

September 22nd:
RANGERS (0) 1   CELTIC (1) 1
  Findlay (63)   Collins (21)

RANGERS: Brown; Young, Little; McColl, Woodburn, Cox; Waddell, Findlay, Gardiner, Thornton, Hubbard

CELTIC: Devanney; Fallon, Rollo; Evans, Boden, Baillie; Collins, Walsh, McPhail, Peacock, Tully

Attendance: 86,000

Collins' goal was the most memorable feature of a most satisfying match. It was the more remarkable in that it was scored when Celtic had only 10 players on the field, McPhail having gone off with a nasty head cut in the 18th minute. Brown did very well even to touch Collins's sudden shot from 25 yards. Fallon could have allowed Young's high lob to go past for a goal-kick; instead he sent his clearance right into the path of Findlay who scored with a fine raking shot.

September 29th:
DUNDEE (1) 1   RANGERS (0) 0
  Steel (6)

DUNDEE: Brown; Follon, Frew; Gallacher, Cowie, Boyd; Hill, Pattillo, Flavell, Steel, Christie

RANGERS: Brown; Young, Little; McColl, Woodburn, Cox; Rutherford, Findlay, Gardiner, Thornton, Waddell

Attendance: 31,000

October 6th: Scotland beat Ireland 3-0 in Belfast. Young, Cox, Woodburn and Waddell were in the team.

October 10th:

RANGERS (0) 1	EAST FIFE (0) 1
Waddell (76)	J. Stewart (70)

RANGERS: Brown; Young, Little; McColl, Woodburn, Rae; Waddell, Findlay, Gardiner, Johnson, Rutherford

EAST FIFE: Curran; Finlay, S. Stewart; Christie, Aird, McLennan; J. Stewart, Fleming, Gardiner, Bonthrone, Duncan

Attendance: 20,000

October 20th:

RANGERS (0) 2	HEARTS (0) 0
Findlay (59), Waddell (70)	

RANGERS: Brown; Young, Little; McColl, Woodburn, Cox; Waddell, Findlay, Thornton, Johnson, Rutherford

HEARTS: Brown; Parker, Gordon; Armstrong, Milne, Laing; Liddell, Conn, Bauld, Urquhart, Williams

Attendance: 35,000

League Positions

	P	W	D	L	F	A	Pts
1 East Fife	9	6	1	2	22	14	14
2 Hibernian	8	5	3	0	23	9	13
3 St Mirren	8	4	1	3	15	14	9
4 Third Lanark	8	3	2	3	16	13	8
5 Hearts	8	3	2	3	13	12	8
10 RANGERS	5	2	2	1	8	4	6

November 3rd:

HIBERNIAN (0) 1	RANGERS (1) 1
Smith (84)	Findlay (21)

HIBERNIAN: Younger; Govan, Howie; Buchanan, Paterson, Combe; Smith, Johnstone, Reilly, Turnbull, Ormond

RANGERS: Brown; Young, Little; McColl, Woodburn, Cox; Waddell, Findlay, Thornton, Johnson, Prentice

Attendance: 50,000

Rangers took the lead in the 21st minute. Hibs dominated the 2nd half, and 9 minutes from time Turnbull's shot hit a defender, and Smith crashed in an unsavable rocket. Reilly, Waddell and Thornton all missed chances in the closing minutes.

November 9th: Rangers swopped Eddie Rutherford for Hearts' Colin Liddell.

November 10th:

RANGERS (1) 5	ST MIRREN (0) 1
Johnson (35),	Blyth (60)
Thornton 3 (59, 71, 89),	
Findlay (69)	

RANGERS: Brown; Young, Little; McColl, Woodburn, Cox; Waddell, Findlay, Thornton, Johnson, Liddell

ST MIRREN: Lynch; Lapsley, Cunningham; Neilson, Telfer, Martin; Rice, Blyth, Stewart, Gemmell, Reid

Attendance: 20,000

November 17th:

RAITH ROVERS (1) 3	RANGERS (0) 1
Brander (7), Maule (52),	Liddell (62)
McEwan (59)	

RAITH ROVERS: Johnstone; Wilkie, McNaught; Young, Colville, Leigh; Wood, McEwan, Copland, Maule, Brander

RANGERS: Brown; Young, Little; McColl, Woodburn, Cox; Waddell, Findlay, Thornton, Johnson, Liddell

Attendance: 21,000

November 24th:

RANGERS (2) 3	STIRLING ALBION (0) 0
Bain o.g. (15),	
Waddell (22),	
Johnson (71)	

RANGERS: Brown; Young, Little; McColl, Woodburn, Cox; Waddell, Findlay, Thornton, Johnson, Liddell

STIRLING ALBION: Jenkins; J. Henderson, Hadden; Bain, Paton, Mitchell; McFarlane, Brown, G. Henderson, Smith, Anderson

Attendance: 20,000

November 28th: Wales beat Scotland 1-0 at Hampden Park. Young, Cox, Woodburn and Waddell were in the team.

December 1st:

RANGERS (0) 1	THIRD LANARK (0) 1
Thornton (55)	Henderson (61)

RANGERS: Brown; Young, Little; McColl, Woodburn, Cox; Waddell, Paton, Thornton, Johnson, Liddell

THIRD LANARK: Miller; Balunas, Archibald; Mooney, Samuel, Harrower; Smellie, Mason, Dick, Henderson, McLeod

Attendance: 20,000

December 5th: George Young played in the Rest of Britain XI against Wales. Wales won 3-2. Sammy Cox was the reserve player.

December 8th:

MORTON (0) 0   RANGERS (1) 1
           McColl (40)

MORTON: Cowan; Mitchell, Westwater; Little, Batton, Hunter; Cupples, Orr, Linwood, McGarritty, Alexander

RANGERS: Brown; Young, Little; McColl, Woodburn, Prentice; Waddell, Paton, Thornton, Cox, Liddell

Attendance: 14,000

December 15th:

RANGERS (1) 3   MOTHERWELL (0) 0
 Thornton (4),
 Liddell (70), Cox (87)

RANGERS: Brown; Young, Little; McColl, Woodburn, Prentice; Waddell, Paton, Thornton, Cox, Liddell

MOTHERWELL: Johnstone; Kilmarnock, Shaw; McLeod, Paton, Redpath; Hunter, Forrest, Kelly, Aitken, Aitkenhead

Attendance: 35,000

December 22nd:

PARTICK THISTLE (0) 1 RANGERS (1) 3
 Davidson (60 pen)   Paton (31),
           Cox 2 (71, 72)

PARTICK THISTLE: Ledgerwood; McGowan, Gibb; Thomson, Davidson, Mathers; Anderson, Crawford, Stott, Sharp, Walker

RANGERS: Brown; Young, Little; Pryde, Woodburn, Prentice; Waddell, Paton, Thornton, Cox, Liddell

Attendance: 31,000

December 29th:

RANGERS (1) 3   QUEEN OF THE
 Thornton 2 (39, 69), SOUTH (1) 2
 Young (79 pen)   Rothera (43),
           Patterson (75)

RANGERS: Brown; Young, Little; McColl, Woodburn, Prentice; Waddell, Paton, Thornton, Cox, Liddell

QUEEN OF THE SOUTH: Henderson; Sharp, Binning; McBain, Aird, Greenock; Oakes, Rothera, Patterson, Neilson, Johnstone

Attendance: 28,000

League Positions

	P	W	D	L	F	A	Pts
1 Hibernian	17	11	4	2	50	18	26
2 East Fife	18	11	3	4	46	33	25
3 Hearts	17	10	3	4	46	25	23
4 RANGERS	14	8	4	2	29	13	20
5 Aberdeen	16	6	5	5	37	32	17

January 1st:

CELTIC (1) 1   RANGERS (2) 4
 Tully (20)   Liddell (15),
           Paton 2 (21, 62),
           Waddell (71)

CELTIC: Bell; Fallon, Jack; Evans, Stein, Baillie; Collins, Walsh, J. Weir, Peacock, Tully

RANGERS: Brown; Young, Shaw; McColl, Woodburn, Prentice; Waddell, Paton, Thornton, Cox, Liddell

Attendance: 45,000

Rangers gained a richly deserved victory in view of the fact that they played with 10 men for almost the last half-hour of the match after Shaw had been carried off on a stretcher suffering from a leg injury after a tackle by Tully.

January 2nd:

RANGERS (0) 1   DUNDEE (2) 2
 Thornton (59)   Steel (n.a.)
           Christie (n.a.)

RANGERS: Brown; Young, Little; McColl, Woodburn, Pryde; Waddell, Paton, Thornton, Cox, Liddell

DUNDEE: Brown; Follon, Cowan; Gallacher, Merchant, Boyd; Hill, Pattillo, Flavell, Steel, Christie

Attendance: 35,000

January 5th:

EAST FIFE (1) 2   RANGERS (1) 1
 Young o.g. (6),   Thornton (12)
 Bonthrone (52)

EAST FIFE: Curran; Weir, S. Stewart; Whyte, Finlay, McLennan; J. Stewart, Fleming, Gardiner, Bonthrone, Duncan

RANGERS: Brown; Young, Little; McColl, Woodburn, Prentice; McCulloch, Paton, Thornton, Cox, Liddell

Attendance: 17,000

January 12th:

RANGERS (1) 1   AIRDRIE (0) 0
 Thornton (16)

RANGERS: Brown; Young, Little; McColl, Woodburn, Prentice; Waddell, Paton, Thornton, Cox, Liddell

AIRDRIE: Fraser; Cosh, T. Brown; Cairns, Murray, Shankland; Quinn, McMillan, Lennox, Welsh, McCulloch

Attendance: 45,000

January 19th:
HEARTS (1) 2   RANGERS (0) 2
  Rutherford (16),   Findlay 2 (71, 74)
  Wardhaugh (53)

HEARTS: Brown; Parker, McKenzie; Glidden, Milne, Laing; Rutherford, Conn, Bauld, Wardhaugh, Urquhart

RANGERS: Brown; Young, Little; McColl, Woodburn, Prentice; McCulloch, Findlay, Thornton, Paton, Liddell

Attendance: 49,000

January 26th:
ST MIRREN (0) 0   RANGERS (3) 5
                    Paton (5),
                    Lapsley o.g. (22),
                    Liddell 2 (39, 85),
                    Thornton (83)

ST MIRREN: Crabtree; Lapsley, Drinkwater; Neilson, Telfer, Johnston; Blyth, Gemmell, Crowe, Stewart, Lesz

RANGERS: Brown; Young, Little; McColl, Woodburn, Prentice; McCulloch, Findlay, Thornton, Paton, Liddell

Attendance: 32,000

February 2nd:
RANGERS (1) 3   ABERDEEN (1) 2
  Thornton (37),   Prentice o.g. (31),
  Paton (68),   Baird (48)
  Young (77 pen)

RANGERS: Brown; Young, Little; McColl, Woodburn, Prentice; McCulloch, Findlay, Thornton, Paton, Liddell

ABERDEEN: Martin; Shaw, Emery; Anderson, Thomson, Harris; Boyd, Yorston, Rodger, Baird, Pearson

Attendance: 40,000

February 13th:
RANGERS (1) 2   HIBERNIAN (1) 2
  McCulloch (28),   Turnbull (4 pen),
  Young (67 pen)   Reilly (65)

RANGERS: Brown; Young, Little; McColl, Woodburn, Prentice; McCulloch, Findlay, Thornton, Paton, Liddell

HIBERNIAN: Younger; Govan, Howie; Combe, Paterson, Gallacher; Smith, Johnstone, Reilly, Turnbull, Ormond

Attendance: 45,000

February 16th:
AIRDRIE (0) 0   RANGERS (1) 1
                    Thornton (44)

AIRDRIE: Fraser; T. Brown, Murray; Cairns, Rodger, Shankland; W. Brown, McMillan, Quinn, Welsh, McCulloch

RANGERS: Brown; Young, Little; McColl, Woodburn, Prentice; McCulloch, Findlay, Thornton, Paton, Liddell

Attendance: 23,000

February 20th: Billy Williamson was transferred to St Mirren.

February 27th:
RANGERS (1) 1   RAITH ROVERS (0) 0
  Thornton (1)

RANGERS: Brown; Little, Cox; McColl, Stanners, Prentice; Waddell, Simpson, Thornton, Paton, Liddell

RAITH ROVERS: Johnstone; McLure, McNaught; Young, Colville, Leigh; Maule, McEwan, Penman, Kelly, McIntyre

Attendance: n.a.

March 1st:
STIRLING ALBION (1) 1   RANGERS (2) 5
  Bertolini (14)   Prentice (31),
                    Waddell (45),
                    Rae (46),
                    Cox (58 pen),
                    Thornton (75)

STIRLING ALBION: Jenkins; McCabe, Hadden; Smith, Paton, Rutherford; Bertolini, Chalmers, Henderson, Dick, Anderson

RANGERS: Brown; Little, Cox; Pryde, McColl, Prentice; Waddell, Boyd, Thornton, Rae, Liddell

Attendance: 14,000

League Positions

	P	W	D	L	F	A	Pts
1 Hibernian	27	18	5	4	84	29	41
2 RANGERS	25	15	6	4	55	25	36
3 East Fife	26	15	3	8	60	42	33
4 Hearts	26	13	6	7	61	43	32
5 Raith Rovers	27	12	5	10	38	29	29

March 15th:
RANGERS (1) 1   MORTON (0) 0
  Thornton (26)

RANGERS: Brown; Little, Cox; McColl, Young, Prentice; Waddell, Boyd, Thornton, Johnson, Liddell

MORTON: Cowan; Mitchell, Whigham; Little, Thom, Hunter; Garth, Gourlay, Cupples, Gibson, McVinish

Attendance: 30,000

March 22nd:

MOTHERWELL   (1) 2   RANGERS   (1) 1
  Watson (44), Sloan (83)   Simpson (65)

MOTHERWELL: Johnstone; Kilmarnock, Shaw; Cox, Paton, Redpath; Sloan, Humphries, Kelly, Watson, Aitkenhead

RANGERS: Brown; Young, Little; McColl, Woodburn, Prentice; Waddell, Simpson, Thornton, Johnson, Liddell

Attendance: 22,200

March 29th:

QUEEN OF THE   RANGERS   (2) 2
  SOUTH   (2) 2   Marshall (9),
  Patterson 2 (3, 27)   Thornton (30)

QUEEN OF THE SOUTH: Henderson; Hall, Binning; McBain, Waldie, Greenock; Oakes, Rothera, Patterson, J. Brown, Johnstone

RANGERS: Brown; Young, Little; McColl, Woodburn, Cox; Waddell, Neillands, Thornton, Marshall, Liddell

Attendance: n.a.

April 5th: England beat Scotland 2-1 at Hampden Park. Brown, Young and Woodburn were in the team.

April 16th:

THIRD LANARK   (0) 1   RANGERS   (1) 1
  Harrower (20)   Prentice (6)

THIRD LANARK: Robertson; Balunas, Cairns; Mooney, Samuel, Harrower; Goodall, Mason, Dick, Henderson, McLeod

RANGERS: Brown; Young, Little; McColl, Woodburn, Cox; Waddell, Neillands, Thornton, Prentice, Liddell

Attendance: 15,000

April 19th:

ABERDEEN   (0) 1   RANGERS   (1) 1
  Rodger (47)   Liddell (35)

ABERDEEN: Martin; Smith, Shaw; Samuel, Thomson, Harris; Newlands, Yorston, Rodger, Baird, Hather

RANGERS: Niven; Young, Shaw; McColl, Woodburn, Cox; Waddell, Neillands, Gardiner, Prentice, Liddell

Attendance: 20,000

Scottish League Division A

	P	W	D	L	F	A	Pts
1 Hibernian	30	20	5	5	92	36	45
2 RANGERS	30	16	9	5	61	31	41
3 East Fife	30	17	3	10	71	49	37
4 Hearts	30	14	7	9	69	53	35
5 Raith Rovers	30	14	5	11	43	42	33
6 Partick Thistle	30	12	7	11	48	51	31
7 Motherwell	30	12	7	11	51	57	31
8 Dundee	30	11	6	13	53	52	28
9 Celtic	30	10	8	12	52	55	28
10 Queen of South	30	10	8	12	50	60	28
11 Aberdeen	30	10	7	13	65	58	27
12 Third Lanark	30	9	8	13	51	62	26
13 Airdrie	30	11	4	15	54	69	26
14 St Mirren	30	10	5	15	43	58	25
15 Morton	30	9	6	15	49	56	24
16 Stirling Albion	30	5	5	20	36	99	15

April 30th: Scotland beat the U.S.A. 6-0 at Hampden Park. Young, Cox and Woodburn were in the team. Cox was carried off injured in the 78th minute of the match.

May 25th: Scotland beat Denmark 2-1 in Stockholm. Young, Cox and Thornton were in the side. Thornton scored one of the goals.

May 30th: Scotland lost to Sweden by 3-1 in Stockholm. Young, Cox and Thornton were in the team.

LEAGUE CUP

August 11th:

EAST FIFE   0   RANGERS   0

EAST FIFE: Curran; Finlay, S. Stewart; Christie, Aird, McLennan; J. Stewart, Fleming, Gardiner, Black, Duncan

RANGERS: Brown; Little, Cox; McColl, Woodburn, Rae; Waddell, Findlay, Simpson, Paton, Prentice

Attendance: 18,500

August 15th:

RANGERS   (0) 2   ABERDEEN   (1) 1
  Rutherford (65),   Yorston (37)
  Paton (75)

RANGERS: Brown; Young, Little; McColl, Woodburn, Cox; Waddell, Findlay, Simpson, Paton, Rutherford

ABERDEEN: Martin; Emery, Shaw; Harris, Thomson, Lowrie; Delaney, Yorston, Hamilton, Hay, Pearson

Attendance: 50,000

August 18th:
QUEEN OF THE   RANGERS (1) 3
  SOUTH   (0) 0   Simpson 2 (7, 85),
                            Waddell (75)

QUEEN OF THE SOUTH: Henderson; Sharp,
Binning; Rothera, Aird, McBain; Inglis, Patterson,
Houliston, McKeown, Oakes

RANGERS: Brown; Young, Little; McColl,
Woodburn, Rae; Waddell, Findlay, Simpson, Paton,
Rutherford

Attendance: 19,000

August 25th:
RANGERS   (2) 4   EAST FIFE   (0) 1
  Simpson 2 (25, 72),   Gardiner (50)
  Waddell (40 pen),
  Findlay (74)

RANGERS: Brown; Young, Little; McColl,
Woodburn, Cox; Waddell, Findlay, Simpson, Paton,
Rutherford

EAST FIFE: Curran; Finlay, S. Stewart; Christie,
Aird, McLennan; J. Stewart, Fleming, Gardiner,
Bonthrone, Matthew

Attendance: 25,000

August 29th:
ABERDEEN   (1) 2   RANGERS   (1) 1
  Delaney (33), Hay (77)   Simpson (5)

ABERDEEN: Martin; Emery, Rodger; Lowrie,
Thomson, Harris; Bogan, Yorston, Delaney, Hay,
Hather

RANGERS: Brown; Young, Little; McColl,
Woodburn, Cox; Waddell, Findlay, Simpson, Thornton,
Rutherford

Attendance: n.a.

September 1st:
RANGERS   (4) 5   QUEEN OF THE
  Thornton 3 (28, 42, 70),   SOUTH   (1) 2
  McColl (30), Simpson (43)   Greenock (34),
                           Brown (52)

RANGERS: Brown; Young, Little; McColl,
Woodburn, Cox; Waddell, Findlay, Simpson, Thornton,
Rutherford

QUEEN OF THE SOUTH: Henderson; Sharp,
Binning; McBain, Rothera, Greenock; Inglis, Patterson,
Houliston, Brown, Oakes

Attendance: 40,000

League Cup Section Table

	P	W	D	L	F	A	Pts
RANGERS	6	4	1	1	15	6	9
East Fife	6	3	1	2	10	9	7
Queen of South	6	2	0	4	11	16	4
Aberdeen	6	2	0	4	10	15	4

September 15th: Quarter-Final First Leg
DUNFERMLINE   (0) 1   RANGERS   (0) 0
  Mays (69)

DUNFERMLINE: Moodie; Kirk, McSeveney;
Whyte, Clarkson, Baikie; McGairy, McAuley, Mays,
Wright, Smith

RANGERS: Brown; Young, Little; McColl,
Woodburn, Rae; Waddell, Findlay, Gardiner, Thornton,
Rutherford

Attendance: 20,000

September 19th: Quarter-Final Second Leg
RANGERS   (2) 3   DUNFERMLINE   (1) 1
  Findlay 2 (13, 25),   Wright (n.a.)
  Gardiner (57)

RANGERS: Brown; Young, Little; McColl,
Woodburn, Cox; Waddell, Findlay, Gardiner,
Thornton, Paton

DUNFERMLINE: Moodie; Kirk, McSeveney;
Whyte, Clarkson, Baikie; McGairy, McAuley, Mays,
Wright, Smith

Attendance: 45,000

Clarkson missed a penalty

Rangers won 3-2 on aggregate

October 13th: Semi-Final   At Hampden Park
CELTIC   (0) 0   RANGERS   (2) 3
                          Thornton (15),
                          Johnson (44),
                          Findlay (53)

CELTIC: Bonnar; Fallon, Rollo; Evans, Boden,
Baillie; Weir, Collins, McPhail, Peacock, Tully

RANGERS: Brown; Young, Little; McColl,
Woodburn, Cox; Waddell, Findlay, Thornton, Johnson,
Rutherford

Attendance: 83,235

Rangers' standard of play in the first half must have been a
revelation to the thousands who had been lamenting their
recent displays. It was an infringement by Baillie on
Waddell that led to Rangers' first goal, Thornton heading
in from Young's free-kick. In the 44th minute Boden was
injured and as he lay unconscious Johnson, with one of his
cannonball shots, scored Rangers' 2nd goal. Boden, much
too late in trying to tackle Waddell, contributed to his
injury. The Celtic centre-half did not reappear until 12
minutes of the second half had gone and by that time
Rangers were 3 goals up, Findlay having headed a splendid

goal in the 53rd minute after Waddell bamboozled Rollo and crossed with precision. Brown was beaten twice in the match and did not lose a goal – Tully hit the bar in the first half and Boden did likewise, from outside-left, in the 2nd.

October 27th: Final	At Hampden Park
DUNDEE (0) 3	RANGERS (1) 2
Flavell (47), Pattillo (69),	Findlay (21),
Boyd (89)	Young (88)

RANGERS: Brown; Young, Little; McColl, Woodburn, Cox; Waddell, Findlay, Thornton, Johnson, Rutherford

DUNDEE: Brown; Follon, Cowan; Gallacher, Cowie, Boyd; Toner, Pattillo, Flavell, Steel, Christie

Attendance: 92,325 *Referee*: J. A. Mowat (Burnside)

Dundee's victory was their first major success since they won the Scottish Cup nearly 41 years before. They achieved their win with a display of cultured football coupled with an ability to fight back. Though Dundee scored their winning goal only in the last minute of the match they were far more than 1 goal the better side.

SCOTTISH CUP

February 9th: Second Round	
RANGERS (2) 6	ELGIN CITY (0) 1
Paton (20), Waddell (44),	Simpson (79)
Liddell (48), Findlay 2 (51, 89),	
Thornton (84)	

RANGERS: Brown; Young, Little; McColl, Woodburn, Prentice; Waddell, Findlay, Thornton, Paton, Liddell

ELGIN CITY: Craig; Law, MacLauchlan; Young, Roy, Studd; Grieve, Middleton, Simpson, McCraw, Logie

Attendance: 36,324

February 23rd: Third Round	
ARBROATH (0) 0	RANGERS (1) 2
	Thornton 2 (3, 52)

ARBROATH: Dorward; Stirling, Malcolm; Grant, Gray, Till; McBain, Box, Gallacher, Murray, Rennett

RANGERS: Brown; Young, Little; McColl, Woodburn, Prentice; McCulloch, Cox, Thornton, Paton, Liddell

Attendance: 13,510

March 8th: Fourth Round	
RANGERS (1) 1	MOTHERWELL (0) 1
Thornton (7)	Sloan (87)

RANGERS: Brown; Little, Cox; McColl, Young, Prentice; Waddell, Rae, Thornton, Paton, Liddell

MOTHERWELL: Johnstone; Kilmarnock, Shaw; Cox, Paton, Redpath; Sloan, Humphries, Kelly, Watson, Aitkenhead

Attendance: 82,000

March 12th: Fourth Round Replay	
MOTHERWELL (0) 2	RANGERS (1) 1
Aitkenhead (49 pen),	Thornton (11)
Humphries (81)	

MOTHERWELL: Johnston; Kilmarnock, Shaw; Cox, Paton, Redpath; Sloan, Humphries, Kelly, Watson, Aitkenhead

RANGERS: Brown; Little, Cox; McColl, Young, Prentice; McCulloch, Waddell, Thornton, Paton, Liddell

Attendance: 35, 632

APPEARANCES

	League	League Cup	Scottish Cup	Glasgow Cup	Charity Cup	Friendlies	St Mungo's
Brown	29	10	4	1	2	1	1
Young	29	9	4	1	2	4	1
Little	28	10	4	1	2	1	1
McColl	29	10	4	1	2	4	1
Woodburn	27	10	2	1	2	3	-
Cox	24	8	3	1	-	4	1
Waddell	23	10	3	1	-	4	1
Findlay	14	10	1	1	-	1	1
Thornton	28	6	4	-	-	1	1
Prentice	19	1	4	-	2	3	1
Liddell	23	-	4	-	2	3	-
Niven	1	-	-	-	-	3	-
Shaw	2	-	-	-	-	3	-
Rae	2	3	1	-	-	-	-
Pryde	3	-	-	-	-	-	-
Simpson	3	6	-	1	2	-	1
Rutherford	4	8	-	1	-	1	-
Gardiner	4	2	-	-	-	2	-
Hubbard	1	-	-	-	2	-	-
Johnson	9	2	-	-	-	1	-
Paton	15	5	4	1	-	-	-
Marshall	1	-	-	-	-	-	-
McCulloch	6	-	2	-	1	-	-
Stanners	1	-	-	-	-	-	-
Boyd	2	-	-	-	-	-	-
Neillands	3	-	-	-	-	3	-
Scobie	-	-	-	-	-	2	-
Frame	-	-	-	-	1	-	-

GOALSCORERS

League: Thornton 17, Findlay 9, Liddell 6, Waddell 6,
          Paton 5, Cox 4 (1 pen), Young 3 (all pens),
          Johnson 2, Prentice 2, Own Goals 2, McColl 1,
          McCulloch 1, Rae 1, Simpson 1, Marshall 1,
          Rutherford 1
League Cup: Simpson 6, Findlay 5, Thornton 4,
              Waddell 2 (1 pen), Rutherford 1, Paton 1,
              McColl 1, Gardiner 1, Johnson 1,
              Young 1

Scottish Cup: Thornton 5, Findlay 2, Paton 1,
                Waddell 1, Liddell 1
Glasgow Cup: Rutherford 1
Charity Cup: Liddell 2, McColl 1, Simpson 1
Friendlies: Prentice 4, Gardiner 3, Johnson 1, Findlay 1
St Mungo's: Findlay 1

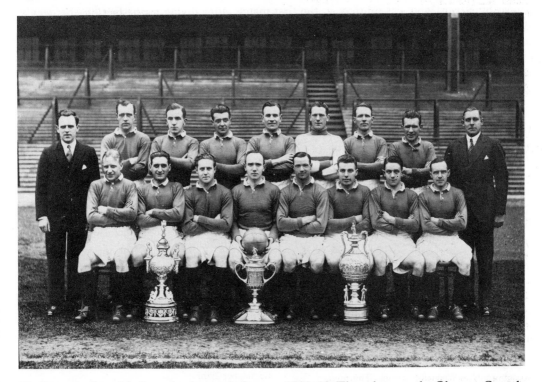

The Rangers Scottish Cup winning pool of season 1929–30. They also won the Glasgow Cup, the
Charity Cup and the Scottish League Championship. Back row: D. Meiklejohn, T. Marshall,
A. Archibald, J. Fleming, T. Hamilton, J. Buchanan, T. Craig. Front row: J. Kerr (trainer),
G. Brown, D. Gray, R. Mcdonald, T. Muirhead (capt.), R. McPhail, R. Hamilton,
W. G. Nicholson, A. Morton, and W. Struth (manager).

Season 1952–53

Rangers completed the League and Cup Double. The League Championship was won on goal average from Hibernian, Waddell scoring the goal which took the Title back to Ibrox in a hard-fought draw against Queen of the South at Palmerston. Their final average was 2.05 as against Hibs' 1.82. Grierson and Simpson scored 44 goals between them. The 80 goals scored was Rangers' best post-war total. Niven, Little, Grierson and Prentice played in all of the matches.

Abroath, Dundee, Morton, Celtic and Hearts were beaten in Rangers' march to the Scottish Cup Final. Prentice scored the winning goal against his old team in the Semi-Final. He also scored in the first match of the Final but missed the replay through injury. His replacement, Simpson, scored the goal which won the Cup. The Final will long be remembered for the courage shown by Niven, who was injured, in the first match, after diving at the feet of Aberdeen's Buckley. Young had to take over in goal for 18 minutes. Sammy Cox missed the Final after being injured in the Scotland v England match at Wembley.

After a disastrous opening match which cost goalkeeper Brown his first-team place Rangers reached the Semi-Final of the League Cup, losing to Kilmarnock to a fluke goal attributed to Jack 2 minutes from time.

League: Champions
League Cup: Semi-Finalists
Scottish Cup: Winners

SCOTTISH LEAGUE DIVISION A

August 5th: Derek Grierson joined Rangers from Queens Park.

September 6th:
ST MIRREN (1) 2   RANGERS (2) 3
  Stewart (24),   Grierson 2 (21, 70),
  Blyth (83)   Thornton (30)

ST MIRREN: Lornie; Lapsley, Cunningham; Neilson, Telfer, Reid; Rice, McGill, Stewart, Gemmell, Blyth

RANGERS: Niven; Young, Little; McColl, Woodburn, Cox; Waddell, Grierson, Thornton, Prentice, Liddell

Attendance: 45,000

September 20th:
CELTIC (2) 2   RANGERS (0) 1
  Walsh (4), Rollo (10)   Liddell (72)

CELTIC: Bonnar; Boden, Meechan; Evans, Stein, Baillie; Rollo, Walsh, Fallon, Tully, Peacock

RANGERS: Niven; Young, Little; McColl, Woodburn, Cox; McCulloch, Grierson, Thornton, Prentice, Liddell

Attendance: 48,000

If only for the fact that they scored one of the finest goals ever seen in Scottish football, Celtic deserved their victory. In 4 minutes, after Fallon had fallen over the ball some 30 yards from Rangers' goal, Walsh's speed enabled him to beat McColl to the ball, his intelligent control baffled Woodburn and his accuracy and power of shot from 18 yards gave Niven no chance.

September 27th:
RANGERS (3) 4   THIRD LANARK (0) 1
  Thornton 2 (5, 66),   Cuthbertson (65)
  Grierson 2 (14, 19)

RANGERS: Niven; Young, Little; McColl, Woodburn, Cox; McCulloch, Grierson, Thornton, Prentice, Hubbard

THIRD LANARK: Robertson; Balunas, Harrower; Duncan, Mooney, Kennedy; Henderson, Docherty, Cutherbertson, Dick, McLeod

Attendance: 25,000

October 11th:
RANGERS (1) 1
Grierson (22)

HIBERNIAN (1) 2
Reilly (29),
Turnbull (82)

RANGERS: Niven; Young, Little; McColl, Woodburn, Cox; McCulloch, Grierson, Simpson, Prentice, Liddell

HIBERNIAN: Younger; Govan, Howie; Gallacher, Paterson, Combe; Smith, Johnstone, Reilly, Turnbull, Ormond

Attendance: 60,000

8 minutes from the end, when a draw seemed inevitable, Turnbull collected a square pass from Smith, steadied himself and from 25 yards shot the dead ball over Niven's head with terrific force. Man for man there was no comparison in the forward lines, but what Rangers lacked in skill they made up for in spirit and endeavour.

October 18th: Scotland beat Wales 2-1 in Cardiff. Young captained the team which also included Cox.

October 18th:
EAST FIFE (2) 3
Duncan 2 (3, 57),
Bonthrone (42)

RANGERS (1) 2
Thornton (40),
Grierson (55)

EAST FIFE: Curran; Emery, S. Stewart; Whyte, Finlay, Christie; J. Stewart, Fleming, Gardiner, Bonthrone, Duncan

RANGERS: Niven; Little, Shaw; McColl, Woodburn, Prentice; McCulloch, Grierson, Simpson, Thornton, Liddell

Attendance: 19,000

October 29th: Joe Johnson was transferred to Lincoln City.

November 1st:
RANGERS (2) 3
Liddell (22),
Simpson (25),
Paton (44)

QUEEN OF THE
SOUTH (0) 1
Johnstone (53)

RANGERS: Niven; Young, Little; McColl, Woodburn, Cox; Paton, Grierson, Simpson, Prentice, Liddell

QUEEN OF THE SOUTH: Henderson; Sharp, Binning; McBain, Smith, Greenock; Oakes, Rothera, Patterson, J. Brown, Johnstone

Attendance: 20,000

League Positions

	P	W	D	L	F	A	Pts
1 East Fife	9	7	1	1	26	15	15
2 Celtic	9	5	3	2	18	11	13
3 St Mirren	9	5	2	2	19	11	12
4 Hibernian	7	5	0	2	20	14	10
5 Aberdeen	9	4	2	3	28	21	10
13 RANGERS	6	3	0	3	14	11	6

November 5th: Scotland, including Young and Cox, drew 1-1 with Ireland at Hampden Park.

November 8th:
FALKIRK (0) 1
Morrison (59)

RANGERS (2) 2
Prentice (1),
Simpson (44)

FALKIRK: McInnes; McDonald, Rae; Gallacher, McKenzie, Hunter; Brown, R. Morrison, Weir, Plumb, Joyner

RANGERS: Niven; Young, Little; McColl, Woodburn, Cox; McCulloch, Grierson, Simpson, Prentice, Liddell

November 15th:
CLYDE (3) 4
Galletly 2 (2, 37),
Buchanan 2 (30, 88)

RANGERS (4) 6
Simpson 3 (6, 60, 74),
Prentice (14),
Waddell (39),
Grierson (44)

CLYDE: Wilson; Lindsay, Haddock; Campbell, Keogh, Long; Galletly, Baird, Buchanan, Robertson, Ring

RANGERS: Niven; Young, Little; McColl, Woodburn, Cox; Waddell, Grierson, Simpson, Prentice, Hubbard

Attendance: 28,000

November 22nd:
RANGERS (1) 3
Prentice (16),
Grierson 2 (56, 60)

RAITH ROVERS (2) 2
Copland 2 (25, 36)

RANGERS: Niven; Young, Little; McColl, Woodburn, Cox; McCulloch, Grierson, Simpson, Prentice, Hubbard

RAITH ROVERS: Stewart; McNaught, Condie; Young, Colville, Williamson; Maule, McIntyre, Copland, McEwan, Penman

Attendance: 25,000

December 6th:
RANGERS (2) 4
McCulloch 2 (12, 79),
Simpson (36),
Young (69 pen)

ABERDEEN (0) 0

RANGERS: Niven; Young, Little; McColl,
Woodburn, Cox; McCulloch, Grierson, Simpson,
Prentice, Hubbard

ABERDEEN: Martin; Mitchell, Smith; Harris,
Young, Allister; Boyd, Rodger, Buckley, Hay, Hather

Attendance: 35,000

December 13th:

HEARTS (1) 2	RANGERS (1) 2
Glidden (44),	Simpson (14)
Conn (88)	Grierson (52)

HEARTS: Watters; Parker, Laing; Glidden, Milne,
Armstrong; Blackwood, Conn, Bauld, Wardhaugh,
Urquhart

RANGERS: Niven; Young, Little; McColl,
Woodburn, Cox; Waddell, Grierson, Simpson, Prentice,
Hubbard

Attendance: 26,000

December 20th:

RANGERS (2) 4	ST MIRREN (0) 0
Simpson 4 (23, 44, 46, 49)	

RANGERS: Niven; Young, Little; McColl,
Woodburn, Cox; Waddell, Grierson, Simpson, Prentice,
Hubbard

ST MIRREN: Park; Lapsley, Ashe; Moore, Neilson,
Johnston; Rice, McGill, Williamson, Gemmell,
Anderson

Attendance: 30,000

December 27th:

AIRDRIE (1) 2	RANGERS (0) 2
Baird (42)	Grierson (54),
McCulloch (65)	Simpson (56)

AIRDRIE: Fraser; Pryde, Cross; Cairns, Rodger,
Shankland; Seawright, McMillan, Baird, Quinn,
McCulloch

RANGERS: Niven; Young, Little; McColl,
Woodburn, Cox; Waddell, Grierson, Simpson, Prentice,
Hubbard

Attendance: 20,000

League Positions

	P	W	D	L	F	A	Pts
1 East Fife	16	10	3	3	41	29	23
2 Hibernian	15	10	1	4	46	28	21
3 Celtic	16	8	5	3	32	22	21
4 St Mirren	17	8	5	4	26	20	21
5 RANGERS	13	8	2	3	37	22	18

January 1st:

RANGERS (0) 1	CELTIC (0) 0
Simpson (53)	

RANGERS: Niven; Young, Little; McColl,
Woodburn, Cox; Waddell, Grierson, Simpson, Prentice,
Hubbard

CELTIC: Hunter; Haughney, Meechan; Evans, Stein,
Rollo; Collins, Fernie, McIlroy, Peacock, Tully

Attendance: 73,000

There was little sustained attacking play on either side.
Evans, Stein and Rollo mopped up almost every inside-
forward move and only the sprightly little Hubbard's darts
and the crosses of Waddell were dangerous to Celtic.

January 3rd:

THIRD LANARK (0) 0	RANGERS (1) 2
	Prentice 2 (4, 73)

THIRD LANARK: Robertson; Balunas, Phillips;
Kennedy, Forsyth, Mooney; Brown, Liddell, Dobbie,
Henderson, McLeod

RANGERS: Niven; Young, Little; McColl,
Woodburn, Cox; Waddell, Grierson, Paton, Prentice,
Hubbard

Attendance: 20,581

January 10th:

RANGERS (1) 2	PARTICK THISTLE (0) 2
Paton (37),	Howitt (64), Crawford (67)
Grierson (50)	

RANGERS: Niven; Young, Little; McColl,
Woodburn, Rae; McCulloch, Grierson, Paton, Prentice,
Hubbard

PARTICK THISTLE: Bell; McGowan, Gibb;
Thomson, Davidson, Mathers; McKenzie, Howitt,
Stott, Crawford, Walker

Attendance: 20,000

January 17th:

HIBERNIAN (0) 1	RANGERS (0) 1
Turnbull (50 pen)	Grierson (65)

HIBERNIAN: Younger; Clark, Howie; Buchanan,
Paterson, Combe; Smith, Johnstone, Reilly, Turnbull,
Ormond

RANGERS: Niven; Young, Little; McColl,
Woodburn, Cox; McCulloch, Grierson, Simpson,
Prentice, Hubbard

Attendance: 60,500

Hibs contributed 75% of the football in a tense, exciting,
match. Their one failing was the inability to shoot
accurately. Niven was a superb goalkeeper on the
occasions on which Hibs did unleash worthy shots. Reilly,
at his elusive best, Buchanan and Niven were the best
players afield.

January 31st:

RANGERS (3) 4	EAST FIFE (0) 0
McColl 2 (12, 44),	
Simpson (32), Grierson (54)	

RANGERS: Niven; Young, Little; McColl, Woodburn, Cox; Waddell, Grierson, Simpson, Prentice, Hubbard

EAST FIFE: Curran; Emery, Weir; Whyte, Finlay, Christie; Stewart, Fleming, Gardiner, Bonthrone, Duncan

Attendance: 52,000

February 14th:

DUNDEE (1) 1	RANGERS (0) 1
Ziesing (12)	Cowie o.g. (63)

DUNDEE: Brown; Follon, Cowan; Gallacher, Cowie, Boyd; Toner, A. Henderson, Ziesing, Steel, Flavell

RANGERS: Niven; Young, Little; McColl, Woodburn, Cox; Waddell, Grierson, Simpson, Prentice, Hubbard

Attendance: 24,000

February 28th:

RANGERS (4) 4	FALKIRK (0) 0
Prentice (14),	
Simpson 3 (33, 38, 43)	

RANGERS: Niven; Young, Little; McColl, Woodburn, Cox; Waddell, Grierson, Simpson, Prentice, Hubbard

FALKIRK: McFeat; McDonald, Rae; Gallacher, McKenzie, Hunter; Delaney, J. Brown, Weir, Campbell, G. Brown

Attendance: 35,000

League Positions

	P	W	D	L	F	A	Pts
1 Hibernian	22	15	2	5	73	41	32
2 East Fife	23	12	6	5	51	39	30
3 RANGERS	20	12	5	3	52	26	29
4 St Mirren	24	10	6	8	40	38	26
5 Clyde	25	11	4	10	68	61	26

March 7th:

RANGERS (1) 1	CLYDE (1) 2
Young (21 pen)	Baird (23 pen),
	Ring (69)

RANGERS: Niven; Young, Little; McColl, Woodburn, Cox; McCulloch, Grierson, Simpson, Prentice, Hubbard

CLYDE: Wilson; Murphy, Haddock; Anderson, Henderson, Keogh; Buchanan, Baird, McPhail, Robertson, Ring

Woodburn was ordered off

Attendance: 55,000

March 18th:

RAITH ROVERS (3) 3	RANGERS (0) 1
A. Young 2 (10 pen, 32),	Simpson (41)
Kelly (41)	

RAITH ROVERS: Johnstone; McLure, McNaught; Leigh, Colville, Williamson; Maule, Young, Copland, Kelly, Penman

RANGERS: Niven; Young, Little; McColl, Woodburn, Cox; Paton, Grierson, Simpson, Prentice, Hubbard

Attendance: 18,000

March 21st:

RANGERS (1) 4	MOTHERWELL (1) 1
Grierson 2 (34, 77),	Kelly (5)
McCulloch (69),	
Simpson (71)	

RANGERS: Niven; Young, Little; McColl, Woodburn, Cox; McCulloch, Grierson, Simpson, Prentice, Hubbard

MOTHERWELL: Johnston; Reid, Shaw; Cox, Paton, Redpath; Dawson, Humphries, Kelly, Forrest, Aitkenhead

Attendance: 35,000

March 28th:

ABERDEEN (1) 2	RANGERS (1) 2
Yorston (21),	Grierson (20),
Rodger (60)	Gardiner (87)

ABERDEEN: Martin; Mitchell, Shaw; Glen, Young, Allister; Rodger, Yorston, Buckley, Smith, Hather

RANGERS: Niven; Young, Little; McColl, Woodburn, Rae; McCulloch, Grierson, Gardiner, Prentice, Hubbard

Attendance: 30,000

April 6th:

RANGERS (1) 3	HEARTS (0) 0
Simpson (31), Prentice (70),	
McColl (77)	

RANGERS: Niven; Young, Little; McColl, Woodburn, Rae; Waddell, Grierson, Simpson, Prentice, Hubbard

HEARTS: Watters; Parker, Adie; Laing, Dougan, Armstrong; Rutherford, Conn, Bauld, Wardhaugh, Urquhart

Attendance: 40,000

April 11th:

PARTICK THISTLE (0) 1	RANGERS (2) 2
McInnes (74)	Gardiner (42),
	Young (45 pen)

C

PARTICK THISTLE: Ledgerwood; McGowan, Gibb; Crawford, Davidson, Mathers; McKenzie, McInnes, Stott, Sharp, Walker

RANGERS: Niven; Young, Little; McColl, Stanners, Cox; Waddell, Grierson, Gardiner, Prentice, Hubbard

Attendance: 25,500

April 15th:

RANGERS	(4) 8	AIRDRIE	(0) 2

Grierson 4 (20, 29, 48, 88),   Baird 2 (71, n.a.)
Prentice (26), Cross o.g. (33),
Paton (73), Young (79 pen)

RANGERS: Niven; Young, Little; McColl, Stanners, Cox; Waddell, Grierson, Paton, Prentice, Hubbard

AIRDRIE: Fraser; Pryde, Cross; Cairns, Rodger, T. Brown; McGurn, McMillan, Baird, Shankland, McCulloch

Attendance: 20,000

April 18th: Scotland drew 2-2 with England at Wembley. Young and Cox were in the team. Cox was carried off injured.

April 20th:

MOTHERWELL	(0) 0	RANGERS	(1) 3

Paton 2 (35, 88),
Young (83 pen)

MOTHERWELL: Johnstone; Kilmarnock, Shaw; Cox, Paton, Redpath; Sloan, Humphries, Kelly, Forrest, Aitkenhead

RANGERS: Niven; Young, Little; McColl, Stanners, Pryde; Waddell, Grierson, Paton, Prentice, Hubbard

Attendance: 30,720

April 22nd: Willie Thornton was wanted by East Fife as manager in succession to Scot Symon who had joined Preston North End.

May 2nd:

RANGERS	(1) 3	DUNDEE	(1) 1

Grierson 2 (25, 77),   Gallacher (40)
Simpson (63)

RANGERS: Niven; Young, Little; McColl, Woodburn, Pryde; Waddell, Grierson, Simpson, Prentice, Hubbard

DUNDEE: Brown; Follon, Cowan; Ziesing, Cowie; Boyd; Christie, Gallacher, Flavell, Steel, Walker

Attendance: 45,000

May 2nd: Marshall, Forbes, Bobby Simpson and Scobie were all given free transfers.

May 6th: Scotland were beaten 2-1 by Sweden at Hampden Park. Young and Little were in the team.

May 7th:

QUEEN OF THE SOUTH	(1) 1	RANGERS	(0) 1

Patterson (41)   Waddell (75)

QUEEN OF THE SOUTH: Henderson; Sharp, Binning; Sweeney, Smith, Greenock; Oakes, Black, Patterson, Neilson, Baxter

RANGERS: Niven; Young, Little; Dunlop, Woodburn, Pryde; Waddell, Grierson, Simpson, Prentice, Hubbard

Attendance: 17,000

Scottish League Division A

	P	W	D	L	F	A	Pts
1 RANGERS	30	18	7	5	80	39	43
2 Hibernian	30	19	5	6	93	51	43
3 East Fife	30	16	7	7	72	48	39
4 Hearts	30	12	6	12	59	50	30
5 Clyde	30	13	4	13	78	78	30
6 St Mirren	30	11	8	11	52	58	30
7 Dundee	30	9	11	10	44	37	29
8 Celtic	30	11	7	12	51	54	29
9 Partick Thistle	30	10	9	11	55	63	29
10 Queen of South	30	10	8	12	43	61	28
11 Aberdeen	30	11	5	14	64	68	27
12 Raith Rovers	30	9	8	13	47	53	26
13 Falkirk	30	11	4	15	53	63	26
14 Airdrie	30	10	6	14	53	75	26
15 Motherwell	30	10	5	15	57	80	25
16 Third Lanark	30	8	4	18	52	75	20

LEAGUE CUP

August 9th:

HEARTS	(2) 5	RANGERS	(0) 0

Conn 2 (11, 34),
Wardhaugh 2 (59, 72),
Bauld (81)

HEARTS: Watters; Parker, McKenzie; Glidden, Milne, Laing; Rutherford, Conn, Bauld, Wardhaugh, Urquhart

RANGERS: Brown; Young, Little; McColl, Woodburn, Cox; Waddell, Grierson, Thornton, Marshall, Liddell

Attendance: 41,000

August 13th:

RANGERS	(1) 2	MOTHERWELL	(0) 0

Thornton (20),
Liddell (55)

RANGERS: Niven; Young, Little; McColl, Woodburn, Cox; Waddell, Grierson, Thornton, Prentice, Liddell

MOTHERWELL: Johnstone; Kilmarnock, Shaw; Cox, Paton, Redpath; Sloan, Humphries, Kelly, Forrest, Aitkenhead

Attendance: 50,000

August 16th:
RANGERS (2) 3   ABERDEEN (0) 1
   Grierson 2 (15, 20),   Buckley (51)
   Thornton (90)

RANGERS: Niven; Young, Little; McColl, Woodburn, Cox; Waddell, Grierson, Thornton, Prentice, Liddell

ABERDEEN: Martin; Mitchell, Shaw; Smith, Thomson, Harris; Rodger, Yorston, Buckley, Baird, Hather

Attendance: 40,000

August 23rd:
RANGERS (1) 2   HEARTS (0) 0
   Thornton (11),
   Liddell (62)

RANGERS: Niven; Young, Little; McColl, Woodburn, Cox; Waddell, Grierson, Thornton, Prentice, Liddell

HEARTS: Watters; Parker, McKenzie; Glidden, Milne, Laing; Cumming, Whittle, Bauld, Wardhaugh, Urquhart

Attendance: 70,000

August 27th:
MOTHERWELL (2) 3   RANGERS (2) 3
   Humphries (n.a.), Forrest (33), Prentice (n.a.),
   Paton (89)   Thornton (30),
                Paton (83)

MOTHERWELL: Johnston; Kilmarnock, Shaw; Cox, Paton, Redpath; Sloan, Humphries, Kelly, Forrest, Aitkenhead

RANGERS: Niven; Young, Little; McColl, Woodburn, Cox; Waddell, Paton, Thornton, Prentice, Liddell

Attendance: 35,000

August 31st:
ABERDEEN (1) 1   RANGERS (0) 2
   Yorston (11)   Waddell (73),
                Thornton (86)

ABERDEEN: Martin; Mitchell, Smith; Anderson, Thomson, Wallace; Boyd, Rodger, Dunbar, Yorston, Hather

RANGERS: Niven; Young, Little; McColl, Woodburn, Cox; Waddell, Paton, Thornton, Prentice, Liddell

Attendance: 35,000

League Cup Section Table

	P	W	D	L	F	A	Pts
RANGERS	6	4	1	1	12	9	9
Hearts	6	3	1	2	12	7	7
Motherwell	6	3	1	2	11	9	7
Aberdeen	6	0	1	5	7	16	1

September 13th: Quarter-Final First Leg
RANGERS 0   THIRD LANARK 0

RANGERS: Niven; Young, Little; McColl, Woodburn, Cox; Waddell, Grierson, Thornton, Prentice, Liddell

THIRD LANARK: Robertson; Balunas, Harrower; Docherty, Samuel, Mooney; Henderson, Mason, Heron, Dick, McLeod

Attendance: 50,000

September 17th: Quarter-Final Second Leg
THIRD LANARK (0) 0   RANGERS (1) 2
                Grierson (13),
                Thornton (60)

THIRD LANARK: Robertson; Balunas, Harrower; Docherty, Samuel, Mooney; Dobbie, Mason, Heron, Dick, McLeod

RANGERS: Niven; Young, Little; McColl, Woodburn, Cox; Waddell, Grierson, Thornton, Prentice, Liddell

Attendance: 42,000

October 4th: Semi-Final   At Hampden Park
RANGERS (0) 0   KILMARNOCK (0) 1
                Jack (88)

RANGERS: Niven; Young, Little; McColl, Woodburn, Cox; Waddell, Paton, Thornton, Grierson, Hubbard

KILMARNOCK: Niven; Collins, Hood; Russell, Thyne, Middlemass; Henaughan, Harvey, Mays, Jack, Murray

Attendance: 45,715

Though the goal that won the match was a fortuitous score, Kilmarnock deserved their surprising victory. They gave no sign of being a team from an inferior grade of football in a match that was fast and exciting throughout. Lack of finishing punch was their only failing. Niven, especially for his excellent saving of several fine efforts from Grierson, and Thyne whose mastery of Thornton on the ground and in the air was remarkable, were Killie's outstanding defenders.

SCOTTISH CUP

January 24th: First Round
RANGERS   (3) 4   ARBROATH   (0) 0
  Hubbard (6), Prentice (15),
  McCulloch (27), Simpson (68)

RANGERS: Niven; Young, Little; McColl,
Woodburn, Cox; McCulloch, Grierson, Simpson,
Prentice, Hubbard

ARBROATH: Robertson; Stirling, Malcolm; Box,
Gray, Grant; McBain, Caldwell, Gallacher, McKenzie,
O'Donnell

Attendance: 44,000

February 7th: Second Round
DUNDEE   (0) 0   RANGERS   (0) 2
                             Hubbard (59),
                             Grierson (60)

DUNDEE: Brown; Follon, Cowan; Gallacher, Cowie,
Boyd; Burrell, Toner, Flavell, Steel, Christie

RANGERS: Niven; Young, Little; McColl,
Woodburn, Cox; Waddell, Grierson, Simpson, Prentice,
Hubbard

Attendance: 43,024

February 21st: Third Round
MORTON   (1) 1   RANGERS   (2) 4
  Gourlay (16)   Simpson (7),
                             Grierson 2 (42, 89),
                             Prentice (82)

MORTON: Cowan; Batton, Quinn; Farquhar, Thom,
Little; Hannigan, Gourlay, Linwood, Gibson, Hope

RANGERS: Niven; Young, Little; McColl,
Woodburn, Cox; Waddell, Grierson, Simpson, Prentice,
Hubbard

Attendance: 23,000

March 14th: Fourth Round
RANGERS   (1) 2   CELTIC   (0) 0
  Prentice (10),
  Grierson (88)

RANGERS: Niven; Young, Little; McColl,
Woodburn, Cox; Paton, Grierson, Simpson, Prentice,
Hubbard

CELTIC: Hunter; Haughney, Meechan; Evans, Stein,
McPhail; Collins, Fernie, McGrory, Walsh, Tully

Attendance: 95,000

Young, who was a superb constructive player and Little,
consistently successful against Collins, formed with their
centre-half a barrier which Celtic found difficult to
penetrate. 2 minutes from the end Grierson showed his
rivals how to score when he cut through with Simpson's
headed pass, enticed Hunter from his goal and slid the ball
into the net.

April 4th: Semi-Final   At Hampden Park
RANGERS   (1) 2   HEARTS   (1) 1
  Grierson (37),   Wardhaugh (11)
  Prentice (75)

RANGERS: Niven; Young, Little; McColl,
Woodburn, Cox; Waddell, Grierson, Simpson, Prentice,
Hubbard

HEARTS: Watters; Parker, Adie; Laing, Dougan,
Armstrong; Rutherford, Conn, Bauld, Wardhaugh,
Cumming

Attendance: 116,262

In the first half Hearts were so superior that they seemed
destined to reach their first Scottish Cup Final in 46 years.
Rangers scored the winning goal in the 75th minute when
Prentice, from the edge of the penalty area, shot a low ball:
a slight deflection from an opponent surprised Watters
who nevertheless got both hands to the ball but failed to
save. Hearts had little service from Cumming after the
19th minute of the second half when he suffered a leg
injury in a tussle with Young.

April 25th: Final   At Hampden Park
RANGERS   (1) 1   ABERDEEN   (0) 1
  Prentice (8)   Yorston (80)

RANGERS: Niven; Young, Little; McColl, Stanners,
Pryde; Waddell, Grierson, Paton, Prentice, Hubbard

ABERDEEN: Martin; Mitchell, Shaw; Harris, Young,
Allister; Rodger, Yorston, Buckley, Hamilton, Hather

Attendance: 129,762

Aberdeen never had a better chance of beating Rangers.
Once again Rangers could thank their defenders for saving
the day. Buckley might have had three or four goals but for
ill-luck and the magnificent goalkeeping of Niven. Niven
saved a certain score when he dived at the feet of Buckley in
the 27th minute but he paid for his courage. He was carried
off with a head injury and Young replaced him in goal for
the rest of the half. Niven returned at the start of the
second half wearing a protective leather helmet. Near the
end, after Yorston had headed a long overdue equalising
goal from Hather's cross, Niven leapt to clutch shots from
Buckley and Hamilton which might have beaten a
goalkeeper who had not suffered injury.

April 29th: Final Replay   At Hampden Park
RANGERS   (1) 1   ABERDEEN   (0) 0
  Simpson (42)

RANGERS: Niven; Young, Little; McColl,
Woodburn, Pryde; Waddell, Grierson, Simpson, Paton,
Hubbard

ABERDEEN: Martin; Mitchell, Shaw; Harris, Young,
Allister; Rodger, Yorston, Buckley, Hamilton, Hather

Attendance: 113,700

After Rangers had been practically locked in their own half
of the field they broke out 3 minutes from half-time.
Attractive ground passing by Hubbard, Paton and
Grierson enabled Simpson to have a clear sight of goal and
his well-placed ground shot went into the corner of the net.
McColl played his heart out with penetrating runs and
passes into Aberdeen's half. Grierson and Simpson were
the best of a forward line that played like a spluttering
candle.

APPEARANCES

	League	League Cup	Scottish Cup
Niven	30	8	7
Young	29	9	7
Little	30	9	7
McColl	29	9	7
Woodburn	27	9	6
Cox	23	9	5
Waddell	16	9	5
Grierson	30	7	7
Thornton	4	9	-
Prentice	30	7	6

	League	League Cup	Scottish Cup
Liddell	6	8	-
McCulloch	12	-	1
Hubbard	24	1	7
Simpson	21	-	6
Shaw	1	-	-
Paton	6	3	3
Rae	3	-	-
Gardiner	2	-	-
Stanners	3	-	1
Pryde	3	-	2
Dunlop	1	-	-
Brown	-	1	-
Marshall	-	1	-
McMillan	-	-	-
Woods	-	-	-

GOALSCORERS

League: Grierson 23, Simpson 21, Prentice 8, Young 5
            (all pens), Paton 5, Thornton 4, McCulloch 3,
            McColl 2, Own Goals 2, Gardiner 2,
            Waddell 2, Liddell 2

League Cup: Thornton 6, Grierson 3, Liddell 2,
                Prentice 1, Paton 1, Waddell 1

Scottish Cup: Grierson 5, Prentice 5, Simpson 3,
                  Hubbard 2, McCulloch 1

A Rangers squad from the early thirties. Sam English who was involved in the fatal clash with the
Celtic goalkeeper Thomson is in the back row fourth from left. Also in the back row, extreme
right, is Jerry Dawson. While in the front row fourth from left is Meiklejohn and Alan Morton
is second from extreme right in the front row.

Season 1953–54

After the highs of the previous season Rangers finished only 4th in the League behind Celtic, Hearts and Partick Thistle. Goal average put them ahead of Hibernian, East Fife, Dundee and Clyde who all finished on 34 points. Hearts and Aberdeen were the only teams to leave Ibrox with both points, but Rangers' away form was dreadful. Only 13 of the 30 matches were won.

It took 7 matches to reach the Semi-Final of the Scottish Cup against Aberdeen but injuries to Brown and Little, early in the match, proved fateful and Aberdeen ran out winners by 6 clear goals, 3 of which were scored in the final 7 minutes.

A similar fate befell the Ibrox men in the League Cup. The Section was won in great style but this time Partick Thistle triumphed in the Semi-Final.

A tour of Canada and North America was undertaken in the close season. 7 of the 9 matches were won and the only defeat was at the hands of Chelsea in the second-last match in Toronto. Jock Shaw and Willie Thornton finished their playing careers after the tour. Thornton took over the managership of Dundee.

At the end of the season Bill Struth announced that he was to stand down as manager of the club after 34 years, and former player Scot Symon, the manager of Preston North End, was named as his successor.

> League: Fourth
> League Cup: Semi-Finalists
> Scottish Cup: Semi-Finalists

SCOTTISH LEAGUE DIVISION A

September 5th:
RANGERS (3) 3   PARTICK THISTLE (0) 0
  Grierson (2), Paton (12),
  Prentice (24)

RANGERS: Niven; Young, Little; McColl, Woodburn, Cox; Waddell, Grierson, Paton, Prentice, Hubbard

PARTICK THISTLE: Ledgerwood; McGowan, Gibb; Thomson, Davidson, Mathers; McKenzie, Howitt, Wright, Sharp, McInnes
Attendance: 50,000

September 9th: The Scottish League beat the Irish League 4-0. Niven, Young, Cox and Prentice were in the team.

September 19th:
RANGERS (1) 1   CELTIC (1) 1
  Paton (21)   Duncan (23)

RANGERS: Niven; Caldow, Little; McColl, Woodburn, Cox; Waddell, Grierson, Paton, Prentice, Hubbard

CELTIC: Bell; Haughney, Fallon; Evans, Stein, Peacock; Collins, Walsh, McPhail, Tully, Duncan
Attendance: 59,000

September 26th:
STIRLING ALBION (1) 2   RANGERS (0) 0
  Woodburn o.g. (38),
  Whitehead (77)

STIRLING ALBION: Jenkins; Ferguson, Forsyth; Bain, Milligan, Whitehead; Chalmers, Smith, Williamson, Swanson, Anderson

RANGERS: Niven; Young, Little; McColl, Woodburn, Cox; Waddell, Grierson, Paton, Prentice, Hubbard

Woodburn was ordered off
Attendance: 24,000

October 3rd: Scotland beat Ireland 3-1 in Belfast. Young, Cox and Waddell were in the team. Simpson played for Ireland.

October 17th:
RANGERS   (1) 2   EAST FIFE   (0) 0
   Simpson (2), Grierson (72)

RANGERS: Niven; Young, Little; McColl, Woodburn, Cox; Waddell, Grierson, Simpson, Prentice, Liddell

EAST FIFE: Curran; Emery, S. Stewart; Christie, Finlay, McLennan; J. Stewart, Fleming, Bonthrone, Gardiner, Matthew

Attendance: 40,000

October 24th:
DUNDEE   (1) 1   RANGERS   (0) 0
   Henderson (31)

DUNDEE: Brown; Frew, Cowan; Gallacher, Malloy, Cowie; Burrell, Henderson, Turnbull, Steel, Christie

RANGERS: Niven; Young, Little; McColl, Woodburn, Cox; Waddell, Grierson, Simpson, Prentice, Liddell

Attendance: 34,000

October 31st:
RANGERS   (0) 0   HEARTS   (0) 1
                                 Urquhart (82)

RANGERS: Niven; Young, Little; McColl, Stanners, Cox; Waddell, Findlay, Simpson, McMillan, Liddell

HEARTS: Watters; Adie, McKenzie; Parker, Dougan, Armstrong; Rutherford, Conn, Wardhaugh, Cumming, Urquhart

Attendance: 30,000

League Positions

	P	W	D	L	F	A	Pts
1 Queen of South	9	7	1	1	26	12	15
2 Dundee	9	4	3	2	13	11	11
3 Celtic	8	4	2	2	12	6	10
4 Hearts	9	4	2	3	18	13	10
5 Raith Rovers	9	4	2	3	19	16	10
14 RANGERS	6	2	1	3	6	5	5

November 4th: Scotland drew 3-3 with Wales at Hampden Park. Young and Cox were in the team.

November 7th:
ABERDEEN   (0) 1   RANGERS   (1) 1
   Allister (70 pen)   Simpson (43)

ABERDEEN: Martin; Mitchell, Smith; Allister, Young, Glen; Boyd, Yorston, Buckley, Kelly, Hather

RANGERS: Niven; Young, Little; McColl, Stanners, Cox; Waddell, Paton, Simpson, Thornton, Hubbard

Attendance: 26,000

November 14th:
RANGERS   (3) 8   HAMILTON
   Thornton 4 (9, 29, 46, 62),   ACADEMICALS   (1) 1
   Waddell 2 (19 pen, 67),   Shearer (23)
   Hubbard (74), Simpson (77)

RANGERS: Niven; Young, Little; McColl, Stanners, Cox; Waddell, Paton, Simpson, Thornton, Hubbard

HAMILTON: Houston; Bathgate, Hunter; Wilson, Simpson, Lindsay; Crawford, Shearer, Rae, Barrett, Cunning

Attendance: 25,000

November 21st:
RAITH ROVERS   (0) 1   RANGERS   (1) 2
   A. Young (83)   Thornton (35),
                                 Simpson (54)

RAITH ROVERS: Drummond; Kirk, McNaught; Williamson, Colville, Leigh; McEwan, A. Young, Copland, Kelly, Scott

RANGERS: Brown; Young, Little; McColl, Stanners, Cox; Waddell, Paton, Simpson, Thornton, Hubbard

Attendance: 18,000

November 28th:
RANGERS   (0) 1   CLYDE   (1) 1
   Thornton (62)   Ring (40)

RANGERS: Brown; Young, Little; McColl, Stanners, Cox; Waddell, Paton, Simpson, Thornton, Hubbard

CLYDE: Wilson; Murphy, Haddock; Campbell, Anderson, Baird; Hill, Robertson, Buchanan, McPhail, Ring

Attendance: 35,000

December 12th:
QUEEN OF THE   RANGERS   (0) 1
SOUTH   (0) 2   McColl (49)
   Brown 2 (48, 58)

QUEEN OF THE SOUTH: Henderson; Sharp, Binning; McBain, Smith, Greenock; Black, McGill, Brown, Rothera, Oakes

RANGERS: Brown; Young, Little; McColl, Woodburn, Cox; Waddell, Paton, Simpson, Thornton, McCulloch

Attendance: 18,500

December 19th:
PARTICK THISTLE   (0) 0   RANGERS   (1) 1
                                 Thornton (38)

PARTICK THISTLE: Ledgerwood; McGowan, Gibb; Crawford, Davidson, Mathers; McKenzie, Howitt, Sharp, Wright, McInnes

RANGERS: Brown; Cox, Little; McColl, Woodburn, Rae; Waddell, Grierson, Thornton, Prentice, McCulloch

Attendance: 20,000

December 26th:
RANGERS   (1) 3   HIBERNIAN   (0) 0
  Gardiner 2 (38, 51),
  Prentice (65)

RANGERS: Brown; Young, Little; McColl, Woodburn, Cox; Waddell, Grierson, Gardiner, Prentice, McCulloch

HIBERNIAN: Hamilton; Howie, Paterson; Gallacher, Ward, Combe; McDonald, Johnstone, Reilly, Turnbull, Ormond

Attendance: 28,000

League Positions

	P	W	D	L	F	A	Pts
1 Queen of South	17	11	2	4	46	25	24
2 Dundee	16	8	5	3	22	17	21
3 Hearts	17	8	4	5	39	26	20
4 Celtic	15	8	3	4	33	17	19
5 Aberdeen	16	8	3	5	40	22	19
6 Clyde	16	8	2	6	33	38	18
8 RANGERS	13	6	3	4	23	11	15

January 1st:
CELTIC   (0) 1   RANGERS   (0) 0
  Mochan (60)

CELTIC: Bonnar; Haughney, Meechan; Stein, Evans, Peacock; Higgins, Fernie, McPhail, Collins, Mochan

RANGERS: Brown; Young, Little; McColl, Woodburn, Cox; Waddell, Grierson, Gardiner, Prentice, McCulloch

Attendance: 65,000

A magnificent display by Rangers' defence almost baulked Celtic of a thoroughly deserved victory. Never had Woodburn in particular served his club more capably. It was cruel luck for Woodburn that his only mistake enabled Mochan to score 15 minutes after half-time, and even that error was partly caused by Young's failure to clear.

January 2nd:
RANGERS   (3) 3   STIRLING ALBION   (1) 1
  Paton (23),   Jackson (8)
  Prentice (40),
  McCulloch (44)

RANGERS: Brown; Young, Little; McColl, Woodburn, Cox; Waddell, Paton, Gardiner, Prentice, McCulloch

STIRLING ALBION: Kyle; Ferguson, Whitehead; Bain, Milligan, Smith; Jackson, Chalmers, Kelly, Williamson, Allan

Attendance: 28,000

January 9th:
ST MIRREN   (0) 0   RANGERS   (1) 1
                              Paton (14)

ST MIRREN: Park; Lapsley, Cunningham; Neilson, Mallan, Johnston; Blyth, Wilson, Telfer, Gemmell, Anderson

RANGERS: Brown; Young, Little; McColl, Woodburn, Cox; Waddell, Paton, Gardiner, Grierson, McCulloch

Attendance: 37,500

January 14th: Alex Scott signed from Bo'ness United.

January 16th:
RANGERS   (1) 3   AIRDRIE   (0) 0
  Thornton (26),
  Gardiner 2 (51, 64)

RANGERS: Brown; Young, Little; McColl, Woodburn, Cox; Waddell, Grierson, Gardiner, Thornton, McCulloch

AIRDRIE: Fraser; Pryde, T. Brown; Cairns, McGuire, Shankland; Quigley, Quinn, Baird, McMillan, W. Brown

Attendance: 19,000

January 23rd:
EAST FIFE   (0) 2   RANGERS   (1) 1
  Fleming 2 (55,59)   Grierson (36)

EAST FIFE: Curran; Emery, S. Stewart; Christie, Finlay, McLennan; J. Stewart, Fleming, Gardiner, Bonthrone, Matthew

RANGERS: Brown; Young, Little; McColl, Woodburn, Cox; Waddell, Grierson, Gardiner, Thornton, McCulloch

Attendance: 16,000

February 1st: The S.F.A. Council decided that any Rangers' players chosen for the World Cup preparation must remain in this country and couldn't take part in the club's tour of Canada and the U.S.A.

February 3rd: Rangers announced that their tour was off.

February 6th:
RANGERS   (2) 2   DUNDEE   (0) 0
  Grierson (27),
  McCulloch (31)

RANGERS: Brown; Young, Little; McColl, Woodburn, Cox; Waddell, Paton, Gardiner, Grierson, McCulloch

DUNDEE: Henderson; Follon, Frew; Ziesing, Malloy, Cowie; Hill, Toner, Merchant, Steel, Christie

Attendance: 30,000

February 15th: Rangers announced that their tour was on again.

February 20th:
HEARTS (2) 3   RANGERS (3) 3
  Bauld (10), Wardhaugh (44),   Waddell (1),
  Conn (88)   Gardiner (3),
                           Adie o.g. (22)

HEARTS: Watters; Parker, Adie; Laing, Glidden, Cumming; Souness, Conn, Bauld, Wardhaugh, Urquhart

RANGERS: Brown; Young, Little; McColl, Woodburn, Rae; Waddell, Grierson, Gardiner, Prentice, Paton

Attendance: 49,000

League Positions

	P	W	D	L	F	A	Pts
1 Hearts	25	14	6	5	63	38	34
2 Celtic	22	12	3	7	45	26	27
3 Aberdeen	23	12	3	8	57	39	27
4 Queen of South	23	12	3	8	58	42	27
5 Clyde	24	11	4	9	49	57	26
7 RANGERS	20	10	4	6	36	18	24

March 3rd: John Laurence joined the Rangers Board.

March 6th:
HAMILTON   RANGERS (1) 1
ACADEMICALS (0) 1   Little (25)
  Martin (89)

HAMILTON: Houston; Shearer, J. Young; Barrett, Scott, Martin; W. Young, Walker, Todd, Brown, Crawford

RANGERS: Niven; Caldow, Little; McColl, Stanners, Cox; Waddell, Grierson, Simpson, Prentice, Hubbard

Attendance: 18,000

March 17th:
RANGERS (0) 2   RAITH ROVERS (1) 2
  Caldow (50 pen),   McNeill (7), Kelly (59)
  Paton (55)

RANGERS: Brown; Caldow, Little; McColl, Young, Cox; McCulloch, Paton, Simpson, Prentice, Liddell

RAITH ROVERS: Drummond; Kirk, McLure; Young, Colville, Leigh; McEwan, McNeill, Copland, Kelly, Duncan

Attendance: 12,000

March 27th:
FALKIRK (3) 4   RANGERS (0) 3
  Sinclair 2 (10, 15),   Simpson 2 (51, 68),
  McCrae (13, 65)   Grierson (80)

FALKIRK: McFeat; Ralston, Sievwright; Black, McKenzie, J. Hunter; Sinclair, Morrison, Aikman, McCrae, Kelly

RANGERS: Brown; Caldow, Little; McColl, Woodburn, Cox; Waddell, Grierson, Simpson, Prentice, Hubbard

Attendance: 16,000

March 29th:
CLYDE (0) 2   RANGERS (3) 5
  Ring (50),   Simpson 2 (20, 70),
  Baird (87 pen)   Prentice 2 (32, 75),
                 Grierson (44)

CLYDE: Wilson; A. Murphy, Ferrier; Baird, E. Murphy, Keogh; Hill, Robertson, Buchanan, McPhail, Ring

RANGERS: Brown; Young, Little; McColl, Woodburn, Cox; Waddell, Grierson, Simpson, Prentice, Hubbard

Attendance: 29,919

April 1st: Bill Struth announced his decision to stand down as manager of the club although he would continue as a Director. The Press were tipping Scot Symon as his successor.

April 3rd: England beat Scotland 4-2 at Hampden Park. Sammy Cox captained the team.

April 3rd:
RANGERS (2) 2   QUEEN OF THE
  Simpson (16), McColl (19)   SOUTH (0) 0

RANGERS: Brown; Caldow, Little; McColl, Stanners, Rae; Waddell, Paton, Simpson, Prentice, Grierson

QUEEN OF THE SOUTH: Henderson; Sharp, Binning; J. Brown, Smith, Greenock; Black, McGill, Patterson, Rothera, Oakes

Attendance: 10,000

April 14th:
RANGERS (0) 1   ST MIRREN (0) 1
  Simpson (47)   Telfer (65 pen)

RANGERS: Brown; Caldow, Cox; McColl, Woodburn, Paton; Waddell, Rodger, Simpson, Rae, Hubbard

ST MIRREN: Park; Lapsley, Mallan; Moore, Telfer, Johnston; McMaster, Neilson, Anderson, Gemmell, McGugan

Attendance: 12,000

April 17th:
RANGERS   (1) 1   ABERDEEN   (1) 3
  Paton (23)   Leggat (40),
                               Buckley (52),
                               Allister (81 pen)

RANGERS: Brown; Caldow, Cox; McColl, Woodburn, Rae; Waddell, Paton, Simpson, Grierson, Hubbard

ABERDEEN: Martin; Smith, Caldwell; Allister, Young, Glen; Leggat, Hamilton, Buckley, O'Neill, Hather

Attendance: 34,000

April 21st:
RANGERS   (2) 3   FALKIRK   (0) 0
  Caldow (20 pen),
  Simpson (25), Grierson (55)

RANGERS: Brown; Caldow, Cox; Rae, Stanners, Prentice; Waddell, Paton, Simpson, Grierson, Hubbard

FALKIRK: Slater; Sievwright, Rae; Black, Ralston, Hunter; Sinclair, Dunlop, Aikman, Morrison, Kelly

Attendance: 22,000

April 21st: The Scottish World Cup Pool was announced. George Young was dropped and there was no Rangers' player in the pool.

April 24th:
AIRDRIE   (1) 2   RANGERS   (0) 0
  McMillan (37 pen),
  Quigley (75)

AIRDRIE: Walker; Pryde, Gordon; Elliot, Baillie, Docherty; Baird, McMillan, Quigley, Welsh, McCulloch

RANGERS: Brown; Rae, Cox; Neillands, Woodburn, Prentice; Waddell, Paton, Simpson, Grierson, Hubbard

Attendance: 8,000

April 27th:
HIBERNIAN   (0) 2   RANGERS   (1) 2
  Turnbull (27), Ogilvie (37)   Grierson (12),
                                 Paton (28)

HIBERNIAN: Miller; MacFarlane, Paterson; Buchanan, Ward, Campbell; Johnstone, Preston, Thomson, Turnbull, Ogilvie

RANGERS: Brown; Cox, Rae; Neillands, Woodburn, Prentice; Waddell, Grierson, Paton, Simpson, Liddell

Attendance: 17,300

May 5th: Willie Thornton accepted the Dundee managership. He took up the post after Rangers' Canadian and U.S.A. Tour.

June 15th: Scot Symon was appointed as Rangers' new manager.

Scottish League Division A

	P	W	D	L	F	A	Pts
1 Celtic	30	20	3	7	72	29	43
2 Hearts	30	16	6	8	70	45	38
3 Partick Thistle	30	17	1	12	76	54	35
4 RANGERS	30	13	8	9	56	35	34
5 Hibernian	30	15	4	11	72	51	34
6 East Fife	30	13	8	9	55	45	34
7 Dundee	30	14	6	10	46	47	34
8 Clyde	30	15	4	11	64	67	34
9 Aberdeen	30	15	3	12	66	51	33
10 Queen of South	30	14	4	12	72	58	32
11 St Mirren	30	12	4	14	44	54	28
12 Raith Rovers	30	10	6	14	56	60	26
13 Falkirk	30	9	7	14	47	61	25
14 Stirling Albion	30	10	4	16	39	62	24
15 Airdrie	30	5	5	20	41	92	15
16 Hamilton	30	4	3	23	29	94	11

LEAGUE CUP

August 8th:
RAITH ROVERS   (0) 0   RANGERS   (2) 4
                               Young (20 pen),
                               Prentice (22),
                               Simpson (70),
                               Grierson (89)

RAITH ROVERS: Johnstone; McLure, McNaught; Young, Colville, Leigh; McEwan, McDonald, Copland, Kelly, Penman

RANGERS: Niven; Young, Little; McColl, Woodburn, Cox; Waddell, Grierson, Simpson, Prentice, Hubbard

Attendance: 24,807

August 12th:
RANGERS   (2) 4   HEARTS   (1) 1
  Simpson (8), Hubbard (10)   Bauld (42)
  Young (84 pen), Grierson (90)

RANGERS: Niven; Young, Little; McColl, Woodburn, Cox; Waddell, Grierson, Simpson, Prentice, Hubbard

HEARTS: Watters; Farquhar, McKenzie; Laing, Dougan, Armstrong; Blackwood, Conn, Bauld, Wardhaugh, Urquhart

Attendance: n.a.

August 15th:

RANGERS   (3) 5   HAMILTON
  Grierson 3 (19, 29, 49),   ACADEMICALS   (1) 1
  Paton 2 (23, 55)   Cunning (37)

RANGERS: Niven; Young, Little; McColl, Woodburn, Cox; Waddell, Grierson, Paton, Prentice, Hubbard

HAMILTON: Ritchie; Bathgate, Johnstone; Wilson, Martin, Jeffrey; Young, Todd, Rae, Brown, Cunning

Attendance: 35,000

August 22nd:
RANGERS   (1) 3   RAITH ROVERS   (1) 1
  McCulloch (38),   Kelly (17)
  Paton 2 (48, 72)

RANGERS: Niven; Young, Little; McColl, Woodburn, Cox; McCulloch, Grierson, Paton, Prentice, Hubbard

RAITH ROVERS: Johnstone; Kirk, McNaught; Leigh, Colville, Williamson; McEwan, Young, Copland, Kelly, McIntyre

Attendance: 38,000

August 26th:
HEARTS   (1) 1   RANGERS   (0) 1
  Bauld (22)   Grierson (78)

HEARTS: Watters; Parker, McKenzie; King, Dougan, Armstrong; Conn, Wardhaugh, Bauld, Cumming, Urquhart

RANGERS: Niven; Young, Little; McColl, Woodburn, Cox; Waddell, Grierson, Paton, Prentice, Hubbard

Attendance: n.a.

August 29th:
HAMILTON   RANGERS   (2) 5
  ACADEMICALS   (0) 0   Paton 4 (15, 27, 46, 89),
                            Waddell (72)

HAMILTON: Ritchie; Bathgate, Johnstone; Wilson, G. Scott, Martin; Young, Shearer, J. Scott, Brown, Cunning

RANGERS: Niven; Young, Little; McColl, Woodburn, Cox; Waddell, Grierson, Paton, Prentice, Hubbard

Attendance: 25,000

League Cup Section Table

	P	W	D	L	F	A	Pts
RANGERS	6	5	1	0	22	4	11
Hearts	6	2	2	2	11	9	6
Raith Rovers	6	3	0	3	8	11	6
Hamilton	6	0	1	5	3	20	1

September 12th: Quarter-Final First Leg
RANGERS   (1) 4   AYR UNITED   (1) 2
  Prentice 3 (14, 62, 83),   Hutton (10),
  Grierson (60)   Finnie (60)

RANGERS: Niven; Caldow, Little; McColl, Woodburn, Cox; Waddell, Grierson, Paton, Prentice, Hubbard

AYR UNITED: Round; Rodger, Leckie; W. Fraser, McNeill, Cairns; Japp, Finnie, J. Fraser, Hutton, McKenna

Attendance: 30,000

September 16th:
AYR UNITED   (2) 3   RANGERS   (1) 2
  McKenna (n.a.),   Waddell (34 pen),
  Fraser (28 pen),   Paton (55)
  Hutton (78)

AYR UNITED: Round; Rodger, Leckie; W. Fraser, McNeill, Cairns; Japp, Finnie, J. Fraser, Hutton, McKenna

RANGERS: Niven; Caldow, Little; McColl, Woodburn, Cox; Waddell, Grierson, Paton, Prentice, Hubbard

Attendance: 20,000

Rangers won 6-5 on aggregate

October 10th: Semi-Final   At Hampden Park
PARTICK THISTLE   (2) 2   RANGERS   (0) 0
  Wright (32), Howitt (45)

PARTICK THISTLE: Ledgerwood; McGowan, Gibb; Crawford, Davidson, Kerr; McKenzie, Howitt, Sharp, Wright, Walker

RANGERS: Niven; Young, Little; McColl, Woodburn, Cox; Waddell, Grierson, Paton, Prentice, Hubbard

Attendance: 48,064

Midway through the first half, Thistle, with the strong wind behind them, decided to start testing Niven from long range. The change of tactics brought 2 goals, the first scored by Wright from a rebound after McKenzie had hit a post and the 2nd by Howitt after Kerr had nonplussed Niven with a huge punt which dropped just under the crossbar. Rangers swept into the attack after the interval and forced a series of corners. That was however the limit of their threat as Ledgerwood was in magnificent form.

SCOTTISH CUP

January 30th: First Round
RANGERS   (0) 2   QUEENS PARK   (0) 0
  Waddell (50), Gardiner (87)

RANGERS: Brown; Young, Little; McColl, Woodburn, Cox; Waddell, Paton, Gardiner, Grierson, McCulloch

QUEENS PARK: H. Weir; I. Harnett, M. T. Dewar; R. Cromar, J. Valentine, W. Hastie; C. Church, R. McKinven, M. Murray, R. Dalziel, W. Omand

Attendance: 34,000

February 13th: Second Round
RANGERS   (0) 2   KILMARNOCK   (1) 2
  Grierson (50),   Murray (25),
  Gardiner (52)   Henaughan (56)

RANGERS: Brown; Young, Little; McColl, Woodburn, Cox; Waddell, Paton, Gardiner, Grierson, McCulloch

KILMARNOCK: Brown; Collins, Hood; Russell, Thyne, Middlemass; Murray, Harvey, Jack, Curlett, Henaughan

Attendance: 40,000

February 17th: Second Round Replay

KILMARNOCK	(0) 1	RANGERS	(2) 3
Jack (67)		Paton 2 (7, 59),	
		McCulloch (32)	

KILMARNOCK: Brown; Collins, Milloy; Russell, Thyne, Middlemass; Murray, Harvey, Jack, Curlett, Henaughan

RANGERS: Brown; Young, Little; McColl, Woodburn, Rae; Waddell, Grierson, Paton, Prentice, McCulloch

Attendance: 33,535

February 27th: Third Round

THIRD LANARK	0	RANGERS	0

THIRD LANARK: Robertson; Balunas, Harrower; Kennedy, Forsyth, Muir; Barclay, Docherty, Kerr, Dick, McLeod

RANGERS: Niven; Young, Little; McColl, Woodburn, Cox; Waddell, Findlay, Paton, Grierson, McCulloch

Attendance: 45,591

March 3rd: Third Round Replay

RANGERS	(2) 4	THIRD LANARK	(1) 4
Prentice 2 (1, 7),		Kerr 2 (22, n.a.),	
Simpson 2 (55, n.a.)		Docherty 2 (56, 87 pen)	
	After Extra Time		

RANGERS: Niven; Young, Little; McColl, Woodburn, Cox; Waddell, Grierson, Simpson, Prentice, McCulloch

THIRD LANARK: Robertson; Balunas, Harrower; Kennedy, Forsyth, Muir; Barclay, Docherty, Kerr, Dick, McLeod

Young missed a penalty

Attendance: 17,000

March 8th: Third Round Second Replay   At Ibrox

RANGERS	(1) 3	THIRD LANARK	(1) 2
Caldow (29 pen),		Kerr (15),	
Paton (48), Prentice (63)		Docherty (88)	

RANGERS: Niven; Caldow, Little; McColl, Young, Cox; McCulloch, Paton, Simpson, Prentice, Liddell

THIRD LANARK: Robertson; Balunas, Murray; Kennedy, Forsyth, Muir; Barclay, Docherty, Kerr, Dick, McLeod

Attendance: 31,000

March 13th: Fourth Round

RANGERS	(2) 4	BERWICK	
Simpson (36), Paton (41),		RANGERS	(0) 0
Liddell (63), Caldow (76 pen)			

RANGERS: Niven; Caldow, Little; McColl, Young, Cox; McCulloch, Paton, Simpson, Prentice, Liddell

BERWICK RANGERS: Devanney; Hogg, McColl; Taggart, Cassidy, Mitchell; Younger, Muir, Kingsmore, McGovern, Blaickie

Attendance: 60,245

April 10th: Semi-Final   At Hampden Park

ABERDEEN	(2) 6	RANGERS	(0) 0
O'Neill 3 (14, 23, 83),			
Leggat (70), Allister (88 pen),			
Buckley (89)			

ABERDEEN: Martin; Mitchell, Caldwell; Allister, Young, Glen; Leggat, Hamilton, Buckley, O'Neill, Hather

RANGERS: Brown; Caldow, Little; McColl, Woodburn, Cox; Waddell, Grierson, Simpson, Prentice, Hubbard

Attendance: 110,939

Outclassed though they were, Rangers enjoyed little luck. Brown was injured in the 2nd minute of the match and was not himself thereafter. Little too was hurt early in the first half, and 25 minutes from the end, with the score only 2-0, hobbled painfully along the left touchline and crossed and both Prentice and Simpson struck the crossbar, in quick succession, with shots that completely beat Martin. The Ibrox team had no forward to compare with Hamilton or O'Neill, who in his first match after a serious head injury scored 3 goals.

Hubbard, a popular winger of Rangers in the fifties.

APPEARANCES

	League	League Cup	Scottish Cup	Glasgow Cup	Charity Cup	Friendlies
Niven	9	9	4	4	3	3
Young	20	7	6	4	3	1
Little	25	9	8	4	-	2
McColl	27	9	8	4	-	2
Woodburn	21	9	7	4	-	1
Cox	28	9	7	4	3	1
Waddell	29	8	6	3	3	3
Grierson	21	9	6	4	3	2
Paton	19	7	6	4	-	1
Prentice	18	9	5	4	3	-
Hubbard	14	9	1	4	-	1
Caldow	8	2	3	-	-	1
Simpson	18	2	4	-	3	2
Liddell	5	-	2	-	-	1
Stanners	8	-	-	-	3	1
Findlay	1	-	1	-	-	1
McMillan	2	-	-	-	-	-
Thornton	8	-	-	-	-	2
Brown	21	-	4	-	-	-
Rae	8	-	1	-	3	2
McCulloch	9	1	7	1	3	1
Gardiner	8	-	2	-	-	1
Rodger	1	-	-	-	-	-
Neillands	2	-	-	-	3	-
Shaw	-	-	-	-	-	1
McKenzie	-	-	-	-	-	1
Pryde	-	-	-	-	-	1

GOALSCORERS

League: Simpson 11, Grierson 8, Thornton 8, Paton 7, Gardiner 5, Prentice 5, Waddell 3 (1 pen), Caldow 2 (both pens), McCulloch 2, McColl 2, Little 1, Own Goals 1

League Cup: Paton 9, Grierson 7, Prentice 4, Young 2 (both pens), Simpson 2, Waddell 2 (1 pen), Hubbard 1, McCulloch 1

Scottish Cup: Paton 4, Prentice 3, Gardiner 2, Simpson 2, Caldow 2 (both pens), Liddell 1, McCulloch 1, Grierson 1, Waddell 1, Own Goals 1

Glasgow Cup: Paton 5, Prentice 3, Hubbard 1, Grierson 1

Charity Cup: Prentice 1, Simpson 1, Own Goals 1

Friendlies: Thornton 1, Paton 1, McCulloch 1

Tour Matches: Simpson 10, Hubbard 7 (1 pen), Paton 6, Young 4 (1 pen), McCulloch 3, Thornton 2, Prentice 2, McColl 1, Waddell 1

N.B. Table does not include Tour Match appearances.

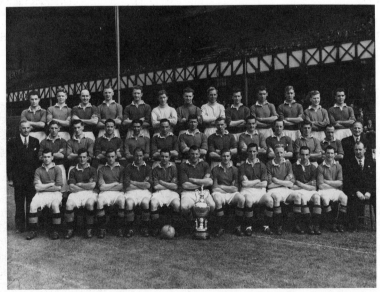

Rangers team group at the start of Season 1954/55. Scott Symon (manager) is at left of picture. George Young is readily identifiable, guarding the silverware.

Season 1954–55

Scot Symon's first season in charge was not particularly successful by Ibrox standards. The team finished 3rd in the Championship – 8 points behind Aberdeen and 4 behind Celtic. Only 2 points were dropped at home where the team remained undefeated, but 6 of the last 7 away games were lost, Rangers' disastrous run starting at Easter Road on Christmas Day. 29 players were used during the campaign and Irishman Billy Simpson finished as top scorer with 19 goals in his 25 appearances. The *sine die* suspension of Woodburn, which finished the career of this great player, seemed particularly harsh – even by the standards of the time. Alex Scott burst onto the scene, scoring a hat-trick on his debut.

An own goal saw Rangers through at Dens Park in a Fifth Round Scottish Cup Replay but Aberdeen proved too strong at Pittodrie in the next Round. One consolation was that nearly 130,000 spectators watched Rangers' 3 ties.

Rangers' League Cup challenge ended at the Quarter-Final Stage, Motherwell winning 3-2 on aggregate. Motherwell went on to reach the Final in which they were beaten by Hearts.

League: Third
League Cup: Quarter-Finalists
Scottish Cup: Sixth Round

SCOTTISH LEAGUE DIVISION A

August 12th: Billy Ritchie was signed from Bathgate Thistle.

September 2nd: Bobby Cunning was signed from Hamilton Academicals for £2,500.

September 11th:
RANGERS (1) 1   HIBERNIAN (0) 1
  Grierson (20)   Preston (70)

RANGERS: Niven; Young, Little; McColl, Woodburn, Rae; McCulloch, Grierson, Gardiner, Prentice, Hubbard

HIBERNIAN: Younger; Higgins, MacFarlane; Buchanan, Paterson, Combe; Smith, Johnstone, Preston, Turnbull, Ormond

Attendance: 50,000

September 14th: The S.F.A. suspended Willie Woodburn *sine die*.

September 18th:
CELTIC (0) 2   RANGERS (0) 0
  Walsh (59), Higgins (89)

CELTIC: Bonnar; Haughney, Fallon; Evans, Stein, Peacock; Higgins, Boden, Walsh, Fernie, Mochan

RANGERS: Niven; Young, Little; McColl, Stanners, Rae; McCulloch, Grierson, Simpson, Prentice, Hubbard

Attendance: 45,000

September 28th: Johnny Little was called up to the Army. He was ordered to report on October 7th.

October 2nd:
EAST FIFE (2) 2   RANGERS (1) 7
  Fleming (18),   Gardiner (10),
  Bonthrone (29),   Young (46 pen),
                    Grierson 2 (57, 88),
                    McCulloch (80),
                    Paton 2 (76, 80)

EAST FIFE: Curran; Emery, S. Stewart; Christie, Finlay, Whyte; Wilson, Fleming, Gardiner, Bonthrone, Matthew

RANGERS: Niven; Young, Little; McColl, Stanners, Rae; McCulloch, Paton, Gardiner, Grierson, Waddell

Attendance: 16,500

October 9th:
RANGERS   (1) 6   STIRLING ALBION   (1) 1
   Grierson 2 (7, 89),   Kelly (38)
   Gardiner 4 (66, 68, 75, 81)

RANGERS: Brown; Young, Gordon McKenzie;
McColl, George McKenzie, Rae; McCulloch, Paton,
Gardiner, Grierson, Waddell

STIRLING ALBION: Mitchell; Gibson, Whitehead;
Bain, Milligan, Smith; Chalmers, Docherty, Kelly,
McGill, Brander

Attendance: 20,000

**October 16th: Scotland beat Wales 1-0 in Cardiff.
Young and Waddell were in the team.**

October 16th:
PARTICK THISTLE   (2) 2   RANGERS   (2) 5
   Mathers 2 (33 pen, 45 pen)   Simpson 3 (13, 17, 46),
                                Hubbard (58 pen),
                                Grierson (73)

PARTICK THISTLE: Brodie; Brown, Gibb; Harvey,
Kerr, Mathers; McKenzie, Howitt, Smith, Wright,
McParland

RANGERS: Brown; Little, Gordon McKenzie;
McColl, Stanners, Rae; McCulloch, Paton, Simpson,
Grierson, Hubbard

Attendance: 35,741

October 23rd:
RANGERS   (1) 3   DUNDEE   (0) 0
   Grierson (9),
   Hubbard (78 pen), Rae (83)

RANGERS: Brown; Young, McKenzie; McColl,
Stanners, Rae; Waddell, Paton, Simpson, Grierson,
Hubbard

DUNDEE: Brown; Follon, Irvine; Gallacher, Malloy,
Cowie; Walker, Henderson, Flavell, Dunsmuir, Hill

Attendance: 30,000

October 30th:
ST MIRREN   (0) 2   RANGERS   (1) 1
   Telfer (59 pen),   Hubbard (43 pen)
   McDonald (86)

ST MIRREN: Lornie; Lapsley, Cunningham;
Neilson, Telfer, Johnston; McGuigan, Holmes,
McDonald, Gemmell, Callan

RANGERS: Niven; Young, Little; McColl, Stanners,
Rae; Waddell, Paton, Simpson, Grierson, Hubbard

Attendance: 35,300

League positions
	P	W	D	L	F	A	Pts
1 Aberdeen	8	6	0	2	21	6	12
2 Celtic	7	5	2	0	19	8	12
3 Clyde	8	5	2	1	25	14	12
4 RANGERS	7	4	1	2	23	10	9
5 St Mirren	7	4	1	2	16	15	9

**November 3rd: Scotland drew 2-2 with Ireland at
Hampden Park. Young and Waddell were in the
team.**

November 6th:
RANGERS   (3) 6   KILMARNOCK   (0) 0
   Simpson 2 (20, 82),
   Brand 2 (30, 84), Paton (41),
   Hubbard (71 pen)

RANGERS: Niven; Little, Cox; McColl, Young, Rae;
Brand, Paton, Simpson, Grierson, Hubbard

KILMARNOCK: Brown; Collins, Hood; Russell,
Thyne, Rollo; Mays, Harvey, Toner, Curlett, Murray

Attendance: 40,000

November 13th:
FALKIRK   (0) 0   RANGERS   (2) 3
                          Prentice (14),
                          Simpson 2 (17, 85)

FALKIRK: Slater; Parker, Rae; Black, Ralston,
Campbell; Ormond, Morrison, Davidson, McCrae,
Plumb

RANGERS: Niven; Young, Cox; McColl, Stanners,
Rae; Brand, Paton, Simpson, Prentice, Hubbard

Attendance: 20,000

November 20th:
CLYDE   (1) 1   RANGERS   (0) 1
   Robertson (12)   Gardiner (86)

CLYDE: Wilson; Murphy, Haddock; Gallacher,
Anderson, Laing; Hill, Robertson, Buchanan,
Carmichael, Ring

RANGERS: Brown; Little, Cox; McColl, Young, Rae;
McCulloch, Paton, Gardiner, Simpson, Waddell

Attendance: 32,000

November 27th:
RANGERS   (1) 1   RAITH ROVERS   (0) 0
   Hubbard (26 pen)

RANGERS: Brown; Little, Cox; McColl, Young, Rae;
Waddell, Grierson, Gardiner, Prentice, Hubbard

RAITH ROVERS: Drummond; McLure, McNaught;
Young, Colville, Leigh; Kirk, Thomson, Copland,
Buchan, Duncan

Attendance: 25,000

December 4th:

QUEEN OF THE SOUTH (1) 1	RANGERS (1) 2
Baxter (7)	Simpson 2 (15, 49)

QUEEN OF THE SOUTH: Henderson; Sharp, Binning; Brown, Smith, Greenock; Black, McGill, Briscoe, Patterson, Baxter

RANGERS: Brown; Little, Cox; McColl, Young, Rae; Waddell, Paton, Simpson, Brand, Hubbard

Attendance: 12,500

December 11th:

RANGERS (2) 3	ABERDEEN (0) 1
Simpson 2 (38, 72), Grierson (41)	Buckley (82)

RANGERS: Brown; Little, Cox; McColl, Young, Rae; Waddell, Paton, Simpson, Grierson, Hubbard

ABERDEEN: Martin; Mitchell, Smith, Allister, Young, Glen; Leggat, Yorston, Buckley, Wishart, Hather

Attendance: 45,800

December 14th: Willie Findlay joined Albion Rovers. No fee was involved.

December 18th:

HEARTS (0) 3	RANGERS (2) 4
Conn (50), Urquhart (56), Bauld (69)	Grierson 2 (7, 9), Simpson 2 (82, 88)

HEARTS: Duff; Parker, Adie; Mackay, Glidden, Cumming; Souness, Conn, Bauld, Wardhaugh, Urquhart

RANGERS: Niven; Little, Cox; McColl, Stanners, Prentice; Rodger, Paton, Simpson, Grierson, Hubbard

Attendance: 35,000

December 25th:

HIBERNIAN (2) 2	RANGERS (0) 1
Combe (5), Ormond (25)	Grierson (88)

HIBERNIAN: Younger; Ward, Paterson; Grant, Plenderleith, Turnbull; Smith, Johnstone, Reilly, Combe, Ormond

RANGERS: Niven; Little, Cox; McColl, Young, Rae; Waddell, Paton, Simpson, Grierson, Hubbard

Attendance: 43,000

League positions

	P	W	D	L	F	A	Pts
1 Aberdeen	16	13	0	3	39	13	26
2 RANGERS	15	10	2	3	44	18	22
3 Celtic	15	8	6	1	44	20	22
4 St Mirren	15	10	2	3	38	25	22
5 Hibernian	16	10	1	5	37	29	21

January 1st:

RANGERS (1) 4	CELTIC (1) 1
Simpson (9), Hubbard 3 (72, 80, 89 pen)	Fernie (32)

RANGERS: Niven; Little, Cox; Pryde, Young, Rae; McCulloch, Prentice, Simpson, Grierson, Hubbard

CELTIC: Bell; Haughney, Meechan; Evans, Stein, Peacock; Boden, Tully, Walsh, Fernie, Collins

Attendance: 65,000

In the 9th minute Stein sliced a clearance straight to the feet of Grierson, who promptly and accurately gave Simpson a scoring chance which he gratefully accepted. Easily as Rangers won in the end, it should be noted that only 3 minutes of the first half were left when Simpson had his side's 2nd shot. 10 minutes earlier on practically the only occasion on which Walsh beat Young, the centre-half brought him down and Fernie lobbed the free-kick over the defensive wall and away from the searching fingers of Niven. In 72 minutes Hubbard jinked past Haughney, Stein and Bell before he walked the ball into the net. 7 minutes later Simpson, closely challenged by Stein, chipped his pass so precisely that Hubbard, intelligently placed in the centre, had merely to direct the ball into a gaping goal. A minute from time Hubbard completed his hat-trick when he converted a penalty after Grierson had been brought down in the box.

January 3rd:

MOTHERWELL (1) 2	RANGERS (0) 0
McSeveney (20), Williams (83)	

MOTHERWELL: McIntyre; Kilmarnock, Shaw; Cox, Mason, Redpath; Sloan, Aitken, McSeveney, Humphries, Williams

RANGERS: Niven; Little, Cox; Pryde, Young, Rae; McCulloch, Prentice, Simpson, Grierson, Hubbard

Attendance: 25,000

January 8th:

RANGERS (0) 2	EAST FIFE (0) 0
Gardiner (58), Simpson (73)	

RANGERS: Niven; Caldow, Little; Pryde, Young, Prentice; McCulloch, Paton, Gardiner, Simpson, Hubbard

EAST FIFE: Curran; S. Stewart, Emery; Christie, Finlay, McLennan; J. Stewart, Gardiner, Wright, Leishman, Matthew

Attendance: 20,000

January 12th: Jimmy Millar was signed from Dunfermline Athletic for £5,000.

January 29th:
DUNDEE   (2) 2   RANGERS   (0) 1
  Christie (3),   Simpson (50)
  Merchant (30)

DUNDEE: Brown; Gray, Craig; Gallacher, Malloy, Cowie; Chalmers, Henderson, Merchant, Roy, Christie

RANGERS: Niven; Little, Cox; McColl, Young, Prentice; Waddell, Paton, Simpson, Millar, Hubbard

Attendance: 25,000

February 12th:
RANGERS   (0) 1   ST MIRREN   (0) 1
  McCulloch (52)   Wilson (84)

RANGERS: Niven; Cox, Little; McColl, Young, Rae; McCulloch, Paton, Millar, Simpson, Hubbard

ST MIRREN: Lornie; Lapsley, Johnston; Neilson, Telfer, Holmes; McGugan, Wilson, Anderson, Gemmell, Callan

Attendance: 40,000

February 26th:
KILMARNOCK   (1) 1   RANGERS   (0) 0
  Flavell (31)

KILMARNOCK: Brown; Baillie, Rollo; Curlett, Dougan, Mackay; Murray, Toner, Flavell, Beattie, Henaughan

RANGERS: Brown; Caldow, Little; McColl, Young, Pryde; Rodger, Paton, Simpson, Neillands, Hubbard

Attendance: 24,000

League positions

	P	W	D	L	F	A	Pts
1 Aberdeen	23	19	1	3	58	18	39
2 Celtic	22	13	7	2	61	29	33
3 Clyde	23	10	8	5	53	39	28
4 St Mirren	22	11	6	5	47	37	28
5 RANGERS	21	12	3	6	52	25	27

March 5th:
STIRLING ALBION   (0) 0   RANGERS   (0) 2
                        Prentice (70),
                        Gardiner (89)

STIRLING ALBION: Mitchell; Gibson, Erskine; Docherty, Williamson, Smith; Laird, Rattray, Andrews, McGill, Brander

RANGERS: Niven; Caldow, Gordon McKenzie; McColl, Young, Prentice; McCulloch, Paton, Gardiner, Simpson, Cunning

Attendance: 9,000

March 9th:
RANGERS   (1) 4   FALKIRK   (1) 1
  Gardiner (12)   McCrae (30)
  Scott 3 (49, 73, 86)

RANGERS: Niven; Caldow, Gordon McKenzie; McColl, Young, Prentice; Scott, Paton, Gardiner, Simpson, Cunning

FALKIRK: Slater; Parker, Sievwright; Grant, McKenzie, Campbell; Taylor, Morrison, Davidson, McCrae, Sinclair

Attendance: 8,000

March 12th:
RANGERS   (0) 1   CLYDE   (0) 0
  Simpson (70)

RANGERS: Niven; Caldow, McKenzie; McColl, Young, Prentice; Scott, McMillan, Gardiner, Simpson, Cunning

CLYDE: Hewkins; Murphy, Haddock; Granville, Anderson, Laing; Hill, Robertson, McPhail, Brown, Ring

Attendance: 60,000

March 19th:
RAITH ROVERS   (1) 1   RANGERS   (0) 0
  Copland (10)

RAITH ROVERS: G. Stewart; Kirk, McLure; Young, McNaught, Leigh; Rutherford, J. Stewart, Copland, Kelly, Scott

RANGERS: Niven; Caldow, McKenzie; Pryde, Young, Prentice; McCulloch, Simpson, Gardiner, Rae, Hubbard

Attendance: 14,500

March 26th:
RANGERS   (0) 1   QUEEN OF THE
  Hubbard (85 pen)   SOUTH   (0) 0

RANGERS: Niven; Caldow, McKenzie; McColl, Young, Prentice; Scott, Woods, Simpson, Grierson, Hubbard

QUEEN OF THE SOUTH: Henderson; Sharp, Whitehead; McBain, Smith, Gibson; Baxter, Black, Patterson, Rothera, Oakes

Attendance: 15,000

April 2nd:
ABERDEEN   (1) 4   RANGERS   (0) 0
  Buckley 3 (19, 48, 75),
  Leggat (89)
ABERDEEN: Morrison; Mitchell, Caldwell; Allister, Young, Glen; Leggat, Yorston, Buckley, Wishart, Hather

RANGERS: Niven; Caldow, McKenzie; McColl, Young, Prentice; Scott, Paton, Gardiner, Rae, Waddell

Attendance: 30,000

April 9th:
RANGERS   (1) 2   HEARTS   (0) 1
  Hubbard (27),   Parker (75 pen)
  Simpson (89)
RANGERS: Niven; Caldow, Little; McColl, Young, Prentice; Scott, McMillan, Simpson, Grierson, Hubbard

HEARTS: Duff; Parker, Adie; Armstrong, Glidden, Cumming; Souness, Whittle, Wardhaugh, Blackwood, Urquhart

Attendance: 30,000

April 11th:
RANGERS   (0) 3   PARTICK THISTLE   (0) 1
  Hubbard 2 (51, 60 pen),   Smith (59)
  Simpson (70)
RANGERS: Niven; Caldow, Little; McColl, Young, Prentice; Scott, McMillan, Simpson, Grierson, Hubbard

PARTICK THISTLE: Ledgerwood; Kerr, Donlevy; Harvey, Thomson, Wright; McKenzie, Howitt, Smith, Crowe, McParland

Attendance: n.a.

April 30th:
RANGERS   (1) 2   MOTHERWELL   (0) 0
  Hubbard (20),
  McMillan (75)
RANGERS: Niven; Caldow, Little; McColl, Young, Prentice; Scott, McMillan, Simpson, Grierson, Hubbard

MOTHERWELL: Weir; Kilmarnock, Shaw; Mason, Paton, Cameron; Sloan, Humphries, Hunter, Aitken, Williams

Attendance: 30,000

Scottish League Division A

	P	W	D	L	F	A	Pts
1 Aberdeen	30	24	1	5	73	46	49
2 Celtic	30	19	8	3	76	37	46
3 RANGERS	30	19	3	8	67	33	41
4 Hearts	30	16	7	7	74	45	39
5 Hibernian	30	15	4	11	64	54	34
6 St Mirren	30	12	8	10	55	54	32
7 Clyde	30	11	9	10	59	50	31
8 Dundee	30	13	4	13	48	48	30
9 Partick Thistle	30	11	7	12	49	61	29
10 Kilmarnock	30	10	6	14	46	58	26
11 East Fife	30	9	6	15	51	62	24
12 Falkirk	30	8	8	14	42	54	24
13 Queen of South	30	9	6	15	38	56	24
14 Raith Rovers	30	10	3	17	49	57	23
15 Motherwell	30	9	4	17	42	62	22
16 Stirling Albion	30	2	2	26	29	105	6

May 4th: Young was in the Scotland team which beat Portugal at Hampden Park.

May 12th: Max Murray was signed from Queens Park.

May 15th: Scotland drew 2-2 with Yugoslavia in Belgrade. Young was in the team.

May 19th: Jim Rodger was freed. Also Gordon McKenzie, and George McKenzie.

June 14th: Sammy Baird was signed from Preston North End for £12,000.

LEAGUE CUP

August 14th:
STIRLING ALBION   (0) 0   RANGERS   (2) 5
                          Prentice 2 (36, 55),
                          Simpson 3 (37, 77, 82)
STIRLING ALBION: Jenkins; Gibson, Whitehead; Bain, McQueen, Smith; Chalmers, Williamson, Kelly, Christie, Brander

RANGERS: Niven; Young, Little; McColl, Woodburn, Rae; Waddell, Grierson, Simpson, Prentice, Liddell

August 18th:
RANGERS   (1) 1   PARTICK THISTLE   (1) 1
  Davidson o.g. (39)   Crowe (16)
RANGERS: Niven; Young, Little; McColl, Woodburn, Rae; Waddell, Grierson, Simpson, Prentice, Liddell

PARTICK THISTLE: Ledgerwood; Kerr, Gibb; Crawford, Davidson, Mathers; Harvey, Howitt, Crowe, Wright, McInnes

August 21st:
RANGERS   (0) 1   CLYDE   (2) 3
  Grierson (77)   Hill (23),
                          Carmichael (32),
                          Buchanan (54)

RANGERS: Niven; Caldow, Little; McColl, Woodburn, Rae; Waddell, Grierson, Paton, Prentice, Liddell

CLYDE: Wilson; Murphy, Haddock; Gallacher, Anderson, Keogh; Hill, Robertson, Buchanan, Carmichael, Ring

Attendance: 45,000

August 28th:
RANGERS   (0) 2   STIRLING ALBION   (0) 0
  Paton (85),
  Hubbard (87 pen)

RANGERS: Niven; Young, Little; McColl, Woodburn, Rae; McCulloch, Paton, Simpson, Prentice, Hubbard

STIRLING ALBION: Jenkins; Gibson, Whitehead; Bain, Milligan, Smith; Chalmers, Rattray, Kelly, Paterson, Brander

Woodburn was ordered off 30 seconds from time following an incident with Paterson

Attendance: 30,000

September 1st:
PARTICK THISTLE   (0) 1   RANGERS   (1) 2
  Howitt (60)   Prentice (19),
                          Simpson (80)

PARTICK THISTLE: Ledgerwood; Kerr, Gibb; Harvey, Davidson, Mathers; McKenzie, Howitt, Wright, Crawford, Henderson

RANGERS: Niven; Young, Little; McKenzie, Woodburn, Rae; McCulloch, Paton, Simpson, Prentice, Hubbard

Attendance: 26,883

September 4th:
CLYDE   (0) 1   RANGERS   (0) 2
  Buchanan (68)   Simpson (64),
                          Paton (89)

CLYDE: Watson; Murphy, Haddock; Granville, Anderson, Gallacher; Hill, Robertson, Buchanan, Carmichael, Ring

RANGERS: Niven; Young, Little; McKenzie, Woodburn, McColl; McCulloch, Paton, Simpson, Prentice, Hubbard

Attendance: 32,700

League Cup Section Table

	P	W	D	L	F	A	Pts
RANGERS	6	4	1	1	13	6	9
Partick Thistle	6	3	1	2	16	8	7
Clyde	6	2	0	4	10	10	4
Stirling Albion	6	2	0	4	5	20	4

September 22nd: Quarter-Final First Leg
MOTHERWELL   (1) 2   RANGERS   (0) 1
  Aitken (5), Hunter (49)   Prentice (50)

MOTHERWELL: Weir; Kilmarnock, Shaw; Cox, Paton, Redpath; Hunter, Aitken, Bain, Humphries, Williams

RANGERS: Niven; Young, Little; Menzies, Stanners, Rae; McCulloch, Grierson, Gardiner, Prentice, Cunning

Attendance: 24,000

September 25th: Quarter-Final Second Leg
RANGERS   (0) 1   MOTHERWELL   (1) 1
  Paton (56)   Bain (6)

RANGERS: Niven; Young, Little; McColl, Stanners, Rae; Waddell, Grierson, Paton, Prentice, Cunning

MOTHERWELL: Weir; Kilmarnock, Shaw; Cox, Paton, Redpath; Hunter, Aitken, Bain, Humphries, Williams

Attendance: 47,000

Motherwell won 3-2 on aggregate

SCOTTISH CUP

February 5th: Fifth Round
RANGERS   0   DUNDEE   0

RANGERS: Niven; Cox, Little; McColl, Young, Rae; Brand, Paton, Simpson, Prentice, Hubbard

DUNDEE: Brown; Gray, Craig; Gallacher, Malloy, Cowie; Chalmers, Henderson, Merchant, Roy, Christie

Attendance: 58,000

February 9th: Fifth Round Replay
DUNDEE   (0) 0   RANGERS   (0) 1
                          Gallacher o.g. (80)

DUNDEE: Brown; Gray, Craig; Gallacher, Malloy, Cowie; Chalmers, Henderson, Merchant, Roy, Christie

RANGERS: Niven; Cox, Little; McColl, Young, Rae; McCulloch, Paton, Gardiner, Simpson, Hubbard

Attendance: 25,600

February 19th: Sixth Round
ABERDEEN   (1) 2   RANGERS   (1) 1
  Hather (7), Wishart (51) Neillands (11)

ABERDEEN: Martin; Mitchell, Smith; Allister, Young, Glen; Hamilton, Yorston, Buckley, Wishart, Hather

RANGERS: Niven; Little, Cox; McColl, Young, Rae; McCulloch, Paton, Millar, Neillands, Hubbard

Attendance: 44,647

APPEARANCES

	League	League Cup	Scottish Cup	Glasgow Cup	Charity Cup	Friendlies
Niven	22	8	3	4	3	4
Young	28	7	3	3	1	4
Little	21	8	3	3	2	2
McColl	26	6	3	4	3	7
Woodburn	1	6	-	2	-	-
Rae	19	7	3	-	3	5
Waddell	11	4	-	-	-	3
Grierson	18	5	-	2	-	4
Simpson	25	5	2	1	3	6
Prentice	18	8	1	2	3	4 + 1 sub
Liddell	-	3	-	-	-	-
Caldow	11	1	-	1	3	5
Paton	19	5	3	3	1	3
McCulloch	12	4	2	4	-	1
Hubbard	23	3	3	2	3	6
Gordon McKenzie	9	-	-	1	-	2
Menzies	-	1	-	2	-	-
Stanners	7	2	-	2	2	5
Gardiner	11	1	1	1	-	2

	League	League Cup	Scottish Cup	Glasgow Cup	Charity Cup	Friendlies
Cunning	3	2	-	2	-	-
George McKenzie	1	2	-	2	-	-
McMillan	4	-	-	2	3	2
Neillands	1	-	1	1	-	-
Brown	8	-	-	-	-	3
Cox	12	-	3	-	-	1
Rodger	2	-	-	-	-	1
Scott	7	-	-	-	3	4
Pryde	5	-	-	-	-	1
Walker	-	-	-	-	-	2
Woods	1	-	-	-	-	-
Millar	2	-	1	-	-	-
Brand	3	-	1	-	-	-

GOALSCORERS

League: Simpson 19, Hubbard 13 (8 pens), Grierson 11, Gardiner 9, Scott 3, Paton 3, Prentice 2, Brand 2, McCulloch 2, Young 1 (pen), Rae 1, McMillan 1

League Cup: Simpson 5, Prentice 4, Paton 3, Grierson 1, Hubbard 1 (pen), Own Goals 1

Scottish Cup: Neillands 1, Own Goals 1

Glasgow Cup: McCulloch 2, Gardiner 2, Paton 1, Prentice 1

Charity Cup: Simpson 3, McMillan 1, Hubbard 1, Scott 1, Paton 1

Friendlies: Hubbard 4 (1 pen), Simpson 3, Waddell 2, Grierson 2, Scott 2, McMillan 2, Prentice 1

The Rangers squad of players from 1967. Back row: Scot Symon (manager), Watson, Provan, McKinnon, Sorensen, Martin, Ritchie, Hynd, Jardine, Persson, Leith. Front row: White (asst. manager), Henderson, A. Smith, Willoughby, Ferguson, Greig, D. Smith, Penman, Johansen, Johnstone, Kinnear.

Season 1955–56

Rangers became League Champions for the 29th time. Reconstruction meant that Division A had been extended to 18 clubs. Only 1 of the first 6 matches was won, but the Ibrox men put together a run of 23 unbeaten matches to take the Flag by 6 points from Aberdeen. 2 of only 4 defeats all season came after the Title had been won. McColl, Scott and Hubbard played in all 34 games. Controversial South African centre-forward Don 'The Rhino' Kichenbrand was introduced into the team and he finished as leading League scorer with 23 goals in his 25 matches, including 5 against Queen of the South in the match at Ibrox. The total goals scored was a healthy 85 with 4 players reaching double figures. Rangers' other South African, winger Johnny Hubbard, scored 33 goals in 59 competitive matches.

In the Scottish Cup Rangers gained revenge over Aberdeen for the previous year's defeat. A Kichenbrand goal at Dens Park eliminated Dundee for the second successive year, but Rangers were well beaten by Hearts, the eventual winners, in the Seventh Round tie at Tynecastle.

Rangers reached the Semi-Final of the League Cup, but despite the fact that opponents Aberdeen had to play with only 10 men for over half an hour after Leggat was stretchered off, they could not pull back the 2-goal first-half deficit. The irony was that previous to that match Rangers had scored 32 goals in their 8 matches in the Tournament. A 4-1 home defeat by Celtic in the Section was avenged with interest only 4 days later.

Willie Waddell and Sammy Cox were amongst the players given free transfers.

League: Champions
League Cup: Semi-Finalists
Scottish Cup: Seventh Round

SCOTTISH LEAGUE DIVISION A

August 11th: Willie Gardiner was transferred to Leicester City.

September 10th:
RANGERS 0   STIRLING ALBION 0

RANGERS: Niven; Caldow, Little; McColl, Thomson, Rae; Scott, Simpson, Murray, Baird, Hubbard

STIRLING ALBION: Mitchell; Gibson, McNichol; Smith, Milligan, Rankin; Pattison, McGill, Kerr, Philliben, Liddell
Attendance: 25,000

September 24th:
RANGERS 0   CELTIC 0

RANGERS: Niven; Caldow, Little; McColl, Young, Rae; Scott, Baird, Simpson, Prentice, Hubbard

CELTIC: Beattie; Boden, Fallon; Fernie, Evans, Peacock; Docherty, Collins, Haughney, Smith, Mochan
Attendance: 47,000

The wind, the rain, the slippery turf and the skidding ball all combined to make the players' task difficult. There was no doubt however who contributed most of the football in the match. Fernie, the individualist, proved that even in difficult conditions the ball can be mastered.

September 26th: Don Kichenbrand was signed from Delfos. Hearts had tried to sign him 2 years previously.

October 8th: Young played for Scotland in a 2-1 defeat by Ireland in Belfast.

October 8th:
RANGERS   (0) 4   AIRDRIE   (0) 4
   Murray (65),   McCulloch 2 (51, 83)
   Hubbard 2 (75, 84),   Reid (63), Rankin (70)
   Baird (85)

RANGERS: Niven; Caldow, Rae; McColl, Stanners,
Prentice; Scott, Millar, Murray, Baird, Hubbard

AIRDRIE: Walker; Miller, Shanks; McNeill, Quigley,
Price; Reid, Rankin, Baird, Welsh, McCulloch

Attendance: 25,000

October 15th:
PARTICK THISTLE   (1) 1   RANGERS   (0) 3
   Sharp (34)   Hubbard (51),
                            Scott (75)
                            Baird (81)

PARTICK THISTLE: Ledgerwood; Kerr, Gibb;
Mathers, Davidson, Baird; McKenzie, Harvey, Sharp,
Bell, McParland

RANGERS: Niven; Caldow, Little; McColl, Young,
Prentice; Scott, Simpson, Kichenbrand, Baird, Hubbard

Attendance: 36,000

October 22nd:
STIRLING ALBION   (2) 2   RANGERS   (2) 2
   Smith (21), Swanson (31)   Scott (27),
                            Kichenbrand (34)

STIRLING ALBION: Robertson; Gibson, Erskine;
Swanson, Williamson, Rankin; McBlain, Smith,
Timmins, Vandermotten, Liddell

RANGERS: Niven; Caldow, Little; Baird, McColl,
Prentice; Scott, Simpson, Kichenbrand, Queen,
Hubbard

Attendance: 15,000

October 29th:
QUEEN OF THE   RANGERS   (0) 1
   SOUTH   (2) 2   Simpson (90)
   Black (10), Patterson (53)

QUEEN OF THE SOUTH: Henderson; Sharp,
Binning; Sweeney, Smith, Gibson; Black, McGill,
Patterson, Rothera, Baxter

RANGERS: Niven; Caldow, Little; McColl, Young,
Rae; Scott, Baird, Kichenbrand, Simpson, Hubbard

Attendance: 15,500

League positions

	P	W	D	L	F	A	Pts
1 Queen of South	8	6	0	2	20	10	12
2 Celtic	8	4	2	2	16	10	10
3 Raith Rovers	8	4	2	2	17	14	10
4 Aberdeen	5	4	1	0	15	5	9
5 Falkirk	8	4	1	3	15	17	9
11 RANGERS	6	1	4	1	10	9	6

November 5th:
FALKIRK   (1) 1   RANGERS   (2) 2
   Wright (25)   Paton (3), Scott (8)

FALKIRK: Slater; Parker, Rae; Campbell, Colville,
McIntosh; Sinclair, Ormond, Wright, McCrae, O'Hara

RANGERS: Niven; Caldow, Little; McColl, Young,
Rae; Scott, Paton, Kichenbrand, Simpson, Hubbard

Attendance: 20,000

**November 9th: Scotland beat Wales 2-0 at Hampden
Park. Young was in the team.**

November 12th:
RANGERS   (1) 4   HEARTS   (1) 1
   Baird (15),   Young (12)
   Kichenbrand 2 (63, 79),
   Simpson (67)

RANGERS: Niven; Caldow, Little; McColl, Young,
Rae; Scott, Baird, Kichenbrand, Simpson, Hubbard

HEARTS: Duff; Parker, Kirk; Mackay, Glidden,
Cumming; Hamilton, Conn, Whittle, Young, Urquhart

Attendance: 51,000

November 19th:
KILMARNOCK   (0) 1   RANGERS   (1) 2
   Beattie (58)   Kichenbrand (44),
                          Baird (52)

KILMARNOCK: Brown; Watson, Rollo; Curlett,
Mackay, Taggart; Mays, Harvey, Flavell, Beattie,
Henaughan

RANGERS: Niven; Caldow, Little; McColl, Young,
Rae; Scott, Simpson, Kichenbrand, Baird, Hubbard

Attendance: 25,600

November 26th:
RANGERS   (2) 2   MOTHERWELL   (0) 2
   Hubbard (10 pen),   Aitkenhead (75),
   Kichenbrand (18)   Gardiner (82)

RANGERS: Niven; Caldow, Rae; McColl, Young,
Prentice; Scott, Simpson, Kichenbrand, Baird, Hubbard

MOTHERWELL: Weir; Kilmarnock, Shaw;
Humphries, Paton, McFadyen; Sloan, Aitken,
McSeveney, Gardiner, Aitkenhead

Attendance: 30,000

December 3rd:
RANGERS   (2) 4   RAITH ROVERS   (0) 0
   Kichenbrand (9),
   Simpson 2 (39, 85),
   Scott (75)

RANGERS: Niven; Caldow, Little; McColl, Young,
Rae; Scott, Simpson, Kichenbrand, Baird, Hubbard

RAITH ROVERS: Drummond; Polland, Weir; Young, McNaught, McMillan; McEwan, Murney, Copland, Thomson, Scott

Attendance: 26,000

December 10th:
ABERDEEN 0   RANGERS 0

ABERDEEN: Morrison; Mitchell, MacFarlane; Allister, Clunie, Glen; Boyd, Wishart, Davidson, Hay, Hather

RANGERS: Niven; Caldow, Little; McColl, Young, Rae; Scott, Simpson, Kichenbrand, Baird, Hubbard

Attendance: 18,000

December 12th: Bobby Shearer signed from Hamilton Academicals for £2,000.

December 15th: Duncan Stanners was transferred to Stirling Albion.

December 17th:
RANGERS (2) 4   HIBERNIAN (1) 1
  Hubbard 2 (20, 65 pen)   Ormond (17)
  Kichenbrand (37),
  Simpson (80)

RANGERS: Niven; Caldow, Little; McColl, Young, Rae; Scott, Simpson, Kichenbrand, Baird, Hubbard

HIBERNIAN: Younger; MacFarlane, Paterson; Thomson, Plenderleith, Preston; Smith, Combe, Reilly, Turnbull, Ormond

Attendance: 50,000

December 23rd: Johnny Woods was loaned to Hamilton Academicals until the end of the season.

December 24th:
RANGERS (2) 6   DUNFERMLINE (0) 0
  Kichenbrand 2 (27, 82),
  Baird 2 (39, 77), Scott (81),
  Hubbard (87)

RANGERS: Niven; Caldow, Little; McColl, Young, Rae; Scott, Simpson, Kichenbrand, Baird, Hubbard

DUNFERMLINE: Jenkins; Laird, Mackie; Samuel, Duthie, Reilly; Peebles, O'Brien, Dickson, Miller, Forrest

Attendance: 25,000

League positions

	P	W	D	L	F	A	Pts
1 Celtic	16	10	3	3	34	17	23
2 Hearts	15	10	1	4	38	21	21
3 RANGERS	14	7	6	1	34	15	20
4 Hibernian	15	9	2	4	38	27	20
5 Falkirk	16	8	4	4	36	28	20

December 31st:
CLYDE (0) 0   RANGERS (0) 4
                      Scott (53),
                      Simpson (65),
                      Kichenbrand (72),
                      Baird (77)

CLYDE: Watson; A. Murphy, Haddock; Gallacher, E. Murphy, Anderson; McHard, Currie, Hill, Robertson, Ring

RANGERS: Niven; Caldow, Little; McColl, Elliot, Rae; Scott, Simpson, Kichenbrand, Baird, Hubbard

Attendance: 31,000

January 2nd:
CELTIC (0) 0   RANGERS (1) 1
                      Kichenbrand (27)

CELTIC: Beattie; Haughney, Fallon; Evans, Stein, Peacock; McVittie, Fernie, Sharkey, Collins, Mochan

RANGERS: Brown; Caldow, Little; McColl, Elliot, Rae; Scott, Simpson, Kichenbrand, Baird, Hubbard

Attendance: 47,000

Celtic and Rangers continued to provide the unpredictable. Rangers were handicapped for 60 minutes of the game by an injury to Rae who had to go to the wing. Beattie was involved in the foolish loss of a goal in the 27th minute. Kichenbrand was faster than Stein in chasing a high punt by Simpson. Beattie rushed out some 18 yards from his line and Kichenbrand accurately lobbed the ball past him into the unguarded net. Rangers were lucky when 3 minutes from time Caldow pulled Mochan down in the box and escaped punishment.

January 7th:
RANGERS (1) 3   DUNDEE (1) 1
  Hubbard 2 (4 pen, 58),   Ritchie (21)
  Scott (63)

RANGERS: Brown; Caldow, Little; McColl, Young, Rae; Scott, Simpson, Kichenbrand, Baird, Hubbard

DUNDEE: Brown; Reid, Irvine; Black, Merchant, Cowie; Stables, Henderson, Ritchie, Smith, Christie

Attendance: n.a.

January 21st:
RANGERS (1) 3   EAST FIFE (0) 0
  Baird (13), Hubbard (58 pen),
  Kichenbrand (71)

RANGERS: Brown; Caldow, Little; McColl, Young, Rae; Scott, Simpson, Kichenbrand, Baird, Hubbard

EAST FIFE: Steedman; Adie, S. Stewart; Christie, Finlay, McLennan; J. Stewart, Leishman, Wright, Bonthrone, Matthew

Attendance: 30,000

January 28th:
AIRDRIE   (0) 0   RANGERS   (2) 4
                              Baird 3 (10, 62, 88),
                              Hubbard (22)

AIRDRIE: Walker; Miller, McNeill; Price, Quigley,
Slingsby; Rankin, McMillan, Baird, Welsh, McCulloch

RANGERS: Niven; Shearer, Little; McColl, Young,
Rae; Scott, Simpson, Kichenbrand, Baird, Hubbard

Attendance: 20,000

Hubbard missed a penalty

February 7th: Jimmy Millar returned from Cyprus.

February 11th:
RANGERS   (0) 1   PARTICK THISTLE   (0) 0
   Kichenbrand (84)

RANGERS: Niven; Shearer, Caldow; McColl, Young,
Rae; Scott, Simpson, Kichenbrand, Baird, Hubbard

PARTICK THISTLE: Smith; McGowan, Gibb;
Kerr, Davidson, Wright; McKenzie, Thomson, Sharp,
Crowe, Ewing

Attendance: 45,000

February 25th:
ST MIRREN   (0) 0   RANGERS   (0) 1
                              Kichenbrand (57)

ST MIRREN: Lornie; Lapsley, Mallan; Neilson,
Telfer, Johnston; McGill, Hendry, Holmes, Brown,
Laird

RANGERS: Niven; Shearer, Little; McColl, Young,
Rae; Scott, Simpson, Kichenbrand, Baird, Hubbard

Attendance: 43,000

League positions

	P	W	D	L	F	A	Pts
1 RANGERS	21	14	6	1	51	16	34
2 Hearts	23	14	5	4	69	28	33
3 Aberdeen	23	13	7	3	65	33	33
4 Hibernian	23	14	3	6	63	36	31
5 Celtic	23	12	6	5	45	25	30

March 7th:
RANGERS   (3) 8   QUEEN OF THE
   Kichenbrand 5 (15, 19, 57, 67, 80),   SOUTH   (0) 0
   Simpson 2 (37, 52), Scott (49)

RANGERS: Niven; Shearer, Caldow; McColl, Young,
Rae; Scott, Simpson, Kichenbrand, Baird, Hubbard

QUEEN OF THE SOUTH: Henderson; Sharp,
Binning; Sweeney, Gibson, Whitehead; Black, McGill,
Patterson, Jenkins, McGuire

Attendance: 30,000. This was the first Scottish League
match played under floodlights.

March 10th:
RANGERS   (3) 4   FALKIRK   (0) 0
   McColl (17), Simpson (34),
   Baird (37), Rae (85)

RANGERS: Niven; Shearer, Caldow; McColl, Young,
Rae; Scott, Simpson, Kichenbrand, Baird, Hubbard

FALKIRK: Slater; Parker, McIntosh; Campbell,
McKenzie, Fletcher; Ormond, Currie, McCrae, Wright,
O'Hara

Attendance: 45,000

**March 12th: Scotland beat the South Africans 2-1 at
Ibrox in an unofficial International. Kichenbrand
and Hubbard were in the South African team and
Hubbard scored their goal from the penalty spot.**

March 17th:
HEARTS   (0) 1   RANGERS   (0) 1
   Bauld (76)   Hubbard (70 pen)

HEARTS: Duff; Kirk, McKenzie; Mackay, Glidden,
Cumming; Young, Urquhart, Bauld, Wardhaugh,
Crawford

RANGERS: Niven; Shearer, Caldow; McColl, Young,
Prentice; Scott, Simpson, Kichenbrand, Baird, Hubbard

Attendance: 45,000

March 21st:
RANGERS   (2) 4   ST MIRREN   (0) 1
   Kichenbrand 3 (8, 42, 67),   Straiton (82)
   Prentice (50)

RANGERS: Niven; Shearer, Caldow; McColl, Young,
Rae; Scott, Prentice, Kichenbrand, Baird, Hubbard

ST MIRREN: Lornie; Lapsley, Mallan; Melrose,
Telfer, Johnston; McGill, Hendry, Straiton, Gemmell,
Callan

Attendance: 30,000

March 24th:
RANGERS   (2) 3   KILMARNOCK   (1) 2
   Kichenbrand 2 (19, 72),   Curlett (29),
   Hubbard (39 pen)   Fletcher (55)

RANGERS: Niven; Shearer, Caldow; McColl, Young,
Rae; Scott, Simpson, Kichenbrand, Baird, Hubbard

KILMARNOCK: Brown; Collins, Watson; Stewart,
Dougan, Mackay; Mays, Fletcher, Curlett, Beattie,
Murray

Attendance: 30,000

March 31st:
MOTHERWELL   (1) 1   RANGERS   (1) 2
   Quinn (6 pen)   Murray 2 (15, 57)

MOTHERWELL: Weir; Kilmarnock, McSeveney;
Mason, Paton, Forrest; Kerr, Quinn, Gardiner, Aitken,
Rae

RANGERS: Niven; Shearer, Caldow; McColl, Young, Prentice; Scott, Simpson, Murray, Baird, Hubbard

Attendance: 27,500

April 2nd:

DUNDEE (0) 0	RANGERS (3) 3
	Hubbard 2 (19, 41)
	Simpson (38)

DUNDEE: Brown; Gray, Irvine; Black, Stevenson, Cowie; Stables, Gallacher, Merchant, O'Hara, Christie

RANGERS: Niven; Shearer, Little; McColl, Young, Rae; Scott, Simpson, Murray, Baird, Hubbard

Attendance: 18,500

April 7th:

RAITH ROVERS (0) 0	RANGERS (0) 5
	Murray 2 (47, 81),
	Hubbard 2 (48 pen, 84),
	Leigh o.g. (58)

RAITH ROVERS: Stewart; Polland, Bain: Young, McNaught, Leigh; Carr, McEwan, Copland, Kelly, McMillan

RANGERS: Niven; Shearer, Little; McColl, Young, Prentice; Scott, Simpson, Murray, Baird, Hubbard

Attendance: 20,000

April 9th:

EAST FIFE (2) 2	RANGERS (1) 1
Matthew (31),	Baird (25)
Bonthrone (33)	

EAST FIFE: Curran; Adie, S. Stewart; Christie, Finlay, McLennan; J. Stewart, Leishman, Plumb, Bonthrone, Matthew

RANGERS: Niven; Shearer, Little; McColl, Young, Prentice; Scott, Simpson, Kichenbrand, Baird, Hubbard

Attendance: 10,000

April 14th: Scotland drew 1-1 with England at Hampden Park. Young was in the team.

April 18th:

| RANGERS (0) 1 | ABERDEEN (0) 0 |
| Scott (63) | |

RANGERS: Niven; Shearer, Little; McColl, Young, Rae; Scott, Simpson, Murray, Baird, Hubbard

ABERDEEN: Morrison; Mitchell, Caldwell; Wilson, Young, Allister; Leggat, Yorston, Buckley, Wishart, Boyd

Attendance: 45,000

April 21st:

HIBERNIAN (2) 2	RANGERS (1) 2
Turnbull (26), Reilly (40)	Murray (13),
	Baird (58)

HIBERNIAN: Younger; MacFarlane, Paterson; Buchanan, Grant, Combe; Smith, Turnbull, Reilly, Harrower, Ormond

RANGERS: Niven; Shearer, Little; McColl, Young, Rae; Scott, Simpson, Murray, Baird, Hubbard

Attendance: 30,000

April 25th:

| DUNFERMLINE (0) 1 | RANGERS (0) 0 |
| Dickson (51) | |

DUNFERMLINE: Mackin; Laird, Duthie; Samuel, Colville, Mailer; Peebles, Miller, Dickson, O'Brien, Anderson

RANGERS: Niven; Shearer, Little; McColl, Young, Rae; Scott, Simpson, Murray, Baird, Hubbard

Attendance: n.a.

April 28th:

| RANGERS (0) 0 | CLYDE (0) 1 |
| | Innes (78) |

RANGERS: Niven; Caldow, Little; McColl, Young, Shearer; Scott, Simpson, Kichenbrand, Baird, Hubbard

CLYDE: Watson; A. Murphy, Haddock; Walters, Keogh, Clinton; Kemp, Robertson, McHard, Innes, Ring

Attendance: 25,000

Scottish League Division A

	P	W	D	L	F	A	Pts
1 RANGERS	34	22	8	4	85	27	52
2 Aberdeen	34	18	10	6	87	50	46
3 Hearts	34	19	7	8	99	47	45
4 Hibernian	34	19	7	8	86	50	45
5 Celtic	34	16	9	9	55	39	41
6 Queen of South	34	16	5	13	69	73	37
7 Airdrie	34	14	8	12	85	96	36
8 Kilmarnock	34	12	10	12	52	45	34
9 Partick Thistle	34	13	7	14	62	60	33
10 Motherwell	34	11	11	12	53	59	33
11 Raith Rovers	34	12	9	13	58	75	33
12 East Fife	34	13	5	16	61	69	31
13 Dundee	34	12	6	16	56	65	30
14 Falkirk	34	11	6	17	58	75	28
15 St Mirren	34	10	7	17	57	70	27
16 Dunfermline	34	10	6	18	42	82	26
17 Clyde	34	8	6	20	50	74	22
18 Stirling Albion	34	4	5	25	23	82	13

April 28th: Rangers' free transfers included Waddell, Cox, Pryde, McMillan, Neillands and Woods.

May 7th: Hamish McMillan joined Queen of the South.

May 10th: Bobby Brown was transferred to Falkirk for £2,2000.

LEAGUE CUP

August 13th:

FALKIRK   (0) 0   RANGERS   (3) 5
                            Scott (2),
                            Murray (16),
                            Hubbard 2 (18, 63),
                            McMillan (47)

FALKIRK: Slater; Parker, Rae; McKenzie, Colville, Grant; Ormond, Campbell, Davidson, McCrae, O'Hara

RANGERS: Niven; Caldow, Little; McColl, Young, Prentice; Scott, McMillan, Murray, Simpson, Hubbard

Attendance: 21,000

August 17th:

RANGERS   (3) 4   FALKIRK   (3) 3
Hubbard 2 (30, 42 pen),   Ormond (9),
Scott (43), Murray (89)   Sinclair (17),
                            Morrison (22)

RANGERS: Niven; Caldow, Little; McColl, Young, Prentice; Scott, Simpson, Murray, McMillan, Hubbard

FALKIRK: Slater; Parker, Rae; Fletcher, Colville, Campbell; Sinclair, Morrison, Ormond, McCrae, O'Hara

Attendance: 30,000

August 20th:

QUEEN OF THE   RANGERS   (1) 2
  SOUTH   (1) 1   Hubbard (30),
McGuire (35)   Scott (51)

QUEEN OF THE SOUTH: Henderson; Sharp, Binning; King, Smith, Whitehead; Black, McGill, Patterson, Jenkins, McGuire

RANGERS: Niven; Caldow, Little; McColl, Young, Prentice; Scott, Simpson, Murray, Baird, Hubbard

Attendance: 15,000

August 27th:

RANGERS   (1) 1   CELTIC   (3) 4
Fallon o.g. (35)   McPhail (16),
                            Smith 2 (28, 41),
                            Mochan (52)

RANGERS: Niven; Caldow, Little; McColl, Young, Baird; Scott, Simpson, Murray, McMillan, Hubbard

CELTIC: Bonnar; Haughney, Fallon; Evans, Stein, Peacock; Collins, Fernie, Mochan, Smith, McPhail

Attendance: 75,000

This was a brilliant display by Celtic at Ibrox. McPhail scored the first goal in 16 minutes, whipping round Caldow and smashing a right-foot shot over Niven's head. 12 minutes later Smith increased Celtic's lead when he scored from a Mochan pass. 10 minutes from half-time Fallon and Scott collided as they went for a Baird free-kick, and Scott received the congratulations for a goal which may have been unwittingly scored by the back. In another 6 minutes McPhail's astute pass was glided round the struggling Baird by Smith, and from 22 yards Smith shot so powerfully that Niven, though he had anticipated the direction, could not prevent a goal. 7 minutes after the interval Mochan took Celtic's total to 4 when he scored with a bullet-like right-foot shot.

August 31st:

CELTIC   (0) 0   RANGERS   (1) 4
                            Baird 2 (4, 49),
                            Simpson (77),
                            Murray (80)

CELTIC: Bonnar; Haughney, Fallon; Evans, Stein, Peacock; Collins, McVittie, Mochan, Smith, McPhail

RANGERS: Niven; Caldow, Little; McColl, Young, Rae; Scott, Simpson, Murray, Baird, Hubbard

Attendance: 61,000

An injury to Stein, 10 minutes from half-time, handicapped the home side. He had to go to outside-left, Evans taking over at centre-half. That apart, this was sweet revenge for Rangers. They took the lead in the 4th minute when Baird, taking a return pass from Simpson, shot a splendid goal from 20 yards. Celtic missed an opportunity to level when McVittie completely missed his kick 5 yards out, and when Collins shot from close range the ball struck the crossbar, ran along the goal-line, and was cleared. Rangers increased their lead in the 49th minute when Celtic half-cleared and Baird rushed in and shot with his left foot from 8 yards past a helpless Bonnar. The limping Stein nearly scored with a glancing header from a Mochan corner. Rangers were well on top in the closing 15 minutes and scored twice more through Simpson in the 76th minute when he collected a long upfield punt, eluded both Peacock and Bonnar and sent the ball into the empty net. 3 minutes later Murray scored a 4th. Near the end Scott struck the post and crossbar in quick succession.

Attendance: n.a.

September 3rd:

RANGERS   (2) 6   QUEEN OF THE
Arnison 2 (3, 60),   SOUTH   (0) 0
Hubbard (16),
Simpson (62),
Scott 2 (81, 89)

RANGERS: Niven; Caldow, Little; McColl, Young, Rae; Scott, Simpson, Arnison, Baird, Hubbard

QUEEN OF THE SOUTH: Henderson; Sharp, Binning; King, Smith, Cruikshank; Oakes, Black, Patterson, Jenkins, McGuire

Attendance: 45,000

League Cup Section Table

	P	W	D	L	F	A	Pts
RANGERS	6	5	0	1	22	8	10
Celtic	6	4	1	1	16	9	9
Falkirk	6	2	1	3	12	15	5
Queen of South	6	0	0	6	3	21	0

September 14th: Quarter-Final First Leg
HAMILTON   RANGERS   (1) 2
  ACADEMICALS   (0) 1   Hubbard (30),
  Hamilton (48)   Simpson (80)

HAMILTON ACADEMICALS: Johnston; Shearer,
Quinn; Barrett, Boyd, Martin; Rutherford, Hamilton,
Miller, Reid, Armit

RANGERS: Niven; Caldow, Little; McColl, Young,
Rae; Scott, Baird, Simpson, Prentice, Hubbard

Attendance: 18,000

September 17th: Quarter-Final Second Leg
RANGERS   (3) 8   HAMILTON
  Scott 3 (15, 57, 78),   ACADEMICALS   (0) 0
  Simpson 2 (40, 75),
  Prentice (36),
  Hubbard 2 (50, 64)

RANGERS: Niven; Caldow, Little; McColl, Young,
Rae; Scott, Baird, Simpson, Prentice, Hubbard

HAMILTON: Johnston; Shearer, Quinn; Barrett,
Boyd, Martin; Rutherford, Hamilton, Richmond, Armit,
Reid

Attendance: 30,000. Rangers won 10-1 on aggregate.

October 1st: Semi-Final   At Hampden Park
ABERDEEN   (2) 2   RANGERS   (0) 1
  Leggat (4), Wishart (40)   Hubbard (51)

ABERDEEN: Martin; Paterson, Mitchell; Wilson,
Clunie, Glen; Leggat, Yorston, Buckley, Wishart,
Hather

RANGERS: Niven; Caldow, Little; McColl, Young,
Rae; Scott, Arnison, Millar, Baird, Hubbard

Attendance: 80,000

Aberdeen were somewhat fortunate to keep their goal
intact in the second half. McColl struck the angle of the
post and crossbar, and Millar's left-foot shot was diverted
by Martin onto the upright. That Rangers failed to score
against a team who were a player short and who had to face
a wind that grew in strength is the measure of their
forwards' shortcomings. Aberdeen played some exquisite
football and Mitchell, Clunie and Glen were magnificent
players for them in their moments of stress. Caldow,
Young and Hubbard were outstanding for Rangers.
Leggat, the scorer of the first goal was outstanding until
injured and carried off on a stretcher, with over half an
hour remaining.

SCOTTISH CUP

February 4th: Fifth Round
RANGERS   (1) 2   ABERDEEN   (0) 1
  Scott (20)   Leggat (80)
  Kichenbrand (74)

RANGERS: Niven; Shearer, Little; McColl, Young,
Rae; Scott, Simpson, Kichenbrand, Baird, Hubbard

ABERDEEN: Martin; McFarlane, Caldwell; Allister,
Glen, Brownlie; Leggat, Yorston, Allan, Wishart,
Hather

Attendance: 66,000

February 18th: Sixth Round
DUNDEE   (0) 0   RANGERS   (1) 1
                            Kichenbrand (35)

DUNDEE: Brown; Gray, Irvine; Gallacher, Black,
Cowie; Stables, Henderson, Merchant, O'Hara, Christie

RANGERS: Niven; Shearer, Little; McColl, Young,
Rae; Scott, Simpson, Kichenbrand, Baird, Hubbard

Attendance: 42,000

March 3rd: Seventh Round
HEARTS   (2) 4   RANGERS   (0) 0
  Bauld 2 (38, 72),
  Crawford (37), Conn (64)

HEARTS: Duff; Kirk, McKenzie; Mackay, Glidden,
Cumming; Young, Conn, Bauld, Wardhaugh, Crawford

RANGERS: Niven; Shearer, Little; McColl, Young,
Rae; Scott, Simpson, Kichenbrand, Baird, Hubbard

Attendance: 49,000

APPEARANCES

	League	League Cup	Scottish Cup	Glasgow Cup	Charity Cup	Friendlies
Niven	31	9	3	3	–	9
Caldow	26	9	–	2	1	6 + 1 sub
Little	25	9	3	3	1	9
McColl	34	9	3	3	1	10
Young	29	9	3	3	–	8
Prentice	10	5	–	–	–	1 + 3 sub
Scott	34	9	3	3	1	10
McMillan	–	3	–	–	–	–
Murray	8	5	–	–	–	4 + 1 sub
Simpson	32	8	3	3	1	9
Hubbard	34	9	3	3	1	9
Baird	33	7	3	3	1	10
Rae	27	5	3	3	–	9 + 1 sub
Arnison	–	2	–	1	–	–
Millar	1	1	–	1	–	–
Pryde	–	–	–	1	–	–
Kichenbrand	25	–	3	1	1	6 + 3 sub
Shearer	16	–	3	–	1	6
Ritchie	–	–	–	–	1	–
Elliot	2	–	–	–	1	1
Stanners	1	–	–	–	–	1
Waddell	–	–	–	–	–	1
Queen	1	–	–	–	–	0 + 1 sub
Brown	3	–	–	–	–	1
Grierson	–	–	–	–	–	0 + 1 sub
Thomson	1	–	–	–	–	–
Paton	1	–	–	–	–	–

GOALSCORERS

League: Kichenbrand 23, Hubbard 17 (6 pens), Baird 14, Simpson 10, Scott 9, Murray 6, Own Goals 2, Paton 1, McColl 1, Rae 1, Prentice 1

League Cup: Hubbard 10 (1 pen), Scott 8, Simpson 5, Murray 3, Arnison 2, Baird 2, McMillan 1, Prentice 1, Own Goals 1

Scottish Cup: Kichenbrand 2, Scott 1

Glasgow Cup: Hubbard 3 (1 pen), Scott 2, Arnison 2, McColl 1, Kichenbrand 1, Own Goals 1

Charity Cup: Kichenbrand 1

Friendlies: Simpson 5, Baird 3, Hubbard 3, Kichenbrand 2, Queen 1, McColl 1, Grierson 1, Murray 1, Shearer 1

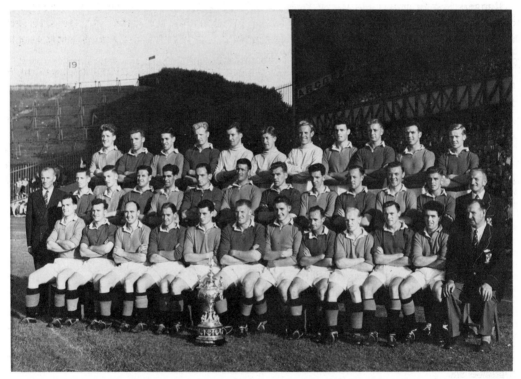

Rangers team group, 1955–56. Back row: Walker, Simpson, Boyd, Gardiner, Ritchie, Niven, Brown, Lawrie, Menzies, Neillands, Woods. Middle row: Scott Symon (manager), Little, Elliot, Waddell, Pryde, McColl, Stanners, Prentice, Murray, Paton. Front row: McCulloch, Grierson, Rae, Cox, Queen, Young, Smith, Hubbard, Cunning, McMillan, Scott, Smith (trainer).

Season 1956–57

Rangers won their 30th League Championship. Trailing to Hearts all season, mainly due to fixture congestion, they put together a run of 16 matches without defeat including 9 straight away wins to take the Flag by 2 points from the Edinburgh team. Kilmarnock, the only team to beat them both home and away, finished 3rd, 15 points behind. Rangers staged a remarkable recovery against Queens Park in a crucial match. From being 1-4 down at one stage they rallied to win 6-4. Runners-up Hearts were beaten home and away. They scored 96 goals in the 34 matches – Murray and Simpson shared 50 of them. Niven, McColl and Shearer were ever-presents.

Rangers first European Cup venture ended at the first hurdle. They should have built up a comfortable lead in the first match at Ibrox but could only manage a 2-1 win. After a rough-house in Nice in which Logie and Bravo were ordered off, the tie went to a play-off and Rangers were to rue missed chances in both of the previous encounters.

After a fine 4-goal Scottish Cup win over Hearts they were knocked out of the competition by Celtic. The first match at Parkhead ended in an amazing 4-4 draw but Celtic won the replay at Ibrox with some ease.

Rangers failed to qualify for the Final stages of the League Cup. Despite impressive wins over Aberdeen and East Fife the 3 points they dropped to Celtic proved decisive.

They won the Glasgow Cup in fine style, beating Celtic – in a 7-goal thriller – Partick Thistle and Clyde. They also won the Charity Cup. Celtic were again beaten together with Clyde and Queens Park. The Semi-Final match against Clyde was George Young's last match as a Rangers player. Prentice and Paton were transferred during the season.

League: Champions
League Cup: Failed to Qualify
Scottish Cup: Sixth Round
European Cup: First Round (after Play-off)

SCOTTISH FIRST DIVISION

September 5th: Young played for the Scottish League against the Irish League. The Scots won 7-1.

September 8th:
AIRDRIE (1) 3   RANGERS (2) 3
Price (41), McCulloch (51),   Murray 2 (11, 19),
Welsh (67)   Hubbard (72)

AIRDRIE: Walker; Miller, McNeill; Price, Quigley, Quinn; Duncan, McMillan, Baird, Welsh, McCulloch

RANGERS: Niven; Caldow, Little; McColl, Young, Shearer; Scott, Paton, Murray, Simpson, Hubbard

Attendance: 18,000

September 15th:
RANGERS (0) 0   KILMARNOCK (1) 1
                  Curlett (8)

RANGERS: Niven; Shearer, Little; McColl, Young, Logie; Scott, Simpson, Murray, Grierson, Hubbard

KILMARNOCK: Brown; Collins, A. Stewart; R. Stewart, Dougan, Mackay; Muir, Harvey, Curlett, Beattie, Burns

Attendance: 30,000

September 18th: John Prentice was transferred to Falkirk for £2,500.

September 21st: Willie Paton was transferred to Ayr United for £1,000.

83

September 22nd:

CELTIC   (0) 0   RANGERS   (1) 2
                                 Murray (32),
                                 Scott (71)

CELTIC: Beattie; Haughney, Fallon; Evans, Jack,
Peacock; Higgins, Collins, McPhail, Fernie, Mochan

RANGERS: Niven; Shearer, Little; McColl, Young,
Logie; Scott, Grierson, Murray, Baird, Hubbard

Attendance: 53,000

The speed of Scott and the skill of Hubbard troubled the
Celtic defence throughout. 19 free-kicks were awarded
against Rangers in the match for infringements other than
offside, a high proportion of them against Baird. Before
Murray headed the first goal in 32 minutes Celtic were
deprived of scores only by superb saves by Niven. Midway
through the second half Scott went racing through the
centre of Celtic's defence and shot low and hard past
Beattie. Young was a majestic figure in defence for
Rangers.

**September 26th: The Scottish League beat the
League of Ireland 3-1. Young and Scott were in the
team.**

September 29th:

RANGERS   (1) 3   AYR UNITED   (1) 1
Hubbard (24 pen),   McMillan (35)
Scott 2 (46, 60)

RANGERS: Niven; Shearer, Little; McColl, Young,
Logie; Scott, Grierson, Murray, Baird, Hubbard

AYR UNITED: Round; Boden, Paterson; Traynor,
Gallacher, Haugh; Japp, Paton, Price, McMillan, Beattie

Attendance: 25,000

October 6th:

ST MIRREN   (1) 1   RANGERS   (2) 2
Lapsley (3)   Baird (15), Scott (24)

ST MIRREN: Forsyth; Lapsley, Moore; Dallas,
Telfer, Holmes; Rodger, Flavell, Humphries, Gemmell,
McGill

RANGERS: Niven; Shearer, Caldow; McColl, Young,
Logie; Scott, Simpson, Murray, Baird, Hubbard

Attendance: 30,000

October 13th:

RANGERS   (3) 4   PARTICK THISTLE   (0) 1
Simpson 2 (4, 19),   Ewing (82)
Baird (33),
Hubbard (67 pen)

RANGERS: Niven; Shearer, Caldow; McColl, Young,
Logie; Scott, Simpson, Murray, Baird, Hubbard

PARTICK THISTLE: Smith; Kerr, Gibb; Harvey,
Davidson, Mathers; Smith, Steel, Hogan, McParland,
Ewing

Attendance: 38,000

**October 20th: Scotland including McColl and Young
drew 2-2 with Wales in Cardiff.**

League positions

	P	W	D	L	F	A	Pts
1 Hearts	8	6	1	1	20	15	13
2 Motherwell	7	5	2	0	21	8	12
3 Raith Rovers	8	3	4	1	22	16	10
4 RANGERS	6	4	1	1	14	7	9
5 East Fife	8	3	3	2	21	17	9

**October 31st: Harry Davis was signed from East
Fife.**

**November 1st: Rain forced the cancellation of the
O.G.C. Nice v. Rangers European Cup Match in
Nice.**

November 3rd:

RANGERS   (3) 5   HIBERNIAN   (1) 3
Scott (15), Murray 2 (20, 43), Ormond 2 (28, 88),
Hubbard (65 pen),   Preston (86)
Simpson (69)

RANGERS: Niven; Shearer, Caldow; McColl, Young,
Logie; Scott, Simpson, Murray, Baird, Hubbard

HIBERNIAN: Wren; MacFarlane, Muir; Grant,
Paterson, Combe; Fraser, Turnbull, Reilly, Preston,
Ormond

Attendance: 45,000

**November 7th: Scotland beat Ireland 1-0 at
Hampden Park. McColl, Young and Scott were in
the team. Scott, making his debut, scored the goal.**

November 10th:

RANGERS   (0) 2   MOTHERWELL   (2) 3
Baird 2 (62, 70)   Aitkenhead (27),
                                Gardiner 2 (42, 44)

RANGERS: Niven; Shearer, Caldow; McColl, Young,
Logie; Scott, Simpson, Murray, Baird, Hubbard

MOTHERWELL: Weir; McSeveney, Holton;
Aitken, Paton, Forrest; J. Hunter, Quinn, Gardiner,
McFadyen, Aitkenhead

Attendance: 62,000

November 17th:

FALKIRK   (0) 0   RANGERS   (2) 2
                                Murray 2 (29, 34)

FALKIRK: Brown; Parker, Rae; Prentice, Ralston,
McIntosh; McCole, Morrison, Ormond, Wright,
O'Hara

RANGERS: Niven; Shearer, Caldow; McColl, Young,
Logie; Scott, Simpson, Murray, Baird, Hubbard

Attendance: 19,000

November 21st: Scotland beat Yugoslavia 2-0 at Hampden Park. McColl, Young, Scott and Baird were in the team. Baird scored one of the goals.

November 24th:
RANGERS   (2) 3   ABERDEEN   (0) 1
  Simpson (2),   Yorston (46)
  Hubbard (30 pen),
  Murray (80)

RANGERS: Niven; Shearer, Caldow; McColl, Davis, Logie; Scott, Simpson, Murray; Baird, Hubbard

ABERDEEN: Martin; Mitchell, Caldwell; Allister, Young, Glen; Boyd, Yorston, Buckley, Hay, Hather

Attendance: 20,000

December 1st:
RANGERS   (2) 6   EAST FIFE   (0) 1
  Scott 2 (13, 85),   Bonthrone (74)
  Baird 2 (35, 65),
  Hubbard 2 (49, 75)

RANGERS: Niven; Shearer, Caldow; McColl, Davis, Logie; Scott, Simpson, Walker, Baird, Hubbard

EAST FIFE: Steedman; Cox, S. Stewart; Fox, Christie, McLennan; J. Stewart, Leishman, Plumb, Bonthrone, Matthew

Attendance: 26,000

December 8th:
RAITH ROVERS (1) 5   RANGERS   (1) 1
  Kelly (19), Urquhart 2 (61, 62), Simpson (14)
  Copland 2 (89, 90)

RAITH ROVERS: Stewart; Polland, Bain; Young, McNaught, Leigh; McEwan, Kelly, Copland, Williamson, Urquhart

RANGERS: Niven; Shearer, Caldow; McColl, Young, Logie; Scott, Simpson, Walker, Baird, Hubbard

Attendance: 20,000

December 15th:
RANGERS   (2) 5   HEARTS   (2) 3
  Hubbard (38),   Wardhaugh 2 (16, 22),
  Davis (42),   Bauld (89)
  Simpson (65),
  Murray 2 (69, 75)

RANGERS: Niven; Shearer, Caldow; McColl, Young, Davis; Scott, Simpson, Murray, Baird, Hubbard

HEARTS: Marshall; Kirk, McKenzie; Mackay, Milne, Cumming; Hamilton, Young, Bauld, Wardhaugh, Crawford

Attendance: 45,000

December 22nd:
KILMARNOCK (1) 3   RANGERS   (0) 2
  Mays 2 (21, 53),   Simpson (51),
  Harvey (47)   Murray (65)

KILMARNOCK: Brown; Collins, Watson; Stewart, Toner, Mackay; Muir, Harvey, Mays, Beattie, Black

RANGERS: Niven; Shearer, Caldow; McColl, Young, Logie; Scott, Simpson, Murray, Baird, Hubbard

Attendance: 21,500

December 29th:
RANGERS   (3) 4   QUEEN OF THE
  Simpson 2 (16, 25),   SOUTH   (0) 0
  Murray 2 (19, 66)

RANGERS: Niven; Shearer, Caldow; McColl, Young, Logie; Scott, Simpson, Murray, Baird, Hubbard

QUEEN OF THE SOUTH: Selkirk; Sharp, Binning; Whitehead, Smith, Greenock; Black, McGill, Patterson, McMillan, Oakes

Attendance: 30,000

League positions

	P	W	D	L	F	A	Pts
1 Hearts	17	13	2	2	46	31	26
2 Motherwell	16	10	3	3	43	26	23
3 RANGERS	15	10	1	4	44	26	21
4 Raith Rovers	17	8	5	4	43	28	21
5 Dundee	14	8	3	2	28	18	19

January 1st:
RANGERS   (1) 2   CELTIC   (0) 0
  Murray (12),
  Simpson (71)

RANGERS: Niven; Shearer, Caldow; McColl, Young, Logie; Scott, Simpson, Murray, Baird, Hubbard

CELTIC: Beattie; Haughney, Meechan; Evans, Jack, Peacock; Smith, Ryan, Mochan, Fernie, Tully

Attendance: 60,000

Celtic were lucky that Rangers did not take much heavier toll of them than the goals scored by Murray and Simpson. Celtic's outstanding player was Jack. Time and again he prevented goals with strong well-timed tackles. Rangers' backs and half-backs gave most of the Celtic players a lesson in going determinedly for the ball. Both Rangers' goals were scored from positions close in on goal, Murray's from Baird's pass and Simpson's from Murray's deflection from Shearer's free-kick. Fernie squandered Celtic's best chance 3 minutes from time when he intercepted a poor back-pass and missed an unguarded goal.

January 2nd:
DUNDEE   (0) 1   RANGERS   (2) 3
  O'Hara (57)   Scott (4),
                    Simpson (7),
                    Young (88 pen)

DUNDEE: Brown; Reid, Cox; Henderson, McKenzie, Cowie; Chalmers, Black, Birse, O'Hara, Christie

RANGERS: Niven; Shearer, Caldow; McColl, Young, Davis; Scott, Simpson, Murray, Baird, Wilson

Attendance: 28,500

January 10th: Rangers exchanged Derek Grierson for Bob Morrison of Falkirk.

January 12th:
AYR UNITED   (0) 1   RANGERS   (0) 0
  Japp (81)

AYR UNITED: Travers: Paterson, Thomson; Traynor, Brice, Telfer; Japp, Paton, Price, Whittle, McMillan

RANGERS: Niven; Shearer, Caldow; McColl, Young, Davis; Scott, Simpson, Murray, Baird, Hubbard

Attendance: n.a.

January 19th:
RANGERS   (1) 1   ST MIRREN   (0) 0
  Murray (45)

RANGERS: Niven; Shearer, Caldow; McColl, Young, Davis; Scott, Simpson, Murray, Baird, Hubbard

ST MIRREN: Forsyth; Lapsley, Johnston; Wilson, Telfer, Holmes; McGill, Gemmell, Cunningham, Thomson, McCulloch

Attendance: 33,000

January 26th:
PARTICK THISTLE   (0) 0   RANGERS   (2) 3
                                    Murray 2 (2, 39),
                                    Simpson (78)

PARTICK THISTLE: W. Smith; Kerr, Baird; Harvey, Davidson, Mathers; McKenzie, Smith, Wright, McIntosh, Ewing

RANGERS: Niven; Shearer, Little; McColl, Young, Davis; Scott, Simpson, Murray, Baird, Hubbard

Attendance: 33,000

February 9th:
RANGERS   (1) 2   DUNFERMLINE   (1) 1
  Murray (22), Simpson (63)   McKinlay (15)

RANGERS: Niven; Shearer, Caldow; McColl, Davis, Logie; Scott, Simpson, Murray, Baird, Hubbard

DUNFERMLINE: Mackin; Burns, Duthie; Mailer, Colville, Reilly; McKinlay, Tighe, Dickson, O'Brien, Anderson

Attendance: 40,000

February 25th:
RANGERS   (1) 3   QUEENS PARK   (1) 3
  Murray (4), Morrison (52),   Cromar 2 (7, 57),
  Hubbard (69 pen)   Herd (49)

RANGERS: Niven; Shearer, Caldow; McColl, Davis, Baird; Wilson, Simpson, Murray, Morrison, Hubbard

QUEENS PARK: F. Crampsey; I. Harnett, W. Hastie; R. Cromar, J. Valentine, A. Glen; G. Herd, W. Omand, A. McEwan, H. Devine, C. Church

Attendance: 19,000

March 2nd:
HIBERNIAN   (2) 2   RANGERS   (0) 3
  Turnbull (25 pen)   Murray 2 (52, 65),
  Harrower (29)   Morrison (89)

HIBERNIAN: Wren; Muir, Paterson; Nichol, Plenderleith, Hughes; Smith, Turnbull, Reilly, Preston, Harrower

RANGERS: Niven; Shearer, Caldow; McColl, Davis, Baird; Wilson, Simpson, Murray, Morrison, Hubbard

Attendance: 40,000

League positions

	P	W	D	L	F	A	Pts
1 Hearts	26	18	5	3	66	40	41
2 RANGERS	23	16	2	5	61	34	34
3 Motherwell	24	15	4	5	60	37	34
4 Raith Rovers	25	13	7	5	70	40	33
5 Kilmarnock	25	11	9	5	44	28	31

March 9th:
MOTHERWELL   (2) 2   RANGERS   (1) 5
  Gardiner (31),   Murray 2 (22, 85),
  Sloan (45)   Morrison (63),
                             Hubbard (69),
                             Wilson (79)

MOTHERWELL: Weir; McSeveney, Holton; Brims, Paton, Forrest; S. Reid, Quinn, Sloan, Gardiner, McCann

RANGERS: Niven; Shearer, Caldow; McColl, Davis, Baird; Wilson, Simpson, Murray, Morrison, Hubbard

Attendance: 29,000

March 14th: The Scottish League beat the English League 3-2 at Ibrox. Caldow and McColl were in the team.

March 16th:
RANGERS   (0) 1   FALKIRK   (0) 1
  Murray (82)   Merchant (69)

RANGERS: Niven; Shearer, Caldow; McColl, Young, Logie; Wilson, Simpson, Murray, Baird, Hubbard

FALKIRK: Slater; Parker, Rae; Wright, Irvine, Prentice; Murray, Grierson, Merchant, Moran, O'Hara

Hubbard missed a penalty

Attendance: 30,000

March 20th:
RANGERS (4) 4   DUNDEE (0) 0
  Ferguson o.g. (9),
  Simpson (17), Murray (33),
  Baird (39)

RANGERS: Niven; Shearer, Caldow; McColl, Young,
Davis; Wilson, Simpson, Murray, Baird, Hubbard

DUNDEE: Ferguson; Reid, Cox; Henderson,
Ferguson, Black; Chalmers, Cousin, Birse, O'Hara,
Christie

Attendance: 25,000

March 23rd:
ABERDEEN (0) 1   RANGERS (0) 2
  Davidson (64)   Hubbard (65),
                         Simpson (70)

ABERDEEN: Martin; Caldwell, Hogg; Allister,
Young, Glen; Leggat, Yorston, Davidson, Wishart,
Hather

RANGERS: Niven; Shearer, Caldow; McColl, Young,
Davis; Scott, Simpson, Murray, Baird, Hubbard

Attendance: n.a.

March 30th:
EAST FIFE (0) 0   RANGERS (2) 3
                         Morrison 2 (20, 38),
                         Simpson (86)

EAST FIFE: McQueen; Wilkie, S. Stewart; Skinner,
Christie, Cox; J. Stewart, Leishman, Plumb, Bonthrone,
Matthew

RANGERS: Niven; Shearer, Caldow; McColl, Young,
Davis; Scott, Morrison, Simpson, Baird, Hubbard

Attendance: 12,000

April 2nd:
RANGERS (2) 3   RAITH ROVERS (0) 1
  Morrison (10),   Copland (70)
  Scott (26), Simpson (53)

RANGERS: Niven; Shearer, Caldow; McColl, Young,
Davis; Scott, Morrison, Simpson, Baird, Hubbard

RAITH ROVERS: Drummond; Polland, Bain;
Young, McNaught, Leigh; McEwan, Kelly, Copland,
Williamson, Buchan

Attendance: 50,000

**April 6th: Scotland were beaten 2-1 by England at
Wembley. Caldow, McColl and Young were in the
team**.

April 13th:
HEARTS (0) 0   RANGERS (1) 1
                       Simpson (35)

HEARTS Marshall; Kirk, McKenzie; Parker, Milne,
Mackay; Wardhaugh, Conn, Bauld, Young, Crawford

RANGERS: Niven; Shearer, Caldow; McColl, Young,
Davis; Scott, Simpson, Murray, Baird, Hubbard

Attendance: n.a.

April 17th:
RANGERS (3) 3   AIRDRIE (1) 2
  Simpson (6),   McLean (27),
  Baird 2 (12, 29)   Baird (75)

RANGERS: Niven; Shearer, Caldow; McColl, Young,
Davis; Scott, Simpson, Murray, Baird, Hubbard

AIRDRIE: Walker; Kilmarnock, Shanks; Price,
Quigley, Quinn; Rankin, Welsh, Baird, Duncan,
McLean

Attendance: 25,000

April 22nd:
QUEENS PARK (4) 4   RANGERS (3) 6
  Herd (14), Devine 3 (18, 38, 40) Murray 2 (19, 60),
                         Simpson (78),
                         Scott (88),
                         Hubbard (40, 43)

QUEENS PARK: F. Crampsey; I. Harnett, W.
Hastie; R. Cromar, J. Robb, A. Glen; G. Herd, W.
Omand, A. McEwan, H. Devine, T. Heron

RANGERS: Niven; Shearer, Caldow; McColl, Young,
Davis; Scott, Simpson, Murray, Baird, Hubbard

Cromar missed a 3rd-minute penalty

Attendance: 33,786

**April 23rd: The *Sine Die* suspension was lifted on
Willie Woodburn**.

April 27th:
QUEEN OF THE SOUTH (0) 0 RANGERS (1) 3
                         Hubbard (15 pen),
                         Murray 2 (52, 58)

QUEEN OF THE SOUTH: Morrow; Sharp, Binning;
Whitehead, Smith, Greenock; Black, McGill, Patterson,
McMillan, Oakes

RANGERS: Niven; Shearer, Caldow; McColl, Young,
Davis; Scott, Simpson, Murray, Baird, Hubbard

Attendance: 14,500

April 29th:
DUNFERMLINE (1) 3   RANGERS (0) 4
  Duthie (44 pen),   Scott 2 (50, 51),
  Anderson (64), Dickson (82) Hubbard (80),
                         Simpson (89½)

DUNFERMLINE: Mackin; Laird, Duthie; Samuel,
Colville, Mailer; McKinlay, Peebles, Dickson, Hume,
Anderson

RANGERS: Niven; Shearer, Caldow; McColl, Young,
Davis; Scott, Simpson, Murray, Baird, Hubbard

Simpson's goal 10 seconds from time relegated Dunfermline.

Attendance: n.a.

Scottish First Division

	P	W	D	L	F	A	Pts
1 RANGERS	34	26	3	5	96	48	55
2 Hearts	34	24	5	5	81	48	53
3 Kilmarnock	34	16	10	8	57	39	42
4 Raith Rovers	34	16	7	11	84	58	39
5 Celtic	34	15	8	11	58	43	38
6 Aberdeen	34	18	2	14	79	59	38
7 Motherwell	34	16	5	13	72	66	37
8 Partick Thistle	34	13	8	13	53	51	34
9 Hibernian	34	12	9	13	69	56	33
10 Dundee	34	13	6	15	55	61	32
11 Airdrie	34	13	4	17	77	89	30
12 St Mirren	34	12	6	16	58	72	30
13 Queens Park	34	11	7	16	55	59	29
14 Falkirk	34	10	8	16	51	70	28
15 East Fife	34	10	6	18	59	82	26
16 Queen of the S.	34	10	5	19	54	96	25
17 Dunfermline	34	9	6	19	54	74	24
18 Ayr United	34	7	5	22	48	89	19

May 2nd: John Valentine signed from Queens Park. Arnison, Elliot and McCulloch were among the players given free transfers.

May 8th: Scotland beat Spain 4-2 at Hampden Park. Caldow, McColl and Young were in the team.

May 19th: Scotland beat Switzerland 2-1 in Basle. Caldow, Young and McColl were in the team.

May 22nd: Scotland beat World Champions Germany 3-1 in Stuttgart. Caldow and McColl were in the team.

May 26th: Spain beat Scotland 4-1 in Madrid. Caldow was in the team. This was to be George Young's last International match but he was dropped by the selectors amid much controversy.

June 6th: Rangers signed full-back Hugh Neil from Falkirk.

LEAGUE CUP

August 11th:
RANGERS   (0) 3   EAST FIFE   (0) 0
Simpson 2 (46, 82),
Hubbard (74 pen)

RANGERS: Niven; Shearer, Little; McColl, Young, Rae; Scott, Simpson, Murray, Baird, Hubbard

EAST FIFE: Watters; Adie, S. Stewart; Cox, Christie, McLennan; J. Stewart, Leishman, Plumb, Bonthrone, Matthew

Attendance: 51,000

August 15th:
CELTIC   (1) 2   RANGERS   (1) 1
Collins (38),   Murray (44)
Tully (68)

CELTIC: Beattie; Haughney, Fallon; Evans, Jack, Peacock; Higgins, Collins, McPhail, Fernie, Tully

RANGERS: Niven; Shearer, Little; McColl, Young, Rae; Scott, Simpson, Murray, Baird, Hubbard

Attendance: 45,000

Niven might have been beaten on three occasions had Evans, Peacock and Fernie been accurate in finishing. Then in the 38th minute McPhail guided a Haughney pass into Collins's path and Niven was decisively beaten. Shortly after a fine angular shot by Scott hit the crossbar. Murray equalised just on half-time after a goalmouth scramble. In the 65th minute Young upset Higgins and Haughney shot the penalty kick over the crossbar. 3 minutes later Tully hooked a lobbed shot past Niven for a 2nd Celtic goal.

August 18th:
ABERDEEN   (0) 2   RANGERS   (1) 6
Wishart (46),   Simpson 2 (59, 60),
Yorston (54)   Murray 2 (9, 64),
                    Shearer (55),
                    Hubbard (67)

ABERDEEN: Morrison; Mitchell, Hogg; Allister, Young, Glen; Boyd, Yorston, Davidson, Wishart, Hather

RANGERS: Niven; Caldow, Little; McColl, Young, Shearer; Scott, Simpson, Murray, Baird, Hubbard

Attendance: 35,000

August 25th:
EAST FIFE   (1) 1   RANGERS   (0) 4
Leishman (15)   Murray (59),
                    Simpson (68),
                    Hubbard (81 pen),
                    Rae (87)

EAST FIFE: Watters; Adie, S. Stewart; Cox, Christie, McLennan; J. Stewart, Leishman, Plumb, Bonthrone, Matthew

RANGERS: Ritchie; Caldow, Little; McColl, Young, Rae; Scott, Shearer, Murray, Simpson, Hubbard

Attendance: 18,000

August 29th:
RANGERS   0   CELTIC 0

RANGERS: Niven; Caldow, Little; McColl, Young, Shearer; Scott, Paton, Murray, Simpson, Hubbard

CELTIC: Beattie; Haughney, Fallon; Evans, Jack, Peacock; Tully, Collins, McPhail, Fernie, Mochan

Attendance: 84,000

Celtic made a promising start and Mochan twice had Niven in difficulty within 5 minutes with accurate crosses. Celtic were much more dangerous and the energetic and clever play of their forwards gave the home defence many moments of anxiety. Towards the interval a tremendous shot by McColl from 35 yards was only a foot wide. At the start of the second half Fallon baulked Rangers of a goal when he headed an overhead kick from Scott off the line. In the 52nd minute a Mochan shot struck the post. Near the end Peacock started a splendid Celtic move with a pass to Tully. The outside-right transferred the ball to McPhail, who in turn sent it to Fernie 2 yards from goal but the inside-left lofted high over when scoring looked easier.

September 1st:

RANGERS   (1) 4   ABERDEEN   (1) 1
  Simpson 2 (37, 77),   Davidson (14)
  Hubbard (61 pen),
  Scott (73)

RANGERS: Niven; Caldow, Little; McColl, Young, Shearer; Scott, Paton, Murray, Simpson, Hubbard

ABERDEEN: Martin; Mitchell, Hogg; Allister, Young, Glen; Leggat, Yorston, Davidson, Hay, Hather

Attendance: 48,000

League Cup Section Table

	P	W	D	L	F	A	Pts
Celtic	6	5	1	0	10	5	11
RANGERS	6	4	1	1	18	6	9
Aberdeen	6	1	0	5	11	18	2
East Fife	6	1	0	5	5	15	2

SCOTTISH CUP

February 2nd: Fifth Round

HEARTS   (0) 0   RANGERS   (3) 4
                                     Hubbard (26 pen),
                                     Murray (27),
                                     Scott (30),
                                     Simpson (80)

HEARTS: Brown; Parker, Kirk; Mackay, Glidden, Cumming; Young, Conn, Bauld, Wardhaugh, Crawford

RANGERS: Niven; Shearer, Caldow; McColl, Young, Davis; Scott, Simpson, Murray, Baird, Hubbard

Attendance: 47,484

February 16th: Sixth Round

CELTIC   (2) 4   RANGERS   (2) 4
  McPhail (10),   Morrison (7),
  Higgins (15),   Simpson (14),
  Collins (75), Fernie (81)   Hubbard (83 pen),
                                     Murray (85)

CELTIC: Beattie; Haughney, Fallon; Evans, Jack, Peacock; Higgins, Fernie, McPhail, Mochan, Collins

RANGERS: Niven; Shearer, Caldow; McColl, Davis, Baird; Scott, Simpson, Murray, Morrison, Hubbard

Attendance: 50,000

This was an exhilarating match with 4 goals inside 9 minutes of the first half and 4 more in the period of 11 minutes in the 2nd. In the 7th minute Morrison directed Simpson's pass away from Beattie. In the 10th minute Celtic equalised with a rasping shot by McPhail. 4 more minutes and Fallon was penalised for impeding Scott, and the wingers' free-kick was headed into the net from 14 yards by Simpson. In exactly quarter of an hour Celtic equalised for the 2nd time when Collins moved to the right touchline and enabled Higgins to dart through and score. Early in the second half Fallon made the save of the day by heading over the crossbar a Scott corner-kick propelled beyond Beattie's reach by Simpson. Celtic scored 2 brilliant goals in the 75th and 81st minutes. For the first Fernie sent a corner to the edge of the penalty area. McPhail with a remarkable leap directed it for goal and Collins hooked the ball chest-high past a bewildered defence. Then McPhail twice beat Davis on the right and passed low and true to Fernie who emulated Collins by swivelling and shooting home in the one movement. With 7 minutes remaining for play Baird pumped the ball upfield, and Hubbard in attempting to jump was clumsily barged by Jack. The little winger converted the penalty kick himself. 2 minutes later Rangers were on equal terms when Murray side-footed home Hubbard's corner-kick.

February 20th: Sixth Round Replay

RANGERS   (0) 0   CELTIC   (2) 2
                                     Higgins (15),
                                     Mochan (35)

RANGERS: Niven; Shearer, Caldow; McColl, Davis, Baird; Scott, Simpson, Murray, Morrison, Hubbard

CELTIC: Beattie; Haughney, Fallon; Evans, Jack, Peacock; Higgins, Fernie, McPhail, Mochan, Collins

Attendance: 88,000

On a heavily sanded, frost-affected pitch Celtic played almost all of the football in the match. Higgins scored the opening goal in the 15th minute. Both he and Baird stumbled as the winger cut in but Higgins managed to keep his feet and with his left foot shot low past Niven. 10 minutes from half-time Collins chipped the ball shrewdly to Mochan, who from the edge of the penalty area swung his famous left foot and sent the ball screeching under the crossbar.

EUROPEAN CUP

October 24th: First Round
RANGERS (1) 2   O.G.C. NICE (France) (1) 1
  Murray (40),   Faivre (23)
  Simpson (61)

RANGERS: Niven; Shearer, Caldow; McColl, Young, Logie; Scott, Simpson, Murray, Baird, Hubbard

O.G.C. NICE: Colonna; Bonvin, Nani; Ferry, Gonzales, Nuremberg; Foix, Muro, Bravo, Diratz, Faivre

Attendance: 65,000

Rangers, much the more powerful side from the point of view of physique and therefore the better equipped for the conditions, should have established a much more imposing lead than they did through the goals scored by Murray and Simpson against that by Faivre. Fine goalkeeping by Colonna, resolute and often desperate defence by his outfield colleagues and inefficient shooting by Rangers kept the Scottish club's lead to the narrowest possible. All of the players and officials had disappeared after the referee had blown for time when it was discovered that there was still 6 or 7 minutes left to play. Back came the participants. Caldow had to be got out of the bath, but the score remained the same.

November 14th: First Round Second Leg
O.G.C. NICE (0) 2   RANGERS (1) 1
  Bravo (60), Foix (62)   Hubbard (40 pen)

O.G.C. NICE: Colonna; Bonvin, Martinez; Ferry, Gonzales, Nuremberg; Foix, Ujlaki, Bravo, Muro, Faivre

RANGERS: Niven; Shearer, Caldow; McColl, Young, Logie; Scott, Simpson, Murray, Baird, Hubbard

Attendance: 5,000

Overnight torrential rain had turned the pitch into a sea of mud. Rangers were the better team but their attacks were stopped time and again by crude tackling. In the 40th minute Gonzales swung his right foot at Murray and brought him down in the penalty box. The French players from the goalkeeper to the outside-left surrounded the referee but the official was in no mood to change his mind. Hubbard placed the ball and scored with his customary simple shot into the right-hand corner of the net. In the 60th minute Bravo floundered with the ball in front of Niven, watched it break to Muro and as he fell he half-hit a shot past Niven. Two minutes later Foix scored a second from a cross by Faivre. Rangers should have had the game won without dispute in the second half as Baird and Murray made many openings.

(3-3 on aggregate)

November 28th: First Round Play-Off   In Paris
RANGERS (0) 1   O.G.C. NICE (1) 3
  Bonvin o.g. (50)   Foix (43), Muro (52),
                         Faivre (n.a.)

RANGERS: Niven; Shearer, Caldow; McColl, Davis, Logie; Scott, Simpson, Murray, Baird, Hubbard

O.G.C. NICE: Colonna; Bonvin, Martinez; Ferry, Gonzales, Nuremberg; Foix, Ujlaki, Bravo, Muro, Faivre

Attendance: 15,000

Rangers might have been 3 ahead at half-time but for some great saves by Colonna. Just before half-time, however, Ujlaki sent a splendid pass between Logie and Baird and Foix ran in to score a splendid goal from 12 yards. 5 minutes after the restart Rangers equalised. Baird took the ball down to the left corner flag, cut in, and shot low and hard across the goal. Colonna dived to gather the ball but Bonvin got there a split second before him and in attempting to turn the ball away for a corner kick, he succeeded only in lofting it over his own goalkeeper. 2 minutes later a defensive blunder allowed Muro to run through and score, and then Faivre added a third.

APPEARANCES

	League	League Cup	Scottish Cup	Glasgow Cup	Charity Cup	Friend- lies	Euro- pean Cup
Niven	34	5	3	2	2	3	3
Caldow	30	4	3	2	1	3	3
Little	5	6	–	2	1	–	–
McColl	34	6	3	3	1	3	3
Young	28	6	1	3	1	2	2
Shearer	34	6	3	3	2	3	3
Logie	16	–	–	2	–	3	3
Davis	20	–	3	–	2	1	1
Scott	29	6	3	3	1	3	3
Paton	1	2	–	–	–	–	–
Murray	30	6	3	3	1	3	3
Simpson	32	6	3	2	1	3	3
Hubbard	33	6	3	3	2	3	3
Grierson	3	–	–	1	–	–	–
Baird	32	3	3	3	1	3	3
Walker	2	–	–	–	–	–	–
Wilson	6	–	–	–	1	–	–
Morrison	5	–	2	–	2	–	–
Rae	–	3	–	–	–	–	–
Ritchie	–	1	–	1	–	–	–
Millar	–	–	–	–	1	–	–
Valentine	–	–	–	–	1	–	–
Kichenbrand	–	–	–	–	1	–	–

GOALSCORERS

League: Murray 29, Simpson 21, Hubbard 15 (5 pens), Scott 12, Baird 9, Morrison 6, Davis 1, Young 1 (pen), Wilson 1, Own Goals 1

League Cup: Simpson 7, Murray 4, Hubbard 4 (3 pens), Rae 1, Scott 1, Shearer 1

Scottish Cup: Murray 2, Simpson 2, Hubbard 2 (2 pens), Scott 1, Morrison 1

Glasgow Cup: Hubbard 4 (3 pens), Murray 3, Grierson 2, Simpson 1, Scott 1

Charity Cup: Baird 2, Morrison 2, Kichenbrand 1

Friendlies: Wilson 1, Scott 1, Walker 1, Morrison 1

European Cup: Murray 1, Simpson 1, Hubbard 1 (pen), Own Goal 1

The Rangers' squad in 1954. Back row: Simpson, Rodger, Rae, McKenzie, Woodburn, Niven, Neal, Brown, Carmichael, Liddell, Menzies, Woods, Neillands. Middle row: Symon (manager), Simpson, Elliot, Waddell, Pryde, McColl, Stanners, Prentice, McCulloch, Paton, Caldow, Hubbard, Craven (asst. trainer). Front row: McMillan, Grierson, MacMillan, Cox, McIntosh, Young, McKenzie, Little, Gardner, Findlay, Brand, Smith (trainer). Foreground: Glasgow Cup.

Season 1957–58

The Ibrox team finished second in the League, 13 points behind run-away winners Hearts who lost only one match all season and scored a record 132 goals. 3 of Rangers' first 4 home matches were lost and 12 goals conceded but the signing of the experienced Willie Telfer from St Mirren bolstered the defence and the team went undefeated for 5 months in the League following his arrival. They ran Hearts close in both matches. They were 2 goals up at one stage in the home match before the Edinburgh side came back to win 3-2, and they also lost to a last-minute goal in the return at Tynecastle. That match was only one of two away matches lost all season. The other was against Hibs in Lawrie Reilly's last match. Murray and Hubbard finished joint top scorers on 19, Hubbard's total including an incredible 12 penalties.

Rangers overcame French Champions St Etienne to reach the Second Round of the European Cup but A.C. Milan, with a number of world-class players in their side, showed that the European game required more than just physical effort. Their 4 goals in the final 15 minutes at Ibrox left the 85,000 crowd stunned.

Rangers reached the Semi-Final of the Scottish Cup having won all 4 previous ties away from home, but a controversial decision by referee Davidson when he chalked off Murray's late equaliser in the Replay with Hibs put paid to their hopes.

They reached the Final of the League Cup for the 4th time. Having qualified from their Section on goal average from Raith Rovers, they beat Kilmarnock on aggregate in the Quarter-Final and easily beat Brechin City in the Semi-Final. Their problem in finding a replacement for George Young was cruelly exposed in the Final as Celtic inflicted their heaviest ever defeat.

The Glasgow Cup was won after 5 matches including 2 replays, but Rangers were beaten by Clyde in the Final of the Charity Cup.

> League: Runners-Up
> League Cup: Finalists
> Scottish Cup: Semi-Finalists
> European Cup: Second Round

SCOTTISH FIRST DIVISION

September 7th:

RANGERS	(3) 4	QUEEN OF THE SOUTH	(1) 2
Simpson 2 (7, 43), Shearer (28), Hubbard (80 pen)		Patterson 2 (43, 62)	

RANGERS: Ritchie; Little, Caldow; Shearer, McColl, Baird; Scott, Simpson, Kichenbrand, Murray, Hubbard

QUEEN OF THE SOUTH: Henderson; Smith, Binning; Rae, Elliot, Whitehead; Black, McGill, Patterson, King, Oakes

Attendance: 25,000

September 17th: The Scottish League beat the League of Ireland 5-1 in Dublin. Caldow, McColl, Baird and Scott were in the team.

September 21st:
RANGERS (1) 2   CELTIC (1) 3
  Simpson 2 (39, 68)   Collins (19,
                                    McPhail (54),
                                    Wilson (64)

RANGERS: Ritchie; Shearer, Caldow; McColl, Valentine, Austin; Scott, Simpson, Murray, Baird, Hubbard

CELTIC: Beattie; Donnelly, Fallon; Fernie, Evans, Peacock; Sharkey, Collins, McPhail, Smith, Tully

Attendance: 60,000

Celtic were fortunate to withstand Rangers' furious efforts to equalise – Fernie kicked a Simpson header off the goal-line and Murray headed against the base of a post. Celtic took the lead in the 19th minute. Fallon's drive was aimed for the head of McPhail who flicked the ball past Valentine in the jump, Collins took the ball in his stride, darted inward and past Shearer and baffled the outcoming Ritchie with a perfectly placed low shot. Rangers equalised 6 minutes from the interval when Scott for once escaped the close marking of Fallon and crossed a ball that Beattie surprisingly did not try to cut out and he was beaten where he stood when Simpson made contact. 9 minutes after half-time a free-kick conceded by young Austin cost Rangers a goal. Collins lofted a ball to McPhail who, standing on the extreme of the free-kick line-up, directed his header over the hands of Ritchie. 10 minutes later Wilson headed a McPhail cross decisively past Ritchie. Simpson gave Rangers late hope by beating Beattie to a backheader by Murray and driving the ball under the diving goalkeeper.

October 5th: Scotland drew 1-1 with Ireland in Belfast. Caldow, McColl and Baird were in the team. Simpson represented Ireland and he scored their goal.

October 9th: The Scottish League beat the Irish League 7-0 at Ibrox. Caldow, McColl and Baird were in the team. McColl scored one of the goals.

October 12th:
ST MIRREN (1) 1   RANGERS (2) 3
  Lapsley (42 pen)   Baird (24),
                                  Hubbard (35),
                                  Murray (88)

ST MIRREN: Lornie; Lapsley, Wilson; Higgins, Telfer, Buchanan; Murray, Neilson, McKay, Gemmell, McGill

RANGERS: Niven; Shearer, Caldow; McColl, Valentine, Davis; Scott, Simpson, Murray, Baird, Hubbard

Attendance: 30,000

October 26th:
RANGERS (2) 2   HEARTS (1) 3
  Simpson 2 (17, 22)   Wardhaugh (45),
                                  Bauld (49),
                                  Young (67)

RANGERS: Niven; Caldow, Little; McColl, Moles, Millar; Scott, Simpson, Kichenbrand, Baird, Hubbard

HEARTS: Brown; Kirk, Thomson; Mackay, Glidden, Cumming; Young, Murray, Bauld, Wardhaugh, Blackwood

Attendance: 60,000

League positions

	P	W	D	L	F	A	Pts
1 Hearts	7	6	1	0	32	5	13
2 Raith Rovers	8	4	3	1	14	9	11
3 Hibernian	8	5	1	2	15	10	11
4 Clyde	6	5	0	1	18	7	10
5 Kilmarnock	6	5	0	1	17	11	10
13 RANGERS	4	2	0	2	11	9	4

November 2nd:
QUEENS PARK (1) 2   RANGERS (0) 4
  Devine (41), Smith (89)   Baird (50),
                                  Kichenbrand (64),
                                  Hubbard (68 pen),
                                  Simpson (80)

QUEENS PARK: F. Crampsey; I. Harnett, W. Hastie; R. Cromar, D. Fergus, J. Chalmers; J. Smith, J. Robb, A. McEwan, J. H. Devine, C. Church

RANGERS: Niven; Caldow, Little; McColl, Moles, Millar; Scott, Simpson, Kichenbrand, Baird, Hubbard

Attendance: 35,000

November 6th: Billy Simpson scored Ireland's winning goal in an historic 3-2 victory against England at Wembley.

Caldow and Scott were in the Scotland team which beat Switzerland 3-2 in a World Cup Qualifier at Hampden Park.

November 9th:
RANGERS (1) 3   KILMARNOCK (3) 4
  Hubbard 2 (15, 54 pen),   Beattie 2 (6, 32),
  Kichenbrand (50)   Mays (30),
                                  Curlett (58)

RANGERS: Niven; Caldow, Little; McColl, Moles, Millar; Scott, Simpson, Kichenbrand, Baird, Hubbard

KILMARNOCK: Brown; Collins, J. Stewart; R. Stewart, Toner, Kennedy; Muir, Curlett, Mays, Beattie, Black

Attendance: 40,000

November 13th: Scotland drew 1-1 with Wales at Hampden Park. Caldow and Scott were in the team.

November 15th: Willie Telfer was signed from St Mirren for £10,000.

November 16th:

RANGERS (0) 2	CLYDE (0) 0
Baird 2 (62, 64)	

RANGERS: Ritchie; Little, Caldow; Millar, Telfer, Davis; Scott, Simpson, Murray, Baird, Hubbard

CLYDE: McCulloch; Murphy, Haddock; Walters, Finlay, Clinton; Herd, Currie, Keogh, Robertson, Ring

Attendance: 54,000

November 23rd:

FALKIRK (0) 0	RANGERS (2) 4
	Hubbard 4 (12, 42 pen, 55, 89 pen)

FALKIRK: Slater; Parker, McIntosh; Thomson, Irvine, Prentice; Sinclair, Grierson, Wright, Moran, O'Hara

RANGERS: Ritchie; Little, Caldow; McColl, Telfer, Davis; Scott, Millar, Murray, Baird, Hubbard

Attendance: 22,000

November 30th:

RANGERS (1) 3	EAST FIFE (3) 3
Murray (34), Baird (66),	Matthew (6),
Davis (70)	Mochan (25),
	Ingram (36)

RANGERS: Ritchie; Little, Caldow; McColl, Telfer, Davis; Scott, Millar, Murray, Baird, Hubbard

EAST FIFE: McCluskey; Wilkie, Cox; Christie, Bowie, Neilson; Ingram, Bonthrone, Duchart, Mochan, Matthew

Attendance: 20,000

December 2nd: Rangers were reported to be interested in Ted Phillips of Ipswich town.

December 7th:

MOTHERWELL (0) 2	RANGERS (1) 2
Gardiner 2 (46, 51)	Baird (33),
	Murray (53)

MOTHERWELL: Wylie; Holton, McFadyen; Forrest, Shaw, Aitken; Hunter, McCann, McSeveney, Gardiner, St John

RANGERS: Ritchie; Shearer, Caldow; McColl, Telfer, Baird; Scott, Millar, Murray, Brand, Hubbard

Attendance: 25,000

December 14th:

DUNDEE (0) 1	RANGERS (1) 2
Cousin (89)	Cowie o.g. (14),
	Hubbard (59 pen)

DUNDEE: Brown; Reid, Cox; Black, McKenzie, Cowie; Christie, Cousin, Henderson, Sneddon, Robertson

RANGERS: Niven; Shearer, Caldow; McColl, Telfer, Baird; Scott, Millar, Murray, Simpson, Hubbard

Attendance: 20,000

December 16th: Ritchie, Little, Morrison and George Young played for a Glasgow Select against a Kilmarnock Select in a match in aid of the Muirkirk Disaster Fund.

December 21st:

RANGERS (3) 5	THIRD LANARK (0) 1
Shearer (32),	Allan (87)
Murray 2 (39, 47),	
Wilson (45), Brand (64)	

RANGERS: Ritchie; Shearer, Caldow; McColl, Telfer, Baird; Scott, Millar, Murray, Brand, Wilson

THIRD LANARK: Robertson; Cosker, Brown; Smith, Lewis, Kelly; McInnes, Craig, Allan, Gray, Callan

Attendance: 22,000

December 26th: Rangers transferred Sandy Thomson to East Stirling.

December 28th:

ABERDEEN (1) 1	RANGERS (1) 2
W. Hogg (19)	Brand (23), Scott (74)

ABERDEEN: Morrison; Caldwell, J. Hogg; Brownlie, Clunie, Glen; Ewen, W. Hogg, Davidson, Wishart, Hather

RANGERS: Ritchie; Shearer, Caldow; McColl, Telfer, Baird; Scott, Millar, Murray, Brand, Wilson

Attendance: 20,000

League positions

	P	W	D	L	F	A	Pts
1 Hearts	17	14	2	1	71	14	30
2 Hibernian	17	11	1	5	39	24	23
3 Clyde	17	10	0	5	46	26	20
4 Raith Rovers	17	8	4	5	32	22	20
5 Celtic	14	8	3	3	31	17	19
7 RANGERS	13	8	2	3	38	23	18

January 1st:

CELTIC (0) 0	RANGERS (1) 1
	Scott (19)

CELTIC: Beattie; Fallon, Kennedy; Smith, Evans, Peacock; McVittie, Colrain, Ryan, Wilson, Mochan

RANGERS: Ritchie; Shearer, Caldow; McColl, Telfer, Baird; Scott, Millar, Murray, Brand, Wilson

Attendance: 50,000

Rangers dis-allowed goal against Hibs in their Scottish Cup semi-final replay in season 1957–58. Rangers lost by 2 goals to 1.

Rangers line-up for season 1957–58. Back row: B. McIlroy, R. Brand, R. Orr, J. Currie, G. Niven, J. Little, N. Martin, W. Moles, A. Austin, D. Wilson, S. McCorquodale. Centre row: S. Symon (manager), J. Millar, W. Smith, W. Simpson, J. Valentine, S. Baird, W. Paterson, W. Telfer, H. Davis, W. Hogg, H. Neil, M. Murray, J. Craven (asst. trainer). Front row: G. Duncan, A. Scott, J. Queen, R. Shearer, A. McEwan, I. McColl, W. Stevenson, E. Caldow, A. Matthew, J. Hubbard, D. Provan, D. Kinnear (trainer).

A remarkable save by Ritchie midway through the second half was the principal factor in Rangers' success. McVittie's shot was placed carefully and cleverly far to the right of the goalkeeper, but with nimbleness and courage he dived headlong and collared the ball when all of the Celtic legions were crying 'goal'. Rangers seemed the more able to master the difficult conditions. The Murray-led line was always the more dangerous. Scott, who scored the goal in the 19th minute, Millar and Wilson were forwards of distinction.

January 2nd:
RANGERS   (2) 2   PARTICK THISTLE   (0) 0
  Murray (24), Scott (34)

RANGERS: Ritchie; Shearer, Caldow; McColl, Telfer, Baird; Scott, Millar, Murray, Brand, Wilson

PARTICK THISTLE: Thomson; Hogan, Baird; Mathers, Davidson, Donlevy; Smith, Harvey, Ewing, Wright, McParland

Attendance: n.a.

Millar was carried off with a broken collar bone.

January 4th:
QUEEN OF THE SOUTH (0) 1 RANGERS (0) 1
  Tasker (54)   Murray (58)
QUEEN OF THE SOUTH: W. Smith; A. Smith, Binning; Whitehead, Elliot, Greenock; Black, Knox, Crosbie, Tasker, Oakes

RANGERS: Ritchie; Shearer, Caldow; McColl, Telfer, Baird; Scott, Queen, Murray, Brand, Wilson
Attendance: 13,000

January 11th:
RANGERS   (1) 3   HIBERNIAN   (0) 1
  Muir o.g. (42),   Smith (89)
  Baird (68), Simpson (74)

RANGERS: Ritchie; Shearer, Caldow; McColl, Telfer, Baird; Scott, Simpson, Murray, Brand, Wilson

HIBERNIAN: Leslie; Grant, Muir; Hughes, Paterson, Baxter; Smith, Frye, Reilly, Turnbull, McLeod
Attendance: 47,000

January 18th:
AIRDRIE   (3) 3   RANGERS   (3) 4
  McGill (27), Ormond (28),   Brand (7), Scott (20),
  McMillan (43)   Murray (39),
                               Simpson (53)
AIRDRIE: Walker; Kilmarnock, Shanks; Price, Baillie, Quinn; McMillan, McGill, Caven, Rankin, Ormond

RANGERS: Ritchie; Shearer, Caldow; McColl, Telfer, Baird; Scott, Simpson, Murray, Brand, Wilson
Attendance: 15,000

January 22nd: Davie Wilson was called up by the Army.

February 22nd:
RANGERS   (2) 5   QUEENS PARK   (1) 1
  Brand (11), Murray 2 (27, 87), Cromar (42 pen)
  Hubbard 2 (60 pen, 75)

RANGERS: Ritchie; Shearer, Caldow; McColl, Telfer, Baird; Duncan, Simpson, Murray, Brand, Hubbard

QUEENS PARK: F. Crampsey; I. Harnett, J. Kerr; R. Cromar, R. McKinven, D. Holt; C. Church, J. Coates, A. McEwan, W. Omand, E. Perry
Attendance: 20,000

League positions

	P	W	D	L	F	A	Pts
1 Hearts	24	21	2	1	100	17	44
2 RANGERS	19	13	3	3	54	29	29
3 Clyde	21	14	1	6	52	36	29
4 Celtic	21	11	6	4	43	24	28
5 Hibernian	24	12	3	9	51	42	27

March 5th: Don Kichenbrand was transferred to Sunderland.

March 8th:
CLYDE   (1) 1   RANGERS   (2) 3
  Coyle (40)   Brand (13),
                             Duncan 2 (30, 52)
CLYDE: McCulloch; Murphy, Haddock; Walters, Finlay, Clinton; Herd, Currie, Coyle, Robertson, Ring

RANGERS: Ritchie; Shearer, Caldow; McColl, Telfer, Baird; Duncan, Millar, Murray, Brand, Wilson
Attendance: 32,000

March 10th:
KILMARNOCK (2) 3   RANGERS (1) 3
  Burns (13), McBride 2 (23, 50) Hubbard 2
                                  (27 pen, 76 pen)
                                  Murray (84)
KILMARNOCK: Brown; Collins, Stewart; Falls, Toner, Kennedy; Henaughan, McBride, Chalmers, Black, Burns

RANGERS: Ritchie; Shearer, Caldow; McColl, Telfer, Baird; Duncan, Millar, Murray, Brand, Hubbard
Attendance: 20,000

March 19th:
RANGERS   (0) 3   FALKIRK   (1) 2
  McColl (50), Brand (59),   Baird o.g. (33),
  Millar (88)   Moran (74)

RANGERS: Ritchie; Shearer, Caldow; McColl, Telfer, Baird; Duncan, Millar, Murray, Brand, Hubbard

FALKIRK: Slater; Irvine, Lachlan; Wright, Prentice, McMillan; Murray, Grierson, McCole, Moran, Sinclair

Attendance: 25,000

March 22nd:
EAST FIFE   (0) 0   RANGERS   (0) 1
                                        Brand (60)

EAST FIFE: McCluskey; Stirrat, Cox; Christie, Bowie, Mochan; Neilson, Ford, Gillan, Reilly, Matthew

RANGERS: Ritchie; Shearer, Caldow; McColl, Telfer, Baird; Scott, Millar, Murray, Brand, Hubbard

Attendance: 12,000

March 26th: The Scottish League were beaten 4-1 by the English League at Newcastle. Caldow, McColl and Baird were in the team.

March 29th:
RANGERS   (2) 2   MOTHERWELL   (2) 2
  Millar (24), Duncan (32)   St John 2 (1, 30)

RANGERS: Ritchie; Shearer, Caldow; McColl, Telfer, Baird; Duncan, Millar, Murray, Brand, Hubbard

MOTHERWELL: H. Weir; Campbell, McSeveney; Aitken, Martis, McCann; Rae, Quinn, St John, Forrest, A. Weir

Attendance: 38,000

April 12th:
THIRD LANARK   (1) 1   RANGERS   (2) 5
  McInnes (33)   Hubbard 2
                                        (17 pen, 60 pen),
                                        Brand (21),
                                        Simpson 2 (86, 89)

THIRD LANARK: Ramage; Smith, Brown; Higgins, Lewis, Slingsby; W. Craig, R. Craig, Allan, Gray, McInnes

RANGERS: Ritchie; Shearer, Caldow; McColl, Telfer, Baird; Duncan, Millar, Simpson, Brand, Hubbard

Attendance: 25,000

April 16th:
RANGERS   (2) 4   RAITH ROVERS   (1) 1
  Hubbard (2),   Shearer o.g. (25)
  Murray 2 (43, 55),
  Millar (54)

RANGERS: Ritchie; Shearer, Caldow; McColl, Telfer, Baird; Brand, Millar, Murray, Davis, Hubbard

RAITH ROVERS: Drummond; Polland, Lockerbie; Young, McNaught, Leigh; McEwan, Kerray, Kelly, Baxter, McMillan

Attendance: 16,000

April 19th: Scotland were beaten 4-0 by England at Hampden Park. McColl was in the team. Caldow was selected but had to withdraw with an injury on the eve of the match.

April 21st:
HIBERNIAN   (0) 3   RANGERS   (0) 1
  Aitken (50),   Murray (79)
  Reilly (56),
  Baxter (87)

HIBERNIAN: Leslie; Grant, McClelland; Turnbull, Plenderleith, Baxter; Fraser, Aitken, Reilly, Preston, Ormond

RANGERS: Ritchie; Shearer, Little; McColl, Telfer, Baird; Brand, Millar, Murray, Simpson, Hubbard

Attendance: 24,000

April 23rd:
RAITH ROVERS   (1) 1   RANGERS   (2) 3
  J. Williamson (24)   Millar 2 (12, 65),
                                        Baird (13)

RAITH ROVERS: Thorburn; Polland, Lockerbie; Young, McNaught, Leigh; McEwan, Kelly, T. Williamson, J. Williamson, Baxter

RANGERS: Ritchie; Shearer, Little; McColl, Telfer, Baird; Brand, Millar, Simpson, Davis, Hubbard

Attendance: n.a.

April 26th:
RANGERS   (3) 5   ABERDEEN   (0) 0
  Murray 3 (32, 34, 80),
  Brand 2 (41, 52)

RANGERS: Ritchie; Shearer, Caldow; McColl, Telfer, Baird; Scott, Millar, Murray, Brand, Hubbard

ABERDEEN: Morrison; Walker, Hogg; Burns, Clunie, Brownlie; Ewen, Leggat, Davidson, Wishart, Hather

Attendance: 10,000

April 28th:
RANGERS   (0) 1   ST MIRREN   (0) 0
  Murray (66)

RANGERS: Ritchie; Shearer, Caldow; McColl, Telfer, Baird; Duncan, Millar, Murray, Brand, Hubbard

ST MIRREN: Forsyth; Lapsley, McTurk; Neilson, Buchanan, Gregal; Bryceland, Ryan, Wilson, Gemmell, Miller

Attendance: n.a.

April 30th:
HEARTS   (0) 2   RANGERS   (1) 1
  Wardhaugh 2 (68, 89)   Brand (16)

HEARTS: Marshall; Kirk, G. Thomson; Cumming, Milne, Bowman; Paton, Murray, Young, Wardhaugh, Crawford

RANGERS: Ritchie; Shearer, Little; McColl, Telfer, Davis; Duncan, Wilson, Murray, Brand, Hubbard

Attendance: n.a.

May 3rd:

RANGERS	(1) 1		AIRDRIE	(0) 2
Hubbard (23 pen)			Storrie 2 (59, 74)	

RANGERS: Ritchie; Shearer, Little; McColl, Telfer, Baird; Scott, Wilson, Simpson, Brand, Hubbard

AIRDRIE: Walker; Neil, Shanks; Quinn, Baillie, Quigley; Rankin, Price, Sharkey, Storrie, Ormond

Attendance: 10,000

May 1st: Walker, Logie, Melrose, Morrison, Wright and Robertson were given free transfers.

May 5th:

PARTICK THISTLE	(1) 1	RANGERS	(2) 2
Ewing (7)		Murray (30),	
		Wilson (35)	

PARTICK THISTLE: Renucci; Collins, Brown; Mathers, Harvey, Donlevy; L. Thomson, Bell, Keenan, McParland, Ewing

RANGERS: Ritchie; Shearer, Little; Davis, Telfer, Smith; Scott, Millar, Murray, Simpson, Wilson

Attendance: 6,500

May 7th: Scotland drew 1-1 with Hungary at Hampden Park. Caldow was in the team.

May 10th:

RANGERS	(0) 0		DUNDEE	(1) 1
			Cousin (43)	

RANGERS: Ritchie; Shearer, Caldow; McColl, Telfer, Smith; Scott, Millar, Murray, Davis, Wilson

DUNDEE: Liney; Hamilton, Cox; Henderson, McKenzie, Curlett; Robertson, Bonthrone, Cousin, Sneddon, McGeachie

Attendance: 10,000

Scottish First Division

	P	W	D	L	F	A	Pts
1 Hearts	34	29	4	1	132	29	62
2 RANGERS	34	22	5	7	89	49	49
3 Celtic	34	19	8	7	84	47	46
4 Clyde	34	18	6	10	84	61	42
5 Kilmarnock	34	14	9	11	60	55	37
6 Partick Thistle	34	17	3	14	69	71	37
7 Raith Rovers	34	14	7	13	66	56	35
8 Motherwell	34	12	8	14	68	67	32
9 Hibernian	34	13	5	16	59	60	31
10 Falkirk	34	11	9	14	64	82	31
11 Dundee	34	13	5	16	49	65	31
12 Aberdeen	34	14	2	18	68	76	30
13 St Mirren	34	11	8	15	59	66	30
14 Third Lanark	34	13	4	17	69	88	30
15 Queen of the S.	34	12	7	17	61	72	29
16 Airdrie	34	13	2	19	71	92	28
17 East Fife	34	10	3	21	45	88	23
18 Queens Park	34	4	1	29	41	114	9

May 12th: Billy Hogg was signed on a free transfer from Aberdeen.

May 19th: Rangers made an offer for Alec Parker of Falkirk.

May 30th: Rangers signed Andy McEwan from Queens Park.

June 1st: Caldow represented Scotland in a 2-1 win over Poland in Warsaw.

June 8th: Caldow represented Scotland in a 1-1 draw against Yugoslavia in a World Cup match in Vasteraas, Sweden.

June 11th: Caldow represented Scotland in a 2-3 defeat by Paraguay in a World Cup match in Norrkoping, Sweden.

June 15th: Caldow and Baird were in the Scotland team beaten 1-2 by France in a World Cup match in Orebro, Sweden. Baird scored Scotland's goal.

LEAGUE CUP

August 10th:

RANGERS	(2) 6		ST MIRREN	(0) 0
Murray 3 (20, 30, 71),				
Simpson 3 (52, 80, 84)				

RANGERS: Niven; Shearer, Caldow; McColl, Valentine, Davis; Scott, Simpson, Murray, Baird, Wilson

ST MIRREN: Forsyth; Higgins, Wilson; Buchanan, Telfer, Clark; Devine, Bryceland, McKay, Gemmell, McCulloch

Attendance: 55,000

August 14th:
PARTICK THISTLE   (0) 0   RANGERS   (0) 1
Baird (53)

PARTICK THISTLE: Ledgerwood; Kerr, Baird; Harvey, Davidson, Mathers; McKenzie, Smith, Gilmour, Wright, Ewing

RANGERS: Niven; Shearer, Caldow; McColl, Valentine, Davis; Scott, Simpson, Murray, Baird, Wilson

Attendance: 35,000

August 17th:
RANGERS   (2) 4   RAITH ROVERS   (0) 3
Scott (6), Leigh o.g. (12),   Urquhart 2 (56, 70),
Murray (49), Simpson (55)   Kelly (85)

RANGERS: Niven; Shearer, Caldow; McColl, Davis, Millar; Scott, Simpson, Murray, Baird, Hubbard

RAITH ROVERS: Drummond; Polland, Knox; Young, McNaught, Leigh; McEwan, Kelly, Copland, Williamson, Urquhart

Attendance: 47,000

August 24th:
ST MIRREN   (0) 0   RANGERS   (3) 4
Scott (11),
Murray 2 (43, 69),
Baird (45)

ST MIRREN: Forsyth; Higgins, Wilson; Neilson, Telfer, Leishman; Miller, Gemmell, Flavell, Johnston, McGill

RANGERS: Niven; Shearer, Caldow; McColl, Valentine, Davis; Scott, Simpson, Murray, Baird, Hubbard

Attendance: 23,000

August 28th:
RANGERS   (0) 0   PARTICK THISTLE   (3) 3
Ewing 2 (8, 10),
Henderson (14)

RANGERS: Niven; Shearer, Caldow; McColl, Valentine, Davis; Scott, Simpson, Murray, Morrison, Hubbard

PARTICK THISTLE: Ledgerwood; Kerr, Baird; Wright, Davidson, Mathers; McKenzie, Henderson, Hogan, McIntosh, Ewing

Attendance: 35,000

August 31st:
RAITH ROVERS   (3) 4   RANGERS   (3) 3
Urquhart (8), Kerray 2 (13, 34),Scott 2 (7, 25),
McEwan (80)   Hubbard (26 pen)

RAITH ROVERS: Drummond; Polland, E. Kelly; Young, McNaught, Leigh; McEwan, Kerray, Williamson, B. Kelly, Urquhart

RANGERS: Niven; Shearer, Caldow; McColl, Davis, Baird; Scott, Simpson, Kichenbrand, Murray, Hubbard

Attendance: 24,000

League Cup Section Table

	P	W	D	L	F	A	Pts
RANGERS	6	4	0	2	18	10	8
Raith Rovers	6	4	0	2	16	10	8
St Mirren	6	3	0	3	5	14	6
Partick Thistle	6	1	0	5	4	9	2

September 12th: Quarter-Final First Leg
KILMARNOCK   (1) 2   RANGERS   (0) 1
Muir (19), Caldow o.g. (82)   Kichenbrand (83)

KILMARNOCK: Brown; Collins, J. Stewart; R. Stewart, Toner, Mackay; Muir, Beattie, Mays, Black, Burns

RANGERS: Ritchie; Shearer, Caldow; McColl, Moles, Baird; Scott, Simpson, Kichenbrand, Millar, Hubbard

Attendance: 26,800

September 14th: Quarter-Final Second Leg
RANGERS   (1) 3   KILMARNOCK   (1) 1
Hubbard (23 pen),   Black (39)
Scott (76),
Simpson (80)

RANGERS: Ritchie; Shearer, Caldow; McColl, Moles, Davis; Scott, Simpson, Murray, Baird, Hubbard

KILMARNOCK: Brown; Collins, J. Stewart; R. Stewart, Toner, Mackay; Muir, Beattie, Mays, Black, Burns

Attendance: 66,000

Rangers won 4–3 on aggregate

September 28th: Semi-Final   At Hampden Park
RANGERS   (2) 4   BRECHIN CITY   (0) 0
Melrose 2 (25, 89),
Shearer (40 pen),
Paterson o.g. (85)

RANGERS: Ritchie; Shearer, Caldow; McColl, Valentine, Millar; Wilson, Robertson, Kichenbrand, Melrose, Murray

BRECHIN: Robertson; Paterson, Hodge; Stormont, Christie, Stewart; McRae, Fowler, Warrender, Scott, Duncan

Attendance: 28,453

In view of the fact that both teams played below full strength because of injuries it was perhaps not expected that the game would produce football of outstanding merit. Brechin held out for 25 minutes. Kichenbrand was obstructed just outside the penalty area and when McColl, with the free-kick, placed the ball accurately into the penalty area Melrose headed it neatly into the net. 15 minutes later Paterson pulled down Murray in the penalty area and Shearer scored from the spot. For all their pressure Rangers did not score again until the 85th minute when Paterson turned a Wilson cross past his own keeper. In the last minute Kichenbrand headed on to Melrose who scored from close range. The best player of all was McColl who excelled in both defence and attack.

October 19th: Final　　　　　At Hampden Park
CELTIC　(2) 7　　　　　RANGERS　(0) 1
　Wilson (23),　　　　　　Simpson (58)
　McPhail 3 (53, 69, 81),
　Mochan 2 (44, 74),
　Fernie (89 pen)

CELTIC: Beattie; Donnelly, Fallon; Fernie, Evans, Peacock; Tully, Collins, McPhail, Wilson, Mochan

RANGERS: Niven; Shearer, Caldow; McColl, Valentine, Davis; Scott, Simpson, Murray, Baird, Hubbard

Attendance: 82,293

Referee: J. A. Mowat (Rutherglen)

Celtic proved conclusively the value of concentration on discipline and on the arts and crafts of the game to the exclusion of the so-called power play. Not since the brilliant Coronation Cup days at Hampden Park had Celtic played football of such quality. In the first 20 minutes Celtic might have scored at least 4 goals. First Collins and then Tully hit the wood around Niven. They opened the scoring in 23 minutes when McPhail headed down to Wilson and the inside-right, without waiting for the ball to touch the ground, bulged the net from 12 yards. Next the crossbar stopped another 30-yard free-kick by Collins. Mochan scored a 2nd in the second-last minute of the first half. McPhail, after engaging in a heading movement with Wilson, lofted the ball over Shearer to the galloping outside-left. Mochan cut in and from the near touchline hurtled his shot into the far corner of the net. Rangers started the second half with Murray, a knee bandaged, at outside-left. In the 53rd minute McPhail made it 3–0 when he headed in a Collins cross. 5 minutes later Simpson, with an exhilarating dive and header, scored from McColl's cross. In the final 21 minutes McPhail (now toying with Valentine), Mochan, McPhail again and Fernie from a penalty-kick completed the humiliation.

SCOTTISH CUP

February 1st: First Round
COWDENBEATH　(1) 1　　　RANGERS　(0) 3
　Gilfillan (7)　　　　　　Simpson (50),
　　　　　　　　　　　　　Murray 2 (62, 87)

COWDENBEATH: Barrie; Duncan, Clark; Moore, Campbell, Murphy; Mulhall, Craig, Miller, Reid, Gilfillan

RANGERS: Ritchie; Shearer, Caldow; McColl, Telfer, Baird; Scott, Simpson, Murray, Brand, Wilson

Attendance: 16,806

February 15th: Second Round
FORFAR　(0) 1　　　　　RANGERS　(4) 9
　Craig (79)　　　　　　Murray 3 (28, 52, 75),
　　　　　　　　　　　　Brand 2 (27, 59)
　　　　　　　　　　　　Simpson 2 (33, 58),
　　　　　　　　　　　　Hubbard (7),
　　　　　　　　　　　　McColl (63)

FORFAR: Mowat; Steen, Berrie; Dudman, Muirhead, Miller; Cord, Weir, Craig, Harrow, Dick

RANGERS: Ritchie; Shearer, Caldow; McColl, Telfer, Baird; Scott, Simpson, Murray, Brand, Hubbard

Attendance: 8,066

March 3rd: Third Round
DUNFERMLINE　(1) 1　　　RANGERS　(2) 2
　McWilliams (13)　　　　Murray (31),
　　　　　　　　　　　　Brand (39)

DUNFERMLINE: Beaton; Duthie, Sweeney; Bain, Colville, Mailer; Peebles, McWilliams, Dickson, Watson, Napier

RANGERS: Ritchie; Shearer, Caldow; McColl, Telfer, Baird; Scott, Simpson, Murray, Brand, Hubbard

Attendance: 24,000

March 15th: Quarter-Final
QUEEN OF THE　　　　　RANGERS　(2) 4
　SOUTH　(2) 3　　　　　Murray 2 (6, 63),
　Black (30),　　　　　　Millar 2 (19, 52)
　Patterson 2 (43, 57)

QUEEN OF THE SOUTH: W. Smith; A. Smith, Binning; Whitehead, Elliot, Greenock; Black, Crosbie, Patterson, Ewing, Oakes

RANGERS: Ritchie; Shearer, Caldow; McColl, Telfer, Baird; Duncan, Millar, Murray, Brand, Wilson

Attendance: 23,000

April 5th: Semi-Final　　　At Hampden Park
RANGERS (1) 2　　　　　HIBERNIAN　(2) 2
　Millar (3), Murray (77)　Preston (32),
　　　　　　　　　　　　Aitken (37)

RANGERS: Ritchie; Shearer, Caldow; McColl, Telfer, Baird; Scott, Millar, Murray, Brand, Wilson

HIBERNIAN: Leslie; Grant, McClelland; Turnbull, Paterson, Baxter; Fraser, Aitken, Baker, Preston, Ormond

Attendance: 76,727

An astonishing feature of the game at Hampden was the deterioration in the standard of Rangers' forward play after the first 20 minutes. A goal ahead through Millar within 3 minutes of the start Rangers gave every indication that they would pass easily into the Final. They had the Hibs defence fully extended and it seemed only a matter of time before they emphasised their outfield superiority with goals. The goals were not forthcoming, however, and the longer the game lasted the more remote they appeared as Hibs, having scored through Preston and Aitken in the 32nd and 37th minutes, tightened their defence. Only 13 minutes remained for play when Murray equalised for Rangers.

April 9th: Semi-Final Replay   At Hampden Park
HIBERNIAN   (1) 2   RANGERS   (0) 1
   Turnbull (18 pen),   Baird (54 pen)
   Fraser (53)

HIBERNIAN: Leslie; Grant, McClelland; Turnbull, Paterson, Baxter; Fraser, Aitken, Baker, Preston, Ormond

RANGERS: Ritchie; Shearer, Caldow; McColl, Telfer, Baird; Duncan, Millar, Murray, Brand, Wilson

Attendance: 74,000

With only 2 minutes remaining for play, Rangers, who had pressed almost continuously after the interval, scored an equalising goal. McColl swept the ball into the goalmouth and in the ensuing scramble Murray bodied the ball past Leslie and over the line. In response to an appeal by Hibs, referee Davidson consulted a linesman and then awarded a free-kick to the Edinburgh side, apparently on the grounds that Leslie had been impeded in his efforts to clutch the ball. Masters in the outfield for most of the game, the Ibrox forwards, apart from Wilson, played like novices in the goal area. Their finishing was slipshod. Baker was much livelier than in the previous game and Telfer consequently had to cover more ground in keeping his youthful opponent in check. Hibs opened the scoring after 18 minutes. A Leslie clearance spun off McColl's head to Telfer whose backheader to Ritchie was well out of his reach. Baker and Ritchie reached the ball simultaneously and when the centre-forward fell the referee awarded a penalty with which Turnbull scored. 8 minutes after the interval Fraser scored Hibs' second from the rebound off an Aitken shot. A minute later Brand was sandwiched by Paterson and Baxter, and from the resultant penalty Baird scored. The nearest Rangers came to scoring was when shots from Millar and Brand squirmed out of Leslie's hands but on each occasion the goalkeeper was given time to recover.

EUROPEAN CUP

September 4th: First Round First Leg
RANGERS   (1) 3   ST ETIENNE (France)   (1) 1
   Kichenbrand (19),   Mekloufi (14)
   Scott (47), Simpson (82)

RANGERS: Niven; Shearer, Caldow; McColl, Davis, Baird; Scott, Simpson, Kichenbrand, Murray, Hubbard

ST ETIENNE: Abbes; R. Tylinski, Wicart; Domingo, M. Tylinski, Bordas; Njo-Lea, Mekloufi, Fevrier, Goujon, Lefevre

Attendance: 85,000

Rangers should have won by half a dozen goals and rendered their visit to France a mere formality. Mekloufi scored the opening goal after 14 minutes after a brilliant run through a retreating defence. Kichenbrand equalised 5 minutes later with a back-header. The Ibrox team took a 2-1 lead within 2 minutes of the re-start when Scott scored. R. Tylinski was injured in a tackle with Kichenbrand after 58 minutes and hobbled on the wing for the remainder of the match. A Hubbard cross headed down to Simpson by Kichenbrand gave Simpson Rangers' 3rd goal 8 minutes from time. Niven, though he had not a tenth of the work of Abbes, effected several saves of splendour, one from Lefevre when the game was dangerously poised at 2-1, with 10 minutes left, being of special value to his side.

September 25th: First Round
ST ETIENNE   (1) 2   RANGERS   (0) 1
   Oleksiak (11),   Wilson (61)
   Fevrier (87)

ST ETIENNE: Abbes; M. Tylinski, Wicart; Domingo, R. Tylinski, Fevrier; Njo-Lea, Mekloufi, Goujon, Oleksiak, Lefevre

RANGERS: Ritchie; Shearer, Caldow; McColl, Valentine, Millar; Scott, Simpson, Murray, Baird, Wilson

Attendance: 35,000

Hubbard, who had been suffering from influenza, was unable to play and his place was taken by Wilson who scored his side's only goal. Oleksiak scored a splendid goal from 14 yards as early as the 11th minute. Njo-Lea had been allowed to run unchallenged from 20 yards and when his cross from the edge of the 18-yard line came over, Oleksiak met the ball on the half-volley. Simpson was injured on the forehead before half-time and had to leave the field in order to have stitches inserted in the wound. Scott was the most dangerous forward, and it was from one of his corner kicks that Wilson stooped low to head the equaliser. 15 minutes from the end Rangers were awarded a penalty when Wilson was charged in the back by Wicart. Amid exploding fireworks, some of which were thrown onto the pitch, McColl took the kick but Abbes pulled off a magnificent one-handed save. Fevrier scored a 2nd goal with only 3 minutes left for play.

Rangers won 4-3 on aggregate

November 27th: Second Round First Leg

RANGERS (1) 1   A.C. MILAN

                         (Italy) (0) 4

   Murray (31)   Grillo 2 (75, 83),

                         Baruffi (81), Bean (86)

RANGERS: Ritchie; Little, Caldow; McColl, Telfer, Millar; Scott, Simpson, Murray, Baird, Hubbard

A.C. MILAN: Buffon; Maldini, Zagatti; Fontana, Zannier, Bergamaschi; Baroldo, Schiaffino, Bean, Grillo, Baruffi

Attendance: 85,000

Rangers deservedly led at half-time by a Murray goal. For 45 minutes Schiaffino, the Milan captain, strolled seemingly unconcernedly but when the second half started this tall, brilliant ball player began increasing his pace. 15 minutes from time Murray received a word of warning from the referee for a rash foul on the Milan goalkeeper and within seconds Grillo, accelerating as all of his colleagues did from that moment, shot the equalising goal after dribbling through the home defence. Milan stunned the crowd by scoring 3 more goals between the 81st and 86th minutes. Milan had magnificent players in their goalkeeper and centre-half in defence, and in Schiaffino and Grillo once both decided that the competition was serious. Ritchie, Little, Caldow, Telfer and Hubbard were the only Rangers players possessing the class and temperament for the occasion.

December 11th: Second Round Second Leg

A.C. MILAN (1) 2   RANGERS (0) 0

   Baruffi (30), Galli (48)

A.C. MILAN: Buffon; Maldini, Zagatti; Fontana, Zannier, Beraldo; Galli, Leidholm, Bean, Grillo, Baruffi

RANGERS: Niven; Shearer, Caldow; McColl, Telfer, Baird; Scott, Millar, Kichenbrand, Wilson, Hubbard

Attendance: 2,000

Milan was a rain-lashed city and as a result of the deluge the game started 10 minutes late. The football itself became largely farcical, the water-logged ground frequently baffling defenders and attackers alike. Rangers' defence, McColl and Telfer especially, played with considerable spirit in view of their increasingly hopeless task. Milan did not look likely to lose at any time and goals scored by Baruffi and Galli ensured the overall rout.

(A.C. Milan won 6-1 on aggregate).

APPEARANCES

	League	League Cup	Scottish Cup	Glasgow Cup	Charity Cup	Friend-lies	Euro-pean Cup
Ritchie	28	3	6	1	2	1	2
Little	12	-	-	2	2	1	1
Caldow	30	10	6	5	-	-	4
Shearer	27	10	6	3	2	1	3
McColl	33	10	6	5	1	1	4
Baird	32	8	6	5	2	1	4
Scott	23	9	4	4	1	1	4
Simpson	16	9	3	4	-	1	3
Kichenbrand	5	3	-	2	-	-	3
Murray	27	9	6	3	2	1	3
Hubbard	24	7	2	4	1	1	3
Valentine	2	6	-	1	-	-	1
Austin	1	-	-	-	-	-	-
Niven	6	7	-	4	-	-	2
Davis	8	8	-	2	2	-	1
Moles	4	2	-	2	-	-	-
Millar	25	3	3	4	1	-	3
Wilson	12	3	4	1	1	-	2
Telfer	27	-	6	2	2	1	1
Brand	22	-	6	1	-	1	-
Queen	1	-	-	-	-	-	-
Duncan	8	-	2	-	1	-	-
Smith	1	-	-	-	1	-	-
Morrison	-	1	-	-	-	-	-
Hogg	-	-	-	-	1	-	-
Robertson	-	1	-	-	-	-	-
Melrose	-	1	-	-	-	-	-

GOALSCORERS

League: Murray 19, Hubbard 19 (12 pens), Simpson 11, Brand 11, Baird 8, Millar 5, Scott 4, Duncan 3, Kichenbrand 2, Wilson 2, Shearer 2, Davis 1, McColl 1, Own Goals 1

League Cup: Murray 6, Simpson 6, Scott 5, Baird 2, Hubbard 2 (2 pens), Melrose 2, Own Goals 2, Kichenbrand 1, Shearer 1 (pen) 1, Shearer 1 (pen)

Scottish Cup: Murray 9, Brand 3, Simpson 3, Millar 3, Hubbard 1, McColl 1, Baird 1 (pen)

Glasgow Cup: Kichenbrand 3, Simpson 3, Brand 3, Baird 2, Scott 1, Millar 1, Own Goals 1

Charity Cup: Murray 1

Friendlies: Murray 1

European Cup: Kichenbrand 1, Scott 1, Simpson 1, Wilson 1, Murray 1

Season 1958–59

Rangers won their 31st Championship. They went into the last day of the season with a 2-point advantage over Hearts and exactly the same goal average and although they were beaten at home by Aberdeen, Celtic's win over Hearts at Parkhead ensured that the League Flag returned to Ibrox. Again their season got off to a slow start but a run of 27 games with only 1 defeat hauled them to the top of the table. The inspirational signing of Ian McMillan from Airdrieonians signalled the start of this run. The 5-0 thrashing of Hearts in December was the most impressive of their 21 victories; and although they conceded 51 goals their attack managed 92. Ralph Brand finished top scorer on 21, 4 ahead of Murray. Niven, Shearer and Scott played in all of the matches.

After a great Scottish Cup win over Hearts at Ibrox, Celtic upset the form book by beating Rangers at Parkhead in the Third Round.

Rangers were drawn in the same League Cup Section as Hearts and although they beat them well in the first match of the season, a defeat by Raith Rovers and a last-minute defeat by Hearts at Tynecastle, in a match in which their young debutant goalkeeper, Norrie Martin, was carried off with a fractured skull, prevented their qualification to the later stages.

In the absence of European football Rangers undertook a number of Friendlies against top-class opposition and they recorded impressive victories against Napoli (Italy) and Grasshoppers (Switzerland) under the Ibrox floodlights. Arsenal were also comprehensively beaten at Highbury. Rangers undertook a short two-match tour of Denmark at the end of the season

Both Billy Simpson and Johnny Hubbard left the club during the season.

League: Champions
League Cup: Failed to Qualify from Section
Scottish Cup: Third Round

SCOTTISH FIRST DIVISION

July 17th: Rangers signed Andy Matthew from East Fife for £4,500.

July 21st: Former Scotland B International Bill Paterson was signed from Newcastle United for £3,500.

August 20th:

RANGERS	(0) 2	THIRD LANARK	(2) 2
Baird (50 pen),		R. Craig (15),	
Millar (58)		Gray (19)	

RANGERS: Niven; Shearer, Caldow; McColl, Telfer, Baird; Scott, Millar, McEwan, Brand, Wilson

THIRD LANARK: Ramage; Smith, Brown; Kelly, Lewis, Robb; W. Craig, R. Craig, Dick, Gray, McInnes
Attendance: 35,000

August 23rd: Cardiff City made a transfer bid for Johnny Hubbard.

September 3rd: The Scottish League beat the Irish League 5-0 in Belfast. Caldow was in the team.

September 6th:

CELTIC	(1) 2	RANGERS	(1) 2
Collins (28),		Hubbard (41 pen),	
Smith (63)		Brand (76)	

CELTIC: Beattie; McKay, Mochan; Fernie, McNeill, Peacock; Smith, Tully, Conway, Collins, Auld

103

RANGERS: Niven; Shearer, Caldow; McColl, Telfer, Davis; Scott, Brand, Murray, Wilson, Hubbard

Attendance: 50,000

Rangers were awarded a penalty in the 41st minute. It looked a soft award as McNeill appeared to slide in a foot from just the rear of Wilson and prod the ball away just as the inside-left drew back his foot to shoot, and Brand seemed to throw himself towards Beattie as the goalkeeper bent to pick up the ball. Hubbard converted the penalty. 27 minutes from time Scott fouled Mochan, the free-kick reached Conway, he transferred it to Smith who warded off Telfer's tackle attempt and ran in and beat the advancing Niven. Brand made the score 2-2 13 minutes later, Collins having opened the scoring for Celtic in the 28th minute.

September 9th: John Valentine was transferred to St Johnstone.

September 13th:
RANGERS   (1) 2   PARTICK THISTLE   (1) 1
  Hubbard (29 pen),   Mathers (37 pen)
  Brand (49)

RANGERS: Niven; Shearer, Caldow; McColl, Paterson, Davis; Scott, Brand, Murray, Wilson, Hubbard

PARTICK THISTLE: Ledgerwood; Hogan, Baird; Mathers, Davidson, Donlevy; McKenzie, Wright, Kerr, Smith, McParland

Attendance: 41,000

September 20th:
AIRDRIE   (0) 5   RANGERS   (1) 4
  Black 2 (62, 75),   Hubbard 3 (19, 54
  Ormond 2 (64, 71),   pen, 88),
  Rankin (56 pen)   Hogg (86)

AIRDRIE: Wallace; Neil, Miller; Quinn, Baillie, Johnstone; Sharkey, McGill, Black, Rankin, Ormond

RANGERS: Niven; Shearer, Caldow; McColl, Telfer, Davis; Scott, Hogg, Simpson, Wilson, Hubbard

Attendance: 18,000

September 24th: The Scottish League beat the League of Ireland 1-0 at Ibrox. Caldow was in the team.
September 27th:
RANGERS   (0) 1   DUNDEE   (0) 2
  Baird (88)   Telfer o.g. (60),
                         Hill (67)

RANGERS: Niven; Shearer, Caldow; McColl, Telfer, Davis; Scott, Hubbard, Wilson, Baird, Matthew

DUNDEE: Brown; Reid, Cox; Henderson, Gabriel, Cowie; McGeachie, Cousin, Hill, Sneddon, Robertson

Attendance: 32,000

October 2nd: Ian McMillan was signed from Airdrie for £10,000.

October 4th:
DUNFERMLINE   (1) 1   RANGERS   (2) 7
  Dickson (9)   Brand (7), Hubbard 3
                           (23, 71 pen, 89),
                           Baird (70),
                           Duncan (80),
                           Scott (83)

DUNFERMLINE: Beaton; Thomson, Sweeney; A. Smith, Colville, Rattray; Peebles, Burns, Dickson, Harvey, Melrose

RANGERS: Niven; Shearer, Caldow; McColl, Telfer, Davis; Duncan, Baird, Scott, Brand, Hubbard

Attendance: 11,000

October 8th: The Scottish League drew 1-1 with the English League at Ibrox. Caldow and Baird were in the team. Baird scored from the penalty spot.

October 11th:
RANGERS   (1) 2   ST MIRREN   (0) 1
  Duncan (24), Brand (85)   Wilson (56)

RANGERS: Niven; Shearer, Caldow; McColl, Telfer, Davis; Duncan, Baird, Scott, Brand, Hubbard

ST MIRREN: Forsyth; Lapsley, McTurk; Doonan, McGugan, Thomson; Ryan, Bryceland, Wilson, Gemmell, McCulloch

Attendance: 40,000

October 18th:
RANGERS   (2) 4   RAITH ROVERS   (2) 4
  McMillan 2 (36, 66),   Kerray (42),
  Baird (41), Scott (59)   Dobbie (43),
                           Urquhart (71),
                           McEwan (82)

RANGERS: Niven; Shearer, Little; McColl, Telfer, Davis; Duncan, McMillan, Scott, Baird, Hubbard

RAITH ROVERS: Thorburn; Polland, Williamson; Ward, McNaught, Baxter; McEwan, Kerray, Dobbie, Young, Urquhart

Attendance: 25,000

October 18th: Scotland beat Wales 3-0 in Cardiff. Caldow was in the side.

October 25h:
STIRLING ALBION   (1) 2   RANGERS   (1) 2
  Gilmour (13), Kilgannon (63)   Brand (19),
                                 McMillan (77)

STIRLING ALBION: Smith; Gibson, Pettigrew; McKechnie, Menzies, Pierson; Benvie, Kilgannon, Gilmour, Spence, McPhee

RANGERS: Niven; Shearer, Caldow; Davis, Telfer, Stevenson; Scott, McMillan, Hogg, Brand, Matthew

McMillan missed a penalty

Attendance: 17,000

League positions

	P	W	D	L	F	A	Pts
1 Hearts	8	6	2	0	30	13	14
2 Motherwell	9	5	3	1	27	12	13
3 Aberdeen	9	6	0	3	24	9	12
4 Airdrie	9	6	0	3	21	19	12
5 Celtic	9	5	1	3	24	16	11
7 RANGERS	9	3	4	2	26	20	10

November 1st:
RANGERS (1) 4   HIBERNIAN (0) 0
  Simpson 4 (29, 52, 83, 88)

RANGERS: Niven; Shearer, Caldow; Davis, Telfer, Stevenson; Scott, McMillan, Simpson, Brand, Matthew

HIBERNIAN: Leslie; Grant, Muir; Hughes, Plenderleith, Baxter; McLeod, Allison, Baker, Preston, Ormond

Attendance: 17,000

November 5th: Scotland drew 2-2 with Ireland at Hampden Park. Caldow put through his own goal for Ireland's opener.

November 8th:
CLYDE (1) 1   RANGERS (2) 4
  Robertson (10)   Davis (14),
                     Simpson (18),
                     Brand 2 (53, 55)

CLYDE: McCulloch; Murphy, Haddock; Reilly, Sim, Walters; Herd, Robertson, Coyle, Innes, Ring

RANGERS: Niven; Shearer, Caldow; Davis, Telfer, Stevenson; Scott, McMillan, Simpson, Brand, Matthew

Attendance: 20,000

November 15th:
RANGERS (2) 3   FALKIRK (0) 0
  Simpson 2 (39, 42),
  Scott (79)

RANGERS: Niven; Shearer, Caldow; Davis, Telfer, Stevenson; Scott, McMillan, Simpson, Brand, Matthew

FALKIRK: Slater; Richmond, Hunter; Wright, Prentice, McMillan; Murray, White, Grierson, Moran, Lachlan

Attendance: 35,000

November 22nd:
KILMARNOCK (0) 0   RANGERS (1) 3
                      Wilson (2),
                      Brand 2 (49, 71)

KILMARNOCK: J. Brown; Collins, Watson; Beattie, Dougan, Mackay; H. Brown, Henaughan, McBride, Black, Muir

RANGERS: Niven; Shearer, Caldow; Davis, Telfer, Stevenson; Scott, McMillan, Simpson, Brand, Wilson

Attendance: 24,000

November 29th:
MOTHERWELL (2) 2   RANGERS (1) 2
  Quinn (35), St John (43)   Brand (8),
                               Hubbard (48)

MOTHERWELL: H. Weir; McSeveney, Stewart; Aitken, Martis, McCann; A. Weir, W. Reid, St John, Quinn, Hunter

RANGERS: Niven; Shearer, Caldow; Davis, Telfer, Stevenson; Scott, McMillan, Simpson, Brand, Hubbard

Attendance: 32,977

December 6th:
QUEEN OF THE SOUTH (2) 3 RANGERS (3) 6
  Oakes (1), McGill (19),   Brand 3 (14, 18, 86),
  Patterson (89)   Scott (20),
                             Murray (55),
                             McMillan (69)

QUEEN OF THE SOUTH: Gebbie; Sharp, Binning; Greenock, Smith, Ewing; Black, Patterson, McGill, King, Oakes

RANGERS: Niven; Shearer, Caldow; Davis, Paterson, Stevenson; Scott, McMillan, Murray, Brand, Wilson

Attendance: 10,000

December 13th:
RANGERS (5) 5   HEARTS (0) 0
  Brand 2 (3, 34),
  Murray 3 (11, 17, 23)

RANGERS: Niven; Shearer, Caldow; Davis, Telfer, Stevenson; Scott, McMillan, Murray, Brand, Matthew

HEARTS: Brown; Kirk, Thomson; Bowman, Robertson, Cumming; Young, Murray, Bauld, Wardhaugh, Crawford

Attendance: 60,000

December 20th:
ABERDEEN (0) 1   RANGERS (1) 3
  Baird (79)   Murray (41),
                 Brand (50),
                 Scott (82)

ABERDEEN: Ogston; Clydesdale, Hogg; Burns, Clunie, Glen; Cooper, Little, Baird, Davidson, Hather

RANGERS: Niven; Shearer, Caldow; Davis, Telfer, Stevenson; Scott, McMillan, Murray, Brand, Matthew

Attendance: 17,000

December 27th:

THIRD LANARK	(0) 2	RANGERS	(1) 3
Hilley (50), Goodfellow (82)		Murray 2 (55, 75), Brand (17)	

THIRD LANARK: Ramage; Caldwell, Brown; Kelly, McCallum, Robb; Hilley, Goodfellow, Lewis, Gray, McInnes

RANGERS: Niven; Shearer, Caldow; Orr, Telfer, Stevenson; Scott, McMillan, Murray, Brand, Matthew

Attendance: 23,000

League positions

	P	W	D	L	F	A	Pts
1 RANGERS	18	11	5	2	59	29	27
2 Airdrie	18	12	2	4	40	28	26
3 Hearts	18	10	5	3	58	31	25
4 Motherwell	17	9	6	2	50	25	24
5 Dundee	18	9	5	4	36	28	23

January 1st:

RANGERS	(2) 2	CELTIC	(1) 1
Matthew (19), Caldow (63 pen)		Peacock (15)	

RANGERS: Niven; Shearer, Caldow; McColl, Telfer, Stevenson; Scott, McMillan, Murray, Brand, Matthew

CELTIC: Beattie; McKay, Mochan; Smith, Evans, Peacock; McVittie, Jackson, Colrain, Divers, Auld

Attendance: 55,000

Peacock began the scoring in 15 minutes with a low shot which was deflected by Telfer past Niven. 4 minutes later Rangers equalised through Matthew after Beattie had saved from the outside-left. Caldow shot the home team ahead from the penalty-spot after Mochan armed away a shot from Scott with no apparent danger to Beattie. 10 minutes from time it was touch and go whether the referee would abandon the match as a dreadful gale was sweeping over the pitch which had long since become a quagmire. Celtic made tremendous efforts to neutralise Rangers' 2-1 lead. 5 minutes from time they were awarded a penalty. Auld had to search for the penalty-spot in the morass but his shot struck the crossbar and was cleared.

January 3rd:

PARTICK THISTLE	(1) 2	RANGERS	(0) 0
Smith 2 (31, 76)			

PARTICK THISTLE: Freebairn; Hogan, Baird; Wright, Harvey, Donlevy; Smith, Wilson, Kerr, McParland, Ewing

RANGERS: Niven; Shearer, Caldow; McColl, Telfer, Stevenson; Scott, McMillan, Murray, Brand, Matthew

Attendance: 37,000

January 21st:

RANGERS	(0) 2	AIRDRIE	(0) 1
Davis (63), McMillan (82)		Sharkey (48)	

AIRDRIE: Wallace; Neil, Miller; Quinn, Baillie, Johnstone; McCulloch, McGill, Sharkey, Rankin, Ormond

Attendance: 30,000

January 24th:

RANGERS	(1) 1	DUNFERMLINE	(0) 0
Murray (16)			

RANGERS: Niven; Shearer, Caldow; Davis, Telfer, Stevenson; Scott, McMillan, Murray, Brand, Matthew

DUNFERMLINE: Connachan; Duthie, Sweeney; Bain, Colville, Mailer; Peebles, A. Smith, Dickson, McWilliam, Melrose

Attendance: 28,000

January 28th:

DUNDEE	(0) 1	RANGERS	(1) 3
Sneddon (77)		Murray 2 (37, 65), Millar (62)	

DUNDEE: Brown; Hamilton, Cox; Henderson, Gabriel, Cowie; Curlett, Bonthrone, Cousin, Sneddon, Robertson

RANGERS: Niven; Shearer, Caldow; Davis, Telfer, Stevenson; Scott, McMillan, Murray, Millar, Matthew

Attendance: 16,000

February 7th:

ST MIRREN	(0) 1	RANGERS	(2) 3
Gemmell (70)		Matthew (7), Scott (38), Murray (50)	

ST MIRREN: Forsyth; Lapsley, Riddell; Neilson, McGugan, Holmes; Laird, Bryceland, Baker, Gemmell, Wilson

RANGERS: Niven; Shearer, Caldow; Davis, Telfer, Stevenson; Scott, McMillan, Murray, Wilson, Matthew

Attendance: 25,000

February 18th:

RAITH ROVERS	(2) 2	RANGERS	(0) 2
McEwan 2 (2, 18)		Matthew 2 (49, 69)	

RAITH ROVERS: Drummond; Polland, McFarlane; Leigh, McNaught, Baxter; McEwan, Conn, Dobbie, Kerray, Gardner

RANGERS: Niven; Shearer, Caldow; Davis, Telfer, Stevenson; Scott, McMillan, Murray, Millar, Matthew

Attendance: 8,000

February 21st:
RANGERS (0) 3   STIRLING ALBION (0) 0
   Caldow (49 pen),
   Wilson (66), Murray (88)

RANGERS: Niven; Shearer, Caldow; McColl, Telfer, Stevenson; Scott, Millar, Murray, Wilson, Matthew

STIRLING ALBION: Stewart; Hailstones, Pettigrew; McKechnie, Sinclair, Kilgannon; McGill, Spence, Gilmour, Benvie, McPhee

Attendance: 23,000

League positions

	P	W	D	L	F	A	Pts
1 RANGERS	26	17	6	3	75	37	40
2 Motherwell	26	13	8	5	67	43	34
3 Hearts	25	14	5	6	71	43	33
4 Airdrie	26	14	2	10	53	50	30
5 Partick Thistle	26	13	4	9	47	38	30

March 3rd: Billy Simpson was transferred to Stirling Albion.

March 4th:
HIBERNIAN (0) 2   RANGERS (2) 2
   Fox (46), Preston (67)   Matthew (17),
                        McMillan (39)

HIBERNIAN: Wren; Grant, McClelland; Baxter, Paterson, Preston; Frye, Aitken, Fox, Gibson, Ormond

RANGERS: Niven; Shearer, Caldow; Davis, Paterson, Stevenson; Scott, McMillan, Murray, Baird, Matthew

Attendance: 32,000

March 7th:
RANGERS (1) 3   CLYDE (1) 1
   McMillan (35),   Robertson (31)
   Scott (63),
   Murray (79)

RANGERS: Niven; Shearer, Caldow; Davis, Telfer, Stevenson; Scott, McMillan, Murray, Brand, Wilson

CLYDE: McCulloch; Murphy, Haddock; Walters, Finlay, White; Herd, Currie, McHard, Robertson, Ring

Attendance: 33,000

March 14th:
FALKIRK (4) 5   RANGERS (2) 5
   Wright 3 (6, 20, 89),   Murray 2 (17, 25),
   Moran (16), White (27)   Caldow (49 pen),
                        Brand (53),
                        McMillan (79)

FALKIRK: Slater; Richmond, Rae; Price, Prentice, McMillan; Murray, Wright, White, Moran, Oliver

RANGERS: Niven; Shearer, Caldow; Davis, Telfer, Stevenson; Scott, McMillan, Murray, Brand, Wilson

Attendance: 15,000

March 21st:
RANGERS (1) 1   KILMARNOCK (0) 0
   Scott (32)

RANGERS: Niven; Shearer, Caldow; Davis, Telfer, Stevenson; Scott, McMillan, Murray, Brand, Wilson

KILMARNOCK: Brown; Collins, Watson; Beattie, Dougan, Stewart; Muir, Henaughan, Wentzel, Black, Burns

Attendance: 30,000

March 28th:
RANGERS (1) 2   MOTHERWELL (0) 1
   Brand (40),   St John (68)
   Murray (88)

RANGERS: Niven; Shearer, Caldow; Davis, Telfer, Stevenson; Scott, McMillan, Murray, Brand, Wilson

MOTHERWELL: H. Weir; McSeveney, Forrest; Aitken, Martis, McCann; S. Reid, Quinn, St John, Hunter, A. Weir

Attendance: 50,000

April 6th:
RANGERS (1) 3   QUEEN OF THE
                              SOUTH (1) 1
   Brand (24), McMillan (66),   Garrett (44)
   Caldow (89 pen)

RANGERS: Niven; Shearer, Caldow; Davis, Telfer, Stevenson; Scott, McMillan, Murray, Brand, Wilson

QUEEN OF THE SOUTH: Gebbie; Elliot, Hyndmarsh; Patterson, Smith, Montgomerie; Black, Knox, Ewing, Garrett, Oakes

Attendance: 15,000

April 11th:
HEARTS (1) 2   RANGERS (0) 0
   Cumming (32), Rankin (75)

HEARTS: Marshall; Kirk, Lough; Thomson, Milne, Cumming; Blackwood, Murray, Young, Rankin, Hamilton

RANGERS: Niven; Shearer, Provan; Davis, Telfer, Stevenson; Scott, McMillan, Murray, Millar, Wilson

Attendance: 30,000

April 11th: Scotland were beaten 1-0 by England at Wembley. Caldow was in the team.

April 16th: Johnny Hubbard was transferred to Bury for £6,000.

April 18th:
RANGERS   (1) 1   ABERDEEN   (1) 2
 Brand (24)   Davidson 2 (42, 50)

RANGERS: Niven; Shearer, Caldow; Davis, Telfer, Stevenson; Scott, McMillan, Murray, Brand, Matthew

ABERDEEN: Martin; Caldwell, Hogg; Brownlie, Clunie, Glen; Ewen, Davidson, Baird, Wishart, Hather

Attendance: 41,000

Scottish First Division

	P	W	D	L	F	A	Pts
1 RANGERS	34	21	8	5	92	51	50
2 Hearts	34	21	6	7	92	51	48
3 Motherwell	34	18	8	8	83	50	44
4 Dundee	34	16	9	9	61	51	41
5 Airdrie	34	15	7	12	64	62	37
6 Celtic	34	14	8	12	70	53	36
7 St Mirren	34	14	7	13	71	74	35
8 Kilmarnock	34	13	8	13	58	51	34
9 Partick Thistle	34	14	6	14	59	66	34
10 Hibernian	34	13	6	15	68	70	32
11 Third Lanark	34	11	10	13	74	83	32
12 Stirling Albion	34	11	8	15	54	64	30
13 Aberdeen	34	12	5	17	63	66	29
14 Raith Rovers	34	10	9	15	60	70	29
15 Clyde	34	12	4	18	62	66	28
16 Dunfermline	34	10	8	16	68	87	28
17 Falkirk	34	10	7	17	58	79	27
18 Queen of the S.	34	6	6	22	38	101	18

April 30th: Rangers freed McEwan and Moles.

May 6th: Caldow was in the Scotland team which beat Germany 3-2 at Hampden Park.

May 27th: Caldow was in the Scotland team which beat Holland 2-1 in Amsterdam.

June 3rd: Scotland were beaten 1-0 by Portugal in Lisbon. Caldow and Scott were in the team.

LEAGUE CUP

August 9th:
RANGERS   (3) 3   HEARTS   (0) 0
 Wilson (5), Hubbard (22),
 Milne o.g. (45)

RANGERS: Niven; Shearer, Caldow; McColl, Telfer, Baird; Scott, Millar, Murray, Wilson, Hubbard

HEARTS: Marshall; Kirk, Thomson; Cumming, Milne, Bowman; Hamilton, Murray, Young, Wardhaugh, Crawford

Attendance: 60,000

August 13th:
RAITH ROVERS   (1) 3   RANGERS   (0) 1
 Dobbie (29), Urquhart (84),   Hubbard (64 pen)
 Williamson (87)

RAITH ROVERS: Thorburn; Polland, Lockerbie; Leigh, McNaught, Baxter; McEwan, Ward, Dobbie, Williamson, Urquhart

RANGERS: Niven; Shearer, Caldow; McColl, Telfer, Baird; Scott, Millar, Murray, Wilson, Hubbard

Baird was ordered off

Attendance: 12,000

August 16th:
RANGERS   (1) 2   THIRD LANARK   (1) 2
 Brand (39), Murray (63)   McInnes (22),
                                W. Craig (58)

RANGERS: Niven; Shearer, Caldow; McColl, Telfer, Baird; Scott, Wilson, Murray, Brand, Hubbard

THIRD LANARK: Ramage; Smith, Brown; Kelly, Lewis, Robb; W. Craig, R. Craig, Allan, Gray, McInnes

Attendance: 38,000

August 23rd:
HEARTS   (0) 2   RANGERS   (0) 1
 Bauld (46),   Hubbard (47 pen)
 Milne (90)

HEARTS: Marshall; Kirk, Thomson; Murray, Milne, Bowman; Paton, Blackwood, Bauld, Wardhaugh, Crawford

RANGERS: Martin; Shearer, Caldow; McColl, Telfer, Baird; Scott, Millar, Murray, Wilson, Hubbard

Martin was carried off

Attendance: 42,000

August 27th:
RANGERS   (4) 6   RAITH ROVERS   (0) 0
 Murray (5), Simpson 3 (10, 37, 69),
 Wilson (15), Hubbard (88 pen)

RANGERS: Niven; Shearer, Caldow; McColl, Telfer, Davis; Scott, Simpson, Murray, Wilson, Hubbard

RAITH ROVERS: Thorburn; Young, Lockerbie; Leigh, McGregor, Baxter; McEwan, Kerray, Dobbie, Ward, Urquhart

Attendance: 25,000

August 30th:
THIRD LANARK   (0) 0   RANGERS   (1) 3
                               Murray 3 (11, 85, 89)

THIRD LANARK: Ramage; Smith, Brown; Kelly, Cosker, Robb; Hilley, Craig, Dick, Gray, McInnes

RANGERS: Niven; Shearer, Caldow; McColl, Telfer, Davis; Scott, Simpson, Murray, Wilson, Hubbard

Attendance: 28,000

League Cup Section Table

	P	W	D	L	F	A	Pts
Hearts	6	5	0	1	16	10	10
RANGERS	6	3	1	2	16	7	7
Raith Rovers	6	2	0	4	10	18	4
Third Lanark	6	1	1	4	11	18	3

SCOTTISH CUP

January 31st: First Round
FORFAR (1) 1   RANGERS (1) 3
  Caldow o.g. (18)   Murray (7),
                            Millar (57),
                            Scott (75)

FORFAR: McKay; Steen, Berrie; Brown, Ogilvie, Buchan; Rodger, Cormie, Craig, Brodie, Dick

RANGERS: Niven; Shearer, Caldow; Davis, Telfer, Stevenson; Scott, McMillan, Murray, Millar, Matthew

Attendance: 9,813

February 14th: Second Round
RANGERS (2) 3   HEARTS (1) 2
  Kirk o.g. (19),   Murray (12),
                            Hamilton (89)
  Matthew 2 (7, 47)

RANGERS: Niven; Shearer, Caldow; Davis, Telfer, Stevenson; Scott, McMillan, Murray, Brand, Matthew

HEARTS: Marshall; Kirk, Thomson; Cumming, Milne, Mackay; Young, Murray, Bauld, Wardhaugh, Hamilton

Attendance: 55,000

February 28th: Third Round
CELTIC (1) 2   RANGERS (0) 1
  Divers (44), McVittie (47)   Murray (90)

CELTIC: Haffey; McKay, Mochan; Smith, Evans, Peacock; McVittie, Jackson, Lochead, Wilson, Divers

RANGERS: Niven; Shearer, Caldow; Davis, Telfer, Stevenson; Scott, McMillan, Murray, Wilson, Matthew

Attendance: 42,500

Rangers were hot favourites for the match, but Divers headed Celtic into the lead a minute before the interval. McVittie added a 2nd shortly after the restart. Divers might have scored 3 but for ill-luck. 11 minutes from time Haffey pulled off a save in a million when he diverted a fast-flying header from Murray one-handed. Murray's headed goal after a minute of overtime proved meaningless.

Appearances

	League	League Cup	Scottish Cup	Glasgow Cup	Charity Cup	Friendlies
Niven	34	5	3	3	1	5
Shearer	34	6	3	3	1	5
Caldow	32	6	3	3	1	5
McColl	12	6	-	2	-	1+1sub
Telfer	31	6	3	3	1	3
Baird	6	4	-	2	-	1
Scott	34	6	3	3	1	5
Millar	5	3	2	-	-	1+1sub
McEwan	1	-	-	-	-	-
Brand	25	1	-	2	1	6
Wilson	15	6	1	1	-	1
Davis	28	2	3	3	1	5
Murray	22	6	3	1	1	5
Hubbard	8	6	-	3	-	1
Paterson	3	-	-	-	-	2
Hogg	2	-	-	-	-	-
Simpson	6	2	-	1	-	1
Matthew	18	-	3	-	1	5
Duncan	3	-	-	2	-	-
Little	1	-	-	-	-	1
McMillan	26	-	3	1	1	5
Stevenson	26	-	3	-	1	5
Orr	1	-	-	-	-	-
Provan	1	-	-	-	-	-
Martin	-	1	-	-	-	-
Neil	-	-	-	-	-	1
Ritchie	-	-	-	-	-	1

GOALSCORERS

League: Brand 21, Murray 17, McMillan 9, Hubbard 9 (4 pens), Scott 8, Simpson 7, Matthew 5, Baird 4 (1 pen), Caldow 4 (4 pens), Wilson 2, Davis 2, Duncan 2, Hogg 1, Millar 1

League Cup: Murray 5, Hubbard 4 (3 pens), Simpson 3, Wilson 2, Brand 1, Own Goals 1

Scottish Cup: Murray 2, Matthew 2, Millar 1, Scott 1, Own Goals 1

Glasgow Cup: Murray 1, Hubbard 1 (pen), Scott 1

Charity Cup: Brand 1

Friendlies: Millar 5, Brand 3, Murray 2, Wilson 2, Caldow 2 (2 pens), Matthew 1 (pen), Hubbard 1 (pen), Davis 1

Season 1959–60

Rangers finished 3rd in the Championship behind Hearts and Kilmarnock. Their League form appeared to suffer as a result of their European Cup involvement. They lost 9 matches during the season including 6 at home. Indeed, after beating Stirling Albion at Ibrox on December 26th, they didn't win another home match for the rest of the season. Celtic were beaten both home and away. Stevenson was their only ever-present and Millar finished top scorer on 21.

They had a great run to the Semi-Final of the European Cup where Eintracht Frankfurt once again emphasised the class needed to take the top prize. Eintracht, who looked invincible, were themselves well beaten by Real Madrid in the most famous of all European Finals.

Rangers won the Scottish Cup for the first time in 7 years. Berwick, Arbroath, Stenhousemuir, Hibernian and Celtic were beaten in the run-up to the Final. Millar scored the two goals which beat Kilmarnock in a rather one-sided match in which Rangers could afford the luxury of missing a penalty. McColl replaced the injured Davis in this match and so collected his 5th winners medal.

Rangers failed to qualify from their League Cup Section, finishing 2nd to a Motherwell team including St John, Hunter, Quinn and Weir who were to beat them 4 times during the season.

They won both the Glasgow Cup and the Charity Cup, beating Partick Thistle in the Final of both competitions.

> League: Third
> League Cup: Failed to Qualify from Section
> Scottish Cup: Winners
> European Cup: Semi-Finalists

SCOTTISH FIRST DIVISION

August 19th:
STIRLING ALBION (0) 2   RANGERS (2) 3
Spence (70), Caldow o.g. (73)   Millar 2 (7, 32), Wilson (63)

STIRLING ALBION: McCallum; Hannah, Pettigrew; McKechnie, Sinclair, Johnstone; Grant, Benvie, Simpson, Spence, Napier

RANGERS: Niven; Shearer, Caldow; Davis, Paterson, Stevenson; Duncan, McLean, Millar, Baird, Wilson

Attendance: n.a.

August 22nd: Davie Meiklejohn died.

September 2nd: Niven represented the Scottish League in a 4-1 victory over the League of Ireland.

September 5th:
RANGERS (1) 3   CELTIC (0) 1
Wilson (9), Scott (65),   Jackson (72)
Millar (76)

RANGERS: Niven; Shearer, Little; Davis, Telfer, Stevenson; Scott, Wilson, Millar, Baird, Matthew

CELTIC: Haffey; McNeill, Kennedy; McKay, Evans, Peacock; McVittie, Jackson, Conway, Divers, Auld

Attendance: 65,000

Davie Wilson scored in the 9th minute, Millar having beaten Evans in the jump for a long corner-kick by Matthew which passed right across Haffey's front. In 65 minutes Millar sent another cross over to the far post and Haffey, by this time not fully fit after a clash with Baird, unwisely used only his left hand to try to stop Scott's header. Jackson scored Celtic's goal in 72 minutes with a fine left-foot shot but 4 minutes later Millar turned and twisted his way all of 40 yards, Evans chasing hard after him, before he shot Rangers' third goal.

September 12th:
HIBERNIAN   (0) 0   RANGERS   (0) 1
                                         Millar (78)
HIBERNIAN: Wilson; Grant, McLelland; Young, Plenderleith, Hughes; Scott, Frye, Baker, Aitken, McLeod

RANGERS: Niven; Shearer, Little; Davis, Telfer, Stevenson; Scott, Wilson, Millar, Baird, Matthew
Attendance: 38,000

September 19th:
RANGERS   (0) 0   AYR UNITED   (3) 3
                                         McGhee 2 (16, 39),
                                         Elliot (43)
RANGERS: Niven; Shearer, Little; Davis, Telfer, Stevenson; Scott, McMillan, Millar, Baird, Matthew

AYR UNITED: Hamilton; Burn, Paterson; McIntyre, McLean, Elliot; McGuinness, McMillan, Price, Paton, McGhee
Attendance: 32,000

September 26th:
PARTICK THISTLE   (0) 0   RANGERS   (1) 3
                                         Matthew (45),
                                         McMillan (67),
                                         Scott (82)
PARTICK THISTLE: Freebairn; Hogan, Baird; Harvey, Davidson, Donlevy; McKenzie, McParland, Smith, Ewing, Fleming

RANGERS: Niven; Shearer, Little; Davis, Telfer, Stevenson; Scott, McMillan, Wilson, Baird, Matthew
Attendance: 30,500

September 29th: Rangers and Manchester United agreed a fee for Eric Caldow.

October 3rd: Caldow played for Scotland in a 4-0 victory over Ireland in Belfast.

October 3rd:
RANGERS   (1) 4   DUNFERMLINE   (1) 1
  Millar (5),   Dickson (28)
  McMillan 2 (64, 71),
  Scott (74)
RANGERS: Niven; Shearer, Little; Davis, Telfer, Stevenson; Scott, McMillan, Millar, Wilson, Matthew

DUNFERMLINE: Connachan; Sweeney, Williamson; Mailer, Colville, Miller; Peebles, Rowan, Dickson, Smith, Melrose
Attendance: 25,000

October 6th: Caldow called off his transfer to Manchester United.

October 10th:
DUNDEE   (0) 1   RANGERS   (1) 3
  Robertson (64)   Baird (28 pen),
                                         Millar (48),
                                         Matthew (66)
DUNDEE: Liney; Hamilton, Cox; Gabriel, Smith, Curlett; McGeachie, Cousin, Hill, Henderson, Robertson

RANGERS: Niven; Shearer, Little; McColl, Telfer, Stevenson; Scott, McMillan, Millar, Baird, Matthew
Attendance: 22,000

October 14th: Niven, Stevenson and Scott represented the Scottish League in a 7-1 win over the Irish League at Ibrox. Scott scored two of the goals.

October 17th:
RANGERS   (0) 1   ST MIRREN   (2) 3
  Millar (52)   Baker 2 (20, 49),
                                         Bryceland (34)
RANGERS: Niven; Shearer, Little; Davis, Telfer, Stevenson; Scott, McMillan, Millar, Baird, Matthew

ST MIRREN: Forsyth; Wilson, Riddell; Neilson, McGugan, Gregal; Rodger, Bryceland, Baker, Gemmell, Miller
Attendance: 45,000

October 24th:
ABERDEEN   (0) 0   RANGERS   (1) 5
                                         Brand (20),
                                         Millar (48),
                                         Scott 2 (50, 85),
                                         McMillan (70)
ABERDEEN: Russell; Cadenhead, Hogg; Baird, McConnachie, Brownlee; Ewan, Little, Davidson, Wishart, Mulhall

RANGERS: Niven; Shearer, Caldow; Davis, Paterson, Stevenson; Scott, McMillan, Millar, Brand, Matthew

Attendance: 25,000

October 31st:
RANGERS   (0) 0   HEARTS   (1) 2
                                         Davis o.g. (8),
                                         Blackwood (85)
RANGERS: Niven; Shearer, Caldow; Davis, Paterson, Stevenson; Scott, McMillan, Millar, Brand, Matthew

HEARTS: Marshall; Kirk, Thomson; Bowman, Cumming, Higgins; Smith, Crawford, Young, Blackwood, Hamilton
Attendance: 70,000

League positions

	P	W	D	L	F	A	Pts
1 Hearts	10	8	2	0	36	17	18
2 RANGERS	10	7	0	3	23	13	14
3 Clyde	10	4	4	2	19	14	12
4 Third Lanark	10	6	0	4	28	22	12
5 St Mirren	10	5	1	4	31	19	11

November 4th: Scotland drew 1-1 with Wales at Hampden Park. Caldow was in the team.

November 7th:
RANGERS   (3) 6   CLYDE   (0) 0
  Caldow (24 pen), Baird (29),
  McMillan (34), Millar 3 (68, 69, 84)

RANGERS: Niven; Caldow, Little; Davis, Telfer, Stevenson; Scott, McMillan, Millar, Baird, Wilson

CLYDE: Thomson; Walters, Haddock; White, Sim, McPhail; A. Wilson, Herd, Coyle, Currie, Boyd

Attendance: 32,000

November 14th:
ARBROATH   (0) 0   RANGERS   (2) 4
                            Millar 4 (30,
                              38, 73, 80)

ARBROATH: Williamson; McLevy, Young; Brown, Fraser, Wright; Shirreffs, Easson, Dunn, Grierson, Murray

RANGERS: Niven; Caldow, Little; Davis, Paterson, Stevenson; Scott, McMillan, Millar, Baird, Wilson

Attendance: 9,000

November 21st:
RANGERS   (2) 2   RAITH ROVERS   (2) 3
  Wilson (2), Scott (14)   Kerray 2 (16, 56),
                            Baxter (17)

RANGERS: Niven; Shearer, Little; Davis, Telfer, Stevenson; Scott, McMillan, Millar, Baird, Wilson

RAITH ROVERS: Drummond; Polland, Mochan; Young, McNaught, Baxter; Wallace, Conn, Kerray, Spence, Urquhart

Attendance: 30,000

November 24th: Rangers signed Stan Anderson from Hamilton Accies for £8,000.

November 28th:
MOTHERWELL   (1) 2   RANGERS   (1) 1
  St John (2), Weir (48)   Baird (30)

MOTHERWELL: Mackin; McSeveney, W. Reid; Aitken, Martis, McCann; S. Reid, Quinn, St John, Hunter, Weir

RANGERS: Niven; Shearer, Little; Davis, Telfer, Stevenson; Scott, McMillan, Millar, Baird, Wilson

Attendance: 22,000

December 1st: Rangers made a bid of £12,000 for Jim Baxter of Raith Rovers.

December 5th:
RANGERS   (2) 5   KILMARNOCK   (0) 0
  Wilson (2), McMillan 2 (20, 82),
  Scott (46), Murray (75)

RANGERS: Niven; Shearer, Little; Davis, Paterson, Stevenson; Scott, McMillan, Murray, Wilson, Hume

KILMARNOCK: J. Brown; Watson, Mackay; Beattie, Toner, O'Connoe; Wentzel, McInally, T. Brown, Black, Muir

Attendance: 20,000

December 12th:
THIRD LANARK   (0) 0   RANGERS   (0) 2
                              Cunningham o.g.
                                (63),
                              Millar (70)

THIRD LANARK: Robertson; Lewis, Caldwell; Reilly, Moles, Cunningham; D. Hilley, Goodfellow, Rankin, Gray, Fraser

RANGERS: Niven; Shearer, Little; Davis, Paterson, Stevenson; Scott, McMillan, Millar, Wilson, Hume

Both McMillan and Shearer missed penalties.

Attendance: 24,000

December 19th:
AIRDRIE   (0) 0   RANGERS   (2) 5
                            Stevenson (32),
                            Scott 2 (39, 65),
                            Hume (49),
                            Millar (80)

AIRDRIE: Leslie; Millar, Shanks; Quinn, J. Stewart, Quigley; Sharkey, McGill, Baillie, Duncan, A. Stewart

RANGERS: Niven; Shearer, Little; Davis, Paterson, Stevenson; Scott, McMillan, Millar, Wilson, Hume

Attendance: 20,000

December 26th:
RANGERS   (2) 3   STIRLING ALBION   (0) 0
  Scott (15), Wilson (28),
  Hume (64)

RANGERS: Niven; Shearer, Little; Davis, Paterson, Stevenson; Scott, McMillan, Millar, Wilson, Hume

STIRLING ALBION: Morrison; McKechnie, Pettigrew; Pierson, Little, Johnstone; Colquhoun, Martin, Grant, McPhee, Rowan

Attendance: 21,000

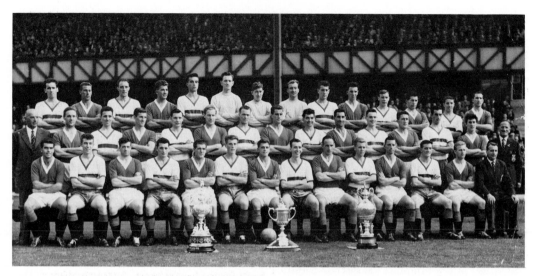

The successful squad of season 1960–61, League Champions and League Cup Winners. Back row: Anderson, Millar, Currie, Hume, McKinnon, Martin, Niven, Ritchie, Grant, Murray, Penman, Matthew, Henderson, Brand. Middle row: Symon (manager), Franks, Evans, Stevenson, More, Baird, McLean, Paterson, King, Davis, Hynd, Telfer, Provan, Baxter, Craven (asst. trainer). Front row: Scott, Cassidy, McMillan, Queen, Shearer, Young, Caldow, Bowie, McColl, Brown, Little, Watson, Wilson, Kinnear (trainer).

Rangers played Fiorentina from Italy in the first leg of the Cup Winners Cup Final at Ibrox on May 17th, 1961. Here trainer Davie Kinnear, assistant trainer Joe Craven, manager Scot Symon and Director, John Wilson jnr, watch the Italians in training.

League positions

	P	W	D	L	F	A	Pts
1 Hearts	18	13	3	2	52	30	29
2 RANGERS	18	13	0	5	51	18	26
3 Kilmarnock	18	11	1	6	32	31	23
4 Hibernian	18	10	2	6	68	44	22
5 Dundee	18	9	3	6	37	29	21

January 1st:
CELTIC (0) 0   RANGERS (0) 1
                           Millar (89½)

CELTIC: Haffey; McKay, Kennedy; McNeill, Evans, Peacock; Auld, Smith, Carroll, Mochan, Byrne

RANGERS: Niven; Shearer, Little; Davis, Paterson, Stevenson; Brand, Baird, Millar, Wilson, Hume

Attendance: 50,000

Less than half a minute from time at Celtic Park Millar gave Rangers their 5th successive win. Evans had dived low to head out from his penalty area and Baird immediately prodded the ball forward to Millar who shot high and hard with his left foot as Haffey, somewhat hesitatingly, left his goal to narrow the angle. Celtic prevailed upon the referee to consult the linesman, on the stand side, appealing that Miller had been offside, but the score stood. Just before Millar's goal Davis cleared on the goal-line a header from Carroll that had beaten his goalkeeper. In the 15th minute of the second half Haffey diverted for a corner-kick, a penalty kick shot hard to his right by Little.

January 2nd:
RANGERS (0) 1   HIBERNIAN (1) 1
  McMillan (52)   Baker (44)

RANGERS: Niven; Shearer, Little; Davis, Paterson, Stevenson; Brand, McMillan, Millar, Baird, Hume

HIBERNIAN: Muirhead; Grant, McLelland; Young, Hughes, Baxter; McLeod, Johnstone, Baker, Preston, Ormond

Attendance: 56,000

January 9th:
AYR UNITED (2) 2   RANGERS (2) 4
  Price (11), McGhee (26)   Millar 2 (19, 53),
                           Hume (17),
                           McMillan (50)

AYR UNITED: Hamilton; Burn, Thomson; McIntyre, McLean, Elliot; Fulton, McMillan, Price, Paton, McGhee

RANGERS: Niven; Shearer, Little; Davis, Paterson, Stevenson; Scott, McMillan, Millar, Wilson, Hume

Attendance: 23,000

January 16th:
RANGERS (0) 1   PARTICK THISTLE (1) 1
  Caldow (69 pen)   Fleming (23)

RANGERS: Niven; Caldow, Little; Davis, Paterson, Stevenson; Scott, McMillan, Millar, Wilson, Hume

PARTICK THISTLE: Freebairn; Hogan, Baird; Wright, Harvey, Donlevy; Fleming, Smith, Nimmo, McParland, Devine

Attendance: 35,000

January 23rd:
DUNFERMLINE (0) 0   RANGERS (1) 5
                           Millar (6),
                           Scott 2 (48, 68),
                           McMillan (73),
                           Wilson (74)

DUNFERMLINE: Connachan; Fraser, Miller; Smith, Stevenson, Mailer; Peebles, Benvie, Dickson, Wardhaugh, Melrose

RANGERS: Niven; Caldow, Little; Baird, Paterson, Stevenson; Scott, McMillan, Millar, Wilson, Hume

Attendance: 16,000

February 1st: Scotland drew 2-2 with the Scottish League in an International trial match at Ibrox. Caldow played for Scotland and Niven, Little and Scott for the League team. Scott scored one of the goals.

February 9th:
RANGERS (0) 0   DUNDEE (0) 0

RANGERS: Niven; Caldow, Little; Davis, Paterson, Stevenson; Scott, Baird, Millar, Wilson, Hume

DUNDEE: Liney; Hamilton, Cox; Gabriel, Smith, Cowie; Penman, McGeachie, Cousin, Gilzean, Robertson

Attendance: n.a.

League positions

	P	W	D	L	F	A	Pts
1 Hearts	26	18	6	2	79	39	42
2 RANGERS	24	16	3	5	63	22	35
3 Kilmarnock	24	17	1	6	49	33	35
4 Dundee	25	12	6	7	47	36	30
5 Clyde	25	11	8	6	58	49	30

March 1st:
RANGERS (2) 2   ABERDEEN (1) 2
  Caldow (30 pen),   Wishart (43),
  Scott (32)   Davidson (49)

RANGERS: Niven; Caldow, Little; Davis, Paterson, Stevenson; Scott, McMillan, Millar, Wilson, Hume

ABERDEEN: Harker; Kinnell, Hogg; Baird, Clunie, Burns; Cumming, Little, Davidson, Wishart, Mulhall

March 5th:
HEARTS (0) 2   RANGERS (0) 0
  Cumming (81), Young (82)

HEARTS: Marshall; Kirk, Thomson; Cumming, Milne, Higgins; Smith, Murray, Young, Crawford, Hamilton

RANGERS: Niven; Caldow, Little; Davis, Paterson, Stevenson; Scott, McMillan, Millar, Brand, Wilson

Attendance: 45,000

March 19th:
RANGERS (1) 1   ARBROATH (0) 1
McMillan (41)   Grierson (71)

RANGERS: Niven; Caldow, Little; Davis, Paterson, Stevenson; Scott, McMillan, Murray, Wilson, Hume

ARBROATH: Williamson; McLevy, Young; Crawford, Fraser, McLean; Sheriffs, Easson, Dunn, Grierson, Quinn

Attendance: 15,000

March 23rd: Niven, Caldow, Little and Scott represented the Scottish League against the English League at Highbury. The English League won 1-0.

March 26th:
RAITH ROVERS (0) 1   RANGERS (0) 2
Urquhart (85)   McMillan (72),
     Baird (86)

RAITH ROVERS: Thorburn; Stevenson, Mochan; Polland, McGregor, Baxter; Wallace, French, Lawson, Spence, Urquhart

RANGERS: Ritchie; Caldow, Little; Davis, Paterson, Stevenson; Scott, McMillan, Millar, Baird, Wilson

Attendance: 11,000

March 28th: Rangers signed Albert Franks from Newcastle United for £7,000.

April 9th: Scotland drew 1-1 with England at Hampden Park. Caldow was in the team. Niven was also selected for his first full cap but had to withdraw through injury.

April 16th:
KILMARNOCK (1) 1   RANGERS (1) 1
Black (40)   Caldow (35 pen)

KILMARNOCK: Brown; Richmond, Watson; Beattie, Toner, Kennedy; Stewart, McInally, Kerr, Black, Muir

RANGERS: Niven; Caldow, Little; McColl, Paterson, Stevenson; Scott, McMillan, Millar, Baird, Wilson

Attendance: 24,500

April 18th:
RANGERS (0) 0   MOTHERWELL (2) 2
     Aitken (22),
     Hunter (40)

RANGERS: Niven; Shearer, Little; Franks, Paterson, Stevenson; Brand, McMillan, Millar, Baird, Wilson

MOTHERWELL: H. Weir; McSeveney, Strachan; Aitken, Martis, McCann; Young, Quinn, St John, Hunter, A. Weir

Attendance: 30,000

Alex Scott, prominent in the Rangers sides of the late fifties and early sixties.

April 25th:
ST MIRREN (0) 1   RANGERS (0) 1
Baker (70)   Wilson (72)

ST MIRREN: Walker; Wilson, McTurk; Doonan, McGugan, Gregal; Rodger, Bryceland, Baker, Gemmell, Miller

RANGERS: Niven; Caldow, Little; McColl, Paterson, Stevenson; Scott, McMillan, Millar, Baird, Wilson

Attendance: 14,000

April 25th: Rangers gave free transfers to Neil, Duncan, McIlroy and Orr.

April 27th:
CLYDE (4) 4   RANGERS (1) 1
Boyd (4),   Brand (43 pen)
McLaughlin 2 (17, 32)
Herd (24)

CLYDE: McCulloch; Walters, Haddock; White, Finlay, Clinton; Wilson, Herd, McLaughlin, Robertson, Boyd

RANGERS: Niven; Shearer, Little; Franks, Telfer, Anderson; Brand, McLean, Grant, Stevenson, Matthew

Attendance: 10,000

April 30th:
RANGERS (0) 0   AIRDRIE (0) 0

RANGERS: Niven; Caldow, Little; McColl, Paterson, Stevenson; Scott, McMillan, Millar, Brand, Wilson

AIRDRIE: Beaton; Neil, Shanks; McNeil, Baillie, Quinn; McCulloch, Rankin, Sharkey, Duncan, Stewart

Attendance: 13,000

May 7th:
RANGERS (1) 1   THIRD LANARK (1) 2
Wilson (20)   Harley 2 (40, 81)

RANGERS: Niven; Caldow, Little; McColl, Paterson, Stevenson; Scott, Franks, Millar, Brand, Wilson

THIRD LANARK: Robertson; McGillivray, Brown; Reilly, Robb, Cunningham; Goodfellow, Hilley, Harley, Gray, McInnes

Attendance: 8,500

Scottish First Division

		P	W	D	L	F	A	Pts
1	Hearts	34	23	8	3	102	51	54
2	Kilmarnock	34	24	2	8	67	45	50
3	RANGERS	34	17	8	9	72	38	42
4	Dundee	34	16	10	8	70	49	42
5	Motherwell	34	16	8	10	71	61	40
6	Clyde	34	15	9	10	77	69	39
7	Hibernian	34	14	7	13	106	85	35
8	Ayr	34	14	6	14	65	73	34
9	Celtic	34	12	9	13	73	59	33
10	Partick Thistle	34	14	4	16	54	78	32
11	Raith Rovers	34	14	3	17	64	62	31
12	Third Lanark	34	13	4	17	75	83	30
13	Dunfermline	34	10	9	15	72	80	29
14	St Mirren	34	11	6	17	78	86	28
15	Aberdeen	34	11	6	17	54	72	28
16	Airdrie	34	11	6	17	56	80	28
17	Stirling	34	7	8	19	55	72	22
18	Arbroath	34	4	7	23	38	106	15

LEAGUE CUP

August 8th:
HIBERNIAN   (1) 1   RANGERS   (3) 6
   Ormond (26)   Brand 4 (25,
                                32, 61, 89),
                              Matthew (39),
                              Millar (74)

HIBERNIAN: Wren; Grant, McLelland; Nicol,
Plenderleith, Baxter; Scott, Fox, Baker, Gibson,
Ormond

RANGERS: Niven; Shearer, Caldow; Davis, Telfer,
Stevenson; Scott, McMillan, Millar, Brand, Matthew
Attendance: 44,700

August 12th:
RANGERS   (1) 1   MOTHERWELL   (1) 2
   Scott (15)   Quinn (8),
                            St John (88)

RANGERS: Niven; Shearer, Caldow; Davis, Telfer,
Stevenson; Scott, McMillan, Millar, Brand, Wilson

MOTHERWELL: H. Weir; McSeveney, Forrest;
Aitken, Martis, McCann; Hunter, Reid, St John, Quinn,
A. Weir

Attendance: 65,000

August 15th:
RANGERS   (2) 2   DUNDEE   (0)
   Brand (20),
   Wilson (34)

RANGERS: Niven; Shearer, Caldow; Davis, Telfer,
Stevenson; Duncan, McMillan, Millar, Brand, Wilson

DUNDEE: Horsburgh; Hamilton, Cox; Curlett,
Gabriel, Cowie; McGeachie, Bonthrone, Cousin,
Henderson, Robertson
Attendance: 37,000

August 22nd:
RANGERS   (3) 5   HIBERNIAN   (1) 1
   Baird (14), Wilson 2 (24, 85),   Aitken (22)
   Millar 2 (33, 67)

RANGERS: Niven; Shearer, Caldow; McColl, Telfer,
Stevenson; Scott, Wilson, Millar, Baird, Matthew

HIBERNIAN: Wilson; Grant, Young; Preston,
Plenderleith, Baxter; Scott, Fox, Baker, Aitken, Ormond
Attendance: 35,000

August 26th:
MOTHERWELL   (0) 2   RANGERS   (1) 1
   St John (64), Hunter (80)   Millar (42)

MOTHERWELL: H. Weir; McSeveney, Forrest;
Aitken, Martis, McCann; Hunter, Reid, St John, Quinn,
A. Weir

RANGERS: Niven; Shearer, Little; Davis, Telfer,
Baird; Scott, Wilson, Millar, Brand, Matthew
Attendance: 33,000

August 29th:
DUNDEE   (0) 2   RANGERS   (1) 3
   Waddell (50),   Millar (34),
   Cousin (82)   Wilson (56),
                           Baird (70)

DUNDEE: Liney; Hamilton, Cox; Gabriel,
McMillan, Henderson; Hill, Cousin, Waddell,
McGeachie, Robertson

RANGERS: Niven; Shearer, Little; Davis, Telfer,
Stevenson; Scott, Wilson, Millar, Baird, Matthew
Attendance: 15,000

League Cup Section Table

	P	W	D	L	F	A	Pts
Motherwell	6	6	0	0	19	8	12
RANGERS	6	4	0	2	18	8	8
Dundee	6	2	0	4	12	17	4
Hibernian	6	0	0	6	9	25	0

SCOTTISH CUP

January 30th: First Round
BERWICK RANGERS   (1) 1   RANGERS   (1) 3
   Whitelaw (40)   Wilson 3 (35, 62, 87)

BERWICK: McQueen; Fleming, Beecham; McLeod,
Rugg, Campbell; Foulis, Kennedy, Purvis, McKenna,
Whitelaw

RANGERS: Niven; Caldow, Little; Davis, Paterson, Stevenson; Scott, McMillan, Millar, Wilson, Hume

Attendance: 16,000

February 13th: Second Round
RANGERS (2) 2   ARBROATH (0) 0
  Scott (6), McMillan (9)

RANGERS: Niven; Caldow, Little; Davis, Paterson, Stevenson; Scott, McMillan, Millar, Wilson, Hume

ARBROATH: Williamson; McLevy, Young; Brown, Fraser, Wright; Shirreffs, Dunn, Easson, Grierson, Quinn

Attendance: 30,000

February 27th: Third Round
STENHOUSEMUIR (0) 0   RANGERS (1) 3
                             Watson o.g. (12),
                             McMillan (56),
                             Wilson (76)

STENHOUSEMUIR: Ross; Watson, Kennedy; Collumbine, Quinn, Richardson; Glegg, Munn, Cairns, Campbell, Cassie

RANGERS: Niven; Caldow, Little; Davis, Paterson, Stevenson; Scott, McMillan, Millar, Wilson, Hume

Attendance: 12,000

March 12th: Fourth Round
RANGERS (1) 3   HIBERNIAN (1) 2
  Baird (42), Wilson (59),   Johnstone (2 pen),
  Millar (72)   McLeod (61)

RANGERS: Niven; Caldow, Little; Davis, Paterson, Stevenson; Scott, Baird, Millar, Brand, Wilson

HIBERNIAN: Muirhead; Grant, McLelland; Young, Plenderleith, Baxter; McLeod, Johnstone, Baker, Buchanan, Ormond

Attendance: 63,000

April 2nd: Semi-Final   At Hampden Park
RANGERS (0) 1   CELTIC (1) 1
  Millar (68)   Chalmers (25)

RANGERS: Niven; Caldow, Little; Davis, Paterson, Stevenson; Scott, McMillan, Millar, Baird, Wilson

CELTIC: Haffey; McKay, Kennedy; McNeill, Evans, Peacock; Chalmers, Colrain, Mochan, Divers, Byrne

Attendance: 79,786

Much of the goalmouth excitement was the result of miskicks and misses. Chalmers headed Celtic's goal in 25 minutes from Colrain's corner-kick when Rangers, not for the first time, left a player unmarked for a cross. Rangers' goal came from a header. 22 minutes from time, during a period of clear Rangers superiority, Wilson crossed hard from the left corner of the field and Millar scored a magnificent goal from no fewer than 15 yards. Haffey

made saves from McMillan, Scott and Millar which saved the day for his side.

April 6th: Semi-Final Replay   At Hampden Park
RANGERS (1) 4   CELTIC (1) 1
  Wilson 2 (27, 71),   Mochan (33)
  Millar 2 (49, 79)

RANGERS: Ritchie; Caldow, Little; Davis, Paterson, Stevenson; Scott, McMillan, Millar, Baird, Wilson

CELTIC: Haffey; McKay, Kennedy; McNeill, Evans, Peacock; Chalmers, Colrain, Mochan, Jackson, Divers

Attendance: 70,977

Few of the 71,000 crowd could have visualised the events of the second half, during which the Celtic defence played like novices. Celtic lost the first goal to Wilson in 27 minutes. The outside-left ran past a dilatory McKay who may have expected Haffey to advance for Baird's free-kick. 6 minutes later Mochan shot an equalising goal. 4 minutes after half-time Peacock struck McMillan on the face as he attempted to drive the ball upfield. The ball rebounded to Millar who, having exchanged a quick ground pass with Scott, sidefooted a leading goal. In 71 minutes Wilson headed almost out of Haffey's hands an orthodox cross by Scott. In 79 minutes Baird, now at right-half for Davis who had to be taken off on a stretcher, dropped a cross into Celtic's goal area for Millar to head in another goal. Millar once again proved to be Evans' bogey man.

April 23rd: Final   At Hampden Park
RANGERS (1) 2   KILMARNOCK (0) 0
  Millar 2 (22, 68)

RANGERS: Niven; Caldow, Little; McColl, Paterson, Stevenson; Scott, McMillan, Millar, Baird, Wilson

KILMARNOCK: Brown; Richmond, Watson; Beattie, Toner, Kennedy; Stewart, McInally, Kerr, Black, Muir

Caldow missed a penalty

Attendance: 108,017

Referee: R. H. Davidson (Airdrie)

Although they took unduly long to win the match, Rangers contributed almost all of the quality football. They frequently dovetailed into smooth attractive play. If the other forwards had been of the standard of Millar and Wilson, the winning margin could have been much greater. The Kilmarnock defence was sadly out of form and the forwards were quite unable to restore the balance. Once in the first half McInally headed for the junction of crossbar and post whereupon Niven was roused to quick action. There practically ends the tale of Kilmarnock's threat to Rangers' goal. After only 15 minutes Toner was injured when Scott somewhat recklessly dived for a Scott cross. The centre-half did not recover fully and 12 minutes after half-time he limped disconsolately to outside-right having again been hurt as Millar tackled him. In 22 minutes Wilson, as he often did, bewildered Richmond and crossed, and Brown failed to prevent Millar getting his head to the ball. Astonishingly the centre-forward had succeeded only in diverting the ball high into the air above his head. He again made contact before Brown and Rangers were in the lead. Two minutes after half-time Caldow shot a penalty-kick high over the crossbar after Kennedy had elbowed Scott in a race for the ball. 22 minutes from time Millar headed his 2nd goal and again the centre-half, by this time Richmond, failed to mark him closely and again Brown, this time on the ground, was surprisingly easily beaten.

EUROPEAN CUP

September 16th: Preliminary Round First Leg
RANGERS   (2) 5   ANDERLECHT
                                    (Belgium)   (0) 2
   Millar (2), Scott (3),   Stockman (50),
   Matthew (48 pen),   De Waele (64)
   Baird 2 (66, 73 pen)

RANGERS: Niven; Shearer, Little; Davis, Telfer, Stevenson; Scott, McMillan, Millar, Baird, Matthew

ANDERLECHT: Meert; Devolelaere, Culot; Hanon, De Koster, Van Wilden; De Waele, Jurion, Stockman, Vandenboer, J. Van den Bosch

Attendance: 80,000

Anderlecht showed how football should not be played. They lost 2 goals to Millar and Scott by the 3rd minute of the match whereupon they proceeded to commit every known infringement. After half an hour Rangers conceded only 2 free-kicks to Anderlecht's 12. At one stage Davis, taking justice into his own hands, chased Jurion who fled at full speed into the other half of the field. Rangers were weak at outside-left. Matthew should have scored 4 goals and Baird's shooting in the second half was dreadful. Matthew scored Rangers' 3rd goal in 48 minutes — he headed the ball past Meert after the goalkeeper had saved his penalty-kick. Stockmann and De Waele scored for Anderlecht in 50 and 64 minutes and Baird for Rangers in 66 and 73 (from a penalty-kick). The crowd of 80,000 can have had little to remember but Anderlecht's bad behaviour and the astonishing referee who tolerated it.

September 23rd: Preliminary Round Second Leg
ANDERLECHT   (0) 0   RANGERS   (0) 2
                             Matthew (65),
                             McMillan (74)

ANDERLECHT: Meert; Devolelaere, Culot; Hanon, De Koster, Van Wilden; Lippims, Jurion, Stockman, Vandenboer, J. Van den Bosch

RANGERS: Niven; Shearer, Little; Davis, Telfer, Stevenson; Scott, McMillan, Wilson, Baird, Matthew

Attendance: 40,000

Rangers won 7-2 on aggregate.

November 11th: First Round
RANGERS   (2) 4   RED STAR
                             (Yugoslavia)   (2) 3
   McMillan (1), Scott (43),   Scherer 2 (16, 68),
   Wilson (74), Millar (89)   Dolinsky (29)

RANGERS: Niven; Caldow, Little; Davis, Telfer, Stevenson; Scott, McMillan, Millar, Baird, Wilson

RED STAR: Hlavaty; Hlozek, Weiss; Matlak, Tichy, Rias; Gajdos, Scherer, Cimra, Kacani, Dolinsky

Matlak was ordered off, Caldow missed a penalty

Attendance: 80,000

Rangers won by a goal scored by Millar in the last few seconds. McMillan scored in 2 minutes. In 40 minutes, with Red Star leading 2-1, Hlavaty, having fisted away a cross from Wilson, was barged to the ground by Baird, and while the keeper lay injured Scott returned the ball into goal and Rangers had equalised. Hlavaty was trundled away on a stretcher. Shortly afterwards an ugly scene developed. Baird played the man, Tichy appeared to strike back and astonishingly Matlak, who had been blameless, was ordered off. 10 Czechs including a head-bandaged goalkeeper started the second half. In 68 minutes in almost the first Red Star attack of the 2nd half the ball was moved from end to end with graceful ease and Scherer scored. 5 minutes later Baird was sent sprawling in the penalty-area but Hlavaty, with a dive to the left, diverted Caldow's kick for a corner. Wilson scored just after this with almost the first opportunity he had been given. Baird twice missed easier chances. The Czech team not surprisingly wilted before Millar scored the winner. Scherer and Dolinsky had scored the first-half Czech goals in 16 and 29 minutes.

November 18th: First Round Second Leg
RED STAR   (0) 1   RANGERS   (0) 1
   Tichy (89)   Scott (70)

RED STAR: Hlavaty; Hlozek, Weiss; Bubernik, Tichy, Rias; Gajdos, Scherer, Cimra, Kacani, Dolinsky

RANGERS: Niven; Shearer, Little; Davis, Telfer, Stevenson; Scott, McMillan, Millar, Baird, Wilson

Millar was ordered off

Attendance: 60,000

Rangers won 5-4 on aggregate

Millar was ordered off 8 minutes from time when, provoked by Tichy's obstructionist tactics, he punched the centre-half in the back. The overall picture was of a stern, efficient, display by Rangers. They defended for 70 of the 90 minutes and were still unfortunate not to win the tie more decisively. The entire Rangers defence played so well that it was not until the 2nd-last minute that Tichy hooked Gadjos's corner-kick into the net. In the previous 88 minutes Rangers had proved themselves complete masters of an ineffectual Red Star forward line. Niven had nothing like the shots to save which were rained in on him in the first leg. Rangers' goal came in 70 minutes. Baird, having discharged his defensive duties for the moment, passed to Wilson who sprinted and crossed to the far post where Scott with deliberation headed into the net. Even after the dismissal of Millar Rangers continued to play as though they had the advantage in numbers, and not until the fortuitous hook from Tichy did they again appear to think of saving the match rather than winning it.

March 9th: Second Round First Leg

SPARTA ROTTERDAM	RANGERS (2) 3
(Holland) (1) 2	Wilson (4), Baird (35),
De Vries 2 (38, 89)	Murray (63)

SPARTA: Van Dijk; Visser, Van Der Lee; Villerius, Schilder, De Koining; Van Ede, Crossan, Fitzgerald, De Vries, Bosselaar

RANGERS: Niven; Caldow, Little; Davis, Paterson, Stevenson; Scott, McMillan, Murray, Baird, Wilson

Attendance: 50,000

Rangers, having won the toss and playing with the wind, were 2 goals up in 35 minutes through Wilson in 4 minutes and Baird 10 minutes before half-time. Both Murray and McMillan had squandered reasonable scoring chances. De Vries gave Sparta hope 7 minutes before the interval — as Niven and Fitzgerald clashed in a jump for Van Ede's cross. 5 minutes after the restart Fitzgerald almost shattered Niven's left-hand post with a 25-yard shot and the goalkeeper, despairingly but successfully, saved with his outstretched left foot the return shot from Van Ede. Minutes before Murray hooked his side's 3rd goal in 63 minutes the Sparta players, not unreasonably, claimed a penalty-kick when Caldow's arm stopped the ball during another time of severe stress in the visitors' penalty area. Later Fitzgerald struck the crossbar. 2 minutes from time De Vries flicked the ball almost out of Niven's hands for Sparta's well-deserved 2nd goal.

16th March: Second Round Second Leg

RANGERS (0) 0	SPARTA
	ROTTERDAM (0) 1
	Van Ede (73)

RANGERS: Ritchie; Caldow, Little; Davis, Paterson, Stevenson; Scott, Baird, Millar, Brand, Wilson

SPARTA: Van Dijk; Visser, Van Der Lee; Verhoeven, Villerius, De Koining; Van Ede, Crossan, Fitzgerald, De Vries, Bosselaar

Attendance: 82,587

Aggregate 3–3

Rangers attacked the Sparta goal for two-thirds of the match but Van Dijk, a cool composed goalkeeper, had but one difficult save to make — and that in the very last minute of the match from Caldow. Sparta had a plan to deal with Scott which entailed the withdrawal of their outside-left Bosselaar to act as an extra guard against the outside-right's speed and thrust. In the 69th minute a 25-yard shot by Baird soared above Van Dijk and rebounded from the crossbar. 11 minutes later Millar fell over the ball some 30 yards from the Sparta goal. Villerius pushed it gracefully out to Fitzgerald and the centre-forward swept his pass all of 20 yards to the right and into the tracks of Van Ede. Little was drawn, the ball was touched inside to De Vries, and the inside-left with a fast low pass let the racing Van Ede straight through for goal against the outrushing Ritchie. The outside-right was within inches of scoring again before Caldow's last despairing effort.

March 30th: Second Round Play-Off at (At Highbury)

RANGERS (1) 3	SPARTA
Verhoeven o.g. (26),	ROTTERDAM (1) 2
Baird (56),	Verhoeven (7),
Van der Lee o.g. (70)	Bosselaar (75 pen)

RANGERS: Niven; Caldow, Little; Davis, Paterson, Stevenson; Scott, McMillan, Millar, Baird, Wilson

SPARTA: Van Dijk; Visser, Van Der Lee; Verhoeven, Villerius, DeKoining; Van Ede, Crossan, Fitzgerald, De Vries, Bosselaar

Attendance: 34,176

Rangers were a goal down after only 7 minutes — Verhoeven headed bullet-like into the net a corner-kick which the defence seemed to leave to one another. Rangers fully deserved to equalise long before half-time but when they did in 26 minutes they had fortune on their side. Baird dummied a low free-kick from Wilson, and Verhoeven miskicked the ball into the net. 11 minutes after half-time Baird, who was striking for goal as often as he could, took a headed clearance from Villerius in his stride 25 yards out and his left-foot shot skidding over the wet turf entirely defeated Van Dijk. 20 minutes from time Van der Lee, crossing to his right to intercept a pass from McMillan to Millar, deflected the ball from all of 12 yards out of the reach of his astonished goalkeeper. In one of the few 2nd-half Sparta attacks Little and Davis made Van Ede the meat of their sandwich and Bosselaar converted the penalty-kick. McMillan continually puzzled his opponents with his tenacious runs and varying tactics.

April 13th: Semi-Final First Leg

EINTRACHT FRANKFURT	RANGERS (1) 1
(Germany) (1) 6	Caldow (29 pen),
Stinka (28),	
Pfaff 2 (52,55),	
Lindner 2 (74, 86)	
Stein (87)	

EINTRACHT: Loy; Lutz, Hofer; Weilbacher, Eigenbrodt, Stinka; Kress, Lindner, Stein, Pfaff, Meier

E

RANGERS: Niven; Caldow, Little; Baird, Paterson, Stevenson; Scott, McMillan, Murray, Millar, Wilson

Attendance: 70,000

Eintracht imposed on Rangers one of their heaviest defeats. Rangers held their opponents to 1-1 at half-time but in the 2nd half Eintracht were faster and more skilful. Rangers had a narrow escape in the 8th minute when Kress shot wide from the penalty-spot after Little had fouled him. The Germans took the lead in the 28th minute, a shot into the roof of the net by their left-hand Stinka leaving Niven helpless. McMillan was brought down shortly afterwards and Caldow made no mistake from the penalty-spot. Eintracht looked a different team in the second half. They were much faster than Rangers, quicker to the tackle and passed with greater precision. They took the lead for the 2nd time only 6 minutes after the interval through Pfaff, their inside-left and captain, after a goalmouth scramble. In the 55th minute the home team made it 3-1, Pfaff scoring direct from a free-kick through a wall of Rangers players. Eintracht were now well on top and Lindner headed a 4th goal in 74 minutes. 4 minutes from time Niven appeared slow to move to a shot from Lindner. The Scots' discomfiture was completed a minute later when Stein dribbled the ball into the net after a splendid solo run of 40 yards.

May 5th: Semi-Final Second Leg
RANGERS (1) 3   EINTRACHT
McMillan 2 (11, 53),   FRANKFURT (3) 6
Wilson (72)   Lindner 2 (8, 28),
                                 Pfaff 2 (20, 88),
                                 Meier 2 (68, 70)

RANGERS: Niven; Caldow, Little; Davis, Paterson, Stevenson; Scott, McMillan, Millar, Baird, Wilson

EINTRACHT: Loy; Lutz, Hofer; Weilbacher, Eigenbrodt, Stinka; Kress, Lindner, Stein, Pfaff, Meier

Attendance: 70,000

Eintracht won 12-4 on aggregate. There was no miracle of Ibrox, no story of Rangers' greatest-ever fightback. Just plain confirmation that the Ibrox side was not in the same class as Eintracht of Frankfurt. As athletes, as football craftsmen, as tacticians the Germans were immeasurably superior and proved it once again by scoring 6 goals. Eintracht were a side of quality. In the 8th minute Stinka broke away and came through with the ball as his forwards fanned out quickly, and as the Rangers defenders fell back expecting a pass he was allowed to advance all of 50 yards before hitting a splendid shot past Niven from well outside the penalty-area. McMillan equalised 3 minutes later. In the 20th minute Eintracht were given a free-kick just outside the penalty-box and Pfaff found a chink in the defensive wall — the ball taking a deflection past Niven. Kress scored a 3rd after Niven had saved brilliantly from Stinka. Niven had 4 or 5 other fine saves before the interval. McMillan appeared in the

game for a few seconds and shot a fine goal in the 53rd minute. Eintracht steadied and Meier shot 2 goals in 2 minutes. Wilson knocked one off with a back-heeler before Pfaff, 2 minutes from time, strode majestically through the middle and shot a 6th.

APPEARANCES

	League	League Cup	Scottish Cup	Glasgow Cup	Charity Cup	European Cup
Niven	33	6	6	3	2	8
Shearer	21	6	-	3	-	3
Caldow	16	4	7	2	2	6
Davis	26	5	6	2	-	8
Paterson	23	-	7	1	2	5
Stevenson	34	5	7	3	2	9
Duncan	1	1	-	1	-	-
McLean	2	-	-	-	-	-
Millar	30	6	7	2	2	7
Baird	19	3	4	3	-	9
Wilson	27	4	7	3	2	8
Little	31	2	7	1	2	9
Telfer	11	6	-	2	-	4
Scott	29	5	7	2	1	9
Matthew	11	5	-	2	-	2
McMillan	26	3	6	2	2	8
McColl	5	1	1	1	2	-
Brand	9	4	1	-	2	1
Murray	2	-	-	-	-	2
Hume	12	-	3	-	1	-
Ritchie	1	-	1	-	-	1
Franks	3	-	-	-	-	-
Anderson	1	-	-	-	-	-
Grant	1	-	-	-	-	-

GOALSCORERS

League: Millar 21, McMillan 13, Scott 12, Wilson 8, Baird 4 (1 pen), Caldow 4 (4 pens), Hume 3, Matthew 2, Brand 2 (1 pen), Murray 1, Stevenson 1, Own Goals 1

League Cup: Millar 5, Brand 5, Wilson 4, Baird 2, Scott 1, Matthew 1

Scottish Cup: Wilson 7, Millar 6, McMillan 2, Scott 1, Baird 1, Own Goals 1

Glasgow Cup: Baird 3, Millar 3, Scott 2, Matthew 1

Charity Cup: Brand 2, Millar 1

European Cup: McMillan 4, Wilson 4, Scott 3, Baird 3 (1 pen), Millar 2, Matthew 2, Own Goals 2, Murray 1, Caldow 1 (pen)

Season 1960–61

Rangers collected their 32nd League Title, pipping Kilmarnock, to whom they had lost both home and away, by one point. Undoubtedly their 2 best league displays of the season were their 5-1 thrashing of Celtic at Parkhead and their 3-1 away win over Hearts — this despite losing goalkeeper Ritchie with a damaged ankle after only 8 minutes. Rangers' physical all-running style had been tempered by the delicate skills of Jim Baxter, signed during the close season from Raith Rovers for a give-away £17,500, which brought out the best in the left-wing partnership of Brand and Wilson. Brand finished top scorer with 24 goals followed by Wilson on 19. Those 2 players were the only ever-presents.

Rangers reached the Final of the newly inaugurated Cup Winners' Cup, disposing of Ferencvaros, Borussia Mönchen-Gladbach and Wolves en route. A missed Caldow penalty and striker Milan's last-minute goal in the first leg at Ibrox were to prove crucial. Millar returned, after a long lay-off with back trouble, for the 2nd leg, but Fiorentina's Swedish International winger Hamrin scored a brilliant goal to clinch the trophy for the Italians.

Rangers also landed the League Cup. Celtic, Third Lanark and Partick Thistle were beaten in the Section and Dundee (over two legs), Queen of the South and Kilmarnock in the later stages. Brand and Scott scored the goals in the Hampden Final in front of a crowd of 82,063. However, their hopes of winning the treble were destroyed by Motherwell with an astonishing 5-2 win in a Quarter-Final Replay at Ibrox.

League: Champions
League Cup: Winners
Scottish Cup: Third Round
Cup Winners' Cup: Finalists

SCOTTISH FIRST DIVISION

June 21st: Jim Baxter was signed from Raith Rovers for a Scottish record fee of £17,500.

August 9th: Doug Baillie was signed from Airdrie for £16,000.

August 24th:

RANGERS (3) 6	PARTICK THISTLE (2) 3
Brown o.g. (11),	Donlevy (19 pen),
Wilson 2 (19, 67),	Smith (29),
Caldow (33 pen),	Hogan (74)
Davis (64), Millar (72)	

RANGERS: Ritchie; Shearer, Caldow; Davis, Paterson, Baxter; Scott, McMillan, Millar, Brand, Wilson

PARTICK THISTLE: Freebairn; Brown, Baird; Wright, Harvey, Donlevy; Smith, McParland, Hogan, Fletcher, Fleming

Attendance: 17,000

September 10th:

CELTIC (0) 1	RANGERS (1) 5
Chalmers (89)	Scott (2), Millar (65),
	Brand (78),
	Wilson (84),
	Davis (86)

CELTIC: Fallon; McKay, Kennedy; Crerand, Kurila, Peacock; Conway, Chalmers, Carroll, Divers, Hughes

RANGERS: Ritchie; Shearer, Caldow; Davis, Paterson, Baxter; Scott, McMillan, Millar, Brand, Wilson

Attendance: 40,000

121

For more than an hour it was anybody's game, but after Rangers scored their 2nd goal in 65 minutes they romped into an unassailable position. Within 2 minutes of the start Rangers scored. Wilson swung in a corner and Fallon punched the ball straight to the feet of Scott, who shot into the net. Before the interval Chalmers hit first the crossbar then the post. In 65 minutes Kurila battered the ball against Wilson from whom it rebounded to Millar who rounded McKay before beating Fallon at the second attempt. In 78 minutes Millar, out on the right with Scott, crossed a ball which Fallon mishandled and Brand scored. 6 minutes later Wilson took a pass from Brand and scored Rangers' 4th, and a minute later Davis, the most accomplished player of all, headed a 5th after a corner-kick. Almost in the last minute Chalmers beat Ritchie from close range.

September 11th: Raith Rovers signed Andy Matthew for £4,500.

September 13th: George Niven was ordered off in a Second XI game with Celtic.

September 17th:
RANGERS (1) 3   AIRDRIE (0) 0
Wilson 2 (30, 61), Brand (64 pen)

RANGERS: Ritchie; Shearer, Caldow; Davis, Paterson, Stevenson; Scott, McMillan, Millar, Brand, Wilson

AIRDRIE: Leslie; Shanks, Keenan; Stewart, Johnstone, McNeill; McCulloch, Storrie, Caven, Rankin, Duncan

Attendance: 25,000

September 24th:
ST JOHNSTONE (1) 2   RANGERS (0) 5
McVittie (19),   Brand (52),
Caldow o.g. (48)   Millar (54),
                           Scott 2 (60, 78),
                           McMillan (76)

ST JOHNSTONE: Taylor; McFadyen, Lachlan; Walker, Little, McKinven; Newlands, Gauld, Gardiner, Innes, McVittie

RANGERS: Ritchie; Shearer, Caldow; Davis, Paterson, Baxter; Scott, McMillan, Millar, Brand, Wilson

Attendance: 19,000

October 1st:
THIRD LANARK (0) 2   RANGERS (3) 4
Goodfellow (48),   Brand 2 (9, 29 pen),
Gray (84)   Scott (17)
                           Wilson (57)

THIRD LANARK: Robertson; McGillivray, Caldwell; Reilly, McCormack, Cunningham; Goodfellow, Hilley, Harley, Gray, McInnes

RANGERS: Ritchie; Shearer, Caldow; Davis, Paterson, Baxter; Scott, McMillan, Millar, Brand, Wilson

Attendance: 32,500

October 5th: Caldow and Wilson played for the Scottish League against the League of Ireland at Celtic Park. The Scots won 5-1.

October 6th: Sammy Baird joined Hibernian for a £6,000 fee.

October 8th:
RANGERS (0) 0   DUNDEE (1) 1
                         Cousin (26)

RANGERS: Ritchie; Shearer, Caldow; Davis, Paterson, Baxter; Scott, McMillan, Millar, Brand, Wilson

DUNDEE: Liney; Reid, Cox; Seith, Ure, Henderson; Penman, McGeachie, Cousin, Gilzean, Robertson

Attendance: 35,000

October 15th:
RANGERS (2) 3   DUNFERMLINE (0) 1
Brand 2 (22, 44),   Peebles (73)
Millar (84)

RANGERS: Ritchie; Shearer, Caldow; Davis, Paterson, Baxter; Scott, McLean, Millar, Brand, Wilson

DUNFERMLINE: Connachan; Williamson, Cunningham; Mailer, Stevenson, Miller; McDonald, Dickson, Wardhaugh, Melrose, Peebles

Attendance: 30,000

League positions

	P	W	D	L	F	A	Pts
1 RANGERS	7	6	0	1	26	10	12
2 Dundee	8	5	1	2	15	11	11
3 Aberdeen	8	3	4	1	18	14	10
4 Third Lanark	8	5	0	3	25	20	10
5 Kilmarnock	8	3	4	1	12	10	10

October 22nd: Scotland were beaten 2-0 by Wales in Cardiff. Caldow and Wilson represented Scotland.

October 26th:
HEARTS (0) 1   RANGERS (1) 3
Smith (61)   Scott (40), Brand (47),
                          Wilson (71)

HEARTS: Marshall; Lough, Holt; Thomson, Milne, Cumming; Smith, Murray, Bauld, McFadzean, Crawford

RANGERS: Ritchie; Shearer, Caldow; Davis, Paterson, Baxter; Scott, McMillan, Millar, Brand, Wilson

Ritchie was carried off after 8 minutes with a chipped ankle bone — Shearer took over in goal.

Attendance: n.a.

November 2nd:
RANGERS (1) 3   RAITH ROVERS (0) 0
  McNaught o.g. (27),
  McMillan (57),
  Wilson (80)

RANGERS: Niven; Shearer, Caldow; Davis, Paterson, Baxter; Scott, McMillan, Millar, Brand, Wilson

RAITH ROVERS: Thorburn; Wilson, Mochan; Polland, McNaught, Duffy; French, Easson, Peebles, Matthew, Urquhart

Attendance: 10,000

November 3rd: Ian McColl was named as the new Scottish team-manager. He continued as a Rangers player.

November 5th:
CLYDE (1) 1   RANGERS (1) 3
  McLaughlin (40)   Scott (27),
                        Baxter (65),
                        Brand (74)

CLYDE: McCulloch; Cameron, Haddock; White, Finlay, Clinton; Herd, Thomson, McLaughlin, Robertson, Steel

RANGERS: Niven; Shearer, Caldow; Davis, Paterson, Baxter; Scott, McMillan, Millar, Brand, Wilson

Attendance: 27,000

November 9th: Caldow, Baxter, Brand and Wilson played for Scotland in a 5-2 victory over Ireland at Hampden Park. Brand scored twice and Caldow converted a penalty.

November 12th:
RANGERS (2) 4   DUNDEE UNITED (0) 0
  McMillan (28),
  Millar 2 (30, 61),
  Scott (47)

RANGERS: Niven; Shearer, Caldow; Davis, Paterson, Baxter; Scott, McMillan, Millar, Brand, Wilson

DUNDEE UNITED: Ugolini; Graham, Briggs; Neilson, Yeats, Fraser; Jackson, Gillespie, Campbell, Irvine, Ormond

Attendance: 25,000

November 19th:
MOTHERWELL (0) 0   RANGERS (1) 1
                               Brand (16)

Match abandoned after 80 minutes due to fog
Attendance: 32,000

November 26th:
RANGERS (2) 2   KILMARNOCK (2) 3
  Wilson (14),   McInally (40),
  McMillan (35)   Kerr (42),
                          Brown (85)

RANGERS: Niven; Shearer, Caldow; Davis, Paterson, Baxter; Scott, McMillan, Millar, Brand, Wilson

KILMARNOCK: McLaughlin; Richmond, Watson; Davidson, Toner, Kennedy; Black, Brown, Kerr, McInally, Muir

Attendance: 50,000

December 3rd:
RANGERS (2) 4   ABERDEEN (0) 0
  Wilson (10), Brand (41),
  McMillan 2 (68, 69)

RANGERS: Niven; Shearer, Caldow; Davis, Paterson, Baxter; Scott, McMillan, Millar, Brand, Wilson

ABERDEEN: Ogston; Bennett, Sim; Fraser, Kinnell, Wishart; Brownlie, Davidson, Little, Cooke, Mulhall

Attendance: 25,132

December 10th:
HIBERNIAN (0) 1   RANGERS (1) 2
  Baird (50 pen)   Wilson (10),
                               Brand (46)

HIBERNIAN: Simpson; Fraser, McClelland; Grant, Easton, Baird; Buchanan, Kinloch, Baker, Preston, McLeod

RANGERS: Niven; Shearer, Caldow; Davis, Paterson, Baxter; Scott, McMillan, Millar, Brand, Wilson

Attendance: 35,000

December 17th:
RANGERS (1) 5   ST MIRREN (0) 1
  Millar 2 (7, 59),   Rodger (47)
  Wilson (75), Brand (82),
  Clunie o.g. (89)

RANGERS: Niven; Shearer, Caldow; Davis, Paterson, Baxter; Scott, McMillan, Millar, Brand, Wilson

ST MIRREN: Brown; Campbell, Wilson; McTavish, Clunie, Thomson; Rodger, Frye, Bryceland, Hume, Miller

Attendance: 34,000

December 24th:
AYR UNITED (1) 1   RANGERS (0) 0
  Price (28)

AYR UNITED: Gallacher; Burn, Thomson; Walker, McLean, Glen; A. McIntyre, Curlett, Price, Fulton, McGhee

RANGERS: Niven; Shearer, Caldow; Davis, Paterson, Baxter; Scott, McMillan, Millar, Brand, Wilson
Attendance: 16,000

League positions

	P	W	D	L	F	A	Pts
1 RANGERS	16	13	0	3	52	18	26
2 Kilmarnock	17	9	6	2	36	26	24
3 Aberdeen	17	7	7	3	37	34	21
4 Third Lanark	17	10	0	7	50	44	20
5 Partick Thistle	17	9	2	6	29	30	20

December 26th:
MOTHERWELL (0) 1   RANGERS (1) 2
  Lindsay (85)   McMillan (32),
                                 Brand (88)

MOTHERWELL: H. Weir; Delaney, I. Weir; McCann, Martis, McPhee; Lindsay, Quinn, St John, Hunter, A. Weir

RANGERS: Niven; Shearer, Caldow; Davis, Paterson, Baxter; Scott, McMillan, Millar, Brand, Wilson
Attendance: 22,000

December 31st:
PARTICK THISTLE (0) 0 RANGERS (2) 3
                                 Wilson (10),
                                 Millar (21),
                                 Brand (57)

PARTICK THISTLE: Freebairn; Muir, Brown; Wright, Harvey, Donlevy; Smith, Closs, McBride, Duffy, McParland

RANGERS: Niven; Shearer, Caldow; Davis, Paterson, Baxter; Scott, McMillan, Millar, Brand, Wilson
Attendance: 31,448

January 2nd:
RANGERS (0) 2   CELTIC (1) 1
  Brand (62),   Divers (28)
  Wilson (80)

RANGERS: Niven; Shearer, Caldow; Davis, Paterson, Baxter; Scott, McMillan, Millar, Brand, Wilson

CELTIC: Haffey; McKay, Kennedy; Crerand, McNeill, Peacock; Chalmers, Divers, Conway, Fernie, Byrne
Attendance: 79,000

Celtic led 1-0 at half-time, Divers having scored in 28 minutes after Baxter had chosen to indulge in frills of ball control almost on his own penalty-spot. Brand equalised in the 62nd minute, a misdirected pass by Scott having been deflected by a Celtic player who inadvertently played both Brand and Wilson onside. An error of judgement by Haffey lost Celtic the match — Scott sent over an orthodox high cross which the goalkeeper missed completely and

Wilson headed into the net. Byrne had been the best winger of the 4 until injured in the the 30th minute of the first-half.

January 7th:
AIRDRIE (1) 1   RANGERS (1) 1
  Storrie (30)   Wilson (20)

AIRDRIE: Leslie; Shanks, Keenan; Quinn, Stewart, McNeill; Sharkey, Storrie, Caven, Rankin, Duncan

RANGERS: Niven; Shearer, Caldow; Davis, Paterson, Baxter; Scott, McMillan, Millar, Brand, Wilson
Attendance: 22,000

January 14th:
RANGERS (1) 1   ST JOHNSTONE (0) 0
  Caldow (30 pen)

RANGERS: Niven; Shearer, Caldow; Davis, Paterson, Baxter; Scott, McMillan, Millar, Brand, Wilson

ST JOHNSTONE: Taylor; McFadyen, Lachlan; Walker, Little, Rattray; McVittie, Docherty, Thomson, Innes, Burns
Attendance: 25,000

January 21st:
RANGERS (2) 4   THIRD LANARK (1) 3
  Brand 3 (14, 33, 53), Harley 2 (23, 58),
  Murray (63)   Hilley (80)

RANGERS: Niven; Shearer, Caldow; Davis, Paterson, Stevenson; Scott, McMillan, Murray, Brand, Wilson

THIRD LANARK: Robertson; McGillivray, Lewis; Reilly, McCormick, Cunningham; Goodfellow, Hilley, Harley, Gray, McInnes
Attendance: 36,000

January 24th: Willie Henderson signed professional terms.

January 28th:
ST MIRREN (1) 1   RANGERS (1) 1
  Clunie (19)   Murray (33)

ST MIRREN: Brown; Campbell, Wilson; Stewart, Clunie, Riddell; Henderson, Bryceland, Kerrigan, Gemmell, Miller

RANGERS: Niven; Shearer, Caldow; Davis, Paterson, Baxter; Scott, Penman, Murray, Brand, Wilson
Attendance: 30,000

February 8th:
DUNDEE (1) 4   RANGERS (1) 2
  Wishart (45),   Murray 2 (20,58)
  Cousin (52),
  Gilzean 2 (63, 90)

DUNDEE: Liney; Hamilton, Cox; Seith, Ure, Cowie; Crichton, Gilzean, Cousin, Wishart, Robertson

RANGERS: Niven; Provan, Caldow; Davis, Paterson, Baxter; Scott, Penman, Murray, Brand, Wilson
Attendance: 22,000

February 18th:
DUNFERMLINE 0   RANGERS 0

DUNFERMLINE: Herriot; Fraser, Sweeney; Mailer, Williamson, Miller; McDonald, Smith, Dickson, Melrose, Peebles

RANGERS: Niven; Shearer, Caldow; Davis, Paterson, Baxter; Scott, McMillan, Murray, Brand, Wilson
Attendance: 18,000

League positions

	P	W	D	L	F	A	Pts
1 RANGERS	25	18	3	4	68	29	39
2 Kilmarnock	25	13	7	5	56	39	33
3 Motherwell	24	12	5	7	51	37	29
4 Aberdeen	24	11	7	6	55	50	29
5 Third Lanark	24	12	2	8	67	61	26

March 4th:
RAITH ROVERS (0) 2   RANGERS (2) 3
Fox (55 pen),   Brand 2 (8, 35),
Wallace (70)   Wilson (78)

RAITH ROVERS: Thorburn; McDonald, McNaught; Stein, Polland, Leigh; Wallace, Fox, Buchanan, Benvie, Urquhart

RANGERS: Niven; Shearer, Caldow; Davis, Baillie, Stevenson; Scott, McMillan, McLean, Brand, Wilson
Attendance: 12,000

March 8th:
RANGERS (0) 3   HEARTS (0) 0
Brand (69), McLean 2 (75, 85)

RANGERS: Niven; Shearer, Caldow; McKinnon, Baillie, Stevenson; Scott, McMillan, McLean, Brand, Wilson

HEARTS: Marshall; Kirk, Holt; Bowman, Milne, Cumming; Smith, Murray, Davidson, Blackwood, Crawford
Attendance: 30,000

March 11th:
RANGERS (0) 2   CLYDE (0) 1
Wilson (53),   Colrain (59)
McLean (85)

RANGERS: Niven; Shearer, Caldow; McKinnon, Baillie, Stevenson; Henderson, McMillan, McLean, Brand, Wilson

CLYDE: McCulloch; Cameron, T. Wilson; Sim, Finlay, Clinton; McLean, Herd, McLaughlin, Robertson, Colrain
Attendance: 22,000

March 18th:
DUNDEE UNITED (1) 1   RANGERS (1) 1
Boner (14)   Brand (37)

DUNDEE UNITED: Ugolini; Cairns, Gordon; Neilson, Yeats, Briggs; Boner, Gillespie, Mochan, Howieson, Ormond

RANGERS: Niven; Shearer, Caldow; Davis, Paterson, Stevenson; Henderson, McMillan, Scott, Brand, Wilson
Attendance: 17,000

March 22nd: Shearer, Caldow, Brand and Wilson were all in the Scottish League team which beat the English League 3-2 at Ibrox. Caldow scored the winner from the penalty spot.

It was reported that Jimmy Millar who was injured against St Johnstone on January 14th had a slipped disc.

March 25th:
RANGERS (0) 2   MOTHERWELL (1) 2
Scott (55),   St John (19),
Murray (64)   Quinn (71)

RANGERS: Niven; Shearer, Caldow; Davis, Paterson, Baxter; Scott, McLean, Murray, Brand, Wilson

MOTHERWELL: Weir; Delaney, Strachan; Aitken, Martis, McCann; Hunter, Quinn, St John, Stevenson, Roberts
Attendance: 42,000

April 1st:
KILMARNOCK (2) 2   RANGERS (0) 0
Kerr (31), Muir (39)

KILMARNOCK: McLaughlin; Richmond, Watson; Beattie, Toner, Kennedy; Brown, Black, Kerr, McInally, Muir

RANGERS: Ritchie; Shearer, Caldow; Stevenson, Paterson, Baxter; Scott, Wilson, Baillie, Brand, Hume
Attendance: 29,000

April 8th:
ABERDEEN (3) 6   RANGERS (1) 1
Cummings 3 (14, 19, 49),   Scott (28)
Little (18), Brownlie (58),
Cooke (67)

ABERDEEN: Harker; Cadenhead, Hogg; Baird, Kinnell, Fraser; Cummings, Brownlie, Little, Cooke, Mulhall

RANGERS: Ritchie; Shearer, Caldow; Davis, Baillie, Stevenson; Scott, Brand, McLean, Penman, Wilson

Attendance: 20,000

April 11th:
RANGERS   (1) 1   HIBERNIAN   (0) 0
  McMillan (36)

RANGERS: Ritchie; Shearer, Provan; Davis, Paterson, Baxter; Henderson, McMillan, Scott, Brand, Wilson

HIBERNIAN: Simpson; Fraser, McClelland; Grant, Easton, Baird; Scott, Preston, Baker, Baxter, McLeod

Simpson saved his 7th penalty of the season from Scott. Henderson was carried off with torn ankle ligaments.

Attendance: 45,000

April 19th: Ian McColl announced that he intended to retire as a player after appearing in almost 600 matches for the club.

April 29th:
RANGERS   (4) 7   AYR UNITED   (1) 3
  Scott 3 (18, 25, 53),   A. McIntyre (44),
  Wilson 2 (33, 75),   Fulton (61),
  Brand 2 (41, 88)   Christie (86)

RANGERS: Ritchie; Shearer, Caldow; Davis, Paterson, Baxter; Wilson, McMillan, Scott, Brand, Hume

AYR UNITED: Gallacher; Burn, G. McIntyre; W. McIntyre, Glen, Curlett; Fulton, Gibson, Christie, A. McIntyre, Bradley

Attendance: 45,000

Scottish First Division

	P	W	D	L	F	A	Pts
1 RANGERS	34	23	5	6	88	46	51
2 Kilmarnock	34	21	8	5	77	45	50
3 Third Lanark	34	20	2	12	100	80	42
4 Celtic	34	15	9	10	64	46	39
5 Motherwell	34	15	8	11	70	57	38
6 Aberdeen	34	14	8	12	72	72	36
7 Hibernian	34	15	4	15	66	69	34
8 Hearts	34	13	8	13	51	51	34
9 Dundee United	34	13	7	14	60	58	33
10 Dundee	34	13	6	15	61	53	32
11 Partick Thistle	34	13	6	15	59	69	32
12 Dunfermline	34	12	7	15	65	81	31
13 Airdrie	34	10	10	14	61	71	30
14 St Mirren	34	11	7	16	53	58	29
15 St Johnstone	34	10	9	15	47	63	29
16 Raith Rovers	34	10	7	17	46	67	27
17 Clyde	34	6	11	17	55	77	23
18 Ayr United	34	5	12	17	51	81	22

April 30th: Queen and Grant were among those given free transfers.

May 3rd: Shearer, Caldow, Baxter, Brand and Wilson were all in the Scotland team which beat Eire 4-1 at Hampden in a World Cup Qualifying match. Brand scored twice.

May 7th: Scotland beat Eire 3-0 in Dublin in the return. Shearer, Caldow, Baxter, Brand and Wilson again represented Scotland. Brand scored one of the goals.

May 14th: Scotland were beaten 4-0 by Czechoslovakia in a World Cup Qualifier. Rangers had six players in the team — Shearer, Caldow, Baxter, McMillan, Brand and Wilson.

May 22nd: Jim Christie was signed from Ayr United for £11,000. He had made only 10 first-team appearances for that club.

LEAGUE CUP

August 13th:
RANGERS   (1) 3   PARTICK THISTLE   (0) 1
  Scott (20),   McParland (88)
  Millar 2 (60, 78)

RANGERS: Niven; Caldow, Little; Davis, Paterson, Stevenson; Scott, McMillan, Millar, Baxter, Wilson

PARTICK THISTLE: Freebairn; Hogan, Baird; Wright, Harvey, Donlevy; Smith, McParland, Wardlaw, Fleming, Ewing

Attendance: 50,000

August 17th:
THIRD LANARK   (2) 2   RANGERS   (0) 1
  Hilley (30 secs),   Millar (50)
  Caldow o.g. (14)

THIRD LANARK: Robertson; McGillivray, Caldwell; Reilly, Robb, Cunningham; Goodfellow, Hilley, Harley, Gray, McInnes

RANGERS: Ritchie; Caldow, Little; Davis, Paterson, Stevenson; Scott, Baxter, Millar, Brand, Wilson

Attendance: n.a.

August 20th:
RANGERS   (1) 2   CELTIC   (3) 3
  Miller (36),   Carroll (15),
  Brand (61)   Divers (25),
                             Hughes (44)

RANGERS: Ritchie; Shearer, Caldow; Davis, Baillie, Baxter; Scott, Baird, Millar, Brand, Wilson

CELTIC: Haffey; McKay, Kennedy; Crerand, McNeill, Peacock; Carroll, Chalmers, Hughes, Divers, Mochan

Attendance: 60,000

Hughes, only seventeen, caused havoc in Rangers' defence. Before Carroll scored the first goal in 15 minutes, Rangers might have had a penalty for McKay impeding Wilson. In 25 minutes Divers shot a 2nd goal when Baillie was baffled by Hughes. 9 minutes from half-time McNeill lost the ball when he tried to dribble round Millar and the Ranger scored with a ground shot which went through Haffey's legs. Just on half-time Mochan for once beat Shearer, and Carroll carried on the attack on the left before passing to Hughes, who suddenly wheeled and shot the goal of the game. In the second-half Haffey, who had broken a toe earlier, was in constant peril, but he was beaten only once — by Brand.

August 27th:
PARTICK THISTLE (0) 1 RANGERS (2) 4
  Smith (50)   McMillan 2 (22, 85),
                            Millar (28),
                            Brand (48)
PARTICK THISTLE: Freebairn; Hogan, Baird; Wright, Harvey, Donlevy; McKenzie, McParland, Smith, Wilson, Fleming

RANGERS: Ritchie; Shearer, Caldow; Davis, Paterson, Baxter; Scott, McMillan, Millar, Brand, Wilson

Attendance: 25,000

August 31st:
RANGERS (2) 3   THIRD LANARK (0) 2
  Millar 2 (26, 70),   Gray (47),
                         Goodfellow (72)
RANGERS: Ritchie; Shearer, Caldow; Davis, Paterson, Baxter; Scott, McMillan, Millar, Brand, Wilson

THIRD LANARK: Robertson; McGillivray, Caldwell; Reilly, Robb, Cunningham; Goodfellow, Hilley, Harley, Gray, McInnes

Robb missed a penalty

Attendance: n.a.

September 3rd:
CELTIC (1) 1   RANGERS (0) 2
  Chalmers (2)   Davis (48), Brand (70)
CELTIC: Fallon; McKay, Kennedy; Crerand, Kurila, Peacock; Carroll, Chalmers, Hughes, Divers, Mochan

RANGERS: Ritchie; Shearer, Caldow; Davis, Paterson, Baxter; Scott, McMillan, Millar, Brand, Wilson

Attendance: n.a.

Rangers were indeed fortunate to be only one goal down at the interval — a goal by Chalmers after only 2 minutes, which they claimed, with some justification, should have

been disallowed on the grounds of offside. Paterson, taking the minimum of risks and blocking the middle successfully if unattractively, kept Rangers in the game. Shortly after half-time Davis headed the equaliser — Brand dummied the ball and deceived Fallon. 20 minutes from time Millar beat Kurila in the air and enabled Brand to shoot from 16 yards, so fast that Fallon was beaten where he stood.

League Cup Section Table

	P	W	D	L	F	A	Pts
RANGERS	6	4	0	2	15	10	8
Celtic	6	3	1	2	11	8	7
Third Lanark	6	3	0	3	12	10	6
Partick Thistle	6	1	1	4	6	16	3

September 14th: Quarter-Final First Leg
RANGERS (0) 1   DUNDEE (0) 0
  Scott (51)
RANGERS: Ritchie; Shearer, Caldow; Davis, Paterson, Baxter; Scott, McMillan, Millar, Brand, Wilson

DUNDEE: Liney; Hamilton, Cox; Seith, Smith, Ure; Penman, McGeachie, Gilzean, Cowie, Robertson

Attendance: n.a.

September 21st:
DUNDEE (0) 3   RANGERS (2) 4
  Cousin 2 (48, 57),   Wilson (21),
  Penman (75 pen)   McMillan 2 (39, 81),
                         Brand (84)
DUNDEE: Liney; Hamilton, Reid; Seith, Smith, Ure; Penman, Cousin, Waddell, Gilzean, Robertson

RANGERS: Ritchie; Shearer, Caldow; Davis, Paterson, Baxter; Scott, McMillan, Millar, Brand, Wilson

Attendance: n.a.

Rangers won 5-3 on aggregate

October 19th: Semi-Final   At Celtic Park
RANGERS (5) 7   QUEEN OF THE
  Brand 3 (2, 30, 61),   SOUTH (0) 0
  Millar 2 (16, 19),
  McMillan (44), Scott (72)
RANGERS: Ritchie; Shearer, Caldow; Davis, Paterson, Baxter; Scott, McMillan, Millar, Brand, Wilson

QUEEN OF THE SOUTH: Farm; Kerr, Scott; Patterson, Mattison, King; Black, Ward, Elliot, Broadis, Smith

Attendance: 17,000

Rangers disposed of Queen of the South with almost contemptuous ease. At half-time they led 5-0. Millar's 2nd goal was worth all of the others, his full-blooded shot from the edge of the penalty area completing a perfectly delightful run by Wilson in which the outside-left tricked both Patterson and Kerr, the latter by means of a back-heel flick, and then laid on the chance for the centre-forward. The Second Division club could hardly have hoped to match Rangers; nevertheless their pathetic attempts to tackle were in the first instance the cause of their heavy defeat. Baxter conceded half of the free-kicks which were awarded in the match. None of his infringements was especially reprehensible; he merely showed an inclination throughout not to be beaten.

October 29th: Final   At Hampden Park
RANGERS   (1) 2   KILMARNOCK   (0) 0
  Brand (37), Scott (74)

RANGERS: Niven; Shearer, Caldow; Davis, Paterson, Baxter; Scott, McMillan, Millar, Brand, Wilson

KILMARNOCK: J. Brown; Richmond, Watson; Beattie, Toner, Kennedy; H. Brown, McInally, Kerr, Black, Muir

Attendance: 82,063   *Referee*: T. Wharton (Clarkston)

For the first 20 minutes Kilmarnock, the wind in their favour, gave Rangers' forwards hardly a glimpse of their goal. Toner displayed such judgement in his interceptions and such shrewd sense of position that the Millar-Brand combination rarely succeeded, but in the 37th minute those 2 players joined in a swift, accurate passing movement and Brand swerved round Brown before he shot unerringly with his left foot. Wilson in particular made the opposing full-back look most ordinary, and both Caldow and Baxter wisely directed their passes to their outside-left. Scott made victory certain 16 minutes from time. His left-foot sweep of the ball from the corner of the penalty area, surely meant as a cross, drifted over Brown's arms.

SCOTTISH CUP

February 11th: Second Round
DUNDEE   (0) 1   RANGER   (4) 5
  Cousin (51)   Murray 2 (8, 86),
                         Brand 2 (13, 27),
                         Scott (43)

DUNDEE: Liney; Hamilton, Cox; Ure, Smith, Stuart; Penman, Gilzean, Cousin, Wishart, Robertson

RANGERS: Niven; Shearer, Caldow; Davis, Paterson, Baxter; Scott, McMillan, Murray, Brand, Wilson

Attendance: 32,000

February 25th: Third Round
MOTHERWELL   (1) 2   RANGERS   (2) 2
  St John (42),   Murray 2 (30, 31)
  McCann (69)

MOTHERWELL: H. Weir; Delaney, McSeveney; Aitken, Martis, McCann; Lindsay, Quinn, St John, Hunter, Roberts

RANGERS: Niven; Shearer, Caldow; Davis, Paterson, Baxter; Scott, McMillan, Murray, Brand, Wilson

Attendance: 33,000

March 1st: Third Round Replay
RANGERS   (2) 2   MOTHERWELL   (2) 5
  Wilson (16),   McPhee (10),
  McMillan (29)   Delaney (41),
                         Roberts 2 (53, 89),
                         St John (68)

RANGERS: Niven; Shearer, Caldow; Davis, Paterson, Stevenson; Scott, McMillan, Murray, Brand, Wilson

MOTHERWELL: Weir; Delaney, McSeveney; Aitken, Martis, McCann; Hunter, Quinn, St John, McPhee, Roberts

Attendance: 80,000

The Army would not release Baxter for this match

CUP WINNERS CUP

September 28th: First Round First Leg
RANGERS   (0) 4   FERENCVAROS
  Davis (52),   (Hungary)   (1) 2
  Millar 2 (57, 86),   Orosz (17),
  Brand (73)   Friedmansky (79)

RANGERS: Ritchie; Shearer, Caldow; Davis, Paterson, Baxter; Scott, McMillan, Millar, Brand, Wilson

FERENCVAROS: Horvath; Thoman, Kiss; Kocsis, Gerendas, Vilezsa; Friedmansky, Orosz, Albert, Rakosi, Fenyvesi

Attendance: 36,000

Rangers defeated Ferencvaros in a very uninspiring match. In 17 minutes, after McMillan had hit a post and Brand had a shot saved, Orosz wheeled on a pass from Albert and shot the ball low into the net past an unsighted Ritchie. Davis equalised after 52 minutes with a header from a Scott free-kick. Five minutes later Brand and Millar executed a fine cross-field passing move which ended with the latter scoring. In 73 minutes Brand added a 3rd goal. Friedmansky scored for the visitors 6 minutes later but Millar restored Rangers' 2-goal lead 4 minutes from time.

October 12th: First Round Second Leg
FERENCVAROS   (1) 2   RANGERS   (0) 1
  Orosz (18),   Wilson (61)
  Friedmansky (48)

FERENCVAROS: Horvath; Kiss, Gerendas; Dalnoki, Vilezsai, Kocsis; Dalnoki, Orosz, Friedmansky, Rakosi, Fenyvesi

RANGERS: Ritchie; Shearer, Caldow; Davis, Paterson, Baxter; Scott, McMillan, Millar, Brand, Wilson

Attendance: 25,000

The Hungarians started without their Internationalist centre-forward Albert, who was injured. Playing fast, open football the home team took the lead after 18 minutes. Dalnoki crossing to the unmarked Rakosi and he at once passed to Orosz who scored a splendid goal. In 48 minutes they increased their lead when Friedmansky scored from a pass from Orosz. Rangers' superior stamina played its part when the Hungarians began to show signs of their first-half exertions and Wilson scored after 61 minutes when Horvath and Kiss both hesitated in clearing a cross from McMillan. Rangers continued to dominate until the end of the game which was hard rather than skilful. The roving Millar, although not on the score sheet, gave the home defenders a most uncomfortable afternoon.

Rangers won 5-4 on aggregate

15th November: Second Round First Leg

BORUSSIA-MÖNCHEN-GLADBACH	RANGERS	(2) 3
(Germany) (0) 0	Millar (22), Scott (25), McMillan (57)	

BORUSSIA: Dresbach; Pfeffier, De-Lange; Muelhausen, Frontzek, Kablitz; Bruntz, Brulles, Kohn, Fender, Bedfstig

RANGERS: Niven; Shearer, Caldow; Davis, Paterson, Baxter; Scott, McMillan, Millar, Brand, Wilson

Attendance: 50,000

After early chances were squandered by Wilson and Brand in particular, Millar in 22 minutes and Scott in 25 minutes emphasised Rangers' superior ball control and pace. Millar's goal was conjured for him by McMillan, who, in a bewildering run baffled no fewer than 4 outfield defenders, enticed the goalkeeper from his line and left Millar to finish. Scott emulated his partner by taking on almost the entire defence himself and completed an exhilarating run perfectly with a left-foot shot. In 29 minutes Muelhausen shot a penalty-kick, awarded against Caldow, straight at Niven. When McMillan shot a glorious goal in 57 minutes, Borussia were in a hopeless situation.

November 30th: Second Round Second Leg

RANGERS	(5) 8	BORUSSIA
Baxter (2), Brand 3 (16, 43, 52), Pfeffier o.g. (36), Millar 2 (44, 54), Davis (66)		MÖNCHEN-GLADBACH (0) 0

RANGERS: Niven; Shearer, Caldow; Davis, Paterson, Baxter; Scott, McMillan, Millar, Brand, Wilson

BORUSSIA: Jansen; Pfeffier, De-Lange; Jansen, Goebbels, Frontzek; Brungs, Brulles, Kohn, Muelhausen, Fender

Attendance: 38,174

Rangers played with their opponents who took their thrashing like sportsmen. Borussia lost a goal in the second minute to Baxter. Rangers led 5-0 at half-time, Brand, Pfeffier (own goal), McMillan and Millar having added the goals. Brand, Millar and Brand again scored in the first 20 minutes of the second half. Niven deserved some sympathy — throughout the match, which was played in torrential rain, he was not once extended to save. Rangers entertained the 38,000 crowd continually with their clever, close passing game.

(Rangers won 11-0 on aggregate).

March 29th: Semi-Final First Leg

RANGERS	(1) 2	WOLVES
Scott (33), Brand (84)		(England) (0) 0

RANGERS: Ritchie; Shearer, Caldow; Davis, Paterson, Baxter; Scott, Wilson, Baillie, Brand, Hume

WOLVES: Finlayson; Stuart, Showell; Clamp, Slater, Flowers; Deeley, Murray, Farmer, Mason, Durandt

Attendance: 80,000

Rangers had a serious upset after only 9 minutes' play when iron-man Davis suffered a leg-muscle injury and had to go disconsolately to outside-right for the remainder of the match. Wilson took his place in defence as part of the re-arrangements. After Wolves' inside-right Murray had struck the crossbar, Scott beat Flowers for speed in the inside-right position and shot a magnificent goal from some 20 yards. For the rest of the half Rangers were under extreme pressure and both Shearer and Caldow kicked shots off the line with Ritchie beaten. The pattern continued in the second half. Rangers had only one forward near Finlayson when Clamp, over on the left and in full control of the ball and the situation, chose to cut across field and attempted to pass to his right wing. This proved to be extreme folly, for the ball struck another Wolves player and was diverted to Brand who accepted the gift with alacrity and shot low and hard past Finlayson, with his one scoring chance, 6 minutes from time.

April 19th: Semi-Final Second Leg

WOLVES	(0) 1	RANGERS	(1) 1
Broadbent (65)		Scott (45)	

WOLVES: Finlayson; Stuart, Showell; Clamp, Slater, Flowers; Deeley, Mason, Murray, Broadbent, Durandt

RANGERS: Ritchie; Shearer, Caldow; Davis, Paterson, Baxter; Wilson, McMillan, Scott, Brand, Hume

Attendance: 45,163

For almost the first half-hour Rangers survived somewhat fortunately a furious attempt by Wolves to cut down the deficit. The match was played in heavy snow and the ground was slippery and treacherous. Deeley, Mason, Murray and Durandt all missed simple scoring chances in the first quarter of an hour. When Wilson showed that he had the mastery of Showell, Rangers were more than prepared to favour attack. In the 2nd-last minute of the first half Brand, having temporarily switched positions with Scott, eluded a weak tackle by Slater, and Scott trailed his thrusting pass in on Finlayson and carefully placed a right-foot shot away from the keeper. Within a minute Ritchie had pulled off the save of the match from a Flowers piledriver from 30 yards. 20 minutes after the restart Broadbent put new heart into Wolves by flicking a cross-shot from Durandt past Ritchie. Rangers' defence stood firm to the end with Shearer and Paterson outstanding.

Rangers won 3-1 on aggregate

May 17th: Final First Leg
RANGERS   (0) 0   FIORENTINA
                         (Italy) (1) 2
                         Milan 2 (11, 90)
RANGERS: Ritchie; Shearer, Caldow; Davis, Paterson, Baxter; Wilson, McMillan, Scott, Brand, Hume

FIORENTINA: Albertosi; Robotti, Casteletti; Gonfiantini, Orzan, Rimbaldo; Hamrin, Micheli, Da Costa, Milan, Petris
Attendance: 80,000

Rangers can claim with some justification that the superior football crafts of their opponents proved less of a stumbling block than their opponents' mastery of the arts of body checking, tripping and almost every other infringement of the football rule book. Rangers failed to realise, at an early stage, that the high cross into the goalmouth was not a device likely to outwit the tall Italian defenders, and they persisted with this tactic throughout the match. In 11 minutes Davis, in attempting a pass-back to his goalkeeper, half-hit the ball. Petris got to it before the outrushing Ritchie and slipped it inside to Milan who glided the ball expertly into the empty net. 6 minutes later Rangers were awarded a soft penalty when McMillan fell in the box after a challenge by Orzan. After heated arguments between the referee, the Italian players and an over-enthusiastic Italian who had run onto the field, Caldow stepped up to take the kick and shot wide of the target. Fiorentina were quite content to let Rangers do the bulk of the attacking and to reply on long passes to their wingers, Hamrin and Petris, who had the legs of their respective opponents. Fiorentina's 2nd goal arrived in the final minute of the match. Milan dispossessed Shearer and square-passed to Hamrin, who flicked it over for the inside-left to score from close range.

May 27th: Final Second Leg
FIORENTINA (1) 2   RANGERS   (0) 1
  Milan (12), Hamrin (83)   Scott (60)

FIORENTINA: Albertosi; Robotti, Castelletti; Gonfiantini, Orzan, Rimbaldo; Hamrin, Micheli, Da Costa, Milan, Petris

RANGERS: Ritchie; Shearer, Caldow; Davis, Paterson, Baxter; Scott, McMillan, Millar, Brand, Wilson
Attendance: 40,000

The pattern of the match was almost identical to the one in Glasgow, the Italian defensive marking being too sound for the Rangers forwards. To counter any surprises caused by the return of Millar, Fiorentina had 2 players with the full-time task of dealing with the centre-forward. In the 60th minute Scott took up a position in the centre of the field and hit a low cross from Wilson straight to the corner of the net from 16 yards. That goal wiped out a 12th-minute effort from Milan, which had apparently made the home side's task simple. In that minute Hamrin cut the ball back into the path of the outside-left after he had beaten both Baxter and Caldow and Milan breasted the ball over the line. Rangers were much the better team after Scott had opened their account. Millar was unfortunate not to make the score 2-1. Seven minutes from time it was the Swede Hamrin who made certain that Fiorentina would win both home and away. He sped away on the right, cut past three Rangers defenders, and from an almost impossible angle shot a magnificent second goal for his side.

Fiorentina won 4-1 on aggregate

Ian McColl, a Rangers stalwart in the fifties.

APPEARANCES

	League	League Cup	Scottish Cup	Glasgow Cup	Charity Cup	Friend-lies	Cup Win'rs Cup
Ritchie	12	8	-	-	-	-	6
Shearer	33	8	3	-	1	2	8
Caldow	33	10	3	1	-	1	8
Davis	31	10	3	1	-	1	8
Paterson	30	9	3	1	1	1	8
Baxter	27	10	2	1	-	-	8
Scott	33	10	3	1	1	2	8
McMillan	28	8	3	1	-	1	7
Millar	21	10	-	1	-	2	5
Brand	34	9	3	-	-	2	8
Wilson	34	10	3	1	1	2	8
Stevenson	8	2	1	1	1	2	-
McLean	6	-	-	-	1	1	-
Niven	22	2	3	1	1	1	2
Murray	5	-	3	-	-	-	-
Penman	3	-	-	-	1	-	-
Provan	2	-	-	-	1	1	-
Baillie	5	1	-	-	-	1	1
McKinnon	2	-	-	-	1	1	-
Henderson	3	-	-	-	-	-	-
Hume	2	-	-	-	1	-	3
Little	-	2	-	1	-	-	-
Baird	-	1	-	-	-	-	-
Martin	-	-	-	-	-1	-	-

GOALSCORERS

League: Brand 24 (2 pens), Wilson 19, Scott 12, Millar 10, McMillan 8, Murray 4, McLean 3, Own Goals 3, Davis 2, Caldow 2 (2 pens), Baxter 1

League Cup: Brand 9, Millar 9, Scott 4, McMillan 4, Wilson 1, Davis 1, Own Goals 1

Scottish Cup: Murray 4, Brand 2, Wilson 1, Scott 1, McMillan 1

Glasgow Cup: Millar 2

Charity Cup: McLean 2, Scott 1

Friendlies: Brand 3, Wilson 1, Millar 1, Mclean 1

Cup Winners Cup: Brand 5, Millar 5, Scott 4, Davis 2, Wilson 1, McMillan 1, Baxter 1, Own Goals 1

Eric Caldow exchanges pennants with Fiorentina's captain Orzan before the start of the European Cup Winner's Cup Final first leg at Ibrox on 17th May, 1961.

Season 1961–62

By dropping 7 points in their last 7 matches, Rangers surrendered the League Title to Dundee, who had led from the start. 22 matches were won and their 84 goals scored was the highest in the Division. Davie Wilson scored a remarkable 6 goals from the centre-forward position in an away match against Falkirk. Henderson and Greig broke into the team during the season. Ritchie and Shearer were the only ever-presents and Brand finished as top scorer with 23. Ian McMillan scored the club's 4,000th League goal.

Both A.S. Monaco of France and A.S.K. Vorwaerts of East Germany were beaten in the European Cup. Because the authorities refused the East Germans visas for this country the home leg had to be played in Malmo, Sweden. This particular match had to be abandoned at half-time due to fog and was rescheduled for the following morning at 9 a.m. A crowd of only 1,781 turned up to watch the match. Rangers were eliminated from the competition by Standard Liège. The Belgians' 4-1 lead in the first match proved too much to pull back at Ibrox. Henderson was caught up in a traffic jam on his way to the ground and had to sit the game out.

Both the Scottish Cup and League Cup were won. 22 goals were scored in Rangers' run to the Scottish Cup Final. Falkirk, Arbroath, Aberdeen (after a replay), Kilmarnock and Motherwell were beaten along the way. The Final against St Mirren was a rather one-sided affair and the 2-0 score gave little indication of Rangers' superiority.

Dundee were one of the teams beaten in the League Cup Qualifying Section. Rangers came back from being 2-0 down against St Johnstone in the Semi-Final at Parkhead to win by a Wilson goal in Extra-Time. The Final against Hearts went to a replay. Baillie for Paterson was the only team change and the Cup was won for the fourth time with 3 goals in the first 20 minutes.

An end-of-season tour of Russia proved very successful — the team returning undefeated to a huge reception at Renfrew Airport.

> League: Runners-up
> League Cup: Winners
> Scottish Cup: Winners
> European Cup: Quarter-Finalists

SCOTTISH FIRST DIVISION

August 23rd:
RANGERS (1) 3   HIBERNIAN (0) 0
Wilson (19),
Brand 2 (52 pen, 69)

RANGERS: Ritchie; Shearer, Caldow; Davis, Paterson, Baxter; Scott, McMillan, Millar, Brand, Wilson

HIBERNIAN: Simpson; Fraser, Grant; Baxter, Easton, Baird; Stevenson, Gibson, Kinloch, Preston, McLeod

Attendance: 40,000

September 9th:
PARTICK THISTLE (0) 1   RANGERS (2) 4
Muir (88)   Wilson (15),
                      Millar (28),
                  Scott (59), Brand (63)

PARTICK THISTLE: Freebairn; Muir, Brown; Cunningham, McKinnon, Donlevy; Williamson, McParland, McBride, Duffy, Ewing

RANGERS: Ritchie; Shearer, Caldow; Davis, Paterson, Baxter; Scott, McMillan, Millar, Brand, Wilson

Attendance: 31,500

September 16th:
RANGERS (1) 2   CELTIC (1) 2
  Christie (5), Baxter (88)   Divers (28),
                          Fernie (48)

RANGERS: Ritchie; Shearer, Caldow; Davis, Paterson, Baxter; Scott, McMillan, Christie, Brand, Wilson

CELTIC: Haffey; McKay, Kennedy; Crerand, McNeill, Price; Chalmers, Jackson, Hughes, Divers, Fernie

Attendance: 70,000

Two people were killed and 60 injured when the crowd broke a stairway barrier at the end of the match.

Rangers were the superior team in the first half. Christie, chasing every ball, was a constant menace to the Celtic defenders as he sought to add to the goal he headed from a cross by Wilson after 5 minutes' play. Divers, taking the home defence by surprise after 28 minutes' play, scored from a pass by Chalmers. 3 minutes after the interval Celtic took the lead when Fernie was in position to jab the ball past Ritchie from close range after Shearer blocked a shot from Chalmers. 2 minutes from the end Rangers equalised through Baxter with a shot from 25 yards.

September 23rd:
ST MIRREN (1) 1   RANGERS (1) 1
  Nelson (5)   Scott (13)

ST MIRREN: Brown; Campbell, Wilson; Stewart, Clunie, McTavish; Rodger, Henderson, Kerrigan, Nelson, Miller

RANGERS: Ritchie; Shearer, Caldow; Davis, Paterson, Baxter; Scott, McMillan, Millar, Brand, Wilson

Attendance: 34,000

September 30th:
RANGERS (1) 4   SITRLING ALBION (1) 1
  McMillan (17),   Addison (21)
  Millar (57, 61),
  Brand (71)

RANGERS: Ritchie; Shearer, Caldow; Davis, Paterson, Baxter; Scott, McMillan, Millar, Brand, Wilson

STIRLING ALBION: Wren; McGuiness, Pettigrew; Myles, Johnstone, McGregor; Sinclair, Kilgannon, Addison, Spence, Lawlor

Attendance: 30,000

October 7th: Scotland beat Ireland 6-1 in Belfast. Caldow, Baxter, Scott, Brand and Wilson all represented Scotland. All of the goals were scored by Rangers players. Wilson scored 2, Scott scored 3 and Brand got the other.

October 14th:
RANGERS (3) 6   RAITH ROVERS (0) 0
  McMillan (28), Brand 4 (30, 70, 88, 89),
  Wilson (35)

RANGERS: Ritchie; Shearer, Provan; Davis, Paterson, Stevenson; Scott, McMillan, Millar, Brand, Wilson

RAITH ROVERS: Cunningham; McDonald, Mochan; Stein, Forsyth, Clinton; Malcolm, White, Adamson, Benvie, Watson

Attendance: 34,500

McMillan's goal was Rangers' 5,000th in the League

October 21st:
MOTHERWELL (1) 2   RANGERS (0) 2
  Quinn (38 pen), McPhee (85)   Wilson (77),
                          Brand (89)

MOTHERWELL: H. Weir; McSeveney, Thomson; Aitken, W. McCallum, McCann; McPhee, Quinn, Roberts, Hunter, A. Weir

RANGERS: Ritchie; Shearer, Caldow; Davis, Paterson, Baxter; Scott, McMillan, Millar, Brand, Wilson

Attendance: 24,500

League positions

	P	W	D	L	F	A	Pts
1 Dundee	9	8	0	1	27	14	16
2 Kilmarnock	9	6	1	2	22	16	13
3 RANGERS	7	4	3	0	22	7	11
4 Celtic	9	5	1	3	20	12	11
5 Third Lanark	9	5	1	3	22	14	11

November 4th:
THIRD LANARK (0) 0   RANGERS (1) 3
                          Brand (21),
                          Christie 2 (66, 80)

THIRD LANARK: Robertson; McGillivray, Caldwell; Robb, McCormack, Lewis; Goodfellow, Hilley, Harley, Gray, McInnes

RANGERS: Ritchie; Shearer, Caldow; Davis, Paterson, Baxter; Scott, McMillan, Christie, Brand, Wilson

Attendance: 25,000

November 11th:
RANGERS (0) 1   DUNDEE (0) 5
  Brand (84)   Gilzean 4 (46, 48, 73, 86),
                          Penman (88)

RANGERS: Ritchie; Shearer, Caldow; Davis, Paterson, Baxter; Scott, McMillan, Christie, Brand, Wilson

DUNDEE: Liney; Hamilton, Cox; Seith, Ure,
Wishart; Smith, Penman, Cousin, Gilzean, Robertson
Attendance: 35,000

November 18th:
RANGERS   (3) 4   FALKIRK   (0) 0
  Wilson (25), Millar 3 (38, 43, 69)
RANGERS: Ritchie; Shearer, Provan; McKinnon,
Baillie, Stevenson; Henderson, Greig, Millar, Brand,
Wilson

FALKIRK: Whigham; Rae, Hunter; Pierson,
Thomson, McIntosh; Reid, Murray, Lowry, Oliver,
Ormond
Attendance: 33,000

November 25th:
DUNDEE UNITED   (1) 2   RANGERS   (1) 3
  Mochan 2 (19, 74)   Caldow (25 pen),
                            Greig (51),
                            Murray (66)

DUNDEE UNITED: Brown; Cairns, Briggs; Gordon,
Smith, Fraser; Boner, Brodie, Carlyle, Gillespie,
Mochan

RANGERS: Ritchie; Shearer, Caldow; Davis, Baillie,
Baxter; Henderson, Greig, Murray, Brand, Hume
Attendance: 20,000

December 2nd:
RANGERS   (1) 2   ST JOHNSTONE   (0) 0
  Wilson (45), Brand (63)
RANGERS: Ritchie; Shearer, Provan; Davis, Baillie,
Stevenson; Henderson, McMillan, Murray, Brand,
Wilson

ST JOHNSTONE: Taylor; McFadyen, Lachlan;
McKinven, J. Ferguson, Rattray; Rankine, Wright,
Gilfillan, A. Ferguson, Bell
Attendance: 22,000

December 16th:
DUNFERMLINE   (0) 1   RANGERS   (0) 0
  Melrose (79)
DUNFERMLINE: Connachan; Fraser, Cunningham;
Mailer, Williamson, Miller; McDonald, Smith, Dickson,
Melrose, Peebles

RANGERS: Ritchie; Shearer, Caldow; Davis, Baillie,
Stevenson; Scott, Greig, Millar, Brand, Wilson
Attendance: 16,000

December 23rd:
RANGERS   (1) 2   ABERDEEN   (2) 4
  Brand (29), Greig (77)   Brownlie (14 secs),
                            Mulhall (43),
                            Cooke (54),
                            Kinnell (60 pen)

RANGERS: Ritchie; Shearer, Caldow; Davis, Baillie,
Baxter; Henderson, Greig, Scott, Brand, Hume

ABERDEEN: Ogston; Bennett, Hogg; Burns, Kinnell,
Fraser; Callachan, Brownlie, Little, Cooke, Mulhall
Attendance: 28,000

December 30th:
KILMARNOCK   (0) 0   RANGERS   (1) 1
                            Millar (16)
KILMARNOCK: McLaughlin; Richmond, Watson;
Beattie, Toner, Davidson; Muir, Yard, Black, McInally,
McIlroy

RANGERS: Ritchie; Shearer, Caldow; Davis, Baillie,
Baxter; Scott, Greig, Millar, Brand, Wilson
Attendance: 20,000

League positions

	P	W	D	L	F	A	Pts
1 Dundee	16	13	2	1	50	25	28
2 Celtic	16	10	2	4	44	19	22
3 RANGERS	15	9	3	3	38	19	21
4 Partick Thistle	17	10	1	6	37	32	21
5 Dunfermline	17	8	4	5	37	22	20

January 6th:
HIBERNIAN   (0) 0   RANGERS   (0) 0
HIBERNIAN: Simpson; Grant, McLelland; Preston,
Young, Baxter; Stevenson, Gibson, Baker, Falconer,
McLeod

RANGERS: Ritchie; Shearer, Caldow; Davis, Baillie,
Baxter; Scott, McMillan, Millar, Brand, Wilson
Attendance: 35,000

January 10th:
RANGERS   (0) 2   HEARTS   (0) 1
  Holt o.g. (48), Scott (51)   Davidson (59)
RANGERS: Ritchie; Shearer, Caldow; Davis, Baillie,
Baxter; Scott, McMillan, Millar, Brand, Wilson

HEARTS: Marshall; Kirk, Holt; Cumming, Polland,
Higgins; Ross, Hamilton, Davidson, Wallace, Gordon
Attendance: n.a.

January 13th:
RANGERS   (1) 4   ST MIRREN   (0) 0
  Caldow (27 pen), McMillan (47),
  Henderson (62), Murray (64)
RANGERS: Ritchie; Shearer, Caldow; Davis, Baillie,
Baxter; Henderson, McMillan, Murray, Brand, Wilson

ST MIRREN: Brown; Doonan, Wilson; Tierney,
Clunie, McTavish; Henderson, McLean, McDonald,
Nelson, Rodger
Attendance: 36,000

January 20th:
STIRLING ALBION   (0) 0   RANGERS   (3) 6
                                        Brand 2 (14, 77),
                                        Millar 3 (28, 35, 89),
                                        Caldow (56 pen)
STIRLING ALBION: J. Brown; D. Brown,
McGuiness; Rowan, Weir, Johnstone; Kilgannon,
Sinclair, Park, Maxwell, Bence

RANGERS: Ritchie; Shearer, Caldow; Davis, Baillie,
Baxter; Henderson, McMillan, Millar, Brand, Wilson
Attendance: 20,000

January 24th:
RANGERS   (0) 2   PARTICK THISTLE   (1) 1
  Brand (63), Millar (65)   Smith (27)

RANGERS: Ritchie; Shearer, Caldow; Davis, Baillie,
Baxter; Henderson, McMillan, Millar, Brand, Wilson

PARTICK THISTLE: Gray; Hogan, Brown; Harvey,
McKinnon, Cunningham; Ewing, McBride, Smith,
Duffy, McParland

Attendance: n.a.

January 31st:
AIRDRIE   (1) 2   RANGERS   (4) 5
  Newlands 2 (32, 89)   Greig 2 (3, 44),
                                Millar 2 (23, 51),
                                Brand (30)
AIRDRIE: Dempster; Shanks, McNeil; Reid,
Hannah, Stewart; Newlands, Storrie, Tees, Hume,
Duncan

RANGERS: Ritchie; Shearer, Caldow; Davis,
Paterson, Baxter; Henderson, Greig, Millar, Brand,
Wilson

Attendance: 12,000

February 3rd:
RANGERS   (0) 4   AIRDRIE   (0) 0
  Brand 2 (55, 71),
  Millar (88), Greig (89)
RANGERS: Ritchie; Shearer, King; Davis, Paterson,
Baxter; Scott, Greig, Millar, Brand, Wilson

AIRDRIE: Dempster; Shanks, Keenan; Reid,
Hannah, Stewart; Duncan, Murray, Conway, Tees,
Newlands

Attendance: 22,000

February 10th:
RAITH ROVERS   (0) 1   RANGERS   (2) 3
  Fox (71)   Brand 2 (9, 59),
                                Scott (23)
RAITH ROVERS: Thorburn; Wilson, Mochan; Stein,
Forsyth, Maguire; Adamson, Fox, Price, Clinton,
Watson

RANGERS: Ritchie; Shearer, King; Davis, Baillie,
Baxter; Scott, McMillan, Murray, Brand, Wilson
Attendance: 13,000

**February 15th: George Niven was transferred to
Partick Thistle.**

February 24th:
HEARTS   (0) 0   RANGERS   (0) 1
                                McMillan (64)
HEARTS: Marshall; Kirk, Holt; Polland, Cumming,
Higgins; Ferguson, Blackwood, Wallace, Gordon,
Hamilton

RANGERS: Ritchie; Shearer, Caldow; Davis, Baillie,
Baxter; Henderson, McMillan, Millar, Brand, Hume
Attendance: 30,000

League positions

	P	W	D	L	F	A	Pts
1 Dundee	24	18	3	3	62	36	39
2 RANGERS	24	17	4	3	65	24	38
3 Celtic	25	14	6	5	64	31	34
4 Hearts	26	14	5	7	47	37	33
5 Dunfermline	25	14	4	7	59	35	32

February 28th:
RANGERS   (2) 2   MOTHERWELL   (1) 1
  Millar (3), Scott (37)   Delaney (26)
RANGERS: Ritchie; Shearer, Caldow; Davis, Baillie,
Stevenson; Scott, McMillan, Millar, Brand, Murray

MOTHERWELL: Wylie; McSeveney, McCallum;
Aitken, Martis, McCann; Young, Quinn, Delaney,
Roberts, McPhee

Attendance: 40,000

Ritchie saved a penalty from Quinn two minutes from time

March 3rd:
RANGERS   (1) 3   THIRD LANARK   (0) 1
  Brand (26), Baxter (58),   Harley (78)
  Scott (74)
RANGERS: Ritchie; Shearer, Caldow; Davis, Baillie,
Baxter; Scott, Greig, Millar, Brand, Henderson

THIRD LANARK: Robertson; McGillivray,
Cunningham; Reilly, McCormack, Robb; Goodfellow,
Hilley, Harley, Gray, Fletcher

Attendance: 35,000

March 17th:
FALKIRK   (0) 1   RANGERS   (1) 7
  Duchart (50)   Wilson 6 (24, 47, 52,
                                55, 63, 82),
                                Scott (58)
FALKIRK: Whigham; Rae, Hunter; Thomson,
Milne, Pierson; Wilson, Harrower, Oliver, Duchart,
Tulloch

RANGERS: Ritchie; Shearer, Caldow; Millar, Davis, Baxter; Scott, McMillan, Wilson, Brand, Henderson
Attendance: 18,000

March 21st: Caldow, Scott, Millar, Brand and Wilson played for the Scottish League in a 4-3 victory over the English League at Villa Park. Wilson scored 3 goals and Brand got the other.

March 22nd: George McLean was transferred to Norwich City.

March 14th:
DUNDEE   0   RANGERS   0
DUNDEE: Liney; Hamilton, Cox; Seith, Ure, Brown; Smith, Penman, Waddell, Cousin, Robertson

RANGERS: Ritchie; Shearer, Caldow; Davis, Baillie, Baxter; Scott, McMillan, Millar, Brand, Wilson
Attendance: 35,000

March 24th:
RANGERS   (0) 0   DUNDEE UNITED   (1) 1
                                  Carlyle (15)

RANGERS: Ritchie; Shearer, Caldow; Millar, Davis, Baxter; Scott, McMillan, Wilson, Brand, Henderson

DUNDEE UNITED: Ugolini; Gordon, Briggs; Neilson, Roe, Fraser; Carlyle, Millar, Gillespie, Irvine, Mochan

Attendance: 28,000

March 31st: While Rangers were beating Motherwell in the Semi-Final of the Scottish Cup at Hampden Park, Jim Baxter was playing for the British Army against the Belgian Army.

April 4th:
ST JOHNSTONE   (0) 0   RANGERS   (1) 4
                                        Wilson (30),
                                        Greig 2 (50, 72),
                                        Brand (75)

ST JOHNSTONE: Taylor; McFadyen, Lachlan; Little, G. Ferguson, Donlevy; McIntyre, Wright, McKinven, A. Ferguson, McVittie

RANGERS: Ritchie; Shearer, Caldow; Davis, McKinnon, Baxter; Henderson, Greig, Murray, Brand, Wilson
Attendance: 15,500

April 7th:
RANGERS   (1) 1   DUNFERMLINE   (0) 0
   Murray (17)

RANGERS: Ritchie; Shearer, Caldow; Davis, McKinnon, Baxter; Scott, McMillan, Murray, Greig, Wilson

DUNFERMLINE: Herriot; Fraser, Cunningham; Thomson, McLean, Miller; McDonald, McLindon, Paton, Melrose, Peebles
Attendance: 41,000

April 9th:
CELTIC   (1) 1   RANGERS   (0) 1
   Hughes (43)   Wilson (78)

CELTIC: Haffey; Donnelly, Kennedy; McKay, McNeill, Clark; Chalmers, Carroll, Hughes, Divers, Brogan

RANGERS: Ritchie; Shearer, Caldow; Davis, McKinnon, Baxter; Henderson, Greig, Millar, Brand, Wilson

Rangers were outplayed for most of the game but were able to salvage the point which kept them ahead of the table. On a surface made treacherous by heavy rain Celtic adopted the proper tactics of moving the ball swiftly from man to man and employing their wingers to full advantage. The only Rangers forward who caused any discomfort to them was the diminutive Henderson. It was appropriate that Hughes should score Celtic's only goal of the game in 43 minutes for he frequently perplexed Rangers' defence. McKinnon had an unhappy match against him. In 78 minutes the persistent Wilson warded off the challenge of Haffey, who had rushed out to intercept, and trundled the ball into the net. Rangers deserved this goal, if only for their pluck.

April 14th: Caldow, Baxter, Scott and Wilson represented Scotland against England at Hampden Park. Wilson and Caldow, with a penalty, scored the goals in a 2-0 victory.

April 25th:
ABERDEEN   (0) 1   RANGERS   (0) 0
   Cummings (49)

ABERDEEN: Ogston; Shewan, Hogg; Brownlie, Kinnell, Fraser; Cummings, Little, Winchester, Cooke, Mulhall

RANGERS: Ritchie; Shearer, Caldow; Davis, McKinnon, Baxter; Henderson, McMillan, Millar, Brand, Wilson
Attendance: n.a.

April 27th: Johnny Little was given a free transfer.

April 28th:
RANGERS   (0) 1   KILMARNOCK   (0) 1
   Wilson (83)   Kerr (67)

RANGERS: Ritchie; Shearer, Caldow; Davis, McKinnon, Baxter; Scott, McMillan, Murray, Brand, Wilson

KILMARNOCK: McLaughlin; King, Richmond; Murray, McGrory, O'Connor; Brown, McInally, Kerr, Sneddon, Black

Attendance: n.a.

Scottish First Division

		P	W	D	L	F	A	Pts
1	Dundee	34	25	4	5	80	46	54
2	RANGERS	34	22	7	5	84	31	51
3	Celtic	34	19	8	7	81	37	46
4	Dunfermline	34	19	5	10	77	46	43
5	Kilmarnock	34	16	10	8	74	58	42
6	Hearts	34	16	6	12	54	49	38
7	Partick Thistle	34	16	3	15	60	55	35
8	Hibernian	34	14	5	15	58	72	33
9	Motherwell	34	13	6	15	65	62	32
10	Dundee United	34	13	6	15	70	71	32
11	Third Lanark	34	13	5	16	59	60	31
12	Aberdeen	34	10	9	15	60	73	29
13	Raith Rovers	34	10	7	17	51	73	27
14	Falkirk	34	11	4	19	45	68	26
15	Airdrie	34	9	7	18	57	78	25
16	St Mirren	34	10	5	19	52	80	25
17	St Johnstone	34	9	7	18	35	61	25
18	Stirling Albion	34	6	6	22	34	76	18

May 2nd: Caldow, Baxter, Scott, Brand and Wilson played for Scotland against Uruguay at Hampden Park. Baxter and Brand scored the goals in a 3-2 defeat.

June 24th: Billy Stevenson quit Ibrox and flew to Australia.

LEAGUE CUP

August 12th:
THIRD LANARK   (0) 0   RANGERS   (2) 2
                         Wilson 2 (9, 35)

THIRD LANARK: Robertson; McGillivray, Lewis; Reilly, McCormick, Robb; Bryce, Goodfellow, McCallum, Gray, McInnes

RANGERS: Ritchie; Shearer, Caldow; Davis, Paterson, Baxter; Scott, McMillan, Millar, Brand, Wilson

Attendance: 37,000

August 16th:
RANGERS   (2) 4   DUNDEE   (2) 2
  Brand 2 (4, 5½),   Penman (28),
  Wilson (72), Millar (85) Cousin (39)

RANGERS: Ritchie; Shearer, Caldow; Davis, Paterson, Baxter; Scott, McMillan, Millar, Brand, Wilson

DUNDEE: Liney; Hamilton, Cox; Seith, Ure, Wishart; McGeachie, Penman, Waddell, Cousin, Robertson

Attendance: 40,000

August 19th:
AIRDRIE   (1) 1   RANGERS   (1) 2
  Storrie (18)   Brand (25), Davis (89)

AIRDRIE: Beaton; Shanks, Kiernan; Hosie, Johnston, McNeil; Newlands, Storrie, Caven, Rankin, Duncan

RANGERS: Ritchie; Shearer, Caldow; Davis, Paterson, Baxter; Scott, McMillan, Millar, Brand, Wilson

Attendance: 20,000

August 26th:
RANGERS   (3) 5   THIRD LANARK   (0) 0
  Wilson 2 (15, 72), Brand (52),
  Millar (44), McGillivray o.g. (16)

RANGERS: Ritchie; Shearer, Caldow; Davis, Paterson, Baxter; Scott, McMillan, Millar, Brand, Wilson

THIRD LANARK: Robertson; McGillivray, Lewis; Reilly, McCormick, Cunningham; Goodfellow, Hilley, Harley, Gray, McInnes

Attendance: 35,000

August 30th:
DUNDEE   (1) 1   RANGERS   (1) 1
  Robertson (3)   Brand (30)

DUNDEE: Liney; Hamilton, Cox; Seith, Ure, Wishart; Smith, Penman, Gilzean, Cousin, Robertson

RANGERS: Ritchie; Shearer, Caldow; Davis, Paterson, Baxter; Scott, McMillan, Christie, Brand, Wilson

September 2nd:
RANGERS   (2) 4   AIRDRIE   (1) 1
  Greig (10), Christie (40), Storrie (20)
  Brand 2 (70, 75)

RANGERS: Ritchie; Shearer, Caldow; Stevenson, Paterson, Baxter; Scott, Greig, Christie, Brand, Wilson

AIRDRIE: Dempster; Shanks, Keenan; Rankin, Johnstone, McNeil; Newlands, Storrie, Tees, Caven, Duncan

Attendance: 32,000

League Cup Section Table

	P	W	D	L	F	A	Pts
RANGERS	6	5	1	0	18	5	11
Dundee	6	2	2	2	14	10	6
Third Lanark	6	2	2	2	10	14	6
Airdrie	6	0	1	5	5	18	1

September 13th: Quarter-Final First Leg

RANGERS   (2) 3   EAST FIFE   (0) 1
Davis (25), Christie 2 (34, 60)   Dewar (71)

RANGERS: Ritchie; Shearer, Caldow; Davis, Paterson, Baxter; Scott, Greig, Christie, Brand, Wilson

EAST FIFE: Donnelly; Stirrat, Morrison; Brown, Young, Bryce; Markie, Dewar, Yardley, Stewart, Ross

September 20th: Quarter-Final Second Leg

EAST FIFE   (0) 1   RANGERS   (2) 3
Dewar (86)   Wilson (5), Scott (17), Brand (88)

EAST FIFE: Donnelly; Stirrat, Morrison; Brown, Young, Bryce; Markie, Dewar, Yardley, Stewart, Ross

RANGERS: Ritchie; Shearer, Caldow; Davis, Paterson, Baxter; Scott, McMillan, Christie, Brand, Wilson

Attendance: 15,000

Rangers won 6-2 on aggregate

October 11th: Semi-Final   At Parkhead

RANGERS   (0) 3   ST JOHNSTONE   (2) 2
Wilson 2 (46, 103),   Gardiner (31),
Caldow (78 pen)   Bell (44)
       After Extra Time

Attendance: 41,000

RANGERS: Ritchie; Shearer, Caldow; Stevenson, Paterson, Baxter; Scott, McMillan, Millar, Brand, Wilson

ST JOHNSTONE: Taylor; McFadyen, Lachlan; Little, Ferguson, McKinven; McVittie, Walker, Gardiner, Bell, Henderson

Not until after 13 minutes of extra-time when Wilson scored the decisive goal was there a sign of relaxation of tension from which almost all of the Rangers players appeared to be suffering. Gardiner opened the scoring after 31 minutes' play when he headed past Ritchie from a free-kick by Little. Bell put his side further ahead just before the interval when, with a pass from Gardiner, he ran 20 yards unchallenged before shooting into the net. Rangers began the second half in determined fashion and within a minute scored. Scott crossed from the wing, Millar headed down and Wilson prodded into the net off the far post. The equalising goal was scored in 78 minutes when Scott was pulled down by Lachlan and Caldow beat Taylor with the penalty kick.

October 28th: Final   At Hampden Park

RANGERS   (1) 1   HEARTS   (0) 1
                After Extra Time
Millar (15)   Cumming (78 pen)

RANGERS: Ritchie; Shearer, Caldow; Davis, Paterson, Baxter; Scott, McMillan, Millar, Brand, Wilson

HEARTS: Marshall; Kirk, Holt; Cumming, Polland, Higgins; Ferguson, Elliot, Wallace, Gordon, Hamilton

Attendance: 90,000   *Referee*: R. H. Davidson (Airdrie)

Rangers had the advantage of a strong wind in the first half but they rarely achieved a good shot. The goal Millar scored in 15 minutes was accidental in that his shot-cum-cross from nearly 30 yards was allowed by Cumming to pass towards Marshall who apparently was not aware that he would be called upon to save. Had the sprightly Hamilton, easily the best forward of the 10, been able to conserve some of his energy for the late dour struggle, Hearts would probably have won. Davis and Paterson frequently profited from their physique. Davis seemed astounded when the referee awarded a penalty-kick in the 78th minute for his bustling Gordon out of the line of the ball as Hamilton crossed into goal. It was in extra-time, with the limping Millar on the right-wing and Scott at centre-forward, that Rangers gave Hearts most trouble. Millar deceived Marshall with a cross which floated against a post and Scott, more than once, almost scored.

December 18th: Final Replay   At Hampden Park

RANGERS   (3) 3   HEARTS   (1) 1
Millar (7), Brand (15),   Davidson (8)
McMillan (19)

RANGERS: Ritchie; Shearer, Caldow; Davis, Baillie, Baxter; Scott, McMillan, Millar, Brand, Wilson

HEARTS: Cruikshank; Kirk, Holt; Cumming, Polland, Higgins; Ferguson, Davidson, Bauld, Blackwood, Hamilton

Attendance: 47,500   *Referee*: R. H. Davidson (Airdrie)

Rangers convincingly defeated Hearts in a fog-threatened match. Baxter and McMillan inspired their colleagues with smooth ground-passing. Millar headed the opening goal from Scott's cross in the 7th minute after a succession of escapes for Hearts who most unexpectedly equalised in the next minute when Davidson headed a free-kick out of Ritchie's reach. But in the 15th and 19th minutes Brand and McMillan headed and shot further goals for Rangers, the pace and thrust of whose wingers constantly menaced Hearts. McMillan suffered a leg injury midway through the second half and much of the rhythm departed from Rangers' play. Nevertheless they struck the crossbar or post 3 times thereafter — Scott, Brand and Wilson were the unlucky players and Cruikshank had to make half-a-dozen saves to Ritchie's one. Baillie was commanding. He was not beaten once on the ground or in the air by the various Hearts players pitted against him.

SCOTTISH CUP

December 13th: First Round
FALKIRK (1) 1   RANGERS (1) 2
  Caldow o.g. (14)   Millar (7),
                                 Wilson (53)

FALKIRK: Whigham; Rae, Hunter; Pierson, Thomson, McIntosh; Reid, Murray, Oliver, Innes, Duchart

RANGERS: Ritchie; Shearer, Caldow, Davis, Baillie, Stevenson; Scott, McMillan, Millar, Brand, Wilson

Attendance: n.a.

January 27th: Second Round
RANGERS (4) 6   ARBROATH (0) 0
  Millar 3 (25, 43, 81),
  Brand 2 (28, 84), Glasgow o.g. (26)

RANGERS: Ritchie; Shearer, Caldow; Davis, Paterson, Baxter; Henderson, McMillan, Millar, Brand, Wilson

ARBROATH: Thomson; Glasgow, Lough; Robertson, Fraser, Kennedy; Matthew, McMillan, Easson, Gourlay, Gillespie

Attendance: 31,908

February 17th: Third Round
ABERDEEN (1) 2   RANGERS (1) 2
  Kinnell (23 pen),   Caldow (39 pen),
  Little (84)   Brand (79)

ABERDEEN: Ogston; Bennett, Hogg; Burns, Kinnell, Fraser; Ewen, Little, Cummings, Cooke, Mulhall

RANGERS: Ritchie; Shearer, Caldow; Davis, Baillie, Baxter; Henderson, Greig, Millar, Brand, Wilson

Caldow missed a penalty

Attendance: n.a.

February 21st: Third Round Replay
RANGERS (3) 5   ABERDEEN (1) 1
  McMillan (14),   Cummings (10)
  Millar 2 (15, 76)
  Wilson (23), Brand (62)

RANGERS: Ritchie; Shearer, Caldow; Davis, Baillie, Baxter; Henderson, McMillan, Millar, Brand, Wilson

ABERDEEN: Ogston; Bennett, Hogg; Brownlee, Kinnell, Fraser; Ewen, Little, Cummings, Cooke, Mulhall

Attendance: 57,000

March 10th: Fourth Round
KILMARNOCK (1) 2   RANGERS (1) 4
  Kerr (11), Black (78)   Caldow (44 pen),
                                 McMillan 2 (62, 81),
                                 Brand (88)

KILMARNOCK: McLaughlin; Richmond, Watson; Davidson, Toner, Beattie; Brown, Black, Kerr, Sneddon, McIlroy

RANGERS: Ritchie; Shearer, Caldow; Davis, Baillie, Baxter; Scott, McMillan, Millar, Brand, Wilson

Attendance: 36,500

March 31st: Semi-Final   At Hampden Park
RANGERS (2) 3   MOTHERWELL (0) 1
  Murray 2 (38, 41),   Roberts (52)
  Wilson (89)

RANGERS: Ritchie; Shearer, Caldow; Davis, Paterson, McKinnon; Henderson, McMillan, Murray, Brand, Wilson

MOTHERWELL: Wylie; McSeveney, Thomson; Aitken, Martis, McCann; Hunter, Quinn, Delaney, McPhee, Roberts

Attendance: 84,321

McCann was carried off on a stretcher in the 15th minute after a tackle by Shearer. Having been in the pavilion for 20 minutes, he returned 10 minutes from half-time but was unable to do more than occupy a position on the right wing. Yet not until Wilson scored Rangers' 3rd goal in the 88th minute was Motherwell's bid for a replay extinguished. Murray scored the first goal in the 38th minute. Rangers' best forwards throughout the match were the wingers. It was Wilson who made Murray's first goal and Henderson who contrived the second in 41 minutes. Newcomer McKinnon was clearly the most accomplished Rangers half-back. Roberts shot a well-deserved goal from Delaney's pass in 52 minutes. As the crowd were making for the exits Wilson, cutting in from the wing, evaded 2 tackles and shot a magnificent goal with his right foot.

April 21st: Final   At Hampden Park
RANGERS (1) 2   ST MIRREN (0) 0
  Brand (40), Wilson (57)

RANGERS: Ritchie; Shearer, Caldow; Davis, McKinnon, Baxter; Henderson, McMillan, Millar, Brand, Wilson

ST MIRREN: Williamson; Campbell, Wilson; Stewart, Clunie, McLean; Henderson, Bryceland, Kerrigan, Fernie, Beck

Attendance: 126,930   *Referee*: T. Wharton (Clarkston)

After Wilson put Rangers 2 ahead in the 57th minute the probability of them increasing this lead was the one remaining factor of special interest. In the hour that elapsed until then only superlative defence — by Williamson and Clunie in particular — and the inability of

Rangers to score more than one goal from dozens of attractive opportunities had kept the final a contest. Henderson, the youngest player of the 22, provided most of the entertainment. St Mirren held out until the 40th minute. Wilson's shot was passing across goal when his namesake and Brand challenged for the ball which the inside-left prodded over the line after he had fallen.

EUROPEAN CUP

September 5th: Preliminary Round First Leg
A.S. MONACO   (0) 2   RANGERS   (2) 3
   Hess (60), Carlier (72 pen)   Baxter (10),
                                    Scott 2 (25, 85)

A.S. MONACO: Hernandez; Novak, Artelesa; Biancher, Ludo, Hidalgo; Djibrill, Hess, Dovis, Theo, Carlier

RANGERS: Ritchie; Shearer, Caldow; Davis, Paterson, Baxter; Scott, McMillan, Millar, Brand, Wilson

Attendance: 7,000

Rangers were both brilliant and careless and the final score gives no indication of their superiority. They baffled and bewildered the home defenders with remarkable ball control and passing accuracy. Rangers lost 2 goals inside 12 minutes and had to dispense with their fineries and fight for the goal which would give them a tremendous moral advantage for the second leg. The match will be remembered as Baxter's finest for the club. The left-half would continually bring the ball from defence to attack and scored their first goal after 10 minutes with a 20-yard shot which rose no more than a foot from the ground. Scott scored a 2nd in 25 minutes after a lob from Baxter had been only partially cleared by Hernandez. Monaco's Hess hooked home after 60 minutes. Their 2nd goal came from a penalty-kick taken by Carlier after Hess had been brought down by both Shearer and Paterson. Ritchie cleverly blocked his shot but he followed up to score. Scott headed the winner 5 minutes from the end.

September 12th: Preliminary Round Second Leg
RANGERS   (0) 3   A.S. MONACO   (1) 2
   Christie 2 (48, 67), Scott (81)   Hess 2 (18, 77)

RANGERS: Ritchie; Shearer, Caldow; Davis, Paterson, Baxter; Scott, McMillan, Christie, Brand, Wilson

A.S. MONACO: Garafalo; Novak, Thomas; Artelesa, Ludo, Biancher; Djibrill, Hess, Dovis, Hidalgo, Carlier

Attendance: 65,000

Rangers won 6-4 on aggregate

Monaco neutralised Rangers' lead of a goal as early as the 18th minute. Scott, who caused the French team most worry, scored the decisive goal 9 minutes from time. Ludo called for the ball from a throw-in. With only Christie in

the vicinity he unwisely tried to dribble round the centre-forward. The ball rebounded past him off Christie's legs and Scott, racing in from the wing, ran all of 40 yards prodding the ball in front of him before he enticed the goalkeeper out and made the score 3-2. 2 minutes earlier Monaco had lost Dovis injured. Just before the centre-forward was assisted off they had scored a 2nd goal headed by Hess, when Carlier beat Shearer and crossed as he ran. Christie, with almost his first unchallenged kick of the ball, scored Rangers' first goal in 48 minutes when Brand head-flicked to him a free-kick taken by Scott. Christie scored his 2nd goal 22 minutes after half-time when he intercepted Novak's weak back pass.

November 15th: First Round First Leg in East Berlin
   ASK VORWAERTS   (1) 1   RANGERS   (2) 2
   Kohle (27)   Caldow (26 pen),
                              Brand (44)

ASK VORWAERTS: Spickenagel; Kalinke, Krampe; Prufke, Kiupel, Korner; Hoge, Kohle, Vogt, Noldner, Wirth

RANGERS: Ritchie; Shearer, Caldow; Davis, Paterson, Baxter; Scott, McMillan, Millar, Brand, Wilson

Attendance: 20,000

Rangers had little difficulty in winning the first match of their tie with Vorwaerts. Brand recovered the form which had been missing from his displays of the last few weeks but the main burden of attack fell on Millar, whose fitness was suspect. 2 minutes before half-time Baxter delighted a sporting and appreciative crowd of 20,000 by bringing the ball deep into the German lines, outflanking 2 defenders and making such a splendid cross that Brand had a simple task of heading in a goal which made the score 2-1. Earlier in the 27th minute Kohle had gone striding through to score a goal which Ritchie might have saved, and immediately afterwards Scott was brought down by Krampe. Caldow scored with the penalty.

November 22nd: First Round Second Leg
RANGERS   1   ASK VORWAERTS   0
   Henderson (36)

Attendance: 4,000

Abandoned after 45 minutes due to fog

The East Germans were refused visas and the match was played in Malmo, Sweden.

November 23rd: First Round Second Leg (Re-arranged Match) in Malmo, Sweden
RANGERS   (0) 4   ASK VORWAERTS   (0) 1
   Kalinke o.g. (50),   Caldow o.g.
   McMillan 2 (63, 80),
   Henderson (83)

RANGERS: Ritchie; Shearer, Caldow; Davis, Paterson, Baxter; Henderson, McMillan, Millar, Brand, Wilson

ASK VORWAERTS: Spickenagel; Kalinke, Krampe; Unger, Kiupel, Korner; Hoge, Karrow, Vogt, Noldner, Wirth

Attendance: 1,781

Rangers won 6-2 on aggregate

Paterson pulled a muscle and is likely to be out of action for 3/4 weeks. Wilson aggravated a previous thigh muscle injury and might miss next week's World Cup Qualifying Decider with the Czechs in Brussels. The Rangers forwards took all of 67 minutes to find a way past the East Germans, but once they scored goals came easily and in the end Vorwaerts were a tired and dispirited team. 5 minutes after the start of the second half Kalinke miskicked a cross from Henderson through his own goal, and after 63 minutes McMillan scored the first of 2 splendid goals with a drive from 18 yards. The inside-right scored with a similar shot from the same distance 10 minutes from time. 7 minutes from the end Henderson scored his first goal in a European tie. Caldow had once again the misfortune to score against his own side with the score 2-0 — miskicking a cross from Wirth past Ritchie.

February 7th: Quarter-Final First Leg
STANDARD LIEGE (2) 4   RANGERS (1) 1
  Claesson (6),   Wilson (19)
  Crossan 2 (42, 50),
  Vliers (54)

STANDARD LIEGE: Nicolay; Vliers, Marchal; Bonga-Bonga, Spronck, Houff; Semmeling, Sztani, Claesson, Crossan, Paeschen

RANGERS: Ritchie; Shearer, King; Davis, Paterson, Baxter; Henderson, Greig, Millar, Brand, Wilson

Attendance: 37,000

Rangers had King at left-back in place of Caldow, who was withdrawn with an injured toe just before the kick-off. They had two 18-year olds, Henderson and Greig, on the right-wing. The most annoying aspect of the defeat was that Standard were slow in defence and not particularly inspiring in attack although they took their goals smartly when the opportunities arose. Within 6 minutes Claesson scored after a shot from Paeschen bounced off Ritchie's chest. Wilson scored a splendid goal after 19 minutes with a shot from 12 yards from a Millar pass. Crossan hit a glorious 2nd goal past Ritchie from 20 yards and Rangers were 2-1 down at half-time. 5 minutes after the restart Paterson, a most uncertain centre-half, was beaten in the air by Sztani and Crossan again scored with a snap shot from 14 yards. Rangers were in serious trouble 4 minutes later. Paterson clashed with Claesson on the 18-yard line and the free-kick by Vliers struck Davis on the thigh and sped past Ritchie.

February 14th: Quarter-Final Second Leg
RANGERS (1) 2   STANDARD LIEGE (0) 0
  Brand (28), Caldow (88 pen)

RANGERS: Ritchie; Shearer, Caldow; Davis, Baillie, Baxter; Scott, McMillan, Millar, Brand, Wilson

STANDARD LIEGE: Nicolay; Vliers, Theilen; Bonga-Bonga, Marchal, Houff; Semmeling, Sztani, Claesson, Crossan, Paeschen

Attendance: 76,000

Standard Liège won 4-3 on aggregate

The pitch was slippery and mistakes inevitable yet the pitch proved no excuse for the poor football both sides played. In the 28th minute Brand scored with one of the few shots of power and accuracy. Early in the second half McMillan struck the crossbar. 2 minutes from time Rangers were awarded a penalty-kick for handling from which Caldow scored. Henderson was held up in traffic and missed the game. His replacement, Scott, was played out of the game by Theilen.

APPEARANCES

	League	League Cup	Scottish Cup	Glasgow Cup	Friendlies	European Cup
Ritchie	34	11	7	-	4	6
Shearer	34	11	7	1	4	6
Caldow	29	11	7	-	4	5
Davis	33	9	7	1	4	6
Paterson	11	10	2	-	1	5
Baxter	29	11	5	-	1	6
Scott	23	11	2	-	4	4
McMillan	24	9	6	1	4	5
Millar	23	7	6	1	4	5
Brand	33	11	7	-	4	6
Wilson	29	11	7	-	4	6
Christie	3	4	-	-	-	1
Provan	3	-	-	-	-	-
Stevenson	5	2	1	-	-	-
McKinnon	6	-	2	1	3	-
Baillie	16	1	4	-	-	1
Henderson	15	-	5	1	2 sub	2
Greig	11	2	1	1	3	1
Murray	8	-	1	1	2 sub	-
Hume	3	-	-	1	-	-
King	2	-	-	1	-	1
Martin	-	-	1	-	-	-

George Niven, the Rangers goalkeeper in the fifties.

GOALSCORERS

*League:*Brand 23 (1 pen), Wilson 15, Millar 15, Scott 7, Greig 7, McMillan 4, Christie 3, Caldow 3 (3 pens), Murray 3, Baxter 2, Henderson 1, Own Goals 1

League Cup: Brand 9, Wilson 8, Millar 4, Christie 3, Davis 2, Scott 1, McMillan 1, Greig 1, Caldow 1 (pen), Own Goals 1

Scottish Cup: Brand 6, Millar 6, Wilson 4, McMillan 3, Murray 2, Caldow 2 (2 pens), Own Goals 1

Glasgow Cup: Shearer 1

Friendlies: Brand 2, Davis 2, McMillan 1, Wilson 1, Henderson 1

European Cup: Scott 3, Christie 2, Brand 2, McMillan 2, Caldow 2 (2 pens), Wilson 1, Henderson 1, Baxter 1, Own Goals 1

Eric Caldow, the victorious Rangers' captain in the 1964 Scottish Cup Final shows the Cup to the fans. Bob Kelly, the Celtic Chairman looks on.

Season 1962-63

Both the League Championship and the Scottish Cup were won. Only 2 league matches were lost during the season — away to Dundee United in November and to runners-up Kilmarnock 6 months later. 9 points separated the top two. Kilmarnock were beaten 6-1 at Ibrox in December. Celtic were beaten 4-0 in the Ne'erday game. George McLean was signed from St Mirren for a record fee between Scottish clubs and both Alec Scott and Max Murray were transferred south of the border. Shearer was the only player to appear in all 34 League matches. Millar scored 27 goals, Wilson 23 and Brand 19.

Rangers reached the Semi-Final of the League Cup but a goal by Kilmarnock's Black, 8 minutes from time, won the match for his team after Rangers had led 2-1 at one stage.

In the Scottish Cup, Rangers' tie with Dundee proved to be their most difficult in their march to the Final. A goal from Brand, two minutes from time, won the replay at Ibrox which was watched by a crowd of 81,190. The Final against Celtic also went to a replay but after the first match, in which Celtic goalkeeper Haffey was the hero for his team, Celtic were not only defeated but completely outclassed. Brand scored 12 goals in the competition including 2 in the replayed Final.

Seville were beaten in the First Round of the Cup Winners' Cup. The second leg of the tie developed into a pitched battle with a number of Rangers players being assaulted. The eventual trophy winners, Tottenham Hotspur, proved too strong in the second round and ran out 8-4 aggregate winners.

Jim Baxter, Willie Henderson and Davie Wilson all played major roles in Scotland's win over England at Wembley after Eric Caldow was carried off in the 6th minute with a triple fracture of the left leg.

    League: Champions
    League Cup: Semi-Finalists
    Scottish Cup: Winners
    Cup Winners Cup: Second Round

SCOTTISH FIRST DIVISION

August 22nd:
RANGERS (1) 3   ST MIRREN (0) 0
    Wilson o.g. (3), Brand (50),
    Millar (81)

RANGERS: Ritchie; Shearer, Caldow; Davis, McKinnon, Baxter; Henderson, McMillan, Millar, Brand, Scott

ST MIRREN: Williamson; Murray, Wilson; Campbell, Clunie, McTavish; Kerrigan, Bryceland, Beck, McLean, Robertson

Attendance: 46,000

September 8th:
CELTIC (0) 0   RANGERS (0) 1
                        Henderson (84)

CELTIC: Haffey; McKay, Kennedy; Crerand, McNeill, Price; Lennox, Gallagher, Hughes, Murdoch, Byrne

RANGERS: Ritchie; Shearer, Caldow; Davis, McKinnon, Baxter; Henderson, Greig, Millar, Brand, Wilson

Attendance: 72,000

With 6 minutes remaining for play Henderson, operating on the left flank, had the better of a tackle with McKay, shook himself free of the back's despairing clutch at his jersey and shot from about 10 yards. It was not a powerful shot and Haffey had it covered but in the goalmouth flurry the ball was deflected the other way. Kennedy, with a despairing lunge, could do no more than batter it into the net. McKinnon was less than comfortable against Hughes who, however, seldom got the ball in open space. After half-an-hour's play Crerand seriously tested Ritchie from long range. Then he strode powerfully into Rangers' penalty-area where Brand, in hot pursuit, tripped him. After some delay while several Rangers players argued that the ball was not placed exactly on the spot, Crerand took the responsibility. Ritchie saw the ball coming all the way and pushed it round his left-hand post.

September 14th: Bobby Hume was transferred to Middlesbrough for £10,000.

September 15th:
RANGERS	(2) 2	PARTICK THISTLE	(1) 1
Millar 2 (41, 45)		McBride (26)	

RANGERS: Ritchie; Shearer, Caldow; Greig, McKinnon, Baxter; Henderson, McMillan, Millar, Brand, Wilson

PARTICK THISTLE: Niven; Hogan, Brown; Ferguson, Harvey, Cunningham; Smith, Whitelaw, McBride, Duffy, McParland

Attendance: 52,000

September 21st: Rangers freed Bill Paterson.

September 22nd:
HIBERNIAN	(1) 1	RANGERS	(2) 5
McCreadie (38)		Millar 2 (14, 61),	
		Baxter (17),	
		Wilson 2 (63, 70 pen)	

HIBERNIAN: Simpson; Fraser, McCelland; Preston, Easton, Baxter; E. Stevenson, Baker, McCreadie, Byrne, McLeod

RANGERS: Ritchie; Shearer, Caldow; Greig, McKinnon, Baxter; Henderson, McMillan, Millar, Brand, Wilson

Attendance: 27,000

September 29th:
RANGERS	(0) 1	DUNDEE	(0) 1
Millar (55)		Roberston (73)	

RANGERS: Ritchie; Shearer, Caldow; Davis, McKinnon, Baxter; Henderson, Greig, Millar, Brand, Wilson

DUNDEE: Liney; Hamilton, Cox; Seith, Ure, Wishart; Smith, Penman, Cousin, Gilzean, Robertson

Attendance: 57,000

October 6th:
QUEEN OF THE SOUTH	(0) 0	RANGERS	(1) 4
		Millar 2 (35, 58),	
		Brand 2 (70, 75)	

QUEEN OF THE SOUTH: Farm; Kerr, Morrison; Irving, Rugg, Murphy; Hannigan, Frye, Garrett, Anderson, McLean

RANGERS: Ritchie; Shearer, Caldow; Davis, McKinnon, Baxter; Henderson, Greig, Millar, Brand, Wilson

Attendance: 20,000

October 13th:
RANGERS	(3) 5	AIRDRIE	(2) 2
Millar 2 (15, 43),		Duncan (11),	
Wilson (31 pen),		Murray (35)	
McMillan (59), Greig (71)			

RANGERS: Ritchie; Shearer, Caldow; Greig, McKinnon, Baxter; Henderson, McMillan, Millar, Brand, Wilson

AIRDRIE: Samson; Shanks, Keenan; Stewart, Hannah, Reid; Murray, Rowan, Tees, Duncan, Coats

Attendance: 28,000

October 19th: Liverpool signed Billy Stevenson for £20,000.

October 20th: Scotland beat Wales 3-2 in Cardiff. Caldow, Baxter, Henderson and Wilson were in the team. Caldow scored with a penalty and Henderson scored what proved to be the winner.

October 23rd:
THIRD LANARK	(1) 1	RANGERS	(2) 4
Gray (5)		Henderson 2 (13, 49),	
		Wilson (30),	
		Brand (70)	

THIRD LANARK: McKinlay; McGillivray, Cunniningham; Stenhouse, McCormick, Lewis; Goodfellow, Reilly, Dennison, Gray, Curran

RANGERS: Ritchie; Shearer, Caldow; Davis, McKinnon, Baxter; Henderson, McMillan, Millar, Brand, Wilson

Wilson missed a penalty

Attendance: 20,000

October 27th:
ABERDEEN	(1) 2	RANGERS	(2) 3
Cummings 2 (16, 53)		Millar (2), Wilson (4),	
		Greig (81)	

ABERDEEN: Ogston; Bennett, Hogg; Kinnell, Coutts, Smith; Cummings, Allan, Winchester, Cooke, Little

RANGERS: Ritchie; Shearer, Caldow; Davis, McKinnon, Baxter; Henderson, Greig, Millar, Brand, Wilson
Attendance: 40,000

League positions

	P	W	D	L	F	A	Pts
1 RANGERS	9	8	1	0	28	8	17
2 Hearts	8	6	2	0	26	10	14
3 Celtic	9	6	1	2	19	7	13
4 Dunfermline	9	6	1	2	21	9	13
5 Partick Thistle	9	6	1	2	21	11 , 13

November 3rd:
RANGERS   (1) 1   DUNFERMLINE   (1) 1
  Wilson (19 pen)   Cunningham (32 pen)
RANGERS: Ritchie; Shearer, McKinnon; Davis, Baillie, Baxter; Henderson, Greig, Millar, Brand, Wilson

DUNFERMLINE: Herriot; Callaghan, Cunningham; Thomson, McLean, Miller; Sinclair, Smith, McLindon, Melrose, Peebles
Attendance: 38,000

November 7th: Scotland beat Ireland 5–1 at Hampden Park. Caldow, Baxter and Henderson played. Henderson scored one of the goals.

November 10th:
DUNDEE UNITED   (1) 2   RANGERS   (1) 1
  Carlyle (23), Irvine (83)   Greig (36)
DUNDEE UNITED: Davie; Millar, Briggs; Neilson, Smith, Fraser; Carlyle, Gillespie, Mochan, Irvine, Mitchell

RANGERS: Ritchie; Shearer, Caldow; Davis, Baillie, McKinnon; Henderson, Greig, Millar, Baxter, Wilson
Attendance: 24,000

November 14th: Baxter, Henderson and Millar represented the Scottish League against the Italian League in Rome. Millar scored one of the goals in a 4–3 defeat.

November 17th:
RANGERS   (1) 4   FALKIRK   (0) 0
  Millar 2 (41, 49),
  Wilson (79), Greig (83)
RANGERS: Ritchie; Shearer, Caldow; McKinnon, Baillie, Baxter; Henderson, Greig, Forrest, Millar, Wilson

FALKIRK: Whigham; Rae, Hunter; Pierson, Thomson, McCarry; Henderson, Lambie, Davidson, Fulton, Adams
Attendance: 18,000

November 21st: Max Murray joined West Bromwich Albion for £15,000.

November 24th:
RANGERS   (1) 3   CLYDE   (1) 1
  Brand 2 (38, 50),   Muir (13)
  Millar (70)
RANGERS: Ritchie; Shearer, Caldow; Davis, Baillie, Baxter; Henderson, McMillan, Millar, Brand, Wilson

CLYDE: McCulloch; McDonald, Finnigan; White, Malloy, McHugh; McLean, Hood, Grant, Colrain, Muir
Attendance: 26,000

December 1st:
MOTHERWELL   (1) 1   RANGERS   (0) 1
  McBride (20)   Davis (87)
MOTHERWELL: Wylie; Thomson, R. McCallum; Aitken, Martis, Roberts; Lindsay, McBride, Russell, McCann, Weir

RANGERS: Ritchie; Shearer, Caldow; Davis, McKinnon, Greig; Scott, McMillan, Millar, Brand, Wilson
Attendance: 18,000

December 8th:
RANGERS   (4) 6   KILMARNOCK   (1) 1
  Wilson (3), Millar (10),   Black (38)
  Brand 3 (23, 44, 69),
  Henderson (77)
RANGERS: Ritchie; Shearer, Caldow; Davis, McKinnon, Baxter; Henderson, McMillan, Millar, Brand, Wilson

KILMARNOCK: McLaughlin; Richmond, Watson; O'Connor, McGrory, Beattie; Brown, Sneddon, Kerr, Hamilton, Black
Attendance: 40,000

December 15th:
RANGERS   (4) 4   RAITH ROVERS   (1) 2
  Wilson (11),   Caven (1),
  Brand 3 (16 pen, 22, 33)   Adamson (52)
RANGERS: Ritchie; Shearer, McKinnon; Davis, Baillie, Baxter; Henderson, McMillan, Forrest, Brand, Wilson

RAITH ROVERS: Thorburn; Stevenson, Haig; Stein, Forsyth, Clinton; Connor, Smith, Caven, Aitken, Adamson
Attendance: 16,000

December 19th: Rangers invited offers for Baxter, Scott, King and Penman.

December 29th:
ST MIRREN   (0) 0   RANGERS   (2) 2
                                    Scott (7), Millar (35)

ST MIRREN: Williamson; Murray, Wilson; R. Campbell, Clunie, McTavish; Ross, McLean, White, Beck, Robertson

RANGERS: Ritchie; Shearer, Caldow; Davis, McKinnon, Baxter; Scott, McMillan, Millar, Brand, Wilson

Attendance: 21,000

League positions

	P	W	D	L	F	A	Pts
1 RANGERS	17	13	3	1	50	16	29
2 Partick Thistle	17	13	2	2	37	16	28
3 Aberdeen	17	10	4	3	43	18	24
4 Hearts	16	9	6	1	42	19	24
5 Celtic	18	9	4	5	33	17	22

January 1st:
RANGERS   (1) 4   CELTIC   (0) 0
Davis (12), Millar (68),
Greig (70), Wilson (80)

RANGERS: Ritchie; Shearer, Caldow; Davis, McKinnon, Baxter; Scott, Greig, Millar, Brand, Wilson

CELTIC: Haffey; McKay, Kennedy; Crerand, McNeill, Price; Chalmers, Murdoch, Hughes, Gallagher, Brogan

Attendance: 55,000

This was a fine display from Rangers. They took the lead with a freakish goal by Davis in the 12th minute. But in 12 minutes from the 68th to the 80th, Millar, Greig and Wilson severely punished a defence that had been vulnerable throughout. Rangers — Davis, Baxter, Millar and Wilson in particular — played much splendid football on a ground which was iron-hard and slippery. Brogan was far and away the best Celtic player. The outside-left received nothing of the service, however, on which Wilson prospered. Davis's scoring shot struck Crerand and was diverted out of Haffey's reach and he could not hold Brand's shot before Millar scored. The goalkeeper had not the slightest chance of saving the 3rd or 4th goals.

January 10th: Rangers agreed to swop Willie Penman for Bobby Hope of West Bromwich Albion.

January 16th: Penman called off the deal.

January 23rd: George McLean was signed from St Mirren for a record fee of £26,500.

February 7th: Alex Scott was transferred to Everton for £46,000.

February 12th: Rangers chairman John Wilson died.

February 26th: John Lawrence was appointed as Rangers chairman.

League positions

	P	W	D	L	F	A	Pts
1 RANGERS	18	14	3	1	54	16	31
2 Partick Thistle	19	14	3	2	40	18	31
3 Kilmarnock	21	11	5	5	58	28	27
4 Aberdeen	20	11	4	5	45	24	26
5 Celtic	21	11	4	6	41	23	26

March 9th:
DUNFERMLINE   (1) 1   RANGERS   (0) 2
Sinclair (44)   Wilson (73),
                                   Millar (89)

DUNFERMLINE: Herriot; Callaghan, Cunningham; Thomson, McLean, Miller; Peebles, Sinclair, Smith, Paton, Melrose

RANGERS: Ritchie; Shearer, Caldow; Greig, McKinnon, Baxter; Henderson, McLean, Millar, Brand, Wilson

Attendance: 22,500

March 16th:
RANGERS   (5) 5   DUNDEE UNITED   (0) 0
Millar 4 (8, 17, 19, 28),
Brand (26)

RANGERS: Ritchie; Shearer, Caldow; Greig, McKinnin, Baxter; Henderson, McLean, Millar, Brand, Wilson

DUNDEE UNITED: Davie; Millar, Briggs; Neilson, Smith, Fraser; Carlyle, Gillespie, Howieson, Irvine, Mitchell

Attendance: 32,000

March 23rd:
FALKIRK   (0) 0   RANGERS   (0) 2
                                   Henderson (52),
                                   McLean (59)

FALKIRK: Whigham; Rae, Hunter; McCarry, Thomson, Pierson; Maxwell, Fulton, Bain, Harrower, Ormond

RANGERS: Ritchie; Shearer, Caldow; Greig, McKinnon, Baxter; Henderson, McLean, Millar, Brand, Wilson

Attendance: 16,500

March 27th:
HEARTS   (0) 0   RANGERS   (1) 5
                                   Millar 2 (35, 87),
                                   McLean (59),
                                   Wilson 2 (78, 89)

HEARTS: Cruikshank; Polland, Holt; Ferguson, Barry, Higgins; Rodger, W. Hamilton, Wallace, Gordon, J. Hamilton

RANGERS: Ritchie; Shearer, Caldow; Greig, McKinnon, Baxter; Henderson, McLean, Millar, Brand, Wilson

Attendance: 35,000

April 4th: Willie Penman was transferred to Newcastle United for £11,500.

April 6th: Jim Baxter scored both of Scotland's goals in a 2-1 win against England at Wembley. Eric Caldow was carried off with a broken leg after a collision with Bobby Smith. Henderson and Wilson were also in the team.

April 10th:
RANGERS (2) 3   HIBERNIAN (0) 1
  Wilson 2 (14, 20), Brand (88)   Baker (89)

RANGERS: Ritchie; Shearer, Provan; Greig, McKinnon, Baxter; Henderson, McLean, Millar, Brand, Wilson

HIBERNIAN: Simpson; Cameron, McClelland; Grant, Toner, Leishman; M. Stevenson, Byrne, Baker, Preston, E. Stevenson

Attendance: 25,000

April 17th:
PARTICK THISTLE (1) 1   RANGERS (3) 4
  Duffy (35)   Wilson 4 (10, 28, 40, 48)

PARTICK THISTLE: Niven; Muir, Brown; Closs, Harvey, Cunningham; Cowan, Fleming, Smith, Duffy, McParland

RANGERS: Ritchie; Shearer, Provan; Greig, McKinnon, Baxter; Henderson, McLean, Millar, Brand, Wilson

Attendance: n.a.

April 20th:
RAITH ROVERS (2) 2   RANGERS (0) 2
  McGrogan (1),   Haig o.g. (52),
  Stevenson (24 pen)   Millar (55)

RAITH ROVERS: Thorburn; Stevenson, Haig; Wilson, Bolton, Burrows; Lourie, McDonald, Gilfillan, Menzies, McGrogan

RANGERS: Ritchie; Shearer, Provan; Greig, McKinnon, Baxter; Henderson, McLean, Millar, Brand, Wilson

Attendance: 10,000

April 27th:
RANGERS (3) 5   HEARTS (1) 1
  Baxter 2 (6, 61), Holt o.g. (25), Ferguson (12)
  Brand (45), Wilson (69)

RANGERS: Ritchie; Shearer, Provan; Greig, McKinnon, Baxter; Henderson, McLean, Millar, Brand, Wilson

HEARTS: Marshall; Shevlane, Holt; Ferguson, Barry, Higgins; J. Hamilton, W. Hamilton, Wallace, Gordon, Cumming

Attendance: 40,000

April 29th:
RANGERS (1) 1   MOTHERWELL (0) 1
  Wilson (26)   McBride (69)

RANGERS: Ritchie; Shearer, Provan; Greig, McKinnon, Baxter; Henderson, McLean, Forrest, Brand, Wilson

MOTHERWELL: Wylie; Delaney, M. Thomson; Aitken, Martis, McCann; Lindsay, Roberts, McBride, I. Thomson, Weir

Attendance: n.a.

May 6th:
AIRDRIE (0) 0   RANGERS (1) 2
                          Baxter (42),
                          Brand (47)

AIRDRIE: Samson; Jonquin, Keenan; Rowan, Hannah, Reid; McColl, Newlands, Tees, Murray, Shanks

RANGERS: Ritchie; Shearer, Provan; Greig, McKinnon, Baxter; Henderson, Watson, Millar, Brand, Wilson

Attendance: 6,500

May 8th: Scotland beat Austria 4-1 at Hampden Park. The match was abandoned by the referee in the 83rd minute because of the violent play of the Austrians. Baxter, Henderson, Millar and Henderson played. Wilson scored 2 goals.

May 11th:
RANGERS (1) 1   THIRD LANARK (0) 0
  Brand (37)

RANGERS: Ritchie; Shearer, Provan; Greig, McKinnon, Baxter; Henderson, McMillan, Millar, Brand, Wilson

THIRD LANARK: Robertson; McGillivray, Davis; Spence, Little, Baird; Bryce, Goodfellow, Cunningham, McMorran, Curran

Attendance: 34,000

May 13th:
KILMARNOCK   (0) 1   RANGERS   (0) 0
  Yard (63)

KILMARNOCK: Forsyth; Richmond, Watson;
Murray, McGrory, Beattie; Brown, McInally, Yard,
Black, McIlroy

RANGERS: Martin; Shearer, Provan; Davis, Baillie,
Hunter; Watson, Greig, Forrest, Brand, Wilson

Attendance: 12,000

May 18th:
RANGERS   (0) 3   QUEEN OF THE
  Millar 2 (49, 86), Brand (70)| SOUTH   (1) 1
                              McKinnon o.g. (13)

RANGERS: Ritchie; Shearer, Provan; Davis,
McKinnon, Baxter; Henderson, Willoughby, Millar,
Brand, Wilson

QUEEN OF THE SOUTH: Wright; Morrison, Kerr;
Irvine, Rugg, Murphy; Gardiner, Hannigan, Martin,
Anderson, Law

Rugg missed a penalty

Attendance: 17,000

May 22nd:
CLYDE   (1) 1   RANGERS   (1) 3
  Currie (6)   Willoughby 2 (12, 63),
                      Brand (75)

CLYDE: McCulloch; Gray, Blain; Murray, Fraser,
White; McLean, Hood, Currie, Reid, McHigh

RANGERS: Ritchie; Shearer, Provan; Greig,
McKinnon, Baxter; Watson, Willoughby, Millar, Brand,
Wilson

Attendance: 6,000

May 25th:
DUNDEE   0   RANGERS   0

DUNDEE: Slater; Hamilton, Stuart; Seith, Ure,
Brown; Penman, Cousin, Waddell, Wishart, Houston

RANGERS: Ritchie; Shearer, Provan; Greig,
McKinnon, Baxter; Watson, McMillan, Millar, Brand,
Wilson

Attendance: 18,000

May 27th:
RANGERS   (1) 2   ABERDEEN   (2) 2
  Wilson 2 (17, 69)   Kinnell (7), Little (25)

RANGERS: Ritchie; Shearer, Provan; Greig,
McKinnon, Baxter; Watson, Willougby, Millar, Brand,
Wilson

ABERDEEN: Ogston; Shewan, Hogg; Brownlee,
Coutts, Fraser; Cummings, Kinnell, Little, Cooke,
Smith

Attendance: n.a.

Scottish First Division

	P	W	D	L	F	A	Pts
1 RANGERS	34	25	7	2	94	28	57
2 Kilmarnock	34	20	8	6	92	40	48
3 Partick Thistle	34	20	6	8	66	44	46
4 Celtic	34	19	6	9	76	44	44
5 Hearts	34	17	9	8	85	59	43
6 Aberdeen	34	17	7	10	70	47	41
7 Dundee United	34	15	11	8	67	52	41
8 Dunfermline	34	13	8	13	50	47	34
9 Dundee	34	12	9	13	60	49	33
10 Motherwell	34	10	11	13	60	63	31
11 Airdrie	34	14	2	18	52	76	30
12 St Mirren	34	10	8	16	52	72	28
13 Falkirk	34	12	3	19	54	69	27
14 Third Lanark	34	9	8	17	56	68	26
15 Queen of the South	34	10	6	18	36	75	26
16 Hibernian	34	8	9	17	47	67	25
17 Clyde	34	9	5	20	49	83	23
18 Raith Rovers	34	2	5	27	35	118	9

**June 4th: Scotland were beaten 4-3 by Norway in
Oslo. Baxter, Henderson and Wilson were in the
team.**

**June 9th: Eire beat Scotland 1-0 in Dublin. Baxter,
Henderson, Millar and Wilson were in the team.**

**June 11th: Raith Rovers turned down a bid of £4,000
for centre-half John Bolton.**

**June 13th: Scotland beat Spain 6-2 in Madrid.
Baxter, Henderson and Wilson were in the team.
Wilson and Henderson both scored.**

LEAGUE CUP

August 11th:
HIBERNIAN   (0) 1   RANGERS   (1) 4
  M. Stevenson (59)   Henderson (36),
                          Brand 2 (70 pen, 89),
                          Wilson (77)

HIBERNIAN: Simpson; Grant, McClelland; Preston,
Easton, Baxter; Scott, McLeod, Baker, M. Stevenson, E.
Stevenson

RANGERS: Ritchie; Shearer, Caldow; Davis,
McKinnon, Baxter; Scott, Henderson, Millar, Brand,
Wilson

Attendance: 36,500

August 15th:
RANGERS   (3) 5   THIRD LANARK   (0) 2
  Millar 3 (5, 32, 43),   Grant 2 (70, 82)
  Scott (55), Wilson (80)

RANGERS: Ritchie; Shearer, Caldow; Davis,
McKinnon, Baxter; Scott, Henderson, Millar, Brand,
Wilson

THIRD LANARK: Robertson; McGillivray, Cunningham; Reilly, McCormick, Robb; Bryce, Stenhouse, Grant, Gray, Goodfellow

Attendance: 25,000

August 18th:
ST MIRREN (0) 2 RANGERS (0) 1
 Campbell (51), McLean (53) Murray (81)

ST MIRREN: Williamson; Murray, Wilson; Campbell, Clunie, McTavish; Kerrigan, Bryceland, Beck, McLean, Robertson

RANGERS: Ritchie; Shearer, Caldow; Davis, McKinnon, Baxter; Scott, Henderson, Murray, Brand, Wilson

Attendance: 37,000

August 25th:
RANGERS 0 HIBERNIAN 0

RANGERS: Ritchie; Shearer, Caldow; Davis, McKinnon, Baxter; Henderson, McMillan, Millar, Brand, Scott

HIBERNIAN: Simpson; Davin, McClelland; Preston, Easton, Baxter; M. Stevenson, Baker, Fraser, Byrne, E. Stevenson

Attendance: 45,000

August 29th:
THIRD LANARK (2) 2 RANGERS (3) 5
 Bryce (18), Grant (32) Miller 3 (28, 55, 62),
 Scott 2 (37, 42)

THIRD LANARK: McKinlay; McGillivray, Cunningham; Reilly, McCormick, Robb; Stenhouse, Bryce, Grant, Gray, Goodfellow

RANGERS: Ritchie; Shearer, Caldow; Davis, McKinnon, Baxter; Henderson, Greig, Millar, Brand, Scott

Attendance: n.a.

September 1st:
RANGERS (1) 4 ST MIRREN (0) 0
 Millar (40), Greig 3 (50, 80, 84)

RANGERS: Ritchie; Shearer, Caldow; Davis, McKinnon, Baxter; Henderson, Greig, Millar, Brand, Wilson

ST MIRREN: Williamson; Murray, Riddell; Campbell, Clunie, McTavish; Robertson, Bryceland, Kerrigan, Beck, Fernie

Attendance: 47,000

League Cup Section Table

	P	W	D	L	F	A	Pts
RANGERS	6	4	1	1	19	7	9
Hibernian	6	3	2	1	13	10	8
St Mirren	6	2	2	2	8	12	6
Third Lanark	6	0	1	5	9	20	1

September 12th: Quarter-Final First Leg
DUMBARTON (1) 1 RANGERS (2) 3
 Carr (42) Millar (8), Greig (38),
 Wilson (48 pen)

DUMBARTON: Robertson; Govan, Jardine; Kilgannon, Harra, Wilson; Morrison, Millar, Campbell, Black, Carr

Ritchie; Shearer, Caldow; Davis, McKinnon, Baxter; Henderson, Greig, Millar, Brand, Wilson

Attendance: 19,000

September 19th: Quarter-Final Second Leg
RANGERS (1) 1 DUMBARTON (1) 1
 Greig (20) Newlands (10)

RANGERS: Ritchie; Shearer, Caldow; Greig, McKinnon, Baxter; Scott, McMillan, Millar, Brand, Wilson

DUMBARTON: Robertson; Govan, Jardine; Kilgannon, Harra, Wilson; Morrison, Millar, Hodgson, Newlands, Carr

Attendance: 17,500

Rangers won 4-2 on aggregate

October 10th: Semi-Final   At Hampden Park
RANGERS (2) 2 KILMARNOCK (2) 3
 Brand 2 (17, 22) McIlroy (15),
 Kerr (44),
 Black (82)

RANGERS: Ritchie; Shearer, Caldow; Davis, McKinnon, Baxter; Henderson, Greig, Millar, Brand, Wilson

KILMARNOCK: McLaughlin; Richmond, Watson; O'Connor, McGrory, Beattie; Brown, Black, Kerr, Sneddon, McIlroy

Attendance: 76,000

A goal headed by Black from a Sneddon corner-kick 8 minutes from time knocked out Rangers, who down a goal after 15 minutes but, one up after 22, were level at the start of the second half. Brand after 17 and 22 minutes scored his side's goals but he handled a net-bound Greig shot that would have put his team 3-1 ahead. In less than a minute Kerr and Black had exchanged passes through a defence still bemused by Brand's blunder, and Kerr, having enticed Ritchie out, coolly equalised. Davis made 2 splendid efforts to win the match late in the second half. McIlroy headed the opening goal in 15 minutes. Throughout the match Kilmarnock with much less of the ball made much better use of it.

SCOTTISH CUP

March 13th: Second Round
AIRDRIE	(0) 0			RANGERS	(3) 6
					Brand (6 pen),
					Wilson 3 (7, 22, 71),
					Henderson (49),
					Thomson o.g. (88)

AIRDRIE:	Samson; Jonquin, Keenan; Hosie,
Thomson, Reid; McColl, Rowan, Tees, Murray,
Duncan

RANGERS:	Ritchie; Shearer, Caldow; Greig,
McKinnon, Baxter; Henderson, McMillan, Millar,
Brand, Wilson

Attendance: 17,823

March 20th: Third Round
RANGERS	(4) 7		EAST STIRLING	(1) 2
Brand 4 (6, 27, 38, 87),		Coburn (36),
Wilson (11), Millar (56),		Sandeman (53)
McLean (65)

RANGERS:	Ritchie; Shearer, Caldow; Greig,
McKinnon, Baxter; Henderson, McLean, Millar, Brand,
Wilson

EAST STIRLING:	Swan; McNab, McQueen;
Collumbine, Craig, Frickleton; Hamill, Sandeman,
Coburn, Kemp, McIntosh

Attendance: 35,000

March 30th: Fourth Round
DUNDEE	(1) 1			RANGERS	(0) 1
Penman (44 pen)			Brand (54)

DUNDEE:	Slater; Hamilton, Cox; Seith, Ure,
Wishart; Smith, Penman, Cousin, Gilzean, Robertson

RANGERS:	Ritchie; Shearer, Caldow; Greig,
McKinnon, Baxter; Henderson, McLean, Millar, Brand,
Wilson

Attendance: 36,839

April 3rd: Fourth Round Replay
RANGERS	(1) 3			DUNDEE	(1) 2
Hamilton o.g. (15),			Gilzean 2 (34, 46)
Brand 2 (74 pen, 88)

RANGERS:	Ritchie; Shearer, Caldow; Greig,
McKinnon, Baxter; Henderson, McLean, Millar, Brand,
Wilson

RANGERS:	Slater; Hamilton, Cox; Seith, Ure,
Wishart; Smith, Penman, Cousin, Gilzean, Robertson

Attendance: 81,190

April 13th: Semi-Final		At Hampden Park
RANGERS	(4) 5		DUNDEE UNITED (2) 2
Millar 3 (24, 26, 44),			Gillespie (29),
Brand (36),				Mitchell (34)
McLean (86)

RANGERS:	Ritchie; Shearer, Provan; Greig,
McKinnon, Baxter; Henderson, McLean, Millar, Brand,
Wilson

DUNDEE UNITED:	Davie; Gordon, Briggs;
Neilson, Smith, Fraser; Millar, Gillespie, Mochan,
Brodie, Mitchell

Attendance: 56,391

Most of the excitement was crammed into the period
between the 24th and 36th minutes when 5 goals were
scored. In the 24th minute Greig, a magnificent half-back,
at last found a response from his forwards and Millar
completed the movement with a neatly taken goal. 2
minutes later McLean, with a cute back-heeler, laid on a
chance which Millar promptly accepted. Undaunted,
United swept into attack and in 29 minutes Gillespie
scored a brilliant goal from the edge of the penalty-area.
Rangers' defence obviously thought that he would cross
the ball but instead he shot and Ritchie was completely
beaten low at his left-hand post. 5 minutes later the teams
were on level terms. In a flurry in the goalmouth the ball
broke to Mitchell, who promptly despatched it beyond
Ritchie. 9 minutes before the interval Brand burst through
and scored a neat goal from close range. Then in 44
minutes came the most spectacular goal of all as the ball
came back off the crossbar from a shot by McLean, Millar
outjumped 4 opponents and headed crisply out of Davie's
reach. 4 minutes from the end McLean scored a great
goal with a full-blooded drive from 25 yards.

May 4th: Final			At Hampden Park
RANGERS	(1) 1		CELTIC	(1) 1
Brand (43)				Murdoch (45)

RANGERS:	Ritchie; Shearer, Provan; Greig,
McKinnon, Baxter; Henderson, McLean, Millar, Brand,
Wilson

CELTIC:	Haffey; McKay, Kennedy; McNamee,
McNeill, Price; Johnstone, Murdoch, Hughes, Divers,
Brogan

Attendance: 129,527	*Referee*: T. Wharton (Clarkston)

Haffey was the man of the match although in the rain and
wind of Hampden this was hardly a goalkeeper's day. His
diverting of a second-half shot of Brand was the best of the
many he made. He was beaten twice — when Brand flicked
past him Henderson's cross in 43 minutes for Rangers' goal
and when midway in the second half the little outside-right
floated a cross over his outstretched arms and onto the top
of the crossbar. Murdoch scored the Celtic goal just on
half-time. McLean was injured for most of the second half
but it was when he was banished to outside-left and Wilson
moved to centre-forward that Rangers looked most
dangerous. Baxter was not permitted to exert his usual
influence. McNamee along with McNeill, a commanding
centre-half, and the cool Price formed the superior half-
back line.

Season 1963–64 was a successful one for trophy collecting. Top picture shows a jubilant Jim Baxter with the League Cup after defeating Morton, 5-0. Bottom picture shows Bobby Shearer displaying the Scottish Cup after defeating Dundee by 3-1.

F

May 15th: Final Replay   At Hampden Park
RANGERS   (2) 3   CELTIC   (0) 0
   Brand 2 (7, 71), Wilson (44)

RANGERS: Ritchie; Shearer, Provan; Greig,
McKinnon, Baxter; Henderson, McMillan, Millar,
Brand, Wilson

CELTIC: Haffey; McKay, Kennedy; McNamee,
McNeill, Price; Craig, Murdoch, Divers, Chalmers,
Hughes

Attendance: 120,263   *Referee*: T. Wharton

Rangers not only defeated but completely outclassed
Celtic. McMillan's recall to the top class led to a feast of
fine football in the first-half. Henderson had never played
so successfully against Kennedy. The outside-right's cross
after Millar had passed down the touch-line was swept past
Haffey in the seventh minute by Brand. In the last minute
of the first-half Millar passed to Brand who, as McKay
retreated, closed in and shot. Haffey could not hold the
fast, low shot and Wilson took the easy scoring chance in
his stride. Once Brand, with his left foot from 25 yards, had
surprised Haffey with a shot which dropped as it came to
the goalkeeper, Rangers toyed with their opponents.

EUROPEAN CUP WINNERS CUP

September 5th: First Round First Leg
RANGERS   (2) 4   SEVILLE   (0) 0
   Millar 3 (12, 16, 63),
   Brand (64)

RANGERS: Ritchie; Shearer, Caldow; Davis,
McKinnon, Baxter; Henderson, Greig, Millar, Brand,
Wilson

SEVILLE: Mut; Manuel, Lugue; Ruiz-Sosa,
Campanal, Achucarro; Canario, Dieguez, Areta, Mateos,
Moya

Attendance: 65,000

Seville were 2 goals in arrears with only 16 minutes played
— both were scored by Millar from crosses by Henderson.
In the 63rd and 64th minutes Millar and Brand bored
through the middle and put Rangers 4 goals ahead. After
that they tended to slacken off and indulge in close and
intricate play. The occasional display of bad manners by
one or two of the dispirited Seville team enlivened the
proceedings.

September 26th: Second Round Second Leg
SEVILLE   (2) 2   RANGERS   (0) 0
   Dieguez (6), Mateos (9)

SEVILLE: Mut; Manuel, Lugue; Ruiz-Sosa,
Campanal, Achucarro; Canario, Dieguez, Areta, Mateos,
Moya

RANGERS: Ritchie; Shearer, Caldow; Davis,
McKinnon, Baxter; Henderson, Greig, Millar, Brand,
Wilson

Attendance: 25,000

Dieguez opened the scoring after only 6 minutes and
Mateos made it two 3 minutes later. However, Rangers
managed to weather the opening storm. The Portuguese
referee had to stop the game 2 minutes before full-time
because of incidents involving all 22 players after the
Spanish centre-forward attacked Rangers' inside-
right Greig. The spectators showed their disapproval
of this by throwing hundreds of cushions onto the
field. Rangers' casualties included Baxter who was
kicked, Greig who was punched, Wilson who was
butted and McKinnon who was bitten.

October 31st: Second Round First Leg
TOTTENHAM HOTSPUR   (4) 5   RANGERS   (2) 2
   White (5), Greaves (23),   Henderson (9),
   Allen (36), Shearer o.g. (43),   Millar (44)
   Norman (78)
TOTTENHAM: Brown; Baker, Henry; Blanchflower,
Norman, Mackay; Medwin, White, Allen, Greaves,
Jones

RANGERS: Ritchie; Shearer, Caldow; Davis,
McKinnon, Baxter; Henderson, McMillan, Millar,
Brand, Wilson

Attendance: 58,859

Only 5 minutes after the start Tottenham gained the much
sought-after quick lead and they were cruising long before
half-time. 2 minutes from the interval Rangers, 3 goals
down, were given much-needed encouragement by Millar
who headed a goal from Henderson, the scorer of his side's
first goal. Almost all of the second half saw Rangers run
into the ground with the superb passing and switching of
positions of Blanchflower, Mackay, White and Greaves.
Ritchie made several wonderful saves, notably from
terrific shots by Mackay, Allen, Greaves and Jones. The
only reward for almost constant Tottenham attack in the
2nd half was a goal from Norman 12 minutes from time.
White headed Spurs' first from a Greaves corner in 5
minutes. In the 36th minute, after Greaves had scored a
2nd, Allen shot a fine 3rd Spurs goal despite a fine effort
from Shearer to kick the ball off the goal-line, and 7
minutes later a Shearer own goal made it 4.

December 11th: Second Round Second Leg
RANGERS   (0) 2   TOTTENHAM
                                        HOTSPUR   (1) 3
   Brand (47), Wilson (74)   Greaves (8),
                                        Smith 2 (50, 89)

RANGERS: Ritchie; Shearer, Caldow; Davis,
McKinnon, Baxter; Henderson, McMillan, Millar,
Brand, Wilson

TOTTENHAM: Brown; Baker, Henry; Blanchflower, Norman, Mackay; Medwin, White, Smith, Greaves, Jones

Attendance: 80,000

Tottenham Hotspur won 8-4 on aggregate

Any slender hopes Rangers had of winning the tie on aggregate vanished in the 8th minute when Greaves, one of the greatest goalscorers of the century, strode through after a dummy by Smith and gave the English club a 4-goal lead. Brand headed an equalising goal from Henderson's cross in the 2nd minute of the 2nd half, but 3 minutes later Smith shot White's cross over Ritchie's head. In the 74th minute the referee awarded a free-kick against Baker, and Wilson scored. One minute from time Smith headed Mackay's cross away from Ritchie and Rangers' ordeal was over. Brown, Tottenham's Scottish International goal-keeper, made several fine saves, notably from Millar and Wilson.

GOALSCORERS

League: Millar 27, Wilson 23 (3 pens), Brand 19 (1 pen), Henderson 5, Greig 5, Baxter 4, Own Goals 3, Davis 2, McLean 2, Willoughby 2, Scott 1, McMillan 1

League Cup: Millar 8, Greig 5, Brand 4 (1 pen), Wilson 3 (1 pen), Scott 3, Henderson 1, Murray 1

Scottish Cup: Brand 12 (2 pens), Wilson 5, Millar 4, McLean 2, Own Goals 2, Henderson 1

Glasgow Cup: Wilson 1, Millar 1, Henderson 1, Brand 1

Friendlies: Brand 2, Millar 1, Baxter 1

Cup Winners Cup: Millar 4, Brand 2, Henderson 1, Wilson 1

APPEARANCES

	League	League Cup	Scottish Cup	Glasgow Cup	Friendlies	Cup Winners Winners
Ritchie	33	9	7	2	3	4
Shearer	34	9	7	2	3	4
Caldow	20	9	4	2	1	4
Davis	16	8	-	-	2	4
McKinnon	32	9	7	2	3	4
Baxter	32	9	7	2	2	4
Henderson	27	8	7	2	2	4
McMillan	12	2	2	1	2+1 sub	2
Millar	31	8	7	2	3	4
Brand	32	9	7	2	3	4
Wilson	33	7	7	2	3	4
Scott	4	6	-	-	1+1sub	-
Greig	27	5	7	2	2	2
Baillie	6	-	-	1	-	-
Forrest	4	-	-	-	-	-
McLean	9	-	5	-	-	-
Provan	12	-	3	-	1	-
Watson	5	-	-	-	1	-
Martin	1	-	-	-	-	-
Hunter	1	-	-	-	-	-
Willoughby	3	-	-	-	-	-
Murray	-	1	-	-	sub	-
King	-	-	-	-	1	-
Penman	-	-	-	-	sub	-

John Greig, no stranger to trophies in his long career at Ibrox as player and manager.

Season 1963–64

For the first time under Scot Symons's managership the club won the treble. The Championship was won by 6 points from Kilmarnock. Rangers lost 3 matches at Ibrox and only one away —against St Johnstone in the last match of the season. 25 of the 34 matches were won. Celtic were beaten home and away. Indeed, all 5 matches against Celtic in 3 competitions were won. Ritchie and Greig did not miss a match but a serious injury restricted Wilson to 16 league appearances. Forrest finished as top scorer with 21, 2 ahead of Brand.

Both Celtic and Kilmarnock were knocked out in the League Cup Section matches, and after comfortable wins in both the Quarter-Final and Semi-Final run-away Second Division leaders, Morton, were overpowered in the second half of the Final. Jim Forrest scored 4 goals and his cousin Alec Willoughby the other in a 5-0 win watched by 105,907.

Goals from Forrest and Henderson put Celtic out in the Fourth Round of the Scottish Cup and a Wilson goal eliminated Dunfermline in the Semi-Final. Despite a heroic display by Dundee's goalkeeper Bert Slater, goals by Millar and Brand in the final 90 seconds ensured that the Cup would return to Ibrox for the 3rd successive season.

Rangers had the misfortune to draw Real Madrid in the Preliminary Round of the European Cup and ended up on the wrong end of a 7-0 aggregate score line.

Rangers met Everton over 2 legs in an unofficial British Championship Decider but the loss of Baxter, with an injury in the first match, badly affected the team, Everton winning 4-2 on aggregate.

> League: Champions
> Scottish Cup: Winners
> League Cup: Winners
> European Cup: Preliminary Round

SCOTTISH FIRST DIVISION

August 5th: Jim Baxter re-signed.

August 7th: Stoke City made a £70,000 bid for Baxter.

August 21st:

DUNDEE (0) 1   RANGERS (1) 1
Seith (47)   Brand (pen) (12)

DUNDEE: Slater; Hamilton, Cox; Seith, Ryden, Stuart; Penman, Houston, Cousin, Gilzean, Robertson

RANGERS: Ritchie; Shearer, Provan; Greig, McKinnon, Baxter; Henderson, McLean, Forrest, Brand, Wilson

Attendance: 34,500

September 4th: The Scottish League beat the Irish League 4-1 in Belfast. Greig, Baxter, Henderson, Brand and Wilson were in the team. Brand scored two of the goals.

September 7th:

RANGERS (0) 2   CELTIC (1) 1
McLean (52), Brand (65)   Chalmers (11)

RANGERS: Ritchie; Shearer, Provan; Greig, McKinnon, Baxter; Henderson, McLean. Forrest, Brand, Wilson

CELTIC: Haffey; McKay, Gemmell; Clark, McNeill, O'Neill; Lennox, Turner, Divers, Chalmers, Brogan

Attendance: 55,000

Of the 3 matches since the start of the season, this was the liveliest and the most entertaining, Rangers proving once again how difficult they are to beat. With 2 minutes to go in the first half Chalmers got his head to a well-directed cross by Lennox and was chagrined to see it rebound to safety from the post. Celtic scored in 11 minutes when McKay and Turner made the opening from which Chalmers scooped the ball past Ritchie. Haffey effected a brilliant point-blank save from Baxter but had no chance when McLean levelled the scores. The tall inside-right galloped into an open space in pursuit of a ball released perfectly by Forrest and guided it out of Haffey's reach. In the 65th minute Brand raced into ideal position for a pass from Forrest and again Haffey was powerless to prevent a score.

September 14th:
PARTICK THISTLE   (0) 0   RANGERS   (2) 3
                                  Forrest 3 (24, 28, 51)

PARTICK THISTLE: Niven; Hogan, Muir; McParland, Harvey, Cunningham; Cowan, Hainey, Yard, Duffy, Hume

RANGERS: Ritchie; Shearer, Provan; Greig, McKinnon, Baxter; Henderson, Millar, Forrest, Brand, Wilson

Attendance: 35,000

September 21st:
RANGERS   (1) 5   HIBERNIAN   (0) 0
  McLean (8),
  Brand 2 (72, 89), Forrest (67),
  Henderson (88)

RANGERS: Ritchie; Shearer, Provan; Greig, McKinnon, Baxter; Henderson, McLean, Forrest, Brand, Wilson

HIBERNIAN: Simpson; Fraser, McClelland; Grant, Easton, Preston; Scott, Martin, Baker, Byrne, Stevenson

Attendance: 50,000

September 28th:
THIRD LANARK   (0) 0   RANGERS   (1) 5
                                  Forrest 4 (5, 52, 58, 75),
                                  Baxter (64)

THIRD LANARK: Paul; McGillivray, Davis; Dickson, McCormick, McLeod; Graham, Cunningham, Murray, Brownlee, Buckley

RANGERS: Ritchie; Shearer, Provan; Greig, McKinnon, Baxter; Henderson, Millar, Forrest, McLean, Wilson

Attendance: 25,000

October 5th:
RANGERS   (3) 4   FALKIRK   (0) 0
  McLean 3 (3, 20, 48),
  Henderson (45)

RANGERS: Ritchie; Shearer, Provan; Greig, McKinnon, Baxter; Henderson, Willoughby, Forrest, McLean, Brand

FALKIRK: Whigham; Lambie, Hunter; Pierson, Rae, Fulton; O'Donnell, Redpath, Irving, Maxwell, Stewart

Attendance: 25,000

October 12th: Scotland were beaten 2-1 by Ireland in Belfast. Provan and Henderson were in the team.

October 12th:
ST MIRREN   (0) 0   RANGERS   (3) 3
                                  Brand (1½),
                                  Willoughby (35),
                                  Forrest (39)

ST MIRREN: Dempster; Murray, Wilson; Campbell, Clunie, McTavish; Kerrigan, Carroll, White, Beck, Robertson

RANGERS: Ritchie; Shearer, Hynd; Greig, McKinnon, Baxter; Brand, Willoughby, Forrest, Millar, Watson

Attendance: 25,000

October 18th: Rangers announced that they were to send manager Scot Symon to Madrid to study the play, training plans and tactical techniques of Real Madrid.

October 19th:
RANGERS   (1) 3   EAST STIRLING   (1) 1
  Watson (45),   Hamill (28)
  Forrest 2 (59, 68)

RANGERS: Ritchie; Shearer, Provan; Greig, McKinnon, Baxter; Henderson, Millar, Forrest, Brand, Watson

EAST STIRLING: Swan; Laird, McQueen; Collumbine, Craig, McPhee; Hamill, Kilgannon, Kemp, Sandeman, McIntosh

Attendance: 20,000

League positions
	P	W	D	L	F	A	Pts
1 RANGERS	8	7	1	0	26	3	15
2 Kilmarnock	9	7	1	1	20	9	15
3 Dundee	9	6	2	1	23	10	14
4 Dunfermline	9	5	3	1	19	9	13
5 Hearts	9	5	2	2	20	13	12

October 23rd: Jim Baxter made an appearance as substitute for Masopust for the Rest of the World team against England at Wembley.

October 30th:
RANGERS   (2) 2   QUEEN OF THE
  Forrest (16), Brand (25)   SOUTH   (0) 0

RANGERS: Ritchie; Shearer, Provan; Greig, McKinnon, Baxter; Henderson, Willoughby, Forrest, Brand, Traill

QUEEN OF THE SOUTH: Farm; Morrison, Kerr; Irving, Rugg, Murphy; Hannigan, Currie, Thomson, Gardner, Coates

Attendance: 15,000

November 2nd:
AIRDRIE   (0) 0   RANGERS   (2) 4
                         Willoughby (14),
                         Forrest (45),
                         Baxter (49),
                         Watson (74)

AIRDRIE: Samson; Black, Keenan; Caldwell, Stewart, Rowan; McColl, Hastings, Whitelaw, Newlands, Jeffrey

RANGERS: Ritchie; Shearer, Provan; Greig, McKinnon, Baxter; Henderson, Willoughby, Forrest, Brand, Watson

Attendance: 20,000

November 7th: Scotland beat Norway 6-1 at Hampden Park. Provan, Baxter and Henderson were in the team.

November 9th:
RANGERS   (0) 0   ABERDEEN   (0) 0

RANGERS: Ritchie; Shearer, Provan; Greig, McKinnon, Millar; Henderson, Willoughby, Forrest, Brand, Watson

ABERDEEN: Ogston; Shewan, Hogg; Kinnell, Coutts, Smith; Kerrigan, Cooke, Graham, Winchester, Hume

Attendance: 34,000

November 16th:
KILMARNOCK   (0) 1   RANGERS   (0) 1
  McIlroy (55)   Brand (70 pen)

KILMARNOCK: Forsyth; King, Watson; O'Connor, McGrory, Beattie; Black, McInally, McFadzean, Sneddon, McIlroy

RANGERS: Ritchie; Shearer, Provan; Greig, McKinnon, Baxter; Henderson, Millar, Forrest, Brand, Watson

Attendance: 30,000

November 20th: Scotland beat Wales 2-1 at Hampden Park. Baxter and Henderson were in the team.

November 23rd:
DUNFERMLINE   (0) 1   RANGERS   (2) 4
  Peebles (67)   Watson 2 (14, 69),
                             Henderson (29),
                             Forrest (61)

DUNFERMLINE: Herriot; W. Callaghan, Lunn; Thomson, McLean, Miller; Edwards, Peebles, Dickson, Kerray, T. Callaghan

RANGERS: Ritchie; Shearer, Provan; Greig, Baillie, McKinnon; Henderson, Millar, Forrest, Brand, Watson

Attendance: 21,000

November 30th:
RANGERS   (0) 0   HEARTS   (3) 3
                         White 2 (3, 44),
                         Wallace (45)

RANGERS: Ritchie; Shearer, Provan; Greig, Baillie, McKinnon; Henderson, McMillan, Forrest, Brand, Watson

HEARTS: Cruikshank; Shevlane, Holt; Polland, Barry, Higgins; Hamilton, Wallace, White, Gordon, Traynor

Attendance: 24,000

December 7th:
DUNDEE UNITED   (1) 2   RANGERS   (1) 3
  Irvine (16), Mitchell (84)   McLean 2 (18, 50),
                               Brand (72)

DUNDEE UNITED: Davie; Millar, Briggs; Neilson, Smith, Fraser; Irvine, Howieson, Davidson, Gillespie, Mitchell

RANGERS: Ritchie; Shearer, Provan; Greig, McKinnon, Wood; Forrest, McMillan, Millar, McLean, Brand

Attendance: 20,000

December 14th:
MOTHERWELL   (1) 3   RANGERS   (1) 3
  McCann 2 (42, 55),   Provan (33 pen),
  Hunter (60)   Greig (57),
                             Brand (63)

MOTHERWELL: Wylie; Thomson, McCallum; Aitken, Delaney, Murray; Carlyle, McCann, McBride, Hunter, Lindsay

RANGERS: Ritchie; Shearer, Provan; Greig, Baillie, Wood; Henderson, McLean, Millar, Brand, Forrest

Attendance: 16,500

December 21st:
RANGERS   (1) 2   ST JOHNSTONE   (0) 3
  Brand (36),   Ferguson 3 (53, 60, 76)
  Provan (72 pen)

RANGERS: Ritchie; Shearer, Provan; Greig, McKinnon, Wood; Henderson, McMillan, Millar, McLean, Brand

ST JOHNSTONE: Fallon; McFadyen, Richmond; Townsend, McKinven, McCarry; Flanagan, Craig, McIntyre, Ferguson, Kemp

Attendance: 14,000

December 28th:
RANGERS (1) 2   DUNDEE (0) 1
  Forrest (30), Provan (64 pen)   Penman (79)

RANGERS: Ritchie; Provan, Caldow; Davis, McKinnon, Wood; Henderson, Greig, Millar, McLean, Forrest

DUNDEE: Slater; Hamilton, Cox; Seith, Stuart, Wishart; Smith, Penman, Waddell, Cousin, Robertson
Attendance: 43,000

League positions

	P	W	D	L	F	A	Pts
1 Kilmarnock	18	13	3	2	41	20	29
2 RANGERS	18	12	4	2	47	17	28
3 Celtic	18	10	5	3	52	20	25
4 Dunfermline	17	9	6	2	37	16	24
5 Dundee	18	10	4	4	44	23	24

January 1st:
CELTIC (0) 0   RANGERS (0) 1
                     Millar (65)

CELTIC: Fallon; Young, Gemmell; Clark, McNeill, Kennedy; Johnstone, Murdoch, Chalmers, Divers, Hughes

RANGERS: Ritchie; Provan, Caldow; Davis, McKinnon, Baxter; Henderson, Greig, Millar, McLean, Brand
Attendance: n.a.

Celtic had several chances to score but a mixture of bad luck, hesitancy at the vital moment and fine saves by Ritchie thwarted all their efforts. The players who most often sparked life into the match were the two outside-rights. In 9 minutes Johnstone beat Ritchie with a left-foot shot which hit a post. In 21 minutes Celtic might have had a penalty when McKinnon brought down Chalmers. Henderson too struck a post with a hard shot. The decisive goal was scored by Millar in 65 minutes from Henderson's free-kick, taken from just outside the penalty area. Brand drove the ball against a defender, and when it came out to Millar the centre-forward turned quickly and hooked it past Fallon.

January 2nd:
RANGERS (2) 4   PARTICK THISTLE (2) 3
  Brand 2 (22, 76),   Hainey 2 (42, 43),
  Greig (34),   Hogan (82)
  Millar (79)

RANGERS: Ritchie; Provan, Caldow; Davis, McKinnon, Baxter; Henderson, Greig, Millar, Brand, Forrest

PARTICK THISTLE: Niven; Hogan, Tinney; Closs, Harvey, Cunningham; Cowan, Hainey, Staite, Duffy, McParland
Attendance: 30,000

January 4th:
HIBERNIAN (0) 0   RANGERS (1) 1
                     Millar (20)

HIBERNIAN: Simpson; Fraser, McClelland; Leishman, Cameron, Baxter; Scott, Hamilton, Martin, O'Rourke, Stevenson

RANGERS: Ritchie; Shearer, Provan; Davis, McKinnon, Baxter; Henderson, Greig, Millar, Brand, Forrest
Attendance: 18,000

January 18th:
RANGERS (2) 2   THIRD LANARK (1) 1
  Brand 2 (24, 37)   Brownlee (21)

RANGERS: Ritchie; Shearer, Provan; Greig, McKinnon, Baxter; Henderson, McLean, Millar, Brand, Traill

THIRD LANARK: Paul; Lewis, Davis; Cunningham, McCormick, Geddes; Graham, Brownlee, Murray, McMorran, Buckley
Attendance: 17,000

February 1st:
FALKIRK (0) 0   RANGERS (1) 1
                     Brand (7)

FALKIRK: Whigham; Thomson, Hunter; Pierson, Rae, Fulton; Foley, Davidson, Wilson, Maxwell, Gourlay

RANGERS: Ritchie; Shearer, Provan; Greig, McKinnon, Baxter; Henderson, McLean, Forrest, Brand, Traill
Attendance: 16,000

February 8th:
RANGERS (1) 2   ST MIRREN (0) 3
  Millar (41), Wilson (78)   Queen (54), Beck (55),
                         Allan (75)

RANGERS: Ritchie; Shearer, Provan; Greig, McKinnon, Baxter; Henderson, McLean, Millar, Brand, Wilson

ST MIRREN: Beattie; Murray, Wilson; Clark, Clunie, Ross; T. Robertson, Allan, Queen, Beck, J. Robertson
Attendance: 25,000

February 19th:
EAST STIRLING (0) 0   RANGERS (2) 5
                      Wilson 2, Forrest 2,
                      Millar o.g.

EAST STIRLING: Arrol; Millar, McQueen; Collumbine, Craig, Frickleton; Hamill, Munro, Roxburgh, Sandeman, McIntosh

RANGERS: Ritchie; Shearer, Provan; Greig,
McKinnon, Baxter; Henderson, McMillan, Forrest,
Brand, Wilson
Attendance: 6,000

February 22nd:

QUEEN OF THE	RANGERS (3) 4
SOUTH (0) 1	Forrest 2 (16, 73),
Byrne (82)	Wilson (35),
	Willoughby (43)

QUEEN OF THE SOUTH: Ball; Morrison, Kerr;
Franks, Plenderleith, Currie; Hannigan, Rodger, Coates,
Elliot, Byrne

RANGERS: Ritchie; Shearer, Provan; Greig,
McKinnon, Baxter; Henderson, McMillan, Forrest,
Willoughby, Wilson
Attendance: 9,500

February 29th:

RANGERS (1) 4	AIRDRIE (0) 1
Baxter (16 pen), Greig (53),	Murray (88)
Forrest 2 (73, 79)	

RANGERS: Ritchie; Shearer, Provan; Greig,
McKinnon, Baxter; Henderson, McMillan, Forrest,
Brand, Wilson

AIRDRIE: Samson; Jonquin, Keenan; Stewart,
Hannah, Reid; Ferguson, Hastings, Rowan, Murray,
Newlands
Attendance: 26,500

League positions

	P	W	D	L	F	A	Pts
1 RANGERS	27	20	4	3	71	26	44
2 Kilmarnock	27	19	5	3	65	31	43
3 Celtic	27	16	6	5	74	25	38
4 Hearts	27	15	8	4	61	30	38
5 Dundee	27	16	5	6	79	37	37

March 11th:

ABERDEEN (1) 1	RANGERS (0) 1
Winchester (37)	Baxter (51 pen)

ABERDEEN: Ogston; Shewan, Hogg; Burns, Coutts,
Smith; Lister, Morrison, Kerrigan, Winchester, Thom

RANGERS: Ritchie; Shearer, Provan; Greig, Baillie,
Baxter; Henderson, McMillan, Forrest, Brand, Wilson
Attendance: 22,000

March 14th:

RANGERS (2) 2	KILMARNOCK (0) 0
McLean (26), Wilson (38)	

RANGERS: Ritchie; Shearer, Provan; Greig,
McKinnon, Baxter; Brand, McMillan, Millar, McLean,
Wilson

KILMARNOCK: Forsyth; King, Watson;
McFadzean, McGrory, Beattie; Brown, McInally, Black,
Sneddon, McIlroy
Attendance: 46,000

**March 17th: Greig, Baxter and Wilson represented
the Scottish League against the English League at
Sunderland. The match ended 2-2**.

March 21st:

RANGERS (2) 2	DUNFERMLINE (0) 1
Wilson (4), McMillan (15)	Sinclair (60)

RANGERS: Ritchie; Shearer, Provan; Greig,
McKinnon, Baxter; Brand, McMillan, Millar, McLean,
Wilson

DUNFERMLINE: Herriot; W. Callaghan, Lunn;
Thomson, McLean, Miller; Edwards, Peebles, Smith,
Kerray, Sinclair
Attendance: 30,000

April 1st:

HEARTS (1) 1	RANGERS (1) 2
Wallace (33)	Brand (17),
	Millar (67)

HEARTS: Cruikshank; Shevlane, Holt; Polland,
Barry, Higgins; Hamilton, Ferguson, Wallace,
Sandeman, Traynor

RANGERS: Ritchie; Shearer, Provan; Greig,
McKinnon, Baxter; Henderson, McLean, Millar, Brand,
Wilson

Attendance: n.a.

April 4th:

RANGERS (2) 2	DUNDEE UNITED (0) 0
Brand (17), McLean (42)	

RANGERS: Ritchie; Shearer, Provan; Greig,
McKinnon, Baxter; Henderson, McLean, Millar, Brand,
Wilson

DUNDEE UNITED: Davie; Millar, Gordon;
Neilson, D. Smith, Briggs; Gillespie, Howieson, Young,
Irvine, R. Smith
Attendance: 28,000

**April 11th: Scotland beat England 1-0 at Hampden
Park. Greig, Baxter, Henderson and Wilson were in
the team**.

April 18th:

RANGERS (0) 5	MOTHERWELL (1) 1
Greig (49),	Mc Bride (41)
Brand 2 (61, 68),	
Millar (78),	
McLean (86)	

RANGERS: Ritchie; Shearer, Provan; Greig, McKinnon, Baxter; Henderson, McLean, Millar, Brand, Wilson

MOTHERWELL: Murdoch; Delaney, McCallum; Murray, Martis, Moore; Coakley, Baillie, McBride, McCann, Weir

Attendance: 39,000

April 29th:
ST JOHNSTONE (1) 1   RANGERS (0) 0
  McIntrue (17)

ST JOHNSTONE: Fallon; McFadyen, Coburn; McCarry, McKinven, Renton; McIntyre, Hawshaw, Donnelly, Ferguson, Kemp

RANGERS: Ritchie; Shearer, Provan; Greig, McKinnon, McLean; Henderson, McMillan, Millar, Brand, Wilson

Millar was ordered off

Attendance: 12,000

Scottish First Division

	P	W	D	L	F	A	Pts
1 RANGERS	34	25	5	4	85	31	55
2 Kilmarnock	34	22	5	7	77	40	49
3 Celtic	34	19	9	6	89	34	47
4 Hearts	34	19	9	6	74	40	47
5 Dunfermline	34	18	9	7	64	33	45
6 Dundee	34	20	5	9	94	50	45
7 Partick Thistle	34	15	5	14	55	54	35
8 Dundee United	34	13	8	13	65	49	34
9 Aberdeen	34	12	8	14	53	53	32
10 Hibernian	34	12	6	16	59	66	30
11 Motherwell	34	9	11	14	51	62	29
12 St Mirren	34	12	5	17	44	74	29
13 St Johnstone	34	11	6	17	54	70	28
14 Falkirk	34	11	6	17	54	84	28
15 Airdrie	34	11	4	19	52	97	26
16 Third Lanark	34	9	7	18	47	74	25
17 Queen of the South	34	5	6	23	40	92	16
18 East Stirling	34	5	2	27	37	91	12

May 12th: Scotland drew 2-2 with West Germany in Hanover. Greig, Baxter, Henderson and Wilson were in the team.

LEAGUE CUP

August 10th:
CELTIC (0) 0   RANGERS (1) 3
                     Forrest 2 (29, 62),
                     McLean (56)

CELTIC: Haffey; McKay, Gemmell; McNamee, McNeill, Price; Johnstone, Turner, Hughes, Chalmers, Murdoch

RANGERS: Ritchie; Shearer, Provan; Greig, McKinnon, Baxter; Henderson, McLean, Forrest, Brand, Wilson

Attendance: 60,000

Celtic had opportunities to win in the first 25 minutes but the match ended with Rangers completely on top and even toying with their opponents. In 19 minutes Forrest swooped on the ball, drew Haffey from his goal and gave Rangers a lead as unexpected as it was undeserved. Baxter was supremely confident throughout, making the opening for McLean to score Rangers' 2nd goal in 56 minutes. 6 minutes later it was all over when Forrest, anticipating the dummy sold by Brand as Henderson crossed, slammed the ball past Haffey.

August 14th:
RANGERS (1) 5   QUEEN OF THE
  McLean (5),   SOUTH (0) 2
  Wilson 2 (72, 74),   Steele (71),
  Forrest 1 (78), Provan (87)   McDonald (89)

RANGERS: Ritchie; Shearer, Provan; Greig, McKinnon, Baxter; Henderson, McLean, Forrest, Brand, Wilson

QUEEN OF THE SOUTH: Farm; Morrison, Kerr; Irving, Rugg, McNaught; McDonald, Hannigan, Thomson, Gardner, Steele

Attendance: 30,800

August 17th:
KILMARNOCK (1) 1   RANGERS (1) 4
  McInally (14)   Henderson (39),
                          McLean (48),
                          Brand 2 (76, 82)

KILMARNOCK: Forsyth; King, Richmond; Murray, McGrory, O'Connor; Brown, McInally, Hamilton, McFadzean, Black

RANGERS: Ritchie; Shearer, Provan; Greig, McKinnon, Baxter: Henderson, McLean, Forrest, Brand, Wilson

Attendance: 35,000

August 24th:
RANGERS (1) 3   CELTIC (0) 0
  Wilson (38), Brand (54 pen),
  Forrest (61)

RANGERS: Ritchie; Shearer, Provan; Greig, McKinnon, Baxter; Henderson, McLean, Forrest, Brand, Wilson

CELTIC: Haffey; McKay, Gemmell; Clark, McNeill, Price; Gallagher, Turner, Divers, Chalmers, Jeffrey

Attendance: 65,000

Celtic's lack of punch in attack was again apparent. In the first half Rangers made poor use of a strong wind. Against the run of play Rangers scored 7 minutes before the interval when Wilson got his head to a corner-kick by Henderson. They took command of the game in 54 minutes when Brand scored with a penalty-kick after Forrest had his feet pulled from him by McNeill, who had an unstable afternoon. He was again outwitted in 61 minutes by Forrest, who with a quick wheel 10 yards out shot past Haffey. This 3rd reverse took much of the heart out of Celtic, and before the close it was obvious that there was only one team.

August 28th:

QUEEN OF THE	RANGERS (4) 5
SOUTH (0) 2	Forrest 4 (10, 36,
McDonald 2 (67, 87)	40, 78),
	Wilson (34)

QUEEN OF THE SOUTH: Farm; Morrison, Kerr; Irving, Rugg, Murphy; Hannigan, Gardner, Thomson, McDonald, Muir

RANGERS: Ritchie; Shearer, Provan; Greig, McKinnon, Baxter; Henderson, McLean, Forrest, Brand, Wilson

Attendance: 10,000

August 31st:

RANGERS (1) 2	KILMARNOCK (0) 2
Wilson (42), Forrest (46)	Brown (88), Beattie
	(90)

RANGERS: Ritchie; Shearer, Provan; Greig, Baillie, Baxter; Henderson, McLean, Forrest, Brand, Wilson

KILMARNOCK: Forsyth; King, Richmond; Murray, McGrory, Beattie; Brown, Mason, McFadzean, Sneddon, Black

Attendance: 32,000

League positions

	P	W	D	L	F	A	Pts
RANGERS	6	5	1	0	22	7	11
Kilmarnock	6	2	2	2	9	9	6
Celtic	6	2	2	2	6	9	6
Queen of the South	6	0	1	5	8	20	1

September 11th: Quarter-Final First Leg

EAST FIFE (0) 1	RANGERS (1) 1
Dewar (60)	Forrest (45)

EAST FIFE: Donnelly; Smith, Orphant; Aitken, Young, Wright; Wyles, McWatt, Dewar, I. Stewart, J. Stewart

RANGERS: Ritchie; Shearer, Provan; Greig, McKinnon, Baxter; Henderson, McLean, Forrest, Brand, Wilson

Attendance: 14,000

September 18th: Quarter-Final Second Leg

RANGERS (2) 2	EAST FIFE (0) 0
Brand (37 pen), Forrest (42)	

RANGERS: Ritchie; Shearer, Provan; Greig, McKinnon, Baxter; Henderson, McLean, Forrest, Brand, Wilson

EAST FIFE: Donnelly; Smith, Orphant; Walker, Young, Wright; McWatt, Aitken, Dewar, I. Stewart, J. Stewart

Attendance: 25,000

Rangers won 3-1 on aggregate

October 2nd: Semi-Final	At Hampden Park
RANGERS (2) 3	BERWICK
	RANGERS (1) 1
Wilson (13), Brand (39),	Bowron (35)
Forrest (78)	

RANGERS: Ritchie; Shearer, Provan; Greig, McKinnon, Baxter; Henderson, Millar, Forrest, Brand, Wilson

BERWICK: Mealyou; Hogg, Robertson; Spence, McKay, Gilchrist; Williamson, Cunningham, Bowron, Boyce, Peacock

Attendance: 16,000

Rangers had most of the play but most of the early shots went straight at Mealyou. The Berwick Rangers defence which was under almost constant pressure refused to crumble. Shearer was outstanding for Rangers — he, Greig and Henderson linked up perfectly. Wilson went off near the end with an ankle injury. In 13 minutes Wilson scored from close range, after an attempt by Henderson had been blocked. In 35 minutes Bowron slipped neatly past McKinnon and scored from 10 yards. Almost immediately Brand restored Rangers' lead. In the 78th minute Forrest scored his 20th goal of the season from a pass by Henderson.

October 26th: Final	At Hampden Park
RANGERS (0) 5	MORTON (0) 0
Forrest 4 (52, 59, 88, 89),	
Willoughby (65)	

RANGERS: Ritchie; Shearer, Provan; Greig, McKinnon, Baxter; Henderson, Willoughby, Forrest, Brand, Watson

MORTON: Brown; Boyd, Mallan; Reilly, Kiernan, Strachan; Adamson, Campbell, Stevenson, McGraw, Wilson

Attendance: 105,907   *Referee*: H. Phillips (Wishaw)

52 minutes elapsed before Forrest scored the first goal, but after that came the deluge. Forrest with his speed and perfect balance on the ground and in the air made Kiernan look ponderous. Rangers missed a number of chances to go ahead. Then in the 52nd minute Willoughby pushed a diagonal pass through on the right and Brown, obviously believing that Mallan would get to the ball before Henderson, came far out of his goal in expectation of a

back-pass. But the winger won the race and passed to Forrest who skilfully back-heeled the ball across the goal-line. 7 minutes later Forrest smartly pulled down Watson's cross and shot a 2nd. Willoughby took a pass from Forrest and hit the 3rd in 65 minutes and Morton were now sunk. 5 minutes from time McGraw hit the crossbar from 18 yards. But Rangers were not finished yet and 2 simple goals by Forrest in the last 2 minutes brought their tally to 5.

SCOTTISH CUP

January 11th: First Round
STENHOUSEMUIR (0) 1   RANGERS (2) 5
  M. Russell (85)   Millar (5),
                       Greig 2 (19, 70),
                       Provan (55 pen),
                       Brand (89)

STENHOUSEMUIR: R. Russell; Erskine, M. Russell; Orr, Hannah, Morrison; Waters, Sibbald, Dakers, Bryce, Henderson

RANGERS: Ritchie; Provan, Caldow; Davis, McKinnon, Baxter; Henderson, Greig, Millar, Brand, Watson

Attendance: 10,384

January 25th: Second Round
RANGERS (4) 9   DUNS (0) 0
  Millar 4 (14, 55, 68, 85),
  Brand 3 (15, 74, 79), McLean (17),
  Henderson (23)

RANGERS: Ritchie; Shearer, Provan; Greig, McKinnon, Baxter; Henderson, McLean, Millar, Brand, Traill

DUNS: Wilson; Fairbairn, Lough; Curle, McLeod, Brimms; Hughes, Finlay, Buchanan, Kelly, Whitelaw

Attendance: 17,350

February 15th: Third Round
RANGERS (1) 3   PATRICK THISTLE (0) 0
  Wilson 2 (26, 72),
  Forrest (48)

RANGERS: Ritchie; Shearer, Provan; Greig, McKinnon, Baxter; Henderson, McMillan, Forrest, Brand, Wilson

PARTICK THISTLE: Niven; Muir, Tinney; Closs, Harvey, Cunningham; Cowan, Hainey, Fleming, Duffy, McParland

Attendance: 60,000

March 7th: Fourth Round
RANGERS (1) 2   CELTIC (0) 0
  Forrest (44), Henderson (46)

RANGERS: Ritchie; Shearer, Provan; Greig, McKinnon, Baxter; Henderson, McMillan, Forrest, Brand, Wilson

CELTIC: Fallon; Young, Gemmell; Murdoch, McNeill, Kennedy; Brogan, Johnstone, Chalmers, Divers, Hughes

Attendance: 84,724

March 28th: Semi-Final   At Hampden Park
RANGERS (1) 1   DUNFERMLINE (0) 0
  Wilson (44)

RANGERS: Ritchie; Shearer, Provan; Greig, McKinnon, Baxter; Brand, McMillan, Millar, McLean, Wilson

DUNFERMLINE: Herriot; W. Callaghan, Lunn; Thomson, Miller, T. Callaghan; Kerray, Peebles, Dickson, Smith, Sinclair

Attendance: 67,823

There was no lack of incidents in a fast and furious game. Rangers just deserved the verdict. Without Henderson and Forrest the attack was anything but rhythmic. The score came just before the interval. As Baxter floated the ball into the Dunfermline penalty-area Brand and Wilson were there to meet it and the outside-left jabbed it past Herriot. Midway through the second half Shearer in rapid succession cleared twice almost on the goal-line. At that stage an equalising goal would not have been unmerited, but from then on Rangers more or less dominated the game and were unfortunate when a header by Wilson rebounded from the post.

April 25th: Final   At Hampden Park
RANGERS (0) 3   DUNDEE (0) 1
  Millar 2 (71, 89), Brand (90)   Cameron (72)

RANGERS: Ritchie; Shearer, Provan; Greig, McKinnon, Baxter; Henderson, McLean, Millar, Brand, Wilson

DUNDEE: Slater; Hamilton, Cox; Seith, Ryden, Stuart; Penman, Cousin, Cameron, Gilzean, Robertson

Attendance: 120,982   *Referee*: H. Phillips (Wishaw)

At the end Henderson wept, Wilson donned a bowler hat and Brand threw a bucketful of water over his colleagues. Rangers' triumph justified their jubilation. It was their 3rd successive win and the 18th in the long and distinguished history of the club. It completed an outstanding season with a clean sweep of the Scottish honours. Rangers might have had it won long before the last frantic minute but for Slater's breathtakingly brave goalkeeping. Millar and Brand hammered away at the weak line of Ryden's uncertainty only to be frustrated time and again by Slater's instinctive anticipation and intelligent sense of position. It was not pretty football that won the day. It was relentless aggression. Dundee resisted stoutly for 71 minutes but then Henderson struck the first blow. Ryden missed his corner-kick and Millar's header sailed into the net past Slater who was distracted by Brand moving in front of him. Right from the kick-off Cameron, for once free of McKinnon's shadow, got hold of a partial clearance and, skilfully bringing the ball under control, hooked a left-foot shot high into the net past Ritchie from 12 yards. Suddenly in the space of the last minute the game was won and lost. Rangers were awarded a free-kick and Baxter pushed the ball straight to Henderson, who had moved over from the right touchline. The winger ran past Hamilton into the penalty area, his cross was directed precisely onto the head of Millar, who was completely unmarked, and the ball floated in past Dundee's disorganised defenders. Half a minute later, Henderson beat Cox and crossed to Wilson whose shot was turned away by Slater. Brand was in position to return the ball to goal and it struck a post before rolling over the line.

EUROPEAN CUP

September 25th: Preliminary Round First Leg
RANGERS   (0) 0   REAL MADRID   (0) 1
                                            Puskas (87)

RANGERS: Ritchie; Shearer, Provan; Greig, McKinnon, Baxter; Henderson, McLean, Forrest, Brand, Wilson

REAL MADRID: Araquistain; Casado, Isidro; Muller, Santamaria, Zoco; Amancio, F. Ruiz, Di Stefano, Puskas, Gento

Attendance: 80,000

One flash of genius 3 minutes from the end nullified the almost constant pressure of the Scottish Champions. Shearer was well out of his beat when Gento fastened onto a ball out of defence and raced halfway up the field before crossing to Puskas who shot high into the net. This move, so simply accomplished, was in marked contrast to the laboured methods of Rangers. Rangers were unlucky 5 minutes before the interval when a header by Brand which had Araquistain beaten was headed off the goal-line by Casado. Soon afterwards Forrest was just off target after good work by Henderson. The famed trio of Di Stefano, Puskas and Gento were seen only in spasms. Henderson had the beating of Casado. Baxter was a pale shadow of the player he could be. McKinnon was steady as a rock and Provan a tough and dominating full-back.

October 9th: Preliminary Round Second Leg
REAL MADRID   (4) 6   RANGERS   (0) 0
   Puskas 3 (3, 24, 49),
   Evariste (12), Gento (19), Ruiz (82)

REAL MADRID: Araquistain; Casado, Isidro; Muller, Santamaria, Zoco; Evaristo, F. Ruiz, Di Stefano, Puskas, Gento

RANGERS: Ritchie; Shearer, Provan; Greig, McKinnon, Baxter, Henderson, Willoughby, Forrest, McLean, Watson

Attendance: 80,000

Real Madrid won 7-0 on aggregate

Real Madrid inflicted humiliation on Rangers. In 24 minutes Puskas, Gento and Di Stefano had scored or helped to score 4 goals. Rangers' forward line averaged only 20 years. They made their expected thrust for a quick goal and they could have scored if Forrest had killed a splendid pass from Shearer and scored a first-minute goal. The rout started in the 3rd minute when Puskas jumped to a cross from Gento, took the ball on his chest, brought it to his feet, then hit it powerfully home via the underside of the crossbar. Shortly after Puskas, with one swerve of his body, pulled the Rangers defence one way and left the ball for Evaristo to make the score 2-0. The 3rd goal came after 19 minutes — a rocket shot from Gento. Puskas then showed that Gento had no monopoly in power shooting with an even more vicious drive from the same distance. Ritchie, who had watched 4 shots fly past him, allowed a 5th to roll along the ground from Puskas 4 minutes after the re-start. Ruiz scored a 6th, 8 minutes from time, from an inch-perfect pass from Di Stefano.

APPEARANCES

	League	League Cup	Scottish Cup	Glasgow Cup	Friendlies	European Cup
Ritchie	34	10	6	2	2	2
Shearer	31	10	5	1	2	2
Provan	33	10	6	1	2	2
Greig	34	10	6	1	2	2
McKinnon	32	9	6	2	2	2
Baxter	26	10	6	1	2	1
Henderson	30	10	5	2	2	2
McLean	19	8	3	1	2	1
Forrest	24	10	2	1	2	1
Brand	31	10	6	1	1	2
Wilson	16	9	4	-	1	-
Millar	22	1	4	1	-	2
Willoughby	6	1	-	-	1	-
Hynd	1	-	-	-	-	-
C. Watson	7	1	1	1	1	1
Traill	3	-	1	1	-	-
Baillie	4	1	-	-	-	sub
McMillan	10	-	3	1	-	1
Wood	4	-	-	-	-	1
Caldow	3	-	1	2	-	-
Davis	4	-	1	2	-	-
Hunter	-	-	-	1	-	-

GOALSCORERS

League: Forrest 21, Brand 19 (2 pens), McLean 10, Millar 6, Wilson 6, Baxter 4 (2 pens), Watson 4, Greig 4, Henderson 3, Willoughby 3, Provan 3 (3 pens), McMillan 1, Own Goals 1

League Cup: Forrest 16, Wilson 6, Brand 5 (2 pens), McLean 3, Provan 1, Henderson 1, Willoughby 1

Scottish Cup: Brand 6, Millar 5, Wilson 4, Forrest 2, Greig 2, Henderson 2, McLean 1, Provan 1 (pen)

Friendlies: Greig 1, Own Goals 1

Glasgow Cup: McLean 1

The successful Rangers squad of season 1963–64. Back row: Henderson, Marshall, Christie, W. Wood, Greig, Ritchie, McFarlane, Martin, Murray, B. Watson, Penman, (trialist), Hume. Middle row: Binny, King, Hunter, McKinnon, Evans, Paterson, Sutherland, Bailie, Hynd, Davies, Neil, Provan, Pickering, Baxter, Joe Craven. Front row: S. Symon (manager), Scott, Setterington, McMillan, Willoughby, Caldow, Mooney, Shearer, C. Watson, Millar, Forrest, Brand, Burnside, Wilson, Kinnear.

Season 1964–65

Rangers got off to a bad start in the League — only one win in their first 7 matches — and never recovered, finishing a disappointing 5th behind Kilmarnock, Hearts, Dunfermline and Hibs. This was their worst placing in the Division for 39 years. Henderson missed much of the season with bunion trouble and Baxter, who was transferred to Sunderland at the season's end for £72,500, missed almost 4 months with a broken leg. Provan, Greig and McKinnon never missed a match. Jim Forrest finished top scorer with 30 League goals — 56 in all competitions. Bobby Shearer was freed at the end of the season.

In the European Cup Rangers beat Red Star of Yugoslavia in the First Round in a play-off at Highbury after a last-minute goal by McKinnon in Belgrade had thrown them a lifeline. Rapid Vienna were beaten both home and away in the next round but the price of victory was high. Baxter's right leg was broken 20 seconds from time in the Prater Stadium after one of his greatest-ever games for the club. European and World Club Champions Internazionale Milan were drawn in the Quarter-Final of the competition, but 3 mad minutes in the San Siro Stadium, in which 3 goals were lost, eventually decided the tie despite the fact that Rangers came so close in the return.

Baxter made his return to first-team action in the Third-Round Scottish Cup tie at Easter Road but it was no triumphant return, a goal by Willie Hamilton, 2 minutes from time, giving Hibs victory.

Rangers did win the League Cup. The Qualifying Section was won without the loss of a match. Dunfermline were beaten 5-2 on aggregate in the Quarter-Final. Dundee United were beaten, after extra-time in the Semi-Final, and Forrest scored 2 goals against one by Johnstone to win the Final against Celtic. Baxter captained the team in the Final in which both Caldow and Wood made their only League-Cup appearance of the season.

League: Fifth
League Cup: Finalists
Scottish Cup: Third Round
European Cup: Quarter-Finalists

SCOTTISH FIRST DIVISION

August 19th:
RANGERS 0   DUNFERMLINE 0

RANGERS: Ritchie; Hynd, Provan; Greig, McKinnon, Baxter; Henderson, McLean, Forrest, Brand, Wilson

DUNFERMLINE: Herriot; Thomson, W. Callaghan, McLean, Miller; Sinclair, Ferguson, McLaughlin, Melrose, Peebles

Attendance: n.a.

September 5th:
CELTIC (1) 3   RANGERS (0) 1
Chalmers 2 (35, 50),   Wilson (82)
Hughes (56)

CELTIC: Fallon; Young, Gemmell; Brogan, Cushley, Kennedy; Johnstone, Divers, Chalmers, Gallagher, Hughes

RANGERS: Ritchie; Hynd, Provan; Greig, McKinnon, Baxter; Henderson, McLean, Forrest, Brand, Wilson

Gallagher missed a penalty

Attendance: 58,000

This was a splendid win for Celtic. They recorded an emphatic victory over Rangers after 90 minutes of excitement on a pitch soaked by incessant heavy rain. Rangers' defence was too often outwitted by the massive Hughes and the diminutive Johnstone. After 8 minutes' play Gallagher failed with a penalty-kick after Provan impeded Johnstone but the overdue goal came in 35 minutes when Chalmers got his head to a ball crossed by Johnstone after Divers had made the opening. Early in the second half McLean struck the crossbar. In 50 minutes Celtic scored again when Ritchie was unable to clutch a ball crossed by Johnstone, and as it spun loose Chalmers slammed it into the net. 6 minutes later Hughes took on the entire Rangers' defence in a dribble from left to right into the penalty-area and when he shot from 12 yards Ritchie allowed the greasy ball to squirm through his fingers and roll over the line. After 82 minutes' play Wilson scored from an acute angle after combination by Henderson and Baxter.

September 12th:
RANGERS (0) 1   PARTICK THISTLE (0) 1
  McLean (74)   Ewing (82)

RANGERS: Martin; Hynd, Provan; Greig, McKinnon, Baxter; Henderson, Willoughby, Forrest, McLean, Wilson

PARTICK THISTLE: Niven; Hogan, Tinney; Davis, Harvey, Cunningham; Ewing, Hainey, Staite, Fleming, McParland

Attendance: 34,000

September 19th:
DUNDEE (1) 4   RANGERS (1) 1
  Stuart (32),   Forrest (4)
  Robertson 2 (54, 85),
  Cousin (70)

DUNDEE: Donaldson; Hamilton, Totten; Houston, Ryden, Stuart; Penman, Cameron, Waddell, Cousin, Robertson

RANGERS: Martin; Shearer, Provan; Greig, McKinnon, Baxter; Henderson, Millar, Forrest, Brand, Wilson

Attendance: 28,600

September 23rd: The Scottish League drew 2-2 with the League of Ireland in Dublin. Greig, Henderson and Millar were in the team.

September 26th:
RANGERS (3) 9   AIRDRIE (0) 2
  Greig (33),   Rowan (48),
  Forrest 3 (35, 82, 88)   Murray (62)
  Brand 3 (38, 70, 84),
  Wilson (69), Baxter (80 pen)

RANGERS: Ritchie; Hynd, Provan; Greig, McKinnon, Baxter; Henderson, Millar, Forrest, Brand, Wilson

AIRDRIE: Samson; Caldwell, Keenan; Reid, Hannah, Wishart; Ferguson, Murray, Rowan, Hastings, McColl

Attendance: 20,000

September 25th: Rangers swopped Doug Baillie for Findlay McGillivray of Third Lanark. Thirds also received a £12,000 cash adjustment.

October 3rd: Scotland were beaten 3-2 by Wales in Cardiff. Greig and Baxter were in the team.

October 8th:
ST JOHNSTONE (0) 0   RANGERS (0) 1
                  Baxter (75)

ST JOHNSTONE: Fallon; McFadyen, Coburn; McCarry, McKinven, Renton; Flanagan, Harrower, Whitelaw, Kerray, Kemp

RANGERS: Ritchie; Shearer, Provan; Greig, McKinnon, Baxter; Forrest, McLean, Millar, Brand, Wilson

Attendance: n.a.

October 10th:
RANGERS (1) 2   HIBERNIAN (1) 4
  Johnston 2 (8, 52)   Cormack 2 (42, 55),
                  Hamilton (80),
                  Quinn (84)

RANGERS: Ritchie; Shearer, Provan; Greig, McKinnon, Baxter; Watson, Millar, Forrest, Brand, Johnston

HIBERNIAN: Wilson; Fraser, Parke; Stanton, McNamee, Baxter; Cormack, Hamilton, Scott, Quinn, Martin

Attendance: 40,000

October 17th:
HEARTS (0) 1   RANGERS (1) 1
  Wallace (89)   Hamilton o.g. (30)

HEARTS: Cruikshank; Shevlane, Holt; Polland, Anderson, Higgins; Ford, Hamilton, Wallace, Gordon, Traynor

RANGERS: Ritchie; Provan, Caldow; Greig, McKinnon, Wood; Forrest, Brand, Millar, Baxter, Johnston

Attendance: 35,000

October 21st: Scotland beat Finland 3-1 at Hampden Park. Greig and Baxter were in the team.

League positions

	P	W	D	L	F	A	Pts
1 Kilmarnock	8	7	1	0	14	3	15
2 Hearts	9	6	3	0	29	11	15
3 Hibernian	9	7	0	2	22	14	14
4 Dunfermline	9	5	2	2	22	10	12
5 Morton	9	5	2	2	13	7	12
10 RANGERS	8	2	3	3	16	15	7

October 27th:
ST MIRREN   (0) 0   RANGERS   (1) 7
                         Forrest 4 (26, 57, 63, 76),
                         Baxter (74),
                         Millar (78), Brand (83)
ST MIRREN: Liney; Murray, Wilson; Ross, Clunie,
Gray; McIntyre, Beck, Queen, Gemmell, Robertson

RANGERS: Ritchie; Provan, Caldow; Greig,
McKinnon, Wood; Brand, Millar, Forrest, Baxter,
Johnston
Attendance: 15,000

October 31st:
RANGERS   (0) 6   CLYDE   (0) 1
Millar 2 (53, 79),   McLean (89 pen)
Forrest (62), Greig (64),
Johnston (71), Wood (75)
RANGERS: Ritchie; Provan, Caldow; Greig,
McKinnon, Wood; Brand, Millar, Forrest, Baxter,
Johnston

CLYDE: McCulloch; Gray, Mulheron; Glasgow,
Fraser, White; Bryce, Gilroy, Hood, McLean, Hastings
Attendance: 29,000

November 7th:
RANGERS   (0) 2   ABERDEEN   (0) 2
Baxter (64), Forrest (75)   Kerrigan (54),
                                Morrison (71)
RANGERS: Ritchie; Provan, Caldow; Greig,
McKinnon, Wood; Brand, Millar, Forrest, Baxter,
Johnston

ABERDEEN: Ogston; Bennett, Shewan; Burns,
McCormick, Smith; Lister, Cooke, Morrison, Kerrigan,
Kerr
Attendance: 30,000

**November 11th: Rangers signed Thorolf Beck from
St Mirren for £20,000**

November 14th:
KILMARNOCK   (0) 1   RANGERS   (0) 1
Beattie (74)   Baxter (62)
KILMARNOCK: Forsyth; King, Watson; Murray,
McGrory, Beattie; McLean, McInally, Hamilton,
McFadzean, Sneddon

RANGERS: Ritchie; Provan, Caldow; Greig,
McKinnon, Wood; Brand, Millar, Forrest, Baxter,
Johnston
Attendance: 30,000

November 21st:
RANGERS   (0) 1   MOTHERWELL   (0) 0
Forrest (89½)
RANGERS: Ritchie; Provan, Hynd; Greig,
McKinnon, Wood; Wilson, Millar, Forrest, Baxter,
Johnston

MOTHERWELL: Wylie; Thomson, R. McCallum;
Murray, Delaney, W. McCallum; Lindsay, McCann,
McBride, Weir, Hunter
Attendance: 33,000

**November 21st: Rangers announced that Willie
Henderson would be out for the rest of the season
with bunion trouble.**

**November 25th: Scotland beat Northern Ireland 3-2
at Hampden Park. Greig, Baxter and Wilson were in
the team. Wilson scored two of the goals. Baxter
captained the team.**

November 28th:
FALKIRK   (0) 0   RANGERS   (3) 5
                         Forrest 2 (32, 86),
                         Greig (38),
                         Baxter (39),
                         Wilson (75)
FALKIRK: Whigham; Lambie, Hunter; Fulton,
Markie, Scott; O'Donnell, Allan, Gourlay, Moran,
Stewart

RANGERS: Ritchie; Provan, Caldow; Greig,
McKinnon, Wood; Brand, Millar, Forrest, Baxter,
Wilson
Attendance: 13,000

**December 8th: Jim Baxter broke his right leg in the
European Cup match in the Prater Stadium,
Vienna.**

**December 2nd: Ian McMillan rejoined Airdrie for
£5,000.**

December 12th:
DUNDEE UNITED   (0) 1   RANGERS   (1) 3
Dick (58)   Forrest 3 (25, 59, 88)
DUNDEE UNITED: Davie; Millar, Briggs; Neilson,
Smith, Fraser; Dick, Gillespie, Dossing, Berg, Persson

RANGERS: Ritchie; Provan, Caldow; Greig,
McKinnon, Wood; Johnston, Millar, Forrest, Beck,
Wilson
Attendance: 25,000

December 19th:
RANGERS (1) 5   THIRD LANARK (0) 0
Forrest 2 (36, 67),
Beck (58), Wilson 2 (80, 90)

RANGERS: Ritchie; Provan, Caldow; Greig,
McKinnon, Wood; Wilson, Millar, Forrest, Beck,
Johnston

THIRD LANARK: Williams; McKay, C. Baillie;
Little, D. Baillie, Geddes; Halloran, Kilgannon,
Murray, Jackson, Black

Attendance: 22,000

League positions

	P	W	D	L	F	A	Pts
1 Hearts	18	13	4	1	56	23	30
2 Kilmarnock	18	13	4	1	35	15	30
3 Hibernian	17	12	2	3	39	22	26
4 Dunfermline	16	10	2	4	35	18	22
5 Celtic	17	10	2	5	35	25	22
6 RANGERS	16	8	5	3	46	20	21

January 1st:
RANGERS (1) 1   CELTIC (0) 0
Forrest (32)

RANGERS: Ritchie; Provan, Caldow; Greig,
McKinnon, Wood; Wilson, Millar, Forrest, Beck,
Johnston

CELTIC: Simpson; Young, Gemmell; Clark, McNeill,
Kennedy; Johnstone, Murdoch, Hughes, Divers,
Gallagher

Attendance: 64,400

Jimmy Johnstone was ordered off for the second time in
his career and Celtic missed a late penalty. Johnstone was
ordered off for charging down Beck in injury time just
before the interval; Hughes had his name taken for a foul
on Ritchie and Provan after one on Kennedy. Murdoch
shot over the bar a penalty-kick awarded 6 minutes from
time when McKinnon brought down Hughes well inside
the area. Rangers were sluggish and their forwards lacked
ideas. Johnston was the most purposeful of the 5 but the
absence of Baxter's influence could almost be felt. It was
only appropriate that the winning goal should have been
initiated by the young winger. In 32 minutes his corner-
kick was headed forward to Forrest by Millar and the
centre-forward, turning quickly, shot home from about 6
yards. Celtic played their best football when they were a
man short.

January 2nd:
PARTICK THISTLE (1) 1 RANGERS (0) 1
Hainey (29)   Caldow (83 pen)
PARTICK THISTLE: Gray; Campbell, Muir; Davis,
Harvey, McParland; Cowan, Hainey, McLindon,
Ewing, Kilpatrick

RANGERS: Ritchie; Provan, Caldow; Greig,
McKinnon, Wood; Wilson, Millar, Forrest, Beck,
Johnston

Ewing missed a penalty

Attendance: 25,000

January 9th:
RANGERS (2) 4   DUNDEE (0) 0
Forrest 3 (36, 38, 46),
Millar (68)

RANGERS: Ritchie; Provan, Caldow; Greig,
McKinnon, Wood; Wilson, Millar, Forrest, Beck,
Johnston

DUNDEE: Donaldson; Hamilton, Reid; Cousin,
Easton, Stuart; Murray, Penman, Harley, Cooke,
Robertson

Attendance: 28,000

January 16th:
AIRDRIE (0) 0   RANGERS (2) 4
Wilson (14),
Johnston (32),
Caldow (55 pen),
Forrest (62)

AIRDRIE: Samson; Jonquin, Keenan; Reid, Hannah,
Marshall; Ferguson, McMillan, Brown, Murray,
Moonie

RANGERS: Ritchie; Provan, Caldow; Greig,
McKinnon, Wood; Wilson, Millar, Forrest, Beck,
Johnston

Attendance: 18,000

January 30th:
HIBERNIAN (1) 1   RANGERS (0) 0
Martin (32)

HIBERNIAN: Wilson; Fraser, Davis; Stanton,
McNamee, Baxter; Martin, Quinn, Vincent, Hamilton,
Cormack

RANGERS: Ritchie; Provan, Caldow; Greig,
McKinnon, Wood; Henderson, Millar, Forrest, Beck,
Wilson

Attendance: 44,300

February 13th:
RANGERS (1) 1   HEARTS (1) 1
Forrest (23)   Higgins (8)

RANGERS: Ritchie; Provan, Caldow; Greig,
McKinnon, Wood; Henderson, Wilson, Forrest, Brand,
Johnston

HEARTS: Cruikshank; Ferguson, Holt; Polland,
Anderson, Higgins; Jensen, Barry, Wallace, Hamilton,
Traynor

Attendance: 50,000

February 27th:
RANGERS   (0) 1   ST MIRREN   (0) 0
  Wood (55)

RANGERS: Ritchie; Provan, Caldow; Greig,
McKinnon, Hynd; Henderson, Wood, Forrest, Beck,
Johnston

ST MIRREN: Liney; Murray, Riddell; Mitchell,
Clunie, Wilson; Ross, Robertson, Carroll, Queen,
Gemmell

Attendance: 20,000

League positions

	P	W	D	L	F	A	Pts
1 Hearts	26	16	5	5	67	39	37
2 Dunfermline	24	16	3	5	57	25	35
3 Hibernian	25	16	3	6	58	34	35
4 Kilmarnock	26	15	5	6	45	28	35
5 RANGERS	23	12	7	4	58	23	31

March 10th:
CLYDE   (0) 0   RANGERS   (2) 3
                        McLean 2 (25, 32),
                        Greig (53)

CLYDE: McCulloch; Glasgow, White; McHugh,
Fraser, Soutar; Bryce, Gilroy, Knox, McLean, Hastings

RANGERS: Ritchie; Provan, Caldow; Greig,
McKinnon, Hynd; Henderson, Millar, McLean, Baxter,
Wilson

Caldow missed a penalty

Attendance: 18,000

March 13th:
ABERDEEN   (2) 2   RANGERS   (0) 0
  Winchester (2), Kerrigan (27)

ABERDEEN: Ogston; Bennett, Shewan; Burns,
McCormick, Smith; Little, Winchester, Ravn, Kerrigan,
Mortensen

RANGERS: Ritchie; Provan, Caldow; Greig,
McKinnon, Hynd; Henderson, Wood, McLean, Baxter,
Johnston

Attendance: 25,000

**March 17th: The Scottish League drew 2-2 with the
English League at Hampden Park. Caldow and
Greig were in the team.**

March 20th:
RANGERS   (0) 1   KILMARNOCK   (0) 1
  Brand (74 pen)   Mason (50)

RANGERS: Ritchie; Provan, Caldow; Greig,
McKinnon, Wood; Brand, Millar, Forrest, Beck, Wilson

KILMARNOCK: Ferguson; King, McFadzean;
Murray, McGrory, Beattie; McLean, McInally, Black,
Mason, McIlroy

Attendance: 31,000

March 24th:
RANGERS   (0) 2   ST JOHNSTONE   (0) 1
  Wilson (46), Forrest (51)   Hawkshaw (67)

RANGERS: Ritchie; Provan, Caldow; Greig,
McKinnon, Wood; Henderson, Millar, Forrest, Baxter,
Wilson

ST JOHNSTONE: McVittie; McFadyen, Coburn;
Richmond, McKinven, Renton; Hawkshaw, Whitelaw,
Kerray, Duffy, Kemp

Attendance: 5,800

March 30th:
RANGERS   (0) 0   MORTON   (0) 1
                          Adamson (75)

RANGERS: Martin; Provan, Caldow; Greig,
McKinnon, Wood; Henderson, Willoughby, Forrest,
Baxter, Wilson

MORTON: Sorensen; Johansen, Mallon; Smith,
Strachan, Neilson; Stevenson, Bertelsen, Caven,
McGraw, Adamson

Attendance: 25,000

April 3rd:
RANGERS   (4) 6   FALKIRK   (0) 1
  Willoughby 2 (4, 30),
  Forrest 4 (5, 17, 60, 81)

RANGERS: Martin; Provan, Caldow; Greig,
McKinnon, Wood; Henderson, Willoughby, Forrest,
Baxter, Wilson

FALKIRK: Whigham; Lambie, Brown; Pierson, Rae,
Stewart; McKinney, Graham, Baillie, Duncan, Halliday

April 7th:
MORTON   (1) 1   RANGERS   (1) 3
  Stevenson (27)   Forrest (21),
                          Wilson 2 (47, 56)

MORTON: Sorensen; Johansen, Mallon; Smith,
Strachan, Neilsen; Wilson, Stevenson, Bertelesen,
McGraw, Adamson

RANGERS: Martin; Provan, Caldow; Greig,
McKinnon, Wood; Henderson, Willoughby, Forrest,
Baxter, Wilson

McGraw missed a penalty

Attendance: n.a.

**April 10th: Scotland drew 2-2 with England at
Wembley. Greig, Henderson and Wilson were in the
team.**

April 14th:
DUNFERMLINE (2) 3   RANGERS (0) 1
  Sinclair 2 (4, 71), Melrose (14)   Wilson (88)

DUNFERMLINE: Herriot; W. Callaghan, Lunn;
Thomson, McLean, T. Callaghan; Edwards, Smith,
McLaughlin, Melrose, Sinclair

RANGERS: Martin; Provan, Caldow; Greig,
McKinnon, Wood; Henderson, Willoughby, Forrest,
Baxter, Wilson

Both T. Callaghan and Baxter missed penalties
Attendance: n.a.

April 17th:
RANGERS (0) 0   DUNDEE UNITED (0) 1
                 Mitchell (67)

RANGERS: Martin; Provan, Caldow; Greig,
McKinnon, Wood; Henderson, Brand, Forrest, Baxter,
Wilson

DUNDEE UNITED: Mackay; Millar, Briggs;
Neilson, Smith, Wing; Berg, Gillespie, Dossing,
Mitchell, Persson
Attendance: 15,000

April 21st:
MOTHERWELL (1) 1   RANGERS (1) 3
  Hunter (30 secs)   McLean (16),
                       Wood (57),
                       Henderson (81)

MOTHERWELL: Wylie; Delaney, R. McCallum;
Aitken, Martis, W. McCallum; Coakley, McBride,
Donnachie, Hunter, Hume

RANGERS: Martin; Provan, Caldow; Hynd,
McKinnon, Greig; Henderson, Wood, McLean, Brand,
Wilson

April 23rd:
THIRD LANARK (0) 0   RANGERS (1) 1
                       Brand (29)

THIRD LANARK: Williams; Connell, May; Jackson,
Little, Geddes; McGuire, Fyfe, Murray, Kilgannon,
Kirk

RANGERS: Martin; Provan, Caldow; Hynd,
McKinnon, Greig; Henderson, Wood, McLean, Brand,
Wilson

Attendance: 5,000

Scottish First Division

	P	W	D	L	F	A	Pts
1 Kilmarnock	34	22	6	6	62	33	50
2 Hearts	34	22	6	6	90	49	50
3 Dunfermline	34	22	5	7	83	36	49
4 Hibernian	34	21	4	9	75	47	46
5 RANGERS	34	18	8	8	78	35	44
6 Dundee	34	15	10	9	86	63	40
7 Clyde	34	17	6	11	64	58	40
8 Celtic	34	16	5	13	76	57	37
9 Dundee United	34	15	6	13	59	51	36
10 Morton	34	13	7	14	54	54	33
11 Partick Thistle	34	11	10	13	57	58	32
12 Aberdeen	34	12	8	14	59	75	32
13 St Johnstone	34	9	11	14	57	62	29
14 Motherwell	34	10	8	16	45	54	28
15 St Mirren	34	9	6	19	38	70	24
16 Falkirk	34	7	7	20	43	85	21
17 Airdrie	34	5	4	25	48	110	14
18 Third Lanark	34	3	1	30	22	99	7

April 26th: Bobby Shearer was given a free transfer.

**April 28th: Both Baxter and Henderson played in
Stanley Matthew's Testimonial Match. Henderson
played and scored for the World XI and Baxter
played for Matthew's XI.**

**May 6th: Inter Milan were reported to be ready to
bid for Jim Baxter.**

**May 8th: Greig and Henderson played for Scotland
against Spain at Hampden Park. The match ended
0-0.**

**May 23rd: Greig and Henderson played for Scotland
against Poland. The match ended 1-1.**

**May 25th: Sunderland signed Jim Baxter for
£72,500.**

**May 27th: Wilson and Greig scored for Scotland in a
2-1 win in Finland. Henderson also appeared in the
match.**

**June 24th: Kaj Johansen was signed from Morton for
£20,000.**

LEAGUE CUP

August 8th:
RANGERS (2) 4   ABERDEEN (0) 0
  Forrest (27), McLean 2 (35, 52),
  Wilson (79)

RANGERS: Ritchie; Shearer, Provan; Greig,
McKinnon, Baxter; Henderson, McLean, Forrest,
Brand, Wilson

ABERDEEN: Ogston; Bennett, Shewan; Cooke,
Coutts, Smith; Kerrigan, Ronaldson, Kerr, Winchester,
McIntosh
Attendance: 45,000

August 12th:
ST MIRREN   0   RANGERS   0
ST MIRREN: Liney; Murray, Wilson; Clark, Clunie,
Gray; Ross, Carroll, Queen, Beck, Robertson

RANGERS: Ritchie; Shearer, Provan; Greig,
McKinnon, Baxter; Henderson, McLean, Forrest,
Brand, Wilson
Attendance: n.a.

August 15th:
ST JOHNSTONE   (1) 1   RANGERS   (3) 9
   McLindon (32)   McLean 2 (8, 74),
                           Forrest 4 (34, 59, 68,
                           85),
                           Brand 2 (43, 45),
                           Baxter (49)
ST JOHNSTONE: Fallon; McFadyen, Coburn;
McCarry, Richmond, Dickson; Flanagan, McLindon,
Whitelaw, Kerray, Kemp

RANGERS: Ritchie; Shearer, Provan; Greig,
McKinnon, Baxter; Henderson, McLean, Forrest,
Brand, Wilson
Attendance: 15,000

August 22nd:
ABERDEEN   (2) 3   RANGERS   (2) 4
   McIntosh (14), Kerr (24),   Forrest 3 (25, 27, 85),
   Smith (86)   Brand (63)
ABERDEEN: Ogston; Bennett, Shewan; Burns,
Coutts, Smith; Lister, Cooke, Kerr, Winchester,
McIntosh

RANGERS: Ritchie; Hynd, Provan; Watson,
McKinnon, Baxter; Henderson, McLean, Forrest,
Brand, Wilson
Attendance: 26,000

August 26th:
RANGERS   (2) 6   ST MIRREN   (0) 2
   Baxter (16), Forrest (36),   Robertson (52 pen),
   McLean (58), Brand (69),   Beck (60)
   Henderson (75), Wilson (86)
RANGERS: Ritchie; Hynd, Provan; Watson,
McKinnon, Baxter; Henderson, McLean, Forrest,
Brand, Wilson

ST MIRREN: Liney; Murray, Wilson; Clark, Clunie,
Gray; McIntyre, Carroll, Queen, Beck, Robertson
Attendance: 35,000

August 29th:
RANGERS   (3) 3   ST JOHNSTONE   (1) 1
   Forrest 3 (3, 11, 13)   Kemp (41 pen)
RANGERS: Ritchie; Hynd, Provan; Watson,
McKinnon, Baxter; Wilson, McLean, Forrest, Brand,
Johnston

ST JOHNSTONE: Fallon; Richmond, Coburn;
McCarry, McKinven, Renton; Flanagan, Kerray,
McLindon, Harrower, Kemp
Attendance: 22,000

League Cup Section Table

	P	W	D	L	F	A	Pts
RANGERS	6	5	1	0	26	7	11
St Mirren	6	2	3	1	11	12	7
Aberdeen	6	1	3	2	11	15	5
St Johnstone	6	0	1	5	5	19	1

September 14th: Quarter-Final First Leg
DUNFERMLINE   (0) 0   RANGERS   (1) 3
                           Forrest (65),
                           Brand (35),
                           McLean o.g. (71)
DUNFERMLINE: Herriot; Thomson, W. Callaghan;
T. Callaghan, McLean, Miller; Peebles, Smith, Dickson,
Kilgannon, Melrose

RANGERS: Martin; Shearer, Provan; Greig,
McKinnon, Baxter; Henderson, Millar, Forrest, Brand,
Wilson
Attendance: 20,000

September 16th: Quarter-Final Second Leg
RANGERS   (1) 2   DUNFERMLINE   (1) 2
   Millar (38), Forrest (85)   Sinclair (40),
                           McLaughlin (51)
RANGERS: Martin; Shearer, Provan; Greig,
McKinnon, Baxter; Henderson, Millar, Forrest, Brand,
Wilson

DUNFERMLINE: Herriot; Thomson, W. Callaghan;
Smith, McLean, Miller; Edwards, Ferguson,
McLaughlin, Kilgannon, Sinclair

Rangers won 5-2 on aggregate
Attendance: n.a.

September 30th: Semi-Final   At Hampden Park
RANGERS   (0) 2   DUNDEE UNITED   (1) 1
                           After Extra Time
   Forrest 2 (86, 106)   Moran (20)
RANGERS: Ritchie; Shearer, Provan; Greig,
McKinnon, Baxter; C. Watson, Millar, Forrest, Brand,
Wilson

DUNDEE UNITED: Davie; Millar, Briggs; Neilson,
Smith, Fraser; Graham, Rooney, Moran, Gillespie,
Thom
Attendance: 39,584

Moran took his goal cleverly in the 20th minute when he
neatly headed the ball past Ritchie from Rooney's cross.
Rangers made their big effort with about 10 minutes
remaining for play and forced corner after corner. Their

persistence was rewarded 4 minutes from time when Forrest equalised with a powerful shot from close range. The all-important goal came just after the teams turned for the last 15 minutes of extra-time. Forrest deceived several opponents with confidence as he strode through the middle to score and put his team into the Final. In a colourless game Rangers' only consistently good forward was Watson, deputising for the unfit Henderson at outside-right. United like Rangers lacked punch near goal.

October 24th: Final   At Hampden Park
RANGERS (0) 2   CELTIC (0) 1
   Forrest 2 (52, 62)   Johnstone (69)

RANGERS: Ritchie; Provan, Caldow; Greig, McKinnon, Wood; Brand, Millar, Forrest, Baxter, Johnston

CELTIC: Fallon; Young, Gemmell; Clark, Cushley, Kennedy; Johnstone, Murdoch, Chalmers, Divers, Hughes

Attendance: 91,423   *Referee*: H. Phillips (Wishaw)

Behind Rangers' success was the influence of Baxter, who laid on the second goal for Forrest after 62 minutes. The centre-forward, having 10 minutes earlier swooped on the ball after an indecisive clearance by Gemmell, again swept the ball into the net. When Johnstone scored for Celtic in 69 minutes after leading-up work by Clark and Chalmers, the stage was set for a grandstand finish which had the crowd of 91,000 in almost continuous uproar. This will be remembered as one of the great encounters between these two famous clubs. In the first half Provan headed off the line a header by Divers which had Ritchie beaten. Hughes and Johnstone exchanged positions during the match but Baxter, Rangers' captain, cunningly countered this move by switching Provan and Caldow.

SCOTTISH CUP

February 6th: First Round
RANGERS (2) 3   HAMILTON (0) 0
   Brand (15 secs), Millar (20),   ACADEMICALS
   Forrest (64)

RANGERS: Ritchie; Provan, Mathieson; Greig, McKinnon, Wood; Henderson, Millar, Forrest, Brand, Johnston

HAMILTON: Lamont; Frye, Holton; Hinshelwood, Small, Anderson; McClare, Currie, Forsyth, Gilmour, Alexander

Attendance: 22,184

February 20th: Second Round
DUNDEE (0) 0   RANGERS (0) 2
                  Forrest 2 (48, 85)

DUNDEE UNITED: Mackay; Millar, Briggs; Munro, Smith, Wing; Berg, Neilson, Dick, Gillespie, Persson

RANGERS: Ritchie; Provan, Caldow; Greig, McKinnon, Hynd; Henderson, Wood, Forrest, Beck, Johnston

Attendance: 23,000

March 6th: Third Round
HIBERNIAN (1) 2   RANGERS (1) 1
   Hamilton 2 (5, 88)   Hynd (23)

HIBERNIAN: Wilson; Fraser, Davis; Stanton, McNamee, Baxter; Martin, Quinn, Scott, Hamilton, Cormack

RANGERS: Ritchie; Provan, Caldow; Greig, McKinnon, Hynd; Henderson, Millar, Forrest, Baxter, Johnston

Attendance: 47,000

EUROPEAN CUP

September 2nd: First Round Second Leg
RANGERS (1) 3   RED STAR
                   (Yugoslavia) (0) 1
   Brand 2 (10, 89), Forrest (46)   Djazic (55)

RANGERS: Ritchie; Hynd, Provan; Greig, McKinnon, Baxter; Henderson, McLean, Forrest, Brand, Wilson

RED STAR: Dujkovic; Durkovic, Jeftic; Melic, Kop, Popovic; Cebinac, Skbic, Milosevic, Kostic, Djazic

Attendance: 80,000

Rangers began as if they would pound their opponents into the ground. In 10 minutes Brand scored a delightful goal after brilliant combination by Baxter and Wilson. Twice Greig shook the crossbar and once Wilson hit the inside of the far post. Immediately after the interval Rangers caught out the Yugoslav defence. Baxter sent Wilson speeding down the wing and with the opposition hesitating, expecting him to run the ball out of play, he cut it back to Forrest, who scored easily. But 9 minutes later Rangers' defence dithered and Djazic nipped in and scored from 6 yards. Soon afterwards Rangers nearly conceded another when Cebinac hit the post. But Brand brought solace with his last-minute goal from a pass by Baxter.

September 9th: First Round Second Leg
RED STAR (1) 4   RANGERS (1) 2
   Prlincevic 2 (32, 67)   Greig (40),
   Kostic (65), Melic (77)   McKinnon (90)

RED STAR: Dujkovic; Durkovic, Jeftic; Melic, Kop, Popovic; Cebinac, Stojamovic, Prlincevic, Kostic, Djazic

RANGERS: Ritchie; Shearer, Provan; Greig, McKinnon, Baxter; Henderson, Millar, Forrest, Brand, Wilson

Attendance: 70,000

Aggregate 5-5

Rangers held out until Kostic sent a 40-yard lob into their goalmouth after 32 minutes. Ritchie jumped high above the incoming opponents but, challenged late by Prlincevic, dropped the ball and the centre-forward kicked it over the line before there was a possibility of recovery. Red Star had earlier struck the crossbar twice and post once. In 40 minutes Rangers equalised when a lob from Greig, following a corner, hit the inside of a post and finished in the back of the net. For 20 minutes of the 2nd half Rangers held out and then in 2 minutes their lead vanished. Kostic headed a magnificent goal and then Prlincevic hit his 2nd goal. Rangers looked a beaten team when Melic scored a glorious fourth 13 minutes from time and then came McKinnon's goal.

With only 60 seconds to an inevitable defeat, a corner-kick for Rangers was the last thing expected at this stage of the tie. Nevertheless Wilson broke away on the left, jostled with the Red Star right-back and won a corner-kick. Wilson flighted this vital shot, the goalkeeper failed to allow for the outswing and Forrest, jumping high, headed the ball against the crossbar. McKinnon jumped, lunged with his head, and with perfect placing and power hit the ball into the roof of the net. McKinnon had saved the day.

November 4th: Play-Off   At Highbury
RANGERS   (2) 3   RED STAR   (0) 1
  Forrest 2 (12, 36), Brand (73)   Kop (75)

RANGERS: Ritchie; Provan, Caldow; Greig, McKinnon, Wood; Brand, Millar, Forrest, Baxter, Johnston

RED STAR: Dujkovic; Durkovic, Jeftic; Skrbic, Kop, Popovic; Cebinac, Melic, Prlincevic, Kostic, Djazic

Attendance: 34,428

The Scottish Champions took the initiative in attack from the start. Millar, roving the length and breadth of the field, and Baxter, who was given all the room in the world, often puzzled the Yugoslavs with sudden changes in the direction of attack. Their delight in the 4th minute when Forrest had the ball in the net was cut short when the goal was ruled out for offside. But in 12 minutes Forrest did score when Millar headed in a Brand corner. Red Star's first scoring effort was a 20-yard drive from Djazic which hit the bar and went over. Forrest scored again in 36 minutes when he prodded in the rebound after Dujkovic had parried Brand's shot. In 73 minutes Brand put Rangers 3-0 up and safely on the road to Vienna. He took a pass from Baxter, and with the linesman waving play-on, hit the ball into the net off Dujkovic's diving body. 2 minutes later Kop came upfield and headed a cross past Ritchie.

November 18th: Second Round First Leg
RANGERS   (0) 1   RAPID VIENNA
  Wilson (55)   (Austria)   (0) 0

RANGERS: Ritchie; Provan, Caldow; Greig, McKinnon, Wood; Wilson, Millar, Forrest, Baxter, Johnston

RAPID: Veres; Halla, Hoeltt; Skocik, Glencher, Hasil; Schmid, Wolny, Grausam, Floegl, Sietl

Attendance: 60,000

Straight from the kick-off Rapid threw across the face of their penalty-area an almost impenetrable screen. Rangers pierced it only once when, in 55 minutes, Wilson gladly accepted a perfect pass from Baxter inside Hoeltt and shot past Veres from close range. Rapid must have felt satisfied with the way they were able to keep the margin so low. Rapid, of course, were content to hang back and allow the waves of Rangers attacks to break and subside over their tightly disciplined defence. Rangers' goal was in serious danger only once 5 minutes from time when Ritchie dropped Hasil's long hard shot just short of the line and the ball had to be scrambled away for a corner.

December 8th: Second Round Second Leg
RAPID VIENNA   (0) 0   RANGERS   (1) 2
                               Forrest (19),
                               Wilson (55)

RAPID: Veres; Zaglitsch, Hoeltt; Skocik, Glencher, Hasil; Schmid, Wolny, Grausam, Floegl, Seitl

RANGERS: Ritchie; Provan, Caldow; Greig, McKinnon, Wood; Johnston, Millar, Forrest, Baxter, Wilson

Attendance: 70,000

Rangers won 3-0 on aggregate

Rangers had to pay a high price for their great victory. Shortly after the match ended it was learned that Baxter, who only 20 seconds from the end had felt the full force of Skocik's boot on his achilles tendon, would be out of football for some time with a simple fracture of the right leg two inches above the ankle. Baxter was the outstanding player afield. Brilliant from beginning to end, he nursed the ball until he was quite certain that no Rangers player was offside and then released it as the Rapid offside trap misfired. Forrest ran through such a gap in the 19th minute to make the aggregate score 2-0. The vital moment of the game came 10 minutes after the restart. Caldow was badly injured in a tackle with the Rapid outside-right and was taken off the field for treatment. At this moment Johnston suddenly broke into the game. He raced through the middle of the field hotly pursued by three Rapid players and cut the ball back and straight into the tracks of Wilson, who had come across to the inside-right position. Wilson instantly rammed the ball into the net.

February 17th: Third Round First Leg
INTER MILAN   (0) 3   RANGERS   (0) 1
  Suarez (48), Peiro 2 (49, 50)   Forrest (64)

INTER MILAN: Sarti; Burgnich, Facchetti; Tagnin, Guarneri, Malatrasi; Domenghini, Mazzola, Peiro, Suarez, Corso

RANGERS: Ritchie; Provan, Caldow; Wood, McKinnon, Greig; Henderson, Millar, Forrest, Brand, Wilson

Attendance: 49,520

Inside the space of 3 devastating minutes Rangers lost 3 goals to Internazionale after a first-half plan in which man-for-man marking had proved so successful that the half-time score was 0-0. Inter's first stroke of good fortune came when the 2nd half was only 3 minutes old. Millar, back in defence as he had been all through the game, was struck on the head by the ball which rebounded to the feet of Suarez who instantly volleyed it into the roof of the net. The ball was centred, Rangers kicked off and were back in defence immediately. This time Corso, the Italian captain, and their most dangerous player on the night, shot for the top left-hand corner of the goal. The ball was flying at least a yard wide of its target when it struck Peiro on the head and was deflected past Ritchie. This second blow, coming as it did immediately after the first, had the Rangers defenders in a panic, and inside another 60 seconds Peiro hit a dipping shot from 16 yards well out of the reach of Ritchie. The defence was immediately tightened up and Forrest was, soon after, presented with an easy scoring chance but, under pressure from Guarneri, he hit it hastily past a post. In 19 minutes of the 2nd half Forrest was presented with a 2nd chance, this time from a pass by Wood, and he immediately shot into the roof of the net.

March 3rd: Third Round Second Leg
RANGERS (1) 1   INTER MILAN (0) 0
   Forrest (6)

RANGERS: Ritchie; Provan, Caldow; Greig, McKinnon, Hynd; Henderson, Millar, Forrest, McLean, Johnston

INTER MILAN: Sarti; Burgnich, Facchetti; Tagnin, Guarneri, Picchi; Jair, Mazzola, Peiro, Suarez, Domenghini

Attendance: 77,206

Inter Milan won 3-2 on aggregate

Rangers could take some consolation from having beaten Inter. They scored a goal quickly as they knew they must do but their play thereafter was disappointing and lacked both method and spirit. The bitterly cold night was soon warmed when Rangers scored in only 6 minutes. Hynd, who was a last-minute replacement for Wood, shot fiercely from 30 yards, the ball hit Sarti in the chest and bounced to the feet of Forrest who took his chance capably from 6 yards. The closest Rangers got to scoring again was to be as far off as 9 minutes from time when a tremendous 20-yard drive by McLean beat Sarti but shivered the crossbar and rebounded to safety. Once Inter had recovered from the setback of Sarti's early mistake they closed ranks in front of him completely. Picchi took up his customary position between his centre-half and goalkeeper, sweeping up stray danger. Rangers' wingers had a dismal night. Johnston saw almost nothing of the ball and Henderson could make nothing of Facchetti and had no better luck against Peiro after the left-back was injured and went to the wing.

APPEARANCES

	League	League Cup	Scottish Cup	Glasgow Cup	European Cup
Ritchie	25	8	3	-	7
Hynd	10	3	2	1	2
Provan	34	10	3	1	7
Greig	34	7	3	1	7
McKinnon	34	10	3	1	7
Baxter	22	10	1	-	5
Henderson	18	7	3	1	4
McLean	8	6	-	1	2
Forrest	30	10	3	-	7
Brand	17	10	1	1	4
Wilson	27	9	-	1	5
Martin	9	2	-	1	-
Willoughby	5	-	-	-	-
Shearer	3	6	-	-	1
Millar	21	4	2	-	6
C. Watson	1	1	-	-	-
Caldow	26	1	2	1	5
Wood	26	1	2	1	4
Johnston	15	2	3	-	4
Beck	9	-	1	-	-
Mathieson	-	-	1	-	-
R. Watson	-	3	-	-	-

GOALSCORERS

League: Forrest 30, Wilson 10, Brand 6 (1 pen), Baxter 6 (1 pen), McLean 4, Johnston 4, Millar 4, Greig 4, Wood 3, Willoughby 2, Caldow 2 (2 pens), Henderson 1, Beck 1, Own Goals 1

League Cup: Forrest 18, Brand 5, McLean 5, Wilson 2, Baxter 2, Henderson 1, Millar 1, Own Goals 1

Scottish Cup: Forrest 3, Brand 1, Millar 1, Hynd 1

Glasgow Cup: Henderson 1

European Cup: Forrest 6, Brand 3, Wilson 2, Greig 1, McKinnon 1, McLean 1

Season 1965-66

The Championship was lost to Celtic (their first victory in the competition since season 1953–54) after an epic struggle. Only one of the first 17 matches was lost, and despite the fact that Rangers led the table on goal average, with a game in hand, at the end of February, they had a disastrous run in March in which 6 points were dropped. And although they finished the season with 7 straight wins, the Flag went to Parkhead. The defending champions Kilmarnock finished 3rd with 45 points. 23 players made League appearances during the campaign. McLean led the goals table with 25, closely followed by Forrest on 24.

Rangers won the League Cup Qualifying Section, beating Hearts, Aberdeen and Clyde in the process. Airdrie were beaten 9-1 on aggregate in the Quarter-Final and Kilmarnock 6-4 in a sensational Semi-Final in which they had at one time led 6-1 but 2 penalties cost them the Final against Celtic.

A goal by Danish International full-back Kaj Johansen, signed during the close-season from Morton, won the Scottish Cup, for the 19th time, in the replayed Final with Celtic. The Cup triumph was built on strong defence as the team managed only 11 goals in their 7 matches, 5 of them coming in their First Round match with Airdrie.

Benfica — Eusebio and all — were beaten in a Friendly at Ibrox, and a short tour of Denmark was undertaken at the end of the season. Caldow was given a free transfer and joined Stirling Albion.

League: Runners-up
Scottish Cup: Winners
League Cup: Finalists

SCOTTISH FIRST DIVISION

August 10th: Ralph Brand was transferred to Manchester City for £30,000.

August 24th: Rangers signed Jorn Sorensen from Morton in exchange for Craig Watson and a fee.

August 25th:
RANGERS (2) 3   ST JOHNSTONE (0) 2
Johnstone (4),   Whitelaw 2 (47, 49)
Forrest 2 (44, 60)

RANGERS: Ritchie; Johansen, Provan; Watson, McKinnon, Greig; Henderson, Willoughby, Forrest, Sorensen, Johnston

ST JOHNSTONE: McVittie; McFadyen, Coburn; Richmond, McKinven, Renton; Kerray, Duffy, Whitelaw, Maxwell, McGrogan

Attendance: 25,000

September 8th: The Scottish League beat the Irish League 6-2 at Ibrox. Greig and Henderson were in the team. Henderson scored twice.

September 11th:
PARTICK THISTLE (0) 1   RANGERS (0) 1
  Roxburgh (78)   McLean (73)

PARTICK THISTLE: Niven; Campbell, Muir; Harvey, McKinnon, Gibb; Cowan, McParland, Rae, Roxburgh, Kilpatrick

174

RANGERS: Ritchie; Johansen, Provan; Watson, McKinnon, Greig; Henderson, Willoughby, McLean, Sorensen, Johnston

Attendance: 29,789

September 18th:
RANGERS   (2) 2   CELTIC   (1) 1
  Forrest (7), McLean (20 pen)   Hughes (18 pen)

RANGERS: Ritchie; Johansen, Provan; Watson, McKinnon, Greig; Henderson, Sorensen, Forrest, McLean, Johnston

CELTIC: Fallon; Young, Gemmell; Murdoch, McNeill, Clark; Johnstone, Divers, Hughes, Lennox, Auld

Attendance: 76,000

For the last 10 minutes of the game it was touch and go whether Rangers would be able to hold on to their narrow lead. In the last half-hour they were greatly indebted to Ritchie and McKinnon for holding together a defensive structure in which cracks began to appear. All the goals were scored in the first 20 minutes. McLean was fortunate to retain possession in a joust with Young near the line after 7 minutes' play but when he crossed low into the goalmouth Forrest beat Gemmell and Fallon to the ball and prodded it into the net. Celtic equalised in 18 minutes. Greig pulled down Lennox and Hughes scored with the penalty-kick. 2 minutes later Forrest went boring through when he was impeded by McNeill and McLean made as satisfactory a job of the penalty-kick as Hughes had done earlier. Celtic were handicapped in their 2nd-half rally by a leg injury to McNeill. Rangers also had to re-arrange their forces when Sorensen, also with a leg injury, switched to outside-left.

September 25th:
DUNDEE   (1) 1   RANGERS   (0) 1
  Bertelsen (12)   McLean (78)

DUNDEE: Donaldson; Hamilton, Cox; Cooke, Easton, Stuart; Murray, Penman, Bertelsen, McLean, Houston

RANGERS: Ritchie; Johansen, Provan; Hynd, McKinnon, Greig; Henderson, Watson, Forrest, McLean, Johnston

Attendance: 22,000

October 2nd: Greig and Henderson were in the Scotland team which was beaten 3-2 by Northern Ireland in Belfast.

October 2nd:
RANGERS   (2) 6   STIRLING ALBION   (0) 0
  Sorensen (15), Willoughby (39),
  Wood (48), Wilson 2 (65, 78),
  Johnston (80)

RANGERS: Ritchie; Johansen, Provan; Watson, McKinnon, Wood; Wilson, Willoughby, Forrest, Sorensen, Johnston

STIRLING ALBION: Murray; McGuinness, Thomson; Reid, Robb, Sutherland; Hall, Thoms, Fleming, Duncan, Gardner

Attendance: 20,000

October 9th:
ST MIRREN   (1) 1   RANGERS   (2) 6
  Redpath (35)   McLean 2 (21 pen, 67),
                       Forrest 3 (25, 47, 77),
                       Johnston (46)

ST MIRREN: Liney; McLardy, Riddell; Murray, Kiernan, Clark; Robertson, Redpath, Queen, Faulds, Adamson

RANGERS: Ritchie; Johansen, Provan; Wood, McKinnon, Greig; Henderson, Willoughby, Forrest, McLean, Johnston

Attendance: 33,000

October 13th: Greig, Henderson and Johnston were in the Scotland team beaten 2-1 by Poland at Hampden Park.

October 16th:
HIBERNIAN   (0) 1   RANGERS   (1) 2
  Stevenson (62)   Willoughby 2 (38, 81)

HIBERNIAN: Wilson; Fraser, Davis; Stanton, McNamee, Baxter; Cormack, Quinn, Scott, Martin, E. Stevenson

RANGERS: Ritchie; Johansen, Provan; Wood, McKinnon, Greig; Wilson, Willoughby, Forrest, McLean, Johnston

Attendance: 38,000

October 27th:
RANGERS   (0) 2   DUNDEE UNITED   (0) 0
  Johnston (62), Forrest (82)

RANGERS: Ritchie; Johansen, Provan; Wood, McKinnon, Greig; Henderson, Willoughby, Forrest, Sorensen, Johnston

DUNDEE UNITED: Mackay; Millar, Briggs; Neilson, Smith, Wing; Seeman, Munro, Dossing, Gillespie, Persson

Attendance: 19,000

October 30th:
HAMILTON   RANGERS   (3) 7
  ACADEMICALS   (0) 1   Forrest 5 (25, 27, 44, 70, 73)
  Alexander (80)   Henderson (76),
                        Wilson (86)

HAMILTON: Brown; Forrest, Holton; Bowman, Small, McCann; Alexander, Anderson, Forsyth, Gilmour, Frye

RANGERS: Ritchie; Johansen, Provan; Wood, McKinnon, Greig; Henderson, Willoughby, Forrest, Sorensen, Wilson

Wood was carried off

Attendance: 11,000

November 6th:
RANGERS   (1) 3   FALKIRK   (0) 0
   Markie o.g. (22), McLean (49),
   Henderson (56)

RANGERS: Ritchie; Johansen, Provan; Watson, McKinnon, Greig; Henderson, Willoughby, Forrest, McLean, Johnston

FALKIRK: Whigham; Lambie, Brown; Rowan, Markie, Fulton; McManus, Moran, McKinney, Graham, Kirk

Attendance: 17,000

League positions
	P	W	D	L	F	A	Pts
1 RANGERS	10	8	2	0	33	8	18
2 Celtic	9	7	1	1	32	12	15
3 Dundee United	10	7	1	2	34	16	15
4 Dunfermline	10	6	3	1	27	14	15
5 Hibernian	10	6	2	2	37	14	14

November 9th: Scotland beat Italy 1-0 at Hampden Park. Greig, Provan, McKinnon and Henderson were in the team. Greig scored the only goal.

November 13th:
HEARTS   (0) 0   RANGERS   (0) 2
                              Henderson (64),
                              McLean (74)

HEARTS: Cruikshank; Shevlane, Holt; Ferguson, Anderson, Polland; O'Donnell, Kerrigan, Wallace, Traynor, Hamilton

RANGERS: Ritchie; Johansen, Provan; Watson, McKinnon, Greig; Henderson, Willoughby, Forrest, McLean, Johnston

Attendance: 28,000

November 15th: It was announced that in future Ne'erday Old Firm games were to be scrapped.

November 20th:
RANGERS   (3) 5   KILMARNOCK   (0) 0
   McLean 3 (19, 23 pen, 50),
   Johnston 2 (42, 69)

RANGERS: Ritchie; Johansen, Provan; Watson, McKinnon, Greig; Henderson, Willoughby, Forrest, McLean, Johnston

KILMARNOCK: Ferguson; King, Dickson; Murray, McGrory, O'Connor; McLean, McInally, Hamilton, Sneddon, McIlroy

Attendance: 30,000

November 24th: Scotland beat Wales 4-1 at Hampden Park. Greig, McKinnon, Henderson, Forrest and Johnston were in the team. Henderson and Greig both scored.

November 27th:
MOTHERWELL   (0) 0   RANGERS   (1) 3
                              Watson (39),
                              Forrest 2 (78 pen, 89)

MOTHERWELL: McCloy; M. Thomson, R. McCallum; W. McCallum, Martis, Murray; Moffat, I. Thomson, Delaney, Campbell, Hunter

RANGERS: Ritchie; Johansen, Provan; Watson, McKinnon, Greig; Henderson, Willoughby, Forrest, McLean, Johnston

Attendance: 18,000

December 7th: Scotland went down 3-0 to Italy in Naples. Provan, McKinnon, Greig and Forrest were in the team. Henderson pulled out injured just before the kick-off.

December 11th:
RANGERS   (1) 3   MORTON   (0) 1
   McLean (5), Greig 2 (65, 83)   Harper (56)

RANGERS: Ritchie; Johansen, Provan; Watson, McKinnon, Greig; Henderson, Willoughby, Forrest, McLean, Johnston

MORTON: Sorensen; Boyd, Laughlan; McGraw, Strachan, Kennedy; Harper, Stevenson, Halliday, Arnetoft, Watson

Attendance: 22,000

December 18th:
CLYDE   (1) 2   RANGERS   (1) 2
   Hastings (44),   McLean (22),
   Knox (57)   Forrest (68)

CLYDE: Wright; Glasgow, Soutar; McHugh, Fraser, White; Reid, Bryce, Knox, Stewart, Hastings

RANGERS: Ritchie; Hynd, Provan; Watson, McKinnon, Greig; Henderson, Willoughby, Forrest, McLean, Johnston

Attendance: 18,000

December 25th:
RANGERS   (1) 2   DUNFERMLINE   (1) 3
    Forrest (1), McLean (73)   Robertson 2 (32, 67),
                                Paton (53)

RANGERS: Ritchie; Caldow, Provan; Hynd,
McKinnon, Watson; Henderson, Willoughby, Forrest,
McLean, Johnston

DUNFERMLINE: Martin; W. Callaghan, Lunn;
Smith, McLean, Thomson; Edwards, Paton, Fleming,
Ferguson, Robertson

Attendance: 30,000

League positions

	P	W	D	L	F	A	Pts
1 Celtic	15	13	1	1	55	15	27
2 RANGERS	16	12	3	1	50	14	27
3 Dunfermline	16	10	4	2	48	25	24
4 Dundee United	16	10	3	3	45	21	23
5 Hibernian	16	9	3	4	49	23	21

January 2nd:
RANGERS   (1) 4   PARTICK THISTLE   (0) 0
    Johnston (32), Greig (54),
    Willoughby (74), McLean (75)

RANGERS: Ritchie; Johansen, Provan; Watson,
Jackson, Greig; Henderson, Willoughby, Forrest,
McLean, Johnston

PARTICK THISTLE: Niven; Hogan, Muir;
Cunningham, McKinnon, Gibb; McLindon, Roxburgh,
Rae, Hainey, Duncan

Attendance: n.a.

January 3rd:
CELTIC   (0) 5   RANGERS   (1) 1
    Chalmers 3 (49, 62, 90),   Wilson (1½)
    Gallagher (68), Murdoch (79)

CELTIC: Simpson; Craig, Gemmell; Murdoch,
Cushley, Clark; Johnstone, Gallagher, McBride,
Chalmers, Hughes

RANGERS: Ritchie; Provan, Johansen; Hynd,
McKinnon, Greig; Wilson, Setterington, Forrest,
McLean, Johnston

Attendance: 65,000

Celtic, a goal down after little more than a minute, scored 5
times in the 2nd half, 3 of the goals being scored by
Chalmers. Celtic, wearing training boots, strode the
sanded surface of the frostbound pitch with comparative
assurance. Rangers took the lead in 1½ minutes. Greig
shot and the ball broke off a defender to Wilson who
shot past Simpson's reach from an angle. After the
interval the goals came. The deluge began in 49
minutes when McBride dummied Gemmell's cross
and Chalmers shot home from 6 yards. In 62 minutes

Chalmers put Celtic into the lead, heading in
Gallagher's corner-kick. 6 minutes later Hughes
slipped past Provan on the touchline and cut the ball
back to the edge of the area where Gallagher drove
the ball past Ritchie off the underside of the crossbar.
After 79 minutes Murdoch hammered a McBride
pass into the net from 30 yards. Ritchie could do
nothing to prevent Johnstone from hitting a post and
Chalmers from scoring the 5th goal in the final
minute.

January 8th:
ST JOHNSTONE   (0) 0   RANGERS   (0) 3
                            McLean 3 (61, 73, 87)

ST JOHNSTONE: McVittie; Michie, Coburn;
McCarry, McKinven, Renton; Cowan, Kerray,
Anderson, Duffy, Kemp

RANGERS: Ritchie; Johansen, Provan; Watson,
McKinnon, Greig; Wilson, Willoughby, Forrest,
McLean, Johnston

Attendance: 12,500

January 22nd:
STIRLING ALBION   (0) 0   RANGERS   (2) 2
                            Forrest (3),
                            Willoughby (10)

STIRLING: Murray; Dickson, McGuinness; Reid,
Rogerson, Thomson; Grant, Anderson, Fleming,
Gardner, Hall

RANGERS: Ritchie; Johansen, Provan; Watson,
McKinnon, Greig; Henderson, Willoughby, Forrest,
McLean, Johnston

Attendance: 18,000

January 29th:
RANGERS   (3) 4   ST MIRREN   (0) 1
    McLean 2 (21, 40),   Adamson (48)
    Beck (37), Greig (65)

RANGERS: Ritchie; Johansen, Provan; Watson,
McKinnon, Greig; Wilson, Beck, McLean, Sorensen,
Traill

ST MIRREN: Liney; Murray, Clark; Pinkerton,
Kiernan, Gemmell; Aird, McCallum, Hamilton,
Adamson, Robertson

Attendance: 18,000

February 12th:
RANGERS   (1) 2   HIBERNIAN   (0) 0
    McLean (30), Sorensen (90)

RANGERS: Ritchie; Johansen, Provan; Watson,
McKinnon, Greig; Willoughby, Beck, McLean,
Sorensen, Forrest

HIBERNIAN: Wilson; Duncan, Davis; Stanton,
Cousin, Baxter; Scott, Cormack, Stein, O'Rourke,
Stevenson

Attendance: 25,000

February 26th:
RANGERS   (1) 4   HAMILTON
                      ACADEMICALS   (0) 0
   Forrest 2 (24, 88),
   McLean 2 (69, 75)

RANGERS: Ritchie; Johansen, Provan; Watson,
McKinnon, Greig; Henderson, Sorensen, Forrest,
McLean, Johnston

HAMILTON: Lamont; Halpin, Holton; Gaughan,
Small, King; McClare, Hinshelwood, Anderson,
Gilmour, McCann

Attendance: 20,000

League positions
	P	W	D	L	F	A	Pts
1 RANGERS	23	18	3	2	70	20	39
2 Celtic	24	19	1	4	79	24	39
3 Kilmarnock	25	16	2	7	60	35	34
4 Dunfermline	22	14	5	3	65	29	33
5 Hearts	23	11	8	4	42	32	30

March 9th:
FALKIRK   (2) 3   RANGERS   (1) 2
   Moran (10), Graham (41),   Forrest (33),
   Fulton (69)   Markie o.g. (84)

FALKIRK: Whigham; Markie, Hunter; Fulton,
Baillie, Scott; McKinney, Lambie, Moran, Graham,
McManus

RANGERS: Ritchie; Johansen, Caldow; Watson,
McKinnon, Greig; Henderson, Willoughby, Forrest,
Sorensen, Johnston

Attendance: n.a.

March 12th:
RANGERS   (0) 1   HEARTS (0) 1
   Forrest (70)   Anderson (73)

RANGERS: Ritchie; Johansen, Provan; Greig,
McKinnon, Mathieson; Henderson, Willoughby, Millar,
Forrest, Johnston

HEARTS: Cruikshank; Polland, Shevlane; Higgins,
Anderson, Miller; Hamilton, Barry, Wallace, Kerrigan,
Traynor

Attendance: 38,000

**March 16th: The Scottish League beat the English
League 3-1. Greig and McKinnon were in the team.**

March 19th:
KILMARNOCK   (0) 1   RANGERS   (0) 1
   McLean (89)   Forrest (81)

KILMARNOCK: Ferguson; King, McFadzean;
Murray, Beattie, O'Connor; McLean, McInally,
Bertelsen, Queen, McIlroy

RANGERS: Ritchie; Johansen, Provan; Greig,
McKinnon, Mathieson; Henderson, Millar, Forrest,
McLean, Johnston

Attendance: 22,000

March 21st:
DUNDEE UNITED   (0) 1   RANGERS   (0) 0
   Hainey (64)

DUNDEE UNITED: Davie; Millar, Briggs; Neilson,
Smith, Fraser; Munro, Hainey, Dossing, Mitchell,
Persson

RANGERS: Martin; Johansen, Provan; Greig,
McKinnon, Mathieson; Henderson, Millar, Forrest,
McLean, Johnston

Attendance: 16,000

**April 2nd: Scotland were beaten 4-3 by England at
Hampden Park. Greig, McKinnon and Johnston
were in the team.**

April 9th:
RANGERS   (0) 1   ABERDEEN   (0) 0
   Greig (79)

RANGERS: Ritchie; Johansen, Provan; Greig,
McKinnon, Millar; Henderson, Willoughby, Forrest,
Johnston, Wilson

ABERDEEN: Clark; Whyte, Shewan; Petersen,
McMillan, D. Smith; Little, Melrose, Winchester, J.
Smith, Wilson

Attendance: 18,000

April 6th:
RANGERS   (0) 1   DUNDEE   (0) 0
   Greig (66)

RANGERS: Ritchie; Johansen, Provan; Greig,
McKinnon, Millar; Henderson, Willoughby, Forrest,
McLean, Johnston

DUNDEE: Donaldson; R. Wilson, Cox; Murray,
Easton, Stuart; Penman, Cooke, Cameron, McLean,
Kinnonmonth

Attendance: 12,000

April 13th:
ABERDEEN   (1) 1   RANGERS   (1) 2
   Melrose (23)   Johnston (34),
                         Willoughby (58)

ABERDEEN: Clark; Whyte, Shewan; Petersen,
McMillan, D. Smith; Little, Melrose, Winchester, J.
Smith, Wilson

RANGERS: Ritchie; Johansen, Provan; Greig,
McKinnon, Millar; Henderson, Willoughby, Forrest,
Johnston, Wilson

Attendance: 17,000

April 16th:
MORTON   (0) 0   RANGERS   (2) 5
                        Madsen o.g. (29),
                        Johnston (37),
                        Wilson (60),
                        Forrest (62),
                        Greig (83)

MORTON: Sorensen; Boyd, Kennedy; McGraw,
Madsen, Neilsen; Arnetoft, Smith, Campbell, Graham,
Watson

RANGERS: Ritchie; Johansen, Provan; Greig,
McKinnon, Millar; Henderson, Sorensen, Forrest,
Johnston, Wilson

Attendance: 15,000

April 19th:
RANGERS   (2) 2   MOTHERWELL   (1) 1
Sorensen (2), Forrest (25)   Campbell (30)

RANGERS: Ritchie; Johansen, Provan; Greig,
McKinnon, Millar; Henderson, Sorensen, Forrest,
Johnston, Wilson

MOTHERWELL: McCloy, Thomson, R. McCallum;
W. McCallum, Martis, Murray; Coakley, Hunter,
Delaney, Cairney, Campbell

Attendance: 12,000

April 30th:
DUNFERMLINE   (1) 1   RANGERS   (2) 2
Fleming (23)   Watson (4),
                       McLean (43)

DUNFERMLINE: Martin; W. Callaghan, Lunn;
Thomson, McLean, T. Callaghan; Edwards, Smith,
Fleming, Ferguson, Robertson

RANGERS: Ritchie; Johansen, Provan; Greig,
McKinnon, Millar; Henderson, Watson, McLean,
Johnston, Wilson

Attendance: 16,000

**April 30th: Rangers announced that Caldow,
McGillivray and Traill had been given free transfers
and that Jorn Sorensen was returning to Denmark.**

**May 3rd: John Greig was named as Scotland's
Player of the Year.**

May 4th:
RANGERS   (2) 4   CLYDE   (0) 0
Millar (6), Wilson (44),
McLean 2 (53, 70)

RANGERS: Ritchie; Johansen, Provan; Greig,
McKinnon, Millar; Henderson, Watson, McLean,
Johnston, Wilson

CLYDE: McCulloch; Glasgow, Soutar; McHugh,
Fraser, Stewart; Bryce, McFarlane, Gilroy, Knox,
Hastings

Attendance: 10,000

Scottish First Division

	P	W	D	L	F	A	Pts
1 Celtic	34	27	3	4	106	30	57
2 RANGERS	34	25	5	4	91	29	55
3 Kilmarnock	34	20	5	9	73	46	45
4 Dunfermline	34	19	6	9	94	55	44
5 Dundee United	34	19	5	10	79	51	43
6 Hibernian	34	16	6	12	81	55	38
7 Hearts	34	13	12	9	56	48	38
8 Aberdeen	34	15	6	13	61	54	36
9 Dundee	34	14	6	14	61	61	34
10 Falkirk	34	15	1	18	48	72	31
11 Clyde	34	13	4	17	62	64	30
12 Partick Thistle	34	10	10	14	55	64	30
13 Motherwell	34	12	4	18	52	69	28
14 St Johnstone	34	9	8	17	58	81	26
15 Stirling Albion	34	9	8	17	40	68	26
16 St Mirren	34	9	4	21	44	82	22
17 Morton	34	8	5	21	42	84	21
18 Hamilton	34	3	2	29	27	117	8

**May 11th: Scotland were beaten 3-0 by Holland at
Hampden Park. Greig, Provan, McKinnon,
Henderson and Johnston were all in the team.**

**June 18th: Scotland were beaten 1-0 by Portugal at
Hampden Park. Greig was in the team.**

**June 25th: Scotland drew 1-1 with World Champions
Brazil at Hampden Park. Greig and McKinnon were
in the team.**

LEAGUE CUP

August 14th:
HEARTS   (2) 4   RANGERS   (1) 2
Hamilton 2 (37, 44 pen),   Forrest 2 (31, 71 pen)
Wallace 2 (66, 79)

HEARTS: Cruikshank; Ferguson, Holt; Barry,
Anderson, Higgins; Jensen, Gordon, Wallace, Traynor,
Hamilton

RANGERS: Martin; Johansen, Caldow; Greig,
McKinnon, Wood; Watson, Millar, Forrest, Beck,
Johnston

Attendance: 32,859

August 18th:
RANGERS   (1) 3   CLYDE   (0) 0
Willoughby 2 (9, 55), Forrest (87)

RANGERS: Martin; Johansen, Provan; Greig,
McKinnon, Wood; Watson, Willoughby, Forrest,
Wilson, Johnston

CLYDE: McCulloch; Glasgow, Soutar; McHugh,
Fraser, White; Bryce, Gilroy, Stewart, McLean,
Hastings

Attendance: 25,000

August 21st:
ABERDEEN   (0) 2   RANGERS   (0) 0
  Little (87), Ravn (90)

ABERDEEN: Ogston; Bennett, Shewan; Burns,
McMillan, Smith; Scott, Winchester, Ravn, Little,
Wilson

RANGERS: Martin; Johansen, Provan; Watson,
McKinnon, Greig; Wilson, Wood, Forrest, Willoughby,
Johnston

Wilson had to replace the injured Martin in goal in the
65th minute

Attendance: n.a.

August 28th:
RANGERS   (1) 1   HEARTS   (0) 0
  Johnston (3)

RANGERS: Ritchie; Johansen, Provan; Watson,
McKinnon, Greig; Henderson, Willoughby, Forrest,
Wilson, Johnston

HEARTS: Cruikshank; Ferguson, Shevlane; Polland,
Anderson, Cumming; Jensen, Barry, Ford, Traynor,
Hamilton

Attendance: 40,000

September 1st:
CLYDE   (0) 1   RANGERS   (2) 3
  McHugh (90)   Johnston (27),
                       Willoughby (34),
                       Forrest (60)

CLYDE: Wright; Glasgow, Mulheron; McHugh,
Fraser, Staite; Bryce, Gilroy, Stewart, McLean,
Hastings

RANGERS: Ritchie; Johansen, Provan; Watson,
McKinnon, Greig; Wilson, Willoughby, Forrest,
McLean, Johnston

Attendance: 15,000

September 4th:
RANGERS   (1) 4   ABERDEEN   (0) 0
  Forrest (3), McLean 3 (19, 87, 88)

RANGERS: Ritchie; Johansen, Provan; Watson,
McKinnon, Greig; Henderson, Willoughby, Forrest,
McLean, Johnston

ABERDEEN: Ogston; Bennett, Shewan; Burns,
McMillan, Petersen; Little, Miller, White, Smith,
Wilson

Attendance: 45,000

League Cup Section

	P	W	D	L	F	A	Pts
RANGERS	6	4	0	2	13	7	8
Hearts	6	3	1	2	10	7	7
Aberdeen	6	3	1	2	7	8	7
Clyde	6	1	0	5	5	13	2

September 15th: Quarter-Final First Leg
AIRDRIE   (0) 1   RANGERS   (2) 5
  Ferguson (51)   Greig (24),
                        McLean 2 (42, 59),
                        Forrest (56),
                        Willoughby (70)

AIRDRIE: McKenzie; Caldwell, Phillips; Goodwin,
Hannah, Gardner; Ferguson, Murray, Black, Breen,
Ramsey

RANGERS: Ritchie; Johansen, Provan; Watson,
McKinnon, Greig; Henderson, Willoughby, Forrest,
McLean, Johnston

Attendance: 15,000

September 22nd: Quarter-Final Second Leg
RANGERS   (2) 4   AIRDRIE   (0) 0
  Forrest 3 (15, 43, 88), McLean (49)

RANGERS: Ritchie; Johansen, Provan; Watson,
McKinnon, Greig; Henderson, Willoughby, Forrest,
McLean, Johnston

AIRDRIE: McKenzie; Black, Phillips; Goodwin,
Hannah, Reid; Ferguson, McMillan, Marshall, Murray,
Ramsey

Attendance: 9,000

Rangers won 9-1 on aggregate

October 6th: Semi-Final   At Hampden Park
RANGERS   (3) 6   KILMARNOCK   (1) 4
  McLean 3 (14, 42 pen, 52),   McInally (36),
  Willoughby (32),   McLean 3 (71, 83 pen,
  Forrest (66),   89)
  Henderson (68)

RANGERS: Ritchie; Johansen, Provan; Wood,
McKinnon, Greig; Henderson, Willoughby, Forrest,
McLean, Johnston

KILMARNOCK: Ferguson; King, Watson; Murray,
McGrory, Beattie; McLean, McInally, Black, Hamilton,
McIlroy

Attendance: 53.900

The score at Hampden gives a false impression of the trend
of the game which was all in favour of Rangers for 65
minutes during which they cut the Kilmarnock defence to
ribbons with forward play of near brilliance and
established a 6-1 lead. As Rangers slackened off in
confidence of victory they left gaps which the Ayrshire
forwards exploited to the full, and they might even have
snatched a 5th goal but for a sprawling save by Ritchie in

the last minute. Shots from Henderson and Forrest were blocked before McLean fastened onto a rebound in 14 minutes, scoring with a rising shot, and 18 minutes later a rampant Rangers side were rewarded when Willoughby shot powerfully past Ferguson. Kilmarnock broke away in 36 minutes and McInally, although obstructed by Greig, recovered his balance and shot strongly past Ritchie. Just before the interval McGrory brought down Forrest in full cry for goal and McLean scored with the penalty-kick. Only 7 minutes of the 2nd half had gone when McLean got his 3rd goal. In 66 minutes Greig released another perfect pass from which Forrest thumped the ball past Ferguson, who again had no chance of saving 2 minutes later when Henderson, with a left-foot shot, completed a crossfield movement. Young Tommy McLean scored 3 goals in the last 20 minutes — his first from a rebound after Beattie hit the post, his 2nd with a penalty-kick when Johansen tripped McInally.

October 23rd: Final   At Hampden Park
CELTIC   (2) 2   RANGERS   (0) 1
   Hughes 2 (18 pen, 28 pen)   Young o.g. (84)
CELTIC: Simpson; Young, Gemmell; Murdoch, McNeill, Clark; Johnstone, Gallagher, McBride, Lennox, Hughes

RANGERS: Ritchie; Johansen, Provan; Wood, McKinnon, Greig; Henderson, Willoughby, Forrest, Wilson, Johnston

Attendance: 107,600   *Referee*: H. Phillips (Wishaw)

Before Celtic scored, Forrest missed 2 gilt-edged chances. Celtic quickly realised that Hughes could do most damage for them. In 18 minutes McKinnon handled a harmless free-kick and Hughes scored from the spot. 10 minutes later Provan, beaten by Johnstone, gave chase and brought the winger down from behind. Ritchie got a hand to Hughes' shot but could not stop it. Rangers' persistence was at last rewarded with a goal when Henderson took a free-kick just outside the area, and with Greig rushing at the ball it spun past Simpson off Young's face. That was 6 minutes from the end and it was too late for Rangers to salvage the match.

SCOTTISH CUP

February 5th: First Round
RANGERS   (0) 5   AIRDRIE   (0) 1
   Wilson (49),   Marshall (81)
   McLean 3 (62, 75 pen, 85),
   Johnston (64)

RANGERS: Ritchie; Johansen, Provan; Watson, McKinnon, Greig; Wilson, Beck, McLean, Sorensen, Johnston

AIRDRIE: McKenzie; Jonquin, Keenan; Goodwin, Hannah, Ramsey; Ferguson, Reid, Marshall, Murray, Phillips

Attendance: 16,500

February 28th: Second Round
ROSS COUNTY   (0) 0   RANGERS   (2) 2
                         Johnston (25),
                         McLean (26)

ROSS COUNTY: Sutherland; Borley, Brett; McMillan, Greig, McNeill; Thompson, Mackenzie, Donald, Hosie, Mackay

RANGERS: Ritchie; Johansen, Provan; Watson, McKinnon, Greig; Wilson, Sorensen, Forrest, McLean, Johnston

Attendance: 8,500

March 5th: Third Round
RANGERS   (0) 1   ST JOHNSTONE   (0) 0
   Willoughby (72)

RANGERS: Ritchie; Johansen, Provan; Watson, McKinnon, Greig; Henderson, Willoughby, Forrest, Sorensen, Johnston

ST JOHNSTONE: McVittie; Michie, Coburn; McCarry, McKinven, Renton; Cowan, Duffy, Kerray, MacDonald, Kemp

Attendance: 32,000

March 26th: Semi-Final   At Hampden Park
RANGERS   (0) 0   ABERDEEN   (0) 0
RANGERS: Ritchie; Johansen, Provan; Greig, McKinnon, Mathieson; Henderson, Millar, McLean, Sorensen, Johnston

ABERDEEN: Clark; Whyte, Shewan; Petersen, McMillan, Smith; Little, Melrose, Winchester, Ravn, Wilson

Attendance: 49,360

The display was unworthy of the attendance of over 49,000. The strong downfield wind was a troublesome factor throughout. The general standard of passing and finishing was low, and although there was more excitement in the 2nd half during which Rangers were facing the wind, it was completely unproductive. On pressure in the 2nd half Rangers should have won. Aberdeen were the more composed side but seldom looked deadly in attack.

March 29th: Semi-Final Replay   At Hampden Park
RANGERS   (1) 2   ABERDEEN   (1) 1
   Forrest (8), McLean (80)   Melrose (39)

RANGERS: Ritchie; Johansen, Provan; Greig, McKinnon, Millar; Henderson, Willoughby, Forrest, McLean, Johnston

ABERDEEN: Clark; Whyte, Shewan; Petersen, McMillan, Smith; Little, Melrose, Winchester, Ravn, Wilson

Attendance: 40,852

A goal scored by McLean 10 minutes from time earned Rangers a Scottish Cup Final place against Celtic. It was a hard struggle for Rangers although they went into the lead after only 8 minutes. A poor Smith clearance went only as far as Willoughby. He pushed the ball forward to Forrest who hit a well-taken goal with a shot from about 20 yards that dipped as it swept past Clark's flying body. From then until the interval Aberdeen commanded a fair share of the ball and they equalised 6 minutes from half-time. McKinnon missed a tackle on Wilson who slipped the ball out to Melrose on his left. The inside-right ran in and shot home with his left foot from a narrow angle. Forrest and Henderson came closest to breaking a deadlock which seemed certain to be carried into a period of extra-time. The winning goal came when Provan struck a pass down the touchline which sent Johnston free of his marker and McLean was on the spot to prod his cross home from close range.

April 23rd: Final   At Hampden Park
RANGERS (0) 0   CELTIC (0) 0

RANGERS: Ritchie; Johansen, Provan; Greig, McKinnon, Millar; Henderson, Watson, Forrest, Johnston, Wilson

CELTIC: Simpson; Young, Gemmell; Murdoch, McNeill, Clark; Johnstone, McBride, Chalmers, Gallagher, Hughes

Attendance: 126,599 *Referee*: T. Wharton (Clarkston)

Both forward lines were endowed with insufficient imagination to break down defences too sophisticated and practised in their art to be deceived by their naive advances. McBride had a header brilliantly touched away by Ritchie but Celtic's leading scorer was, for the most part, an anonymous figure. McNeill sent a header thudding against a crossbar. McKinnon and McNeill and their attendant sweepers Greig and Clark were impregnable. Rangers may have proved, at least to themselves, that Celtic were by no means invincible.

April 27th: Final Replay   At Hampden Park
RANGERS (0) 1   CELTIC (0) 0
  Johansen (70)

RANGERS: Ritchie; Johansen, Provan; Greig, McKinnon, Millar; Henderson, Watson, McLean, Johnston, Wilson

CELTIC: Simpson; Craig, Gemmell; Murdoch, McNeill, Clark; Johnstone, McBride, Chalmers, Auld, Hughes

Attendance: 96,862   *Referee*: T. Wharton (Clarkston)

Rangers won the Scottish Cup for the 19th time in their history. The vital goal was scored by their Danish right-back Johansen 20 minutes from the end. It was a goal worthy of winning any trophy. Johnston wriggled his way to the bye-line and when McLean missed the ball a few yards out it ran to Henderson. The winger's shot was cleared off the line by Murdoch out to Johansen who let fly from 25 yards and the ball flew low and hard into the net. Rangers' triumph, against all the predicted odds, was built on a magnificent defence. The outstanding figure was Millar, always there when he was needed. This was Celtic's 4th successive game in which they failed to score. Johnstone made life a misery for Provan but Hughes was once more subdued. Auld, returning after suspension, laid on chances, of which Chalmers missed 2 and Hughes the other.

APPEARANCES

	League	League Cup	Scottish Cup	Glasgow Cup	Friendlies
Ritchie	33	7	7	1	3
Johansen	32	10	7	1	3
Provan	33	9	7	1	3
Watson	21	8	5	1	2
McKinnon	33	10	7	1	3
Greig	32	10	7	1	3
Henderson	28	6	5	1	3
Willoughby	23	9	2	1	0+2S
Forrest	30	10	4	1	1+1S
Sorensen	12	-	4	1	2+1S
Johnston	31	10	7	1	3
McLean	24	5	5	-	3
Hynd	4	-	-	-	-
Wood	5	5	-	-	0+1S
Wilson	12	5	4	-	2
Caldow	2	1	-	-	-
Jackson	1	-	-	-	0+1S
Beck	2	1	1	-	-
Traill	1	-	-	-	-
Mathieson	3	-	1	-	-
Millar	10	1	4	-	2
Martin	1	3	-	-	-
Setterington	1	-	-	-	-

Ralph Brand, a favourite with the fans in the sixties.

GOALSCORERS

League: McLean 25 (3 pens), Forrest 24 (1 pen), Johnston 9, Greig 7, Willoughby 6, Wilson 6, Sorensen 3, Henderson 3, Own Goals 3, Watson 2, Wood 1, Beck 1, Millar 1

League Cup: Forrest 10 (1 pen), McLean 9 (1 pen), Willoughby 5, Johnston 2, Greig 1, Henderson 1, Own Goals 1

Scottish Cup: McLean 5 (1 pen), Johnston 2, Wilson 1, Willoughby 1, Forrest 1, Johansen 1

Glasgow Cup: Forrest 2, Henderson 1, Sorensen 1

Friendlies: Forrest 3, McLean 2, Sorensen 2, Millar 1, Wilson 1

The Rangers team squad for season 1965–66. Back row: Willoughby, Stewart, C. Watson, Paterson, B. Watson, McGillivray, W. Ritchie, Marten, McFarlane, McLardy, Beck, W. Jardine, Mathieson, W. Smith, Traill. Middle row: Johansen, Donnelly, Greig, Jackson, McKinnon, D. Ritchie, Provan, Simpson, Hynd, Sutherland, McLean, McCartney, Wood, Joe Craven (asst. trainer). Front row: S. Symon (manager), Henderson, Paul, Millar, Reid, Forrest, Setterington, Caldow, Semple, Brand, J. Jardine, Johnston, Vint, Wilson, Davie Kinnear (trainer).

Season 1966–67

Despite collecting 55 points for the second successive season and scoring 92 goals, Rangers again finished as runners-up behind Celtic. Only three matches were lost — Dunfermline beating them home and away. They had a sequence of 12 straight wins but 5 points were dropped in the final 5 matches. Two half-backs, Dave Smith and Alex Smith, were bought at the beginning of the season for a total of £80,000. Dave Smith was the only player to appear in all 34 matches and Alex Smith finished top scorer with 19. Willoughby scored 16 goals in his 11 appearances. Jardine was introduced into the team after the Scottish Cup defeat.

Rangers reached the League Cup Final but although they outplayed Celtic, 2 penalty claims were turned down and an apparently genuine score by Watson was obscurely disallowed and Celtic took the Cup with Lennox's 19th-minute goal. Hibs and Kilmarnock were beaten in the Section and Aberdeen after a replay in the Semi-Final. McLean and Forrest each scored 6 goals in the competition. Both were transferred after the Berwick defeat. Forrest went to Preston North End and McLean joined Dundee, in part exchange for Andy Penman. Jimmy Millar was freed at the end of the season.

The Scottish Cup run ended at Berwick in the First Round. Scot Symon's quote after the match says it all: 'Our prestige has received a shattering blow. This is the worst result in the club's history and it's there now in the record books and these players took part in the game. That cannot be forgotten'.

Rangers reached the Final of the Cup Winners Cup for the second time, beating Glentoran, holders Borussia Dortmund, Real Saragossa and Slavia Sofia along the way, but lost to Bayern Munich in extra-time to a goal by Roth. The lack of a first-class finisher cost them the trophy. The performance in the away match against Borussia Dortmund, when they had to play for 52 minutes with 10 men after Watson was carried off, was one of the finest in the club's long history.

League: Runners-up
League Cup: Finalists
Scottish Cup: First Round
Cup Winners' Cup: Finalists

SCOTTISH FIRST DIVISION

August 9th: Alex Smith was signed from Dunfermline for £35,000.

August 12th: Dave Smith was signed from Aberdeen for £45,000.

September 10th:
RANGERS (3) 6   PARTICK THISTLE (0) 1
A. Smith (7),   Flanagan (85)
McLean 4 (27, 54, 57, 89),
D. Smith (31)

RANGERS: Ritchie; Johansen, Provan; Millar, McKinnon, D. Smith; Wilson, A. Smith, Forrest, McLean, Johnston

184

PARTICK THISTLE: Niven; West, Muir; Cunningham, McKinnon, Gibb; Gallagher, McParland, Roxburgh, Flanagan, Duncan

Attendance: 20,000

September 17th:
CELTIC (2) 2   RANGERS (0) 0
  Auld (1), Murdoch (4)

CELTIC: Simpson; Gemmell, O'Neill; Murdoch, McNeill, Clark; Johnstone, Lennox, McBride, Auld, Hughes

RANGERS: Ritchie; Provan, Greig; Millar, McKinnon, D. Smith; Wilson, A. Smith, Forrest, McLean, Johnston

Attendance: 65,000

Rangers' defence was run through twice before they even took guard. Murdoch in the first minute whipped a long ball through the middle to Lennox who beat McKinnon to it and crossed for Auld to hit it past Ritchie and in off a post. Barely 3 minutes had elapsed when Murdoch put Celtic further ahead with a clever goal. After a shot from him had been blocked on the 18-yard line he regained possession and coolly chipped the ball into the top corner of the net well out of Ritchie's reach. Things might have been different if Johnston had not unaccountably headed wide of the target, an easy chance, in the 63rd minute. Celtic moved with a smooth efficiency in attack and defence which Rangers never achieved.

September 24th:
RANGERS (0) 3   ABERDEEN (0) 0
  Henderson (52),
  Johnston (67),
  McLean (72)

RANGERS: Ritchie; Johansen, Provan; Millar, McKinnon, D. Smith; Henderson, Greig, McLean, A. Smith, Johnston

ABERDEEN: Clark; Whyte, Shewan; Millar, McMillan, Petersen; Smith, Melrose, Winchester, Watt, Wilson

Attendance: 30,000

October 1st:
DUNDEE UNITED (1) 2   RANGERS (0) 3
  Dossing (44),   Johansen (55),
  Mitchell (86)   A. Smith (80)
                  Setterington (83)

DUNDEE UNITED: Davie; Millar, Briggs; Neilson, Smith, Wing; Dossing, Hainey, Mitchell, Gillespie, Persson

RANGERS: Ritchie; Johansen, Provan; Greig, McKinnon, D. Smith; Henderson, A. Smith, McLean, Setterington, Johnston

Attendance: 17,000

October 8th:
RANGERS (1) 5   FALKIRK (0) 0
  Provan (22 pen), Millar (62),
  Henderson (76), Johnston (78),
  A. Smith (89)

RANGERS: Ritchie; Johansen, Provan; Greig, McKinnon, D. Smith; Henderson, A. Smith, Forrest (Millar), Johnston, Wilson

FALKIRK: Calder; Markie, Hunter; Lambie, Baillie, Fulton; Cowan, Moran, Vincent, Graham, McKinney

Attendance: 25,000

October 15th:
HEARTS (0) 1   RANGERS (0) 1
  Anderson (80)   Millar (53)

HEARTS: Cruikshank; Shevlane, Peden; Anderson, Polland, Miller; Hamilton, Murphy, Wallace, Gordon (Clunie), Traynor

RANGERS: Ritchie; Johansen, Provan; Greig, McKinnon, D. Smith; Henderson, A. Smith, Millar, Johnston, Wilson

Attendance: 30,000

October 22nd: Scotland drew 1-1 with Wales in Cardiff. Greig, McKinnon and Henderson were in the team.

October 22nd: It was rumoured that Rangers were after Ferenc Puskas as coach.

League positions

	P	W	D	L	F	A	Pts
1 Celtic	7	7	0	0	26	6	14
2 Kilmarnock	7	5	1	1	12	7	11
3 Aberdeen	8	4	2	2	12	11	10
4 RANGERS	6	4	1	1	18	6	9
5 Dunfermline	8	3	3	2	21	15	9

November 1st: Rangers offered Eddie Turnbull of Aberdeen the post as assistant manager.

November 2nd:
ST MIRREN (0) 1   RANGERS (5) 6
  Adamson (60)   A. Smith (3),
                  Provan (12 pen),
                  Henderson 2 (15, 63),
                  Johnston 2 (25, 35)

ST MIRREN: Thorburn; Murray, Gemmell; Clark, Clunie, Pinkerton; Aird, Hamilton, Taylor, Hutton, Adamson

RANGERS: Martin; Johansen, Provan; Greig, McKinnon, D. Smith; Henderson, Watson (Wilson), Forrest, A. Smith, Johnston

Attendance: 10,000

November 2nd: Turnbull turned down the offer.

November 5th:
RANGERS   (2) 5   MOTHERWELL   (1) 1
   Forrest 2 (14, 56),   Moffat (37)
   Setterington (38),
   A. Smith 2 (70, 74)

RANGERS: Martin; Johansen, Provan; Greig,
McKinnon, D. Smith; Henderson, A. Smith, Forrest,
Setterington, Johnston

MOTHERWELL: McCloy; Whiteford, W.
McCallum; R. McCallum, Martis, Murray; Moffat,
Campbell, Deans, Cairney, Hunter

Attendance: 28,000

November 9th:
RANGERS   (1) 3   KILMARNOCK   (0) 0
   A. Smith (30),
   Setterington (53),
   Provan (71 pen)

RANGERS: Martin; Johansen, Provan; Greig,
McKinnon, D. Smith; Henderson, A. Smith (Wilson),
Forrest, Setterington, Johnston

KILMARNOCK: Ferguson; King, M. Watson;
O'Connor, McGrory, Dickson; McLean, McInally,
Bertelsen, Queen (C. Watson), Brown

Attendance: 35,000

November 12th:
ST JOHNSTONE   (1) 1   RANGERS   (0) 1
   Townsend (15)   Forrest (47)

ST JOHNSTONE: Donaldson; Coburn, Smith;
Townsend, Ryden, McPhee; Kemp, Whitelaw,
Kilgannon, McCarry, MacDonald

RANGERS: Martin; Johansen, Provan; Greig,
McKinnon, D. Smith; Henderson, Millar, Forrest,
Setterington, Johnston

Attendance: 15,000

**November 16th: Scotland beat Northern Ireland 2-1
at Hampden Park. Greig, McKinnon and Henderson
were in the team.**

**November 17th: Bobby Seith was appointed as
Rangers' trainer-coach.**

November 19th:
RANGERS   (2) 4   AYR UNITED   (0) 0
   A. Smith 2 (17, 56),
   Forrest (28), Provan (73 pen)

RANGERS: Martin; Johansen, Provan; Greig,
McKinnon, D. Smith; Henderson, Watson, Forrest, A.
Smith, Johnston

AYR UNITED: Miller; Malone, Murphy; Thomson,
Monan, McAnespie; McMillan, Oliphant, Black,
Hawkshaw, Grant

Attendance: 22,000

November 26th:
HIBERNIAN   (1) 1   RANGERS   (0) 2
   O'Rourke (30)   Forrest 2 (55, 72)

HIBERNIAN: Allan; Duncan, Davis; Stanton,
McNamee, Cousin; O'Rourke, Quinn, Scott, Cormack,
McGraw

RANGERS: Martin; Johansen, Provan; Greig,
McKinnon, D. Smith; Henderson, Watson, Forrest, A.
Smith, Johnston

Attendance: 25,798

December 3rd:
DUNFERMLINE   (2) 3   RANGERS   (1) 2
   Ferguson 2 (20, 78),   Forrest (6),
   Edwards (29 pen)   A. Smith (53)

DUNFERMLINE: Martin; W. Callaghan, Lunn;
Thomson, McLean, Barry; Edwards, Fleming, Delaney,
Ferguson, Robertson

RANGERS: Martin; Johansen, Provan; Greig,
McKinnon, D. Smith; Henderson, Watson, Forrest, A.
Smith, Johnston

Attendance: 18,000

December 10th:
RANGERS   (2) 4   STIRLING ALBION   (0) 0
   Greig (21),
   Forrest (33),
   Henderson 2 (75, 87)

RANGERS: Martin; Johansen, Provan; Greig,
McKinnon, D. Smith; Henderson, A. Smith, Forrest,
Setterington, Johnston

STIRLING: Murray; Dickson, Caldow; Grant,
Rogerson, Thomson; Kerray, McKinnon (Laing),
Caven, Peebles, Hall

Attendance: 20,000

December 17th:
RANGERS   (1) 3   AIRDRIE   (0) 0
   A. Smith 2 (41, 89),
   Keenan o.g. (54)

RANGERS: Martin; Johansen, Provan; Greig,
McKinnon, D. Smith; Henderson, A. Smith, Forrest,
Setterington (Willoughby), Johnston

AIRDRIE: McKenzie; Jonquin, Keenan; Goodwin,
Black, Ramsey; Ferguson, Fyfe, Marshall, Murray,
Phillips (McPheat)

Attendance: 18,000

League positions

	P	W	D	L	F	A	Pts
1 Celtic	15	13	2	0	55	19	28
2 RANGERS	15	11	2	2	48	13	24
3 Aberdeen	15	10	2	3	34	20	22
4 Clyde	15	9	2	4	31	23	20
5 Dundee	15	8	3	4	30	19	19

December 31st:
RANGERS (0) 2   DUNDEE (0) 2
  McKinnon (66),   Bryce (67),
  A. Smith (85)   Cameron (81)

RANGERS: Martin; Johansen, Provan; Greig,
McKinnon, D. Smith; Henderson, A. Smith, Forrest,
McLean, Johnston

DUNDEE: Arrol; Hamilton, Cox; Murray, Easton,
Stuart; Bryce, Kinnonmonth, Wilson (Cameron),
McLean, Scott

Attendance: 25,000

January 2nd:
PATRICK THISTLE (0) 1   RANGERS (0) 1
  Flanagan (75)   A. Smith (62)

PARTICK THISTLE: Niven; Tinney, Muir;
McParland, McKinnon, Gibb; McLindon, Divers,
Flanagan, Cunningham, Gallagher

RANGERS: Martin; Johansen, Provan; Greig,
McKinnon, D. Smith; Henderson, A. Smith, McLean,
Forrest, Johnston

Attendance: 26,000

January 14th:
RANGERS (0) 3   DUNDEE
  Greig (55), Johnston (67),   UNITED (0) 1
  McLean (69)   Gillespie (83)

RANGERS: Martin; Johansen, Provan; Greig,
McKinnon, D. Smith; Henderson, A. Smith, McLean,
Forrest, Johnston

DUNDEE UNITED: Davie; Millar, Briggs; Neilson,
Smith, Wing; Dossing, Gillespie, Mitchell, Graham,
Berg

Attendance: 35,000

January 18th:
ABERDEEN (1) 1   RANGERS (0) 2
  Johnston (27)   McLean 2 (48, 62)

ABERDEEN: Clark; Whyte, Shewan; Munro,
McMillan, Petersen; Wilson, J. Smith, Winchester,
Melrose, Johnston

RANGERS: Martin; Johansen, Provan; Greig,
McKinnon, D. Smith; Henderson, A. Smith, McLean,
Forrest, Johnston

Attendance: 30,000

January 21st:
FALKIRK (0) 0   RANGERS (1) 1
                A. Smith (35)

FALKIRK: Connachan; Lambie, Hunter; Markie,
Baillie, Baxter; Cowan, Rowan, Fulton, Moran,
McKinney

RANGERS: Martin; Johansen, Provan; Greig,
McKinnon, D. Smith; Henderson, A. Smith, McLean,
Forrest, Johnston

Attendance: 17,000

February 3rd:
RANGERS (2) 5   HEARTS (1) 1
  Willoughby 3 (45, 72, 78),   Ferguson (38)
  Henderson (42), Wilson (67)

RANGERS: Martin; Johansen, Provan; Jardine,
McKinnon, Greig (Jackson); Henderson, Willoughby,
A. Smith, D. Smith, Wilson

HEARTS: Cruikshank; Polland, Holt; Anderson,
Thomson, Miller; Fleming, Ferguson, Kerrigan,
Gordon, Kemp

Attendance: 33,087

**McLean and Forrest were dropped after the
previous week's Scottish Cup defeat by Berwick
Rangers.**

February 7th: Jim Forrest asked for a transfer.

February 8th:
CLYDE (0) 1   RANGERS (2) 5
  Stewart (62)   Henderson (5),
                Willoughby 3 (7, 61, 80),
                Wilson (74)

CLYDE: McCulloch; Soutar, McHugh; Anderson,
Fraser, Staite; McFarlane, Hood, Gilroy, Stewart,
Hastings

RANGERS: Martin; Johansen, Provan; Jardine,
McKinnon, Jackson; Henderson (Paul), Willoughby, A.
Smith, D. Smith, Wilson

February 12th:
KILMARNOCK (0) 1   RANGERS (0) 2
  McIlroy (72)   Wilson (55),
                Willoughby (77)

KILMARNOCK: Ferguson; King, McFadzean;
Murray, McGrory, Beattie; McLean, McInally, Queen,
C. Watson, McIlroy

RANGERS: Martin; Johansen, Provan; Jardine,
McKinnon, Greig; Henderson, Willoughby, A. Smith,
D. Smith, Wilson

Attendance: 28,000

Russian prime minister Alexei Kosygin attended this
match

February 25th:
RANGERS (0) 3   ST MIRREN (0) 0
  Reid 2 (64, 89),
  A. Smith (75)

RANGERS: Martin; Johansen, Provan; Jardine, McKinnon, Greig; Henderson, Reid, A. Smith, D. Smith, Wilson

ST MIRREN: Connachan; Murray, Young; Kiernan, Hannah, Renton; Aird, Hamilton, Kane, Gemmill, Pinkerton

Attendance: 20,000

League positions

	P	W	D	L	F	A	Pts
1 Celtic	24	19	4	1	83	25	42
2 RANGERS	24	18	4	2	72	21	40
3 Aberdeen	25	14	4	7	58	31	32
4 Hibernian	25	15	2	8	50	40	32
5 Clyde	24	13	4	7	43	37	30

March 4th:
MOTHERWELL (1) 1   RANGERS (3) 5
  R. McCallum (31)   Willoughby 4 (2, 25, 56, 80),
                       A. Smith (11)

MOTHERWELL: Wylie; Whiteford, R. McCallum; Campbell, Martis, W. McCallum; Lindsay, Murray, Deans (Thomson), Cairney, Hunter

RANGERS: Martin; Johansen, Provan; Jardine, McKinnon, Greig; Henderson, Willoughby, A. Smith, D. Smith, Wilson

Attendance: 25,000

March 7th:
AIRDRIE (0) 0   RANGERS (0) 1
                        D. Smith (53 pen)

AIRDRIE: McKenzie; Jonquin, Keenan; Goodwin, Black, Ramsay; Irvine, Marshall, Menzies, Murray, Breen

RANGERS: Martin; Johansen, Provan; Jardine, McKinnon, Greig; Henderson, Willoughby, A. Smith, D. Smith, Wilson

Attendance: 18,000

Jonquin was ordered off

March 16th: Jim Forrest joined Preston North End for £38,000.

March 18th:
AYR UNITED (0) 1   RANGERS (3) 4
  Ingram (80)   Willoughby 2 (9, 84),
                         Jardine (19),
                         Oliphant o.g. (11)

AYR UNITED: Anton; Thomson, Murphy; Oliphant, Monan, Mitchell; Grant, McMillan, Ingram, Black, Moore

RANGERS: Martin; Johansen, Provan; Jardine, McKinnon, Greig; Henderson, Willoughby, A. Smith, D. Smith, Wilson

Attendance: 16,000

March 25th:
RANGERS (0) 1   HIBERNIAN (0) 0
  A. Smith (65)

RANGERS: Martin; Johansen, Provan; Jardine, Jackson, Greig; Henderson, Willoughby, A. Smith, D. Smith, Wilson

HIBERNIAN: Allan; Duncan, Davis; Stanton, Madsen, Cousin; O'Rourke, Stein, Scott, McGraw, Stevenson

March 29th:
RANGERS (3) 4   ST JOHNSTONE (3) 3
  Wilson 2 (3, 29)   Whitelaw (29),
  A. Smith (36),   Aitken 2 (25, 44)
  Willoughby (58)

RANGERS: Martin; Johansen, Provan; Jardine, Jackson, Greig; Henderson, Willoughby, A. Smith, D. Smith, Wilson

ST JOHNSTONE: Donaldson; Michie, Coburn; McCarry, Rooney, McPhee; Johnstone, Whitelaw, Wilson, Townsend, Aitken

Attendance: 20,000

April 1st:
RANGERS (0) 0   DUNFERMLINE (0) 1
                        Robertson (51)

RANGERS: Martin; Johansen (Hynd), Provan; Jardine, Jackson, Greig; Henderson, Reid, A. Smith, D. Smith, Wilson

DUNFERMLINE: Martin; Callaghan, Totten; Paton, Fraser, Thomson; Edwards, Kerrigan, Hunter, Ferguson, Robertson

Attendance: 27,000

April 4th: Rangers signed Andy Penman from Dundee. George McLean, valued at £25,000, went to Dens Park. Dundee also received £30,000 in cash.

April 8th:
STIRLING ALBION (0) 0   RANGERS (1) 1
                          Willoughby (36)

STIRLING ALBION: Murray; Cunningham, McGuinness; Reid, Rogerson, Thomson; Peebles, Smith, Grant, Kerray, Hall

RANGERS: Martin; Johansen, Mathieson; Jardine, McKinnon, Greig; Henderson, Willoughby, A. Smith, D. Smith, Wilson

Attendance: 8,500

April 15th: Scotland beat England 3-2 at Wembley. Greig and McKinnon were in the team.

April 22nd:
RANGERS (1) 1   CLYDE (0) 1
  Wilson (45)   Stewart (73)

The season 1968–69 pool. Back row: White (manager), Smith (physiotherapist), Watson, McKinnon, Persson, Sorensen, Martin, Provan, D. Smith, Mathieson, Craven (asst. trainer), Kinnear (trainer), Front row: Henderson, Willoughby, Jardine, A. Smith, Ferguson, Greig, Penman, Semple, Johansen, and Johnston.

A picture from 1973 shows the changes in personnel that can take place in a few years. Back row: Young, Struthers, Scott, Jackson, Hunter, McCloy, Kennedy, Forsyth, Burke, Donaldson, McNichol. Middle row: Craig (physiotherapist), McDonald, Hamilton, O'Hara, Conn, D. Smith, D. Johnston, Miller, Thomson, Mathieson, Fyffe, McDougall, Anderson (trainer). Front row: Wallace (manager), Morris, McLean, MacDonald, Houston, Parlane, Greig, Jardine, Mason, Steel, Young, Denny and Thornton (asst. manager).

RANGERS: Martin; Johansen, Provan; Jardine, McKinnon, Greig; Henderson, Willoughby, A. Smith, D. Smith, Wilson

CLYDE: Wright; Glasgow, Soutar; Anderson, Staite, McHugh; McFarlane, Hood, Gilroy, Stewart, Hastings

Attendance: 25,000

April 29th:
DUNDEE   (1) 1   RANGERS   (0) 1
  Scott (33)   Willoughby (59)
DUNDEE: Arrol; R. Wilson, Cox; Murray, Easton, Stuart; Campbell, J. McLean (Kinnonmonth), J. Wilson, Scott, Bryce

RANGERS: Martin; Johansen, Provan; Jardine, McKinnon, Greig; Henderson, Willoughby, A. Smith, D. Smith, Wilson

Attendance: 20,000

May 6th:
RANGERS   (1) 2   CELTIC   (1) 2
  Jardine (40), Hynd (81)   Johnstone 2 (41, 74)
RANGERS: Martin; Johansen, Provan; Jardine, McKinnon, Greig; Henderson, A. Smith, Hynd, D. Smith, Johnston

CELTIC: Simpson; Craig, Gemmell; Murdoch, McNeill, Clark; Johnstone, Wallace, Chalmers, Auld, Lennox

Attendance: 78,000

Celtic attained the one point which won them the League Championship for the 22nd time. In 40 minutes Dave Smith set off on a long meandering run down the left touchline in search of an opening. He held off one challenge and then pitched the ball across to the unmarked Jardine who drove an unsaveable shot from 25 yards into the net via the underside of the crossbar. Rangers conceded the equaliser 45 seconds later. A Wallace shot was stopped by Martin, the ball bobbed around tantalisingly on the 6-yard line until Lennox pushed it on to a post and Johnstone, following up, shot home the rebound. In 74 minutes Johnstone, having received the ball from a throw-in by Chalmers, made for the penalty area, evading McKinnon's tackle, and in the process veered left as other defenders closed in and then smacked a glorious shot into the roof of the net. Hynd scored the equaliser for Rangers 9 minutes from time when he scliffed home a Henderson cross.

Scottish First Division

	P	W	D	L	F	A	Pts
1 Celtic	34	26	6	2	111	33	58
2 RANGERS	34	24	7	3	92	31	55
3 Clyde	34	20	6	8	64	48	46
4 Aberdeen	34	17	8	9	72	38	42
5 Hibernian	34	19	4	11	72	49	42
6 Dundee	34	16	9	9	74	51	41
7 Kilmarnock	34	16	8	10	59	46	40
8 Dunfermline	34	14	10	10	72	52	38
9 Dundee United	34	14	9	11	68	62	37
10 Motherwell	34	10	11	13	59	60	31
11 Hearts	34	11	8	15	39	48	30
12 Partick Thistle	34	9	12	13	49	68	30
13 Airdrie	34	11	6	17	41	53	28
14 Falkirk	34	11	4	19	33	70	26
15 St Johnstone	34	10	5	19	53	73	25
16 Stirling Albion	34	5	9	20	31	85	19
17 St Mirren	34	4	7	23	25	81	15
18 Ayr United	34	1	7	26	20	86	9

June 11th: Jimmy Millar was freed by Rangers.

June 28th: Davie White, manager of Clyde, was appointed as assistant manager of Rangers.

LEAGUE CUP

August 13th:
RANGERS   (0) 1   HIBERNIAN   (0) 0
  McLean (85)
RANGERS: Ritchie; Johansen, Greig; Millar, McKinnon, D. Smith; Henderson, A. Smith, Forrest, McLean, Wilson

HIBERNIAN: Allan; Duncan, Davis; Stanton, McNamee, Cousin; Cormack, Stein, Scott, McGraw, E. Stevenson

Attendance: 40,000

August 17th:
STIRLING ALBION   (0) 0   RANGERS   (4) 8
                          Wilson (18),
                          McLean 2 (41, 62
                          pen),
                          Forrest 5 (39, 43, 59,
                          64, 85)
STIRLING ALBION: Murray; Caldow, McGuinness; Cunningham, Rogerson, Thomson; Peebles, McKinnon, Grant, Kerray, Hall

RANGERS: Ritchie; Johansen, Greig; Millar, McKinnon, D. Smith; Henderson, A. Smith, Forrest, McLean, Wilson

Attendance: 12,000

August 20th:
RANGERS   (0) 0   KILMARNOCK   (0) 0

RANGERS: Ritchie; Johansen, Provan; Millar, McKinnon, D. Smith; Henderson, A. Smith, Forrest, Greig, Johnston

KILMARNOCK: Ferguson; King, Watson; O'Connor, McGrory, Beattie; McLean, McFadzean, Bertelsen, Queen, McIlroy

Attendance: 50,000

August 27th:
HIBERNIAN (1) 3   RANGERS (1) 2
  Scott (32), McNamee (83),   McLean (25),
  McGraw (88)   A. Smith (68)

HIBERNIAN: Allan; Duncan, Davis; Stanton, McNamee, Cousin; Cormack, Stein, Scott, McGraw, Stevenson

RANGERS: Ritchie; Johansen, Provan; Millar, McKinnon, D. Smith; Henderson, A. Smith, Forrest, McLean, Johnston

Attendance: 32,913

August 31st:
RANGERS (0) 1   STIRLING ALBION (0) 1
  A. Smith (72)   Peebes (48)

RANGERS: Ritchie; Johansen, Provan; Millar, McKinnon, D. Smith; Henderson, A. Smith, Forrest, McLean, Johnston

STIRLING ALBION: Murray; Caldow, McGuinness; Grant, Thomson, Reid; Aitken, Peebles, Orr, Kerray, Symington

Attendance: 14,000

September 3rd:
KILMARNOCK (0) 0   RANGERS (0) 1
    Forrest (74)

KILMARNOCK: Dick; King, Watson; O'Connor, McGrory, Beattie; McLean, McFadzean, Bertelsen, Queen, McIlroy

RANGERS: Ritchie; Johansen, Provan; Millar, McKinnon, D. Smith; Henderson (Wilson), A. Smith, Forrest, McLean, Johnston

Attendance: 28,000

League Cup Section Table

	P	W	D	L	F	A	Pts
RANGERS	6	3	2	1	13	4	8
Hibernian	6	4	0	2	12	9	8
Kilmarnock	6	2	2	2	6	3	6
Stirling Albion	6	0	2	4	3	18	2

September 14th: Quarter-Final First Leg
AYR UNITED (1) 1   RANGERS (1) 1
  Ingram (16)   Johnston (59)

AYR UNITED: Miller; Malone, Murphy; Thomson, Monan, Quinn; Grant, Oliphant, Ingram, McAnespie, Hawkshaw

RANGERS: Ritchie; Provan, Greig; Millar, McKinnon, D. Smith; Wilson, A. Smith, Forrest, McLean, Johnston

Attendance: 14,250

September 21st: Quarter-Final Second Leg
RANGERS (2) 3   AYR UNITED (0) 0
  McLean 2 (16, 65), Greig (38)

RANGERS: Ritchie; Johansen, Provan; Miller, McKinnon, D. Smith; Henderson, Greig, McLean, A. Smith, Johnston

AYR UNITED: Miller; Malone, Murphy; Thomson, Monan, Quinn; Grant, McMillan, Ingram, McAnespie, Hawkshaw

Attendance: 23,000

Rangers won 4-1 on aggregate

October 19th: Semi-Final   At Hampden Park
RANGERS (2) 2   ABERDEEN (1) 2
  Henderson 2 (13, 35)   J. Wilson (23),
    Shewan (70)
    After Extra Time

RANGERS: Ritchie; Johansen, Provan; Greig, McKinnon, D. Smith; Henderson, A. Smith, Millar (Wilson), McLean, Johnston

ABERDEEN: Clark; Whyte, Shewan; Millar, McMillan, Petersen; Little (P. Wilson), Melrose, Winchester, Smith, J. Wilson

Attendance: 38,623

Although Henderson twice gave Rangers the lead in the first half, Aberdeen equalised each time. It was in many ways an extraordinary match. In the last 10 minutes Clark got in the way of shots from McLean and A. Smith. McLean hit the crossbar and Johnston hesitated fatally in dealing with the rebound. In the last minute D. Millar had a shot saved by Ritchie and during the first period of extra time Johnston struck a post. Finally McLean missed a sitter laid on for him by Wilson.

October 24th: Semi-Final Replay   At Hampden Park
ABERDEEN (0) 0   RANGERS (2) 2
    Johnston (3), A. Smith (38)

ABERDEEN: Clark; Whyte, Shewan; Millar, McMillan, Petersen; Little, Melrose, Winchester, Smith, J. Wilson; Sub: P. Wilson

RANGERS: Martin; Johansen, Provan; Greig, McKinnon, D. Smith; Wilson, Watson, McLean, A. Smith, Johnston; Sub: Jardine

Attendance: 38,086

Rangers summarily disposed of Aberdeen in this replay. They were forced to make a number of changes because of injuries to key players. Aberdeen were at full strength. It was Rangers who had all the confidence from the start and in 3 minutes they were a goal ahead. Greig sent a powerful pass 40 yards up the right wing to Wilson who wasted no time in crossing. McLean breasted the ball down and in a goalmouth flurry it broke to Johnston who scored a spectacular goal. 7 minutes before half-time a spell of intense pressure by Rangers was preluded by the 2nd goal when A. Smith, after co-operation by Wilson and Watson, shot past Clark.

October 29th: Final   At Hampden Park
CELTIC   (1) 1   RANGERS   (0) 0
   Lennox (19)

CELTIC: Simpson; Gemmell, O'Neill; Murdoch, McNeill, Clark; Johnstone, Lennox, McBride, Auld, Hughes (Chalmers)

RANGERS: Martin; Johansen, Provan, Greig, McKinnon, D. Smith; Henderson, Watson, McLean, A. Smith, Johnston; Sub: Wilson

Attendance: 94,532   *Referee*: T. Wharton (Clarkston)

Celtic were outplayed by Rangers but retained the League Cup. Their one opportunity was brilliantly taken but for almost all of the remainder of the game Rangers outplayed them and pushed them relentlessly back into defence. 2 claims for a penalty were turned down and Watson had an apparently genuine score obscurely disallowed. In the dying minutes McLean shot over from 5 yards and A. Smith, with the ball at his feet and Simpson beaten, stumbled as he shot and O'Neill was able to clear. Throughout McLean was his most irritatingly cumbersome self. Celtic's goal came after 19 minutes. Auld flighted a cross beyond the far post and McBride headed down and back for Lennox who hammered it past Martin into the net.

SCOTTISH CUP

January 27th: First Round
BERWICK RANGERS   (1) 1 RANGERS   (0) 0
   Reid (35)

BERWICK: Wallace; Haig, Riddell; Craig, Coutts, Kilgannon; Lumsden, Reid, Christie, Dowds, Ainslie

RANGERS: Martin; Johansen, Provan; Greig, McKinnon, D. Smith; Henderson, A. Smith, McLean, Forrest, Johnston (Wilson)

Attendance: 13,283

EUROPEAN CUP WINNERS CUP

September 27th: First Round
GLENTORAN   (0) 1   RANGERS   (1) 1
   Sinclair (90)   McLean (14)

GLENTORAN: Finlay; Creighton, McKeag; Bruce, McCullough, Stewart; Conroy, Sinclair, Thompson, Colrain, Ross

RANGERS: Ritchie; Johansen, Provan; Millar, McKinnon, D. Smith; Henderson, Greig, McLean, A. Smith, Johnston

Attendance: 40,000

October 5th: First Round Second Leg
RANGERS   (2) 4   GLENTORAN   (0) 0
   Johnston (10), D. Smith (44),
   Setterington (70), McLean (78)

RANGERS: Ritchie; Johansen, Provan; Greig, McKinnon, D. Smith; Henderson, A. Smith, McLean; Setterington, Johnston

GLENTORAN: Finlay; Creighton, McKeag; Bruce, McCullough, Stewart; Conroy, Sinclair, Thompson, Colrain, Ross

Attendance: 40,000

Rangers won 5-1 on aggregate

November 23rd: Second Round First Leg
RANGERS   (1) 2   BORUSSIA
   Johansen (12),   DORTMUND   (1) 1
   A. Smith (75)   Trimholdt (31)

RANGERS: Martin; Johansen, Provan; Greig, McKinnon, D. Smith; Henderson, Watson, Forrest, A. Smith, Johnston

BORUSSIA DORTMUND: Wessel; Cyliax, Peehs; Kurrat, Paul, Assauer; Wosab, Trimholdt, Held, Emmerich, Neuberger

Attendance: 65,000

December 6th: Second Round Second Leg
BORUSSIA   (0) 0   RANGERS   (0) 0
   DORTMUND

BORUSSIA DORTMUND: Wessel; Cyliax, Peehs; Kurrat, Paul, W. Sturm; Libuda, Trimholdt, Held, Assauer, Emmerich

RANGERS: Martin; Johansen, Provan; Greig, McKinnon, D. Smith; Henderson, Watson, Forrest, A. Smith, Johnston

Watson was carried off with damaged ligaments after 40 minutes

Rangers won 2-1 on aggregate

March 1st: Third Round First Leg
RANGERS   (2) 2   REAL
   D. Smith (10),   ZARAGOSSA   (0) 0
   Willoughby (27)

RANGERS: Martin; Johansen, Provan; Jardine, McKinnon, Greig; Henderson, Willoughby, A. Smith, D. Smith, Wilson

REAL ZARAGOSSA: Yarza; Irusquieta, Reija; Violeta, Gonzales, Pais; Canario, Santos, Marcellino, Villa, Lapetra

Attendance: 65,000

March 22nd: Third Round Second Leg
REAL ZARAGOSSA (1) 2 RANGERS (0) 0
Lapetra (24),
Santos (86 pen)
After Extra Time
REAL ZARAGOSSA: Yarza; Irusquieta, Reija; Violeta, Gonzales, Pais; Villa, Santos, Marcellino, Bustillo, Lapetra

RANGERS: Martin; Johansen, Provan; Jardine, Jackson, Greig; Henderson, Willoughby, A. Smith, D. Smith, Wilson

Attendance: 35,000

D. Smith missed a penalty

Rangers won on the toss of a coin

April 19th: Semi-Final
SLAVIA SOFIA (0) 0 RANGERS (1) 1
Wilson (31)
SLAVIA: Simenov; Shalamanov, Petrov; Alexiev, Davidov, Manolov; Lukach, Kharalampiev, Crzhev, Vassilev, Mishev

RANGERS: Martin; Johansen, Provan; Jardine, McKinnon, Greig; Henderson, Willoughby, A. Smith, D. Smith, Wilson

Rangers beat Slavia on the bumpy pitch of the Levski National Stadium. The only goal of the game was scored by Wilson in the 31st minute of an uninspiring contest.

May 3rd: Semi-Final Second Leg
RANGERS (1) 1 SLAVIA SOFIA (0) 0
Henderson (32)
RANGERS: Martin; Johansen, Provan; Jardine, McKinnon, Greig; Henderson, A. Smith, Hynd, D. Smith, Johnston

SLAVIA: Simenov; Shalamanov, Petrov; Alexiev, Largov, Manalov; Vrajev, Haralampiev, Vassilev, Davidov, Michev

Attendance: 70,000

Rangers won 2-0 on aggregate

Rangers qualified to meet Bayern Munich in the Final at Nuremberg. The one-goal margin hardly represented Rangers' superiority over a Bulgarian team who offered a spirited challenge but were for the most part slow and ponderous in the build-up. Rangers were rarely out of their opponents' territory in the entire 90 minutes and but for some ill-luck and some breathtaking goalkeeping would have won by a much more comfortable margin.

Time and again Simenov came to his side's rescue with saves that bordered on the miraculous. Hynd challenged and harassed his opponents at every opportunity. Appropriately it was Henderson and Hynd who were responsible for the only goal of the game scored in 32 minutes. Vassilev diverted a shot by Jardine for a corner, and when Johnston's kick came across Hynd headed the ball on to Henderson who, from 20 yards, drove the ball past Simenov into the net.

May 31st: Final   In Nuremberg
RANGERS (0) 0 BAYERN MUNICH (0) 1
Roth (109)
After Extra Time
RANGERS: Martin; Johansen, Provan; Jardine, McKinnon, Greig; Henderson, A. Smith, Hynd, D. Smith, Johnston

BAYERN: Maier; Nowak, Kupferschmidt; Roth, Beckenbauer, Olk; Nafziger, Ohlhauser, Muller, Koulmann, Brenninger

Attendance: 65,000

A goal scored by right-half Roth in the 19th minute of extra time cost Rangers the Cup Winners' Cup. Henderson, the man from whom Rangers expected most, was the biggest disappointment on this disappointing night. He could make nothing of the German left-back. Greig was an inspiring captain. Rangers should have been a goal ahead at half-time, for when in the 33rd minute D. Smith passed the ball to Hynd on the 6-yard line the centre-forward had an excellent chance to score. He did not get enough power into his shot and Maier made a splendid one-handed save.

Sammy Cox, a Rangers stalwart in the fifties.

APPEARANCES

	League	League Cup	Scottish Cup	Cup Winners Cup
Ritchie	6	9	-	2
Johansen	33	10	1	9
Provan	33	10	1	9
Millar	5+1S	9	-	1
McKinnon	31	11	1	8
D. Smith	34	11	1	9
Wilson	17+2S	4+2S	0+1S	3
A. Smith	33	11	1	9
Forrest	17	7	1	2
McLean	9	10	1	2
Johnston	21	9	1	6
Greig	32	7	1	9
Henderson	32	9	1	9
Setterington	6	-	-	1
Watson	4	2	-	2
Willoughby	11+1S	-	-	3
Jardine	14	-	-	5
Jackson	4+1S	-	-	1
Paul	0+1S	-	-	-
Reid	2	-	-	-
Hynd	1+1S	-	-	2
Mathieson	1	-	-	-
Martin	28	2	1	7

GOALSCORERS

League: A. Smith 19, Willoughby 16, McLean 8, Forrest 8, Henderson 8, Wilson 6, Johnston 5, Provan 4 (4 pens), Setterington 3, D. Smith 2 (1 pen), Millar 2, Greig 2, Reid 2, Jardine 2, Own Goals 2, Johansen 1, McKinnon 1, Hynd 1

League Cup: McLean 6 (1 pen), Forrest 6, A. Smith 3, Johnston 2, Henderson 2, Wilson 1, Greig 1

Cup Winners Cup: McLean 2, D. Smith 2, Johnston 1, Setterington 1, Johansen 1, A. Smith 1, Willoughby 1, Wilson 1, Henderson 1

The Rangers team that took part in the 1967 European Cup Winners Cup Final against Bayern Munich. Back row: Jardine, Johansen, Martin, Provan, McKinnon, Greig. Front row: Henderson, A. Smith, Hynd, D. Smith, Johnston.

Season 1967–68

Rangers went through the whole League Season with only one defeat — that coming at Ibrox on the last Saturday; they amassed their highest points total since League re-construction in Season 1955–56; they took 3 of the 4 points from Celtic; they scored 10 goals in a match against Raith Rovers; they led the Table at the end of October, at Christmas and at the beginning of March and yet they still had to surrender the title to their greatest rivals for the 3rd successive season. They signed Alex Ferguson from Dunfermline for £65,000 at the start of the Season and he finished as top scorer with 19 goals. Johnston was next on 18 and Swedish International Orjan Persson contributed 14 out of a total of 93, McKinnon and Dave Smith played in every match.

Missed penalties by Penman and Johansen in both League Cup Section matches with Celtic prevented Rangers' further progress in that competition. Dundee United and Aberdeen were their other Section opponents.

After having beaten Hamilton Academicals and Dundee (after a replay) in the Scottish Cup, Rangers were put out by Hearts in a Third Round Replay at Tynecastle, a late goal from Donald Ford doing the damage.

Teams from both East Germany and West Germany were eliminated in the Fairs Cup but England's Leeds United proved too strong in the Quarter-Final. Too many chances were missed in the first leg at Ibrox. The use of closed circuit television in both ties was an interesting experiment.

Rangers undertook a 4-match Scandinavian Tour at the end of the Season and returned with four victories.

The biggest talking point of the season was the departure of manager Scot Symon after 13 years at the club. During his period in charge the club won 6 League Championships, 5 Scottish Cups and 4 League Cups and were twice in European Finals. Their full League record was as follows: Played 446 Won 295 Drew 81 Lost 70

League: Runners-up
League Cup: Failed to Qualify from Section
Scottish Cup: Third Round
Fairs Cities Cup: Quarter-finalists

SCOTTISH FIRST DIVISION

July 18th: Jimmy Millar joined Dundee United on a free transfer.

July 26th: Danish International goalkeeper Erik Sorensen was signed from Morton.

July 31st: Alex Ferguson was signed from Dunfermline for £65,000.

August 3rd: Swedish International Orjan Persson was signed from Dundee United in a deal which took long-serving Davie Wilson and wing-half Wilson Wood to Tannadice.

September 9th:
PARTICK THISTLE (0) 0 RANGERS (1) 2
Penman 2 (39, 76)

PARTICK THISTLE: Niven; Campbell, Muir; O'Neill, McKinnon, Gibb; Flanagan, Coulston, Rae, Cunningham, Duncan

RANGERS: Sorensen; Johansen, Provan; Jardine, McKinnon, Greig; Henderson, Penman, Ferguson, D. Smith, Johnston

September 16th:
RANGERS (0) 1   CELTIC (0) 0
  Persson (47)

RANGERS: Sorensen; Johansen, Provan (Johnston); Jardine, McKinnon, Greig; Henderson, Penman, Ferguson, D. Smith, Persson

CELTIC: Simpson; Cattenach, Gemmell; Murdoch, McNeill, Clark; Johnstone, Wallace, Chalmers, Auld, Lennox

Attendance: 90,000

After the match it was confirmed that Rangers' Scottish Internationalist left-back Provan, carried off after a tackle on Auld in 4 minutes, would be out of football for some 3 months with a broken leg. In 47 minutes McKinnon began the move which led to the only goal of the game. He lobbed the ball to Persson, who had wandered into the inside-right position. In a devastating run of some 30 yards he beat Gemmell on the inside, swerved past Murdoch and Clark and then again side-stepped Gemmell who had chased back to cover the route to goal. Even then a goal seemed impossible, as the angle was acute and the range about 18 yards but Persson, showing admirable control and coolness, suddenly wheeled round and cracked an unstoppable left-foot shot past Simpson. Thereafter as before, Rangers created — and scorned — more clear-cut chances than Celtic.

September 23rd:
FALKIRK (0) 0   RANGERS (0) 1
                         Penman (83)

FALKIRK: Devlin; Lambie, Hunter; Markie, Baillie, Gibson; Marshall, Moreland, Graham, McLaughlin, McManus

RANGERS: Sorensen; Hynd, Greig; Watson, McKinnon, D. Smith; Persson, Penman, Ferguson, Jardine, Johnston

Attendance: 25,000

September 30th:
RANGERS (0) 1   HEARTS (1) 1
  Ferguson (75)   G. Fleming (22)

RANGERS: Sorensen; Johansen, Greig; Jardine, McKinnon, D. Smith; Henderson, Penman, Ferguson, Persson, Johnston

HEARTS: Garland; Sneddon, Holt; MacDonald, Thomson, Miller; J. Fleming (G. Fleming), Townsend, Ford, Irvine, Traynor

Attendance: 30,000

Penman missed a penalty

October 7th:
MOTHERWELL (0) 0   RANGERS (1) 2
                            Ferguson (20),
                            Greig (74)

MOTHERWELL: McCloy; Whiteford, Mackay; Murray, Martis, W. McCallum; Lindsay, Thomson, Deans, Goldthorpe, Campbell

RANGERS: Sorensen; Johansen, Mathieson; Greig, McKinnon, D. Smith; Henderson (Jardine), Penman, Ferguson, Persson, Johnston

Attendance: 20,500

Henderson missed a penalty and then had to go off with a fractured jaw

October 10th: Billy Ritchie joined Partick Thistle.

October 14th:
CLYDE (0) 1   RANGERS (1) 3
  Stewart (77)   Greig (37),
                         Persson (75),
                         Ferguson (80)

CLYDE: Wright; Glasgow (Anderson), Soutar; McHugh, Fraser, Staite; McFarlane, Hood, Gilroy, Stewart, Hastings

RANGERS: Martin; Johansen, Mathieson; Greig, McKinnon, D. Smith; Persson, Penman, Ferguson, Willoughby, Johnston

Attendance: 25,000

October 21st: Scotland were beaten 1-0 by Northern Ireland in Belfast. Greig and McKinnon were in the team.

October 23rd:
RANGERS (1) 2   DUNDEE (0) 0
  Mathieson (13), Hynd (89)

RANGERS: Martin; Johansen, Mathieson; Greig, McKinnon, D. Smith; Persson (Hynd), Penman, Ferguson, Willoughby, Johnston

DUNDEE: Donaldson; R. Wilson, Cox; Murray, Stewart, Stuart; Campbell (Bryce), J. McLean, S. Wilson, Houston, G. McLean

Attendance: 30,000

October 28th:
RANGERS 0   DUNFERMLINE 0

RANGERS: Martin; Johansen, Mathieson; Greig, McKinnon, D. Smith; Johnston, Watson, Ferguson, Willoughby, Persson; Sub: Penman for Willoughby

DUNFERMLINE: Martin; W. Callaghan, Lunn; Fraser, Barry, Thomson; Edwards, Paton, Gardner, T. Callaghan, Robertson

Attendance: 35,000

League positions

	P	W	D	L	F	A	Pts
1 RANGERS	8	6	2	0	12	2	14
2 Hibernian	8	6	1	1	24	10	13
3 Celtic	7	5	1	1	21	5	11
4 Hearts	8	5	1	2	19	14	11
5 St Johnstone	8	3	4	1	14	9	10

November 1st: On the day Celtic were playing for the World Club Championship in South America. Rangers announced that manager Scot Symon had parted company with the club. Assistant Manager Davie White was named as the new manager. Speaking of his successor Scot Symon said, 'Davie is a very fine man. I wish him all the best. He is with a wonderful club'.

November 2nd: Coach Bobby Seith also quit the club.

November 4th:
ST JOHNSTONE   (2) 2   RANGERS   (1) 3
  Whitelaw (26),   Johnstone (21),
  MacDonald (40)   Ferguson (49),
                             Persson (54)

ST JOHNSTONE: Donaldson; McGillivray, Coburn; Gordon, Rooney, McPhee; Aird, Whitelaw, McCarry, Wilson, MacDonald

RANGERS: Sorensen; Johansen, Mathieson; Greig, McKinnon, D. Smith; Henderson, Penman, Ferguson, Johnston, Persson

Attendance: 16,000

November 11th:
RANGERS   (1) 1   MORTON   (0) 0
  Johnston (90 secs)

RANGERS: Sorensen; Jardine, Mathieson; A. Smith, McKinnon, D. Smith; Henderson, Penman, Ferguson, Johnston, Persson

MORTON: Crawford; Loughlan, Kennedy; Arnetoft, Strachan, Rankin; Stevenson, Bartram, Mason, Jensen, Sweeney

Attendance: 38,000

November 18th:
STIRLING ALBION   (1) 2   RANGERS   (1) 4
  Munro 2 (43, 88)   McKinnon (38),
                            Penman (60),
                            Henderson (74),
                            Persson (76)

STIRLING ALBION: Murray; Cunningham, Corrigan; Grant, Thomson, Orr; Hall, McKinnon, Munro, Peebles, Symington

RANGERS: Sorensen; Johansen, Mathieson; Greig, McKinnon, D. Smith; Henderson, Penman, Ferguson, Johnston, Persson; Sub: Jardine for Mathieson

Attendance: 18,000

November 22nd: Scotland beat Wales 3-2 at Hampden Park. Greig, McKinnon and Johnston were in the team. McKinnon scored the winning goal.

November 25th:
RANGERS   (1) 2   HIBERNIAN   (0) 0
  Greig (36 pen),
  Willoughby (84)

RANGERS: Sorensen; Jardine, Mathieson; Greig, McKinnon, D. Smith; Henderson, Penman, Ferguson, Willoughby, Persson

HIBERNIAN: Wilson; Duncan, Davis; Stanton, Madsen, McGraw; Scott, Quinn, Stein, Cormack, O'Rourke

Attendance: 40,000

Both Ferguson and Stein were sent off for fighting

December 2nd:
RANGERS   (1) 2   AIRDRIE   (0) 1
  Johnston (30),   Fyfe (60)
  Ferguson (78)

RANGERS: Sorensen; Johansen, Mathieson; Greig, McKinnon, D. Smith; Henderson, Penman, Ferguson, Johnston, Persson

AIRDRIE: McKenzie; Jonquin, Caldwell; Goodwin, Black, Whiteford; McLellan, Ramsey, Marshall, Fyfe, Phillips

Attendance: 30,000

December 11th: Jim Baxter was transferred from Sunderland to Nottingham Forest for £100,000.

December 16th:
RANGERS   (5) 10   RAITH ROVERS   (1) 2
  Johnston 2 (3, 89),   Lister (27),
  Persson 2 (6, 84),   D. Smith o.g. (83)
  Greig 2 (17, 75),
  Ferguson 3 (34, 49, 78),
  Willoughby (37)

RANGERS: Sorensen; Johansen, Mathieson; Greig, McKinnon, D. Smith; Penman, Willoughby, Ferguson, Johnston, Persson

RAITH ROVERS: J. Gray; Hislop, A. Gray; Stein, Davidson, Porterfield; Lister, Sneddon, Wallace, Cunningham, Falconer

Attendance: 25,000

December 23rd:

RANGERS (2) 4　　　　KILMARNOCK (0) 1
　Willoughby 2 (18, 20),　　　Cameron (90)
　Johnstone (21), Greig (90)

RANGERS: Sorensen; Jardine, Mathieson; Greig, McKinnon, D. Smith; Penman, Willoughy, A. Smith, Johnston, Persson

KILMARNOCK: McLaughlin; Arthur, McFadzean; Murray, McGrory, Beattie; McLean, Queen, Morrison, Sinclair, Cameron

Attendance: 35,000

December 30th:

ABERDEEN (0) 1　　　　RANGERS (1)4
　Smith (72)　　　　　　Penman (11),
　　　　　　　　　　　　Watson (55),
　　　　　　　　　　　　Johnston (78),
　　　　　　　　　　　　Willoughby (83)

ABERDEEN: Clark; Whyte, Shewan; Petersen, McMillan, Munro; Little, Buchanan, Johnston, Smith, Craig

RANGERS: Sorensen; Johansen, Greig; Watson, McKinnon, D. Smith; Penman, Willoughby, A. Smith, Johnston, Persson

Attendance: 20,000

League positions

	P	W	D	L	F	A	Pts
1 RANGERS	16	14	2	0	42	12	30
2 Celtic	16	13	2	1	47	13	28
3 Hearts	17	10	3	4	38	26	23
4 Hibernian	16	9	2	5	32	20	20
5 Clyde	16	9	1	6	28	23	19

January 1st:

RANGERS (2) 5　PARTICK THISTLE (0) 2
　Hynd 2 (35, 87),　　Rae (59), Gibb (78)
　Johnston 2 (44, 49),
　Penman (72)

RANGERS: Sorensen; Johansen, Mathieson; Greig, McKinnon, D. Smith; Penman, Willoughby, Hynd, Johnston, Semple

PARTICK THISTLE: Niven; Campbell, Muir; O'Neil, McKinnon, Gibb; Rae, McLindon, Coulston, Flanagan, Gallagher

January 2nd:

CELTIC (1) 2　　　　RANGERS (0) 2
　Auld (18), Murdoch (78)　Johnston (55),
　　　　　　　　　　　　Johansen (88)

CELTIC: Fallon; Gemmell, Cattenach; Brogan, McNeill, Clark; Johnstone, Murdoch, Hughes, Lennox, Auld (Quinn)

RANGERS: Sorensen; Johansen, Greig; Jardine, McKinnon, D. Smith; Penman, Watson (A. Smith), Hynd, Johnston, Persson

Attendance: 75,000

Celtic took the lead in 18 minutes when Auld's free-kick was deflected by Jardine into his own goal with Sorensen stranded out of range. 10 minutes after the interval Rangers equalised. Johnston got a second chance at the ball and his shot squeezed between the kneeling knees of Fallon and rolled over the line. With 12 minutes remaining Celtic scored the goal they thought was the winner. Brogan found Murdoch in the area, and he drove a magnificent left-foot shot away from Sorensen. With only 2 minutes remaining Rangers scored an equaliser when Fallon blundered by allowing a speculative drive from Johansen to pass under his body.

January 6th:

RANGERS (1) 2　　　　FALKIRK (0) 0
　Ferguson (23), Penman (53)

RANGERS: Sorensen; Johansen, Mathieson; Greig, McKinnon, D. Smith; Penman, Willoughby, Ferguson, Johnston, Persson

FALKIRK: Devlin; Lambie, Hunter; Scott, Baillie, Gibson; McManus, Markie, Graham, McLaughlin (Vincent), Watson

Attendance: 33,000

January 13th:

HEARTS (1) 2　　　　RANGERS (1) 3
　Irvine (32),　　　　Johnston 2 (38, 50),
　Ford (53)　　　　　Ferguson (61)

HEARTS: Cruikshank; Sneddon, Mann; Anderson, Thomson, Miller; Ford, G. Fleming, J. Fleming, Irvine, Kemp

RANGERS: Sorensen; Johansen, Greig; Watson, McKinnon, D. Smith; Penman, Willoughby, Ferguson, Johnston, Persson

Attendance: 36,000

January 20th:

RANGERS (1) 2　　　　MOTHERWELL (0) 0
　Willoughby (25),
　Greig (81 pen)

RANGERS: Sorensen; Johansen, Greig; Watson (A. Smith), McKinnon, D. Smith; Semple, Penman, Ferguson, Willoughby, Persson

MOTHERWELL: McCloy; Whiteford, Mackay; Forsyth, Martis, W. McCallum; Campbell, McInally, Deans, McCall (Lindsay), Wilson

Attendance: 30,000

February 3rd:
RANGERS (1) 1   CLYDE (0) 0
   Greig (27)

RANGERS: Sorensen; Johansen, Mathieson; Greig, McKinnon, D. Smith; Penman, Willoughby, Ferguson, Johnston, Persson

CLYDE: Wright; Glasgow, Staite; Anderson, Fraser, McHugh; McFarlane, Hood, Knox, Stewart, Hastings
Attendance: 35,000

February 10th:
DUNDEE (2) 2   RANGERS (3) 4
   Scott 2 (3, 21)   Greig (12 pen),
                     Johnston 2 (19, 43),
                     Persson (00)

DUNDEE: Donaldson; Wilson, Houston; Murray, Easton, Stuart; Campbell, J. McLean, G. McLean, Scott, Kinnonmonth

RANGERS: Sorensen; Johansen, Mathieson; Greig, McKinnon, D. Smith; Penman, Willoughby, Ferguson, Johnston, Persson
Attendance: 30,000

March 2nd:
RANGERS (1) 6   ST JOHNSTONE (1) 2
   Ferguson 4 (5, 62 pen,   Whitelaw 2 (20, 59)
    77, 87),
   Willoughby (48),
   Persson (81)

RANGERS: Sorensen; Johansen, Mathieson; Jardine, McKinnon, D. Smith; Henderson, Willoughby, Ferguson, Johnston (Watson), Persson

ST JOHNSTONE: Robertson; Michie, Coburn; McCarry, Ryden, Rennie; Aird (Wilson), McPhee, MacDonald, Whitelaw, Aitken
Attendance: 25,000

League positions
	P	W	D	L	F	A	Pts
1 RANGERS	24	21	3	0	67	21	45
2 Celtic	23	19	3	1	67	18	41
3 Hibernian	24	15	3	6	50	29	33
4 Dunfermline	24	11	5	8	46	30	27
5 Kilmarnock	26	11	5	10	48	48	27

March 6th:
DUNFERMLINE (1) 1   RANGERS (1) 2
   Mitchell (14)   Ferguson (37),
                     Persson (85)

DUNFERMLINE: Martin; W. Callaghan, Lunn; Thomson, Kinloch, T. Callaghan; Lister, Paton, Mitchell, Gardner, Robertson

RANGERS: Sorensen; Johansen, Mathieson; Greig, McKinnon, D. Smith; Henderson, Watson, Ferguson, Willoughby, Persson

Lunn was sent off for fouling Ferguson

March 16th:
RANGERS (2) 5   STIRLING ALBION (0) 0
   Persson 3 (24, 65, 67),
   Ferguson (17),
   Corrigan o.g. (54)

RANGERS: Sorensen; Johansen, Mathieson; Greig, McKinnon, D. Smith; Henderson, Willoughby, Ferguson, Johnston, Persson

STIRLING ALBION: Lowrie; Reid, Corrigan; Henderson, Rogerson, Thomson; McPhee, Peebles, Hughes, Smith, Hall
Attendance: 16,000

March 16th: Rangers' bid for George Gibson of Falkirk was turned down.

March 20th: The Scottish League were beaten 2-0 by the English League at Middlesbrough. Greig, McKinnon and D. Smith were in the team.

March 23rd:
HIBERNIAN (1) 1   RANGERS (1) 3
   Stevenson (32)   Persson (18),
                     Henderson (48)
                     Johnston (64)

HIBERNIAN: Wilson; Blackley, Davis; Cousin, Madsen, McGraw; Marinello, Quinn, Stein, Cormack, Stevenson

RANGERS: Sorensen; Johansen, Mathieson; Greig, McKinnon, D. Smith; Henderson, A. Smith, Ferguson, Johnston, Persson
Attendance: 27,195

March 30th:
AIRDRIE (1) 1   RANGERS (1) 2
   McPheat (11)   Johnston (30),
                   A. Smith (87)

AIRDRIE: McKenzie; Jonquin, Keenan; Goodwin, Black, Whiteford; Madden, Jarvie, McPheat, Ramsay, Phillips

RANGERS: Sorensen; Johansen, Mathieson; Greig, McKinnon, D. Smith; Henderson, A. Smith, Ferguson (Willoughby), Johnston, Persson
Attendance: 17,000

April 3rd:
DUNDEE UNITED   0   RANGERS   0
DUNDEE UNITED: Davie; Rolland, Cameron;
Neilson, Smith, Wood; Seeman, Gillespie, Mitchell, J.
Millar, Wilson

RANGERS: Sorensen; Johansen, Mathieson; Greig,
McKinnon, D. Smith; Henderson, A. Smith, Ferguson,
Johnston, Persson

April 6th:
RANGERS   (0) 4   DUNDEE UNITED   (0) 1
  Ferguson 2 (56, 70),   Graham (78)
  Willoughby (58),
  Johnston (83)
RANGERS: Sorensen; Johansen, Mathieson; Greig,
McKinnon, D. Smith; Henderson, Willoughby,
Johnston, Ferguson, Persson

DUNDEE UNITED: Davie; Rolland, Cameron;
Neilson, Smith, Wood; Hainey, Gillespie (Graham),
Mitchell, Millar, Wilson
Attendance: 25,000

April 13th:
RAITH ROVERS   (0) 2   RANGERS   (2) 3
  Judge 2 (66, 84)   D. Smith (23),
                        Willoughby (38),
                        Penman (83)
RAITH ROVERS: Reid; Hislop, Gray; Bolton,
Polland, Millar; Falconer, Stein, Wallace, Judge,
Gillespie

RANGERS: Sorensen; Johansen, Mathieson; Greig,
McKinnon, D. Smith; Henderson, Willoughby,
Johnston, Ferguson, Persson (Penman)
Attendance: 24,000

April 17th:
MORTON   (2) 3   RANGERS   (0) 3
  Taylor (20), Mason (33),   Greig 2 (48, 70),
  Allan (49)   Johnston (75)
MORTON: Russell; Loughlan, Sweeney; Arnetoft,
Strachan, Rankin; Stevenson, Gray, Allan, Mason,
Taylor

RANGERS: Martin; Johansen, Mathieson; Greig,
McKinnon, D. Smith; Henderson, Penman, Johnston,
Willoughby, Persson
Attendance: 18,500

April 20th:
KILMARNOCK   (1) 1   RANGERS   (1) 2
  McFadzean (11)   Persson (42),
                              Willoughby (78)
KILMARNOCK: Dick; Arthur, King; Murray,
McGrory, Dickson; McLean, Queen, Morrison,
McFadzean, McIlroy

RANGERS: Sorensen; Johansen, Mathieson; Greig,
McKinnon, D. Smith; Henderson, Penman, Ferguson,
Johnston, Persson (Willoughby)
Attendance: 25,000

April 27th:
RANGERS   (1) 2   ABERDEEN   (1) 3
  D. Smith (17),   Johnston 2 (28, 57),
  Ferguson (54)   Taylor (89)
RANGERS: Sorensen; Johansen, Mathieson; Greig,
McKinnon, D. Smith; Henderson, Willoughby,
Ferguson, Johnston, Persson

ABERDEEN: Clark; Whyte, Shewan; Petersen,
McMillan, Buchan; Little, Smith, Johnston, Robb,
Craig (Taylor)
Attendance: 45,000

Scottish First Division

	P	W	D	L	F	A	Pts
1 Celtic	34	30	3	1	106	24	63
2 RANGERS	34	28	5	1	93	34	61
3 Hibernian	34	20	5	9	67	49	45
4 Dunfermline	34	17	5	12	64	41	39
5 Aberdeen	34	16	5	13	63	38	37
6 Morton	34	15	6	13	57	53	36
7 Kilmarnock	34	13	8	13	59	57	34
8 Clyde	34	15	4	15	55	55	34
9 Dundee	34	13	7	14	62	59	33
10 Partick Thistle	34	12	7	15	51	67	31
11 Dundee United	34	10	11	13	53	72	31
12 Hearts	34	13	4	17	56	61	30
13 Airdrie	34	10	9	15	45	58	29
14 St Johnstone	34	10	7	17	43	52	27
15 Falkirk	34	7	12	15	36	50	26
16 Raith Rovers	34	9	7	18	58	86	25
17 Motherwell	34	6	7	21	40	66	19
18 Stirling Albion	34	4	4	26	29	105	12

**May 30th: Scotland drew 0-0 with Holland in
Amsterdam. McKinnon, D. Smith, Henderson and
Greig were in the team. Willie Mathieson was in the
orginal pool of players for the match.**

June 3rd: Benfica made an approach for Penman and Johnston.

June 17th: Alex Reid was freed.

LEAGUE CUP

August 12th:
ABERDEEN　(0) 1　　　RANGERS　(1) 1
　Storrie (82)　　　　　Persson (25)

ABERDEEN:　Clark; Whyte, Shewan; Munro, McMillan, Petersen; P. Wilson, Storrie, Johnston, Buchan, J. Wilson

RANGERS:　Sorensen; Johansen, Provan; Jardine, McKinnon, Greig; Henderson, Penman, Ferguson, D. Smith, Persson

Attendance: 40,000

August 16th:
RANGERS　(0) 1　　　CELTIC　(1) 1
　Penman (88)　　　　Gemmell (38 pen)

RANGERS:　Sorensen; Johansen, Provan; Jardine, McKinnon, Greig; Henderson, Penman, Ferguson, D. Smith, Persson

CELTIC:　Simpson; Craig, Gemmell; Murdoch, McNeill, Clark; Johnstone, Wallace, Chalmers, Auld, Lennox

Attendance: 94,168

Penman missed a penalty in the 60th minute

Although Rangers had most of the pressure and enough scoring chances to win the game, Celtic performed magnificently in defence. With just 2 minutes remaining Penman, who had earlier failed to score with a penalty kick, brought the Ibrox house down when he rammed the ball home directly from a free-kick awarded some 25 yards from goal. In 38 minutes Smith pulled down Lennox from behind and Gemmell sent Sorensen the wrong way with the resultant penalty-kick. In the second half it was almost one-way traffic towards Simpson's goal. In the 60th minute Rangers were awarded a penalty when Auld barged Jardine off the ball. Penman took the kick and Simpson threw himself across goal and saved the ball shoulder high at the post.

August 19th:
RANGERS　(0) 1　　DUNDEE UNITED　(0) 0
　Johansen (72 pen)

RANGERS:　Sorensen; Johansen, Provan; Jardine, McKinnon, Greig; Henderson, Penman, Ferguson, D. Smith, Persson

DUNDEE UNITED:　Mackay; T. Millar, Briggs; J. Millar, Smith, Wood; Seeman, Berg, Hainey, Gillespie, Wilson

Attendance: 55,000

August 26th:
RANGERS　(2) 3　　　ABERDEEN　(0) 0
　Penman 2 (30, 80),
　Jardine (22)

RANGERS:　Sorensen; Johansen, Provan; Jardine, McKinnon, Greig; Henderson, Penman, Ferguson, D. Smith, Persson

ABERDEEN:　Clark; Whyte, Shewan; Munro, McMillan, Petersen; Storrie, Smith, Johnston, Melrose, Taylor

Attendance: 50,000

August 30th:
CELTIC　(0) 3　　　RANGERS　(1) 1
　Wallace (78), Murdoch (83),　Henderson (8)
　Lennox (89)

CELTIC:　Simpson; Craig, Gemmell; Murdoch, McNeill, Clark; Johnstone, Wallace, Chalmers, Auld, Lennox

RANGERS:　Sorensen; Johansen, Provan; Jardine, McKinnon, Greig; Henderson, Penman, Ferguson, D. Smith, Johnston

Attendance: 75,000

Johansen missed a 76th-minute penalty

With 14 minutes to go and Rangers grimly holding on to a one-goal lead Johansen was presented with an opportunity to put his side into a strong position after Henderson was brought down in the penalty-area by a late tackle by Clark but the Dane's kick struck the underside of the bar and came out. 2 minutes later Wallace emerged from a group of players with his right hand held high and the ball in the back of the net. 5 minutes later Lennox teed up the ball for Murdoch on the edge of the penalty-area and the wing-half sent it hurtling into the roof of the net. Lennox scored the third for Celtic.

September 1st:
DUNDEE UNITED　(0) 0　　RANGERS　(0) 3
　　　　　　　　　　Ferguson 2 (52, 84),
　　　　　　　　　　Johnston (86)

DUNDEE UNITED:　Mackay; T. Millar, Briggs; J. Millar, Smith, Gillespie; Berg, Dossing, Hainey, Graham, Mitchell

RANGERS:　Sorensen; Johansen, Provan; Jardine, McKinnon, Greig; Henderson, Penman, Ferguson, D. Smith, Johnston

Attendance: 15,000

League Cup Section Table

	P	W	D	L	F	A	Pts
Celtic	6	5	1	0	14	4	11
RANGERS	6	3	2	1	10	5	8
Dundee United	6	1	1	4	7	8	3
Aberdeen	6	0	2	4	5	19	2

SCOTTISH CUP

January 27th: First Round
RANGERS (1) 3 HAMILTON
Johnston (18), ACADEMICALS (0) 1
Greig 2 (47, 87) Gilchrist (58)

RANGERS: Sorensen; Johansen, Hynd; Greig, McKinnon, D. Smith; Penman, Willoughby, Ferguson, Johnston, Persson

HAMILTON: Lamont; Halpin, Forrest; Gaughan, Small, Wardrop; Horn, Fraser, Vint, Gilchrist, Hunter

Attendance: 27,500

Horn was ordered off

February 17th: Second Round:
DUNDEE (0) 1 RANGERS (0) 1
Campbell (71) Stewart o.g. (60)

DUNDEE: Donaldson; R. Wilson, Houston; Murray, Easton, Stewart; Campbell, J. McLean, S. Wilson, G. McLean, Scott

RANGERS: Sorensen; Johansen, Mathieson; Greig, Hynd, D. Smith; Henderson, Penman, Ferguson, Johnston, Persson

Attendance: 33,000

March 4th: Second Round Replay
RANGERS (1) 4 DUNDEE (0) 1
Persson (5), S. Wilson (52)
Watson 2 (95, 115),
Easton o.g. (113)
After Extra Time

RANGERS: Sorensen; Johansen, Mathieson; Jardine, McKinnon, D. Smith; Henderson, Watson, Ferguson, Johnston, Persson

DUNDEE: Donaldson; R. Wilson, Houston; Murray, Easton, Stewart; Campbell, J. McLean, S. Wilson, G. McLean, Scott (Kinnonmonth)

Attendance: 54,000

March 9th: Third Round
RANGERS (0) 1 HEARTS (1) 1
Persson (50) Irvine (33)

RANGERS: Sorensen; Johansen, Mathieson; Greig, McKinnon, D. Smith; Henderson, Watson, Ferguson, Willoughby, Persson

HEARTS: Cruikshank; Sneddon, Mann; E. Thomson, A. Thomson, Miller; Jensen, Townsend, Moller, Irvine, Traynor

Attendance: 54,000

March 13th: Third Round Replay
HEARTS (0) 1 RANGERS (0) 0
Ford (87)

HEARTS: Cruikshank; Sneddon, Mann; E. Thomson (G. Fleming), Anderson, Miller; Jensen, Townsend, Ford, Irvine, Traynor

RANGERS: Sorensen; Johansen, Mathieson; Greig, McKinnon, D. Smith; Henderson, Watson, Ferguson, Johnston, Persson

Attendance: 44,094

FAIRS CITIES CUP

September 20th: First Round First Leg
DINAMO DRESDEN (0) 1 RANGERS (0) 1
Reidel (66) Ferguson (48)

DRESDEN: Kellenback; Haustein, Sammer; May, Watzlich, Hemp; Hoffman, Riedel, Zeigler, Kreische, Gumz

RANGERS: Sorensen; Johansen, Greig; Jardine, McKinnon, D. Smith; Henderson, Penman, Ferguson, Persson, Johnston

Attendance: 48,000

Rangers owe a debt of gratitude to goalkeeper Sorensen for their drawing at the Heinz Steyer Stadium. After Sorensen had made splendid saves from Hoffman early in the first half he was beaten by Gumz in 35 minutes but the referee had no hesitation giving an offside decision. Ferguson put Rangers into the lead in 48 minutes after splendid work by Jardine and Persson but Dinamo deservedly equalised when Riedel scored 18 minutes later.

October 4th: First Round Second Leg
RANGERS (1) 2 DINAMO DRESDEN (0) 1
Penman (14), Kreische (90)
Greig (91)

RANGERS: Sorensen; Johansen, Mathieson; Greig, McKinnon, D. Smith; Henderson, Penman, Ferguson, Persson, Johnston

DRESDEN: Kallenback; Haustein, Sammer; Pfeifer, Watzlich, Hemp; Hoffman, Walter, Zeigler, Kreische, Gumz

Attendance: 50,000

Rangers deservedly beat Dinamo Dresden but it was not a game in which they distinguished themselves. For almost the entire 90 minutes they had the East Germans confined to deep defence. Kreische scored an equaliser right at the end with a shot which was as unexpected as it was powerful. That goal made the scores level at 2-2 and extra-time looked certain but Rangers threw everything into a grandstand finish and Greig clipped home a glorious winner in injury time. Penman had scored in 14 minutes and the East German defence was stretched on innumerable occasions. Rangers won 3-2 on aggregate.

November 8th: Second Round First Leg
RANGERS   (0) 3   COLOGNE   (0) 0
  Ferguson 2 (54, 73),
  Henderson (68)

RANGERS: Sorensen; Johansen, Mathieson; Greig
(A. Smith), McKinnon, D. Smith; Henderson, Penman,
Ferguson, Johnston, Persson

COLOGNE: Schumacher; Rausch, Reigh; Simmet,
Pott, Hemmersbach; Ruhl, Flohe, Lohr, Overath,
Hornig

Attendance: 54,000

Rangers established a comfortable lead in the first leg of
this second-round tie. In the first half Cologne had the
measure of a Rangers team who for all their pressure were
incapable of turning to account the numerous opportunities
of scoring they created. Their only shot of note in the first
half was from Greig, who had the ill luck to see the ball
rebound from a post. It was a different story after the
interval. The turning point came in 54 minutes when
Ferguson swooped on a ball only parried by the German
goalkeeper as Greig shot and gave Rangers the lead. In 68
minutes Henderson consolidated their lead with a swift
wheel and shot. 5 minutes later Ferguson headed a
spectacular third goal.

November 28th: Second Round Second Leg
COLOGNE   (1) 3   RANGERS   (0) 1
  Overath (30 secs),   Henderson (118)
  Weber (75),
  Ruhl (79)
                  After Extra Time
COLOGNE: Schumacher; Rausche, Pott;
Hemmersbach, Thielen, Weber; Ruhl, Simmet, Lohr
(Flohe), Overath, Hornig

RANGERS: Sorensen; Johansen, Mathieson; Greig,
McKinnon, D. Smith; Henderson, Penman, Ferguson
(Watson), Johnston, Persson

A goal by Henderson after 28 minutes of extra time in the
Mungersdorf Stadium gave Rangers an astonishing
victory. Rangers, who had taken the field with an
apparently impregnable 3-0 lead from the first match, had
been shaken by a goal against them in only 30 seconds
when, after a mistake by McKinnon, Overath clipped the
ball into the net. Then in one of Cologne's infrequent
attacks Weber hit a fierce shot from outside the 18-yard
line and the ball skidded along the turf and into the back of
the net. The Germans were now rejuvenated. In 79
minutes Sorensen was penalised for wasting time. Cologne
were awarded an indirect free kick just outside the 6-yard
line. The ball was touched to Ruhl and the outside-right
shot straight through Rangers' defensive line-up to
equalise. In the last 15 minutes Rangers made a
determined bid for victory and Schumacher made a
magnificent save from Greig before Henderson won the
match for his side. Rangers won 4-3 on aggregate.

March 26th: Quarter-Final First Leg
RANGERS   0   LEEDS UNITED   0

RANGERS: Sorensen; Johansen, Mathieson; Greig,
McKinnon, D. Smith; Henderson, A. Smith, Ferguson,
Johnston, Persson

LEEDS UNITED: Sprake; Reaney, Cooper;
Bremner, Charlton, Hunter; Greenhoff (Belfitt),
Lorimer, Jones, Giles, Madeley

Attendance: 80,000

21,000 watched the match on closed circuit at Elland Road

Rangers' failings up front, especially in the first half, cost
them the chance of taking an invaluable lead to Elland
Road. Henderson moved the ball well and Greig fought
valiantly, but there was little response. Leeds would be
exceptionally pleased with the result. As early as the 2nd
minute they lost Greenhoff with a pulled muscle and
Belfitt came on. Bremner was an inspiring captain —
muddied from head to foot, he was running as strongly at
the end as at the start. Rangers could have gone in at the
interval 2 goals in the lead. A Henderson cross was missed
in front of goal by Johnston and Ferguson, either of whom
could have scored, and a Persson cross eluded Cooper, and
Johnston, all alone, spoon-fed his shot at Sprake. The
second half was disappointing — Sprake saved brilliantly
from Persson 2 minutes from the end but Leeds
themselves had enough chances to make the 2nd leg
virtually a formality.

April 9th: Quarter-Final Second Leg
LEEDS UNITED   (2) 2   RANGERS   (0) 0
  Giles (25 pen), Lorimer (31)

LEEDS UNITED: Harvey; Reaney, Cooper;
Bremner, Charlton, Hunter; Greenhoff, Madeley, Jones,
Giles, Lorimer

RANGERS: Sorensen; Johansen, Mathieson; Greig,
McKinnon, D. Smith; Henderson, Willoughby (Penman),
Ferguson, Johnston, Persson

Attendance: 50,498

43,177 watched the match on closed circuit at Ibrox

Rangers were put out of the Fairs Cities Cup by a
confident Leeds team. They might have had a flying start
—Johnston headed wide after splendid work by Ferguson
after only 3 minutes with Harvey stranded but Leeds
shook them with 2 goals in 6 minutes. Giles scored from
the spot after a handling offence and Lorimer took
advantage of a miscued shot to lash the ball home.
Henderson went close 23 minutes from the end. Penman
replaced Willoughby in the closing quarter but by that
time Rangers' hopes of qualifying for an all-Scottish Semi-
Final had been shattered. Leeds won 2-0 on aggregate.

APPEARANCES

	League	League Cup	Scottish Cup	Fairs Cup
Sorensen	30	6	5	6
Johansen	30	6	5	6
Provan	2	6	-	-
Jardine	9+2S	6	1	1
McKinnon	34	6	4	6
Greig	32	6	4	6
Henderson	20	6	4	6
Penman	24+2S	6	2	4+1S
Ferguson	29	6	5	6
D. Smith	34	6	5	6
Johnston	30	2	4	6
Persson	32	4	5	6
Hynd	3+1S	-	2	-
Watson	7+1S	-	3	0+1S
Mathieson	26	-	4	5
Martin	4	-	-	-
Willoughby	20+2S	-	2	1
A. Smith	6+2S	-	-	1+1S
Semple	2	-	-	-
Jackson	-	-	-	-

GOALSCORERS

League: Ferguson 19 (1 pen), Johnston 18, Persson 14, Greig 11 (2 pen), Willoughby 10, Penman 8, Hynd 3, D. Smith 2, Henderson 2, Mathieson 1, McKinnon 1, Watson 1, Johansen 1, A. Smith 1, Own Goals 1

League Cup: Penman 3, Ferguson 2, Persson 1, Jardine 1, Johansen 1 (pen), Henderson 1, Johnston 1

Scottish Cup: Greig 2, Persson 2, Watson 2, Own Goals 2, Johnston 1

Fairs Cup: Ferguson 3, Henderson 2, Penman 1, Greig 1

John Greig, captain of Rangers over many seasons, shows how a penalty kick should be taken in this Scottish Cup tie against Airdrie.

Season 1968–69

For the 4th successive Season Rangers finished as Runners-up in the Championship to Celtic — this time by a 5-point margin. Big-money signing Colin Stein missed the last 7 League matches of the season as the result of suspension, following his 2nd ordering off in very dramatic circumstances against Clyde, and only 3 of those last 7 matches were won. Rangers did manage to beat Celtic both home and away, but missed penalties again proved costly. 5 of the 6 matches lost were lost by a one-goal margin. Willie Johnston finished top scorer with 17 followed by Penman on 15 and Stein on 13. Stein and Alex MacDonald from St Johnstone were signed for a total of £150,000 and Willoughby, Hynd and Alec Smith were transferred at the end of the season.

Rangers can have had few complaints about losing out to Celtic in the League Cup Qualifying Section.

Both Edinburgh teams and Airdrie were beaten in the early rounds of the Scottish Cup. Aberdeen were thrashed 6-1 in the Semi-Final at Parkhead but Celtic, with ruthless professionalism, took heavy toll of Rangers in the Final in which there is no doubt that the suspended Stein was badly missed.

Rangers reached the Semi-Final of the Fairs Cities Cup, beating Vojvodina, Dundalk, D.W.S. Amsterdam and Atletico Bilbao along the way. The late introduction of Persson in the home leg against Bilbao brought an explosive finish to the match. In the First Leg of the Semi-Final against Newcastle United innumerable chances were missed including a penalty by Penman. Newcastle won the return leg by 2 goals to nil.

League: Runners-up
League Cup: Failed to Qualify from Section
Scottish Cup: Finalists
Fairs Cities Cup: Semi-Finalists

SCOTTISH FIRST DIVISION

July 29th: Rangers' bid of £90,000 for Bobby Hope of West Bromwich Albion was rejected.

September 7th:
RANGERS (0) 2 PARTICK THISTLE (0) 0
Jardine 2 (78, 88)

RANGERS: Martin; Jackson, Mathieson; Greig, McKinnon, Hynd; Henderson, Willoughby, Jardine, D. Smith, Persson

PARTICK THISTLE: Ritchie; Cumming, McLindon; Hansen, McKinnon, O'Neil, Gibson, McParland, Bone, Flanagan, Duncan

Attendance: 30,000

September 7th: Willie Thornton of Partick Thistle was appointed as Rangers' new assistant manager.

September 9th: Rangers were reported to be interested in signing Pantelic of Vojvodina.

September 14th:
CELTIC (1) 2   RANGERS (2) 4
Wallace 2 (28, 66)   Johnston 2 (17, 89),
                      Penman (65),
                      Persson (15)

CELTIC: Simpson; Gemmell, O'Neil; Brogan, McNeill, Clark; Johnstone, Lennox, Wallace, Connelly (Chalmers), Hughes

205

RANGERS: Martin; Jackson, Mathieson; Greig, McKinnon, Hynd; Henderson, Penman, Jardine, Johnston, Persson

Attendance: 75,000

In 89 minutes Johnston headed in a lofted cross by Jardine. In the preceding 10 minutes it was touch and go whether Rangers would be able to hang on to their slender lead. Then Rangers broke quickly from deep defence. From Henderson out to the left, the ball went across the edge of the penalty-area to Johnston who in turn whipped it out to Jardine on the right. The Celtic defence were completely caught out and when the ball came back into the middle there was Johnston to nod it in at Simpson's right-hand post. This was Rangers' first victory in an Old Firm match for exactly 12 months and their first at Parkhead since New Year's Day 1964. With Celtic having to give best to Penman and Greig in midfield, Rangers' strikers, Persson and Johnston, enjoyed a field day. Gemmell had an uncomfortable afternoon against the powerful Swede. In 15 minutes Persson completely flummoxed Simpson with a header which went across Simpson and in at the far post. Two minutes later a peach of a pass from Penman caught McNeill off balance and sent Johnston darting through the middle with only Simpson to beat. This he did by gliding the ball past Simpson as he rushed out to intercept. In 28 minutes Connelly sent a glorious pass out to Johnston who drew Martin to him and then clipped the ball across to the waiting Wallace who had merely to tap it home. Johnstone then struck the bar in the course of producing several mesmeric runs. In 65 minutes Penman hit home a Jardine cross at the 2nd attempt. Wallace immediately reduced the arrears, swivelling round on a Lennox pass and deceiving Martin with a shot which slithered underneath his body.

September 21st:

RANGERS	(0) 3	KILMARNOCK	(1) 3
Johnston (65),		Morrison 2 (30, 58),	
Jardine (72),		Queen (85 pen)	
Henderson (80)			

RANGERS: Martin; Jackson, Johansen; Greig, McKinnon, Hynd; Henderson, Penman, Jardine, Johnstone, Persson

KILMARNOCK: McLaughlin; King, Dickson; Gilmour, McGrory, Arthur: T. McLean, Queen, Morrison, J. McLean, Cook

Attendance: 40,000

September 28th:

HEARTS	(0) 1	RANGERS	(0) 1
Ford (54)		Penman (87)	

HEARTS: Cruikshank; Sneddon, Mann; Townsend, E. Thomson, MacDonald; Traynor (Ford), Hamilton, J. Fleming, Moller, G. Fleming

RANGERS: Martin; Jackson, Mathieson; Greig, McKinnon, Hynd; Henderson, Penman, Jardine, Johnston, Persson

Attendance: 33,000

McKinnon was ordered off after 41 minutes.

October 5th:

RANGERS	(1) 2	FALKIRK	(1) 1
Persson (37),		C. Watson (30)	
Johnston (87)			

RANGERS: Martin; Jackson, Mathieson; Greig (D. Smith), McKinnon, Hynd; Henderson, Penman, Jardine, Johnston, Persson

FALKIRK: Devlin; Cuthbert, McLaughlin; Markie, Baillie, Gibson; Hoggan, Smith, Young, Graham, Watson

Attendance: 30,000

October 12th:

ST JOHNSTONE	(1) 2	RANGERS	(0) 0
Aird 2 (29, 87)			

ST JOHNSTONE: Robertson; Miller, Coburn; Gordon, Rooney, McPhee; Aird, Whitelaw, McCarry, MacDonald, Aitken

RANGERS: Martin; Jackson, Mathieson; Hynd, McKinnon, D. Smith; Henderson (Willoughby), Penman, Jardine, Johnstone, Persson

October 19th:

RANGERS	(2) 3	DUNFERMLINE	(0) 0
Persson (26),			
Jardine (45), Ferguson (86)			

RANGERS: Martin; Jackson, Mathieson; Greig, McKinnon, Hynd; Henderson, Penman, Jardine, Johnston, Persson (Ferguson)

DUNFERMLINE: Martin; W. Callaghan, Totten; Fraser, Barry, Renton; Robertson, Paton, Edwards, Gardner, Mitchell

Attendance: 35,000

October 26th;

RANGERS	(0) 2	ABERDEEN	(2) 3
Ferguson (83),		Johnston (3),	
Henderson (84)		Forrest 2 (13,75)	

RANGERS: Martin; Jackson, Mathieson; Greig, Hynd, D. Smith; Henderson, Penman, Jardine (Ferguson), Johnston, Persson

ABERDEEN: Clark; Whyte, Shewan; Petersen, McMillan, Craig; Johnston, Smith, Forrest, Buchan, Taylor

Attendance: 32,000

Greig missed a penalty

Willie Johnston of Rangers in a tussle with Ian Young of Celtic. Matches between the 'Old Firm' are usually tense and close affairs.

League positions

	P	W	D	L	F	A	Pts
1 Celtic	8	5	2	1	14	8	12
2 St Mirren	8	3	5	0	10	6	11
3 Dundee United	8	5	1	2	15	11	11
4 Dunfermline	8	5	1	2	12	10	11
5 RANGERS	8	4	2	2	17	12	10

October 31st: Colin Stein was signed from Hibernian for a Scottish record fee of £100,000.

November 2nd:
ARBROATH (0) 1			RANGERS (2) 5
   Smith o.g. (56)			 Johnston 2 (15, 29),
					   Stein 3 (62, 63, 66)

ARBROATH: Williamson; Booth, Riddell; Kennedy, Stirling, Finnie; Sellars, Reid, Jack, Bruce, Cant

RANGERS: Martin; Johansen, Mathieson; Greig, McKinnon, D. Smith; Henderson, Penman (Ferguson), Stein, Johnston, Persson

Attendance: 9,653

November 6th: Scotland beat Austria 2-1 in a World Cup Qualifying Match at Hampden Park. McKinnon and Greig were in the team.

November 9th:
RANGERS (2) 6			HIBERNIAN (0) 1
   Johnston (7),			 McBride (66)
   Stein 3 (21, 55, 60),
   Henderson (58),
   Persson (83)

RANGERS: Martin; Johansen, Mathieson; Hynd, Greig, D. Smith; Henderson, Penman (Ferguson), Stein, Johnston, Persson

HIBERNIAN: Allan; Shevlane, Davis; Cousin, Stanton, O'Rourke; Scott, Grant, McBride, Cormack, Stevenson

Attendance: 50,000

November 12th: Charlton offered £50,000 for Alex Ferguson.

November 16th:
ST MIRREN (0) 1			RANGERS (0) 0
   Gilshan (69)

ST MIRREN: Connaghan; Murray, Connell; Fulton, McFadden, Murray; Adamson, Blair (Hainey), Kane, Pinkerton, Gilshan

RANGERS: Martin; Johansen, Mathieson; Hynd, Greig, D. Smith; Henderson, Penman (Jardine), Stein, Johnston, Persson

Attendance: 43,500

November 19th: Alex MacDonald was signed from St Johnstone for £50,000.

November 23rd:
CLYDE (0) 1			RANGERS (0) 1
   Glasgow (87)			 Stein (53)

CLYDE: Wright; Glasgow, Mulheron; Anderson, Fraser, McHugh; McFarlane, Hood, Staite, Burns, Hastings

RANGERS: Martin; Johansen, Mathieson; Greig, McKinnon, D. Smith; Willoughby, MacDonald, Stein, Johnston, Persson

November 30th:
RANGERS (1) 1			AIRDRIE (0) 1
   Stein (25)			 Goodwin (66 pen)

RANGERS: Martin; Johansen, Mathieson; Jackson, McKinnon, Greig; Henderson, MacDonald, Stein, Johnston, Persson

AIRDRIE: McKenzie; Jonquin, Caldwell; Goodwin, Black, Whiteford; Wilson, Fyfe, Marshall, Jarvie, Phillips

Attendance: 20,000

December 7th:
RAITH ROVERS (0) 0			RANGERS (0) 3
					   MacDonald (47),
					   Stein (75),
					   Watson (83)

RAITH ROVERS: Reid; Hislop, Weir; Millar, Polland, Bolton; Wilson, Wallace, Sneddon, Watt, Gillespie

RANGERS: Martin; Johansen, Provan; Greig, McKinnon, D. Smith; Henderson, Watson, Stein, MacDonald, Johnston

Attendance: 15,000

December 11th: Scotland beat Cyprus 5-0 in Nicosia. McKinnon, Greig and Stein were in the team.

December 14th:
RANGERS (1) 2			DUNDEE UNITED (1) 1
   Greig (37),			 Mitchell (45)
   Johnston (57)

RANGERS: Martin; Johansen, Provan; Greig, McKinnon, D. Smith; Henderson (Persson), Watson, Stein, MacDonald, Johnston

DUNDEE UNITED: Mackay; Millar, Cameron; Gillespie, Smith, Wood; Hogg, Reig, Cameron, Mitchell, Rolland

Attendance: 30,000

December 28th:
MORTON (0) 0			RANGERS (1) 2
					   Penman (16),
					   Johnston (74)

MORTON: Russell; Ferguson, Sweeney; Rankin, Gray, Strachan; Coakley, Harper, Mason, Arnetoft, Bartram

RANGERS: Martin; Johansen, Provan; Greig, McKinnon, Watson; MacDonald, Penman, Stein, Johnston, Persson

Attendance: 20,000

League positions

	P	W	D	L	F	A	Pts
1 Celtic	17	11	5	1	39	12	27
2 Dundee United	17	11	3	3	32	21	25
3 Kilmarnock	17	10	4	3	31	16	24
4 Dunfermline	17	10	3	4	36	25	23
5 RANGERS	16	9	4	3	37	18	22

January 1st:
PARTICK THISTLE   (0) 0   RANGERS   (1) 2
                          Johnston (33),
                          Stein (70)

PARTICK THISTLE: Ritchie; Campbell, McLindon; Hansen, McKinnon, Gray; Flanagan, Bone, Divers, O'Neil, Duncan

RANGERS: Martin; Johansen, Provan; Greig, McKinnon, D. Smith; Henderson, Watson, Stein, Johnston, Persson

Attendance: 24,000

January 2nd:
RANGERS   (0) 1   CELTIC   (0) 0
Greig (60 pen)

RANGERS: Martin; Johansen, Provan (Jardine); Greig, McKinnon, Watson; Henderson, Penman, Stein, Johnston, Persson

CELTIC: Fallon; Craig, Gemmell; Brogan, McNeill, Clark; Johnstone, Murdoch, Wallace (Chalmers), Lennox, Hughes

Attendance: 85,000

24 people were taken to hospital after a crush barrier collapsed on a stairway

Celtic followers can have had little complaint. The only goal came after exactly an hour's play, Greig scoring from the spot after McNeill had allegedly deflected a Henderson shot with a hand, in a game largely dominated by Rangers.

January 4th:
KILMARNOCK   (2) 3   RANGERS   (2) 3
  Dickson (14),   Penman (7),
  McLean (41 pen),   Beattie o.g.(27),
  McIlroy (73)   Persson (61)

KILMARNOCK: McLaughlin; King, Dickson; Gilmour, McGrory, Beattie; T. McLean, Queen, Morrison, J. McLean, McIlroy

RANGERS: Martin; Johansen, Mathieson; Greig, McKinnon, Watson; Henderson, Penman, Stein, Johnston, Persson

Attendance: 32,000

Both Stein and Dickson were ordered off

January 5th: Rangers announced that they would listen to offers for Henderson. Newcastle United were reported to be ready to bid £100,000.

January 11th:
RANGERS   (2) 2   HEARTS   (0) 0
  Penman (8), Johnston (28)

RANGERS: Martin; Johansen, Mathieson; Greig, McKinnon, Watson; Henderson, Penman, Stein, Johnston, Persson

HEARTS: Cruikshank; Holt, McAlpine; Anderson, E. Thomson, A. Thomson; Traynor, Ford, Gordon (Hamilton), Fleming, Moller

Attendance: 40,000

January 18th:
FALKIRK   (0) 0   RANGERS   (1) 3
                             Johnston (6),
                             Penman 2 (75, 83)

FALKIRK: Rennie; Lambie, McLaughlin; Smith, Markie, Miller; Graham, Hunter, Rowan, Gibson, Watson

RANGERS: Martin; Johansen, Mathieson; Greig, McKinnon, Watson; Henderson, Penman, Stein, Johnston, MacDonald

Attendance: 22,000

Johnston and Markie were ordered off

January 27th: Willie Johnston was suspended for 21 days for his ordering off at Falkirk. Colin Stein was suspended for 28 days for his ordering off at Kilmarnock.

February 1st:
RANGERS   (1) 3   ST JOHNSTONE   (0) 0
  Penman (26), Ferguson (76),
  Henderson (86)

RANGERS: Martin; Johansen, Mathieson; Greig, McKinnon, Watson; Henderson, Penman, Jardine, Ferguson, MacDonald

ST JOHNSTONE: Robertson; McGillivray, Coburn; Gordon, Rooney, McPhee; Aird, Miller, Whitelaw, Rennie (McCarry), Aitken

Attendance: 28,000

March 5th:
HIBERNIAN   (1) 1   RANGERS   (1) 2
  O'Rourke (19)   Greig (34 pen),
                            Johnston (90)
HIBERNIAN: Wilson; Duncan, Davis; Stanton, Madsen, Blackley; Marinello, O'Rourke, McBride, Cormack, Stevenson

RANGERS: Martin; Johansen, Mathieson; Watson, Greig, D. Smith; Henderson, Penman, Stein, Johnston, Persson

Attendance: 30,000

March 8th:
RANGERS   (2) 6   ST MIRREN   (0) 0
  Johansen (25), Smith (38),
  Greig (61 pen), Ferguson (73),
  Persson (79), Penman (84)
RANGERS: Martin; Johansen, Mathieson; Greig, McKinnon, D. Smith; Henderson, Penman, Stein, Johnston (Ferguson), Persson

ST MIRREN: Thorburn; Duffy, Connell; Fulton, McFadden, Murray; Adamson, Blair, Kane, Pinkerton, Gilshan

Attendance: 33,000

March 11th:
RANGERS   (1) 2   ARBROATH   (0) 0
  Persson (19), Penman (68)
RANGERS: Martin; Johansen, Mathieson; Greig, McKinnon, D. Smith; Henderson, Penman, Stein, Ferguson, Persson

ARBROATH: Hodge; Booth, Hughes; Cargill, Stirling, Reid; Sellars, Cant, Jack, Bruce, Wilkie (Kennedy)

Attendance: 18,000

March 16th:
RANGERS   (4) 6   CLYDE   (0) 0
  Stein 3 (35, 40, 48),
  Smith (3), Penman (30),
  Ferguson (45)
RANGERS: Martin; Johansen, Mathieson; Greig, McKinnon, D. Smith; Henderson, Penman, Stein, Ferguson (Persson), Johnston

CLYDE: McCulloch; Glasgow, Mulheron; Burns, Fraser (Staite), McHugh; Soutar, Hood, Anderson, Stewart, Hastings

Attendance: 35,000

Stein and Mulheron were ordered off in the 88th minute

March 24th:
AIRDRIE   (2) 3   RANGERS   (0) 2
  Menzies (3),   Penman (47),
  Fyfe (50), McPheat (55)   Caldwell o.g. (85)

AIRDRIE: Clarke; Jonquin, Caldwell; Goodwin, Black, Whiteford; Bird, Fyfe, Menzies, McPheat, Wilson

RANGERS: Martin; Johansen, Mathieson; Greig, McKinnon, D. Smith; Henderson, Penman, Stein, Ferguson (MacDonald), Persson

Attendance: 20,000

Stein missed a penalty

March 26th: Colin Stein was suspended from March 27th until May 1st for his ordering off against Clyde.

March 28th: John Greig vowed 'I'll never take another penalty kick'.

March 29th:
RANGERS   (0) 2   RAITH ROVERS   (0) 1
  Penman (46),   Falconer (58)
  Johnston (89)
RANGERS: Martin: Johansen, Mathieson; Greig (Persson), McKinnon, D. Smith; Henderson, Penman, Jardine, Johnston, MacDonald

RAITH ROVERS: Reid; McDonald, Gray; Miller, Polland, Bolton; A. Miller (Stein), Falconer, Wallace, Sneddon, Gillespie

Attendance: 28,000

April 5th:
DUNDEE UNITED   (1) 2   RANGERS   (0) 1
  Scott (32), Cameron (54)   Greig (49)
DUNDEE UNITED: Mackay; Rolland, J. Cameron; Gillespie, Smith, Wood; Hogg, Reid, K. Cameron, Dunne, Scott

RANGERS: Martin; Johansen, Mathieson; Greig, McKinnon, D. Smith; Henderson, Penman, Jardine, Johnston, Persson

Attendance: 20,000

April 9th:
ABERDEEN   0   RANGERS   0
ABERDEEN: McGarr; Whyte, Shewan; Petersen, Boel, M. Buchan; Johnston, Smith, Forrest, Robb, Craig

RANGERS: Martin; Johansen, Mathieson; Greig, McKinnon, D. Smith; Henderson, Jardine (Conn), Ferguson, Johnston, Persson

Attendance: 20,000

April 16th: Scotland drew 1-1 with West Germany at Hampden Park in a World Cup Qualifier. McKinnon and Greig were in the team.

April 19th:
RANGERS (2) 3   MORTON (0) 0
  Sweeney o.g. (15),
  Persson (32), Penman (81)

RANGERS: Neef; Johansen, Mathieson; Greig, McKinnon, D. Smith; Henderson, Penman, Ferguson, Johnston, Persson

MORTON: Neilson; Ferguson, Kerr; Sweeney, Gray, Strachan; Coakley, Allan, Mason, Harper, Bartram

Attendance: 25,000

April 22nd:
DUNDEE (0) 3   RANGERS (1) 2
  Bryce 2 (56, 67),   Greig (22),
  Gilroy (61)   Henderson (82)

DUNDEE: Donaldson; Wilson, Swan; Murray, Easton, Houston; McKay, Scott, Gilroy, Kinnonmonth, Bryce

RANGERS: Martin; Johansen, Provan; Greig, Jackson, D. Smith; Henderson, Conn, Jardine, Ferguson, Persson

Attendance: 7,000

April 28th:
RANGERS (0) 1   DUNDEE (1) 1
  Johnston (90)   Steele (35)

RANGERS: Neef; Johansen, Provan; Greig, McKinnon (Miller), D. Smith; Henderson, Jardine, Penman, Johnston, Persson

DUNDEE: Donaldson; Wilson, Swan; Murray, Easton, Houston; Steele, Scott, Gilroy, Kinnonmonth, Bryce

Attendance: 6,800

April 30th:
DUNFERMLINE 0   RANGERS (2) 3
                          Johnston 2 (19, 43),
                          Penman (82)

DUNFERMLINE: Martin; Callaghan, Lunn; Fraser, Barry, Robertson; McLean, McKimmie (Renton), Edwards, Gardner, Mitchell

RANGERS: Neef; Johansen, Mathieson; Greig, Provan, D. Smith; Henderson, Jardine, Penman, Johnston, Persson

Attendance: 11,700

Scottish First Division

	P	W	D	L	F	A	Pts
1 Celtic	34	23	8	3	89	32	54
2 RANGERS	34	21	7	6	81	32	49
3 Dunfermline	34	19	7	8	63	45	45
4 Kilmarnock	34	15	14	5	50	32	44
5 Dundee United	34	17	9	8	61	49	43
6 St Johnstone	34	16	5	13	66	59	37
7 Airdrie	34	13	11	10	46	44	37
8 Hearts	34	14	8	12	52	54	36
9 Dundee	34	10	12	12	47	48	32
10 Morton	34	12	8	14	58	68	32
11 St Mirren	34	11	10	13	40	54	32
12 Hibernian	34	12	7	15	60	59	31
13 Clyde	34	9	13	12	35	50	31
14 Partick Thistle	34	9	10	15	39	53	28
15 Aberdeen	34	9	8	17	50	59	26
16 Raith Rovers	34	8	5	21	45	67	21
17 Falkirk	34	5	8	21	33	69	18
18 Arbroath	34	5	6	23	41	82	16

May 3rd: Scotland beat Wales 5-3 in Cardiff. Greig and Stein were in the team. Stein scored one of the goals.

May 6th: A Colin Stein goal gave Scotland a 1-1 draw with Northern Ireland at Hampden Park. Greig and Henderson were also in the team. Willie Johnston came on as a substitute.

May 10th: Scotland were beaten 4-1 by England at Wembley. Greig, Henderson and Stein were in the side. Stein scored Scotland's goal.

May 12th: Colin Stein scored 4 goals for Scotland in an 8-0 win over Cyprus at Hampden Park. Greig and Henderson were also in the team. Henderson also scored one of the goals.

May 28th: Jim Baxter, freed by Nottingham Forest, re-joined Rangers for a £10,000 signing-on fee.

May 31st: Alec Willoughby was transferred to Aberdeen for £25,000.

June 22nd: Roger Hynd joined Crystal Palace for £25,000.

June 25th: Alex Smith was transferred to Aberdeen for £25,000.

June 14th: Kaj Johansen announced that he was quitting Ibrox.

LEAGUE CUP

August 10th:
RANGERS (0) 0   CELTIC (2) 2
                          Wallace 2 (9, 35)

RANGERS: Martin; Jackson, Mathieson; Greig, McKinnon, D. Smith; Henderson, A. Smith, Penman, Ferguson, Persson

CELTIC: Simpson; Gemmell, O'Neill; Murdoch, McNeill, Brogan; Connelly (Clark), Johnstone, Wallace, Lennox, Hughes

Attendance: 80,000

August 14th:
PARTICK THISTLE   (0) 1   RANGERS   (2) 5
   Bone (68)   A. Smith 2 (4, 19),
                                    Ferguson 2 (49, 59),
                                    Persson (62)

PARTICK THISTLE: Ritchie; Cumming, Brown; Cunningham, McKinnon, O'Neill; Duncan, Bone, Coulston, Flanagan, Gallagher

RANGERS: Martin; Jackson, Mathieson; A. Smith, McKinnon, Greig; Henderson, Penman, Ferguson, McPhee, Persson

Attendance: 25,000

August 17th:
RANGERS   (1) 2   MORTON (0) 0
   Jackson 2 (28, 84)

RANGERS: Martin; Jackson, Mathieson; A. Smith, McKinnon, Greig; Johnston, Ferguson, Penman, D. Smith, Persson

MORTON: Russell; Thorup, Loughlan; Arnetoft, Strachan, Gray; Harper, Sweeney, Allan, Stevenson, Taylor

Attendance: 40,000

August 24th:
CELTIC   (0) 1   RANGERS   (0) 0
   Wallace (55)

CELTIC: Simpson; Gemmell, O'Neill; Murdoch, McNeill, Brogan; Johnstone, Connelly, Wallace, Lennox, Hughes

RANGERS: Martin; Jackson, Mathieson; Greig, McKinnon, Hynd; Penman, Ferguson, Johnston, D. Smith, Persson

Attendance: 75,000

Martin saved a Gemmell penalty

August 28th:
RANGERS   (1) 2   PARTICK THISTLE   (0) 1
   Henderson (12),   Hansen (89)
   Jardine (88)

RANGERS: Martin; Jackson, Mathieson; Greig, McKinnon, Hynd; Henderson, McPhee, Penman, Persson, Johnston (Jardine)

PARTICK THISTLE: Ritchie; Cumming, McLindon; Hansen, McKinnon, O'Neill; Gallagher, McParland, Bone, Flanagan, Duncan

Attendance: 21,000

August 31st:
MORTON   (0) 0   RANGERS   (2) 5
                                    Jardine 2 (22, 47),
                                    Henderson 2 (37, 88),
                                    Penman (75)

MORTON: Crawford; Thorup, Laughlin; Arnetoft, Strachan, Gray; McNeill (Jensen), Allan, Mason, Sweeney, Taylor

RANGERS: Martin; Jackson, Mathieson; Greig, McKinnon, Hynd; Henderson, Willoughby, Jardine, D. Smith, Persson (Penman)

Attendance: 15,000

League Cup Section Table

	P	W	D	L	F	A	Pts
Celtic	6	6	0	0	20	2	12
RANGERS	6	4	0	2	14	5	8
Partick Thistle	6	2	0	4	8	18	4
Morton	6	0	0	6	2	19	0

SCOTTISH CUP

January 25th: First Round
RANGERS   (0) 1   HIBERNIAN   (0) 0
   Stein (67)

RANGERS: Martin; Johansen, Mathieson; Greig, McKinnon, Watson; Henderson, Penman, Stein, Johnston, Persson (D. Smith)

HIBERNIAN: Allan; Duncan, Davis; Stanton, Madsen, Cousin; Scott (O'Rourke), Quinn, McBride, Cormack, Stevenson

Attendance: 60,000

February 24th: Second Round
RANGERS   (1) 2   HEARTS   (0) 0
   Johnston (32), Persson (49)

RANGERS: Martin; Johansen, Mathieson; Greig, McKinnon, Watson; Henderson, Penman, Stein, Johnston, Persson (D. Smith)

HEARTS: Cruikshank; Holt, McAlpine; Anderson, E. Thomson, A. Thomson; Traynor, J. Fleming, Ford, G. Fleming (Veitch), Jensen

Attendance: 48,000

March 1st: Third Round
RANGERS   (1) 1   AIRDRIE   (0) 0
   Greig (2 pen)

RANGERS: Martin; Johansen, Mathieson; Watson, Greig, D. Smith; Henderson, Penman, Stein, Johnstone (MacDonald), Persson

AIRDRIE: McKenzie; Jonquin, Caldwell; Goodwin, Black, Whiteford; Wilson, Fyfe (Phillips), Marshall, McPheat, Jarvie

Attendance: 46,726

March 21st: Semi-Final   At Parkhead
ABERDEEN (1) 1   RANGERS (2) 6
  Forrest (44)   Penman 2 (14, 51),
                    Henderson (38),
                    Johnston 3 (47, 72, 84)

ABERDEEN: McGarr; Whyte, Shewan; Petersen, Boel, Buchan; Johnston, Smith, Forrest, Robb, Craig; Sub: Hamilton

RANGERS: Martin; Johansen, Mathieson; Greig, McKinnon, D. Smith; Henderson, Penman, Stein, Johnston, Persson; Sub: Ferguson

Attendance: 66,197

Rangers stormed into the Final. It was the left side of Rangers' team that worked particularly well. 2 of Rangers' goals were scored by Penman in 14 and 51 minutes. Rangers' top scorer was Willie Johnston who had goals in 47 minutes when Persson dispossessed Jimmy Smith, in 72 minutes when a Henderson pass found him unmarked 10 yards from goal, and in 84 minutes when he headed in from Penman's cross. Rangers' other goal went to Henderson in 38 minutes when he exploited a clever pass by Dave Smith. Aberdeen, having lost 2 goals, came right back into the match on half-time when fast passes by Robb, Craig and Buchan produced a fine goal by Forrest.

April 26th: Final   At Hampden Park
CELTIC (3) 4   RANGERS (0) 0
  McNeill (2), Lennox (44),
  Connelly (45), Chalmers (76)

CELTIC: Fallon; Craig, Gemmell; Murdoch, McNeill, Brogan (Clark); Connelly, Chalmers, Wallace, Lennox, Auld

RANGERS: Martin; Johansen, Mathieson; Greig, McKinnon, D. Smith; Henderson, Penman, Ferguson, Johnston, Persson; Sub: Jardine

Attendance: 132,870 *Referee*: J. Callaghan (Glasgow)

Celtic, with ruthless professionalism, took heavy toll of their opponents' defensive blunders and technical naivety. Connelly, brought in for the suspended Johnstone, was employed almost solely in midfield. Connelly it was who a minute from the interval intercepted Persson's intended pass to Mathieson near the halfway line and clipped the ball forward to Lennox lurking in the clear. Off Lennox went like a scalded cat, pausing only briefly in his stride just inside the penalty-box to glide the ball in at the far post as Martin came out to narrow the angle. The next minute

Martin attempted a short kick out to Greig. He, not surprisingly lost possession to Connelly, who ambled in on Martin and took the ball past him to put his team 3 up. McNeill opened the scoring in the 2nd minute when he rose unchallenged to Lennox's corner-kick and sent a curving header in off the far post. In 33 minutes Fallon could only push out a powerful Greig shot and Ferguson fell over as he rushed in to meet the rebound. Chalmers scored Celtic's 4th in 76 minutes after Auld had done the initial damage. This was Rangers' first defeat in a Scottish Cup Final for 40 years.

FAIRS CITIES CUP

September 18th: First Round First Leg
RANGERS (1) 2   VOJVODINA (0) 0
  Greig (28 pen),
  Jardine (84)

RANGERS: Martin; Jackson, Mathieson; Greig, McKinnon, Hynd; Henderson, Penman, Jardine, Johnston, Persson

VOJVODINA: Pantelic; Aleksik, Stamevski; Zemco, Brzic, Nikolic; Rakic (Dakic), Trivic, Radosav, Pirmajer, Savic

Attendance: 65,000

October 2nd: First Round Second Leg
VOJVODINA (0) 1   RANGERS (0) 0
  Nikezic (66)

VOJVODINA: Pantelic; Aleksik, Stamevski; Savic, Brzic, Dakic; Ivezik (Nikezic), Radosav, Trivic, Pirmajer, Pusibrk

RANGERS: Martin; Jackson, Mathieson; Greig, McKinnon, Hynd; Henderson, Penman (D. Smith), Jardine, Johnston, Persson

Attendance: 7,000

Greig and Trivic were ordered off

Rangers won 2-1 on aggregate

October 30th: Second Round First Leg
RANGERS (2) 6   DUNDALK (Eire) (1) 1
  Henderson 2 (13, 26),   Murray (43 pen)
  Greig (50),
  Ferguson 2 (55, 90),
  Brennan o.g. (88)

RANGERS: Martin; Johansen, Mathieson; Greig, McKinnon, D. Smith; Henderson, Penman, Ferguson, Johnston, Persson

DUNDALK: Lawless; Murphy, Morrissey; Murray, Brennan, Millington; Turner, O'Connor, Stokes, Hannigan, O'Connell

Attendance: 26,000

Rangers romped home against Dundalk

November 13th: Second Round Second Leg
DUNDALK   (0) 0   RANGERS   (1) 3
                                    Mathieson (45),
                                    Stein 2 (64, 81)

DUNDALK: Lawless; O'Reilly, Brennan; Murray,
Keogh, Millington; Turner, O'Connor, Stokes,
Morrissey, Gilmore

RANGERS: Martin; Johansen, Mathieson; Hynd,
Jackson, D. Smith; Henderson, Ferguson (Conn), Stein,
Johnston, Persson

Without any of their players having to exert themselves
Rangers beat Dundalk 3-0. Dundalk played with an
enthusiasm that was commendable but which was no
compensation for their lack of ability. Rangers won 9-1 on
aggregate.

January 15th: Third Round First Leg
D.W.S. AMSTERDAM   RANGERS   (1) 2
     (Netherlands) (0) 0   Johnston (38),
                                    Henderson (53)

D.W.S. AMSTERDAM: Jongbloed; Flinkevleugel,
Overweg; Soetekeuw, Piljman, Kammingor; Dijkstra,
Van der Vall, Geurtsen, Seeman, Rensenbrink; Sub:
Cornwall for Overweg

RANGERS: Martin; Johansen, Mathieson; Greig,
McKinnon, Watson; Henderson, Penman, Stein,
Johnston, Persson (D. Smith)

Attendance: 18,000

Greig passed a fitness test and he proved to be an inspiring
player throughout. In 38 minutes Johnston put Rangers
into the lead after a splendid move via Henderson and
Persson, and Johnston's shot gave Jongbloed no chance.
That goal gave Rangers tremendous confidence. Persson,
who played in spite of a heavy cold, remained in the
dressing room for the second-half with Dave Smith
coming on as sub. And it was Smith who provided the
perfect pass that gave Henderson the chance to shoot
Rangers into a 2 goal lead in 53 minutes.

January 22nd: Third Round Second Leg
RANGERS   (2) 2   D.W.S. AMSTERDAM   (1) 1
     Smith (8),   Geurtsen (12)
     Stein (22)

RANGERS: Martin; Johansen, Greig; Watson,
McKinnon, D. Smith (Jardine); Henderson, Penman,
Stein, MacDonald, Johnston

D.W.S. AMSTERDAM: Jongbloed; Flinkevleugel,
Overweg; Soetekeuw, Piljman, Kammingor; Dijkstra,
Van der Vall, Geurtsen, Seeman, Rensenbrink

Attendance: 51,000

Rangers completed the elimination of D.W.S. from the
Fairs Cup with the score at 2-1 for Rangers, and 4-1 on
aggregate. The second-half was largely academic as
Rangers never looked like letting their 3-goal lead slip
away.

March 19th: Quarter-Final First Leg
RANGERS   (2) 4   ATLETICO BILBAO   (1) 1
     Ferguson (7),   Clemente (29)
     Penman (27),
     Persson (86), Stein (87)

RANGERS: Martin; Johansen, Mathieson; Greig,
McKinnon, D. Smith; Henderson, Penman, Stein,
Ferguson (Persson), Johnston

BILBAO: Iribar; Zugazaga, Saez; Guatua, Echeberria,
Karrauri; Argoitia, Uriate, Arieta, Clemente, Rojo

Attendance: 63,000

Greig missed a penalty

Rangers left it late. For almost an hour they led 2-1 — a
dangerously narrow margin for the second leg. Then with
scarcely three minutes left for play Persson, who had
substituted for Ferguson with a quarter of an hour to go,
broke clear on Stein's pass and slipped the ball cleverly
past Iribar at his near post. A minute later the compliment
was returned when Stein arrived simultaneously with
Persson's cross and smashed the ball on the run into the
net. Greig shot over the crossbar a penalty kick awarded
after Karrauri had brought down Stein only a minute after
the interval. Rangers' overwhelming pressure was rewarded
after 7 minutes when Ferguson headed in a Henderson
corner and again 20 minutes later as Penman took Smith's
lob and tipped the ball over Iribar's head. In 29 minutes
Clemente took the clearance of a corner-kick and scored
through a screen of players. That goal and Greig's missed
penalty deflated Rangers until Persson brought about the
late transformation scene.

April 2nd: Quarter-Final Second Leg
ATLETICO BILBAO   (1) 2   RANGERS   (0) 0
     Estefano (10), Ibanez (54)

BILBAO: Iribar; Betzeun, Saez; Guatua, Echeberria,
Karrauri; Estefano, Ibanez, Arieta, Uriate, Rojo

RANGERS: Martin; Johansen, Mathieson; Greig,
McKinnon, D. Smith; Henderson, Jackson, Stein,
Ferguson, Johnston

Attendance: 40,000

Johnston and Betzeun were ordered off

Rangers lost the game and also Willie Johnston who was
sent off with Atletico's right-back 10 minutes from the
end. Bilbao scored once in each half. Johnston retaliated
after a foul by Betzeun, there was a flurry of fists and the
referee sent both players off. Rangers held off a final surge
of pressure and were through to the Semi-Final although
they would now be deprived of Johnston's services for the
first leg. After 10 minutes Estefano scored from close range
after Ibanez had made the opening. 9 minutes after the
interval Bilbao again narrowed the gap when Ibanez forced
home a shot during a scrimmage in the Rangers' goal. Then
came the tumultuous moments before Rangers wearily left
the field. Rangers won 4-3 on aggregate.

May 14th: Semi-Final First Leg
RANGERS   0   NEWCASTLE UNITED   0

RANGERS: Neef; Johansen, Provan; Greig, Jackson, D. Smith; Henderson, Penman, Stein, Jardine, Persson

NEWCASTLE: McFaul; Craggs, Clark; Moncur, McNamee, Gibb; Scott, Robson, Davies, Arnetoft, Foggon

Attendance: 70,000

Penman missed a penalty

Innumerable chances to score were there for the taking, most notably perhaps when Rangers were granted a penalty after 34 minutes. Persson was impeded by McFaul. The goalkeeper anticipated Penman's penalty-kick and made a spectacular save. Rangers had most of the pressure but never really worked to a pattern against opponents who were mainly concerned with keeping their goal intact.

May 21st: Semi-Final Second Leg
NEWCASTLE UNITED   (0) 2   RANGERS   (0) 0
   Scott (52), Sinclair (77)

NEWCASTLE: McFaul; Craig, Clark; Moncur, Burton, Gibb; Scott, Robson, Davies, Arnetoft, Sinclair

RANGERS: Neef; Johansen, Mathieson; Greig, McKinnon, D. Smith; Henderson, Penman, Stein, Johnston, Persson

Attendance: 60,000

Rangers' last bid for glory this season ended in disaster. Jim Scott killed Rangers' chance of a Final place in the 52nd minute with a glorious shot that raged into the roof of the net — a goal that came from a chance set up by another Scot, Tommy Gibb. Another exile, Jackie Sinclair, sank Rangers without trace 13 minutes from time with a thundering 2nd goal. The game was over. Newcastle won 2-0 on aggregate.

APPEARANCES

	League	League Cup	Scottish Cup	Fairs Cup
Martin	31	6	5	8
Jackson	10	6	-	5
Mathieson	25	6	5	8
Greig	32	6	5	9
McKinnon	28	6	4	8
Hynd	10	3	-	3
Henderson	31	4	5	10
Willoughby	2+1S	1	-	-
Jardine	14+2S	1+1S	-	3+1S
D. Smith	21+1S	4	3+2S	7+2S
Persson	27+3S	6	5	7+1S
Penman	25	5+1S	5	8
Johnston	28	3	5	9
Johansen	26	-	5	8
Stein	18	-	4	7
MacDonald	8+1S	-	0+1S	1
Provan	7	-	-	1
Watson	10	-	3	2
Ferguson	7+5S	4	1	4
Neef	2	-	-	2
Conn	1+1S	-	-	0+1S
Miller	0+1S	-	-	-
Sorensen	-	-	-	-
A. Smith	-	3	-	-
McPhee	-	2	-	-

GOALSCORERS

League: Johnston 17, Penman 15, Stein 13, Persson 8, Greig 6 (3 pens), Henderson 5, Ferguson 5, Jardine 4, Own Goals 3, D. Smith 2, MacDonald 1, Watson 1, Johansen 1

League Cup: Henderson 3, Jardine 3, A. Smith 2, Ferguson 2, Jackson 2, Penman 1, Persson 1

Scottish Cup: Johnston 4, Penman 2, Stein 1, Persson 1, Greig 1 (pen), Henderson 1

Fairs Cup: Stein 4, Henderson 3, Ferguson 3, Greig 2 (1 pen), Jardine 1, Mathieson 1, Johnston 1, D. Smith 1, Penman 1, Persson 1, Own Goal 1

It's 1976 and Rangers have won the Scottish Cup. The players celebrate and John Greig gives it a big kiss.

H

Season 1969–70

In one of the most dramatic seasons in the club's history Manager Davie White was dismissed following a home European defeat by Gornik Zabre and an indifferent start to the League campaign. Ex-International winger and former Kilmarnock Manager Willie Waddell was lured back from his career in journalism to manage the club. White's League record as manager was: Played 74 Won 51 Drew 13 Lost 10. He had not won any of the major trophies during his time in charge. The team went 11 matches without defeat after the appointment of Waddell but this form nose-dived at the end of the season and only two of the last 10 matches were won. The team again finished as Runners-up, 12 points behind Celtic. 19 matches were won, 7 drawn and 8 lost (6 by one goal). 28 players were used and Stein finished as top scorer with 24. By the end of the season Baxter, Martin, Sorensen, Provan, Setterington, Ferguson, Bobby Watson, Heron and Johansen had all left the club.

After Jim Baxter had masterminded the defeat of Celtic in Rangers' first League Cup encounter at Ibrox, a goalkeeping error by Neef cost them the return. A valuable home point was also thrown away in a 6-goal shared draw with Raith Rovers. This was the 3rd successive season that they had been drawn in the same Qualifying Section, and eliminated by Celtic.

Under Waddell Rangers progressed to the Third Round of the Scottish Cup but Alex MacDonald was ordered off in an ugly match with Celtic, and 2 goals were lost in the last 5 minutes to put them out of the competition.

After beating Steau of Rumania in the First Round of the Cup Winners Cup Rangers were beaten home and away by Gornik of Poland.

League: Runners-Up
League Cup: Failed to Qualify from Section
Scottish Cup: Third Round
Cup Winners Cup: Second Round

SCOTTISH FIRST DIVISION

July 28th: Willie Henderson represented the Rest of Britain versus Wales in Cardiff.

August 30th:
DUNDEE UNITED 0   RANGERS 0

DUNDEE UNITED: Mackay; Rolland, J. Cameron; Gillespie, Smith, Markland; Hogg (Stuart), Reid, K. Cameron, Scott, Wilson

RANGERS: Neef; Johansen, Provan; Greig, McKinnon, Baxter (Penman); Henderson, MacDonald, Stein, Smith, Johnston

Attendance: 20,000

September 3rd:
RANGERS (0) 2   ABERDEEN (0) 0
Provan (75 pen),
Stein (89)

RANGERS: Neef; Johansen, Provan; Greig, McKinnon, Baxter; MacDonald, Jardine, Stein, Penman, Johnston

ABERDEEN: McGarr; Boel, Hermiston; Murray, McMillan, Petersen; Willoughby, Robb, Forrest (Clark), Wilson, Hamilton

Attendance: 45,000

McMillan was ordered off

September 6th:
RANGERS   (2) 2   ST MIRREN   (0) 0
Johnston (27),
Provan (29 pen)

RANGERS: Neef; Johansen (Smith), Provan; Greig,
McKinnon, Baxter; Penman, Jardine, Stein,
MacDonald, Johnston

ST MIRREN: Thorburn; C. Murray, Connell;
Fulton, Young, Cumming; Gilshan, Blair, Adamson,
McLaughlin, Knox

Attendance: 35,000

September 13th:
AYR UNITED   (2) 2   RANGERS   (0) 1
Young (8),   Stein (90)
Ferguson (12)

AYR UNITED: Stewart; Malone, Murphy; Fleming,
Quinn, Mitchell; Young, Ferguson, Ingram, McCulloch,
Rough

RANGERS: Neef; Johansen, Mathieson; Greig,
Provan, Baxter; Penman, Jardine (Smith), Stein,
MacDonald, Johnston

Attendance: 25,225

September 20th:
RANGERS   (0) 0   CELTIC   (0) 1
                         Hood (49)

RANGERS: Neef; Johansen, Provan; Greig,
McKinnon, Baxter; Henderson, Jardine (Watson), Stein,
Smith, Johnston

CELTIC: Fallon; Craig, Gemmell; Clark, McNeill,
Brogan; Johnstone, Hood, Wallace, Hay, Lennox

Attendance: 75,000

Craig was ordered off in the 67th minute

This was Celtic's first League win at Ibrox for 12 years.

September 27th:
PARTICK THISTLE   (0) 1   RANGERS   (1) 2
Bone (82)   Henderson (5),
                          Johnston (85)

PARTICK THISTLE: Dick; Reid, Gray; McLindon,
McKinnon, Rowan; Flanagan, Smith, Bone, Hansen,
Duncan

RANGERS: Neef; Johansen, Provan; Greig,
McKinnon, Baxter; Henderson, Watson, Stein, McPhee,
Johnston

Attendance: 15,000

**September 28th: Harold Davis, coach of Queens
Park, was appointed as assistant trainer at Ibrox.**

October 4th:
ST JOHNSTONE   (0) 1   RANGERS   (0) 3
Connolly (58)   Baxter (48),
                         Stein 2 (74, 89)

ST JOHNSTONE: Donaldson; Lambie, Coburn;
Gordon, Rooney, McPhee; Aird, Hall, McCarry,
Connolly, Aitken

RANGERS: Neef; Johansen, Provan; Greig,
McKinnon, Baxter; Henderson, Watson, Stein, Jardine,
Johnston

Attendance: 20,000

October 11th:
RANGERS   (1) 1   HIBERNIAN   (2) 3
Johnston (39)   Marinello 2 (16, 43),
                         McBride (71)

RANGERS: Martin; Johansen, Heron; Greig,
McKinnon, Baxter; Henderson, Watson, Stein, Jardine,
Johnston

HIBERNIAN: Marshall; Shevlane, Jones; Blackley,
Black, Stanton; Marinello, Hamilton, McBride,
Cormack, Stevenson

Attendance: 54,000

**October 22nd: Greig, McKinnon and Stein played
for Scotland against West Germany in a World Cup
Qualifier in Hamburg. West Germany won the
match 3-2.**

October 25th:
RANGERS   (1) 2   DUNFERMLINE   (0) 0
Penman (3),
Johansen (90)

RANGERS: Neef; Johansen, Heron; Greig,
McKinnon, Watson; Henderson, Penman, Stein,
Johnston, Persson

DUNFERMLINE: Martin; Callaghan, Lunn;
McGarty, Baillie, Thomson; Mitchell, Gardner,
Traynor, Lister, McLean

Attendance: 25,000

October 29th:
MOTHERWELL   (0) 2   RANGERS   (2) 2
McInally (81),   Stein 2 (33, 40)
Donnelly (84)

MOTHERWELL: McCloy; Campbell, Wark;
Forsyth, McCallum, Donnelly; Murphy, McInally,
Muir, Goldthorpe, Wilson

RANGERS: Neef; Johansen, Heron; Greig,
McKinnon, Watson (Smith); Henderson, Penman,
Stein, Johnston, Persson

Attendance: 25,000

November 1st:
RANGERS   (1) 3   DUNDEE   (1) 1
  Penman 2 (26, 74 pen),   Murray (33)
  Johnston (64)

RANGERS: Neef; Johansen, Heron; Greig,
McKinnon, Smith; Henderson, Penman, Stein,
Johnston, Persson

DUNDEE: Donaldson; Wilson, Swan; Selway,
Stewart, Houston; Murray, Gilroy, Wallace,
Kinninmonth, Bryce
Attendance: 30,000

League positions

	P	W	D	L	F	A	Pts
1 Dundee United	10	7	2	1	19	13	16
2 Dunfermline	11	7	2	2	15	11	16
3 Celtic	10	7	1	2	27	14	15
4 Hibernian	10	7	1	2	20	10	15
5 Motherwell	11	5	4	2	21	13	14
6 RANGERS	11	6	2	3	18	11	14

**November 5th: Greig and McKinnon played for
Scotland against Austria in Vienna. Stein appeared
as a substitute. Austria won 2-0.**

November 8th:
AIRDRIE   (0) 1   RANGERS   (2) 3
  Bird (78)   Penman (9),
                           Henderson (27),
                           Johnston (61)

AIRDRIE: Clark; Jonquin, Caldwell; Goodwin,
Delaney, Whiteford; Bird, Jarvie, Marshall, McPheat,
Stewart

RANGERS: Neef; Johansen, Heron; Greig,
McKinnon, Baxter; Henderson, Penman, Stein,
Johnston, Persson
Attendance: 12,200

November 15th:
RANGERS   (2) 5   KILMARNOCK   (1) 3
  Penman (8 pen),   Morrison 2 (7, 58),
  Stein 3 (20, 46, 49),   Mathie (75)
  Dickson o.g. (84)

RANGERS: Neef; Johansen, Heron; Greig,
McKinnon, Baxter; Henderson, Penman, Stein,
Johnston, Persson

KILMARNOCK: McLaughlin; King, Dickson;
Gilmour (Waddell), McGrory, Beattie; T. McLean,
Mathie, Morrison, J. McLean, Cook
Attendance: 30,000

**November 21st: Alex Ferguson was transferred to
Falkirk for £20,000.**

November 22nd:
MORTON   (0) 2   RANGERS   (2) 2
  Osborne (64),   Stein (14),
  O'Neil (71)   Johnston (41)

MORTON: Neilson; Murray (Coakley), Laughton;
McDerment, Gray, Rankin; Collins, Sweeney, Osborne,
Mason, O'Neil

RANGERS: Neef; Johansen, Heron; Greig,
McKinnon, Baxter; Henderson, Penman, Stein,
Johnston, Persson
Attendance: 15,000

**November 27th: Manager Davie White was dismissed
following the Cup Winners' Cup defeat by Gornik.
Willie Thornton was put in charge of the team
pending the appointment of a new manager.**

November 29th:
RANGERS   (2) 3   RAITH ROVERS   (0) 0
  Johnston (8), Stein (36),
  MacDonald (62)

RANGERS: Neef; Johansen, Greig; Smith,
McKinnon, Baxter (Watson); Henderson, Penman,
Stein, MacDonald, Johnston

RAITH ROVERS: Reid; Lindsay, Weir; Bolton,
Polland, Cooper (Sneddon); Brand, McGuire, Judge,
Sinclair, Falconer
Attendance: 23,000

Weir was ordered off

**December 3rd: Willie Waddell was appointed as
Rangers' new manager.**

December 6th:
HEARTS   (1) 1   RANGERS   (1) 2
  Brown (40 secs)   Stein (45),
                           Johnston (72)

HEARTS: Cruikshank; Clunie, Oliver; MacDonald,
Anderson, Thomson; Ford, Fleming, Winchester
(Townsend), Brown, Moller

RANGERS: Neef; Johansen, Greig; Smith,
McKinnon, Baxter; Henderson, Penman, Stein,
MacDonald (Watson), Johnston
Attendance: 24,000

December 13th:
RANGERS   (1) 2   DUNDEE UNITED   (1) 1
  Henderson (13),   Gordon (14)
  Stein (85)

RANGERS: Neef; Johansen, Mathieson; Greig,
McKinnon, Smith; Henderson, Penman, Stein,
Johnston, Persson (Watson)

DUNDEE UNITED: Mackay; Rolland, Cameron; Gillespie, Smith, Henry; Wilson, Reid, Gordon, Mitchell, Scott

Attendance: 41,000

December 20th:
ABERDEEN   (2) 2   RANGERS   (2) 3
  Robb 2 (3, 29)   Stein 2 (10, 40),
                            Johnston (61)

ABERDEEN: McGarr; Hermiston, Kirkland; Murray, Boel, Petersen; Harper, Robb, Forrest, Buchan, Hamilton

RANGERS: Neef; Johansen, Mathieson; Greig, McKinnon, Smith; Henderson, Baxter, Stein, Setterington (Penman), Johnston

Attendance: 22,000

December 27th:
RANGERS   (1) 3   CLYDE   (0) 0
  Setterington (29),
  Penman (68 pen),
  Greig (82)

RANGERS: Neef; Johansen, Mathieson; Greig, McKinnon, Smith; Henderson, Penman (Conn), Stein, Setterington, Johnston

CLYDE: McCulloch; Anderson, Mulheron; Beattie, McHugh, Burns; Glasgow (Soutar), Hulston, Staite, Stewart, Hastings

Attendance: 32,000

Johnston and Beattie were ordered off in the 64th minute

League positions

	P	W	D	L	F	A	Pts
1 Celtic	19	15	1	3	57	22	31
2 RANGERS	19	13	3	4	41	21	29
3 Hibernian	17	12	2	3	33	16	26
4 Dundee United	18	9	5	4	30	29	23
5 Dunfermline	19	9	4	6	24	22	22

January 1st:
RANGERS   (1) 3   PARTICK THISTLE   (0) 1
  Johnston (30),   Rae (62)
  Semple (57),
  Stein (62)

RANGERS: Neef; Johansen, Mathieson; Greig, McKinnon, Smith; Henderson, Penman (Conn), Stein, Semple, Johnston

PARTICK THISTLE: Ritchie; Campbell, Holt; Johnston, Gray, Clark; Rae, Smith, Coulston, Hansen, Duncan

Attendance: 40,000

Penman missed a twice-taken penalty

January 2nd:
CELTIC   0   RANGERS   0

CELTIC: Williams; Hay, Gemmell; Murdoch, McNeill, Brogan; Johnstone, Hood, Wallace, Auld, Hughes

RANGERS: Neef; Johansen, Mathieson; Greig, McKinnon, Smith; Henderson (Jardine), Penman, Stein, Johnston, MacDonald

Attendance: 72,000

Rangers and Celtic were subdued by the frost-bound conditions at Parkhead. As a spectacle the greatest club match in the world shrank to ordinary proportions, but this was not the fault of the players who had to guard against injury on the icy, bone-hard surface.

January 13th: Rangers signed Gordon McQueen from Largs Thistle.

January 17th:
RANGERS   (0) 3   AYR UNITED   (0) 0
  Stein (56),
  Greig (80), I. MacDonald (82)

RANGERS: Neef; Johansen, Mathieson; Greig, McKinnon, Smith; Henderson, Penman (Conn), Stein, A. MacDonald, I. MacDonald

AYR UNITED: Stewart, Malone, Murphy; McAnespie, Fleming, Mitchell; Young, Reynolds, Hood, McCulloch, McCall

Attendance: 32,000

January 31st:
ST MIRREN   (0) 0   RANGERS   (2) 4
                            Greig (16),
                            Stein 2 (36, 68),
                            MacDonald (65)

ST MIRREN: Thorburn; C. Murray, Connell; Fulton, McFadden, Cumming; Lister, Pinkerton, J. Young, Blair (I. Young), Munro

RANGERS: Neef; Johansen, Mathieson; Greig, McKinnon, Smith; Conn, Penman, Stein, MacDonald, Persson

Attendance: 35,000

February 25th:
RANGERS   (1) 3   ST JOHNSTONE   (1) 1
  Semple (7),   Aird (15)
  Greig 2 (53, 75)

RANGERS: Neef; Johansen, Mathieson; Greig, McKinnon, Smith; Henderson, Penman, Stein, MacDonald, Semple

ST JOHNSTONE: Donaldson; Lambie, Coburn; Gordon, Rooney, McPhee; Aird, Hall, McCarry, Connolly (Wilson), Aitken

Attendance: 25,000

Coburn was ordered off

February 28th:
HIBERNIAN   (1) 2   RANGERS   (2) 2
  Graham (10),   Stein (36),
  McBride (64)   Greig (38)

HIBERNIAN: Marshall; Shevlane, McEwan; Blackley, Black, Stanton; Graham, McBride, Cormack, Murphy, Duncan

RANGERS: Neef; Johansen, Mathieson; Greig, McKinnon, Smith; Penman, Jardine, Stein, MacDonald, Johnston

Attendance: 31,322

League positions

	P	W	D	L	F	A	Pts
1 Celtic	26	21	2	3	75	27	44
2 RANGERS	25	17	5	3	56	25	39
3 Hibernian	24	14	5	5	45	25	33
4 Hearts	26	10	10	6	39	28	30
5 Dundee United	26	12	6	8	48	49	30

March 6th: Iain MacDonald went to hospital for a cartilege operation and was ruled out for the rest of the season.

March 7th:
RANGERS   (0) 2   MOTHERWELL   (0) 1
  Stein 2 (61, 68)   Wilson (89)

RANGERS: Neef; Johansen, Mathieson; Greig, McKinnon, Smith; Conn (Penman), K. Watson, Stein, MacDonald, Johnston

MOTHERWELL: MacRae; Campbell, Wark (Murray); Forsyth, McCallum, Donnelly; Muir, McInally, Deans, Murphy, Wilson

Attendance: 31,000

March 11th:
RAITH ROVERS   (2) 2   RANGERS   (1) 1
  Miller (18), Cooper (41)   Penman (26)

RAITH ROVERS: Reid; Brown, Lindsay; Bolton, Buchanan, Sneddon; Miller (McCarthy), Cooper, Judge, McGuire, Wilson

RANGERS: Neef; Johansen, Mathieson; Greig, McKinnon, Smith; Penman, Watson (Jardine), Stein, MacDonald, Johnston

Attendance: 7,000

March 13th: Peter McCloy of Motherwell joined the club in exchange for both Bobby Watson and Brian Heron.

March 14th:
DUNFERMLINE   (1) 2   RANGERS   (1) 1
  McLaren (40),   Stein (27)
  McLean (56)

DUNFERMLINE: Arrol; Callaghan, Lunn; Fraser, McNichol, Renton; Mitchell (Gardner), McLaren, Edwards, McLean, Gillespie

RANGERS: McCloy; Johansen, Mathieson; Greig, McKinnon, Smith; Henderson, Penman (Conn), Stein, Johnston, Semple

Attendance: 12,000

March 21st:
DUNDEE   (1) 2   RANGERS   (0) 1
  Wallace (2), Scott (89)   Stein (64)

DUNDEE: Donaldson; Selway, Johnston; Steele, Easton, Stewart; Campbell, Kinninmonth, Wallace, Scott, Bryce

RANGERS: McCloy; Johansen, Mathieson; Conn, McKinnon, Smith; Henderson, Penman, Stein, Johnston, Semple (Setterington)

Attendance: 17,000

March 25th:
RANGERS   (2) 3   HEARTS   (0) 2
  Penman 2 (12, 58),   Winchester (80),
  Johnston (20)   Irvine (85)

RANGERS: McCloy; Johansen, Provan; Conn, McKinnon, Smith; Henderson, Penman, Stein, Johnston (Jardine), Fyfe

HEARTS: Cruikshank; Clunie, Oliver; Veitch, Anderson, Thomson; Traynor, Townsend, Irvine, Fleming (Winchester), Moller

Attendance: 14,000

March 28th:
RANGERS   (1) 1   AIRDRIE   (0) 1
  Penman (37)   McPheat (49)

RANGERS: McCloy; White, Provan; Conn, McKinnon, Smith; Fyfe, Penman (Jardine), Stein, Setterington, Henderson

AIRDRIE: McKenzie; Jonquin, Keenan; Menzies, Delaney, Whiteford; Wilson, Jarvie, McPheat, Goodwin, Cowan

Attendance: 16,000

March 31st:
CLYDE (1) 1   RANGERS (0) 0
  S. Anderson (28)

CLYDE: McCulloch; E. Anderson, Mulheron; Beattie, McGoldrick, Burns; McFarlane, McVie, Hulston, S. Anderson, Hastings

RANGERS: McCloy; Johansen, Jardine; Conn, Jackson, Smith; Fyfe, Penman, Stein (Setterington), Johnston, Henderson

S. Anderson was ordered off in the 62nd minute

April 4th:
KILMARNOCK (0) 2   RANGERS (1) 2
  J. McLean (51),   Greig (12),
  T. McLean (56 pen)   Henderson (74)

KILMARNOCK: McLaughlin; King, Dickson; Gilmour, Rodman, McGrory; T. McLean, Morrison, Mathie, J. McLean, Cook

RANGERS: McCloy; Jardine, Johansen; Greig, Jackson, Smith (Penman); Henderson, Conn, Stein, MacDonald, Johnston

Attendance: 12.000

Dave Smith was carried off with a broken leg

April 16th: Three lost their jobs in Ibrox shuffle — Lawrie Smith, Harold Davis (after 5 months) and Davie Kinnear (after 26 years). Hearts' assistant manager, Jock Wallace, took over as chief trainer and coach.

April 18th:
RANGERS (0) 0   MORTON (1) 2
                Coakley (5),
                Collins (90)

RANGERS: McCloy; Jardine, Johansen; Greig, Jackson, Conn; Henderson, Fyfe, Setterington (Penman), MacDonald, Persson

MORTON: Neilsen; Ferguson, Sweeney; Anderson, Gray, Rankin; Coakley, Collins, Mason, Allan (Hayes), Jordan

Attendance: 15,000

Willie Henderson, a Rangers' favourite in the sixties.

Scottish First Division

	P	W	D	L	F	A	Pts
1 Celtic	34	27	3	4	96	33	57
2 RANGERS	34	19	7	8	67	40	45
3 Hibernian	34	19	6	9	65	40	44
4 Hearts	34	13	12	9	50	36	38
5 Dundee United	34	16	6	12	62	64	38
6 Dundee	34	15	6	13	49	44	36
7 Kilmarnock	34	13	10	11	62	57	36
8 Aberdeen	34	14	7	13	55	45	35
9 Morton	34	13	9	12	52	52	35
10 Dunfermline	34	15	5	14	45	45	35
11 Motherwell	34	11	10	13	49	51	32
12 Airdrie	34	12	8	14	59	64	32
13 St Johnstone	34	11	9	14	50	62	31
14 Ayr United	34	12	6	16	37	52	30
15 St Mirren	34	8	9	17	39	54	25
16 Clyde	34	9	7	18	34	56	25
17 Raith Rovers	34	5	11	17	32	67	21
18 Partick Thistle	34	5	7	22	41	82	17

April 18th: Scotland beat Northern Ireland 1-0 at Windsor Park, Belfast. McKinnon and Johnston were in the team. Stein made an appearance as substitute.

April 22nd: Scotland drew 0-0 with Wales at Hampden Park. Greig, McKinnon and Stein were in the team.

April 25th: Scotland and England drew 0-0 at Hampden Park. Greig, McKinnon and Stein were in the team.

April 28th: Rangers freed Baxter, Martin, Sorensen, Provan, Laing and McPhee. Persson was placed on the open-to-transfer list.

May 29th: Clyde player Stan Anderson was appointed as assistant trainer at Ibrox.

June 1st: Alfie Conn fractured his leg in a Youth Tournament.

June 3rd: Denis Setterington was transferred to Falkirk for a fee of £10,000.

June 5th: Kai Johansen announced his retirement from football.

LEAGUE CUP

August 9th:
RAITH ROVERS (0) 2   RANGERS (2) 3
  A. Miller (46), Sinclair (89)   Johansen (14),
                             Stein (36),
                             MacDonald (71)

RAITH ROVERS: Reid; McDonald, Gray; Polland, Bolton, D. Millar; A. Millar, Falconer, Wallace, Sinclair, Sneddon

RANGERS: Neef; Johansen, Provan; Greig, McKinnon, Baxter; Henderson (Persson), MacDonald, Stein, Smith, Johnston

Attendance: 21,000

August 13th:

RANGERS (0) 2   CELTIC (1) 1
  Persson (48),   Hood (8)
  Johnston (50)

RANGERS: Neef; Johansen, Provan; Greig, McKinnon, Baxter; Johnston, Watson, Stein, Jardine, Persson

CELTIC: Fallon; Hay, Gemmell; Murdoch (Auld), McNeill, Clark; Connelly, Hood, Wallace, Lennox, Hughes

Attendance: 71,645

The turning point came when in the 3rd and 5th minutes of the second half Rangers levelled the score, then drew ahead Celtic took the lead after 8 minutes' play through Hood who made the most of a careless back-pass by Provan. The equaliser, scored by Persson, and the leading goal nodded in by Johnston from Greig's service after a Baxter free-kick inspired the home side. Masterminds in Rangers' triumph were Baxter and Johnston.

August 16th:

AIRDRIE (0) 0   RANGERS (1) 3
                         Persson (37),
                         Jardine (62),
                         Watson (83)

AIRDRIE: McKenzie; Jonquin, Caldwell; Menzies, Keenan, Whiteford; Jarvie (Stewart), Fyfe, Marshall, McPheat, Wilson

RANGERS: Neef; Johansen, Provan; Greig, McKinnon, Baxter; Johnston (Smith), Watson, Stein, Jardine, Persson

Attendance: 23,000

August 20th:

CELTIC (0) 1   RANGERS (0) 0
  Gemmell (67)

CELTIC: Fallon; Craig, Gemmell; Murdoch, McNeill, Clark; Johnstone, Hood, Wallace, Lennox (Brogan), Hughes

RANGERS: Neef; Johansen, Provan; Greig, McKinnon, Smith; Henderson (Penman), Jardine, Stein, Johnston, Persson

Attendance: 70,000

A blunder by goalkeeper Neef cost Rangers the League Cup Sectional Tie. He failed to hold the ball after Murdoch had taken a free-kick from the angle of the penalty-area and Gemmell bobbed up to nod into the net.

August 23rd:

RANGERS (1) 3   RAITH ROVERS (1) 3
  Polland o.g. (32),   Wallace 2 (40, 70),
  Penman (57),   Sinclair (81)
  MacDonald (82)

RANGERS: Neef; Johansen, Provan; Greig, McKinnon, Smith (Watson); Penman, Jardine, Stein, MacDonald, Johnston

RAITH ROVERS: Reid; Hislop, Gray; D. Millar, Davidson, Polland; A. Millar, Lindsay, Wallace, Sinclair, Wilson

Attendance: 30,000

August 27th:

RANGERS (1) 3   AIRDRIE (0) 0
  Stein (8), Johnston (51),
  Penman (81)

RANGERS: Neef; Johansen, Provan; Greig, McKinnon, Baxter (Henderson); Penman, MacDonald, Stein, Smith, Johnston

AIRDRIE: McKenzie; Jonquin, Caldwell; Goodwin, Whiteford, Menzies; Bird, Jarvie, Marshall, McPheat, Stewart

League Cup Section Table

	P	W	D	L	F	A	Pts
Celtic	6	5	1	0	21	5	10
RANGERS	6	4	1	1	14	7	9
Raith Rovers	6	1	4	1	10	20	3
Airdrie	6	1	5	0	5	18	2

SCOTTISH CUP

January 24th: First Round

RANGERS (2) 3   HIBERNIAN (1) 1
  A. MacDonald 2 (12, 53), Graham (16)
  Penman (39)

RANGERS: Neef; Johansen, Mathieson; Greig, McKinnon, Smith; Henderson, Penman, Stein, A. MacDonald, I. MacDonald (Conn)

HIBERNIAN: Marshall; Shevlane, Schaedler; Blackley, Black, Stanton; Stevenson (McBride), Graham, Cormack, McEwan, Duncan

Attendance: 73,716

February 7th: Second Round

FORFAR ATHLETIC (0) 0 RANGERS (5) 7
                         MacDonald (8),
                         Stein (22),
                         Penman (28),
                         Johansen (30 pen),
                         Greig 2 (42, 58),
                         Jardine (73)

FORFAR: Phillip; McKenzie, Sime; Knox, Milne, Fyfe; Wyles, May, Waddell, Mackle, Stewart

RANGERS: Neef; Johansen, Mathieson; Greig, McKinnon, Smith; Conn, Penman, Stein (Jardine), MacDonald, Johnston

Attendance: 10,800

February 21st: Third Round
CELTIC (1) 3   RANGERS (1) 1
  Lennox (39), Hay (85),   Craig o.g. (5)
  Johnstone (88)

CELTIC: Williams; Craig, Gemmell; Murdoch, McNeill, Brogan; Johnstone, Lennox, Wallace, Hay, Hughes (Hood)

RANGERS: Neef; Johansen, Mathieson; Greig, McKinnon, Smith; Conn (Henderson), Penman, Stein, MacDonald, Johnston

Attendance: 75,000

MacDonald was ordered off in the 62nd minute

In one of the most towsy confrontations between the sides for years few players emerged with any lasting credit. The referee, Mr Tom Wharton, was always in the midst of controversy and there was even severe criticism of his decision to send off Alex MacDonald without a reprimand for Jim Brogan when he became involved in the incident. The torch was put to the powder keg when Jim Craig headed the ball into his own goal in 5 minutes. His misery was mirrored in head-on bewilderment when Willie Johnston ran to him and ruffled the Celtic's full-back in mock congratulations. Colin Stein then supplied the second provocative act by running over to give Craig a 'well done' slap. Hughes having earlier hit the post, Celtic deservedly equalised in 39 minutes with a Lennox shot that deflected off Neef into the net. Davie Hay was fielded at inside-left in place of Bertie Auld and he crowned his day by shooting the magnificent 25-yard match-winning 2nd goal 5 minutes from the end. Celtic's 3rd goal scored by Johnstone a couple of minutes from time merely emphasised the superiority of the Cupholders. MacDonald was sent off in 62 minutes after he went in with a leg outstretched on Williams. Brogan appeared to push MacDonald off his feet, but escaped punishment.

CUP WINNERS CUP

September 17th: First Round First Leg
RANGERS (2) 2   STEAU (Rumania) (0) 0
  Johnston 2 (38, 42)

RANGERS: Neef; Johansen, Provan; Greig, McKinnon, Baxter; Henderson, Jardine, Stein, Johnston, Persson (Smith)

STEAU: Sucvic; Cristache, Satmareanu; Vigu, Dimitriu, Halmageanu; Panteau, Tataru, Voinea, Negrea, Greimiceanu (Stefanescu)

Attendance: 43,346

2 opportunist goals by Johnston gave Rangers a good start for the return trip to Bucharest.

October 1st: First Round Second Leg
STEAU 0   RANGERS 0

STEAU: Sucvic; Cristache, Satmareanu; Halmageanu, Vigu, Dimitriu (Nicola); Negrea, Panteau, Tataru, Voinea, Manea (Stefanescu)

RANGERS: Neef; Johansen, Provan; Greig, McKinnon, Baxter; Henderson, Watson (Smith), Stein, Jardine, Johnston

Attendance: 90,000

Rangers played a splendid defensive game. Steau, although pressing for most of the game, seldom seemed capable of pulling back the 2-goal deficit from the First Leg. When the Rumanian forwards did make any worthwhile scoring efforts they found Neef in inspired form. Once again the outstanding Rangers' player was Greig. He played most of the game behind Johansen and Provan, mopping up when Steau threatened even slight danger. Rangers, as expected, used only 3 forwards — Henderson, Stein and Johnston. Jardine struck the crossbar and seconds later a fierce drive from Negrea met the same fate. Rangers won 2-0 on aggregate.

November 12th: Second Round First Leg
GORNIK (Poland) (2) 3   RANGERS (0) 1
  Lubanski 2 (5, 88),   Persson (55)
  Szoltysik (11)

GORNIK: Koska; Latocha, Florenski; Oslizlo, Gorgon, Wilczek; Szoltysik, Szarynski, Banas, Lubanski, Olek

RANGERS: Neef; Johansen, Heron; Greig, McKinnon, Baxter; Henderson, Penman, Stein, Johnston, Persson

Attendance: 60,000

Rangers, although 2 goals down to Gornik Zabre, returned home not without hope of qualifying for the next round of the tournament.

November 26th: Second Round Second Leg
RANGERS (1) 1   GORNIK (0) 3
  Baxter (18)   Olek (64),
       Lubanski (76),
       Skowronek (81)

RANGERS: Neef; Johansen, Heron; Greig, McKinnon, Baxter; Henderson, Penman, Stein, Johnston, Persson (MacDonald)

GORNIK: Koska; Kuchta, Oslizlo; Gorgon, Latocha, Szoltysik; Wilczek, Olek, Banas, Lubanski, Szarynski (Skowronek)

Attendance: 63,000

3 brilliant goals put Rangers out of the Cup Winners Cup. Gornik held their fire until the last half-hour. They then won as they pleased. Rangers applied most of the pressure and had nearly all of the play until then. They enjoyed the boost of a tremendous goal by Baxter after only 18 minutes' play. Then Gornik mounted their 30-minute offensive. Olek shot the first in the 64th minute from a narrow angle. 14 minutes from the end Lubanski made it 2. He collected the ball at the centre line and his colleagues permitted him to go it alone. He fought off a tackle by McKinnon. Neef, coming out, worked him to the goal-line but Lubanski came back infield and as the Rangers' defenders charged towards him he swivelled again and shot home. 9 minutes from time substitute Skowronek made it 3 when he ran through the middle and curled in an unstoppable shot from outside the 20-yard range. The crowd in the stand rose to Gornik as they came off the field.

APPEARANCES

	League	League Cup	Scottish Cup	Cup Winners
Neef	26	6	3	4
Johansen	33	6	3	4
Provan	10	6	-	2
Greig	30	6	3	4
McKinnon	30	6	3	4
Baxter	14	4	-	4
Henderson	27	2+1S	1+1S	4
A. MacDonald	14	3	3	0+1S
Stein	33	6	3	4
Smith	22+3S	4+1S	3	0+2S

	League	League Cup	Scottish Cup	Cup Winners
Johnston	29	6	2	4
Jardine	10+4S	4	0+1S	2
Penman	25+5S	2+1S	3	2
Mathieson	14	-	3	-
R. Watson	7+4S	2+1S	-	1
McPhee	1	-	-	-
Martin	1	-	-	-
Heron	7	-	-	2
Persson	9	3+1S	-	3
Setterington	4+2S	-	-	-
Semple	4	-	-	-
I. MacDonald	1	-	1	-
Jackson	3	-	-	-
Conn	8+4S	-	2+1S	-
K. Watson	2	-	-	-
McCloy	7	-	-	-
Fyfe	4	-	-	-
White	1	-	-	-
Miller	-	-	-	-

GOALSCORERS

League: Stein 24, Johnston 11, Penman 10 (3 pens), Greig 7, Henderson 4, Provan 2 (2 pens), A. MacDonald 2, Semple 2, Baxter 1, Johansen 1, Setterington 1, I. MacDonald 1, Own Goal 1

League Cup: Persson 3, Stein 2, A. MacDonald 2, Johnston 2, Johansen 1, Penman 1, Jardine 1, Watson 1, Own Goal 1

Scottish Cup: A. MacDonald 3, Penman 2, Greig 2, Stein 1, Jardine 1, Johansen 1 (pen), Own Goal 1

Cup Winners Cup: Johnston 2, Persson 1, Baxter 1

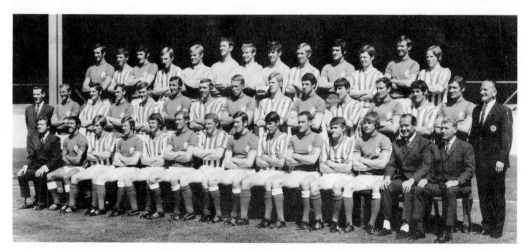

The Rangers squad in season 1969–70.

Season 1970–71

The season was completely overshadowed by the disaster at Ibrox on 2nd January in which 66 people died and 145 were injured.

The team finished 4th in the Championship behind Celtic, Aberdeen and St Johnstone, the Perth side being the only team to complete the double over them. Rangers suffered a total of 9 defeats and managed only 16 wins — their lowest total since League reconstruction in season 1955–56. Their goals total of 58 was also the lowest in that period. McKinnon and Jackson each missed only one game and Colin Stein finished as top scorer with 12 goals.

Rangers met their oldest rivals in the Final of the League Cup, and a fine headed goal from 16-year-old Derek Johnstone took the trophy to Ibrox and put the name of the young centre-forward straight into the record books. Captain John Greig had to miss the Final through injury and Ron McKinnon collected the Cup in his absence.

They disposed of Falkirk, St Mirren, Aberdeen and Hibs to reach the Scottish Cup Final. A Colin Jackson goal beat Aberdeen at Ibrox in front of 60,584 and an Alfie Conn goal in the Semi-Final Replay proved to be conclusive. Smith, Jardine and Conn missed the Final against Celtic through injury, and although Rangers had 3 outstanding chances in the early stages, they had to rely on a late goal from substitute Derek Johnstone to earn them a replay. Jim Denny made his first team debut in the replay, replacing the injured Miller, and although Rangers put up an outstanding performance, the loss of 2 goals in 2 minutes cost them the match.

Although Rangers outplayed Bayern Munich in the two Fairs Cities Cup first-round matches, a controversial goal by German centre-forward Gerd Müller at Ibrox ended their interest in the competition.

League: Fourth
Scottish Cup: Runners-up
League Cup: Winners
Fairs Cities Cup: First Round

SCOTTISH FIRST DIVISION

July 25th: Orjan Persson re-joined Orgryte (Sweden) for a small fee.

August 29th:
ST MIRREN 0   RANGERS 0

ST MIRREN: Connachan; Murray, Connell; Fulton, McFadden, Munro; McKean, Hamilton, Reid, Gilshan, Lister

RANGERS: McCloy; Jardine, Miller; Greig, McKinnon, Jackson; Fyfe, Conn, Stein, MacDonald, Johnston
Attendance: 27,400

September 5th:
RANGERS (1) 2   FALKIRK (0) 0
  Johnston 2 (25 pen, 67)

RANGERS: McCloy; Jardine, Miller; Greig, McKinnon, Jackson; Fyfe, Conn, Stein, MacDonald, Johnston

225

FALKIRK: Rennie; Abel, Totten; Gibson, Markie, Miller; Scott, Ford, Ferguson, McLaughlin, Setterington (Little)

Attendance: 32,000

Greig was ordered off along with Ferguson

September 12th:
CELTIC   (1) 2   RANGERS   (0) 0
  Hughes (6), Murdoch (54)

CELTIC: Williams; McGrain, McNeill, Connelly, Brogan; Murdoch, Hay; Johnstone, Hood, Hughes, Lennox

RANGERS: McCloy; Jardine, McKinnon, Jackson, Miller; Greig, Conn, MacDonald; Fyfe (Penman), Stein, Johnston

Attendance: 73,000

Brogan missed a penalty

This was the 25th time Celtic had met Rangers since Jock Stein had taken over the mangerial reigns at Parkhead five and a half years previously.

September 19th:
RANGERS   (3) 5   COWDENBEATH   (0) 0
  D. Johnstone 2 (23, 88),
  Greig 2 (35, 55),
  MacDonald (12)

RANGERS: McCloy; Jardine, Miller; Greig, McKinnon, Jackson; Henderson, Conn, D. Johnstone, MacDonald, Fyfe

COWDENBEATH: Wylie; McLaughlan, Jack; Ferguson, Kinnell, Moore; Laing (Sharp), Dickson, Mullen, Taylor, Ross

Attendance: 30,000

September 26th:
DUNDEE UNITED   (0) 0   RANGERS   (0) 2
                         Conn (57), Fyfe (59)

DUNDEE UNITED: Mackay; Rolland, Cameron; Markland, Smith, Henry; Wilson, A. Reid, I. Reid, Gordon, Traynor

RANGERS: McCloy; Jardine, Miller; Greig, McKinnon, Jackson; Fyfe, Conn, Stein, MacDonald, Johnston

Attendance: 23,000

September 29th: Colin Stein was fined £25.00 for being sent off in Germany.

October 3rd:
RANGERS   (3) 3   MOTHERWELL   (1) 1
  MacDonald (17),   Lawson (43)
  Stein (27),
  Johnston (34)

RANGERS: McCloy; Jardine, Miller; Conn, McKinnon, Jackson; Henderson, Fyfe, Stein (D. Johnstone), MacDonald, Johnston

MOTHERWELL: MacRae: Whiteford, Wark; Forsyth, McCallum, Watson; McInally, Lawson, Deans, Goldthorpe, Heron; Sub: Martin for Watson

Attendance: 25,000

October 10th:
HEARTS   (0) 0   RANGERS   (1) 1
                         Johnston (22 pen)

HEARTS: Cruikshank; Clunie, Oliver; Anderson, Thomson, Brown; Fleming, Townsend, Ford, Hegarty (Winchester), Lynch

RANGERS: McCloy; Jardine, Miller; Greig, McKinnon, Jackson; Henderson, Conn (Fyfe), Stein, MacDonald, Johnston

Attendance: 32,500

October 17th:
RANGERS   (0) 0   ABERDEEN   (1) 2
                         Jackson o.g. (43),
                         Harper (58)

RANGERS: McCloy; Jardine, Miller; Greig, McKinnon, Jackson; Henderson, Fyfe, Stein, MacDonald (Smith), Johnston

ABERDEEN: Clark; Boel, Hermiston; Murray, McMillan, Buchan; Taylor, Harper, Forrest, Robb, Graham

Attendance: 39,763

League positions

	P	W	D	L	F	A	Pts
1 Celtic	8	7	0	1	18	3	14
2 Aberdeen	9	6	2	1	18	7	14
3 St Johnstone	9	5	3	1	18	8	13
4 Motherwell	9	6	0	3	16	10	12
5 RANGERS	8	5	1	2	13	5	11

October 31st:
RANGERS   (3) 5   AIRDRIE   (0) 0
  Conn (3),
  Johnston 2 (14, 83 pen),
  Stein 2 (28, 68)

RANGERS: McCloy; Jardine, Miller; Conn, McKinnon, Jackson; Henderson, MacDonald, D. Johnstone, Stein, Johnston

AIRDRIE: McKenzie; Jonquin, Caldwell; Menzies, Delaney, Whiteford; Wilson (Cowan), Goodwin, Busby, Jarvie, McPheat

Attendance: 28,788

November 7th:
DUNFERMLINE   (1) 1   RANGERS   (1) 1
  Gardiner (8)   Jackson (38)

DUNFERMLINE: Arrol; Thomson, Lunn; Fraser, Cushley, McNichol; Edwards, Mitchell, Gardner, McLaren, Robertson

RANGERS: McCloy; Jardine, Miller; Greig (MacDonald), McKinnon, Jackson; Henderson, Conn, D. Johnstone, Stein, Johnston

Attendance: 18,000

November 11th: Greig, McKinnon, Stein and Johnston represented Scotland against Denmark at Hampden Park. Jardine appeared as a substitute. Scotland won 1-0.

November 14th:
RANGERS (1) 5   CLYDE (0) 0
  Stein 2 (43, 83),
  Mulheron o.g. (65),
  Johnston (80 pen),
  D. Johnstone (84)

RANGERS: McCloy; Jardine, Miller; Conn (Fyfe), McKinnon, Jackson; Henderson, MacDonald, D. Johnstone, Stein, Johnston

CLYDE: Wallace; Burns, Mulheron; Beattie, McGoldrick, McHugh; Hay, Sullivan, Hulston, Flanagan (McColligan), Hastings

Attendance: 25,915

Wallace was sent off

November 21st:
AYR UNITED (1) 2   RANGERS (0) 1
  Whitehead (34),   Young o.g. (72)
  Young (76)

AYR UNITED: Stewart; McFadzean, Murphy; Fleming, Quinn, Mitchell; Young, Reynolds, McLean, Whitehead, Doyle

RANGERS: McCloy; Jardine, Miller; Conn (D. Johnstone), McKinnon, Jackson; Henderson, MacDonald, Stein, Fyfe, Johnston

Attendance: 19,000

November 24th: Kai Johansen was put up for sale.

November 25th:
HIBERNIAN (1) 3   RANGERS (1) 2
  Blair 2 (31, 70),   D. Johnstone (26),
  Graham (84)   Stein (61)

HIBERNIAN: Baines; R. Duncan, Schaedler; Blackley, Black, Stanton; Graham, O'Rourke, McEwan, Blair, A. Duncan

RANGERS: McCloy; Jardine, Miller; Conn, McKinnon, Jackson; Henderson, MacDonald, D. Johnstone, Stein, Johnston

Attendance: 18,770

Willie Johnston was ordered off in the 75th minute

November 28th:
MORTON (0) 1   RANGERS (1) 2
  Gray (53)   Conn (26), Fyfe (47)

MORTON: Sorensen; Hayes, McDerment; Sweeney, Gray, Rankin; Hannigan, Collins, Osborne (O'Neil), Mason, Anderson

RANGERS: McCloy; Jardine, Miller; Conn, McKinnon, Jackson; Henderson (Smith), MacDonald, D. Johnstone, Stein, Fyfe

Attendance: 15,000

December 5th:
RANGERS 0   DUNDEE 0

RANGERS: McCloy; Jardine, Miller; Conn, McKinnon, Jackson; Henderson, MacDonald, D. Johnstone (Fyfe), Stein, Johnston

DUNDEE: Hewitt; Wilson, Houston; Selway, Phillip, Steele; Gilroy (Duncan), Kinninmonth, Wallace, Scott, Johnston

Attendance: 25,420

December 8th: Willie Johnston was suspended for 6 weeks. Willie Henderson appeared as a substitute for Cruyff for the Rest of Europe against Benfica in a Testimonial match for Mario Coluna in Portugal.

December 12th:
ST JOHNTONE (1) 2   RANGERS (1) 1
  Connolly (7), Rennie (71) Fyfe (34)

ST JOHNSTONE: Donaldson; Lambie, Argue; Rooney, Gordon, Rennie; Aird, Hall, McPhee, Connolly, Aitken

RANGERS: McCloy; Jardine, Miller; Greig, McKinnon, Jackson; Henderson Conn, Stein, Fyfe, MacDonald

Attendance: 10,300

December 19th:
RANGERS (1) 4   KILMARNOCK (0) 2
  Jackson (17),   McLean (69),
  MacDonald (77),   Maxwell (72)
  D. Johnstone (83, 85)

RANGERS: McCloy; Jardine, Miller; Greig, McKinnon, Jackson; Henderson, MacDonald, Stein, Smith, Conn (D. Johnstone)

KILMARNOCK: Hunter; Whyte, Dickson; Gilmour, McGrory, MacDonald; McLean, Maxwell, Morrison, Cairns, Cook

Attendance: 19,450

December 26th:
RANGERS   (0) 1   ST MIRREN   (0) 0
  Greig (76)

RANGERS: McCloy; Jardine, Miller; Greig,
McKinnon, Jackson; Henderson, Stein, D. Johnstone,
Smith, MacDonald

ST MIRREN: Connaghan; Palmer, McLaughlin;
Fulton, McFadden, McQueen; Lister, Knox, Hamilton,
Munro, McKean

Attendance: 25,000

McLaughlin was ordered off

League positions

	P	W	D	L	F	A	Pts
1 Aberdeen	18	15	2	1	42	7	32
2 Celtic	18	15	1	2	42	8	31
3 RANGERS	18	10	3	5	35	16	23
4 St Johnstone	18	9	4	5	34	28	22
5 Dundee	18	8	5	5	28	21	21

January 1st:
FALKIRK   (1) 3   RANGERS   (0) 1
  Miller (10), Roxburgh (56),   Conn (87)
  Hoggan (70)

FALKIRK: Rennie; Abel, McLaughlin; Markie,
Miller, Gibson; Hoggan, Roxburgh, Ferguson, Shirra,
Setterington

RANGERS: McCloy; Jardine, Miller; Conn,
McCallum, Jackson; Fyfe, Parlane, D. Johnstone,
MacDonald, Semple

Attendance: 18,000

**January 2nd: 66 people died and 145 were injured on
Stairway 13 at the end of this match. With a mere 15
seconds of the game remaining Colin Stein equalised
for Rangers. Those down the exit steps made an
attempt to clamber back into the ground and share
the jubilation. They were met by a floodtide of their
happy fellow-supporters sweeping down uncon-
trollably on top of them. In a good-natured match
there had been only 2 arrests — for drunkenness in
an 80,000 all-ticket crowd.**

RANGERS   (0) 1   CELTIC   (0) 1
  Stein (90)   Johnstone (89)

RANGERS: Neef; Jardine, Mathieson; Greig,
McKinnon, Jackson; Henderson (MacDonald), Conn,
D. Johnstone, Smith, Stein

CELTIC: Williams; Craig, Gemmell; Brogan,
Connelly, Hay; Johnstone, Hood, Wallace, Callaghan,
Lennox

Attendance: 80,000

**January 4th: Rangers donated £50,000 to the Lord
Provost's Appeal Fund for the relatives of the
disaster victims.**

January 16th:
RANGERS   (1) 1   DUNDEE UNITED   (0) 1
  Greig (13)   Reid (72)

RANGERS: Neef; Jardine, Mathieson; Greig,
McKinnon, Jackson; Henderson (MacDonald), Conn,
D. Johnstone, Smith, Stein

DUNDEE UNITED: McAlpine; Rolland, Cameron;
W. Smith, D. Smith, Stevenson; Wilson, Reid, Copland,
Devlin, Traynor

Attendance: 27,776

**January 18th: West Ham were reported to be ready
to bid £175,000 for Willie Johnston.**

**January 27th: Scotland beat an Old Firm Select at
Hampden Park in a match in aid of the Ibrox
disaster victims.**

SCOTLAND   (1) 2   OLD FIRM SELECT   (1) 1
  Gemmill, Lorimer   Best

SCOTLAND: Cruikshank; Hay, Gemmell; Stanton,
McKinnon (Craig), Moncur; Lorimer (T. McLean),
Gemmill, Stein, O'Hare, Cooke

OLD FIRM SELECT: Bonetti (Chelsea); Jardine,
Greig; Murdoch, McNeill, Smith; Henderson, Hughes,
Charlton (Manchester United), Johnston, Best
(Manchester United)

Attendance: 81,405

January 30th:
MOTHERWELL   (0) 1   RANGERS   (1) 2
  Muir (84)   Mathieson (42),
                          Stein (64)

MOTHERWELL: Ritchie; Whiteford, Wark; Forsyth,
McCallum, Main; Lawson, McInally, Deans (Martin),
Muir, Heron

RANGERS: Neef; Jardine, Mathieson (MacDonald);
Greig, McKinnon, Jackson; Henderson, Conn, Stein,
Smith, Johnston

Attendance: 20,000

**February 3rd: Belgium beat Scotland 3-0 in Brussels.
McKinnon, Greig and Stein were in the side.**

February 6th:
RANGERS   (1) 1   HEARTS   (0) 0
  Henderson (7)

RANGERS: McCloy; Jardine, Mathieson; Greig,
McKinnon, Jackson; Henderson, Conn (MacDonald),
Stein, Smith, Johnston

HEARTS: Cruikshank; Clunie, Kay; Thomson, Anderson, Brown; Fleming, Townsend, Ford, Hegarty, Winchester

Attendance: 29,398

February 20th:
ABERDEEN 0   RANGERS 0

ABERDEEN: Clark; Boel, Hermiston; Murray, McMillan, Buchan; Taylor, Robb, Forrest, Hamilton (Willoughby), Graham

RANGERS: McCloy; Jardine, Mathieson; Greig, McKinnon, Jackson; Henderson, MacDonald, D. Johnstone (Conn), Smith, Johnston

Attendance: 36,000

February 24th: Sandy Jardine was in the Scotland Under-23 team which drew 2-2 with England at Hampden Park.

February 27th:
RANGERS (1) 1   HIBERNIAN (0) 1
  Greig (41)   Baker (71)

RANGERS: McCloy; Jardine, Mathieson; Greig, McKinnon, Jackson; Henderson, Conn, Stein, MacDonald, Johnston (D. Johnstone)

HIBERNIAN: Marshall; Brownlie, Jones; Stanton, Black, Cropley; Davidson, O'Rourke, Baker, Hazel, Duncan

Attendance: 30,644

League positions

	P	W	D	L	F	A	Pts
1 Aberdeen	26	19	4	3	54	12	42
2 Celtic	25	19	3	3	61	16	41
3 St Johnstone	26	15	4	7	46	36	34
4 RANGERS	25	12	7	6	42	23	31
5 Falkirk	25	10	8	7	34	30	28

March 10th:
AIRDRIE (3) 4   RANGERS (0) 3
  Busby 2 (11, 83),   MacDonald 2 (75, 86),
  Jarvie (34),   Stein (82)
  McCloy o.g. (42)

AIRDRIE: Gourlay; Jonquin, Caldwell; Menzies, Goodwin, D. Whiteford; J. Whiteford, Cowan, Busby, Jarvie, Wilson

RANGERS: McCloy; Jardine, Mathieson; Greig, Jackson, K. Watson; Henderson, A. MacDonald, Stein, Smith, I. MacDonald (Parlane)

Attendance: 15,000

March 13th:
RANGERS (2) 2   DUNFERMLINE (0) 0
  Henderson (12),
  Greig (30)

RANGERS: McCloy; Jardine, Mathieson; Greig, McKinnon, Jackson; Henderson, MacDonald, Stein, Smith (Parlane), Johnston

DUNFERMLINE: McGarr; Thomson, Lunn; Fraser, McNichol, McKimmie; Edwards, Mitchell, McBride, Gardner, Robertson (Millar)

Attendance: 21,580

March 20th:
CLYDE (2) 2   RANGERS (1) 2
  Hay (14), Hastings (25)   Johnston (30),
                        Stein (61)

CLYDE: McCulloch; Anderson, Mulheron; Beattie (Glasgow), McGoldrick, Miller; Sullivan, Hay, Flanagan, Burns, Hastings

RANGERS: McCloy; Jardine, Mathieson; Greig, McKinnon, Jackson; Henderson, A. MacDonald, Stein, Johnston, I. MacDonald

Attendance: 10,500

March 25th: Dave Smith broke his right leg in a training accident.

March 27th:
RANGERS (0) 2   AYR UNITED (0) 0
  Greig (59), Johnston (77)

RANGERS: McCloy; Jardine, Mathieson; Greig, McKinnon, Jackson; Henderson, MacDonald (Penman), Stein, Conn, Johnston

AYR UNITED: Stewart; McFadzean, Murphy; Fleming, Quinn, Mitchell; Doyle, McGovern, Ingram, McCulloch, Rough

Attendance: 15,000

March 28th: Rangers opened their new Social Club.

April 3rd:
RANGERS 0   MORTON 0

RANGERS: McCloy; Jardine, Miller; Greig, McKinnon, Jackson; Henderson, Penman, Parlane, Johnston, I. MacDonald (A. MacDonald)

MORTON: Sorensen; Anderson, Laughton; Sweeney, Gray, Rankin; Hannigan, Collins, Osborne, Thomson, Bartram (Booth)

Attendance: 14,000

April 10th:
DUNDEE (1) 1   RANGERS (0) 0
  Scott (44)

DUNDEE: Donaldson; R. Wilson, Houston; Stewart, Phillip, Steele; Kinninmonth, Gilroy, Wallace, Scott, J. Wilson

RANGERS: McCloy; Jardine, Mathieson; Greig, McKinnon, Jackson; Henderson, Penman (Conn), Stein, D. Johnstone, Johnston

Attendance: 13,000

April 14th:

COWDENBEATH   (1) 1   RANGERS   (2) 3
  Kennedy (12)   Jardine (30),
                                 Greig (43),
                                 Stein (75)

COWDENBEATH: McArthur; McLaughlan, Bostock; Taylor, Kinnell, Moore; Harper, Dickson, Laing, Kennedy, Thomson

RANGERS: McCloy; Alexander, Mathieson; Jardine (Penman), McKinnon, Jackson; Henderson, MacDonald, Stein, Greig, Johnston

Attendance: 6,000

Jardine was put in plaster after the game with a hairline fracture of the right leg

April 17th:

RANGERS   (0) 0   ST JOHNSTONE   (1) 2
                              Hall (8),
                              Connolly (90)

RANGERS: McCloy; Alexander, Mathieson; Greig, McKinnon, Jackson; Henderson, MacDonald, Stein, Semple (Penman), Johnston

ST JOHNSTONE: Donaldson; Lambie, Coburn; Gordon, Rennie, Whitelaw; Aird, Hall (Aitken), Connolly, McPhee, Pearson

Attendance: 17,560

April 21st: Scotland were beaten 2-0 by Portugal in Lisbon. McKinnon and Henderson were in the team.

April 24th:

KILMARNOCK   (1) 1   RANGERS   (1) 4
  McCulloch (11)   Miller (45),
                                Henderson (72),
                                MacDonald (87),
                                Stein (89)

KILMARNOCK: Hunter; Whyte, Dickson; Gilmour, McGrory, MacDonald; McLean, McSherry, McCulloch, Waddell (Morrison), Cook

RANGERS: McCloy; Miller, Mathieson; Greig, McKinnon, Jackson; Henderson, Penman, Stein, MacDonald, Johnston

Attendance: 7,800

Scottish First Division

	P	W	D	L	F	A	Pts
1 Celtic	34	25	6	3	89	23	56
2 Aberdeen	34	24	6	4	68	18	54
3 St Johnstone	34	19	6	9	59	44	44
4 RANGERS	34	16	9	9	58	34	41
5 Dundee	34	14	10	10	53	45	38
6 Dundee United	34	14	8	12	53	54	36
7 Falkirk	34	13	9	12	46	53	35
8 Morton	34	13	8	13	44	44	34
9 Motherwell	34	13	8	13	43	47	34
10 Airdrie	34	13	8	13	60	65	34
11 Hearts	34	13	7	14	41	40	33
12 Hibernian	34	10	10	14	47	53	30
13 Kilmarnock	34	10	8	16	43	67	28
14 Ayr United	34	9	8	17	37	54	26
15 Clyde	34	8	10	16	33	59	26
16 Dunfermline	34	6	11	17	44	56	23
17 St Mirren	34	7	9	18	38	56	23
18 Cowdenbeath	34	7	3	24	33	77	17

May 1st: Johansen and Renton were given free transfers.

May 18th: Scotland were beaten 1-0 by Northern Ireland at Hampden Park. Greig had the misfortune to deflect a shot into his own net.

May 22nd: Greig was in the Scotland team which was beaten 3-1 by England at Wembley.

June 8th: Tommy McLean was signed from Kilmarnock for £60,000.

June 9th: McLean, McKinnon and Stein were in the Scotland team which was beaten 1-0 by Denmark in Copenhagen.

June 14th: Scotland were beaten 1-0 by Russia in Moscow. McKinnon and Stein were in the side.

LEAGUE CUP

August 8th:

RANGERS   (3) 4   DUNFERMLINE   (0) 1
  Stein 2 (2, 79),   McKimmie (64)
  Jardine (6),
  Johnstone (36 pen)

RANGERS: Watson; Jardine, Mathieson; Greig, McKinnon, D. Smith; Henderson, Conn, Stein, MacDonald, Johnston

DUNFERMLINE: Arrol; Callaghan, Lunn; Fraser, McNichol, Renton (Millar); Robertson, McKimmie, McLean, Gardner, McLaren

Attendance: 45,056

August 12th:
MOTHERWELL (0) 0   RANGERS (0) 2
                         Fyfe (85),
                         Henderson (87)

MOTHERWELL: Ritchie; Whiteford, Wark; Forsyth, McCallum, Watson; Campbell, McInally, Muir, Goldthorpe, Heron

RANGERS: McCloy; Jardine, Mathieson (Miller); Greig, McKinnon, Jackson; Henderson, Conn, Stein, Fyfe, Johnston

Attendance: 25,000

August 15th:
RANGERS 0   MORTON 0
RANGERS: McCloy; Jardine, Miller; Greig, McKinnon, Jackson; Henderson, Conn, Stein, Fyfe, Johnston (MacDonald)

MORTON: Neilsen; Murray, McDerment; Sweeney, Rankin, O'Neil; Coakley, Collins, Mason, Hannigan, Clarke

Attendance: 40,000

August 19th:
RANGERS (1) 2   MOTHERWELL (0) 0
  Penman (43), Stein (75)

RANGERS: McCloy; Jardine, Miller; Greig, McKinnon, Jackson; Henderson, Penman, Stein, Johnston, I. MacDonald (Conn)

MOTHERWELL: Ritchie; Whiteford, Wark; Forsyth, McCallum, Watson; Campbell, McInally, Lawson, Goldthorpe, Heron

Attendance: 28,000

April 22nd:
DUNFERMLINE (0) 0   RANGERS (3) 6
                   Johnston 3 (9, 14 pen, 88),
                   Jackson (45),
                   Fyfe (76), Stein (87)

DUNFERMLINE: Arrol; Callaghan, Brown; Thomson, McGarty (McKimmie), McLaren; Robertson, McNichol, McLean, Gardner, Gillespie

RANGERS: McCloy; Jardine, Miller; Greig, McKinnon, Jackson; Fyfe, Conn, Stein, A. MacDonald, Johnston

Attendance: 17,000

August 26th:
MORTON (0) 0   RANGERS (1) 2
                        Johnston (14),
                        Conn (85)

MORTON: Sorensen; Murray, McDerment; Sweeney, Rankin, Campbell; Booth, Collins, Mason, Hannigan, Clarke

RANGERS: McCloy; Jardine, Miller; Conn, McKinnon, Jackson; Fyfe, Semple, Stein, MacDonald, Johnston

Attendance: 18,000

League Cup Section Table

	P	W	D	L	F	A	Pts
RANGERS	6	5	1	0	16	1	11
Morton	6	3	1	2	8	8	7
Motherwell	6	2	1	3	8	8	5
Dunfermline	6	0	1	5	4	19	1

September 9th: Quarter-Final First Leg
HIBERNIAN (0) 1   RANGERS (1) 3
  Duncan (73)   Conn (1),
                        Fyfe 2 (51, 76)

HIBERNIAN: Marshall; Brownlie, Schaedler; Blackley (Cropley), Black, Stanton; Graham, Blair, McBride, McEwan, Duncan

RANGERS: McCloy; Jardine, Miller; Greig, McKinnon, Jackson; Stein, Fyfe, Johnston, Conn, MacDonald

Attendance: 37,355

September 23rd: Quarter-Final Second Leg
RANGERS (2) 3   HIBERNIAN (0) 1
  MacDonald (5),   Graham (98)
  Greig (38), Fyfe (64)

RANGERS: McCloy; Jardine, Miller; Greig, McKinnon, Jackson, Fyfe (Henderson), Conn, Stein, MacDonald, Johnston

HIBERNIAN: Marshall; Jones, Schaedler; Blackley, Black, Stanton; Hamilton, Blair, McBride (Graham), McEwan, Duncan

Attendance: 54,000

McCloy saved a McBride penalty

Rangers won 6-2 on aggregate

October 14th: Semi-Final   At Hampden Park
RANGERS (1) 2   COWDENBEATH (0) 0
  Johnston (45 pen), Stein (64)

RANGERS: McCloy; Jardine, Miller; Greig, McKinnon, Jackson; Henderson, Conn, Stein, MacDonald, Johnston — Fyfe

COWDENBEATH: Wylie; McLaughlan, Jack; Ferguson, Kinnell, Moore; Laing, Dickson (Allan), McCullie, Taylor, Ross

Attendance: 34,000

The full measure of Rangers' power and superiority cannot be assessed by their 2 goal winning margin.

October 24th: Final   At Hampden Park
RANGERS   (1) 1   CELTIC   (0) 0
  D. Johnstone (40)

RANGERS: McCloy; Jardine, Miller; Conn,
McKinnon, Jackson; Henderson, MacDonald, D.
Johnstone, Stein, Johnston — Fyfe

CELTIC: Williams; Craig, Quinn; Murdoch, McNeill,
Hay; Johnstone, Connelly, Wallace, Hood (Lennox),
Macari

Attendance: 106,263 *Referee*: T. Wharton (Glasgow)

Rangers' side, with 2 exceptions, was composed of the men
who had been humiliated on the previous Saturday by
Aberdeen at Ibrox Park. The only goal of the match was
scored after 40 minutes' play. From Henderson's pass
MacDonald slung the ball out to Johnston, operating on
the right wing, and when the cross came over young Derek
Johnstone outleaped both McNeill and Craig and crisply
headed past Williams. McKinnon collected the trophy in
Greig's absence.

SCOTTISH CUP

January 23rd: Third Round
RANGERS   (2) 3   FALKIRK   (0) 0
  Conn (19),
  Johnston 2 (26, 85)

RANGERS: McCloy; Jardine, Mathieson; Greig,
McKinnon, Jackson; Henderson, Conn, Stein, Smith,
Johnston

FALKIRK: Rennie; Abel, McLaughlin; Markie,
Miller, Gibson; Hoggan, Roxburgh, Young, Shirra,
Setterington

Attendance: 41,000

February 13th: Fourth Round
ST MIRREN   (0) 1   RANGERS   (2) 3
  McKean (69)   Stein 2 (19, 60),
                             Johnston (20 pen)

ST MIRREN: Connaghan; Murray, McLaughlin;
McFadden, McQueen (McKean), Fulton; Prentice,
Millar, Knox, Lister, Munro

RANGERS: McCloy; Jardine, Mathieson; Greig,
McKinnon, Jackson; Henderson, Conn, Stein, Smith,
Johnston

Attendance: 36,000

March 6th: Fifth Round
RANGERS   (0) 1   ABERDEEN   (0) 0
  Jackson (67)

RANGERS: McCloy; Jardine, Mathieson; Greig,
McKinnon, Jackson; Henderson, Conn (MacDonald),
Stein, Smith, Johnston

ABERDEEN: Clark; Boel, Hermiston; Murray,
McMillan, Buchan; Taylor (Willoughby), Robb,
Forrest, Harper, Graham

Attendance: 60,584

March 31st: Semi-Final   At Hampden Park
RANGERS   0   HIBERNIAN   0

RANGERS: McCloy; Jardine, Mathieson; Greig,
McKinnon, Jackson; Henderson, Conn, Stein,
MacDonald, Johnston — Penman

HIBERNIAN: Marshall; Brownlie, Jones; Blackley,
Stanton, Pringle; Graham, O'Rourke, Baker, Cropley,
Stevenson — Black

Attendance: 69,429

John Greig earned his team a Semi-Final replay. The game
burst to life in the dying seconds when Joe Baker turned
the ball in at the post but Greig, with a swift header,
cleared desperately on the line. It was a breathtaking finale
to what must otherwise rank as the bore of the season.

April 5th: Semi-Final Replay   At Hampden Park
HIBERNIAN   (1) 1   RANGERS   (1) 2
  O'Rourke (22)   Henderson (16),
                             Conn (62)

HIBERNIAN: Marshall; Brownlie, Jones; Blackley,
Black, Pringle; Graham, O'Rourke, Baker, Cropley,
Stevenson —Black

RANGERS: McCloy; Jardine, Mathieson; Greig,
McKinnon, Jackson; Henderson, MacDonald, Stein,
Conn, Johnston —Penman

Attendance: 54,435

Rangers edged their way into another Scottish Cup Final
with an Alfie Conn goal in the second half. The teams came
up with a stirring and exciting Cup-tie. Willie Henderson
was in International form and Eric Stevenson was Hibs'
star attraction. In 16 minutes Henderson scored the first
goal with a fine shot after Stein had turned the ball back to
him. Marshall got a touch but could not prevent it going in.
Hibs equalised in 22 minutes. McCloy tried to force
Cropley wide but the young inside-forward tenaciously
held onto the ball and cut it back from the bye-line to
O'Rourke who headed into the empty net. The woodwork
saved Hibs in 39 minutes when a Johnston header
rebounded from the underside of the bar. This escape was
cancelled out in the second half when Hibs, striving for the
equaliser, were unlucky when an O'Rourke header
slammed off the crossbar. It was after substantial pressure
that Rangers broke away and scored the winning goal. A
great deal of the credit goes to Stein, who headed down
intelligently to Conn, who controlled it beautifully before
despatching it into the net.

May 8th: Final   At Hampden Park
CELTIC   (1) 1   RANGERS   (0) 1
  Lennox (40)   D. Johnstone (87)

CELTIC: Williams; Craig, Brogan; Connelly, McNeill, Hay; Johnstone, Lennox, Wallace, Callaghan, Hood (Macari)

RANGERS: McCloy; Miller, Mathieson; Greig, McKinnon, Jackson; Henderson, Penman (D. Johnstone), Stein, MacDonald, Johnston

Attendance: 120,092 *Referee*: T. Wharton (Glasgow)

Miller broke his cheekbone in this match and was ruled out of the replay

Derek Johnstone was brought into the team to replace Penman in the final 20 minutes and completed a modern football fairy tale by heading the vital equaliser to give his club another chance.

May 12th: Final Replay   At Hampden Park
CELTIC   (2) 2   RANGERS   (0) 1
  Macari (24), Hood (25 pen)   Craig o.g. (58)

CELTIC: Williams; Craig, Brogan; Connelly, McNeill, Hay; Johnstone, Macari, Hood (Wallace), Callaghan, Lennox

RANGERS: McCloy; Denny, Mathieson; Greig, McKinnon, Jackson; Henderson, Penman (D. Johnstone), Stein, MacDonald, Johnston

Attendance: 103,332 *Referee*: T. Wharton (Glasgow)

Rangers courageously introduced Jim Denny, a 21-year-old novice from the Junior ranks, into the intense heat of an Old Firm duel. Denny was never overwhelmed and certainly his inclusion did not contribute to his team's defeat. Lou Macari and Jimmy Johnstone held the key to Celtic's 21st Cup success. It was largely through their sharpness and trickery that Celtic established command before the interval. In a late rally Rangers almost forced extra time when a Colin Stein shot hit Williams on the chest and rebounded clear.

FAIRS CITIES CUP

September 16th: First Round First Leg
BAYERN MUNICH   (1) 1   RANGERS   (0) 0
  Beckenbauer (22)

BAYERN: Maier; Koppenhoffen, Pumm; Hansen, Beckenbauer, Breitner; Roth, Zobel, Müller, Mrosko, Brenninger

RANGERS: McCloy; Jardine, Miller; Greig, McKinnon, Jackson; Fyfe, Conn, Stein (Henderson), MacDonald, Johnston

Attendance: 27,000

If Rangers were disappointed at the result it should have been over missed chances that would have made them worthy winners. John Greig hit the bar with shattering force from a header and Maier pulled off a number of fine saves. Only Franz Beckenbauer could have scored such a classic goal from nothing in 22 minutes. Forsaking his defensive role he strode to within 20 yards of Rangers' goal and stroked a pass from Breitner with perfect timing and precision along the ground just out of the reach of the diving McCloy. Rangers played coolly and constructively throughout.

September 30th: First Round Second Leg
RANGERS   (0) 1   BAYERN MUNICH   (0) 1
  Stein (81)   Müller (80)

RANGERS: McCloy; Jardine, Miller; Greig, McKinnon, Jackson (D. Johstone); Fyfe (Henderson), Conn, Stein, MacDonald, Johnston

BAYERN: Maier; Handen, Pumm; Schwarzenbeck, Beckenbauer, Koppenhoffer; Roth (Breitner), Zobel, Müller, Mrosko, Brenninger

Attendance: 83,000

Gerd Müller put Rangers out of Europe with a controversial free-kick goal to the dismay and disappointment of the Ibrox crowd. Rangers claimed vehemently that the goal should not have been allowed by the Swiss referee. They appealed to the official that he had signalled an indirect free-kick when McKinnon fouled Müller almost on the 18-yard line. Müller took the kick himself, swerved it past the defensive barrier and the ball went in off the post. Although Colin Stein equalised within a matter of seconds Rangers knew they could not pull back the deficit in the short time that remained. Chances fell to Greig, MacDonald, Henderson and McKinnon but all were cleared or saved. Bayern Munich won 2-1 on aggregate.

APPEARANCES

	League	League Cup	Scottish Cup	Fairs Cup
McCloy	31	9	7	2
Jardine	32	10	5	2
Miller	21	8+1S	1	2
Greig	26	8	7	2
McKinnon	33	10	7	2
Jackson	33	9	7	2
Fyfe	11+3S	6	-	2
Conn	23+2S	9+1S	5	2
Stein	30	10	7	2
A. MacDonald	27+6S	7+1S	4+1S	2
Johnston	25	10	7	2
Henderson	29	6+1S	7	0+2S
D. Johnstone	13+4S	1	0+2S	0+1S
Smith	9+2S	1	3	-
McCallum	1	-	-	-
Parlane	2+2S	-	-	-
Semple	2	1	-	-
Neef	3	-	-	-
Mathieson	14	2	7	-
K. Watson	1	-	-	-

	League	League Cup	Scottish Cup	Fairs Cup
I. MacDonald	3	1	-	-
Penman	3+4S	1	2	-
Alexander	2	-	-	-
B. Watson	-	1	-	-
Denny	-	-	1	-

GOALSCORERS

League: Stein 12, Johnston 9 (4 pens), Greig 8, D. Johnstone 6, A. MacDonald 6, Conn 4, Henderson 3, Fyfe 3, Jackson 2, Own Goals 2, Mathieson 1, Jardine 1, Miller 1

League Cup: Johnston 6 (3 pens), Stein 5, Fyfe 5, Conn 2, Jardine 1, Henderson 1, Penman 1, Jackson 1, A. MacDonald 1, Greig 1, D. Johnstone 1

Scottish Cup: Johnston 3 (1 pen), Stein 2, Conn 2, Jackson 1, Henderson 1, D. Johnstone 1, Own Goal 1

Fairs Cup: Stein 1

The Rangers squad in 1971–72. Back row: Struthers, Conn, Fyfe, Jackson, Neef, McCloy, Watson, D. Johnson, Donaldson, Millar, I. McDonald. Middle row: Wallace (coach), Craig (physiotherapist), Stein, Pirrie, Mathieson, Denny, McKinnon, McCallum, Jardine, Penman, Smith, Walker, Anderson (asst. coach), Craven (trainer). Front row: Waddell (manager), Henderson, Semple, A. MacDonald, Alexander, Greig, Parlane, McLean, Morrison, W. Johnston, and Thornton (asst. manager).

Season 1971–72

After 2 near misses Rangers at last got their hands on a major European trophy.

Their League form was very disappointing. They started badly and finished poorly — winning only 2 of their last 7 matches. They recorded 21 victories but their 11 defeats were their worst of the post-war period. They eventually finished 3rd in the Table — 16 points behind Champions Celtic and 6 behind Runners-up Aberdeen. Peter McCloy was their only ever-present — indeed, he missed only 2 of their 55 competitive matches during the season. Their goals total of 71 was their best for 3 seasons. Alex MacDonald, Colin Stein and Willie Johnston all finished on 11 goals. Dave Smith was named as Scotland's Player of the Year and Willie Henderson was freed at the end of the season.

Rangers failed to qualify from their League Cup Section — losing to Celtic twice at Ibrox — but they did win the Glasgow Cup and they recorded victories over Everton, Tottenham Hotspur and Chelsea in Friendlies.

Rangers reached the Semi-Final of the Scottish Cup but were well beaten by Hibs after a replay, their 3rd replay in the 4 rounds of the competition.

Rangers faced and defeated top-class opposition in every round of the Cup Winners' Cup. The basis of their Cup-winning performance was their spirited away performances. An Alex MacDonald goal at Ibrox saw off the French Cup Winners. After surrendering a 3-goal advantage to Sporting Lisbon, a goal by Henderson in extra time in Lisbon, which counted double, saw them through but not before the referee had forced them to participate in a penalty-kick competition which they lost. The confusion was eventually sorted out and they were confirmed as winners of the tie. Ron McKinnon suffered a double fracture of the right leg in the match in Lisbon. Torino were beaten in the Quarter-Final and German cracks Bayern Munich who included Beckenbauer, Müller, Maier and Breitner in their line-up were beaten in the Semi-Final. In the match at Ibrox, Derek Parlane — making his European debut — replaced the injured John Greig and he went on to play the game of his life, scoring the 2nd goal after a first-minute goal by Sandy Jardine had demoralised the Germans. Goals by Stein and Willie Johnston (2) in Barcelona's Nou Camp stadium appeared to have the Final wrapped up until Moscow Dynamo brought on substitute Eschtrekov after the 3rd goal. The move transformed the match and sparked off a Dynamo revival. Rangers managed to hang on but their fans impatiently anticipated the end of the game and rushed onto the field to be met by baton-wielding Spanish policemen. Rangers, at the time of their greatest triumph, were to find themselves banned from Europe for 2 seasons — later reduced to one after an appeal. The unlucky Colin Jackson missed the Final through injury.

At the end of the season Willie Waddell became General Manager and Jock Wallace took over as Team Manager. During Waddell's spell in charge Rangers had won the European Cup Winners' Cup and the League Cup. Their League record was as follows: Played 88 Won 48 Drew 15 Lost 25

League: Third
League Cup: Failed to Qualify from Section
Scottish Cup: Semi-Finalists
European Cup Winners' Cup: Winners

SCOTTISH FIRST DIVISION

September 4th:
PARTICK THISTLE (3) 3   RANGERS   (1) 2
  Gibson 2 (15, 31),   MacDonald (5),
  Coulston (30)   Stein (58)

PARTICK THISTLE: Rough; Reid, Forsyth; Smith, Campbell, Strachan; Gibson, Coulston, Bone, A. Rae, Lawrie

RANGERS: McCloy; Jardine, Mathieson; Greig, McKinnon, MacDonald; McLean, Penman, Stein, Denny (Conn), Johnston

Attendance: 22,000

September 11th:
RANGERS   (2) 2   CELTIC   (1) 3
  W. Johnston (31 pen),   Macari (8),
  Stein (45)   Dalglish (55)
                         Johnstone (89)

RANGERS: McCloy; Jardine, Mathieson; Greig, Jackson, MacDonald; McLean (Henderson), Penman, Stein, Conn, Johnston

CELTIC: Williams; Brogan, Hay; Murdoch, McNeill, Connelly; Johnstone, Lennox, Dalglish, Callaghan, Macari

Attendance: 69,000

Alfie Conn was ordered off

September 18th:
FALKIRK   (0) 0   RANGERS   (1) 3
                          Stein (7),
                          Greig 2 (78, 82)

FALKIRK: Devlin; Jones, McLaughlin; Markie, Miller, Shirra; Hoggan, Jack, Young, Ferguson, Setterington

RANGERS: McCloy; Jardine, Mathieson; Greig, McKinnon, Jackson; Penman, Conn, Stein, MacDonald, Johnston

Attendance: 20,000

Johnston missed a penalty

September 25th:
RANGERS   (0) 0   ABERDEEN   (1) 2
                          S. Murray (36),
                          Harper (77)

RANGERS: McCloy; Jardine, Mathieson; Greig, Jackson, Smith; Penman, Conn, Stein, MacDonald (McLean), Johnston

ABERDEEN: Geoghegan; Boel, Hermiston; Murray, Young, Buchan; Forrest, Robb, Harper, Willoughby, Miller

Attendance: 41,000

October 2nd:
HEARTS   (1) 2   RANGERS   (0) 1
  Murray (32), Brown (86) W. Johnston (87)

HEARTS: Cruikshank; Sneddon, Kay; Brown, Anderson, Thomson; Townsend, T. Murray, Ford, Winchester, Lynch

RANGERS: McCloy; Jardine, Mathieson; Greig, McKinnon, Jackson; Henderson, McLean (Penman), Stein, MacDonald, Johnston

Attendance: 29,000

October 9th:
RANGERS   (1) 3   EAST FIFE   (0) 0
  Jardine (2 pen), Fyfe (47),
  MacDonald (62)

RANGERS: McCloy; Greig, Mathieson; Jardine, McKinnon, Smith; Henderson, Conn, Stein, Fyfe, MacDonald

EAST FIFE: Gorman; Duncan, Clarke; Cairns, Martis, Thomson (Love); Bernard, Hamilton, Hughes, Honeyman, McQuade

Attendance: 25,000

October 13th: Scotland beat Portugal 2-1 at Hampden Park. Jardine was in the team.

October 16th:
DUNDEE UNITED   (0) 1 RANGERS   (4) 5
  Copland (90)   MacDonald 2 (10, 23),
                          Stein (20),
                          Greig (43), Jardine (53)

DUNDEE UNITED: McAlpine; Rolland, Cameron; Markland, Gray, Henry; Traynor, Reid, Copland, Gordon, Devlin (White)

RANGERS: McCloy; Greig, Mathieson; Jardine, McKinnon, Smith; Henderson, Penman, Stein, Fyfe, MacDonald

Attendance: 17,000

October 23rd:
RANGERS   (0) 4   MOTHERWELL   (0) 0
  Fyfe 2 (53, 87),
  MacDonald (66),
  Jardine (73)

RANGERS: McCloy; Greig, Mathieson; Jardine, McKinnon, Smith; Henderson, Conn, Stein, Fyfe, MacDonald

MOTHERWELL: MacRae; Whiteford, Gillespie; Forsyth, McCallum, Goldthorpe; Campbell, McClymont, Muir, McInally, Lawson

Attendance: 21,000

October 30th:
RANGERS (1) 3   KILMARNOCK (1) 1
Stein (15),   Mathie (3)
MacDonald 2 (67, 79)

RANGERS: McCloy; Greig, Mathieson; Jardine,
McKinnon, Smith; Henderson, Penman, Stein, Fyfe,
MacDonald

KILMARNOCK: Hunter; Whyte, Cairns; Maxwell,
Rodman, McGrory; McSherry, Gilmour, Mathie,
McCulloch, Cook

Attendance: 25,000

Jardine was ordered off

League positions
	P	W	D	L	F	A	Pts
1 Aberdeen	9	8	1	0	26	4	17
2 Celtic	9	8	0	1	27	7	16
3 St Johnstone	9	5	2	2	18	11	12
4 Hearts	9	4	4	1	13	9	12
5 Hibernian	9	5	1	3	18	8	11
7 RANGERS	9	5	0	4	23	12	10

November 6th:
ST JOHNSTONE (0) 1   RANGERS (0) 4
Pearson (87)   Johnston 3 (53 pen,
                                73 pen, 84 pen),
                                MacDonald (55)

ST JOHNSTONE: Donaldson; Coburn, Argue;
Rennie, Gordon, Whitelaw; Aird, Lambie, Pearson,
Connolly, Hall

RANGERS: McCloy; Greig, Mathieson; Jardine,
Jackson, Smith; Henderson, Conn, Stein, Fyfe
(Johnston), MacDonald

Attendance: 20,000

**November 10th: Scotland beat Belgium 1-0 at
Pittodrie. Jardine was in the team.**

November 13th:
RANGERS (1) 2   DUNDEE (3) 3
Johnston 2 (37, 63)   Kinninmonth (5),
                                G. Wallace (12),
                                Johnston (19)

RANGERS: McCloy; Greig, Mathieson; Jardine,
Jackson, Smith; Henderson, Conn, Stein, Johnston,
MacDonald

DUNDEE: Donaldson; Wilson, Johnston; Steele,
Phillip, Ford; Duncan, Kinninmonth, Wallace, Scott,
Wilson

Attendance: 33,200

November 20th:
MORTON (1) 1   RANGERS (2) 2
Osborne (15)   Johnston (6),
                                Greig (27)

MORTON: Sorensen; Hayes, Laughton; Lumsden,
Anderson, Clark; Smith (Gillies), Mason, Osborne,
Murphy, Chalmers

RANGERS: McCloy; Jardine, Mathieson; Greig,
Jackson, Smith; McLean (Conn), Fyfe, Stein,
MacDonald, Johnston

Attendance: 12,500

Anderson was ordered off

November 27th:
AYR UNITED (1) 1   RANGERS (2) 2
Fillipi (36)   Stein (11),
                                Henderson (39)

AYR UNITED: Stewart; Fillipi, Murphy; Fleming,
Quinn, Mitchell; Doyle, Graham, Whitehead,
McGovern (Ingram), Stevenson

RANGERS: McCloy; Jardine, Mathieson; Greig, D.
Johnstone, Smith; Henderson, Conn, Stein,
MacDonald, Johnston

Attendance: 15,000

**December 1st: Holland beat Scotland 2-1 in
Amsterdam. Jardine was in the team.**

December 4th:
RANGERS (0) 1   CLYDE (0) 0
Stein (70)

RANGERS: McCloy; Denny, Mathieson; Jardine, D.
Johnstone, Smith; Henderson, Fyfe, Stein, MacDonald,
Johnston

CLYDE: Cairney; McGoldrick, Swan; Burns,
McHugh, Glasgow; Sullivan, McGrain, McBride,
Hulston (Hastings), Aherne

Attendance: 23,000

December 11th:
DUNFERMLINE (0) 0   RANGERS (1) 2
                                Greig (5),
                                Johnston (90)

DUNFERMLINE: Arrol; Callaghan, Mercer; Fraser,
Cushley, McNicol; Paterson, Thomson, Mitchell, Scott
(Millar), Gillespie

RANGERS: McCloy; Jardine, Mathieson; Greig, D.
Johnstone, Smith; Henderson, McLean, Stein,
MacDonald, Johnston

Attendance: 14,000

**December 15th: Alan Morton and Torry Gillick
died.**

December 18th:
RANGERS (3) 3   AIRDRIE (0) 0
Stein (2), Jardine (33 pen),
Fyfe (37)

RANGERS: McCloy; Jardine, Mathieson (Henderson); Greig, Jackson, Smith; McLean, Conn, Stein, Fyfe, MacDonald

AIRDRIE: McKenzie; Jonquin, Clarke; Menzies, Delaney, D. Whiteford; Wilson, McKay, Busby, Jarvie, Cowan

Attendance: 18,000

December 25th:
HIBERNIAN (0) 0   RANGERS (0) 1
                      Stein (89½)

HIBERNIAN: Herriot; Brownlie, Schaedler; McEwan, Stanton, Blackley; Edwards, Hamilton, O'Rourke, Cropley, Duncan

RANGERS: McCloy; Jardine, Denny; Greig, Jackson, Smith; McLean, Conn, Stein, MacDonald, Johnston

Attendance: 25,000

League positions

	P	W	D	L	F	A	Pts
1 Celtic	17	15	1	1	55	15	31
2 Aberdeen	17	14	2	1	53	10	30
3 RANGERS	17	12	0	5	40	18	24
4 Hibernian	17	10	3	4	30	14	23
5 Dundee	17	8	5	4	30	19	21

January 1st:
RANGERS (0) 2   PARTICK THISTLE (1) 1
  Greig (85),   McQuade (44)
  D. Johnstone (90)

RANGERS: McCloy; Jardine, Denny; Greig, Jackson, Smith; McLean, Johnston, Stein, A. MacDonald, I. MacDonald (D. Johnstone)

PARTICK THISTLE: Rough; Hansen, Forsyth; Glavin, Campbell, Strachan; McQuade, Gibson (T. Rae), Coulston, A. Rae, Lawrie

Attendance: 38,200

January 3rd:
CELTIC (1) 2   RANGERS (0) 1
  Johnstone (35),   Stein (81)
  Brogan (90)

CELTIC: Connaghan; Hay, Brogan; Dalglish, McNeill, Connelly; Johnstone, Lennox, Deans, Callaghan, Hood

RANGERS: McCloy; Jardine, Mathieson; Greig, Jackson, Smith; McLean, D. Johnstone, Stein, MacDonald, Johnston

Attendance: 70,000

Rangers were stunned by an injury-time winner from Brogan. With the game ebbing towards the draw McNeill took a free kick. The ball came to Hood and, as he brought it under control, Brogan began a run into the area which he timed perfectly to meet Hood's lob and glance the ball

home. Rangers hardly deserved to lose. Johnstone opened the scoring in 35 minutes. From the left side of the area Hood flighted the ball to the far side and there was Johnstone standing completely unmarked so that he only had to stoop to beat McCloy with a header. With 9 minutes left Rangers were at last rewarded with the equalising goal. Mathieson pushed the ball forward to Stein. Connaghan put his hands to the shot but could not stop it. Brogan's bolt from the blue of a goal brought the game to its stirring end.

January 8th:
RANGERS (2) 3   FALKIRK (0) 1
  Greig (2), Jackson (9),   Shirra (60)
  I. MacDonald (88)

RANGERS: McCloy; Jardine, Mathieson; Greig, Jackson, Smith; McLean, Johnston, Stein, A. MacDonald, I. MacDonald

FALKIRK: Rennie; Abel, Jones; Bruce (McLeod), Markie, Gibson; Hoggan, Ferguson, Somner, Shirra, Setterington

Attendance: 20,000

January 15th:
ABERDEEN 0   RANGERS 0

ABERDEEN: Geoghegan; G. Murray, Hermiston; S. Murray, Young, M. Buchan; Miller, Robb, Harper, Willoughby, Graham

RANGERS: McCloy; Jardine, Mathieson; Greig, D. Johnstone, Smith; McLean, Johnston, Stein (Jackson), A. MacDonald, I. MacDonald

Attendance: 36,000

January 14th: Willie Henderson walked out of Ibrox — he said that he would not return.

January 22nd:
RANGERS (0) 6   HEARTS (0) 0
  W. Johnston (47), Greig (61),
  D. Johnstone 3 (67, 76, 87),
  Conn (78)

RANGERS: McCloy; Jardine, Mathieson; Greig, Jackson, Smith; McLean, Conn, D. Johnstone, A. MacDonald, Johnston

HEARTS: Garland; Sneddon, Kay; Brown, Anderson, Thomson; Townsend, Renton, Ford, Winchester, Murray (Lynch)

Attendance: 35,000

January 29th:
EAST FIFE (0) 0   RANGERS (1) 1
                      D. Johnstone (35)

EAST FIFE: Gorman; Duncan, McQuade; McLaren (Dailey), Martis, Clarke; Honeyman, Love, Hughes, Hamilton, McPhee

RANGERS: McCloy; Jardine, Mathieson; Greig, Jackson, Smith; McLean, Conn, D. Johnstone, A. MacDonald, Johnston

Attendance: 12,018

Johnston missed a penalty

February 12th:
RANGERS (0) 1   DUNDEE UNITED (0) 0
  Smith (84)

RANGERS: McCloy; Jardine, Mathieson; Greig, Jackson, Smith; McLean, Conn, D. Johnstone, A. MacDonald, I. MacDonald (Denny)

DUNDEE UNITED: McAlpine; Rolland, J. Cameron; Markland, Smith, Gray; Kopel, Knox, K. Cameron, Fleming, Traynor (Copland)

Attendance: 25,000

February 19th:
MOTHERWELL (1) 2   RANGERS (0) 0
  Heron (8), Lawson (65)

MOTHERWELL: MacRae; Muir, Wark; Forsyth, McCallum, Watson (Goldthorpe); Campbell, McInally, McCabe, Lawson, Heron

RANGERS: McCloy; Jardine, Miller; Greig, Jackson, Smith; McLean, Conn, Stein, D. Johnstone, I. MacDonald (A. MacDonald)

Attendance: 16,192

League positions

	P	W	D	L	F	A	Pts
1 Celtic	24	21	2	1	73	18	44
2 Aberdeen	25	18	5	2	67	19	41
3 RANGERS	25	17	1	7	54	24	35
4 Hibernian	25	13	5	7	43	25	31
5 Dundee	24	10	10	4	43	25	30

March 4th:
KILMARNOCK (0) 1   RANGERS (0) 2
  Mathie (55)   Jardine (48),
                         Conn (62)

KILMARNOCK: Hunter; Dickson, Cairns; Maxwell, Rodman, McGrory; McSherry, Gilmour, Mathie, Morrison, Cook

RANGERS: McCloy; Jardine, Mathieson; Greig, Jackson, Smith; McLean, Conn, Stein, MacDonald, Johnston

Attendance: 18,000

March 11th:
RANGERS (1) 2   ST JOHNSTONE (0) 0
  D. Johnstone (39),
  McLean (60)

RANGERS: McCloy; Denny, Mathieson; Greig, Jackson, Smith; McLean, Conn, D. Johnstone, Johnston, I. MacDonald (Fyfe)

ST JOHNSTONE: Robertson; Lambie, Coburn; Rennie, Gordon, Argue; Leslie, Rooney, Pearson, Connolly, Fraser

Attendance: 25,000

March 13th: Henderson was back at Ibrox after his walk out.

March 15th: Rangers' bid of £45,000 for John Connolly of St Johnstone was rejected.

March 15th: The English League beat the Scottish League 3-2 at Middlesbrough. Jardine and Stein were in the team. Stein scored one of the goals.

March 25th:
RANGERS (1) 1   MORTON (0) 2
  Jackson (45)   Chalmers (70),
                     Jackson o.g. (85)

RANGERS: McCloy; Denny, Mathieson; Conn, Jackson, Smith; Penman (Fyfe), D. Johnstone, Stein, A. MacDonald, I. MacDonald

MORTON: Sorensen; Shevlane, Laughton; Lumsden, Anderson, Rankin; Gillies (Osborne), Mason, Chalmers, Murphy, Armstrong

Attendance: 16,000

April 8th:
CLYDE (1) 1   RANGERS (0) 1
  Millar (44)   Johnston (49)

CLYDE: McCulloch; Anderson, McHugh; Houston, McVie, Burns; McGrain, Miller, Flanagan, Hulston (McColligan), Sullivan

RANGERS: McCloy; Jardine, Mathieson; Greig, Jackson, Smith; McLean, Parlane, D. Johnstone, Conn (Fyfe), Johnston

Attendance: 10,000

April 10th:
DUNDEE (0) 2   RANGERS (0) 0
  I. Scott (54), Stewart (57)

DUNDEE: Hewitt; R. Wilson, Johnston; Stewart, Phillip, Houston; Duncan, Ford, I. Scott, J. Scott, Lambie

RANGERS: McCloy; Jardine, Mathieson; Greig, Jackson, Smith; Henderson, McLean, Stein, Parlane, A. MacDonald

Attendance: 12,000

April 22nd:
AIRDRIE (0) 0   RANGERS (3) 3
                    Penman 2 (16, 29),
                    Fyfe (27)

AIRDRIE: McKenzie; Caldwell, Clarke; Menzies, McKinlay, Whiteford; Wilson, Walker, Busby, Jarvie, Cowan

RANGERS: McCloy; Denny, Miller; Conn, Jackson, Smith; Henderson, Penman, Fyfe, D. Johnstone, A. MacDonald

Attendance: 10,000

April 27th:

RANGERS	(2) 3	DUNFERMLINE	(3) 4
A. MacDonald (13, 14),		Mackie (9),	
Stein (59)		Thomson (18)	
		Jardine o.g. (45),	
		Leishman (81)	

RANGERS: McCloy; Jardine, Mathieson; Conn, Jackson, Smith; Henderson, D. Johnstone, Stein, Johnston, A. MacDonald

DUNFERMLINE: Arrol; Callaghan, Lunn; Fraser, McNichol, Leishman; K. Thomson, Mitchell, Mackie, Scott, Gillespie

Attendance: 3,000

April 29th:

RANGERS	(0) 1	HIBERNIAN	(0) 2
D. Johnstone (69)		O'Rourke (52 pen),	
		Auld (72)	

RANGERS: McCloy; Jardine, Mathieson; Penman, Jackson (Denny), Smith; McLean, D. Johnstone, Stein, MacDonald, Johnston

HIBERNIAN: Herriot; Brownlie, Schaedler; Stanton, Black, Blackley; Auld, Hazel, Gordon, O'Rourke, McGhee (McEwan)

Attendance: 10,000

May 1st:

RANGERS	(1) 4	AYR UNITED	(2) 2
Conn (23), Penman (58),		Ingram 2 (22, 40)	
MacDonald (74), Fyfe (86)			

RANGERS: McCoy; Jardine, Mathieson; Conn, D. Johnstone, Smith; McLean (Fyfe), Penman, Stein, A. MacDonald, Johnston

AYR UNITED: A. McLean; McFadzean, Murphy; McAnespie, Quinn, Mitchell; Doyle, Graham, Ingram, McGregor, McCulloch

Attendance: 3,000

'Prime Minister' Ian McMillan, influential in the sixties.

Scottish First Division

	P	W	D	L	F	A	Pts
1 Celtic	34	28	4	2	96	28	60
2 Aberdeen	34	21	8	5	80	26	50
3 RANGERS	34	21	2	11	71	38	44
4 Hibernian	34	19	6	9	62	34	44
5 Dundee	34	14	13	7	59	38	41
6 Hearts	34	13	13	8	53	49	39
7 Partick Thistle	34	12	10	12	53	54	34
8 St Johnstone	34	12	8	14	52	58	32
9 Dundee United	34	12	7	15	55	70	31
10 Motherwell	34	11	7	16	49	69	29
11 Kilmarnock	34	11	6	17	49	64	28
12 Ayr United	34	9	10	15	40	58	28
13 Morton	34	10	7	17	46	52	27
14 Falkirk	34	10	7	17	44	60	27
15 Airdrie	34	7	12	15	44	76	26
16 East Fife	34	5	15	14	34	61	25
17 Clyde	34	7	10	17	33	66	24
18 Dunfermline	34	7	9	18	31	50	23

May 1st: Dave Smith was named as Scotland's Player of the Year.

May 2nd: Rangers freed Henderson, Semple, Morrison, Pirrie and Kenny Watson.

May 24th: Colin Jackson was ruled out of the Cup Winners' Cup Final with an injury.

June 7th: Willie Waddell became Rangers' General Manager. Jock Wallace became Team Manager.

June 16th: Moscow Dynamo's protest was rejected and the result of the Cup Winners' Cup Final stood but Rangers were barred from all U.E.F.A. competitions for 2 seasons by a European Union Disciplinary Committee in Brussels.

LEAGUE CUP

August 14th: At Ibrox

CELTIC	(0) 2	RANGERS	(0) 0
Johnstone (67),			
Dalglish (70 pen)			

CELTIC: Williams; Craig, Hay; Murdoch, McNeill, Connelly; Johnstone, Lennox, Dalglish, Callaghan, Hughes

RANGERS: McCloy; Jardine, Mathieson; Greig, McKinnon, Jackson; McLean, Conn, D. Johnstone (Stein), Johnston, MacDonald

Attendance: 72,500

On this performance Murdoch disproved the old axiom that they never come back. Johnstone's individual genius provided a springboard for attacking operations. In 67 minutes Celtic took the lead — Lennox sending a corner-kick to Johnstone and the winger shooting through a chink in the packed defence. 3 minutes later Hughes was pulled down for what was undoubtedly a penalty. Billy McNeill signalled for young Dalglish to take the kick in his first Old Firm game. He showed no strain and he even took time to lace a boot tighter before he placed the ball away from McCloy. Jackson and McKinnon both played well in defeat.

August 18th:
RANGERS (3) 4   AYR UNITED (0) 0
D. Johnstone 2 (2, 38),
Stein (40), McLean (86 pen)

RANGERS: McCloy; Jardine, Mathieson; Greig, McKinnon, Jackson; McLean, Conn, Stein, D. Johnstone, Johnston

AYR UNITED: Gilmour; McFadzean, Murphy; Quinn, McAleer, Mitchell; Reynolds, McGovern, Lannon, Campbell, Doyle

Attendance: 25,000

August 21st:
RANGERS (0) 2   MORTON (0) 0
D. Johnstone (47),
MacDonald (87)

RANGERS: McCloy; Jardine, Mathieson; Greig, McKinnon, Jackson; McLean, Denny (MacDonald), Stein, D. Johnstone, Johnston

MORTON: Sorensen; Hayes, McDerment; Lumsden, Anderson, Laughton; Booth, Mason, Osborne, Murphy, Nelson

Attendance: 33,000

August 25th:
AYR UNITED (0) 0   RANGERS (2) 4
Stein 2 (39, 76),
MacDonald (6),
D. Johnstone (61)

AYR UNITED: Stewart; Fillipi, Murphy; Fleming, Quinn, Mitchell; Doyle, McGovern, Ingram, Whitehead, Rough

RANGERS: McCloy; Jardine, Mathieson; Greig, McKinnon, Jackson; McLean, MacDonald (Conn), Stein, D. Johnstone, Johnston

Attendance: 15,000

August 28th:
RANGERS (0) 0 CELTIC (0) 3
Dalglish (48), Callaghan (71),
Lennox (82)

RANGERS: McCloy; Jardine, Mathieson; Greig, McKinnon, Jackson; McLean, MacDonald (Conn), Stein, D. Johnstone, Johnston

CELTIC: Williams; Brogan, Hay; Murdoch (Hood), McNeill, Connelly; Johnstone, Lennox, Dalglish, Callaghan, Macari

Attendance: 74,000

Celtic were undisputed masters. They did not have a bad player and Billy McNeill was majestic.

September 1st:
MORTON (0) 0   RANGERS (0) 1
Stein (76)

MORTON: Sorensen; Hayes, McDerment; Lumsden, Anderson, Laughton; Brand, Mason (Lavelle), Osborne, Murphy, Mulhall

RANGERS: McCloy; Jardine, Mathieson; Greig, McKinnon, Jackson; McLean, MacDonald, Stein, D. Johnstone (Penman), Johnston

Attendance: 7,000

League Cup Section Table

	P	W	D	L	F	A	Pts
Celtic	6	5	0	1	13	2	10
RANGERS	6	4	0	2	11	5	8
Morton	6	2	1	3	4	5	5
Ayr United	6	0	1	5	2	18	1

SCOTTISH CUP

February 5th: Third Round
FALKIRK (1) 2   RANGERS (1) 2
Jack (34),   D. Johnstone (42),
Ferguson (72)   Greig (49)

FALKIRK: Donaldson; Jones, Gibson; Cattenach (Harley), Markie, Shirra; Hoggan, Ferguson, Jack, Young, McLeod

RANGERS: McCloy; Jardine, Mathieson; Greig, Jackson, Smith; McLean, Conn, D. Johnstone, MacDonald, Johnston

Attendance: 20,000

February 9th: Third Round Replay
RANGERS (1) 2   FALKIRK (0) 0
Stein (2), McLean (76)

RANGERS: McCloy; Jardine, Mathieson; Greig, D. Johnstone, Smith; McLean, Conn, Stein, A. MacDonald, Johnston

FALKIRK: Donaldson; Jones, Shirra; Markie, Wheatley, Gibson; J. Scott, Ferguson, Jack (McLeod), Young, Harley

Attendance: 43,000

Both Johnston and Jack missed penalties

February 25th: Fourth Round
ST MIRREN (0) 1   RANGERS (0) 4
McLeod (86)   MacDonald (55),
                                 Stein (56),
                                 McLean 2 (62, 89 pen)

ST MIRREN: Stevenson; McLaughlin, Munro; Millar, McQueen, Murray; Borland, McLeod, Prentice, Bryceland, McKean

RANGERS: McCloy; Jardine, Mathieson; Greig, D. Johnstone, Smith; McLean, Conn, Stein, MacDonald, Johnston

Attendance: 29,376

March 18th: Fifth Round
MOTHERWELL   (0) 2   RANGERS   (1) 2
  Heron (59), Campbell (73)   MacDonald (33),
                              Stein (83)

MOTHERWELL: Fallon; Muir, Whiteford; Forsyth, McCallum, Watson; Campbell, McInally, McCabe, Lawson, Heron

RANGERS: McCloy; Jardine, Mathieson; Greig, Jackson, Smith; McLean, D. Johnstone, Stein, MacDonald, Johnston

Attendance: 28,500

March 27th: Fifth Round Replay
RANGERS   (2) 4   MOTHERWELL   (1) 2
  Fallon o.g. (8),   Lawson 2 (1, 65)
  Stein 2 (12, 82),
  McLean (77)

RANGERS: McCloy; Jardine, Mathieson; Greig, Jackson, Smith; McLean, D. Johnstone, Stein, MacDonald, Johnston

MOTHERWELL: Fallon; Muir, Whiteford; Forsyth, McCallum, Watson; Campbell, McInally, McCabe (Goldthorpe), Lawson, Heron

Attendance: 50,000

April 15th: Semi-Final   At Hampden Park
HIBERNIAN   (0) 1   RANGERS   (1) 1
  O'Rourke (48)   MacDonald (41)

HIBERNIAN: Herriot; Brownlie, Schaedler; Stanton, Black, Blackley; Edwards, O'Rourke, Baker, Gordon, Duncan —McEwan

RANGERS: McCloy; Jardine, Mathieson; Greig (Denny), Jackson, Smith; McLean, D. Johnstone, Stein, MacDonald, Johnston

Attendance: 75,884

Greig stayed on the field for 30 pain-wracked minutes before being replaced by Denny. Both Semi-finalists appeared to be affected by tension and played well below their best. One of the few players to enhance his reputation was Derek Johnstone. Dave Smith made a fine contribution too and it was clear that Rangers had expended their energy in their challenge before the interval. Alex MacDonald scored his side's goal in 41 minutes and at that time it looked as if it would take his side through. Hibs were a disappointing side in the first half and Blackley and Black saved many an awkward situation with their timely

interventions. In the second half Stanton was more positive and 3 minutes after the interval he passed for O'Rourke to score the equaliser.

April 24th: Semi-Final Replay   At Hampden Park
RANGERS   (0) 0   HIBERNIAN   (1) 2
                          Stanton (12),
                          Edwards (67)

RANGERS: McCloy; Jardine, Mathieson; Parlane (Denny), Jackson, Smith; McLean, D. Johnstone, Stein, MacDonald, Johnston

HIBERNIAN: Herriot; Brownlie, Schaedler; Stanton, Black, Blackley; Edwards, Hazel, Gordon, O'Rourke, Duncan —Baker

Attendance: 57,457

Hibs, who had been knocked out of the Cup by Rangers in the 3 previous seasons, gained sweet revenge in this replay. They qualified by a margin more comfortable than the 2 goals suggest. Rangers were only a shadow of themselves and they were not allowed to recover after losing a 12th-minute goal to Pat Stanton, Hibs' inspiring captain. Stanton's shot did not have his full force behind it but it struck Jackson's outstretched leg, bounced awkwardly and swerved deceptively past McCloy. Rangers lost young Parlane after 50 minutes through injury. Hazel headed an Edwards free-kick against the crossbar. Rangers survived more heavy pressure but when Gordon swung a cross to Hazel in 67 minutes the latter touched it back for Edwards to shoot a 2nd goal.

CUP WINNERS CUP

September 15th: First Round First Leg
RENNES (France)   (0) 1   RANGERS   (0) 1
  Redon (78)   Johnston (68)

RENNES: Auboir; Cosnard, Cedolin; Chlosta, Cardiet, Garcia (Redon); Keruzore, Terrier, Mosjov (Periault), Betta, Lenoir

RANGERS: McCloy; Jardine, Mathieson; Greig, McKinnon, Jackson; McLean, MacDonald, Stein (Denny), Penman, Johnston

Attendance: 20,000

September 28th: First Round Second Leg
RANGERS   (1) 1   RENNES   (0) 0
  MacDonald (38)

RANGERS: McCloy; Jardine, Mathieson; Greig, McKinnon, Jackson; Henderson, Conn, Stein, MacDonald, Johnston

RENNES: Aubour; Cosnard, Cardiet; Cedolin, Chlosta, Toublant; Terrier, Garcia, Keruzore (Redon), Betta, Lenoir

Attendance: 40,000

Rangers won 2-1 on aggregate

October 20th: Second Round First Leg
RANGERS   (3) 3   SPORTING LISBON   (0) 2
Stein 2 (9, 19),   Chic (70), Gomes (86)
Henderson (28)

RANGERS: McCloy; Greig, Mathieson; Jardine,
McKinnon, Smith; Henderson, Penman (Conn), Stein,
Fyfe, MacDonald

SPORTING: Damas; Laranjiero (Lourenco), Hilario;
Goncalves (Gomes), Calo, Jose Carlos; Chico, Nelson,
Yazalde, Vagner, Dinis

Attendance: 50,000

November 3rd: Second Round Second Leg
SPORTING LISBON   (2) 4   RANGERS   (1) 3
Yazalde (26), Tome (37),   Stein 2 (27, 46),
Gomes (83), Perez (114)   Henderson (100)
                   After Extra Time

SPORTING: Damas; Pedro Gomes, Hilario; Tome,
Talo, Laranjiero; Vagner, Lourenco, Yazalde, Peres,
Dinis (Marinho)

RANGERS: McCloy; Greig, Mathieson; Jardine,
McKinnon (Smith), Jackson; Henderson, Conn, Stein,
Johnston (McLean), MacDonald

Attendance: 60,000

McKinnon was carried off with a double fracture of the
right leg. After some delay it was decided that extra-time
away goals counted double, and Rangers were through

March 8th: Quarter-Final First Leg
TORINO   (0) 1   RANGERS   (1) 1
Toschi (61)   Johnston (12)

TORINO: Castellini; Mozzini, Fossati (Toschi);
Zecchin, Cereser, Agroppi; Rampanti, Ferrini, Pulici,
Sala, Bui

RANGERS: McCloy; Jardine, Mathieson; Greig,
Jackson, Smith; McLean, D. Johnstone, Stein,
MacDonald, Johnston

Attendance: 35,000

Rangers raised their game to frustrate Torino in the
Communale Stadium, to put themselves well within reach
of the Semi-Finals.

March 22nd: Quarter-Final Second Leg
RANGERS   (0) 1   TORINO   (0) 0
MacDonald (46)

RANGERS: McCloy; Jardine, Mathieson; Greig,
Jackson, Smith; McLean, D. Johnstone, Stein,
MacDonald, Johnston

TORINO: Castellini; Lombardo, Fossati (Rossi); Puia,
Cereser, Ferrini; Luppi, Crivelli, Bui (Barberes),
Rampanti, Toschi

Attendance: 65,000

Rangers won 2-1 on aggregate

April 5th: Semi-Final First Leg
BAYERN MUNICH   (1) 1   RANGERS   (0) 1
Breitner (23)   Zobel o.g. (49)

BAYERN: Maier; Hansen, Breitner; Schwarzenbeck,
Beckenbauer, Roth (Schneider); Krauthausen, Zobel,
Müller, Hoeness, Suchnholz

RANGERS: McCloy; Jardine, Mathieson; Greig,
Jackson, Smith; McLean, D. Johnstone, Stein,
MacDonald, Johnston

Attendance: 40,000

This was Rangers' best performance in Europe. They
survived a stricky opening spell, an early setback when
Bayern scored in 23 minutes and some ridiculous
refereeing decisions before levelling a game they were
unlucky not to win. From the start they were aggesssive
and never allowed the German side to settle into their
normal fluid rhythm. Gerd Müller, who was well marked
throughout by Colin Jackson, headed against the crossbar
in 8 minutes but the Bayern goal, quite significantly, came
from a defender. Their International full-back Breitner
shot well away from McCloy from just outside the 6-yard
box after having broken downfield from deep in his own
half. Rangers' defence was magnificent. Dave Smith swept
majestically and Derek Johnstone marked Hoeness out of
the game. Rangers equalised after only 3 minutes of the
second half when Stein took the ball wide of Maier before
shooting hard across the face of the goal. Zobel, back
helping his defence, met it with his head and the ball raged
past his goalkeeper. Rangers finished the game the better
side. Twice, Mathieson, up with his attack, brought out
fine saves from Maier.

April 19th: Semi-Final Second Leg
RANGERS   (2) 2   BAYERN MUNICH   (0) 0
Jardine (1), Parlane (23)

RANGERS: McCloy; Jardine, Mathieson; Parlane,
Jackson, Smith; McLean, D. Johnstone, Stein,
MacDonald, Johnston

BAYERN: Maier; Hansen, Breitner (Rybarczyk);
Schwarzenbeck, Beckenbauer, Roth; Schneider, Zobel,
Müller, Hoeness, Koppenhofer

Attendance: 80,000

Rangers were on the brink of success by decisively beating
Bayern Munich. The advantage of their away goal
counting double never looked like being needed, so
convincing were the Ibrox team. Bayern were demoralised
by a first-minute goal by Sandy Jardine. Derek Parlane,
making his European debut as stand-in for the injured

John Greig, scored the 2nd goal in 23 minutes and played the game of his life. Johnstone and Jackson kept a stranglehold on Muller and Hoeness. Muller was hardly given a kick of the ball. It was a badly placed pass by Beckenbauer that Derek Johnstone picked up in the opening minute. He prodded the ball through to Jardine who hit it with his left foot and its flight obviously deceived Maier who stood still expecting it to go past. In the 5th minute a Stein header rebounded from the crossbar. In the 23rd minute Parlane first-timed a Willie Johnston corner-kick high into the net for the 2nd goal. A minute after the interval McCloy had a brilliant save when he touched a Hoeness shot onto a post. Rangers played well within themselves afterwards.

May 24th: Final   In Barcelona
RANGERS (2) 3   MOSCOW DYNAMO (0) 2
   Stein (24),   Eschtrekov (59),
   W. Johnston 2 (40, 49)   Makovikov (87)

RANGERS: McCloy; Jardine, Mathieson; Greig, D. Johnstone, Smith; McLean, Conn, Stein, MacDonald, Johnston

MOSCOW DYNAMO: Pilgui; Basalev, Dolmatov; Zykov, Dobbonosov (Gerschkovitch), Zhukov; Baidatchini, Jakubik (Estrekov), Sabo, Makovikov, Evryuzhikbin

Attendance: 35,000

Rangers found the rainbow's end when they beat Moscow Dynamo in the Nou Camp Stadium. Rangers' future in Europe may have been jeopardised by hostility that marred a night that should have rated as their finest hour. Intermittent invasions of the field had earlier threatened to have the game abandoned. Then only a minute from time the most highly excited contingent among the 20,000-plus Rangers' supporters impatiently anticipated the end and rushed onto the field. After the match Konstantin Beskov, Dynamo's senior coach, claimed that his players were intimidated by the Rangers' supporters who spilled onto the pitch before play had ended and appealed to the European Football Union to have the game replayed. The Ibrox players were not even accorded the honour of having the trophy presented to them with the medals on the field. This was done somewhat shamefully in an underground dressing-room. Rangers were deserved winners for their performance during the first 50 minutes with Dave Smith conducting the play in remarkably stylish fashion from deep in defence. It was his precise passes that led to the first 2 goals. The first goal came in 24 minutes. From the middle of his own half Smith prodded the ball forward for Stein to run on to it just at the edge of the penalty-area and the centre-forward hit a fierce drive past Pilgui. Smith ventured much further downfield 5 minutes before the interval to set up the 2nd goal. With the Russians retreating before him Smith chipped the ball over onto the head of Willie Johnston who flicked it into the net. 3 minutes after the interval a clearance from McCloy spun to Johnston who ran on unchallenged and

stroked it home. Rangers appeared to have the game wrapped up until the Russians brought on substitute Eschtrekov for Jakubik after the 3rd goal. It transformed the Russians as the replacement scored a goal almost immediately that sparked off a Dynamo revival. In a cliff-hanging finish Smith kicked off the line, Jardine almost scored an own goal and with 3 minutes to go Makavikov scored Dynamo's 2nd goal.

APPEARANCES

	League	League Cup	Scottish Cup	Cup Winners Cup
McCloy	34	6	7	9
Jardine	31	6	7	9
Mathieson	30	6	7	9
Greig	28	6	6	8
McKinnon	7	6	-	4
A. MacDonald	31+1S	4+1S	7	9
McLean	21+1	6	7	6+1S
Penman	10+1	0+1	-	2
Stein	28	5+1S	6	9
Conn	21+2	2+2	3	3+1S
Johnston	23+1	6	7	8
Jackson	24+1S	6	5	7
Smith	30	-	7	6+1S
Henderson	13+2	-	-	3
Fyfe	9+4	-	-	1
Johnstone	16+1	6	7	5
Denny	7+2	1	0+2S	0+1S
I. MacDonald	7	-	-	-
Miller	2	-	-	-
Parlane	2	-	1	1
Neef	-	-	-	-

GOALSCORERS

League: A. MacDonald 11, Stein 11, W. Johnston 11 (4 pens), Greig 8, D. Johnstone 7, Fyfe 6, Jardine 5 (2 pens), Conn 3, Penman 3, Jackson 2, Henderson 1, I. MacDonald 1, Smith 1, McLean 1

League Cup: D. Johnstone 4, Stein 4, A. MacDonald 2, McLean 1 (pen)

Scottish Cup: Stein 5, McLean 4 (1 pen), A. MacDonald 3, D. Johnstone 1, Greig 1, Own Goal 1

Cup Winners Cup: Stein 5, W. Johnston 4, A. MacDonald 2, Henderson 2, Parlane 1, Jardine 1, Own Goal 1

Rangers won the Scottish Cup for the 21st time in 1976 when they defeated Hearts 3-1 at Hampden Park before 85,000 spectators. Here manager Jock Wallace and Chairman Rae Simpson join the players in celebration.

Season 1972–73

After a poor start which saw them lose 3 of their first 5 matches, Rangers lost only one of their remaining 29 games. But even that performance, their best for 5 seasons, wasn't enough to prevent Celtic winning their 8th consecutive League Title. In a season of major changes Colin Stein and Willie Johnston, whose periods of suspension were becoming ever longer, were transferred to English League football and Quinton Young, Joe Mason and Tom Forsyth were brought to Ibrox. Houston, Hamilton and Scott were also signed at the end of the season. Jardine and Mathieson were ever-presents and McCloy missed only one match. Derek Parlane finished as top scorer with 19 goals. At the end of the season Ron McKinnon was given a free transfer.

Rangers reached the Semi-Final of the League Cup. They were forced to take the field without the unfit John Greig. It was a handicap they could not overcome and John Brownlie's 70th-minute goal took Hibs into the Final in which they beat Celtic. Earlier in the competition the Ibrox team suffered embarrassing home defeats at the hands (or feet) of both St Mirren and Stenhousemuir.

In their centenary year and Jock Wallace's first season as team manager Rangers did win the Scottish Cup for the first time since 1966. Dundee United, Hibernian and Airdrie were beaten in the early rounds. 2 goals from Derek Parlane gave Rangers a Semi-Final victory over Ayr United. As a result of a new disciplinary clampdown Parlane received a booking for running off the field to celebrate. Alfie Conn was preferred to Dave Smith for the Final against Celtic and he scored a sensational goal 20 seconds after the interval to put Rangers 2-1 ahead. After Celtic drew level through a penalty, Tom Forsyth stabbed home what proved to be the winning goal in the 60th minute following a McLean free-kick and a Johnstone header which struck a post and rolled agonisingly along the goal-line.

Banned from Europe, Rangers faced the mighty Ajax of Amsterdam over 2 legs for the Super Cup — a new competition between the winners of the European Cup and the European Cup Winners' Cup. Although defeated in both matches, Rangers were far from dishonoured.

> League: Runners-up
> League Cup: Semi-Finalists
> Scottish Cup: Winners

SCOTTISH FIRST DIVISION

September 2nd:
AYR UNITED (2) 2   RANGERS (1) 1
  Doyle (8), Ingram (36)   Johnston (3)

AYR UNITED: McLean; Fillipi, Murphy; McAnespie, Quinn, Fleming; Doyle, Graham (McCulloch), Ingram, McGovern, Stevenson

RANGERS: McCloy; Jardine, Mathieson; Greig, Jackson, D. Johnstone; McLean, Denny, Johnstone, Stein, Fyfe (MacDonald)

Attendance: 14,500

Willie Johnston made a gesture at the Rangers fans

September 9th:
RANGERS (1) 2 PARTICK THISTLE (1) 1
  MacDonald (41),   Forsyth (29 pen)
  Johnston (69)

246

RANGERS: McCloy; Jardine, Mathieson; Greig, Jackson, Smith; McLean, Denny, D. Johnstone, MacDonald, Johnston

PARTICK THISTLE: Rough; Reid, Forsyth; Glavin, Clark, Strachan; McQuade, Coulston, T. Rae, A. Rae, Lawrie (C. Smith)

Attendance: 28,000

Willie Johnston was ordered off

September 16th: At Hampden Park
CELTIC   (2) 3   RANGERS   (0) 1
  Dalglish (2),   Greig (90)
  Johnstone (17),
  Macari (49)

CELTIC: Williams; McGrain, McCluskey; Murdoch, McNeill, Connelly; Johnstone (Hood), Dalglish, Deans, Macari, Callaghan

RANGERS: McCloy; Jardine, Mathieson; Greig, Jackson, Smith; Stein, Denny, Johnstone, MacDonald, Johnston (Conn)

Attendance: 50,416

September 20th: Alfie Conn asked for a transfer.

September 21st: Willie Johnston was banned for 9 weeks for his last ordering-off offence.

September 23rd:
RANGERS   (0) 1   FALKIRK   (0) 0
  McLean (47 pen)

RANGERS: McCloy; Jardine, Mathieson; Greig, Jackson, Smith; McLean, Parlane, Johnstone, MacDonald, Johnston

FALKIRK: Donaldson; Kennedy, Shirra; Markie, McMillan, J. Kennedy; Hoggan, Harley, Scott, Young (Jack), McLeod

Attendance: 12,000

September 30th:
KILMARNOCK   (1) 2   RANGERS   (1) 1
  Morrison 2 (43, 47)   McLean (29)

KILMARNOCK: Stewart; Whyte, Robertson; Gilmour, Rodman, Maxwell; Stevenson, Smith, Morrison, McSherry, Cook

RANGERS: McCloy; Jardine, Mathieson; Greig, Jackson, Smith; McLean, Parlane, Johnstone, Conn (Stein), MacDonald

Attendance: 12,500

October 5th: Colin Stein joined Coventry City in a deal valued at £140,000. Rangers received £90,000 cash plus former Ayr United winger Quinton Young.

October 7th:
RANGERS   (1) 1   MORTON   (0) 1
  Fyfe (23)   Gillies (56)

RANGERS: McCloy; Denny, Mathieson; Greig, Jackson, Donaldson (Parlane); Fyfe, Jardine, Johnstone, MacDonald, Young

MORTON: Sorensen; Hayes, Shevlane; Rankin, Anderson (Osborne), Clark; Mason, Gillies, Christiansen, Murphy, Armstrong

Attendance: 15,000

October 9th: Rangers signed Joe Mason from Morton.

October 11th: Tom Forsyth was signed from Motherwell for £40,000.

October 13th: Rangers made a bid for Ken Mackie of Dunfermline.

October 14th:
MOTHERWELL   (0) 0   RANGERS   (1) 2
                                    Young (10),
                                    Parlane (61 pen)

MOTHERWELL: MacRae; Whiteford, Wark; Watson, McCallum, Goodwin; Gray, Martin, McCabe, Lawson, Heron (McInally)

RANGERS: McCloy; Jardine, Mathieson; Greig, Johnstone, Smith; Conn, Forsyth, Parlane, Mason, Young

Attendance: 17,621

October 14th: Mackie rejected Rangers' move after their £50,000 bid.

October 21st:
ARBROATH   (0) 1   RANGERS   (0) 2
  Pirie (56)   Parlane (83),
                                    Mason (89)

ARBROATH: Marshall; Milne, McAlpine; Cargill, Waddell, Winchester; Sellars, Cant, Pirie, Rylance, Payne

RANGERS: Neef; Jardine, Mathieson; Greig, Johnstone, Smith; Conn, Forsyth, Parlane, Mason, Young

Attendance: 8,400

October 28th:
RANGERS   (2) 5   ST JOHNSTONE   (1) 1
  Johnstone (2),   Muir (13)
  Conn 2 (42, 80),
  Parlane 2 (73, 84)

RANGERS: McCloy; Jardine, Mathieson; Greig, Johnstone, Smith; Conn (Donaldson), Forsyth, Parlane, Mason, Young

ST JOHNSTONE: Donaldson; Lambie, Argue; Smith, Rennie, Rooney; Hall, Muir, Pearson, Mercer (McPhee), Hotson

Attendance: 20,000

League positions

	P	W	D	L	F	A	Pts
1 Celtic	9	7	1	1	23	8	15
2 Dundee United	9	7	0	2	19	11	14
3 Hibernian	9	6	1	2	19	10	13
4 Aberdeen	9	4	3	2	18	12	11
5 RANGERS	9	5	1	3	16	11	11

November 4th:
DUNDEE (1) 1   RANGERS (0) 1
  Wallace (39)   Conn (69)

DUNDEE: Allan; Wilson, Houston; Robinson, Stuart, Ford; Wilson, Duncan, Wallace, J. Scott, I. Scott

RANGERS: McCloy; Jardine, Mathieson; Greig, Johnstone, Smith; Conn, Donaldson, Parlane, Mason, Young

Attendance: 19,600

November 11th:
RANGERS (0) 1   AIRDRIE (0) 0
  Conn (84)

RANGERS: McCloy; Jardine, Mathieson; Greig (Fyfe), Johnstone, Smith; Conn, Donaldson, Parlane, Mason, MacDonald

AIRDRIE: Poulton; Caldwell, Jonquin; Menzies, Montgomery, Whiteford; Wilson, Walker, Busby, McRoberts, Cowan

Attendance: 15,000

November 18th:
HIBERNIAN (1) 1   RANGERS (1) 2
  Stanton (27)   Conn (36), Fyfe (47)

HIBERNIAN: McArthur; Brownlie, Schaedler; Stanton, Black, Blackley; Edwards, O'Rourke, Hazel, Cropley, Duncan

RANGERS: McCloy; Jardine, Mathieson; Greig, Johnstone, Smith; Conn, Fyfe, Parlane, Mason, MacDonald

Attendance: 33,356

November 21st: Willie Johnston said a final no to a move to West Bromwich Albion for £135,000.

November 25th:
RANGERS (1) 3   DUMBARTON (0) 1
  Young (41),   McCormack (59)
  Conn (70), Parlane (80)

RANGERS: McCloy; Jardine, Mathieson; Greig, Johnstone, Smith; Conn, MacDonald, Parlane, Mason (McLean), Young

DUMBARTON: Williams; Menzies, Wilkinson; Jenkins, Cushley, Graham; Wallace, C. McAdam, McCormack, T. McAdam, Wilson

Attendance: 12,000

December 1st: Willie Johnston signed for West Bromwich Albion.

December 2nd:
RANGERS (0) 0   HEARTS (0) 1
                           Ford (88)

RANGERS: McCloy; Jardine, Mathieson; Greig, Johnstone, Smith; Conn, MacDonald, Parlane, Mason (McLean), Young

HEARTS: Garland; Sneddon, Clunie; Thomson, Anderson, Brown; Park, Menmuir, Ford, Carruthers, T. Murray

Attendance: 25,000

December 9th:
DUNDEE UNITED (0) 1   RANGERS (3) 4
  Henry (77)   Conn (20),
                           Parlane 2 (33, 36),
                           Jardine (70)

DUNDEE UNITED: McAlpine; Rolland, Markland (K. Cameron); Copland, D. Smith, Henry; Kopel, Fleming, Knox, Gardner, White

RANGERS: McCloy; Jardine, Mathieson; MacDonald, Johnstone, Smith; McLean, Conn, Parlane, Mason, Young

Attendance: 11,000

December 16th:
RANGERS 0   ABERDEEN 0

RANGERS: McCloy; Jardine, Mathieson; MacDonald, Johnstone, Smith; McLean, Conn (Fyfe), Parlane, Mason, Young

ABERDEEN: Clark; Willoughby, Hermiston; S. Murray, Young, Wilson; Varga, Smith, Mitchell, Jarvie, Miller

Attendance: 19,000

December 23rd:
EAST FIFE (0) 0   RANGERS (4) 4
                          Johnstone 2 (5, 22),
                          Young (41),
                          Parlane (42)

EAST FIFE: McGarr; Duncan, Printy; Borthwick, Martis, Clarke; Hegarty, Hamilton, Honeyman, McIvor (Dailey), McPhee

RANGERS: McCloy; Jardine, Mathieson; MacDonald, Johnstone, Forsyth; McLean, Mason, Parlane, Greig, Young

Attendance: 8,608

December 30th:
RANGERS (0) 2   AYR UNITED (1) 1
  Conn (51), Parlane (81)   McCulloch (33)

RANGERS: McCloy; Jardine, Mathieson; Greig, Jackson, Smith; Conn, Forsyth, Parlane, Mason (MacDonald), Young

AYR UNITED: Stewart; Wells, Murphy; McAnespie, Fleming, Ingram; Doyle, McCulloch, Flynn, Graham, Mitchell

Attendance: 17,653

League positions

	P	W	D	L	F	A	Pts
1 Celtic	16	13	2	1	47	16	28
2 Hibernian	17	12	2	3	45	19	26
3 RANGERS	18	11	3	4	33	17	25
4 Dundee	18	9	5	4	32	20	23
5 Dundee United	18	11	1	6	32	30	23

January 1st:
PARTICK THISTLE (0) 0 RANGERS (1) 1
                        Young (10)

PARTICK THISTLE: Rough; Gray, Ralston; Glavin, McKinnon, Strachan; Gibson (Lawrie), Coulston, Craig, A. Rae, McQuade

RANGERS: McCloy; Jardine, Mathieson; Greig, Johnstone, Smith; McLean, Forsyth, Parlane, MacDonald, Young

Attendance: 18,500

Glavin was ordered off

January 6th:
RANGERS (1) 2   CELTIC (0) 1
  Parlane (24),   Smith o.g. (51)
  Conn (89)

RANGERS: McCloy; Jardine, Mathieson; Greig, Johnstone, Smith; Conn, Forsyth, Parlane, MacDonald, Young

CELTIC: Williams; Hay, Brogan; McCluskey (Hood), McNeill, Connelly; Johnstone, Dalglish, Deans, Callaghan, Macari

Attendance: 67,000

Rangers controlled most of the game and their victory was hard-earned and well-deserved. McCluskey rugby-tackled MacDonald from behind and Parlane needed a lucky rebound from Williams' legs before the penalty ended in the back of the net. Celtic's equalising goal was fortunate because McCloy had Deans' shot covered before a wicked deflection off Smith carried it out of his reach. Conn's persistence finally brought him reward in the last minute when he headed home a Young cross.

January 13th:
FALKIRK (1) 2   RANGERS (2) 4
  McLeod (40), Young (52)   Young 2 (27, 89),
                            Parlane (45 pen),
                            Conn (59)

FALKIRK: Donaldson; S. Kennedy, Cattenach (Setterington); Markie, McMillan, McLeod; Hoggan, Harley, Scott, Ferguson, Young

RANGERS: McCloy; Jardine, Mathieson; Greig, Forsyth, Smith; McLean, Conn, Parlane, MacDonald, Young

Attendance: 14,000

January 20th:
RANGERS (3) 4   KILMARNOCK (0) 0
  Parlane 2 (5, 50),
  Young (33), Greig (37)

RANGERS: McCloy; Jardine, Mathieson; Greig, Johnstone, Smith (Donaldson); McLean, Forsyth, Parlane, MacDonald, Young

KILMARNOCK: Stewart; Whyte, Robertson; Dickson, Maxwell, Sheed; McGovern, Smith, Morrison, McSherry, Cook

Attendance: 14,000

January 27th:
MORTON (0) 1   RANGERS (2) 2
  Gillies (64 pen)   MacDonald (5),
                         Young (23)

MORTON: Baines; Hayes, Shevlane; Lavelle (Christiansen), Anderson, Clark; Osborne, Townsend, Gillies, Murphy, Armstrong

RANGERS: McCloy; Jardine, Mathieson; Greig, Johnstone, Smith; McLean, Forsyth, Conn (Fyfe), MacDonald, Young

Attendance: 16,000

February 10th:
RANGERS (1) 2   MOTHERWELL (0) 1
  Young (13), Jardine (76)   Millar (57 pen)

RANGERS: McCloy; Jardine, Mathieson; Greig, Forsyth, Smith; McLean, Denny, Parlane, MacDonald, Young

MOTHERWELL: MacRae; Whiteford, Wark; Watson, McCallum, Goodwin; Campbell, McCabe, Goldthorpe (Martin), Lawson, Millar

Attendance: 22,000

February 19th:
RANGERS (2) 5   ARBROATH (0) 0
  Young (40), Parlane 2 (42, 57),
  Greig (50), Miller (75)

RANGERS: McCloy; Jardine, Mathieson; Greig, Johnstone, Smith; McLean, Forsyth, Parlane (Mason), Miller, Young

ARBROATH: Marshall; Milne, Rylance; Cargill, Waddell, Winchester; Sellars, McKenzie, Pirie, Stanton, Payne

Attendance: 15,000

League positions

	P	W	D	L	F	A	Pts
1 RANGERS	25	18	3	4	53	22	39
2 Celtic	23	16	4	3	61	25	36
3 Hibernian	23	16	3	4	61	22	35
4 Aberdeen	24	12	7	5	48	26	31
5 Dundee	24	11	7	6	41	28	29

March 3rd:
ST JOHNSTONE (0) 1   RANGERS (1) 2
 Rooney (59)   Miller (11),
                        Mason (84)

ST JOHNSTONE: Donaldson; McManus, Argue; Kinnell, MacDonald, Rennie; Muir, Hall, Pearson, Rooney, Aitken

RANGERS: McCloy; Jardine, Mathieson; MacDonald, Johnstone, Smith; McLean, Forsyth, Parlane, Miller (Mason), Young

Attendance: 12,000

March 10th:
RANGERS (2) 3   DUNDEE (0) 1
 Parlane 2 (37, 86),   Duncan (63)
 MacDonald (41)

RANGERS: McCloy; Denny (Miller), Mathieson; Jardine, Johnstone, Smith; McLean, Forsyth, Parlane, MacDonald, Young

DUNDEE: Allan; Wilson, Houston; Robinson, Stewart, Anderson (Ford); Wilson, Wallace, Duncan, J. Scott, I. Scott

Attendance: 32,500

March 20th:
AIRDRIE (2) 2   RANGERS (3) 6
 Busby 2 (22, 37)   Parlane (8), Greig (17),
                        Johnstone (42),
                        McLean (50),
                        MacDonald (67),
                        Young (80)

AIRDRIE: Poulton; Caldwell, Jonquin; Fraser, Montgomery, Whiteford; McCann, McRoberts, Busby, Cowan, Wilson

RANGERS: McCloy; Jardine, Mathieson; Greig, Johnstone, Smith; McLean, Forsyth, Parlane (Mason), MacDonald, Young

Attendance: 20,000

March 24th:
RANGERS (0) 1   HIBERNIAN (0) 0
 McLean (59)

RANGERS: McCloy; Jardine, Mathieson; Greig, Johnstone, Smith; McLean, Forsyth, Parlane, MacDonald, Young

HIBERNIAN: McArthur; Bremner, McEwan; Stanton, Black, Blackley; Smith, Higgins, Gordon (Hazel), Cropley, Duncan

Attendance: 51,000

Blackley was ordered off

March 31st:
DUMBARTON (1) 1   RANGERS (2) 2
 Mathie (22)   Young (13),
                        Parlane (20)

DUMBARTON: Whigham; McKay (Menzies), Wilkinson; Cushley, Bolton, Graham; Wilson, Wallace, McCormack, Mathie, Heron

RANGERS: McCloy; Jardine, Mathieson; Greig, Johnstone, Smith (Mason); McLean, Forsyth, Parlane, MacDonald, Young

Attendance: 13,000

April 2nd: Stewart Kennedy was signed from Stenhousemuir for £10,000.

April 7th:
HEARTS (0) 0   RANGERS (1) 1
                        Greig (21)

HEARTS: Cruikshank; Sneddon, Oliver; Kay, Anderson, Wood; Aird, Stevenson (Park), Ford, Brown, Carruthers

RANGERS: McCloy; Jardine, Mathieson; Greig, Johnstone, Smith (Conn); McLean, Forsyth, Parlane, MacDonald, Young

Attendance: 24,000

April 14th:
RANGERS (0) 2   DUNDEE UNITED (0) 1
 Greig 2 (58, 69)   Reid (63)

RANGERS: McCloy; Jardine, Mathieson; Greig, Johnstone, MacDonald; McLean, Forsyth, Parlane, Conn, Young

DUNDEE UNITED: Davie; Rolland, Kopel; Copland, D. Smith, W. Smith; K. Cameron, Fleming, Gardner, Reid, Traynor

Attendance: 30,000

April 21st:
ABERDEEN (0) 2   RANGERS (1) 2
 Hermiston (67 pen),   McLean (22),
 Taylor (85)   Conn (89)

ABERDEEN: Clark; Williamson, Hermiston; Thomson, Young, Smith (Boel); Murray, Taylor, Jarvie, Varga, Graham

RANGERS: McCloy; Jardine, Mathieson; Greig, Johnstone, Smith; McLean, Forsyth, Parlane, MacDonald, Conn

Attendance: 32,000

April 28th:
RANGERS (2) 2   EAST FIFE (0) 0
  Young (21), Conn (32)

RANGERS: McCloy; Jardine, Mathieson; Greig, Johnstone, MacDonald; McLean, Forsyth, Parlane, Conn, Young

EAST FIFE: McGarr; Duncan, Printy; Borthwick, Martis, Clarke; Hegarty, Hamilton, Honeyman, Love, McPhee (Dailey)

Attendance: 30,000

Scottish First Division

	P	W	D	L	F	A	Pts
1 Celtic	34	26	5	3	93	28	57
2 RANGERS	34	26	4	4	74	30	56
3 Hibernian	34	19	7	8	74	33	45
4 Aberdeen	34	16	11	7	61	34	43
5 Dundee	34	17	9	8	68	43	43
6 Ayr United	34	16	8	10	50	51	40
7 Dundee United	34	17	5	12	56	51	39
8 Motherwell	34	11	9	14	38	48	31
9 East Fife	34	11	8	15	46	54	30
10 Hearts	34	12	6	16	39	50	30
11 St Johnstone	34	10	9	15	52	67	29
12 Morton	34	10	8	16	47	53	28
13 Partick Thistle	34	10	8	16	40	53	28
14 Falkirk	34	7	12	15	38	56	26
15 Arbroath	34	9	8	17	39	63	26
16 Dumbarton	34	6	11	17	43	72	23
17 Kilmarnock	34	7	8	19	40	71	22
18 Airdrie	34	4	8	22	34	75	16

April 27th: Rangers gave Ron McKinnon a free transfer.

April 28th: Doug Houston was signed from Dundee for £45,000.

May 1st: Johnny Hamilton was signed from Hibernian on a free transfer.

May 2nd: Ally Scott was signed from Queens Park.

May 12th: Scotland beat Wales 2-0 in Cardiff. McCloy, Johnstone and Parlane were in the team.

May 16th: Scotland were beaten 2-1 by Northern Ireland at Hampden Park. McCloy and Johnstone were in the team.

May 19th: Jardine and Johnstone were in the Scotland team which was beaten 1-0 by England at Wembley.

June 5th: Joe Craven died.

June 19th: Matt Taylor became Rangers' new Chairman. John Lawrence was appointed as the club's first Honorary President. John F. Wilson returned to the Board after 6 years.

June 30th: Scotland were beaten 1-0 by Brazil at Hampden Park. McCloy, Jardine, Johnstone and Parlane were in the side. Derek Johnstone had the misfortune to put through his own goal for the only goal of the game.

LEAGUE CUP

August 12th:
RANGERS (0) 2   CLYDEBANK (0) 0
  Conn (68), MacDonald (89)

RANGERS: McCloy; Jardine, Mathieson; Greig, Jackson, Smith; McLean, Johnston, Stein, Conn, MacDonald

CLYDEBANK: McDonald; Abel, Gray; Fallon, Delaney, Hay; Roxburgh (Hall), Love, McPaul, Munro, Currie

Attendance: 26,240

August 16th:
ST MIRREN (0) 0   RANGERS (3) 4
                       Johnston (12),
                       Greig (18),
                       Stein (43), Conn (81)

ST MIRREN: Gilmour; Clelland, Munro; Millar, Ure, McQueen; O'Neill, Blair, Storrie, A. McLeod, McKean

RANGERS: McCloy; Jardine, Mathieson; Greig, Jackson, Smith; McLean, Conn (Denny), Stein, Johnston, MacDonald

Attendance: 12,000

August 19th:
RANGERS (0) 2   AYR UNITED (0) 1
  Johnston (65), Parlane (89)   McLean (46)

RANGERS: McCloy; Jardine, Mathieson; Greig, Jackson, Smith; McLean, Johnston, Stein, Conn, MacDonald (Parlane)

AYR UNITED: Stewart; Fillipi, Murphy; McAnespie, Quinn, Fleming; Doyle, Graham, Ingram, McLean, Stevenson

Attendance: 20,000

Graham was ordered off

August 23rd:
RANGERS (1) 1   ST MIRREN (2) 4
Conn (4)   McLeod 4 (5, 45, 78, 83)

RANGERS: McCloy; Jardine, Mathieson; Greig, D. Johnstone, Smith; Penman, Conn, Stein, Parlane, Johnston

ST MIRREN: Stevenson; Clelland, Jamieson (O'Neill); Millar, McQueen, Johnston; McKean, Blair, Storrie, A. McLeod, Munro

Attendance: 15,000

August 26th:
CLYDEBANK (0) 0   RANGERS (2) 5
                   Greig (21),
                   McLean (24 pen),
                   Smith (55),
                   D. Johnstone (70),
                   Stein (85)

CLYDEBANK: McDonald; Abel, Gray; Fallon (McPaul), Delaney, Hay; Roxburgh, Love, Larnach, Munro, Caskie

RANGERS: McCloy; Jardine, Mathieson; Greig, Jackson, Smith; McLean, D. Johnstone, Stein, MacDonald, Fyfe

Attendance: 9,000

August 30th:
AYR UNITED (0) 1   RANGERS (1) 2
Graham (64)   W. Johnston (25),
                   D. Johnstone (65)

AYR UNITED: A. McLean; Fillipi, Murphy; McAnespie, Quinn, Fleming; Doyle, Graham, Ingram, McGovern, Stevenson

RANGERS: McCloy; Jardine, Mathieson; Greig, D. Johnstone, Smith; McLean, Denny, Johnston, Fyfe, MacDonald

Attendance: 13,000

League Cup Section Table

	P	W	D	L	F	A	Pts
RANGERS	6	5	0	1	16	6	10
Ayr United	6	3	0	3	12	6	6
St Mirren	6	2	1	3	12	15	5
Clydebank	6	1	1	4	6	19	3

September 20th: Second Round First Leg
STENHOUSEMUIR (0) 0   RANGERS (1) 5
                   D. Johnstone 3
                   (36, 69, 70),
                   Parlane (49),
                   Greig (62)

STENHOUSEMUIR: Kennedy; Muir, Rose; Murdoch, Glasgow, Jamieson (Boyle); Wight, Scobie, Hughes, Richardson, Lynn

RANGERS: McCloy; Jardine, Mathieson; Greig, Jackson, Smith; McLean, Parlane, D. Johnstone, MacDonald, Fyfe

Attendance: 3,500

October 4th: Second Round Second Leg
RANGERS (0) 1   STENHOUSEMUIR (1) 2
Fyfe (55)   Hughes (13),
                   Murdoch (77)

RANGERS: McCloy; Jardine, Mathieson; Greig, Jackson, D. Johnstone; Penman, Bonnyman, Fyfe, Parlane (Donaldson), A. MacDonald

STENHOUSEMUIR: Kennedy; Henderson, Rose; Richardson, Muir, Glasgow; Wight, Boyle, Murdoch, Halliday (Scobie), Hughes

Attendance: 6,000

Rangers won 6-2 on aggregate

October 11th: Quarter-Final First Leg
RANGERS (0) 1   ST JOHNSTONE (1) 1
Parlane (57)   Rooney (38)

RANGERS: McCloy; Denny, Mathieson; Greig, D. Johnstone, Donaldson; Fyfe, Jardine, Parlane, Conn, Young

ST JOHNSTONE: Donaldson; Lambie, Argue; Smith, Rennie, Rooney; Aird, Hall, Pearson, Mercer, Aitken

Attendance: 15,000

November 1st: Quarter-Final Second Leg
ST JOHNSTONE (0) 0   RANGERS (1) 2
                   Young (27),
                   Parlane (79 pen)

ST JOHNSTONE: Donaldson; Lambie, Argue; Rennie, Kinnell, Rooney; Aird, Hall, Pearson, McPhee, Aitken

RANGERS: McCloy; Jardine, Mathieson; Greig, D. Johnstone, Smith; Conn, Donaldson, Parlane, MacDonald, Young

Attendance: 12,300

Rangers won 3-1 on aggregate

November 22nd: Semi-Final   At Hampden Park
RANGERS   (0) 0   HIBERNIAN   (1) 1
                              Brownlie (70)

RANGERS: McCloy; Jardine, Mathieson; Jackson, D. Johnstone, Smith; Conn, Fyfe (Young), Parlane, Donaldson, MacDonald

HIBERNIAN: Herriot; Brownlie, Schaedler; Stanton, Black, Blackley; Edwards, O'Rourke, Gordon, Cropley, Duncan —Hazel

Attendance: 46,513

Hibs deservedly won a place in the Scottish League Cup Final. The referee John Gordon booked 5 players —3 from Rangers and 2 from Hibs. John Brownlie's decisive goal in 70 minutes came after he had emerged unscathed through a series of hard tackles. He hit a low shot from just inside the penalty-area that beat McCloy for power and placement. Only in the last seconds when Mathieson hit the bar did Rangers pierce a strong defence. Rangers were forced to take the field without the unfit John Greig. It was a handicap they could not overcome.

SCOTTISH CUP

February 3rd: Third Round
RANGERS   (0) 1   DUNDEE UNITED   (0) 0
   Young (65)

RANGERS: McCloy; Jardine, Mathieson; Greig, Johnstone (Mason), Smith; McLean, Forsyth, Parlane, MacDonald, Young

DUNDEE UNITED: McAlpine; Rolland, Kopel; Copland, D. Smith, W. Smith; Markland, Fleming, Gardner, Knox, Traynor

Attendance: 35,657

February 24th: Fourth Round
RANGERS   (1) 1   HIBERNIAN   (0) 1
   Johnstone (29)   Gordon (60)

RANGERS: McCloy; Jardine, Mathieson; Greig, Johnstone, Smith; McLean, Forsyth, Parlane, Miller (Conn), Young

HIBERNIAN: Herriot; Bremner, Schaedler; Stanton, Black, Blackley; Hamilton, O'Rouke (Higgins), Gordon, Cropley, Duncan

Attendance: 63,889

February 28th: Fourth Round Replay
HIBERNIAN   (0) 1   RANGERS   (1) 2
   Duncan (61)   McLean 2 (7, 72 pen)

HIBERNIAN: Herriot; Bremner, Schaedler; Stanton, Black, Blackley; Hamilton, Higgins, Gordon, Cropley, Duncan

RANGERS: McCloy; Jardine, Mathieson; Greig, Johnstone, Smith; McLean, Forsyth, Parlane, MacDonald, Young

Attendance: 49,000

March 17th: Fifth Round
RANGERS   (0) 2   AIRDRIE   (0) 0
   Parlane (49 pen), Young (60)

RANGERS: McCloy; Jardine, Mathieson; Greig, Johnstone, Smith; McLean, Forsyth, Parlane, MacDonald, Young

AIRDRIE: McKenzie; Jonquin, Clarke (Caldwell); Fraser, Montgomery, Whiteford; Wilson, Hulston, Busby, Cowan, Gallacher

Attendance: 35,500

April 4th: Semi-Final   At Hampden Park
RANGERS   (1) 2   AYR UNITED   (0) 0
   Parlane 2 (41, 58)

RANGERS: McCloy; Jardine, Mathieson; Greig, Johnstone, Smith; McLean, Forsyth, Parlane, MacDonald, Young

AYR UNITED: Stewart; Wells, Murphy; McAnespie, Fleming, Fillipi; Doyle, Graham (Campbell), Ingram, McLean, McCulloch

Attendance: 51,815

Rangers capped a fine season by going back to Hampden on the last climactic afternoon of a long and successful campaign. 2 goals from Derek Parlane gave them victory in this Semi-Final. Rangers might have scored after 3 minutes when Wells cleared a Young header off the line with a suspicion of hand ball. The Rangers' goal had to come and it did 4 minutes before half-time. MacDonald lofted a ball forward, Parlane shrugged off the challenge of McAnespie and hit a low left-foot shot wide of the advancing Stewart. In 58 minutes the Ibrox side scored a wonderful 2nd goal. Greig swept a long ball inside the full-back to McLean, who carried it to the bye-line and crossed. Parlane struck the ball on the volley past Stewart. Parlane was immediately booked by referee Davidson for running off the pitch to salute the ecstatic fans behind the goal.

May 5th: Final   At Hampden Park
CELTIC   (1) 2   RANGERS   (1) 3
   Dalglish (24),   Parlane (34),
   Connelly (54 pen)   Conn (46),
                       Forsyth (60)

CELTIC: Hunter; McGrain, Brogan (Lennox); Murdoch, McNeill, Connelly; Johnstone, Deans, Dalglish, Hay, Callaghan

RANGERS: McCloy; Jardine, Mathieson; Greig, Johnstone, MacDonald; McLean, Forsyth, Parlane, Conn, Young —Smith

Attendance: 122,714 *Referee*: J. R. P. Gordon (Newport-on-Tay)

This was Rangers' first triumph in the competition since 1966. Celtic, attacking first, took the lead in 24 minutes. Dalglish, scampering on to a Deans pass, struck a shot past McCloy and turned in celebration. After 34 minutes Mathieson pushed a shrewd ball forward and MacDonald beat Connelly, drawn wide. His chipped centre to the near post brought Parlane away from his defender for the header that tied the match. 20 seconds after the interval Rangers took the lead. Young passed forward, Parlane flicked on, and Conn, left with a clear run at goal, shot past the advancing Hunter. In the 54th minute Celtic drew level. Greig handled a net-bound shot and Connelly, as cool as ever, struck the penalty home with authority. In the 60th minute Forsyth scored what proved to be the winner. McLean slanted over a free-kick. Johnstone headed against a post and as the ball rolled agonisingly along the goal-line Forsyth stabbed it into the net. John Greig stood in tears at the end.

SUPER CUP

(a competition between the winners of the European Cup and the European Cup Winners Cup)

January 16th:

RANGERS (1) 1	AJAX (2) 3
MacDonald (41)	Rep (34), Cruyff (45), Haan (76)

RANGERS: McCloy; Jardine, Mathieson; Greig, Johnstone, Smith; Conn (McLean), Forsyth, Parlane, MacDonald, Young

AJAX: Stuy; Suurbier, Hulshoff; Blankenberg, Krol, G. Muhren; Haan, A. Muhren, Rep, Cruyff, Keizer

Attendance: 58,000

Rangers failed to cope with the undisputed Champions of the World but this was defeat without the slightest suggestion of dishonour. Ajax were a class apart. In individual skills they were superlative and Cruyff was majestic. The flags of all Rangers' previous European opponents were carried round the ground before the kick-off. Andy Cunningham, one of the legendary figures of the past, set the game in motion. In the 34th minute Ajax went ahead. Cruyff struck a perfectly weighted ball to Rep who drew McCloy off his line before slipping the ball into the net. 7 minutes later Rangers equalised. A long ball from Greig was played on by Conn to MacDonald who shot home on the turn from the edge of the penalty area. Seconds before half-time Ajax took the lead. Cruyff beat Forsyth on the outside and then struck a wicked shot over McCloy's shoulder. McLean came on for Conn shortly after the

restart. In 76 minutes Hulshoff sent Haan clear and with the home defence ball watching he hit the 3rd goal. Twice in the closing stages Greig and Parlane might have scored goals.

January 24th:

AJAX (2) 3	RANGERS (2) 2
Haan (12),	MacDonald (2),
Muhren (37 pen),	Young (35)
Cruyff (79)	

AJAX: Stuy; Suurbier, Hulshoff; Blankenburg, Krol, Haan; Neeskens, G. Muhren, Swart, Cruyff, Keizer

RANGERS: McCloy; Jardine, Mathieson; Greig, Johnstone, Smith; McLean, Forsyth, Parlane, MacDonald, Young

Attendance: 40,000

Ajax took possession of the enormous Super Cup. It took a dubious penalty to ensure Ajax victory against a spirited Rangers side. Twice Rangers were in the lead and twice Ajax came back into the match. Greig was at the heart of every matter, Parlane chased every ball and McCloy pulled off several fine saves. After 2 minutes Rangers took the lead when MacDonald took a loose ball in the penalty area and hit a left-foot shot straight into the top corner of the net. Ajax equalised after 12 minutes when a pass from Cruyff found Haan and he hit a great left-foot shot past McCloy. Rangers took the lead after 35 minutes. McLean took a free-kick over the heads of the defence and Young dived low to head past Stuy. 2 minutes later Ajax were awarded a penalty following a challenge by Mathieson on Neeskens. Muhren hit the kick low and hard past McCloy. 11 minutes from time Cruyff broke from midfield and hit a vicious swerving shot past McCloy. There was never much to choose between the teams on the night. Ajax won 6-3 on aggregate.

Willie Johnston, always a great favourite with the Rangers fans.

APPEARANCES

	League	League Cup	Scottish Cup	Super Cup
McCloy	33	11	6	2
Jardine	34	11	6	2
Mathieson	34	11	6	2
Greig	30	10	6	2
Jackson	7	7	-	-
D. Johnstone	31	8	6	2
McLean	22+2S	6	6	1+1
Denny	6	2+1S	-	-
Johnston	4	5	-	-
Stein	2+1S	5	-	-
Smith	29	9	5	2
MacDonald	27+2S	9	5	2
Parlane	29+1S	6+1S	6	2
Conn	18+2S	7	1+1S	1
Donaldson	3+2S	3+1	-	-
Fyfe	3+3S	6	-	-
Young	26	2+1S	6	2
Forsyth	21	-	6	2
Mason	12+4S	-	0+1S	-
Neef	1	-	-	-
Miller	2+1S	-	1	-
Penman	-	2	-	-
Bonnyman	-	1	-	-

GOALSCORERS

League: Parlane 19 (2 pens), Young 13, Conn 12, Greig 7, McLean 5 (1 pen), MacDonald 4, Johnstone 4, Jardine 2, Miller 2, Mason 2, Fyfe 2, Johnston 2

League Cup: Johnstone 5, Parlane 4 (1 pen), Conn 3, Johnston 3, Greig 3, Stein 2, MacDonald 1, McLean 1 (pen), Smith 1, Fyfe 1, Young 1

Scottish Cup: Parlane 4 (1 pen), Young 2, McLean 2 (1 pen), Johnstone 1, Conn 1, Forsyth 1

Super Cup: MacDonald 2, Young 1

Rangers over the years have made a habit out of winning the Scottish Cup. This occasion was 1978 when the victims were Aberdeen going down by 2 goals to 1 before 61,000 spectators. Goalkeeper Peter McCloy looks very pleased with himself while skipper John Greig keeps a firm grip of the silverware.

Season 1973-74

The 7 points dropped in Rangers first 4 home matches proved costly as the team finished 3rd in the Championship — 5 points behind Celtic and one behind Hibernian. Their longest undefeated sequence of matches was 10 (from October 20th to January 1st). Both matches against Celtic were lost. Derek Johnstone scored the club's 6,000th League goal during the season and John Greig scored their 10,000th goal in all competitions in the same match —against Clyde at Ibrox. Both Johnstone and Greig were presented with silver salvers to commemorate the event. The team scored 67 goals and Derek Parlane finished as top scorer with 14. Sandy Jardine played in all of the League matches and also represented Scotland throughout the season and at the World Cup Finals in West Germany.

Rangers reached the Semi-Final of the League Cup. They topped their Section which included Celtic, beat Dumbarton 8-1 on aggregate in the Second Round and Hibs 2-0 overall in the Quarter-Final. They met Celtic again in the Semi-Final where a Harry Hood hat-trick gave Celtic victory and a much more comfortable win than they could have expected.

After beating Queens Park 8-0 in the Third Round of the Scottish Cup Rangers were well beaten by Dundee, in front of their own supporters, in the next Round. This match was played on a Sunday and attracted a crowd of 64,672.

Rangers' Cup Winners' Cup challenge ended at the 2nd hurdle. Turkish Cup Winners Ankaragucu were beaten 6-0 on aggregate in the First Round but Rangers were decisively beaten by Borussia Monchen-Gladbach in the away leg and despite a fighting 3-2 win at Ibrox went out of the competition.

Arsenal were invited to the Stadium to take part in a match to commemorate the club's centenary. The match attracted 71,000 spectators and Rangers looked to have it won until the London team hit them with two late goals.

League: Third
League Cup: Semi-Finalists
Scottish Cup: Fourth Round
Cup Winners Cup: Second Round

SCOTTISH FIRST DIVISION

September 1st:
RANGERS 0   AYR UNITED 0

RANGERS: McCloy; Jardine, Mathieson; Greig, Johnstone, MacDonald; McLean, Forsyth, O'Hara (Conn), Parlane, Smith (Denny)

AYR UNITED: Stewart; Wells, Murphy; McAnespie, Fleming, Fillipi; Doyle, Graham, Ingram (Bell), McLean, McCulloch (Taylor)

Attendance: 30,000

September 8th:
PARTICK THISTLE (0) 0 RANGERS (0) 1
                          Scott (89)

PARTICK THISTLE: Rough; Hansen, Kellachan; Glavin, Anderson, Clark; Chalmers (McQuade), Craig, Rae, Houston, Lawrie

RANGERS: McCloy; Jardine, Mathieson; Greig (Smith), Johnstone, MacDonald; McLean, Forsyth, O'Hara, Scott, Conn (Parlane)

Attendance: 21,000

September 15th:
RANGERS (0) 0   CELTIC (0) 1
                   Johnstone (69)

RANGERS: McCloy; Jardine, Mathieson; Greig, Johnstone, MacDonald; McLean (Scott), Forsyth, Parlane, Conn, Young

CELTIC: Hunter; McGrain, Brogan; Murray, McNeill, Connelly; Johnstone, Hood (Callaghan), Dalglish, Hay, Wilson

Attendance: 69,000

September 29th:
RANGERS (0) 0   HEARTS (2) 3
                   Prentice (25),
                   Busby 2 (29, 58)

RANGERS: McCloy; Jardine, Mathieson; Greig, Johnstone, MacDonald; McLean (Scott), Forsyth, Parlane, Conn, Young (Houston)

HEARTS: Garland; Sneddon, Clunie; Cant, Anderson, Brown; Aird, Ford, Busby, Stevenson, Prentice

Attendance: 30,000

October 1st: Joe Mason was appointed as Rangers Coach.

October 6th:
ARBROATH (1) 1   RANGERS (1) 2
 Pirie (14)   O'Hara 2 (42, 46)

ARBROATH: Marshall; Milne, Lawson (Carson); Cargill, Waddell, Murray; Sellars, Rylance, Pirie (Butler), Penman, Payne

RANGERS: McCloy; Jardine, Mathieson; Greig, Johnstone, MacDonald; McLean, Forsyth, O'Hara, Scott (Conn), Houston

Attendance: 7,170

October 13th:
RANGERS (0) 0   EAST FIFE (1) 1
                   Hamilton (7)

RANGERS: Kennedy; Jardine, Mathieson; Greig, Johnstone, MacDonald; McLean, Forsyth, Scott (Fyfe), O'Hara, Houston

EAST FIFE: McGarr; Duncan, Clarke; McIvor, Martis, Borthwick; Hamilton, Love, Hegarty (Honeyman), McPhee, Ritchie (O'Connor)

Attendance: 20,000

October 20th:
DUNDEE UNITED (0) 1   RANGERS (0) 3
 Johnstone o.g. (77)   Conn 2 (76, 84),
                         O'Hara (46)

DUNDEE UNITED: McAlpine; Rolland (Knox), Kopel; Copland, D. Smith, W. Smith; Henry, Gray, Gardner (Cameron), Fleming, Traynor

RANGERS: McCloy; Jardine, Mathieson; Greig, Johnstone, MacDonald; McLean, Forsyth, O'Hara, Scott (Conn), Houston (Smith)

Attendance: 10,000

October 27th:
RANGERS (2) 4   HIBERNIAN (0) 0
 Conn (8),
 Jardine 2 (37 pen, 89 pen),
 Greig (86)

RANGERS: McCloy; Jardine, Mathieson; Greig, Johnstone, MacDonald; McLean, Forsyth, O'Hara, Conn, Houston

HIBERNIAN: McArthur; Bremner, Schaedler; Stanton, Black, Blackley; Edwards (Smith), Higgins, Gordon, Cropley, Duncan

Attendance: 30,000

League positions

	P	W	D	L	F	A	Pts
1 Celtic	8	6	1	1	17	6	13
2 Hearts	9	5	3	1	20	10	13
3 Aberdeen	8	4	4	0	10	4	12
4 Ayr United	9	5	2	2	17	11	12
5 Dundee United	8	5	0	3	13	11	10
7 RANGERS	8	4	1	3	10	7	9

November 3rd:
DUNFERMLINE (1) 2   RANGERS (0) 2
 Shaw (20),   Jackson (58),
 Kinninmonth (57)   O'Hara (73)

DUNFERMLINE: Aroll; Evans (Cameron), Wallace; Thomson, Leishman, Kinninmonth; Campbell, Scott, Mackie, Shaw, Gillespie

RANGERS: McCloy; Jardine, Mathieson; Greig, Jackson, MacDonald; McLean, Forsyth, Parlane (O'Hara), Conn, Houston

Attendance: 17,000

Derek Johnstone, a centre-half and a centre-forward for Rangers.

November 10th:
RANGERS   (0) 1   MORTON   (0) 0
  Greig (66)

RANGERS: McCloy; Jardine, Mathieson; Greig,
Jackson, MacDonald; McLean, Forsyth, O'Hara, Conn
(Fyfe), Houston

MORTON: Baines; Hayes, Ritchie; Townsend,
Rankin, Nelson; Osborne (Johnstone), Reid, McIlmoyle,
McCallion, Thomas (Lavelle)

**November 14th: Sandy Jardine was in the Scotland
team which drew 1-1 with West Germany at
Hampden Park.**

November 17th:
RANGERS   (0) 2   FALKIRK   (1) 1
  Greig 2 (65, 69)   Fowler (41)

RANGERS: McCloy; Jardine, Mathieson; Greig,
Jackson, Houston; McLean, Forsyth, Parlane,
Johnstone, MacDonald

FALKIRK: Donaldson; D. Whiteford, Cameron;
Markie, Gibson, Wheateley; Thomas, Fowler, Lawson
(Young), Shirra (Whiteford), McLeod

Attendance: 15,000

November 24th:
CLYDE   (0) 0   RANGERS   (1) 2
                       Jackson (40),
                       MacDonald (67)

CLYDE: Cairney; Anderson, Swan; Beattie
(Gillespie), McHugh, Aherne; Sullivan, Burns, Miller,
McGrain, Boyle (Houston)

RANGERS: McCloy; Jardine, Mathieson; Greig,
Jackson, Houston; McLean, Forsyth, Parlane,
MacDonald, Scott

Attendance: 12,000

December 15th:
RANGERS   (3) 5   ST JOHNSTONE   (1) 1
  Conn (15), Young (35),   Muir (3)
  MacDonald (39),
  Parlane (54), Smith (89)

RANGERS: McCloy; Jardine, Mathieson; Greig,
Johnstone, Smith; Young, Forsyth, Parlane, Conn
(McLean), MacDonald

ST JOHNSTONE: Robertson; Ritchie, Argue;
Kinnell, Cochrane, Crammond; Muir, Smith, Pearson,
McQuade, Aitken

Attendance: 8,200

December 22nd:
DUMBARTON   (0) 0   RANGERS   (2) 2
                          Parlane (14),
                          Young (31)

DUMBARTON: Williams; C. McAdam, Wilkinson;
Watt, Cushley, Ruddy; T. McAdam (Mathie), Wallace,
McCormack, Paterson, Heron

RANGERS: McCloy; Jardine, Mathieson; Greig,
Johnstone, Smith; Young, Forsyth, Parlane (Scott),
O'Hara, MacDonald

Attendance: 7,500

December 29th:
AYR UNITED   (0) 0   RANGERS   (0) 1
                           Parlane (88)

AYR UNITED: A. McLean; Fillipi, Murphy;
McAnespie, Fleming, Mitchell; Graham, Ferguson,
Ingram, G. McLean, McCulloch (Bell)

RANGERS: McCloy; Jardine, Mathieson; Greig,
Johnstone, Smith; Young, Forsyth, Parlane, O'Hara,
MacDonald

Attendance: 16,000

League positions

	P	W	D	L	F	A	Pts
1 Celtic	16	13	2	1	48	12	28
2 RANGERS	15	10	2	3	25	11	22
3 Hibernian	15	9	3	3	31	19	21
4 Hearts	17	8	5	4	30	21	21
5 Aberdeen	14	7	6	1	21	11	20

January 1st:
RANGERS   (1) 1   PARTICK THISTLE   (0) 1
  Parlane (n.a. pen)   Clark (n.a.)

RANGERS: McCloy; Jardine, Mathieson; Greig,
Johnstone, Houston; Young, Forsyth, Parlane,
MacDonald, Scott (Hamilton)

PARTICK THISTLE: Rough; Houston, Kellachan;
Glavin, Campbell, Clark; Chalmers (Gibson), Craig, T.
Rae, Rooney, Lawrie (Coulston)

Attendance: 16,000

January 5th:
CELTIC   (1) 1   RANGERS   (0) 0
  Lennox (27)

CELTIC: Hunter; McGrain, Brogan; McCluskey,
McNeill, Hay; Hood, Murray, Deans, Dalglish, Lennox

RANGERS: McCloy; Jardine, Mathieson; Greig,
Johnstone, Houston; Young, Forsyth, Parlane,
MacDonald, Scott (Hamilton)

Attendance: 55,000

A goal by Bobby Lennox was all that separated the teams.
Rangers showed remarkable stamina and spirit but were a
collection of players without corporate understanding.
Rangers came closest to scoring when Greig sent Hunter
scurrying to stop one low shot at the post. Murray and Hay
were the guiding midfield lights and Dalglish was a class
attacker. Lennox and Deans might have scored the late

goals that could have better reflected the difference in class.

January 12th:
RANGERS (0) 1
McLean (52)
ABERDEEN (1) 1
Purdie (32)

RANGERS: McCloy; Jardine, Mathieson; Greig, Johnstone, Forsyth; McLean, O'Hara, Parlane, MacDonald, Young (Fyfe)

ABERDEEN: Clark; Boel, Hermiston; Thomson (Williamson), Young, Miller; Graham, Smith, Taylor, Henry, Purdie

Attendance: 15,000

January 19th:
HEARTS (1) 2
Busby (29), Brown (65)
RANGERS (3) 4
Parlane 4 (8, 17, 22, 60)

HEARTS: Cruikshank; Kay, Clunie; Cant, Anderson, Brown; Park, Ford, Busby, Stevenson, Prentice

RANGERS: McCloy; Jardine, Mathieson; Greig, Johnstone, Smith; McLean, O'Hara, Parlane, Scott, Morris

Attendance: 20,000

February 2nd:
RANGERS (1) 2
McLean (38),
Parlane (68 pen)
ARBROATH (0) 3
Fletcher 2 (62, 86),
Pirie (64)

RANGERS: Hunter; Jardine, Mathieson; O'Hara, Johnstone, Smith; McLean, Scott (Fyfe), Parlane, Hamilton, Morris (Young)

ARBROATH: Marshall; Donald, Rylance; Walker, Waddell, Murray; Sellars, Cant, Pirie, Penman, Fletcher

Attendance: 15,000

February 9th:
EAST FIFE (0) 0
RANGERS (1) 3
Hamilton (44),
Scott (80),
McLean (86)

EAST FIFE: McGarr; Printy, Gillies; Clarke, Borthwick, Rae; Miller, McIvor, Kinnear, Love, McPhee (Hegarty)

RANGERS: Hunter; Jardine, Mathieson; O'Hara, Jackson, Johnstone; McLean, Scott, Parlane, Hamilton, Morris

Attendance: 8,499

League positions

	P	W	D	L	F	A	Pts
1 Celtic	22	17	2	3	61	19	36
2 Hibernian	22	13	5	4	46	27	31
3 RANGERS	21	12	4	5	36	19	28
4 Ayr United	23	11	6	6	32	24	28
5 Aberdeen	20	8	9	3	28	18	25

February 24th:
RANGERS (3) 3
Young (10)
Parlane 2 (24, 42 pen)
DUNDEE
UNITED (0) 1
Gardner (63)

RANGERS: Hunter; Jardine, Mathieson; Denny, Jackson, Johnstone; McLean, Hamilton, Parlane, Scott (Greig), Young

DUNDEE UNITED: Davie; Holt, Kopel; Copland, D. Smith, W. Smith; Knox, Gardner, Payne (Traynor), Fleming, Rankin (K. Cameron)

Attendance: 15,500

March 2nd:
HIBERNIAN (3) 3
Gordon 2 (10, 13),
Bremner (40)
RANGERS (1) 1
McLean (35)

HIBERNIAN: McArthur; Bremner, Schaedler; Spalding, Black, Blackley; Harper, Stanton, Gordon, Munro, Duncan

RANGERS: McCloy; Jardine, Mathieson; O'Hara, Jackson, Johnstone; McLean, Scott, Parlane (Greig), MacDonald, Young

Attendance: 24,000

March 15th: There was Press speculation that Rangers were to swop Dave Smith for Ian Purdie of Aberdeen.

March 16th:
MORTON (1) 2
Hunter (1),
Reid (89)
RANGERS (0) 3
Jackson 2 (70, 75),
Parlane (86 pen)

MORTON: Baines; Hayes, Ritchie; Townsend, Nelson, Hunter; McGhee (Murray), Reid, McIlmoyle, Hegarty, Hepburn

RANGERS: McCloy; Jardine, Mathieson; O'Hara, Jackson, Johnstone; McLean, Greig, Parlane, MacDonald, Young

Attendance: 9,000

March 19th: Parlane was in the Scottish League team which was beaten 5-0 by the English League at Maine Road, Manchester. Derek Johnstone made an appearance as substitute.

March 23rd:
FALKIRK 0
RANGERS 0

FALKIRK: Donaldson; Whiteford, Cameron; Markie, Gibson (Smith), Wheatley; Hoggan, Fowler, Lawson, Harley (Thomas), Shirra

RANGERS: McCloy; Jardine, Mathieson; Greig, Jackson, Johnstone; McLean, O'Hara, Parlane, MacDonald, Young

Attendance: 10,000

March 27th: Sandy Jardine was in the Scotland team which was beaten 2-1 by West Germany in Frankfurt.

March 30th:
RANGERS   (0) 4   CLYDE   (0) 0
   D. Johnstone (61), Greig (66),
   MacDonald (75), Scott (76)

RANGERS: McCloy; Jardine, Mathieson; Greig (McDougall), Johnstone, Jackson; Young, Scott, Parlane, MacDonald, Morris (Fyfe)

CLYDE: Cairney; Anderson, Swan; McHugh, McVie, Aherne (Harvey); Sullivan, Ferris, Miller, Burns, Boyle

Attendance: 10,000

Derek Johnstone's goal was Rangers 6,000th in League football.
John Greig's goal was Rangers 10,000th in all competitions.

April 2nd:
RANGERS   (1) 3   DUNFERMLINE   (0) 0
   Parlane (35 pen),
   Scott (75), Fyfe (84)

RANGERS: McCloy; Jardine, Greig; McDougall, Johnstone, Jackson; Young, Scott, Parlane, MacDonald, Morris (Fyfe)

DUNFERMLINE: Karlsen; Cameron, Leishman; Evans, MacCallum, Kinninmonth; Scott, McNichol, Mackie, Campbell, Sinclair

Attendance: 7,000

Leishman was ordered off

April 6th:
MOTHERWELL   (0) 1   RANGERS   (2) 4
   MacDonald o.g. (55)   Young 2 (13, 33),
                            Scott (47),
                            Fyfe (60)

MOTHERWELL: Rennie; Watson, Wark; Watson, R. Muir, Millar; Gray (McGuinness), Graham, Pettigrew, Martin, McClymont

RANGERS: McCloy; Jardine, Greig; McDougall (McLean), Johnstone, Jackson; Young, Scott, Parlane, MacDonald, Fyfe

Attendance: 13,346

April 13th:
RANGERS   (0) 1   DUNDEE   (2) 2
   Jardine (69 pen)   J. Scott 2 (19, 43)

RANGERS: McCloy; Jardine, Greig; McDougall, Johnstone, Jackson; Young, Scott, Parlane, MacDonald, Fyfe

DUNDEE: Allan; Gemmell, Johnston; Ford, Stewart (Caldwell), Phillip; Wilson (Wallace), Robinson, Duncan, J. Scott, Lambie

Attendance: 15,000

April 17th:
ABERDEEN   (0) 1   RANGERS   (0) 1
   McDougall o.g. (56)   Greig (75)

ABERDEEN: Clark; Hermiston, McLelland; Thomson, Young, Miller; Smith, Robb, Pirie, Jarvie, Graham

RANGERS: McCloy; Jardine, Greig; McDougall, Johnstone, Jackson; Young, Scott, Parlane, MacDonald, Fyfe

Attendance: 18,000

April 20th:
ST JOHNSTONE   (0) 1   RANGERS   (2) 3
   Smith (74)   Fyfe 2 (2, 36),
                            Young (55)

ST JOHNSTONE: Robertson; Ritchie, Argue (Hotson); Rennie, McDonald, Kinnell; Muir, Smith, Thomson, Hall, Cramond

RANGERS: McCloy; Jardine, Greig; McDougall, Johnstone, Jackson; Young, Scott (McLean), Parlane, MacDonald, Fyfe

Attendance: 7,500

April 23rd: Rangers gave free transfers to Iain MacDonald and Donaldson.

April 24th:
RANGERS   (1) 2   MOTHERWELL   (0) 1
   Scott (31),   Johnstone o.g. (69)
   Parlane (70)

RANGERS: McCloy; Jardine, Greig; MacDonald, Johnstone, Jackson; McLean (Hamilton), Scott, Parlane, MacDonald, Fyfe

MOTHERWELL: Rennie; Millar, Wark; R. Watson, Muir, Goodwin; Kennedy, Graham, Goldthorpe, Martin, McClymont

Attendance: 10,000

April 27th:
RANGERS   (1) 3   DUMBARTON   (0) 1
   Fyfe (8), Scott 2 (52, 56)   Heron (70)

RANGERS: McCloy; Jardine, Greig; McDougall, Johnstone, Jackson; Hamilton, Scott, Parlane (Conn), MacDonald, Fyfe (Morris)

DUMBARTON: Williams; Mullen, Wilkinson; Ruddy, Cushley, Graham; Coleman (Heron), Watt, C. McAdam, Bourke (Mathie), Black

Attendance: 6,000

April 29th:
DUNDEE (1) 2   RANGERS (0) 3
  Duncan 2 (20, 89)   Fyfe 2 (58, 67),
                           Young (80)

DUNDEE: Allan; Wilson, Gemmell; Ford, Caldwell, Phillip; Wallace, Robinson, Duncan, J. Scott, Johnston

RANGERS: McCloy; Jardine, Greig; McDougall, Johnstone, Jackson; Young, Scott, Parlane, McDonald, Fyfe

Attendance: 10,517

Scottish First Division

	P	W	D	L	F	A	Pts
1 Celtic	34	23	7	4	82	27	53
2 Hibernian	34	20	9	5	75	42	49
3 RANGERS	34	21	6	7	67	34	48
4 Aberdeen	34	13	16	5	46	26	42
5 Dundee	34	16	7	11	67	48	39
6 Hearts	34	14	10	10	54	43	38
7 Ayr United	34	15	8	11	44	40	38
8 Dundee United	34	15	7	12	55	51	37
9 Motherwell	34	14	7	13	45	40	35
10 Dumbarton	34	11	7	16	43	58	29
11 Partick Thistle	34	9	10	15	33	46	28
12 St Johnstone	34	9	10	15	41	60	28
13 Arbroath	34	10	7	17	52	69	27
14 Morton	34	8	10	16	37	49	26
15 Clyde	34	8	9	17	29	65	25
16 Dunfermline	34	8	8	18	43	65	24
17 East Fife	34	9	6	19	26	51	24
18 Falkirk	34	4	14	16	33	58	22

May 8th: By Hibernian beating Dundee United 4-1 at Tannadice, Rangers were eliminated from European competition for season 1974-75.

May 11th: Jardine was in the Scotland team which was beaten 1-0 by Northern Ireland at Hampden Park.

May 14th: Scotland beat Wales 2-0 at Hampden Park. Jardine was in the team and he scored one of the goals from the penalty spot.

May 18th: Jardine was in the Scotland team which beat England 2-0 at Hampden Park.

Between June 1st and June 22nd Sandy Jardine played 5 times for Scotland in matches against Belgium (1-2), Norway (2-1), Zaire (2-0), Brazil (0-0)

and Yugoslavia (1-1). The last three matches were in the World Cup Finals in West Germany.

LEAGUE CUP

August 11th:
RANGERS (2) 3   FALKIRK (1) 1
  Scott 2 (13, 23),   Somner (15)
  Conn (68)

RANGERS: McCloy; Jardine, Mathieson; Greig, Johnstone, MacDonald; McLean, Forsyth, Parlane (Conn), Scott, Mason

FALKIRK: Donaldson; Kennedy, Young; Fowler, Markie (Mercer), Wheatley; Hoggan, Whiteford (Thomas), Harley, Somner, McLeod

Attendance: 30,000

August 15th:
ARBROATH (1) 1   RANGERS (0) 2
  Pirie (4)   Conn (70),
                       Parlane (84)

ARBROATH: Marshall; Milne, Rylance; Cargill, Waddell, Murray; Sellars (Reid), Penman, Pirie, Cant, Fletcher

RANGERS: McCloy; Jardine, Mathieson; Greig, Johnstone, MacDonald; McLean, Forsyth, Parlane, Scott (Smith), Mason (Conn)

Attendance: 6,677

August 18th:
RANGERS (0) 1   CELTIC (0) 2
  McNeill o.g. (89)   Lennox (82),
                       Hood (86)

RANGERS: McCloy; Jardine, Mathieson; Greig, Johnstone, MacDonald; McLean (Scott), Forsyth, Parlane, Conn, Young (Smith)

CELTIC: Hunter; McGrain, Brogan; Murray, McNeill, Connelly; Johnstone, McLaughlin (Callaghan), Dalglish (Hood), Hay, Lennox

Attendance: 63,173

Missed chances proved costly for Rangers. 4 times Conn and Young mis-hit shots that would have guaranteed goals. Rangers rather abused their chance of winning while Celtic accepted the fewer opportunities that came their way. It became the day of the substitutes. Hood, the late arrival for Celtic, turned Smith, the Rangers replacement, inside out and crossed for Lennox to shoot home an unexpected goal in the 82nd minute. When Smith drove a free-kick into a defensive wall Celtic used 2 passes to allow Hood to score at the other end. Rangers' only reply was a last-minute own goal from McNeill under pressure from another substitute, Scott.

August 22nd:
RANGERS   (0) 3   ARBROATH   (0) 0
MacDonald (47), Conn (68),
   Smith (81)

RANGERS: McCloy; Jardine, Mathieson; Greig,
Johnstone, MacDonald; McLean, Forsyth, Parlane,
Scott (Conn), Morris (Smith)

ARBROATH: Marshall; Milne, Rylance; Cargill,
Waddell, Murray; Fletcher, Cant, Pirie, Penman
(Donald), Yule (Butler)

Attendance: 12,000

August 25th:
CELTIC   (1) 1   RANGERS   (0) 3
   Lennox (23)   MacDonald (53),
                            Parlane (56),
                            Conn (82)

CELTIC: Hunter; McGrain, Brogan; Murray,
McNeill, Connelly; Johnstone, McLaughlin (Hood),
Dalglish, Hay, Lennox

RANGERS: McCloy; Jardine, Mathieson; Greig,
Johnstone, MacDonald; McLean, Forsyth, Parlane,
Conn, Young

Attendance: 57,000

Jimmy Johnstone was ordered off

It was Alex MacDonald who won the match for Rangers
by scoring the first and making the 2nd and 3rd goals.
After Lennox had opened the scoring for Celtic in the 23rd
minute. MacDonald's vicious volley from Jardine's cross
brought Rangers level. A MacDonald cross, a Conn back-
header and a Parlane lunge took them in front. Conn
scored a 3rd 8 minutes from time. Even in the period after
Johnstone was sent off and Celtic were reduced to 10 men
Dalglish dredged the bottom of his stamina in trying to
equalise and the whole side fought against impossible
odds. Lennox had another goal disallowed.

August 29th:
FALKIRK   (0) 1   RANGERS   (3) 5
   Whiteford (50)   O'Hara (19),
                            McLean (28),
                            Forsyth (39),
                            Conn 2 (80, 89)

FALKIRK: Donaldson; S. Kennedy, Gibson; Markie,
Wheatley, Fowler; Hoggan, Whiteford, Harley, Somner,
Shirra

RANGERS: Kennedy; Jardine, Mathieson;
Donaldson, Johnstone, MacDonald; McLean, Forsyth,
O'Hara, Scott (Conn), Smith

Attendance: 12,000

League Cup Section Table

	P	W	D	L	F	A	Pts
RANGERS	6	5	0	1	17	6	10
Celtic	6	5	0	1	12	7	10
Arbroath	6	2	0	4	9	13	4
Falkirk	6	0	0	6	6	18	0

September 12th: Second Round First Leg
RANGERS   (5) 6   DUMBARTON   (0) 0
   Parlane 3 (45 secs, 8 pen, 22),
   Young 2 (12, 51), Greig (41 pen)

RANGERS: McCloy; Jardine, Mathieson; Greig,
Johnstone, MacDonald; McLean, Forsyth, Parlane,
Conn, Young

DUMBARTON: Taylor; Watt, McQuade; Menzies,
Jenkins, Graham; Coleman, Wallace, McCormack, T.
McAdam, Paterson

Attendance: 25,000

October 10th: Second Round Second Leg
DUMBARTON   (0) 1   RANGERS   (1) 2
   McCormack (76)   Scott (14), Fyfe (59)

DUMBARTON: Williams; McKay, Wilkinson;
Menzies (Graham), Cushley, Ruddy; Coleman, Wallace
(T. McAdam), McCormack, Paterson, Bourke

RANGERS: Kennedy; Jardine, Mathieson; Greig
(Conn), Johnstone, MacDonald (Smith); McLean,
Forsyth, Scott, Fyfe, Houston

Attendance: 6,000

Rangers won 8-1 on aggregate

October 31st: Quarter-Final First Leg
RANGERS   (1) 2   HIBERNIAN   (0) 0
   Greig (7), Schaedler o.g. (68)

RANGERS: McCloy; Jardine, Mathieson; Greig,
Jackson, MacDonald; McLean, Forsyth, O'Hara (Scott),
Conn, Houston

HIBERNIAN: McArthur; Bremner, Schaedler;
Stanton, Black, Blackley; Smith (Hazel), Higgins,
Gordon, Cropley, Duncan

Attendance: 22,000

November 21st: Quarter-Final Second Leg
HIBERNIAN   0   RANGERS   0

HIBERNIAN: McArthur; Brownlie, Schaedler;
Stanton, Black, Blackley; Edwards, O'Rourke, Gordon,
Cropley (Munro), Duncan

RANGERS: McCloy; Jardine, Mathieson; Greig,
Jackson, Houston; McLean, Forsyth, Parlane,
MacDonald, Scott

Attendance: 19,245

Rangers won 2-0 on aggregate

December 5th: Semi-Final   At Hampden Park
CELTIC   (1) 3   RANGERS   (1) 1
  Hood 3 (35, 55, 73)   MacDonald (38)

CELTIC: Hunter; McGrain, Brogan; McCluskey,
McNeill, Murray; Hood, Hay, Wilson, Callaghan,
Dalgish — Connelly, Johnstone

RANGERS: McCloy; Jardine, Mathieson; Greig,
Jackson, Houston; McLean (Johnstone), Forsyth,
Parlane, Conn, MacDonald —Smith

Attendance: 54,864

A Harry Hood hat-trick gave Celtic victory and a much
more comfortable win than they could have expected.

SCOTTISH CUP

January 26th: Third Round
RANGERS   (4) 8   QUEENS PARK   (0) 0
  Parlane 3 (11, 39, 76),
  McLean 3 (59, 80, 87),
  Scott (18), Morris (29)

RANGERS: Hunter; Jardine, Mathieson; Hamilton,
Johnstone, Smith; McLean, O'Hara, Parlane, Scott,
Morris

QUEENS PARK: Lowrie; Dougan, McGowan;
Gibson, Thomson, Hunter; Inglis, Borland, Fallis,
Smith, Mackay

Attendance: 19,000

Parlane missed a penalty

February 17th: Fourth Round
RANGERS   (0) 0   DUNDEE   (0) 3
                          Scott (50),
                          Duncan 2 (70, 76)

RANGERS: McCloy; Jardine, Mathieson; Greig,
Jackson, Johnstone; McLean, O'Hara, Parlane, Scott,
Hamilton (Young)

DUNDEE: Allan; R. Wilson, Gemmell; Ford,
Stewart, Phillip; J. Wilson, Robinson, Duncan, J. Scott,
Lambie

Attendance: 64,672

CUP WINNERS CUP

September 19th: First Round First Leg
ANKARAGUCU (Turkey)   (0) 0   RANGERS   (1) 2
                                Conn (11),
                                McLean (60)
ANKARAGUCU: Baskin; Remzi, Ismail; Mehmet,
Mujdat, Selcuk; Metin, Zafer, Melih, Ali Osman,
Tahsin

RANGERS: McCloy; Jardine, Mathieson; Greig,
Jackson, Smith; McLean, Forsyth, Parlane, Conn,
Young

Attendance: 30,000

October 3rd: First Round Second Leg
RANGERS   (1) 4   ANKARAGUCU   (0) 0
  Greig 2 (18, 83),
  O'Hara (80),
  Johnstone (89)

RANGERS: McCloy; Jardine, Mathieson; Greig,
Johnstone, MacDonald, McLean, Forsyth, O'Hara,
Conn, Houston

ANKARAGUCU: Baskin; Remzi, Ismael, Errian,
Mujdat, Zafer, Mehmet, Metin, Melih, Coskun, Tahsin

Attendance: 30,000

Coskun and Errian were ordered off

Rangers won 6-0 on aggregate

October 24th: Second Round First Leg
BORUSSIA MOENCHEN-   RANGERS   (0) 0
  GLADBACH   (1) 3
  Heynckes 2 (21, 65),
  Rupp (86)

BORUSSIA: Kleff, Vogts, Bonhof, Sieloff, Danner,
Koppel, Wimmer, Kulik, Jensen, Rupp, Heynckes

RANGERS: McCloy, Jardine, Johnstone, Forsyth,
Mathieson, Greig, MacDonald, Houston, McLean,
Parlane (O'Hara), Conn

Attendance: 33,000

McCloy saved a penalty from Heynckes

Rangers lost decisively and so set themselves a near
impossible task to survive the Second Round of the
Competition.

November 7th: Second Round Second Leg
RANGERS   (2) 3   BORUSSIA MOENCHEN-
  Conn (10),   GLADBACH   (1) 2
  Jackson (32),   Jensen 2 (28, 70)
  MacDonald (61)

RANGERS: McCloy, Jardine, Mathieson, Greig,
Jackson, MacDonald, McLean, Forsyth (Young),
O'Hara, Conn, Houston

BORUSSIA: Kleff, Danner, Bonhof, Kulik, Sieloff,
Vogts, Jensen, Koppel, Rupp, Wimmer, Heynckes

Attendance: 40,000

This Rangers' performance was entertaining and at times
quite exhilarating but it was in pursuit of a lost cause.
Faced with a 3-goal handicap, Rangers were forced to
trade goals with a team whose attack was among the best in
Europe. The fans were thus treated to a night of action. It
took Rangers only 10 minutes to open the scoring.

Mathieson sent over a long free-kick, O'Hara struck a fine glancing header onto the post and the ball rebounded to Conn who shot home. But in 28 minutes the Germans scored a goal which left Rangers seeking 4 for victory. Jensen cut inside past Mathieson and, picking up pace all the way, fired a low shot past McCloy. Rangers scored a 2nd goal 4 minutes later when Jackson outjumped the vistors' defence to head home a Houston cross. In 60 minutes Rangers sent on Young as an extra striker for Forsyth and seconds later the move paid a dividend. Young created space for Houston to cross and MacDonald nodded home his side's third. 20 minutes from time Heynckes sent Jensen free again. McCloy saved his first shot but the great Dane netted the rebound. Borussia Monchen-Gladbach won 5-3 on aggregate.

APPEARANCES

	League	League Cup	Scottish Cup	Cup Winners Cup
McCloy	30	9	1	4
Jardine	34	11	2	4
Mathieson	26	11	2	4
Greig	30+2S	10	1	4
D. Johnstone	31	8+1S	2	2
MacDonald	29	11	-	3
McLean	21+3S	11	2	4
Smith	7+2S	1+4S	1	1
Forsyth	18	11	-	4
Parlane	28+1S	8	2	2
Conn	7+4S	5+5S	-	4
Scott	21+3S	6+2S	2	-
Young	19+1S	3	0+1S	1+1S
O'Hara	18+1S	2	2	2+1S
Denny	0+1S	-	-	-
Houston	9+1S	4	-	3
Morris	5+1S	1	1	-
Jackson	18	3	1	2
Fyfe	7+6S	1	-	-
Hamilton	4+3S	-	2	-
McDougall	8+1S	-	-	-
Hunter	3	-	1	-
Kennedy	1	2	-	-
Mason	-	2	-	-
Donaldson	-	1	-	-
Miller	-	-	-	-

GOALSCORERS

League: Parlane 14 (5 pens), Scott 8, Fyfe 7, Young 7, Greig 6, O'Hara 4, Conn 4, Jackson 4, McLean 4, MacDonald 3, Jardine 3 (3 pens), Smith 1, Hamilton 1, Johnstone 1

League Cup: Conn 6, Parlane 5 (1 pen), Scott 3, MacDonald 3, Young 2, Greig 2 (1 pen), Own Goals 2, Smith 1, O'Hara 1, McLean 1, Forsyth 1, Fyfe 1

Scottish Cup: Parlane 3, McLean 3, Scott 1, Morris 1

Cup Winners Cup: Greig 2, Conn 2, McLean 1, O'Hara 1, Johnstone 1, Jackson 1, MacDonald 1

The Rangers squad of 1976 show off the silverware. Back row: Miller, Parlane, M. Henderson, Kennedy, McCloy, Lawrie, Jackson, Watson, Forsyth. Middle row: Craig, McDougall, Brand, Robertson, Stein, Johnstone, Boyd, Armour, O'Hara, Dawson, Mason. Front row: Wallace (manager), McLean, Boyd, Morris, Jardine, Greig, Denny, MacDonald, McKean, Munro, and Hamilton.

Season 1974–75

Rangers won their first League Championship since season 1963–4 and finished 7 points ahead of Runners-up Hibs and 11 points ahead of 3rd-placed Celtic. They won 25 matches and lost only 3 (2 home and 1 away) in what was to be the last Championship before reconstruction and the formation of the Premier League. After drawing at Ayr in the first match of the season they went 12 matches without defeat and after losing to lowly Airdrie on December 21st they went a further 16 matches undefeated before again losing to Airdrie at Ibrox in the last match of the Season. Celtic were beaten both home and away. Rangers scored 86 goals — 19 more than in the previous season. Parlane finished with 17 of the goals and Derek Johnstone and Tommy McLean finished with 14 goals each. Kennedy and Jardine were ever-presents and Jackson missed only one match. Alfie Conn was transferred to Tottenham Hotspur for £140,000 before the Season got underway and Colin Stein returned to the club from Coventry City. Stein it was who scored the goal at Easter Road which clinched the title with four matches remaining.

Rangers drew Hibernian, Dundee and St Johnstone in their League Cup Section. Failure to beat Hibs at Ibrox in the last of their 6 matches caused their elimination from that competition.

Having drawn at Aberdeen in the Third Round of the Scottish Cup, Rangers lost the replay at Ibrox to an extra-time goal by substitute Duncan Davidson.

After failing to qualify for Europe Rangers took part in the Texaco Cup competition but they were beaten both home (1-3) and away (2-0) by Southampton.

Rangers reached the Final of the Drybrough Cup but lost to Celtic on penalties (2-4) after extra time in the Hampden Final.

Rangers undertook a pre-season tour of Sweden with rather mixed results. Following that they took up an invitation to take part in the prestigious Barcelona Tournament. As a reward for winning the Championship they undertook a World Tour which involved playing matches in Norway, Canada, New Zealand and Australia. 9 matches were played and only 2 lost in a gruelling schedule.

Sandy Jardine, who missed the end of the season tour through injury, was voted the Scottish Football Writers' Player of the Year.

League: Champions
League Cup: Failed to Qualify from Section
Scottish Cup: Third Round

SCOTTISH FIRST DIVISION

July 15th: Alfie Conn was transferred to Tottenham Hotspur for £140,000.

August 31st:
AYR UNITED (0) 1   RANGERS (1) 1
  McCulloch (75)   Jardine (30 pen)

AYR UNITED: A. McLean; Wells, McAnespie; Fleming, Murphy, McCulloch; Graham, Lannon (Tait/Bell), Doyle, Ingram, G. McLean

RANGERS: Kennedy; Jardine, Miller; Forsyth, Jackson, Johnstone; McLean, Young, Parlane, Scott, Fyfe

Attendance: 15,000

265

September 7th:
RANGERS (2) 3   PARTICK THISTLE (1) 2
  Young (37),   Craig (6), Coulston (81)
  Fyfe 2 (41, 76)

RANGERS: Kennedy; Jardine, Jackson, Forsyth, Miller; McDougall, Johnstone, MacDonald; Young, Parlane, Fyfe

PARTICK THISTLE: Rough; Hansen (Anderson), Campbell, Clark, Kellachan; Houston, Glavin; Craig, Gibson, Coulston, McQuade (Gray)

Attendance: 20,000

September 14th:
CELTIC (1) 1   RANGERS (0) 2
  Dalglish (31)   McDougall (57),
                         Jackson (75)

CELTIC: Connaghan; McGrain, McCluskey, McNeill, Brogan; Murray, Davidson, Callaghan; Johnstone (Hood), Dalglish, Wilson

RANGERS: Kennedy; Jardine, Jackson, Forsyth, Greig; McDougall (McLean), Johnstone, Young; Parlane, Fyfe, Scott

Attendance: 60,000

Brogan and Parlane were ordered off

This was Rangers' first victory at Parkhead since September 1968.

September 20th: Bobby McKean was signed from St Mirren for £40,000.

September 21st:
RANGERS (3) 3   DUMBARTON (1) 2
  Johnstone 2 (9, 19),   McAdam (44),
  Scott (29)   Cook (57)

RANGERS: Kennedy; Jardine, Jackson, Forsyth, Greig; Johnstone, McKean, McLean (Parlane); Scott, Young, Fyfe (MacDonald)

DUMBARTON: Williams; Mullen, Cushley, Muir, Watt; Ruddy, Wallace, Graham; Cook, Bourke, McAdam

Attendance: 18,000

September 28th:
KILMARNOCK (0) 0   RANGERS (2) 6
                         Jardine (22 pen),
                         Young 2 (39, 62),
                         McKean (49),
                         Johnstone (68),
                         McLean (82)

KILMARNOCK: Stewart; Maxwell, Rodman, McDicken, Robertson; McCulloch, Sheed, McSherry; Fleming, Morrison (Fallis), Smith

RANGERS: Kennedy; Jardine, Jackson, Forsyth, Greig; McKean, Johnstone, MacDonald; McLean, Scott, Young

Attendance: 18,000

October 5th:
RANGERS (1) 2   MORTON (0) 0
  Forsyth (7), McKean (84)

RANGERS: Kennedy; Jardine, Greig; Johnstone, Jackson, Forsyth; McKean, McLean, Parlane, MacDonald, Young

MORTON: Baines; Hayes, Ritchie; Reid, Anderson, Rankin; McGhee, Townsend, Osborne, Lumsden, Skovdam

Attendance: 25,000

October 12th:
DUNFERMLINE (1) 1   RANGERS (3) 6
  Mackie (37)   Parlane 5
                         (4, 7, 60, 71, 75),
                       Johnstone (45)

DUNFERMLINE: Karlsen; R. Campbell, McCallum (Evans), McNichol, Thomson; Sinclair, Scott, Kinninmonth; Mackie, Campbell, Shaw

RANGERS: Kennedy; Jardine, Forsyth, Jackson, Greig (Scott); McKean, Johnstone, MacDonald; McLean, Parlane, Young

Attendance: 18,000

October 19th:
RANGERS (1) 3   CLYDE (0) 1
  Jardine (24), Fyfe (56),   Miller (86)
  Johnstone (87)

RANGERS: Kennedy; Jardine, Jackson, Denny, Miller; Johnstone, McKean, MacDonald; McLean, Fyfe, Young

CLYDE: Cairney; Jim Burns, McVie, Aherne, Swan (John Burns); Sullivan, Miller, Pringle; Harvey (Ferris), Ward, Marshall

Attendance: 20,000

October 26th:
HEARTS (1) 1   RANGERS (0) 1
  Gibson (34)   Jardine (66 pen)

HEARTS: Cruikshank; Sneddon, Clunie, Kay, Anderson, Jeffries; Gibson, Busby, Carruthers (Stevenson), Murray, Callachan (Prentice)

RANGERS: Kennedy; Jardine, Greig; Johnstone, Jackson, Forsyth; McKean, McLean, Fyfe (O'Hara), MacDonald, Young

Attendance: 28,000

League positions

	P	W	D	L	F	A	Pts
1 RANGERS	9	7	2	0	27	9	16
2 Celtic	8	7	0	1	26	9	14
3 Aberdeen	9	7	0	2	22	9	14
4 Dundee United	9	4	3	2	19	10	11
5 Hibernian	8	5	1	2	19	12	11

October 30th: Scotland beat East Germany 3-0 at Hampden Park. Jardine missed a penalty-kick. Derek Johnstone made an appearance as substitute.

November 2nd:
ST JOHNSTONE (1) 1   RANGERS (0) 2
O'Rourke (1)   McLean (53),
                                  Young (84)

ST JOHNSTONE: Robertson; Smith, Rennie, MacDonald, Argue; Kinnell, Cramond, Hall; O'Rourke, Muir, Lambie

RANGERS: Kennedy; Jardine, Jackson, Forsyth, Greig; McKean, MacDonald, Johnstone; McLean, Parlane, Young

Attendance: 13,260

November 9th:
RANGERS (1) 1   DUNDEE (0) 0
McKean (24)

RANGERS: Kennedy; Jardine, Jackson, Forsyth, Greig; Johnstone, McKean, MacDonald; McLean, Parlane, Young

DUNDEE: Allan; Wilson, Stewart, Phillip, Gemmell (Johnston); Ford, Robinson, Caldwell; Hoggan (I. Scott), J. Scott, Hutchinson

Attendance: 25,000

November 11th: An Old Firm Select drew 3-3 with Dunfermline in a match for the dependents of the late John Lunn. The Select's goals were scored by Smith, Parlane and Denis Law, who was guesting.

November 14th: Dave Smith was transferred to Arbroath for £10,000.

November 16th:
MOTHERWELL (0) 0   RANGERS (4) 5
                                  Johnstone (42 secs),
                                  Young (33),
                                  MacDonald (37),
                                  Parlane (41),
                                  McKean (86)

MOTHERWELL: Rennie; W. Watson, R. Watson, Muir, Wark; Goodwin, Millar, Gardner; Graham, Goldthorpe, McIlwraith (Pettigrew)

RANGERS: Kennedy; Jardine, Jackson, Forsyth, Greig; Johnstone (McDougall), McKean, MacDonald; McLean, Parlane, Young

Attendance: 19,409

November 20th: Scotland were beaten 2-1 by Spain at Hampden Park. Jardine was in the team.

November 23rd:
RANGERS (0) 0   HIBERNIAN (0) 1
                                  Harper (75)

RANGERS: Kennedy; Jardine, Jackson, Forsyth, Greig; Johnstone (McDougall), McKean, MacDonald; McLean, Parlane, Young

HIBERNIAN: McArthur; Brownlie, Spalding, Blackley, Bremner; Stanton, Smith, Munro; Duncan, Harper, Cropley

Attendance: 30,000

November 30th:
RANGERS (2) 4   DUNDEE
Parlane (10),   UNITED (0) 2
Jardine 2 (37 pen, 75), Fleming (50),
McLean (59)   Jackson o.g. (68)

RANGERS: Kennedy; Jardine (Denny), Jackson, Forsyth, Greig; McDougall, McKean, MacDonald; McKean, Parlane, Young

DUNDEE UNITED: McAlpine; Rolland, Copland, W. Smith (McLeod), Kopel; Fleming, Narey, Houston; Traynor, Gray, MacDonald (Hegarty)

Attendance: 25,000

December 7th:
ABERDEEN (0) 1   RANGERS (1) 2
Hair (75)   Johnstone (30),
                                  McLean (87)

ABERDEEN: Clark; Hair, Miller, Young, McLelland; Hermiston, Thomson, Purdie; Graham, Jarvie, Street

RANGERS: Kennedy; Jardine, Jackson, Forsyth, Greig; Johnstone, McKean, MacDonald; McLean, Parlane, Young

Attendance: 25,000

December 14th:
RANGERS (1) 3   ARBROATH (0) 0
Parlane 2 (2, 84),
Jackson (73)

RANGERS: Kennedy; Jardine, Jackson, Denny, Greig; Johnstone, McKean, MacDonald; McLean, Parlane, Young

ARBROATH: Wilson; Murray, Cargill, Carson, Buchan; Rylance, Penman, Smith; Sellars, Fletcher (Reid), Yule

Attendance: 20,000

December 21st:
AIRDRIE   (3) 4   RANGERS   (2) 3
  Lapsley (2), Walker (8),   Johnstone (9),
  Jonquin (23 pen), Wilson (87)   Jardine 2 (24 pen, 89)

AIRDRIE: McWilliams; Jonquin, Menzies, Black,
Cowan; Reynolds, Walker, Whiteford; McCann, Wilson,
Lapsley

RANGERS: Kennedy; Jardine, Denny, Jackson,
Greig; McKean (Hamilton), Johnstone, MacDonald;
McLean, Parlane, Young (Fyfe)

Attendance: 19,500

December 28th:
RANGERS   (3) 3   AYR UNITED   (0) 0
  McLean (6), Jardine (8 pen),
  Parlane (31)

RANGERS: Kennedy; Jardine, Jackson, Denny,
Miller; Greig, Johnstone, McDougall; McLean, Parlane,
Scott

AYR UNITED: McGiffen; Fillipi, McDonald
(McAnespie), Murphy, Fleming, Cairns (Dickson);
Graham, McCulloch, Doyle, Ingram, Lannon

Attendance: 22,000

League positions
                  P   W   D   L   F   A   Pts
1 Celtic   18   15   2   1   49   13   32
2 RANGERS   18   14   2   2   50   18   30
3 Hibernian   18   11   4   3   34   16   26
4 Dundee United 18   9   5   4   46   22   23
5 Aberdeen   18   8   4   6   31   24   20

January 1st:
PARTICK THISTLE   (0) 0   RANGERS   (0) 4
                          Jackson (50),
                          McLean (69),
                          McDougall (75),
                          Greig (82)

PARTICK THISTLE: Arrol; J. Hansen, Kellachan;
Campbell, A. Hansen, Anderson (Lawrie); Houston,
Rooney (Mitchell), Joe Craig, Somner, McQuade

RANGERS: Kennedy; Jardine, Greig; McDougall,
Jackson, McLean; Forsyth, Johnstone, Parlane, Miller;
Scott

Attendance: 22,000

Somner was sent off after a clash with McLean

January 4th:
RANGERS   (1) 3   CELTIC   (0) 0
  Johnstone (6), McLean (50),
  Parlane (74)

RANGERS: Kennedy; Jardine, Forsyth, Jackson
(Miller), Greig; McDougall, Johnstone, MacDonald;
McLean, Parlane, Scott (Young)

CELTIC: Hunter; McGrain, McNeill, McCluskey,
Brogan; Glavin, Hood (Johnstone), Murray; Callaghan,
Dalglish, Wilson

Attendance: 70,000

Rangers won well and deservedly. Jock Wallace's match-
winning stroke was to play without a left-back. Greig
moved into a defensive midfield position cutting off
Dalglish's work at source. Both Glavin and Murray were
bogged down in the mud and Wilson tired after a brilliant
first half. Kennedy pulled off a remarkable save from
McGrain and a series of dives at Celtic feet was bravery in
the extreme. Rangers took the lead in the 6th minute,
McLean curling over a cross for Johnstone to head home.
Another cross gave Parlane a goal in the 74th minute and in
between times he scored himself from one of MacDonald's
many well-weighted passes. The story might have been
different if Hood could have trundled the ball over the line
from 3 yards and if Dalglish had placed an 8-yard shot
inside the post — both in the first half.

January 11th:
DUMBARTON   (1) 1   RANGERS   (2) 5
  Muir (39)   McLean 3 (24, 32, 83),
                            Parlane (53),
                            Johnstone (78)

DUMBARTON: McGregor; Muir, Cushley, Ruddy,
Watt (A. Brown); Wallace, Bourke, Menmuir; Cook, T.
McAdam, C. McAdam (Coleman)

RANGERS: Kennedy; Jardine, Forsyth, Denny,
Greig; McDougall, Johnstone, MacDonald; McLean,
Parlane, Scott (Young)

Attendance: 16,000

February 1st:
MORTON   (1) 1   RANGERS   (0) 1
  Hazel (16)   Fyfe (86)

MORTON: Baines; Hayes, Anderson, Rankin,
Ritchie; Lumsden, Lieffson, Skovdam; Osborne, Hazel,
McGhee (Hegarty)

RANGERS: Kennedy; Denny (Fyfe), Jackson,
Forsyth, Miller; Jardine, McDougall, MacDonald;
McLean, Parlane, Young

Attendance: 17,000

**February 5th: Scotland drew 1-1 with Spain in
Valencia. Jardine was in the team and Parlane made
an appearance as substitute.**

February 8th:
RANGERS   (0) 2   DUNFERMLINE   (0) 0
  McLean (46),
  MacDonald (71)

RANGERS: Kennedy; Jardine, Jackson, Forsyth, Miller; McDougall (McKean), O'Hara, MacDonald; McLean, Parlane, Young

DUNFERMLINE: Karlsen; Scott, Thomson, R. Campbell, Wallace; Kinninmonth, Reid, Cameron; Watson, Shaw, Sinclair (Davidson)

Attendance: 23,500

February 15th:
RANGERS (1) 3   KILMARNOCK (2) 3
  Parlane 3 (35, 57, 83)   Provan (29),
                            McDicken (44),
                            Fallis (68)

RANGERS: Kennedy; Jardine, Jackson, Forsyth, Miller; McDougall, Johnstone, Hamilton; McLean (Scott), Parlane, McKean

KILMARNOCK: A. McCulloch; McLean, Rodman, McDicken, Robertson; I. McCulloch (Maxwell), Sheed, Provan; Fleming, Morrison (Fallis), Smith

Attendance: 26,000

February 22nd:
CLYDE (1) 1   RANGERS (2) 2
  Sullivan (25)   McKean (13),
                      O'Hara (42)

CLYDE: Williams; Anderson, Aherne, McVie, Jim Burns (John Burns); Sullivan, Miller, Swan (Ferris); Harvey, Ward, Boyle

RANGERS: Kennedy; Jardine, Jackson, Forsyth, Miller; McKean, MacDonald, Hamilton (McDougall); McLean, Parlane, O'Hara

Attendance: 20,000

March 1st:
RANGERS (1) 2   HEARTS (1) 1
  McKean (2), McLean (89)   Callachan (33)

RANGERS: Kennedy; Jardine, Jackson, Forsyth, Miller; McDougall, McKean, MacDonald; McLean, Parlane, Young

HEARTS: Cruikshank; Kay (Brown), D. Murray, Anderson, Clunie; T. Murray, Aird, Busby; Callachan, Ford (Jeffries), Gibson

Attendance: 38,000

League positions

	P	W	D	L	F	A	Pts
1 RANGERS	26	20	4	2	72	25	44
2 Celtic	26	18	4	4	69	29	40
3 Hibernian	26	14	7	5	46	29	35
4 Dundee United	25	12	6	7	54	33	30
5 Aberdeen	25	11	7	7	45	31	29

March 5th: Rangers signed Colin Stein from Coventry City for £80,000.

March 8th:
RANGERS (1) 1   ST JOHNSTONE (0) 0
  Young (5)

RANGERS: Kennedy; Jardine, Jackson, Forsyth, Greig; McKean, MacDonald, Young; McLean, Parlane, Stein

ST JOHNSTONE: Robertson; G. Smith, Kinnell, MacDonald, S. Smith; Ritchie, Lambie, Crammond; O'Rourke (Thomson), McGregor, Muir

Attendance: 42,500

March 15th:
DUNDEE (1) 1   RANGERS (0) 2
  Hutchinson (1)   McLean (51),
                     Parlane (84)

DUNDEE: Allan; Wilson, Gemmell; Stewart, Ford, Robinson; Anderson, J. Scott, Hutchinson, Wallace, Hoggan

RANGERS: Kennedy; Jardine, Jackson, Forsyth, Greig (Miller); McKean, MacDonald, McLean; Stein, Parlane, Young

Attendance: 30,000

March 22nd:
RANGERS (2) 3   MOTHERWELL (0) 0
  Miller (34),
  Johnstone 2 (45, 51)

RANGERS: Kennedy; Jardine, Jackson, Forsyth, Miller; McKean, Johnstone, MacDonald; McLean (Young), Stein, Parlane

MOTHERWELL: Rennie; W. Watson, R. Watson, McLaren, Wark; Martin, Gardner, Miller; Pettigrew, Graham, Goldthorpe (Taylor)

Attendance: 36,500

McKean was ordered off

March 29th:
HIBERNIAN (1) 1   RANGERS (0) 1
  McLeod (19)   Stein (61)

HIBERNIAN: McArthur; Brownlie, Barry, Stanton, Schaedler; Bremner, Smith, Munro; McLeod, Harper, Duncan

RANGERS: Kennedy; Jardine (Greig), Jackson, Forsyth, Miller; McKean, MacDonald, Johnstone; McLean, Stein, Parlane — Young

Attendance: 38,585

Jardine missed a penalty

Rangers celebrated their first Scottish Championship in 11 years. They won a hard-fought point against Hibs. They took the Title with only 2 matches lost in the League, with 79 goals scored and only 27 conceded and with 4 full matches remaining. Rangers lost an early goal when

Schaedler crossed for McLeod to score with a well-placed header under Kennedy's body. Jardine missed a penalty, striking a post after McKean had been brought down. Then Stein from McKean's cross headed his first goal since his return to the club. Rangers dominated the final stages and hit the bar before the end. The injured Greig came out for the last few seconds.

April 5th:
DUNDEE UNITED (2) 2   RANGERS (1) 2
 Sturrock 2 (26, 37)   McLean (8),
                         Johnstone (65)

DUNDEE UNITED: McAlpine; Copland, Smith, Narey, Flemming; Addison, Kopel (Hegarty), McLeod; Houston, Gray, Sturrock

RANGERS: Kennedy; Jardine, Jackson, Forsyth, Miller; McKean, MacDonald, Johnstone; McLean (O'Hara), Stein (Young), Parlane

Attendance: 12,000

April 12th:
RANGERS (0) 3   ABERDEEN (0) 2
 Johnstone (57), Stein (60),   Williamson (55),
 Miller (76 pen)   Hermiston (61 pen)

RANGERS: Kennedy; Jardine, Jackson, Forsyth, Miller; McKean, Johnstone, MacDonald; McLean (Fyfe), Parlane, Stein

ABERDEEN: Clark; Hermiston, Young, Miller, McLelland; Hair, Smith, Williamson; Robb, Jarvie, Graham

Attendance: 33,000

April 16th: Kennedy, Jardine, Jackson and Parlane represented Scotland in a 1-1 draw with Sweden in Gothenburg. Derek Johnstone made an appearance as substitute.

April 19th:
ARBROATH (0) 1   RANGERS (1) 2
 Yule (85)   Stein (30),
                         Parlane (66)

ARBROATH: Marshall; Milne (Carson), Wells, Cargill, Murray; Penman, Fletcher, Rylance; Payne (Sellars), Bone, Yule

RANGERS: Kennedy; Jardine, Jackson, Forsyth, Miller; McKean, Johnstone, MacDonald; McLean (Fyfe), Stein (Young), Parlane

Attendance: 6,393

April 26th:
RANGERS (0) 0   AIRDRIE (0) 1
                         Wilson (66)

RANGERS: Kennedy; Jardine, Jackson, Forsyth, Greig; McKean (Miller), MacDonald, Johnstone; McLean, Stein (Young), Parlane

AIRDRIE: McWilliams; Jonquin, Menzies, Black, Cowan; Whiteford, Walker, Lapsley; McCann (March), McCulloch, Wilson

Attendance: 63,000

League positions

	P	W	D	L	F	A	Pts
1 RANGERS	34	25	6	3	86	33	56
2 Hibernian	34	20	9	5	69	37	49
3 Celtic	34	20	5	9	81	41	45
4 Dundee United	34	19	7	8	72	43	45
5 Aberdeen	34	16	9	9	66	43	41
6 Dundee	34	16	6	12	48	42	38
7 Ayr United	34	14	8	11	50	61	36
8 Hearts	34	11	13	10	47	52	35
9 St Johnstone	34	11	12	11	41	44	34
10 Motherwell	34	14	5	15	52	57	33
11 Airdrie	34	11	9	14	43	55	31
12 Kilmarnock	34	8	15	11	52	68	31
13 Partick Thistle	34	10	10	14	48	62	30
14 Dumbarton	34	7	10	17	44	55	24
15 Dunfermline	34	7	9	18	46	66	23
16 Clyde	34	6	10	18	40	63	22
17 Morton	34	6	10	18	31	62	22
18 Arbroath	34	5	7	22	34	66	17

May 6th: Sandy Jardine was voted Scotland's Player of the Year.

May 13th: Kennedy, Jardine and Parlane were in the Scotland team which beat Portugal 1-0 at Hampden Park. Jackson made an appearance as substitute.

May 17th: Scotland drew 2-2 with Wales at Ninian Park, Cardiff. Kennedy, Jardine, Jackson and Parlane were in the team. Jackson scored one of the goals.

May 20th: Scotland beat Northern Ireland 3-0 at Hampden Park. Parlane scored one of the goals. Kennedy and Jardine were also in the team.

May 24th: Jardine captained the Scotland team which was beaten 5-1 by England at Wembley. Kennedy and Parlane were also in the side. It was discovered after the match that Jardine had dislocated his pelvic bone. He missed the International in Rumania and also missed the club's World Tour.

June 1st: Derek Parlane was in the Scotland team which drew 1-1 with Rumania in Bucharest.

LEAGUE CUP

August 7th:
RANGERS (2) 3   ST JOHNSTONE (0) 2
   Scott (90 secs),   McGregor 2 (76, 83)
   Jardine (2), Parlane (84)

RANGERS: Kennedy; Jardine, Mathieson; Greig, Jackson, Johnstone; McLean, Fyfe, Parlane, O'Hara (Young), Scott (Miller)

ST JOHNSTONE: Robertson; Ritchie, Argue; Rennie, MacDonald, Cramond; Muir, G. Smith, McGregor, Thomson, Hall

Attendance: 20,000

August 10th:
HIBERNIAN (3) 3   RANGERS (0) 1
   Gordon (4), Duncan (33),   Scott (56)
   Harper (45)

HIBERNIAN: McArthur; Brownlie, Spalding, Blackley, Schaedler; Stanton, Edwards, Higgins; Gordon, Harper, Cropley

RANGERS: Kennedy; Jardine, Forsyth, Johnstone, Mathieson; McLean, MacDonald; Young, Sharp (Denny), Scott, Fyfe

Attendance: 23,539

August 14th:
ST JOHNSTONE (1) 3   RANGERS (2) 6
   Thomson 2 (43, 48)   Young 2 (18, 49),
                 Jardine 2 (44, 60),
                 Scott (64),
                 Forsyth (86)

ST JOHNSTONE: Robertson; Ritchie, Argue; Rennie, MacDonald, Cramond; Muir, G. Smith, McGregor, Thomson (McQuade), Hall

RANGERS: Kennedy; Denny, Miller; Forsyth, Jackson, Johnstone; McLean, Jardine, Young, Fyfe, Scott

Attendance: 6,000

August 17th:
DUNDEE (0) 0   RANGERS (1) 2
                 Jardine (42), Fyfe (84)

DUNDEE: Allan; R. Wilson, Gemmell (Johnston); Ford, Stewart, Phillip; J. Wilson (Duncan), Robinson, Hutchinson, J. Scott, I. Scott

RANGERS: Kennedy; Denny, Miller; Forsyth, Jackson, Johnstone; McLean, Jardine, Young, Fyfe, Scott

Attendance: 18,548

August 24th:
RANGERS (2) 4   DUNDEE (0) 0
   Jardine (25 pen), Scott (44),
   Johnstone 2 (47, 76)

RANGERS: Kennedy; Denny, Miller; Forsyth, Jackson, Johnstone; McLean, Jardine, Young, Fife, Scott

DUNDEE: Allan; R. Wilson, Johnston; Ford, Stewart (Anderson), Gemmell; Caldwell, Robinson, Hutchinson, J. Scott (I. Scott), J. Wilson

Attendance: 35,000

August 28th:
RANGERS (0) 0   HIBERNIAN (0) 1
                 Cropley (90)

RANGERS: Kennedy; Denny, Miller; Forsyth, Jackson, Johnstone; McLean (O'Hara), Jardine, Young (Parlane), Fyfe, Scott

HIBERNIAN: McArthur; Bremner, Schaedler; Stanton, Spalding, Blackley; Edwards (Cropley), Smith, Harper, Gordon, Duncan

Attendance: 55,000

League Cup Section Table

	P	W	D	L	F	A	Pts
Hibernian	6	5	0	1	16	6	10
RANGERS	6	4	0	2	16	9	8
Dundee	6	2	0	4	11	14	4
St Johnstone	6	1	0	5	9	23	2

SCOTTISH CUP

January 25th: Third Round
ABERDEEN (0) 1   RANGERS (0) 1
   Miller (86)   Scott (67)

ABERDEEN: Clark; Thomson, Young, Miller, McLelland; Williamson, Henry, Hair; Graham, Jarvie, Purdie (Davidson)

RANGERS: Kennedy; Jardine, Jackson, Forsyth, Miller; McDougall, Johnstone (McKean), MacDonald; McLean, Parlane, Scott

Attendance: 30,000

February 10th: Third Round Replay
RANGERS (1) 1   ABERDEEN (1) 2
   McKean (30)   Graham (1),
                 Davidson (112)
           After Extra Time

RANGERS: Kennedy; Jardine, Miller; Johnstone (O'Hara), Jackson, Forsyth; McKean, McLean, Parlane, MacDonald, Scott

ABERDEEN: Clark; Hair, McLelland; Thomson,
Young, Miller; Purdie, Henry (Davidson), Jarvie,
Williamson, Graham

Attendance: 52,000

APPEARANCES

	League	League Cup	Scottish Cup
Kennedy	34	6	2
Jardine	34	6	2
Greig	21+1S	1	-
Forsyth	30	5	2
Jackson	33	5	2
Johnstone	27	6	2
McLean	32+1S	6	2
Fyfe	6+4S	6	-
Parlane	30+1S	1+1S	2
Young	22+6S	5+1S	-
MacDonald	29+1S	1	2
McDougall	11+3S	-	1
McKean	25+1S	-	1+1S
Stein	8	-	-
Hamilton	2+1S	-	-
O'Hara	2+2S	1+1S	0+1S
Scott	7+2S	6	2
Miller	15+3S	4+1S	2
Henderson	-	-	-
Denny	6+1S	4+1S	-
Mathieson	-	2	-
Sharp	-	1	-
Hunter	-	-	-
Steele	-	-	-

GOALSCORERS

League: Parlane 17, Johnstone 14, McLean 14, Jardine
            9 (6 pens), McKean 6, Young 6, Fyfe 4,
            McDougall 3, Jackson 3, Stein 3, Miller 2 (1
            pen), Scott 1, Forsyth 1, Greig 1, MacDonald
            1, O'Hara 1
League Cup: Jardine 5 (1 pen), Scott 4, Young 2,
            Johnstone 2, Parlane 1, Forsyth 1, Fyfe 1
Scottish Cup: Scott 1, McKean 1

The Rangers squad in 1978. Back row: A. Miller, D. Parlane, C. Jackson, P. McCloy,
S. Kennedy, T. Forsyth, K. Watson, A. Boyd. Middle row: T. Craig (physiotherapist), E. Morris,
S. Richardson, R. Brand, D. Johnstone, G. Smith, D. Armour, A. Dawson, J. Denny, J. Mason
(trainer). Front row: J. Greig (manager), W. Mackay, C. Robertson, T. McLean, S. Jardine,
J. MacDonald, D. Cooper, A. MacDonald, R. Russell and D. Strickland.

Season 1975–76

Rangers won the first Premier League Championship. They also won the Scottish Cup and the League Cup to give Jock Wallace his first 'treble' as Manager.

They overcame a shaky spell in October and November and put together a run of 21 games without defeat — from December 6th right to the end of the season — to take the title by 6 points from Celtic. Such was Rangers' success that Internationalists Sandy Jardine and Derek Parlane had to spend most of the 2nd half of the season in the role of substitutes. Only 24 goals were conceded in the 36 matches — by far the lowest in the Division. John Greig who was elected as Scotland's Player of the Year for the 2nd time was the only player to appear in every League Match. Derek Johnstone finished as top scorer with 16 of the 60 goals. Martin Henderson was next best with 10.

In the process of reaching the League Cup Final against Celtic, Rangers scored 26 goals in matches against Motherwell, Airdrie, Clyde, Queen of the South and Montrose. The victory over Queen of the South was achieved by an Alex MacDonald goal in extra time of the Quarter-Final Second Leg tie. A fine headed goal by MacDonald was enough to win the Final and for the first time John Greig received the trophy as Captain. Peter McCloy missed the Final as a result of an injury received in the warm-up before the away leg of the European Cup-tie with St Etienne.

Rangers saw off East Fife, Aberdeen (in a fine display at Ibrox), Queen of the South and Motherwell in their run to the Scottish Cup Final. Their Semi-Final tie with Motherwell saw them pull back from 0-2 down at half-time to win an astonishing match with a Derek Johnstone goal with only 2 minutes left of the match. The same player scored after only 42 seconds of the Final against Hearts, which Rangers won with ease, to take the Cup back to Ibrox after a gap of 3 seasons.

Rangers' brief European Cup run was ended by a fine St Etienne team who were desperately unlucky not to win the trophy in Glasgow some months later.

> League: Champions
> League Cup: Winners
> Scottish Cup: Winners
> European Cup: Second Round

SCOTTISH PREMIER LEAGUE

August 23rd: Kenny Watson was signed from Montrose for £30,000.

August 30th:
RANGERS (0) 2   CELTIC (1) 1
Johnstone (56), Young (68)   Dalglish (42)

RANGERS: McCloy; Forsyth, Greig; Jackson, Jardine (O'Hara), McKean; MacDonald, McLean, Stein, Johnstone, Young

CELTIC: Latchford; McGrain, MacDonald, McCluskey, Lynch; McNamara (Connelly), Dalglish, Edvaldsson; Callaghan, Wilson, Lennox (Ritchie)

Attendance: 69,000.

Alex MacDonald was ordered off

The Celtic goal was scored by Kenny Dalglish 3 minutes before half-time. Early in the 2nd half Derek Johnstone equalised. Quinton Young gave Rangers the lead and Alex MacDonald was despatched to the pavilion. McCloy kept Celtic from the equaliser in the last desperate stages when the substitutes Ritchie and Connelly inspired a rally against the 10-man Rangers.

September 6th:
HEARTS   (0) 0   RANGERS   (2) 2
                        Anderson o.g. (7),
                        Murray o.g. (32)
HEARTS: Cruikshank; Clunie, Anderson, Murray, Burrell; Park, Brown, Busby; Hancock (Callaghan), Gibson, Prentice

RANGERS: McCloy; Miller, Forsyth (Denny), Jackson, Greig; McKean (Stein), MacDonald; Young, McLean, Parlane, Johnstone

Attendance: 25,000

September 13th:
RANGERS   (0) 2   ST JOHNSTONE   (0) 0
  Stein (67), Johnstone (76)
RANGERS: McCloy; Jardine, Greig; Jackson, Miller, MacDonald; O'Hara, Johnstone, McKean (Denny), Parlane (Stein), Young

ST JOHNSTONE: Robertson; G. Smith, MacDonald, Kinnell, S. Smith; McLeod, Thomson, Hamilton; Hotson, Muir, O'Rourke

Attendance: 23,000

September 16th: Rae Simpson was appointed as Rangers' chairman in succession to Matt Taylor who had died the week before. Willie Waddell became Vice-Chairman.

September 20th:
RANGERS   (1) 1   HIBERNIAN   (0) 1
  Blackley o.g. (9)   Brownlie (55)
RANGERS: McCloy; Denny, Jackson, Greig, Miller; McKean, Johnstone, MacDonald; McLean (Stein), Parlane, Young (Fyfe)

HIBERNIAN: McArthur; Brownlie, Barry, Blackley, Schaedler; Stanton, Edwards (Higgins), Munro; Smith, Harper, Duncan

Attendance: 37,000

September 27th:
DUNDEE 0   RANGERS 0
DUNDEE: Allan; Martin, Robinson, Stewart, Johnston; Hoggan, Ford, Gordon (Strachan); Sinclair, Wallace, Purdie

RANGERS: McCloy; Miller, Greig; Jackson, Dawson, McDougall; Johnstone, MacDonald, McLean, Parlane, Young

Attendance: 15,087. McCloy saved a penalty from Hoggan

October 4th:
RANGERS   (1) 1   ABERDEEN   (0) 0
  McDougall (15)
RANGERS: McCloy; Jardine, Greig; Jackson, Dawson, McDougall; McLean, Miller, Parlane, Johnstone, Young

ABERDEEN: Geoghegan; Hair, Ward, Miller, McLelland; Thomson, Scott, Jarvie; Williamson (Cooper), Robb, Graham

Attendance: 22,000

October 11th:
AYR UNITED   (2) 3   RANGERS   (0) 0
  McCulloch (28), Ingram (29),
  Graham (58)
AYR UNITED: Sproat; Wells, McAnespie, Fleming, Murphy; Fillipi, Graham, McCulloch; Doyle, Ingram, Phillips

RANGERS: McCloy; Jardine, Greig; Jackson, Dawson, MacDonald; McDougall (Miller), Johnstone, McLean, Parlane (McKean), Scott

Attendance: 18,000

October 18th:
MOTHERWELL   (0) 2   RANGERS   (1) 1
  Pettigrew (75),   Johnstone (8)
  Davidson (84)
MOTHERWELL: Rennie; Millar, McVie, Stevens, Wark; Watson, McAdam, Davidson; Pettigrew, Graham, Taylor

RANGERS: McCloy; Jardine, Forsyth, Jackson, Greig; MacDonald, McKean, Johnstone; McLean, Parlane, Stein

Attendance: 18,925

October 29th: Greig and Jackson were in the Scotland team which beat Denmark 3-1 at Hampden Park. Parlane made an appearance as substitute.

November 1st:
CELTIC   (0) 1   RANGERS   (0) 1
  Wilson (78)   Parlane (75)
CELTIC: Latchford; McGrain, P. McCluskey, MacDonald, Lynch; Dalglish, Edvaldsson; Callaghan, G. McCluskey (Hood), Deans, Wilson

RANGERS: Kennedy; Jardine, Forsyth, Jackson, Greig; McLean, MacDonald; Johnstone, Stein, Parlane, Young

Attendance: 55,000. In a good Old Firm match a draw was a fair result.

League positions

	P	W	D	L	F	A	Pts
1 Celtic	8	5	2	1	16	8	12
2 Hibernian	9	4	3	2	13	9	11
3 RANGERS	9	4	3	2	10	8	11
4 Motherwell	10	3	5	2	17	15	11
5 Hearts	10	4	3	3	12	13	11

November 8th:
RANGERS (0) 1   HEARTS (2) 2
  Henderson (46)   Gibson 2 (13, 28)

RANGERS: Kennedy; Jardine, Forsyth, Jackson, Greig, McKean; Boyd (Johnstone), MacDonald, Fyfe (McLean), Parlane, Henderson

HEARTS: Cruikshank; Jeffries, Anderson, Murray (Kay), Clunie; Aird, Callachan (Park), Brown; Busby, Gibson, Prentice

Attendance: 23,000

November 12th:
RANGERS (1) 4   DUNDEE UNITED (0) 1
  Parlane (30),   Sturrock (61)
  Johnstone (59),
  Jackson (85),
  MacDonald (89)

RANGERS: Kennedy; Denny, Miller; Jardine, Jackson, Forsyth; McLean, McKean (MacDonald), Parlane, Greig, Johnstone (Henderson)

DUNDEE UNITED: McAlpine; Rolland, Kopel; Rennie, Fleming (Sturrock), Narey; Holt, Payne, Hegarty, McAdam, Houston

Attendance: 10,000

November 15th:
ST JOHNSTONE (0) 1   RANGERS (2) 5
  Muir (74)   MacDonald o.g. (20),
                          Parlane (42),
                          McKean (53),
                          McLean (57),
                          Jardine (65)

ST JOHNSTONE: Robertson; G. Smith, Roberts; MacDonald, Cramond, Kinnell; F. Smith, Lambie, O'Rourke, Thomson (McGregor), Muir

RANGERS: Kennedy; Denny, Jackson, Forsyth, Greig; Jardine, MacDonald, McLean; McKean, Johnstone, Parlane

Attendance: 9,500

November 22nd:
HIBERNIAN (1) 2   RANGERS (0) 1
  Stanton 2 (44, 66)   Young (83)

HIBERNIAN: McArthur; Brownlie, Barry, Blackley; Schaedler; Edwards, Bremner, Stanton, Munro; Harper, Duncan

RANGERS: Kennedy; Denny, Jackson, Forsyth, Greig; Jardine, MacDonald, McLean; McKean (Young), Parlane (Henderson), Johnstone

Attendance: 26,547

November 29th:
RANGERS (2) 2   DUNDEE (1) 1
  Henderson 2 (13, 36)   Wallace (14)

RANGERS: Kennedy; Jardine, Forsyth, Jackson, Greig; MacDonald, Hamilton, McLean; McKean, Henderson, Johnstone

DUNDEE: Allan; Caldwell, Ford, Stewart, Gemmell; Johnston, Strachan (Mackie), Gordon; Hoggan (Hutchinson), Wallace, Purdie

Attendance: 16,500

December 6th:
ABERDEEN (0) 1   RANGERS (0) 0
  Jarvie (84)

ABERDEEN: Geoghegan; Williamson, Miller, Thomson, McLelland; Robb, Smith, McMaster; Scott, Jarvie, Graham

RANGERS: Kennedy; Jardine, Forsyth, Jackson, Greig; Hamilton, MacDonald, McLean; McKean, Henderson, Johnstone

Attendance: 19,565

December 13th:
RANGERS (0) 3   AYR UNITED (0) 0
  Jardine (51 pen),
  Henderson (78),
  McKean (88)

RANGERS: Kennedy; Jardine, Forsyth, Jackson, Greig; MacDonald, Hamilton; McLean, McKean, Henderson, Johnstone

AYR UNITED: Sproat; McDonald, McAnespie, Fleming; Murphy; McSherry, Graham, McCulloch; Doyle, Ingram, Robertson

Attendance: 15,500

December 17th: Colin Jackson was in the Scotland team which drew 1-1 with Rumania at Hampden Park.

December 20th:
RANGERS (1) 3   MOTHERWELL (1) 2
  Johnstone 2 (5, 52),   Pettigrew (15),
  Henderson (81)   McLaren (85)

RANGERS: Kennedy; Jardine (Miller), Jackson, Forsyth, Greig; Hamilton, MacDonald; McLean, McKean, Henderson, Johnstone

MOTHERWELL: Rennie; Millar (W. Watson), McVie, Stevens, Wark; R. Watson (McAdam), McLaren, Davidson; Pettigrew, Graham, Marinello

Attendance: 24,000

December 27th:
DUNDEE UNITED   0   RANGERS   0
DUNDEE UNITED: McAlpine; Rolland, Rennie, Narey, Kopel; Fleming, Smith, Holt; Hall (Steele), Hegarty, McAdam

RANGERS: Kennedy; Miller, Forsyth (Fyfe), Jackson, Greig; MacDonald, Hamilton; McLean, McKean, Henderson, Johnstone

Attendance: 11,500

League positions
	P	W	D	L	F	A	Pts
1 Celtic	18	11	3	4	37	21	25
2 RANGERS	18	9	4	5	29	18	22
3 Motherwell	18	8	6	4	34	26	22
4 Hibernian	18	8	6	4	28	23	22
5 Hearts	18	7	7	4	22	20	21

January 1st:
RANGERS   (1) 1   CELTIC   (0) 0
  Johnstone

RANGERS: Kennedy; Miller, Greig; Forsyth, Jackson, MacDonald; McKean (Scott), Hamilton (O'Hara), Henderson, McLean, Johnston

CELTIC: Latchford; McGrain, Lynch; Edvaldsson, MacDonald, McCluskey; McNamara, Dalglish, Deans (Wilson), Callaghan, Lennox (Hood)

Attendance: 57,839

January 3rd:
HEARTS   (0) 1   RANGERS   (0) 2
  Forsyth o.g. (71)   Henderson 2 (55, 86)
HEARTS: Cruikshank; Clunie, Murray; Anderson, Jeffries, Park; Brown, Donaldson (Prentice), Callachan, Busby, Gibson

RANGERS: McCloy; Miller, Jackson, Forsyth, Greig; Hamilton (O'Hara), MacDonald, McLean; McKean, Henderson, Johnstone

Attendance: 23,000

January 10th:
RANGERS   (1) 4   ST JOHNSTONE   (0) 0
  Miller (33 pen),
  Hamilton (76),
  Johnstone (86),
  McKean (88)

RANGERS: McCloy; Miller, Forsyth, Jackson, Greig; Hamilton, MacDonald, McLean; McKean, Henderson, Johnstone

ST JOHNSTONE: Robertson; G. Smith, Anderson, MacDonald, S. Smith; Roberts, O'Rourke, Cramond; Lambie, Hotson, McGregor

Attendance: 17,000

January 17th:
RANGERS   (0) 2   HIBERNIAN   (0) 0
  Parlane (68), McLean (82)
RANGERS: McCloy; Miller, Forsyth, Jackson, Greig; Hamilton, MacDonald, McLean; McKean, Henderson, Parlane

HIBERNIAN: McArthur; Brownlie, Barry, Spalding, Schaedler; Stanton, Smith, Bremner; McLeod (Higgins), Harper, Duncan

Attendance: 39,000

January 31st:
DUNDEE   (0) 1   RANGERS   (0) 1
  Johnston (65)   Johnstone (47)
DUNDEE: Allan; Ford, Phillip, Stewart, McIntosh; Johnston, Laing, Caldwell; Hendrie, Wallace, Hutchinson

RANGERS: McCloy; Forsyth, Jackson, Miller, Hamilton, Greig; MacDonald, McKean; Parlane (Henderson), Johnstone, McLean

Attendance: 14,407

February 7th:
RANGERS   (2) 2   ABERDEEN   (0) 1
  Henderson (24),   Pirrie (77)
  MacDonald (44)
RANGERS: McCloy; Miller, Forsyth, Jackson, Greig; Hamilton (Jardine), MacDonald, McLean; McKean, Henderson (Parlane), Johnstone

ABERDEEN: Geoghegan, Williamson (Pirrie), Miller, Thomson, McLelland, Robb, Smith, McMaster, Scott, Jarvie (Fleming), Graham

Attendance: 35,000

February 21st:
AYR UNITED   (0) 0   RANGERS   (0) 1
                           McKean (52)
AYR UNITED: Sproat; Wells, Fleming, Paton, Murphy; Graham (McCulloch), McDonald (Fillipi), McSherry; Phillips, Ingram, Robertson

RANGERS: McCloy; Miller, Forsyth, Jackson, Greig; MacDonald, Hamilton (Jardine), McLean; McKean, Henderson, Parlane

Attendance: 15,000

February 28th:
MOTHERWELL (0) 0   RANGERS (1) 1
                                    Johnstone (22)

MOTHERWELL: Rennie; Stevens, McLaren, McVie, Wark; Gardner, Davidson, R. Watson; McAdam, Graham, Pettigrew

RANGERS: McCloy; Greig, Forsyth, Jackson, Miller; Hamilton (Jardine), MacDonald, McLean; McKean (Parlane), Henderson, Johnstone

Attendance: 25,241

League positions

	P	W	D	L	F	A	Pts
1 Celtic	26	17	4	5	56	30	38
2 RANGERS	26	16	5	5	43	21	37
3 Hibernian	25	13	6	6	44	29	32
4 Motherwell	26	12	7	7	45	33	31
5 Aberdeen	26	10	7	9	41	36	27

March 13th: The scheduled Celtic v. Rangers match had to be postponed due to a flu epidemic among the Celtic players.

March 17th: Alex MacDonald was in the Scottish League team which was beaten 1-0 by the English League at Hampden Park.

March 20th:
RANGERS (1) 3   HEARTS (0) 1
   Johnstone (16), Greig (55),   Aird (50)
   McLean (76)

RANGERS: McCloy; Miller, Forsyth, Jackson, Greig; Hamilton, Johnstone, MacDonald; McKean, Henderson, McLean

HEARTS: Cruikshank; Brown, Kay; Jeffries, Gallagher, Burrell; Callachan, Fraser (Park), Aird, Shaw, Prentice

Attendance: 25,000

March 27th:
ST JOHNSTONE (0) 0   RANGERS (1) 3
                                    Greig (4),
                                    Johnstone 2 (52, 53)

ST JOHNSTONE: Robertson; G. Smith, MacDonald, Kinnell, Ritchie (Henderson); Anderson, Hamilton, Thomson; O'Rourke, S. Smith, Lambie (McGregor)

RANGERS: McCloy; Miller, Jackson, Forsyth, Greig; MacDonald, McLean, Hamilton; McKean (Jardine), Henderson (Parlane), Johnstone

Attendance: 8,000

April 3rd:
HIBERNIAN (0) 0   RANGERS (1) 3
                                    MacDonald (20),
                                    Henderson (51),
                                    Johnstone (55)

HIBERNIAN: McDonald; Brownlie, Barry (Stanton), Blackley, Schaedler; Bremner, Edwards, Muir; Wilson, Smith, Duncan

RANGERS: McCloy; Miller, Forsyth, Jackson, Greig; MacDonald, Hamilton, McLean; McKean, Henderson (Parlane), Johnstone

Attendance: 18,820

April 7th: Scotland beat Switzerland 1-0 at Hampden Park. Tom Forsyth captained the team which also included MacDonald and Johnstone. McKean made an appearance as substitute.

April 7th: Ian Munro of Hibs joined Rangers in an exchange deal which took Graham Fyfe and Ally Scott to Easter Road.

April 10th:
RANGERS (2) 3   DUNDEE (0) 0
   McKean (14), Greig (35),
   Johnstone (50)

RANGERS: McCloy; Forsyth, Jackson, Miller, Hamilton (Jardine), Greig; MacDonald, McKean; Henderson, McLean (Parlane)

DUNDEE: Allan; Wilson, Caldwell (McPhail); Phillip, Gemmell, Johnstone; Mackie, Robinson (Bavidge), Laing, Wallace, Hutchinson

Attendance: 24,000. Gemmell missed a penalty

April 14th:
ABERDEEN 0   RANGERS 0

ABERDEEN: Clark; Hair, McLelland; Thomson, Garner, Miller; Robb, Williamson, Jarvie, Fleming, Smith

RANGERS: McCloy; Miller, Greig; Forsyth, Jackson, MacDonald; McKean (Parlane), Hamilton, Henderson, McLean (Jardine), Johnstone

Attendance: 17,968. Robb was ordered off

April 16th: Rangers sacked Quinton Young.

April 17th:
RANGERS (1) 2   AYR UNITED (1) 1
   MacDonald (14),   Ingram (50 secs)
   Parlane (70)

RANGERS: McCloy; Miller, Jackson (Jardine), Greig; Hamilton, Forsyth, MacDonald; McKean, Henderson (Parlane), Johnstone, McLean

AYR UNITED: Sproat; McDonald, Fleming, Tait, Murphy; Graham, Fillipi, Cramond; Robertson, Ingram, McSherry (McCulloch)

Attendance: 25,000

April 21st:
RANGERS   (1) 2   MOTHERWELL   (0) 1
McLean (26),   Stevens (54)
Henderson (77)

RANGERS: McCloy; Miller, Greig; Jardine, Forsyth (Denny), MacDonald; McKean, Hamilton, Henderson, McLean, Johnstone

MOTHERWELL: Rennie; McAdam, Wark; R. Watson, McVie, McLaren; Stevens, Pettigrew, Graham, Gardner, Taylor (Davidson)

Attendance: 25,000

April 24th:
DUNDEE UNITED   (0) 0   RANGERS   (1) 1
                                    Johnstone (22 secs)

DUNDEE UNITED: McAlpine; Rolland, Forsyth, Copland, Kopel; Hegarty, Narey, Houston; Hall, Fleming, McAdam

RANGERS: McCloy; Denny, Jackson, Miller, Greig; McLean, Jardine, MacDonald; Henderson, Johnstone, McKean

Attendance: 15,000

April 26th:
CELTIC   0   RANGERS   0

CELTIC: Latchford; McGrain, Lynch; P. McCluskey, Aitken, Edvaldsson (McNamara); Doyle, Dalglish, MacDonald, Burns, Lennox

RANGERS: McCloy; Miller, Greig; Jardine, Johnstone, MacDonald; McKean, Hamilton, Henderson, McLean, Parlane

Attendance: 51,000

May 4th:
RANGERS   0   DUNDEE UNITED   0

RANGERS: Kennedy; Miller, Greig; Jardine, Denny, MacDonald; McKean, Hamilton, Henderson, McLean, Parlane

DUNDEE UNITED: McAlpine; Rolland, Kopel; Forsyth, Houston, Narey; Hall, Fleming, Hegarty, McAdam, Copland

Attendance: 50,000. McAlpine missed a penalty

Scottish Premier League

	P	W	D	L	F	A	Pts
1 RANGERS	36	23	8	5	60	24	54
2 Celtic	36	21	6	9	71	42	48
3 Hibernian	36	20	7	9	55	43	43
4 Motherwell	36	16	8	12	56	48	40
5 Hearts	36	13	9	14	39	45	35
6 Ayr United	36	14	5	17	46	59	33
7 Aberdeen	36	11	10	15	49	50	32
8 Dundee United	36	12	8	16	46	48	32
9 Dundee	36	11	10	15	49	62	32
10 St Johnstone	36	3	5	28	29	79	11

May 4th: John Greig was named Scotland's Player of the Year.

May 6th: Forsyth and Jackson were in the Scotland team which beat Wales 3-1 at Hampden Park.

May 8th: Forsyth and Jackson were in the Scotland team which beat Northern Ireland 3-0 at Hampden Park.

May 15th: Forsyth and Jackson were in the Scotland team which beat England 2-1 at Hampden Park.

June 1st: Vancouver Whitecaps offered Jock Wallace the job as Coach.

LEAGUE CUP

August 9th:
RANGERS   (2) 6   AIRDRIE   (1) 1
Jardine 3 (19 pen, 59, 89 pen),   Jonquin (32 pen)
Stein (40), Parlane (48),
Miller (72 pen)

RANGERS: McCloy; Jardine, Greig; Jackson, Miller, Stein; Johnstone (Denny), MacDonald, McLean, Parlane, Fyfe

AIRDRIE: McWilliams; Jonquin, Menzies, Black, Cowan; Reynolds, Walker, McCulloch; Lapsley (McRoberts), March, Wilson (Clark)

Attendance: 45,000

August 13th:
CLYDE   (0) 0 .   RANGERS   (0) 1
                                    Johnstone (60)

CLYDE: Cairney; Anderson, Swan; Miller, Boyd, Jim Burns; Sullivan, Ward, Boyle, Aherne, Marshall (Archibald)

RANGERS: McCloy; Jardine, Miller; Greig, Jackson, MacDonald; McLean, Stein, Parlane, Johnstone, McKean

Attendance: 25,000

August 16th:
RANGERS   (0) 1   MOTHERWELL   (0) 1
  Greig (72)   Wark (80)

RANGERS: McCloy; Jardine, Jackson, Greig, Miller; McLean, Stein, MacDonald; Parlane, Johnstone, Young

MOTHERWELL: Rennie; Millar, McVie, Stevens, Wark; Gardner (Taylor), Watson, Davidson; McAdam, Pettigrew, Graham

Attendance: 31,500. McCloy saved a Millar penalty

August 20th:
RANGERS   (2) 6   CLYDE   (0) 0
  Parlane 2 (16, 27),
  Jackson (48), Miller (52 pen),
  Young (77), Johnstone (79)

RANGERS: McCloy; Jardine, Miller; Greig, Jackson, MacDonald; McLean, McKean, Parlane, Johnstone, Young

CLYDE: Cairney; Anderson, Swan; Millar, Boyd (Archibald), Jim Burns (Harvey); Sullivan, Ferris, Ward, Aherne, Boyle

Attendance: 15,000

August 23rd:
MOTHERWELL   (1) 2   RANGERS   (1) 2
  R. Watson (39),   Jardine (11),
  Pettigrew (78)   Miller (65 pen)

MOTHERWELL: Rennie; W. Watson, Stevens, McVie, Wark; McAdam, R. Watson, Millar (Davidson); Pettigrew, Graham, Taylor

RANGERS: McCloy; Jardine, Greig, Jackson, Miller, McKean, Johnstone, MacDonald, McLean, Parlane, Young

Attendance: 20,561

August 27th:
AIRDRIE   (0) 1   RANGERS   (2) 2
  McCann (66)   Johnstone (5),
                          Young (19)

AIRDRIE: McWilliams; Jonquin, Cowan; Menzies, Black, Lapsley; McCann, Reynolds, Wilson, Whiteford, Walker

RANGERS: McCloy; Greig, Miller; Forsyth, Jackson, MacDonald; McKean, O'Hara, Stein, Johnstone, Young

Attendance: 12,000

League Cup Section Table

	P	W	D	L	F	A	Pts
RANGERS	6	4	2	0	18	5	10
Motherwell	6	3	2	1	10	6	8
Airdrie	6	2	0	4	7	14	4
Clyde	6	1	0	5	4	14	2

September 10th: Quarter-Final First Leg
RANGERS   (0) 1   QUEEN OF THE
  Johnstone (74)   SOUTH   (0) 0

RANGERS: McCloy; Denny, Miller; Greig, Jackson, MacDonald; McLean (Stein), McKean (O'Hara), Parlane, Johnstone, Young

QUEEN OF THE SOUTH: Ball; Miller, Thorburn, McLaren, Boyd; O'Hara, Dempster, Law; Reid, G. Dickson, Bryce

Attendance: 12,000. Miller missed a penalty after 29 in a row without missing

September 24th: Quarter-Final Second Leg
QUEEN OF THE   RANGERS   (1) 2
  SOUTH   (1) 2   Johnstone (44)
  Dempster (38 pen),   MacDonald (114)
  Bryce (89)
                After Extra Time

QUEEN OF THE SOUTH: Ball; Miller, McChesney, McLaren, Boyd; O'Hara, Dempster, Reid; Donald (Thorburn), G. Dickson, Bryce

RANGERS: McCloy; Miller, Dawson; Greig, Jackson, MacDonald; McLean, McDougall, Parlane, Johnstone, Young

Attendance: 7,500. Rangers won 3-2 on aggregate

October 8th: Semi-Final   At Hampden Park
MONTROSE   (1) 1   RANGERS   (0) 5
  Barr (44 pen)   Parlane (54),
                          Johnstone (57),
                          Miller (69 pen),
                          Scott (74),
                          Jardine (87)

MONTROSE: Gorman; Barr, Lowe; McNicoll, D'Arcy, Markland; Guthrie, Stewart, Cameron, Johnstone, Livingstone

RANGERS: McCloy; Jardine, Dawson; Greig, Jackson, Miller; McLean, McDougall, Parlane, Johnstone, Scott

Attendance: 20,319.

Rangers won well. In a second half of sharp play and physical power, they gained the result which seemed impossible after Montrose took the lead.

October 25th: Final   At Hampden Park
RANGERS   (0) 1   CELTIC   (0) 0
  MacDonald (67)

RANGERS: Kennedy; Jardine, Greig; Forsyth, Jackson, MacDonald; McLean, Stein, Parlane, Johnstone, Young — McKean, Miller

CELTIC: Latchford; McGrain, Lynch; McCluskey, MacDonald, Edvaldsson; Hood, Dalglish, Wilson, Callaghan, Lennox — McNamara, Glavin

Attendance: 58,000.

K

Rangers were adequate most of the time, good in bits and pieces especially in the first part of the second half. The only goal of the match came in the 67th minute. Parlane beat MacDonald well on the left bye-line and his cross was headed away by Edvaldsson in the general direction of Young. Young headed across goal and MacDonald dived forward to head strongly into the net. Forsyth marked Dalglish out of the match. The Rangers' defender needed five stitches in a head cut after colliding with Parlane. This was the first time that John Greig had received the League Cup as captain.

SCOTTISH CUP

January 24th: Third Round
RANGERS   (2) 3   EAST FIFE   (0) 0
  MacDonald (13),
  Henderson (32),
  Hamilton (83)

RANGERS: McCloy; Greig, Forsyth, Jackson, Miller; Hamilton, MacDonald, McLean; McKean, Parlane, Henderson

EAST FIFE: McGarr; McIvor, Clarke; Methven, Stevens, George; Rutherford, Rankin, McPhee, Hegarty, O'Connor (Mellon)

Attendance: 30,000

February 14th:
RANGERS   (1) 4   ABERDEEN   (0) 1
  Johnstone (41),   Smith (70)
  MacDonald (46),
  Henderson (75), Parlane (87)

RANGERS: McCloy; Miller, Greig; Forsyth (Parlane), Jackson, MacDonald; McKean, Hamilton (Jardine), Henderson, McLean, Johnstone

ABERDEEN: Geoghegan; Williamson, McLelland; Smith, Thomson (Hair), Miller; Scott, Robb, Jarvie, McMaster (Pirie), Graham

Attendance: 53,000

March 6th: Fifth Round
QUEEN OF THE   RANGERS   (1) 5
  SOUTH   (0) 0   McKean 2 (37, 84),
                             Johnstone 2 (71, 78),
                             Henderson (75)

QUEEN OF THE SOUTH: Ball; McChesney, Thorburn; Clark, Boyd, McLaren; Dempster, P. Dickson, Reid (Bryce), O'Hara, G. Dickson (Miller)

RANGERS: McCloy; Miller, Greig; Forsyth, Jackson, MacDonald; McKean, Hamilton, Henderson, McLean, Johnstone

Attendance: 18,700

March 31st: Semi-Final   At Hampden Park
MOTHERWELL   (2) 2   RANGERS   (0) 3
  McLaren (36),   Miller (69 pen),
  Pettigrew (44)   Johnstone 2 (80, 88)

MOTHERWELL: Rennie; W. Watson, Wark; R. Watson, McLaren, Stevens; McAdam, Pettigrew, Graham, Gardner, Marinello (Davidson)

RANGERS: McCloy; Miller, Greig; Forsyth, Jackson, MacDonald; McKean (Parlane), Hamilton, Henderson (Jardine), McLean, Johnstone

Attendance: 48,915.

Motherwell held a 2 goal advantage as the game entered its final quarter. Rangers made little impression until the 69th minute when Johnstone fell after a challenge by Rennie. Referee Gordon awarded a penalty from which Miller scored. 11 minutes later the scores were level. McCloy cleared a ball out of his hands, the ball bounced once and Johnstone beat Rennie to it and headed home over the keeper's head. With 2 minutes remaining the Motherwell defence were caught ball-watching from a Greig free-kick into the penalty area. Only Johnstone moved and eased the ball over the line for a dramatic winner.

May 1st: Final   At Hampden Park
HEARTS   (0) 1   RANGERS   (2) 3
  Shaw (83)   Johnstone 2
                               (42 secs, 81),
                             MacDonald (45)

HEARTS: Cruikshank; Brown, Burrell (Aird); Jeffries, Gallagher, Kay; Gibson (Park), Busby, Shaw, Callachan, Prentice

RANGERS: McCloy; Miller, Greig; Forsyth, Jackson, MacDonald; McKean, Hamilton (Jardine), Henderson, McLean, Johnstone — Parlane

Attendance: 85,354 *Referee*: R. H. Davidson (Airdrie)

Rangers won the Scottish Cup for the 21st time and the treble for a 3rd. Johnstone, for the second successive week, scored a goal in the first minute. MacDonald's volley through a ruck of players carried Rangers further ahead just before half-time. In the 2nd half Aird replaced Burrell. Greig cleared off the line at one end, Gallagher twice at the other end. Rangers and Hearts both hit the bar and both scored goals. A simple move with Henderson feeding McKean and the winger turning Brown inside out set up a 3rd goal for Rangers. With 7 minutes left Shaw pulled one back for Hearts.

EUROPEAN CUP

September 17th: First Round First Leg
RANGERS   (2) 4   BOHEMIANS (Eire)   (1) 1
  Fyfe (20),   Flanagan (37)
  Burke o.g. (39),
  O'Hara (50),
  Johnstone (63)

RANGERS: McCloy; Denny, Miller; Greig, Jackson, Johnstone; Fyfe, O'Hara, Parlane, Stein, Young

BOHEMIANS: Smyth; Doran, O'Brien; Kelly, Burke, Fullam; Byrne, P. O'Connor, T. O'Connor, Flanagan, Mitten

Attendance: 24,000

This was a good Ibrox victory in a match played in torrential rain. Fyfe was the tie's major personality — he scored one goal and had a hand in two others.

October 1st: First Round Second Leg
BOHEMIANS   (0) 1   RANGERS   (1) 1
  T. O'Connor (56)   Johnstone (38)

BOHEMIANS: Smyth; Gregg, O'Brien; Kelly, Burke, Fullam; Byrne, T. O'Connor, J. O'Connor, Martin, Mitten

RANGERS: McCloy; Miller, Dawson; Greig, Jackson, Young; McLean, MacDonald, Parlane, Johnstone, Fyfe

Attendance: 8,000

Once Derek Johnstone had scored a goal in the 38th minute to add to the four scored at Ibrox two weeks before, Rangers were absolutely safe. There was quite a lot of incident in the game but not much purpose. Rangers won 5-1 on aggregate.

October 22nd: Second Round First Leg
ST ETIENNE (France)   (1) 2   RANGERS   (0) 0
  P. Revelli (25), Bathenay (89½)

ST ETIENNE: Curkovic; Janvion, Piazza, Lopez, Farison; Larque, Bathenay, Synaeghel; Rochteau, H. Revelli, P. Revelli

RANGERS: Kennedy; Jardine, Miller; Greig, Jackson, Forsyth; McLean, Stein, Parlane, MacDonald, Johnstone

Attendance: 28,394

McCloy was injured during shooting-in practice before the match started

For 89½ minutes it looked as if Rangers would carry a scoreline back to Glasgow which if not ideal would at least be acceptable. But then their concentration lapsed and a badly judged pass-back by MacDonald gave St Etienne the opening they had been denied for so long. Jardine could not reach the ball and Bathenay ran unchallenged into the penalty area to shoot low past Kennedy.

November 5th: Second Round Second Leg
RANGERS   (0) 1   ST ETIENNE   (0) 2
  MacDonald (89)   Rocheteau (63),
                          Revelli (70)

RANGERS: Kennedy; Jardine, Greig; Forsyth, Jackson, MacDonald; McLean, Stein, Parlane, Johnstone, Young

ST ETIENNE: Curkovic; Janvion, Farison, Piazza, Lopez; Bathenay, Rocheteau, Larque; H. Revelli, Synaeghel, Schaer (Santini)

Attendance: 45,000

Rangers were an agony to the 45,000 supporters who spent most of the 2nd half chanting 'What a load of rubbish'. The Ibrox team were outthought, outskilled and outclassed by an accomplished St Etienne side. In the 89th minute MacDonald pulled one back. Only about 10,000 remained in the ground when the Belgian referee blew the final whistle. St Etienne won 4-1 on aggregate.

APPEARANCES

	League	League Cup	Scottish Cup	European Cup
McCloy	24	9	5	2
Kennedy	12	1	-	2
Jardine	18+7S	7	0+3S	2
Miller	25+2S	9	5	3
Greig	36	10	5	4
Jackson	33	10	5	4
MacDonald	34+1S	9	5	3
Forsyth	28	2	5	2
Johnstone	32+1S	10	4	4
McLean	34+1S	9	5	3
Stein	3+3S	5+1S	-	3
Parlane	17+7S	9	1+2S	4
McKean	32+1S	5	5	-
Denny	6+3S	1+1S	-	1
Fyfe	1+2S	1	-	2
O'Hara	1+3S	1+1S	-	1
Scott	1+1S	1	-	-
Young	7+1S	7	-	3
Henderson	23+3S	-	5	-
Dawson	3	2	-	1
McDougall	3+1S	2	-	-
Hamilton	22	-	5	-
Boyd	1	-	-	-
Armour	-	-	-	-
Munro	-	-	-	-

Iain Durrant, a rising midfield star of the mid-eighties.

GOALSCORERS

League: Johnstone 16, Henderson 10, Parlane 5,
McKean 5, MacDonald 4, McLean 4,
Own Goals 4, Greig 3, Young 2,
Jardine 2 (1 pen), Stein 1, McDougall 1,
Jackson 1, Miller 1 (pen), Hamilton 1

League Cup: Johnstone 6, Jardine 5 (2 pens),
Miller 4 (4 pens), Parlane 4, Young 2,
MacDonald 2, Scott 1, Jackson 1, Greig 1,
Stein 1

Scottish Cup: Johnstone 7, MacDonald 3, Henderson 3,
McKean 2, Hamilton 1, Parlane 1,
Miller 1 (pen)

European Cup: Johnstone 2, Fyfe 1, O'Hara 1,
MacDonald 1, Own Goal 1

The May 1978 Scottish Cup Final. John Greig had just landed his *third* treble — Scottish Cup,
League Cup and League — a Scottish record for any one player.

Season 1976-77

Rangers failed to retain their title, finishing 2nd — 9 points behind Celtic. They collected only 8 points from their first 8 matches, drawing 4 of the first 5, and had a total of 10 draws during the season. Their longest winning sequence was 6 matches. Jardine and McLean played in every game. Derek Parlane finished as top scorer with 16 followed by Derek Johnstone with 15. Winger Davie Cooper was signed from Clydebank at the end of the Season for £100,000.

Rangers reached the Semi-Final of the League Cup. They dropped only one point in their Section which included Hibs, Montrose and St Johnstone. Clydebank were beaten after a Quarter-Final marathon which went to 2 Play-offs. Aberdeen proved too strong in the Semi-Final and were 2 goals up in the first 14 minutes. Ally McLeod's team went on to beat Celtic in the Final.

Rangers reached the Scottish Cup Final for the 2nd successive season with wins against Falkirk, Elgin City, Motherwell and Hearts along the road. They lost the Final to Celtic following a controversial penalty incident involving Derek Johnstone. Substitute Chris Robertson hit the bar with a header in the closing stages.

Rangers were knocked out of the European Cup in the First Round by F.C. Zurich of Switzerland. They lost early goals in both matches and paid the price — despite a heroic second-half performance in Switzerland.

Rangers reached the Final of the Tennant Caledonian Tournament but were beaten 2-1 by F.A. Cup holders Southampton.

> League: Runners-up
> League Cup: Semi-Finalists
> Scottish Cup: Finalists
> European Cup: First Round

SCOTTISH PREMIER LEAGUE

September 4th:

CELTIC (0) 2   RANGERS (2) 2
Wilson 2 (54, 87)   Johnstone (9),
                       Parlane (34)

CELTIC: Latchford; McGrain, McCluskey, MacDonald, Lynch; Glavin, Stanton, Burns; Wilson, Dalglish, Doyle

RANGERS: McCloy; Denny, Greig; Forsyth, Miller, Jardine; MacDonald, Munro, McLean, Parlane, Johnstone

Attendance: 57,000

In a great match Rangers took the lead in the 9th minute when McLean's free-kick and MacDonald's header gave Johnstone the present of the first goal. Celtic had hit the bar before Munro's pass to McLean's run gave Parlane a second. Wilson's half-hit goal just after half-time gave some decency to the score. Celtic forced McCloy into serious saves for the next 20 minutes. In the last 10 minutes after Johnstone had abused 2 chances Burns's pass and Wilson's run and shot gave Celtic their 2nd goal. They had deserved no less.

September 8th: Tom Forsyth was in the Scotland team which beat Finland 6-0 at Hampden Park.

September 11th:
RANGERS 0   KILMARNOCK 0

RANGERS: McCloy; Denny, Forsyth, Greig, Miller; Jardine, Munro, MacDonald; McLean (McKean), Johnstone, Henderson (Parlane)

KILMARNOCK: Stewart; McLean, Welsh, Clarke, Robertson; McCulloch, Murdoch, Sheed; Provan, Fallis, Smith

Attendance: 23,430

September 18th:
HIBERNIAN   (0) 1   RANGERS   (1) 1
  Smith (46)   Parlane (34)
HIBERNIAN: McDonald; Brownlie, Stewart,
Blackley, Schaedler (Muir); McNamara, Bremner,
Smith; Murray, Scott, Duncan

RANGERS: McCloy; Jardine, Greig, Forsyth, Miller;
Hamilton, Johnstone, MacDonald; McLean, Parlane,
McKean

Attendance: 19,606

September 25th:
RANGERS   (2) 4   HEARTS   (2) 2
  Hamilton (27),   Gibson (14),
  Miller (41 pen),   Miller o.g. (32)
  Parlane (70), Johnstone (89)
RANGERS: McCloy; Jardine, Jackson, Forsyth,
Miller; Greig, Hamilton, Munro; McLean, Parlane,
Johnstone

HEARTS: Cruikshank; Brown, Gallagher, Clunie,
Kay; Callachan (Cant), Busby, Park; Shaw, Gibson,
Prentice

Attendance: 23,000

October 2nd:
AYR UNITED   (0) 1   RANGERS   (0) 1
  Robertson (81)   Parlane (69)
AYR UNITED: Geoghegan; McDonald, Fleming
(Graham), Rodman, Murphy; McSherry, Fillipi,
McCulloch; Ingram, McCall (Cramond), Robertson

RANGERS: McCloy; Jardine, Jackson, Forsyth,
Miller; Hamilton, MacDonald, McLean (Munro);
Parlane, Johnstone

Attendance: 14,000

October 16th:
RANGERS   (0) 1   ABERDEEN   (0) 0
  MacDonald (77)
RANGERS: Kennedy; Jardine, Jackson, Denny,
Miller; Greig, Hamilton (McKean), MacDonald;
McLean, Parlane, Johnstone (Henderson)

ABERDEEN: Clark; Kennedy, Garner, Miller,
McLelland; Sullivan, Smith, Thomson (Rougvie);
Graham (Campbell), Fleming, Robb

Attendance: 21,800

October 23rd:
MOTHERWELL   (2) 3   RANGERS   (1) 1
  Wark (9),   Hamilton (7)
  Pettigrew 2 (38, 84)
MOTHERWELL: Rennie; McAdam, McVie,
Stevens, Wark; Millar, Davidson, Kennedy; Pettigrew,
Graham, Marinello

RANGERS: Kennedy; Miller, Jackson, Watson,
Greig; Jardine, Hamilton (Henderson), Dawson;
McLean (McDougall), Parlane, McKean

Attendance: 15,857

October 30th:
PARTICK THISTLE   (0) 2   RANGERS   (0) 1
  Somner (74), Whittaker (89)   Watson (53)
PARTICK THISTLE: Rough; Campbell, Anderson,
Marr, Whittaker; J. Hansen, A. Hansen, Craig;
Johnston, Frame (Melrose), Somner

RANGERS: Kennedy; Denny, Jackson, Miller,
Jardine; Greig, Watson, MacDonald; McLean, Parlane,
Henderson (Robertson)

Attendance: 16,900

League positions
	P	W	D	L	F	A	Pts
1 Dundee United	8	6	0	2	16	12	12
2 Celtic	9	4	3	2	19	9	11
3 Aberdeen	8	4	3	1	16	8	11
4 Partick Thistle	8	3	3	2	9	8	9
5 Hibernian	9	1	7	1	10	10	9
6 RANGERS	8	2	4	2	11	11	8

**November 3rd: Rangers signed Jim Steele from
Southampton on a month's loan.**

November 9th:
RANGERS   (2) 3   DUNDEE UNITED   (0) 0
  Jackson (9),
  McKean (12),
  Parlane (46)
RANGERS: Kennedy; Jardine, Greig, Steele, Jackson
(Miller); Watson, McLean, Hamilton; Parlane,
MacDonald, McKean

DUNDEE UNITED: McAlpine; Rolland, Kopel;
Fleming, Forsyth, Narey; Sturrock, Wallace (McAdam),
Hegarty, Holt (Houston), Payne

Attendance: 16,000

November 13th:
KILMARNOCK   (0) 0   RANGERS   (3) 4
                           McKean (20),
                           Jackson 2 (25, 57),
                           Parlane (32)
KILMARNOCK: McCulloch; S. McLean (A.
McLean), Clarke, Welsh, Robertson; Murdoch,
McDicken (Maxwell), Sheed; Provan, Fallis, Smith

RANGERS: Kennedy; Jardine, Jackson (Miller),
Steele, Greig; Hamilton, Watson, MacDonald; McLean,
Parlane, McKean

Attendance: 14,700

November 20th:
RANGERS (1) 1   HIBERNIAN (1) 1
Parlane (25)   Steele o.g. (44)

RANGERS: Kennedy; Jardine, Steele, Jackson, Greig;
Watson, Hamilton (Miller), MacDonald; McLean,
Parlane, McKean

HIBERNIAN: McDonald; Brownlie, Spalding,
Blackley, Schaedler; Bremner, Edwards (Scott),
McNamara; Duncan, Smith, Fyfe

Attendance: 24,621

November 24th:
RANGERS (0) 0   CELTIC (1) 1
    Craig (36)

RANGERS: Kennedy; Jardine, Greig; Steele, Jackson,
Watson; McLean, Hamilton, Parlane, MacDonald,
McKean (Stein)

CELTIC: Latchford; McGrain, Lynch; Stanton,
MacDonald, Aitken; Doyle, Glavin, Craig, Dalglish,
Lennox (Wilson)

Attendance: 43,500

Celtic beat Rangers for the first time since January 1974.
They were awarded a penalty in the 12th minute of the
match when Greig brought down Lennox but the referee
changed his mind after consulting his linesman. As a result
of the tackle Lennox went off to hospital with a broken
ankle. Rangers brought on Colin Stein late in the match,
for his first appearance in more than a year, but it made no
real difference.

November 27th:
HEARTS (0) 0   RANGERS (1) 1
    Parlane (33)

HEARTS: Wilson; Brown, Kay; Gallagher, Clunie,
Jeffries; Busby, Shaw, Aird (Park), Gibson, Prentice

RANGERS: Kennedy; Jardine, Jackson, Steele, Greig;
Hamilton, MacDonald, Watson; McLean, Parlane, Stein

Attendance: 19,000

League positions

	P	W	D	L	F	A	Pts
1 Celtic	13	8	3	2	29	13	19
2 Aberdeen	13	8	3	2	24	12	19
3 Dundee United	14	9	1	4	28	20	19
4 RANGERS	13	5	5	3	20	13	15
5 Motherwell	14	5	3	6	24	25	13

**December 22nd: Motherwell turned down a Rangers'
bid for centre-half Willie McVie.**

December 26th:
RANGERS (0) 1   MOTHERWELL (0) 0
O'Hara (75)

RANGERS: Kennedy; Jardine, Greig, Forsyth,
Jackson, Watson; McLean, O'Hara, Parlane (Miller),
Henderson, Johnstone

MOTHERWELL: Rennie; Millar (O'Rourke), Wark;
McAdam, Watson, Stevens; Marinello, Pettigrew,
Graham, Davidson (Hood), Kennedy

Attendance: 25,000

January 1st:
RANGERS (0) 1   PARTICK THISTLE (0) 0
Johnstone (82)

RANGERS: Kennedy; Jardine, Miller; Forsyth,
Jackson, Watson; McLean, O'Hara, Henderson
(Robertson), McKean, Johnstone

PARTICK THISTLE: Rough; J. Hansen, Whittaker;
Anderson, Campbell, A. Hansen; McQuade, Melrose,
Marr, Craig, Johnston

Attendance: 19,000

January 8th:
RANGERS (1) 3   KILMARNOCK (0) 0
Parlane 2 (34, 67),
O'Hara (84)

RANGERS: Kennedy; Jardine, Forsyth, Jackson
(Henderson), Miller; O'Hara, Johnstone, Watson;
McLean, Parlane, McKean

KILMARNOCK: Stewart; Maxwell, Clarke, Welsh,
Robertson; Murdoch (Sheed), McCulloch, McDicken;
Provan, Fallis, Smith

Attendance: 16,819

January 11th:
CELTIC (0) 1   RANGERS (0) 0
Jackson o.g. (76)

CELTIC: Latchford; McGrain, Lynch; Stanton,
MacDonald, Aitken; Doyle, Glavin, Craig, Dalglish,
Wilson

RANGERS: Kennedy; Jardine, Miller; Forsyth,
Jackson, Watson; McLean, O'Hara, Parlane, McKean,
Johnstone

Attendance: 52,000

Celtic took the points that put them back on top of the
Premier League. The victory came from an unlucky own
goal by Colin Jackson. Rangers might have equalised 2
minutes from the end when Aitken scrambled away a lob
from McLean which had beaten Latchford.

January 19th:
ABERDEEN (1) 3   RANGERS (1) 3
Jarvie (41),   Miller (44 pen),
Scott (60), Smith (65)   MacDonald (80),
    Johnstone (86)

ABERDEEN: Clark; Kennedy, McLelland; Smith,
Garner, Miller; Sullivan, Scott, Harper, Jarvie, Graham

RANGERS: Kennedy; Jardine, Miller; Forsyth, Jackson, Watson; McLean, O'Hara (MacDonald), Parlane (McKean), Greig, Johnstone

Attendance: 21,591

January 19th: Former Rangers great Jerry Dawson died.

January 22nd:
RANGERS   (3) 3   HEARTS   (1) 2
  MacDonald 2 (11, 34),   Gallagher (36),
  Johnstone (29)   Shaw (82)

RANGERS: Kennedy; Jardine, Jackson, Forsyth, Greig; Hamilton, MacDonald, Watson; McLean (McKean), Johnstone, Robertson

HEARTS: Cruikshank; Brown, Gallagher, Fraser, Jeffries; Clunie, Busby, Callachan; Aird, Shaw, Prentice (Park)

Attendance: 19,700

February 5th:
AYR UNITED   (0) 0   RANGERS   (1) 2
                          Johnstone (2),
                          McLean (70)

AYR UNITED: Geoghegan; Wells, Fleming, Paton, Murphy; McSherry, Fillipi, McCulloch; Cramond, McCall (Robertson), Masterton

RANGERS: Kennedy; Jardine, Jackson, Forsyth, Greig; Hamilton (Miller), Watson, MacDonald; McLean, Robertson, Johnstone

Attendance: 12,800

February 12th:
RANGERS   (2) 2   DUNDEE UNITED   (1) 3
  Jackson (17),   Sturrock (38),
  MacDonald (20)   McAlpine (51 pen),
                               Wallace (79)

RANGERS: Kennedy; Jardine, Denny (Miller), Jackson, Greig; Hamilton, Watson, MacDonald; McLean, Robertson (Parlane), Johnstone

DUNDEE UNITED: McAlpine; Fleming, Hegarty, Smith, Kopel; Houston, Rennie, Payne; Sturrock, Wallace, McAdam

Attendance: 16,000

February 16th:
HIBERNIAN   0   RANGERS   0

HIBERNIAN: McDonald; Brownlie, Schaedler; Bremner, Stewart, Blackley; Edwards, McLeod, Smith, Carroll, Fyfe (Scott)

RANGERS: Kennedy; Jardine, Miller; Greig, Jackson (McKean), Watson; McLean, Hamilton, Parlane, MacDonald, Johnstone

Attendance: 12,452

February 19th:
RANGERS   (0) 1   ABERDEEN   (0) 0
  Miller (89 pen)

RANGERS: Kennedy; Jardine, Jackson, Miller, Greig; Hamilton (MacDougall), MacDonald, Watson; McLean (McKean), Parlane, Johnstone

ABERDEEN: Clark; Kennedy, Garner, Miller, McLelland; Smith, Scott (Thomson), Jarvie (Shirra); Sullivan, Harper, Graham

Attendance: 17,000

League positions

	P	W	D	L	F	A	Pts
1 Celtic	22	16	4	2	56	24	36
2 RANGERS	23	11	7	5	36	22	29
3 Dundee United	21	12	4	5	42	27	28
4 Aberdeen	22	10	8	4	37	22	28
5 Hibernian	23	4	14	5	20	23	22

March 5th:
MOTHERWELL   (0) 0   RANGERS   (1) 2
                          MacDonald (19),
                          Watson (90)

MOTHERWELL: Rennie; Watson, Stevens, McAdam, Wark; Millar, Davidson (Hood), McLaren; Pettigrew, O'Rourke, Marinello (Kennedy)

RANGERS: Kennedy; Jardine, Forsyth, Jackson, Greig; McDougall (Miller), MacDonald, Watson; McLean, Parlane (McKean), Robertson

Attendance: 15,468

March 8th:
DUNDEE UNITED   0   RANGERS   0

DUNDEE UNITED: McAlpine; Rolland, Williamson; Fleming, Smith, Narey; Sturrock, Wallace, Hegarty, McAdam, Houston

RANGERS: Kennedy; Jardine, Greig; Forsyth, Jackson, Watson; McLean, McKean, Parlane, MacDonald, Robertson (McDougall)

Attendance: 10,250

March 15th:
PARTICK THISTLE   (1) 4   RANGERS   (1) 3
  Johnston (20), Melrose (54),   Johnstone (32),
  A. Hansen 2 (67, 85 pen)   Watson (59),
                                 Parlane (64)

PARTICK THISTLE: Rough; Mackie, Whittaker; Gibson, Marr, A. Hansen; Melrose, J. Hansen, Love, Somner, Johnston

RANGERS: Kennedy; Jardine, Greig; Forsyth, Morris, Watson; McLean, McKean (Robertson), Parlane, MacDonald, Johnstone

Attendance: 12,000

March 19th:
RANGERS (1) 2   CELTIC (1) 2
Parlane 2 (21, 79)   Aitken 2 (12, 84)

RANGERS: Kennedy; Jardine, Forsyth, Jackson, Greig; McKean, MacDonald, Watson; McLean, Parlane, Johnstone

CELTIC: Latchford; McGrain, Stanton, Edvaldsson, Burns; Glavin, Aitken, Dalglish; Doyle, Craig, Conn

Attendance: 51,500

In the first 20 minutes Celtic's performance was almost brilliant. They scored through Roy Aitken in 12 minutes and should have had a couple more. Alfie Conn curled a shot round Stewart Kennedy after 15 minutes but the ball came back off the post and Rangers took over. Derek Parlane equalised with a great drive from the edge of the penalty area in 21 minutes. It was no real surprise when Parlane grabbed his 2nd goal 11 minutes from time. A neat dummy from Johnstone, a slide-rule pass from McLean, and there was the Rangers' striker in perfect position to hammer the ball past Latchford. 6 minutes from time Celtic equalised. Watson fouled Doyle on the right wing and when the winger's free-kick came over Aitken met it in mid-air and sent a tremendous drive high into the Rangers' net. Alex MacDonald scored what he thought was the winner, but after signalling the goal referee Paterson spotted his linesman with his flag in the air and the score was chalked off. The game finished with two wonder saves, Latchford touching a Greig piledriver round the post and Kennedy throwing himself full length to palm away a Joe Craig shot.

March 23rd:
RANGERS (1) 1   AYR UNITED (0) 1
Johnstone (36)   Masterton (86)

RANGERS: Kennedy; Jardine, Greig; Forsyth, Jackson, Watson; McLean, McKean, Parlane, MacDonald, Johnstone

AYR UNITED: Sproat; Wells, Kelly; Fleming, Tait (McDonald), McAnespie; McSherry, McCall (Phillips), Masterton, Fillipi, McCulloch

Attendance: 7,000

March 26th:
KILMARNOCK (0) 1   RANGERS (0) 0
Robertson (59)

KILMARNOCK: Stewart; Maxwell, Clarke, McDicken, Robertson; McCulloch, Jardine, Sheed (Murdoch); Provan, Fallis, Smith

RANGERS: Kennedy; Jardine, Forsyth, Jackson, Greig; Watson, McLean, MacDonald; McKean (Hamilton), Parlane, Johnstone

Attendance: 8,000

April 2nd:
RANGERS (2) 2   HIBERNIAN (1) 1
Parlane (42), Johnstone (44)   Smith (29)

RANGERS: Kennedy; Jardine, Jackson, Forsyth, Greig; Hamilton, MacDonald, Watson; McLean, Parlane, Johnstone

HIBERNIAN: McDonald; Brownlie, Blackley, Spalding, Schaedler; Bremner, Edwards, Smith; McLeod, Scott, Duncan

Attendance: 11,500

April 9th:
HEARTS (0) 1   RANGERS (1) 3
Busby (89)   Johnstone (29),
        Parlane (58),
        Jardine (86 pen)

HEARTS: Cruikshank; Brown, Gallagher, Clunie, Kay; Shaw, Busby, Park (Bannon); Aird, Gibson, Prentice

RANGERS: Kennedy; Jardine, Jackson, Forsyth, Greig; Watson, Hamilton, MacDonald; McLean, Parlane (McKean), Johnstone

Attendance: 12,500

April 19th:
RANGERS (2) 2   PARTICK THISTLE (0) 1
Johnstone (2),   Johnston (53)
Jardine (23 pen)

RANGERS: Kennedy; Jardine, Greig; Forsyth, Jackson, Watson; McLean, Hamilton, Parlane, MacDonald, Johnstone

PARTICK THISTLE: Rough; J. Hansen, Whittaker; Campbell, Marr, A. Hansen; Johnston, Melrose (McQuade), Gibson, Deans, Craig

Attendance: 4,000

April 16th:
RANGERS (2) 5   AYR UNITED (0) 1
Johnstone (25),   McDonald (53)
MacDonald 2 (34, 72),
Hamilton (62), Miller (68 pen)

RANGERS: Kennedy; Jardine, Forsyth, Jackson (Robertson), Miller; Hamilton, Watson, MacDonald; McLean, Parlane, Johnstone

AYR UNITED: Sproat; Brogan, Fleming, McAnespie, Murphy; McDonald, Fillipi, McCulloch (Christie); Joyce, McCall, Masterton

Attendance: 5,500

April 20th:
RANGERS (0) 4   MOTHERWELL (1) 1
Johnstone (61),   Pettigrew (6)
MacDonald (73),
Parlane (76),
Robertson (79 pen)

RANGERS: Kennedy; Jardine, Miller; Forsyth, Johnstone, Watson; McLean, Hamilton, Parlane, MacDonald, Robertson

MOTHERWELL: Hunter; P. Millar, Wark; McAdam, McLaren, Stevens; J. Miller, Pettigrew, Graham, Davidson, Kennedy

Attendance: 5,000

April 23rd:
DUNDEE UNITED (0) 0   RANGERS (0) 1
                                 Johnstone (51)
DUNDEE UNITED: McAlpine; Rolland (Fleming), Hegarty, Narey, Williamson; Addison, Smith, Houston (Kirkwood); Payne, Sturrock, McAdam

RANGERS: Kennedy; Jardine, Johnstone, Forsyth, Miller (Munro); Hamilton, Watson, MacDonald; McLean, Robertson, Parlane

Attendance: 8,000

April 27th: Forsyth was in the Scotland team which beat Sweden 3-1 at Hampden Park. Jardine made an appearance as substitute.

April 30th:
ABERDEEN (2) 2   RANGERS (1) 1
  Harper (10 pen),   Johnstone (26)
  Davidson (34)
ABERDEEN: McLean; Kennedy, Garner, Miller, McLelland; Davidson (Sullivan), Smith, Jarvie; Fleming (Shirra), Harper, Graham

RANGERS: Kennedy; Jardine, Forsyth, Jackson, Greig; Hamilton, Watson (Armour), MacDonald; McLean, Parlane, Johnstone

Attendance: 13,484. Greig was ordered off

Scottish Premier League
	P	W	D	L	F	A	Pts
1 Celtic	36	23	9	4	79	39	55
2 RANGERS	36	18	10	8	62	37	46
3 Aberdeen	36	16	11	9	56	42	43
4 Dundee United	36	16	9	11	54	45	41
5 Partick Thistle	36	11	13	12	40	44	35
6 Hibernian	36	8	18	10	34	35	34
7 Motherwell	36	10	12	14	57	60	32
8 Ayr United	36	11	8	17	44	68	30
9 Hearts	36	7	13	16	49	66	27
10 Kilmarnock	36	4	9	23	32	71	17

May 10th: Sandy Jardine asked for a transfer.

May 28th: Forsyth and Parlane played for Scotland against Wales at Wrexham. The match ended 0-0.

June 1st: Tom Forsyth was in the Scotland team which beat Northern Ireland 3-0 at Hampden Park.

June 4th: Forsyth was in the Scotland team which beat England 2-1 at Wembley.

June 8th: Davie Cooper was signed from Clydebank for £100,000.

June 15th: Scotland beat Chile 4-2 in Santiago. Forsyth was in the side and Jardine made an appearance as substitute.

June 18th: Forsyth was in the Scotland team which drew 1-1 with Argentina in Buenos Aires.

June 23rd: Brazil beat Scotland 2-0 in the Maracana Stadium in Rio de Janeiro. Forsyth was in the team and Jardine appeared as a substitute.

LEAGUE CUP

August 14th:
RANGERS (3) 5   ST JOHNSTONE (0) 0
  Jardine 2 (8, 31),
  Johnstone (24),
  Miller (65 pen),
  Henderson (75)
RANGERS: McCloy; Miller, Greig; Forsyth, Denny, MacDonald; McLean (McKean), Jardine, Parlane, Munro, Johnstone (Henderson)

ST JOHNSTONE: Robertson; Hamilton, McBean (Mackay); Anderson, Roberts, Rankin; Lambie, Robson (McGregor), Lawson, Thomson, Taylor

Attendance: 25,000

August 18th:
HIBERNIAN (0) 1   RANGERS (1) 1
  Scott (52)   Munro (33)
HIBERNIAN: McDonald; Brownlie, Smith; Bremner, Stewart, Blackley; Fyfe, Edwards, Scott, Muir, Duncan

RANGERS: McCloy; Miller, Greig; Forsyth, Denny, MacDonald; McLean, Jardine, Parlane, Munro, Johnstone

Attendance: 25,000

August 21st:
RANGERS (1) 4   MONTROSE (0) 0
  Johnstone 2 (4, 81),
  Jardine (73),
  MacDonald (77)
RANGERS: McCloy; Miller, Greig; Forsyth, Denny, MacDonald; McLean, Jardine, Parlane, Munro (McKean), Johnstone

MONTROSE: Gorman; Barr, Markland; McNicoll, D'Arcy, Cant (Robb); Lowe (Walker), Knox, Stewart, Johnston, Street

Attendance: 18,000

August 26th:
RANGERS (2) 3 HIBERNIAN (0) 0
Miller (18 pen),
Jardine (28),
McLean (84)

RANGERS: McCloy; Miller, Greig; Forsyth, Denny, MacDonald; McLean, Jardine, Parlane, Munro (Hamilton), Johnstone

HIBERNIAN: McDonald; Brownlie, Smith; Bremner, Stewart, Blackley; Fyfe, McLeod, Scott, Muir, Duncan
Attendance: 35,000

August 28th:
MONTROSE (0) 0 RANGERS (1) 3
Johnstone (7),
Parlane (79),
Jardine (83)

MONTROSE: Gorman; Barr, Markland; McNicoll, D'Arcy, Cant; Street, Knox, Stewart, Johnston (Lowe), Miller

RANGERS: McCloy; Miller, Greig; Forsyth, Denny, MacDonald; McLean, Jardine, Parlane, Munro, Johnstone
Attendance: 7,000

September 1st:
ST JOHNSTONE (0) 0 RANGERS (1) 1
Jardine (10)

ST JOHNSTONE: D. Robertson; Mackay, Smith; Hamilton, Roberts, Rankin; Lambie, Taylor, McGregor, Thomson, Sellars

RANGERS: McCloy; Miller, Greig; Forsyth, Denny, MacDonald; McLean, Jardine, Parlane, McKean, Johnstone
Attendance: 5,000

League Cup Section Table

	P	W	D	L	F	A	Pts
RANGERS	6	5	1	0	17	1	11
Hibernian	6	3	2	1	13	7	8
Montrose	6	1	2	3	5	9	4
St Johnstone	6	0	1	5	4	22	1

September 22nd: Quarter-Final First Leg
RANGERS (1) 3 CLYDEBANK (2) 3
Johnstone (30), Larnach (25),
MacDonald (70), McColl (37 pen),
Hamilton (72) Cooper (78)

RANGERS: McCloy; Jardine, Greig; Forsyth, Jackson, MacDonald; McLean, Hamilton, Parlane, McKean, Johnstone

CLYDEBANK: Gallacher; Hall, Abel; Fallon, Fanning, Hay; Cooper, McColl, Larnach, McCallon, Lumsden
Attendance: 15,000

October 6th: Quarter-Final Second Leg
CLYDEBANK (0) 1 RANGERS (1) 1
Cooper (62) Greig (43)
After Extra Time

CLYDEBANK: Gallacher; Hall, Abel; Fallon, Fanning, Hay; Cooper, McColl, Larnach, McCallon, Lumsden

RANGERS: Kennedy; Jardine, Miller; Greig (Denny), Jackson, Forsyth (Henderson); McKean, Hamilton, Parlane, MacDonald, Johnstone
Attendance: 10,000

October 18th: Quarter-Final Play-Off
RANGERS 0 CLYDEBANK 0
After Extra Time

RANGERS: Kennedy; Jardine, Miller; Greig, Jackson, Denny; McLean (Henderson), McKean, Parlane, MacDonald, Munro (Watson)

CLYDEBANK: Gallacher; Provan (McLaughlin), Abel; Fallon, Fanning, Hay; Cooper, McColl, Larnach, McCallon, Lumsden
Attendance: 15,000. Miller missed a penalty

October 19th: Quarter-Final Second Play-Off
At Firhill Park
RANGERS (1) 2 CLYDEBANK (1) 1
Parlane (7), McKean (60) Cooper (8)

RANGERS: Kennedy; Jardine, Miller; Greig, Watson, Denny; McLean, McKean, Parlane (Henderson), MacDonald (McDougall), Dawson

CLYDEBANK: Gallacher; McLaughlin, Abel; Fallon, Fanning (Provan), Hay; Cooper, Houston (Browning), Larnach, McCallon, Lumsden
Attendance: 12,000

October 27th: Semi-Final At Hampden Park
ABERDEEN (2) 5 RANGERS (1) 1
Scott 3 (3, 14, 73), MacDonald (15)
Harper (63), Jarvie (65)

ABERDEEN: Clark; Kennedy, Williamson; Smith (Thomson), Garner, Miller: Sullivan, Scott, Harper, Jarvie, Bell

RANGERS: Kennedy; Jardine, Miller; Greig, Jackson, Watson; McLean, McKean (Hamilton), Parlane, MacDonald, Henderson
Attendance: 20,990

Aberdeen followed up a Premier League victory over Celtic on Saturday with a Cup demolition of the other half of the Old Firm. They were never going to lose from the 3rd minute when Scott scored the first of his 3 goals.

SCOTTISH CUP

January 29th: Third Round
RANGERS   (2) 3   FALKIRK   (1) 1
  Jardine (20 pen),   Ford (38)
  Johnstone (22),
  MacDonald (55)

RANGERS: Kennedy; Jardine, Forsyth, Jackson, Greig; Watson, Hamilton, MacDonald; McLean, Robertson, Johnstone

FALKIRK: Watson; Gibson (Traynor), Clougherty, Holt, McLaughlin; Cameron, Graham, Mitchell; Cook, Mackie, Ford

Attendance: 18,000

February 26th: Fourth Round
RANGERS   (2) 3   ELGIN CITY   (0) 0
  Jackson (4), McLean (42 pen),
  MacDonald (79)

RANGERS: Kennedy; Jardine, Forsyth, Jackson, Greig; Watson, McDougall, MacDonald; McLean, Parlane, Johnstone

ELGIN CITY: Lawtie; Nicols (McKen), T. Wilson, Finnie, Buchan; Dingwall, Douglas, Davidson; Cowie (I. Wilson), Bavidge, Wells

Attendance: 18,000

March 12th: Quarter-Final
RANGERS   (1) 2   MOTHERWELL   (0) 0
  McKean (6), Watson (89)

RANGERS: Kennedy; Jardine, Forsyth, Jackson, Greig; McKean, MacDonald, Watson; McLean, Parlane, Johnstone

MOTHERWELL: Rennie; Watson, McAdam, Stevens, Wark; Kennedy (O'Rourke), McLaren, Davidson (Marinello); Pettigrew, Graham, Hood

Attendance: 35,500

March 30th: Semi-Final   At Hampden Park
HEARTS   (0) 0   RANGERS   (0) 2
                              Jackson (67),
                              Jardine (84 pen)

HEARTS: Cruikshank; Brown, Kay; Clunie, Gallagher, Fraser; Bannon, Busby, Gibson (Prentice), Park, Shaw —Aird

RANGERS: Kennedy; Jardine, Greig; Forsyth, Jackson, Watson; McLean, Hamilton, Parlane, MacDonald, Johnstone — Miller and Robertson

Attendance: 23,222

This was a dour, unadventurous Cup Semi-Final. Hearts were bankrupt of ideas with which to breach the Rangers' defence. They had no one up front to match the skills of Tommy McLean.

May 7th: Final   At Hampden Park
CELTIC   (1) 1   RANGERS   (0) 0
  Lynch (20 pen)

CELTIC: Latchford; McGrain, Lynch; Stanton, MacDonald, Aitken; Dalglish, Edvaldsson, Craig, Wilson, Conn — Burns, Doyle

RANGERS: Kennedy; Jardine, Greig; Forsyth, Jackson, Watson (Robertson); McLean, Hamilton, Parlane, MacDonald, Johnstone — Miller

Attendance: 54,252 *Referee*: R. Valentine (Dundee)

Controversy raged over Celtic's Scottish Cup-Winning goal. With 20 minutes gone Conn swung over a corner from the left. MacDonald headed back across goal and the ball was only partially cleared by Kennedy. Edvaldsson charged in and his shot beat the goalkeeper, but was handled on the line by Johnstone. Referee Valentine had no hesitation in pointing to the spot despite Rangers' furious protests. Alfie Conn made history by gaining a winners' medal with both Rangers and Celtic.

EUROPEAN CUP

September 15th: First Round First Leg
RANGERS   (1) 1   F.C. ZURICH
  Parlane (30)   (Switzerland)   (1) 1
                              Cucinotta (50 secs)

RANGERS: McCloy; Miller, Greig; Forsyth, Denny, MacDonald; McLean, Jardine, Parlane, McKean, Johnstone

F.C. ZURICH: Grob; Heer, Fischbach; Zigerlig, Chapuisat, Kuhn; Martinelli (Stierli), Cucinotta (Aliesch), Risi, Weller, Botteron

Attendance: 35,000

Rangers lost a first minute goal — needlessly. They equalised before half-time but as the match wore on Zurich grew in stature. After 20 years Rangers had still to learn the lesson that the aggression and power which could override their Scottish neighbours was no recipe for beating European opponents.

September 29th: First Round Second Leg
F.C. ZURICH   (1) 1   RANGERS   (0) 0
  Martinelli (8)

F.C. ZURICH: Grob; Heer, Chapuisat; Zigerlig, Fischbach, Martinelli (Rutschmann); Kuhn, Weller, Cucinotta, Botteron, Schweiler (Stierli)

RANGERS: McCloy; Miller, Greig; Forsyth, Jackson (Denny), Jardine; MacDonald, Hamilton (McKean), McLean, Parlane, Johnstone

Attendance: 28,500. Johnstone was ordered off

The Scottish Champions fought a brave and unrelenting fight to win a tie which had been lost at Ibrox. F.C. Zurich won 2-1 on aggregate.

APPEARANCES

	League	League Cup	Scottish Cup	European Cup
McCloy	5	7	-	2
Kennedy	31	4	5	-
Miller	17+7S	10	-	2
Greig	30	11	5	2
Jardine	36	11	5	2
Jackson	30	4	5	1
Forsyth	25	8	5	2
Denny	5	8+1S	-	1+1S
Watson	30	2+1S	5	-
MacDonald	29+1S	11	5	2
Hamilton	22+1S	2+2S	3	1
McLean	36	10	5	2
Henderson	4+3S	1+4S	-	-
Parlane	31+2S	11	4	2
Munro	3+2S	6	-	-
Johnstone	27	8	5	2
McKean	14+8S	6+2S	1	1+1S
O'Hara	5	-	-	-
Robertson	7+4S	-	1+1S	-
McDougall	1+3S	0+1S	1	-
Dawson	1	1	-	-
Steele	5	-	-	-
Stein	1+1S	-	-	-
Morris	1	-	-	-
Armour	0+1S	-	-	-
Brand	-	-	-	-
A. Boyd	-	-	-	-
G. Boyd	-	-	-	-

GOALSCORERS

League: Parlane 16, Johnstone 15, MacDonald 9, Jackson 4, Miller 4 (4 pens), Hamilton 3, Watson 3, McKean 2, O'Hara 2, Jardine 2 (1 pen), McLean 1, Robertson 1 (pen)

League Cup: Jardine 6, Johnstone 5, MacDonald 3, Parlane 2, Miller 2 (2 pen), Henderson 1, Munro 1, Hamilton 1, Greig 1, McKean 1

Scottish Cup: MacDonald 2, Jackson 2, Jardine 2 (2 pen), Johnstone 1, McKean 1, Watson 1, McLean 1 (pen)

European Cup: Parlane 1

The Skol League Cup was won on 28th October, 1984. Rangers defeated Dundee United by a single goal scored by Ian Fergusson in the 44th minute. The match played in dreadful weather conditions was watched by over 44,000 spectators.

Season 1977–78

Jock Wallace took Rangers to their second 'Treble' in 3 years and then sensationally resigned at the end of the season. After losing the first 2 matches of the season Rangers lost only one of the next 23 and won the title by 2 points from Aberdeen. Hibs were 15 points behind in 3rd place and Celtic were a full 19 points behind in 5th place. Rangers won 24 of the 36 matches and lost only 5, scoring 76 goals in the process. Derek Johnstone, who was named as Scotland's Player of the Year, scored 25 times followed by Gordon Smith — an early-season signing from Kilmarnock — on 20. Jackson, Cooper and Smith missed only one League match. The season was marred by the tragic death of Bobby McKean. He had been at Ibrox since September 1974 and had appeared in 77 League matches + 14 as substitute and scored 13 goals. He won one Scottish Cap against Switzerland at Hampden Park in 1976.

The highlight of Rangers' run to the League Cup Final was the 6-1 thrashing of Aberdeen in the Third Round tie at Ibrox. Forfar gave them a fright in the Semi-Final but by the end of the night they coasted into their 14th Final. The Final against Celtic also went into extra-time before Gordon Smith headed the winning goal 3 minutes from time.

Rangers won the Scottish Cup, beating bogey team Aberdeen in the Final with a magnificent display on the day. Alex MacDonald's header from Russell's chip put them ahead in the 34th minute and a Derek Johnstone header in 58 minutes put them further ahead. Although Billy McNeill's team scored a freaky late goal there was no doubt that the Cup was going to Ibrox. Berwick Rangers, Stirling Albion, Kilmarnock and Dundee United were eliminated in the earlier rounds of the competition.

Rangers beat Switzerland's Young Boys of Berne 3-2 on aggregate in the Preliminary Round of the Cup Winners Cup. As in the previous year, Derek Johnstone found the trip to Switzerland an unhappy experience. Twente of Holland, who included Frans Thijssen and Arnold Muhren in their line-up, proved to be too much of a handful in the next round and Rangers passed out of European contention for another season.

Immediately after Jock Wallace's shock resignation, John Greig was named as his successor. Wallace's League record as team manager had been as follows: Played 210 Won 137 Drew 41 Lost 32. He had taken the club to 3 Championships in his 6 seasons in charge, and under his managership the club had won the Scottish Cup 3 times and the League Cup twice.

League: Champions
League Cup: Winners
Scottish Cup: Winners
Cup Winners' Cup: First Round

SCOTTISH PREMIER LEAGUE

August 2nd: Ian McDougall was transferred to Dundee for £15,000.

August 13th:
ABERDEEN (1) 3   RANGERS (1) 1
Jarvie 2 (11, 60),   Russell (31)
Harper (61)

ABERDEEN: Clark; Kennedy, Garner, Miller, McLelland; Smith (Davidson), Shirra, Jarvie; Fleming, Harper, McMaster

RANGERS: McCloy; Jardine, Forsyth, Jackson, Miller; Russell, MacDonald; Mackay (McKean), Parlane, Robertson, Cooper

Attendance: 21,100

August 15th: Gordon Smith was signed from Kilmarnock for £65,000.

August 20th:
RANGERS (0) 0   HIBERNIAN (1) 2
                             Rae (4), Bremner (89)

RANGERS: McCloy; Jardine, Miller; Forsyth, Jackson, MacDonald; McLean, Russell, Parlane, Robertson, Cooper (Smith)

HIBERNIAN: McDonald; McNamara, Schaedler; Brazil, Stewart, Blackley; Smith, Bremner, Rae, McLeod, Scott

Attendance: 20,800

A group of fans stayed behind after the match chanting their displeasure at the Management.

August 27th:
PARTICK THISTLE (0) 0   RANGERS (1) 4
                                  Miller (44 pen),
                                  Smith 2 (53, 88),
                                  Russell (84)

PARTICK THISTLE: Rough; Hansen (Houston), Whittaker; Gibson, Campbell, Marr; Sheed, Melrose, Somner, Johnston (Anderson), Craig

RANGERS: McCloy; Jardine, Miller; Forsyth, Jackson, MacDonald; McLean, Russell, Johnstone, Smith, Cooper

Attendance: 18,000

September 10th:
RANGERS (0) 3   CELTIC (2) 2
   Smith 2 (53, 81),   Edvaldsson 2 (18, 31)
   Johnstone (65)

RANGERS: McCloy; Jardine, Miller; Forsyth, Johnstone, MacDonald (McLean); McKean, Russell, Parlane (Greig), Smith, Cooper

CELTIC: Latchford; McGrain, Lynch; Edvaldsson, MacDonald, Casey; Doyle, Dowie (McAdam), Glavin, Burns (Lennox), Wilson

Attendance: 48,788

Rangers gave their great rivals two goals of a start, sorted out their own problems at half-time and went on to win the points with a breathtaking display of attacking football.

September 17th:
ST MIRREN (2) 3   RANGERS (1) 3
   Docherty (33),   Jardine (27),
   McGarvey 2 (43, 75 pen)   Cooper (61),
                                 Johnstone (67)

ST MIRREN: Hunter; Young (Beckett), Mowat; Fitzpatrick, Reid, Copland; Docherty, Stark, McGarvey, Richardson (Abercrombie), Hyslop

RANGERS: McCloy; Jardine, Greig (Miller); Forsyth, Jackson, Watson; McKean, Russell, Johnstone, Smith, Cooper

Attendance: 25,000. Forsyth was ordered off

September 21st: Jardine and Forsyth were in the Scotland team which beat Czechoslovakia 3-1 at Hampden Park.

September 24th:
RANGERS (1) 2   AYR UNITED (0) 0
   Smith 2 (25, 49)

RANGERS: Kennedy; Jardine, Forsyth, Jackson, Miller; Russell, MacDonald; McKean, Johnstone, Smith, Cooper

AYR UNITED: Geoghegan; Fillipi, Fleming, McAnespie, Tait; Kelly, Hannah, McCulloch (McSherry); Cramond, McCutcheon (Masterton), McCall

Attendance: 18,000

October 1st:
RANGERS (0) 4   CLYDEBANK (1) 1
   Cooper 2 (53, 87),   Colgan (21)
   Smith 2 (67, 89)

RANGERS: Kennedy; Jardine, Miller; Forsyth, Jackson, MacDonald; McKean (McLean), Russell, Johnstone, Smith, Cooper

CLYDEBANK: Gallacher; Hall, Abel; Fallon, McCormick, Hay; Ronald, McColl, Larnach, McCallan, Colgan (McNaughton)

Attendance: 14,500

October 8th:
DUNDEE UNITED (0) 0   RANGERS (0) 1
                                  Russell (73)

DUNDEE UNITED: McAlpine; Rolland, Kopel; Fleming, Hegarty, Narey; Sturrock, Wallace (Kirkwood), Bourke (Robinson), Addison, Payne

RANGERS: Kennedy; Jardine, Miller; Forsyth, Jackson, MacDonald; McLean, Russell, Johnstone, Smith, Cooper

Attendance: 17,000

October 12th: Jardine and Forsyth were in the Scotland team which beat Wales 2-0 at Anfield to qualify for the World Cup Finals in Argentina.

October 12th: Following the loan of Colin Stein to Kilmarnock, Martin Henderson was loaned to Hibs for 3 months.

October 13th: Alex O'Hara was transferred to Partick Thistle for £25,000.

October 15th:
MOTHERWELL   (0) 1   RANGERS   (4) 4
 O'Rourke (71)   Smith (14),
                         Johnstone 3 (24, 27, 33)

MOTHERWELL: Muir; P. Millar, Stevens, McVie (O'Rourke), Wark; McLaren, J. Miller, O'Neill (Marinello); Davidson, Kennedy, Purdie

RANGERS: Kennedy; Miller, Forsyth, Jackson, Greig; Russell, MacDonald; Smith, McLean, Johnstone, Cooper

Attendance: 20,050

October 22nd:
RANGERS   (1) 3   ABERDEEN   (1) 1
 Jardine (31 pen),   Harper (37 pen)
 Smith (70), MacDonald (73)

RANGERS: Kennedy; Jardine, Greig; Forsyth, Jackson, MacDonald; McLean, Russell, Johnstone, Smith, Cooper

ABERDEEN: Clark; Kennedy, McLelland; Smith, Garner, Miller; Jarvie, Shirra, Harper, Fleming, McMaster (Sullivan)

Attendance: 35,000. McLelland was ordered off

October 29th:
HIBERNIAN   (0) 0   RANGERS   (0) 1
                         Jardine (70 pen)
HIBERNIAN: McDonald; Brownlie (Carroll), Schaedler; Brazil, Stewart, McNamara; McLeod, Higgins, Henderson, Smith, Duncan

RANGERS: Kennedy; Jardine, Greig; Forsyth, Jackson, MacDonald; McLean, Russell, Johnstone, Smith, Cooper

Attendance: 22,750

League positions

	P	W	D	L	F	A	Pts
1 RANGERS	11	8	1	2	26	13	17
2 Aberdeen	11	6	3	2	19	11	15
3 Dundee United	11	6	2	3	15	8	14
4 Partick Thistle	11	6	1	4	15	15	13
5 St Mirren	11	4	3	4	16	17	11

November 5th:
RANGERS   (1) 3   PARTICK THISTLE   (2) 3
 Parlane 2 (22, 48),   Somner (15),
 MacDonald (79)   Melrose (17),
                         Gibson (49)

RANGERS: Kennedy; Jardine, Greig; Forsyth, Jackson (Robertson), MacDonald; McLean, Russell, Parlane, Smith, Cooper

PARTICK THISTLE: Rough; Mackie, Whittaker; Marr, Anderson, Campbell; Melrose (Houston), Somner (Love), O'Hara, Gibson, Craig

Attendance: 28,200

November 12th:
CELTIC   (0) 1   RANGERS   (1) 1
 McAdam (50)   Johnstone (26)

CELTIC: Latchford; Fillipi, Edvaldsson, MacDonald, Lynch; Glavin, Aitken, Conn; Doyle, Craig (Wilson), McAdam

RANGERS: Kennedy; Jardine, Jackson, Forsyth, Greig; Russell, Smith, MacDonald; McLean, Johnstone, Cooper

Attendance: 56,000

Rangers were expected to win but, in the end, a draw was the right result

November 19th:
RANGERS   (0) 2   ST MIRREN   (0) 1
 Johnstone (47),   Stark (62)
 Miller (75 pen)

RANGERS: Kennedy; Jardine, Miller; Greig, Jackson, MacDonald; McLean, Russell, Johnstone, Smith (Parlane), Cooper

ST MIRREN: Hunter; Young, Beckett; Fitzpatrick, Reid, Dunlop; Copland, McGarvey, Stark, Abercrombie (Hyslop), Munro (Leonard)

Attendance: 25,000. Tommy McLean was sent off with Andy Dunlop

November 26th:
AYR UNITED   (0) 0   RANGERS   (1) 5
                         Johnstone 3 (43, 65, 75),
                         Jackson (69),
                         Parlane (85)

AYR UNITED: Sproat; Rodman, Kelly; Fleming, Hyslop, McAnespie; McLaughlin, McCall (McLelland), Masterton, Cramond, Christie

RANGERS: Kennedy; Jardine, Miller; Greig, Jackson, MacDonald; McLean (Parlane), Russell, Johnstone, Smith (McKean), Cooper

Attendance: 15,300

December 10th:
RANGERS (1) 2   DUNDEE UNITED (0) 0
  McLean (3), Smith (67)

RANGERS: Kennedy; Jardine, Greig; Jackson (Parlane), Miller, Russell, MacDonald; McLean (McKean), Smith, Johnstone, Cooper

DUNDEE UNITED: McAlpine; Rolland, Hegarty, Rennie, Kopel; Payne, Narey (Wallace), Fleming; Kirkwood, Sturrock, Bourke (Robinson)

Attendance: 22,000

December 17th:
RANGERS (1) 3   MOTHERWELL (1) 1
  Smith 2 (24, 86),   P. Millar (72)
  Johnstone (51)

RANGERS: Kennedy; Jardine, Greig; Forsyth, Jackson, MacDonald; McKean, Russell, Johnstone, Smith, Cooper

MOTHERWELL: Rennie; P. Millar, Wark; McLaren (Watson), McVie, Stevens; J. Miller (Kennedy), Pettigrew, O'Rourke, Davidson, Purdie

Attendance: 19,500

December 24th:
ABERDEEN (2) 4   RANGERS (0) 0
  Gibson (31), Robb (41),
  Harper (77),
  Jarvie (85)

ABERDEEN: Clark; Kennedy, McLelland; McMaster, Garner, Miller; Sullivan, Jarvie, Harper, Gibson, Robb

RANGERS: Kennedy; Jardine, Greig; Forsyth, Jackson, MacDonald; McLean, Russell, Johnstone, Smith (Parlane), Cooper

Attendance: 21,000

League positions

	P	W	D	L	F	A	Pts
1 RANGERS	18	12	3	3	42	23	27
2 Aberdeen	19	10	4	5	33	19	24
3 Partick Thistle	18	10	3	5	29	26	23
4 Dundee United	18	7	5	6	21	14	19
5 Celtic	17	8	3	6	28	23	19

December 31st:
RANGERS 0   HIBERNIAN 0

RANGERS: Kennedy; Jardine, Greig; Forsyth, Jackson, MacDonald; McLean, Russell, Johnstone (Parlane), Smith, Cooper

HIBERNIAN: McDonald; Brownlie, Smith; McNamara, Stewart, Bremner; Murray, McLeod, Hutchinson, Duncan, McGhee (Paterson)

Attendance: 25,000

January 2nd:
PARTICK THISTLE (0) 1 RANGERS (0) 2
  Frame (69)   Johnstone (55),
                     Smith (74)

PARTICK THISTLE: Rough; Mackie, Whittaker; Campbell, Anderson, Gibson; Houston, O'Hara (Melrose), Marr, Frame, Craig

RANGERS: Kennedy; Jardine, Miller; Forsyth, Jackson, MacDonald; McLean, Russell, Johnstone, Smith, Cooper (Parlane)

Attendance: 30,000

January 7th:
RANGERS (2) 3   CELTIC (0) 1
  Smith (35), Greig (37),   Edvaldsson (64)
  Parlane (87)

RANGERS: Kennedy; Jardine, Greig; Forsyth, Jackson, MacDonald; McLean (Parlane), Russell, Johnstone, Smith, Cooper (Miller)

CELTIC: Latchford; Fillipi, Lynch; Aitken, MacDonald, Munro; Glavin, Edvaldsson, Craig, McAdam, Wilson

Attendance: 51,000.

Celtic were trailing to a brilliant Gordon Smith goal when Joe Craig was pushed in the back by Jackson as he tried to head the ball in at the far post. It looked a clear penalty but the referee said 'no' and was immediately besieged by a posse of Celtic players. While the protests were going on Rangers took a quick free-kick, and with only Latchford and Munro against a 5-man attack John Greig finished off the move by tapping the ball into the net to make it 2-0. Celtic had another penalty claim turned down when Alex MacDonald scooped an Aitken shot off the line with his arm. In the 64th minute Edvaldsson set the game alight when he shot past Kennedy from 12 yards after Aitken had touched on a Glavin free-kick. Shortly afterwards an Aitken shot cannoned back off a post with Kennedy beaten. 3 minutes from time Miller who had replaced Cooper took a throw on the right to Jardine whose shot was fumbled by Latchford, leaving Derek Parlane with an easy job of scoring.

January 14th:
ST MIRREN (0) 0   RANGERS (1) 2
                     Johnstone (21),
                     Smith (73)

ST MIRREN: Hunter; Young, Beckett; Fitzpatrick, Reid, Copland; Torrance, Stark (Docherty), McGarvey, Abercrombie, Munro

RANGERS: Kennedy; Jardine, Greig; Forsyth, Jackson, MacDonald; McKean, Russell, Johnstone, Smith, Cooper

Attendance: 24,300

January 22nd: Rangers offered £400,000 (Derek Parlane + £200,000) for Gordon McQueen of Leeds United.

February 4th:

RANGERS   (0) 1   CLYDEBANK   (0) 0
  Johnstone (82)

RANGERS: McCloy; Jardine, Greig; Miller, Jackson, MacDonald; McLean (McKean), Russell, Johnstone, Smith, Cooper (Parlane)

CLYDEBANK: Gallacher; Hall, Colgan; Fallon, McCormack, Houston; O'Brien, McColl, Murray (Ronald), McCallan, Lumsden

Attendance: 15,195

February 19th:

CLYDEBANK   (0) 0   RANGERS (2) 3
                             Johnstone 2 (6, 37),
                             Cooper (71)

CLYDEBANK: Gallacher; Abel (Gourlay), Colgan; McLaughlin, McCormack, Houston; O'Brien, Lumsden, McCallan (Miller), McColl, Ronald

RANGERS: Kennedy; Miller, Dawson; Greig, Jackson, MacDonald; McLean, Russell, Johnstone, Smith, Cooper

Attendance: 8,000

February 25th:

MOTHERWELL   (2) 3   RANGERS   (2) 5
  O'Rourke (25),   Johnstone 2 (35, 57),
  Davidson 2 (28, 66)   Smith (37),
                            Cooper (48),
                            McVie o.g. (62)

MOTHERWELL: Rennie; Watson, McVie, Stevens, Wark; Millar (Clinging), Davidson, O'Rourke; Marinello, Pettigrew, McLaren (McAdam)

RANGERS: Kennedy; Greig, Jackson, Forsyth, Miller; Russell, Smith, MacDonald; McLean (Parlane), Johnstone, Cooper

Attendance: 20,387

League positions

	P	W	D	L	F	A	Pts
1 RANGERS	25	18	4	3	58	28	40
2 Aberdeen	25	14	6	5	41	21	34
3 Dundee United	23	10	6	7	27	17	26
4 Partick Thistle	23	10	4	9	31	35	24
5 Motherwell	25	9	5	11	33	34	23

March 4th:

RANGERS   (0) 0   ABERDEEN   (2) 3
                             Archibald 2 (23, 78),
                             Harper (38)

RANGERS: Kennedy; Miller, Greig; Forsyth, Jackson, MacDonald; McLean, Russell (Dawson), Johnstone, Smith (Parlane), Cooper

ABERDEEN: Clark; Kennedy, McLelland; McMaster, Garner, Miller; Sullivan, Archibald, Harper, Jarvie, Davidson

Attendance: 34,000

March 16th: Bobby McKean was found dead in his car beside his home at Barrhead.

March 21st:

RANGERS   (0) 2   PARTICK THISTLE   (0) 1
  MacDonald (50),   Somner (74)
  Jardine (89)

RANGERS: Kennedy; Jardine, Greig; Forsyth, Jackson, MacDonald; McLean (Parlane), Hamilton (Miller), Johnstone, Smith, Cooper

PARTICK THISTLE: Rough; Mackie, Whittaker; Marr, McAdam, Anderson; Houston, Gibson, O'Hara, Somner (Melrose), Craig (Love)

Attendance: 18,000

March 25th:

CELTIC   (2) 2   RANGERS   (0) 0
  Glavin (32), MacDonald (39)

CELTIC: Latchford; Sneddon, MacDonald, Edvaldsson, Lynch; Glavin, Aitken, Dowie; Doyle, McAdam, Burns

RANGERS: Kennedy; Jardine, Jackson, Forsyth, Greig; Russell (Miller), Smith, MacDonald; McLean, Johnstone, Cooper (Parlane)

Attendance: 50,000

Celtic salvaged a lot of pride in this match and turned on some of their best football of the season. Rangers found themselves hustled and stretched right from the start. They had no answer to the midfield strength of Dowie and Glavin. After the interval Rangers began to show some urgency and drive. Parlane and Miller replaced Cooper and Russell. Some fine saves from Latchford prevented any chance of a Rangers fightback.

March 29th:

HIBERNIAN   (0) 1   RANGERS   (1) 1
  McLeod (80 pen)   Parlane (36)

HIBERNIAN: McDonald; Brownlie, Smith; McNamara, Stewart, Bremner; Murray, McLeod, Hutchinson, Duncan, Higgins

RANGERS: McCloy; Jardine, Greig; Forsyth, Jackson, MacDonald; McLean (Miller), Hamilton, Johnstone, Smith, Parlane

Attendance: 21,245. Parlane was ordered off

April 1st:
RANGERS   (1) 1   ST MIRREN   (1) 1
Johnstone (45)   McGarvey (44)

RANGERS: McCloy; Jardine, Forsyth, Jackson, Greig; Hamilton (Miller), Smith, MacDonald; McLean (Cooper), Johnstone, Parlane

ST MIRREN: McCulloch; Beckett, Reid, Copland, Munro; Fitzpatrick, Abercrombie, Stark (Leonard); Richardson, Bone (Torrance), McGarvey

Attendance: 20,000

April 8th:
AYR UNITED   (1) 2   RANGERS   (2) 5
McCulloch (5),   Johnstone 2 (30, 69),
McLaughlin (84 pen)   Greig (34),
                             Smith 2 (54, 59)

AYR UNITED: Sproat; Wells, Fleming, Kelly, Connor; McLaughlin, McCulloch, McSherry; Cramond, McCall, Masterton (McLelland)

RANGERS: McCloy; Jardine, Forsyth, Jackson, Greig; Russell (Miller), Smith, MacDonald; McLean (Parlane), Johnstone, Cooper

Attendance: 13,400

April 12th:
RANGERS   (1) 2   AYR UNITED   (1) 1
Johnstone (20)   Cramond (35)

RANGERS: McCloy; Jardine, Greig; Forsyth, Jackson, MacDonald; McLean (Parlane), Russell (Miller), Johnstone, Smith, Cooper

AYR UNITED: Sproat; Wells, Connor; McSherry, Fleming, Kelly (McAllister); Phillips, McLaughlin, McCall (Hyslop), McCulloch, Cramond

Attendance: 12,282

April 15th:
CLYDEBANK   (0) 0   RANGERS   (0) 2
                             Johnstone 2 (56, 81)

CLYDEBANK: Gallacher; Gourlay, Hall; Fallon, Abel, O'Brien (McNaughton); Lumsden, Houston, McCormack, McColl, Colgan

RANGERS: McCloy; Jardine, Jackson, Forsyth, Greig; Russell (Hamilton), Smith (Parlane), MacDonald; McLean, Johnstone, Cooper

Attendance: 9,600

April 17th: Derek Johnstone was named as Scotland's Player of the Year.

April 19th:
DUNDEE UNITED   (0) 0   RANGERS   (1) 1
                             Johnstone (16)

DUNDEE UNITED: McAlpine; Holt, Kopel; Fleming, Hegarty, Narey; Sturrock, Robinson (Kirkwood), Bourke (Dodds), Stewart, Payne

RANGERS: McCloy; Jardine, Greig; Forsyth, Jackson, Watson; McLean, Russell, Johnstone, Smith, Cooper

Attendance: 17,293

April 22nd:
RANGERS   (2) 3   DUNDEE UNITED   (0) 0
Jackson (5),
Jardine (20 pen),
Cooper (75)

RANGERS: McCloy; Jardine, Forsyth, Jackson, Greig; Russell, MacDonald, McLean (Parlane); Johnstone, Smith (Watson), Cooper

DUNDEE UNITED: McAlpine; Stewart, Hegarty, Narey, Kopel; Robinson, Addison, Holt; Bourke, Fleming, Payne (Kirkwood)

Attendance: 29,200

April 24th: Martin Henderson was transferred to Philadelphia Furies for £30,000.

April 28th: Colin Stein and Johnny Hamilton were given free transfers.

April 29th:
RANGERS   (2) 2   MOTHERWELL   (0) 0
Jackson (5), Smith (19)

RANGERS: McCloy; Jardine, Forsyth, Jackson, Greig; Russell, MacDonald; McLean (Watson), Johnstone, Smith, Cooper

MOTHERWELL: Rennie; Watson (Millar), Stevens, McLeod, Kennedy; Mungall, Clinging, McLaren; Pettigrew (Sommerville), Lindsay, Marinello

Attendance: 47,000. Rangers clinched the Title

Scottish Premier League

	P	W	D	L	F	A	Pts
1 RANGERS	36	24	7	5	76	39	55
2 Aberdeen	36	22	9	5	68	29	53
3 Dundee United	36	16	8	12	42	32	40
4 Hibernian	36	15	7	14	51	43	37
5 Celtic	36	15	6	15	63	54	36
6 Motherwell	36	13	7	16	45	52	33
7 Partick Thistle	36	14	5	17	52	64	33
8 St Mirren	36	11	8	17	52	63	30
9 Ayr United	36	9	6	21	36	68	24
10 Clydebank	36	6	7	23	23	64	19

May 13th: Derek Johnstone scored Scotland's goal in a 1-1 draw with Northern Ireland at Hampden Park. Jardine and Forsyth were also in the team.

May 17th: Derek Johnstone scored for Scotland in a 1-1 draw with Wales at Hampden Park.

May 20th: England beat Scotland 1-0 at Hampden Park. Forsyth was in the team.

June 3rd: Forsyth was in the Scotland team which was beaten 3-1 by Peru in Cordoba in the World Cup Finals.

June 7th: Scotland drew 1-1 with Iran in Cordoba. Jardine was in the team and Forsyth made an appearance as substitute.

June 11th: Forsyth was in the Scotland team which beat Holland 3-2 in Mendoza.

May 23rd: Jock Wallace sensationally quit Ibrox.

May 24th: John Greig was named as Rangers' new Manager to succeed Jock Wallace.

June 2nd: Leeds United bid £150,000 for Derek Parlane.

LEAGUE CUP

August 24th: Second Round First Leg
RANGERS   (1) 3   ST JOHNSTONE   (1) 1
  Johnstone 2 (41, 70),   Brogan (34)
  Miller (55 pen)

RANGERS: McCloy; Jardine, Miller; Forsyth, Jackson, Watson; Mackay, Russell, Johnstone, Smith, Cooper

ST JOHNSTONE: Robertson; Mackay, Taylor; O'Brien, Houston, Clunie; Rutherford, Brogan, O'Connor, Thomson, Lawson

Attendance: 10,000

September 3rd: Second Round Second Leg
ST JOHNSTONE   (0) 0   RANGERS   (2) 3
                              Parlane (16),
                              Miller (19 pen),
                              Smith (83)

ST JOHNSTONE: Robertson; Mackay, O'Brien; Houston, Taylor, Anderson; Rutherford, Thomson, Brogan, O'Connor (Salisbury), Lawson

RANGERS: McCloy; Jardine, Miller; Johnstone (Henderson), Jackson (Watson), MacDonald; McKean, Russell, Parlane, Smith, Cooper

Attendance: 11,200. Rangers won 6-1 on aggregate

October 5th: Third Round First Leg
RANGERS   (4) 6   ABERDEEN   (0) 1
  Smith 3 (3, 43, 73),   Davidson (81)
  Johnstone (30), Miller (44 pen),
  MacDonald (85)

RANGERS: Kennedy; Jardine, Miller; Forsyth, Jackson, Macdonald; McLean, Russell, Johnstone, Smith, Cooper

ABERDEEN: Clark; Kennedy, McLelland; Robb, Garner, Miller; Jarvie, Davidson, Harper, Fleming (Sullivan), McMaster

Attendance: 20,000

October 26th: Third Round Second Leg
ABERDEEN   (1) 3   RANGERS   (1) 1
  Smith (38), Jarvie 2 (59, 64)   Smith (32)

ABERDEEN: Clark; Kennedy, McLelland; Smith, Garner, Miller; Jarvie, Shirra (Davidson), Harper, Fleming, McMaster

RANGERS: Kennedy; Jardine, Miller (Parlane); Forsyth, Greig, MacDonald; McLean, Russell, Johnstone, Smith, Cooper

Attendance: 15,600. Rangers won 7-4 on aggregate

November 9th: Quarter-Final First Leg
RANGERS   (2) 3   DUNFERMLINE   (0) 1
  Jackson (34),   Mullin (74)
  McLean 2 (44, 65)

RANGERS: Kennedy; Jardine, Greig; Forsyth, Jackson, MacDonald; McLean, Russell, Johnstone, Smith, Cooper

DUNFERMLINE: Whyte; Scott, Mercer; Thomson, Salton, Meakin; Watson (Mullin), Robertson, Georgeson, Donnell (Dunn), Morrison

Attendance: 10,000

November 16th: Quarter-Final Second Leg
DUNFERMLINE   (1) 1   RANGERS   (2) 3
  Morrison (29)   Greig (14),
                              Jardine (33 pen),
                              Johnstone (79)

DUNFERMLINE: Whyte; Scott, Mercer; Thomson, Salton, Meakin (Dunn); Bowie, Robertson, Georgeson, Donnelly (Mullin), Morrison

RANGERS: Kennedy, Jardine, Greig, Forsyth (Miller), Jackson, MacDonald, McLean, Russell, Johnstone, Smith, Cooper

Attendance: 8,274. Rangers won 6-2 on aggregate

February 27th: Semi-Final   At Hampden Park
FORFAR ATHLETIC   (1,2) 2   RANGERS (1,2) 5
  Brown (44), Rankin (60)   Johnstone 2 (26, 108),
                                  Parlane 2 (83, 100),
                                  MacDonald (95)
                        After Extra Time

FORFAR ATHLETIC: Nicholl; Smith, Rankin; Brown, Knox, Rae; Payne, Clark, Hall, Gallacher, Gavine

RANGERS: Kennedy; Miller, Greig; Forsyth, Jackson, MacDonald; McLean, Russell, Johnstone, Smith, Cooper (Parlane)

Attendance: 12,799

Forfar gave Rangers the fright of their lives at Hampden and came within 7 minutes of causing the biggest football upset of all time. At the end of the night Rangers coasted into their 14th League Cup Final but for a long time their faces were as red as their jerseys. For 90 minutes Forfar had matched Rangers in every department.

March 18th: Final   At Hampden Park
CELTIC   (0) 1   RANGERS   (1) 2
  Edvaldsson (84)   Cooper (38),
                   Smith (117)
           After Extra Time

CELTIC: Latchford; Sneddon, Munro, MacDonald, Lynch (Wilson); Glavin (Doyle), Dowie, Aitken; McCluskey, Edvaldsson, Burns

RANGERS: Kennedy; Jardine, Jackson, Forsyth, Greig; Hamilton (Miller), MacDonald, Smith; McLean, Johnstone, Cooper (Parlane)

Attendance: 60,168   *Refereee*: D. Syme (Rutherglen)

In a tense, tight and untidy Final Rangers opened the scoring in the 38th minute. Glavin and Smith chased a ball to the byeline. The Celtic player decided to shield the ball and let it run for a goal-kick. Smith however managed to get a foot in and whipped the ball across goal for Cooper to send a tremendous drive high into the net. 6 minutes from time Edvaldsson headed in a Sneddon cross to send the match into extra time. Jock Wallace decided to push on both substitutes in the extra period and it was the drive and pace of Miller which brought the winning goal.

SCOTTISH CUP

28th January: Third Round
BERWICK RANGERS (0) 2   RANGERS (2) 4
  I. Smith (58), G. Laing (86)   Jackson 2 (10, 37),
                       Johnstone 2 (61, 87)

BERWICK: Lyle; Bennett, McDowell, D. Smith, G. Laing; Barrowman, Wheatley, Jobson (B. Laing); McLeod (Wight), I. Smith, Tait

RANGERS: Kennedy; Jardine, Forsyth, Jackson, Greig; Russell, MacDonald, McLean; Johnstone (Parlane), Smith, Cooper

Attendance: 10,500

February 18th: Fourth Round
RANGERS   (1) 1   STIRLING ALBION (0) 0
  Johnstone (19)

RANGERS: Kennedy; Jardine (Morris), Miller; Greig, Jackson, MacDonald; McLean, Russell, Johnstone, Smith, Cooper (Parlane)

STIRLING ALBION: Young; Gray, Watson; Clark, Kennedy, Moffat; McPhee (Steadman), Browning (Duffin), Steele, Thomson, Armstrong

Attendance: 15,500

March 11th: Quarter-Final
RANGERS   (2) 4   KILMARNOCK   (0) 1
  Johnstone (41),   McCulloch (82)
  Hamilton (44),
  MacDonald (67), Cooper (78 pen)

RANGERS: Kennedy; Jardine, Greig; Forsyth, Jackson, MacDonald; McLean, Hamilton, Johnstone, Smith, Cooper

KILMARNOCK: Stewart; McLean, Robertson; Jardine, Clarke, McDicken; Provan (Docherty), McDowell (Murdoch), Stein, Maxwell, McCulloch

Attendance: 28,000

April 5th: Semi-Final   At Hampden Park
DUNDEE UNITED   (0) 0   RANGERS   (0) 2
                       Johnstone (70),
                       Greig (78)

RANGERS: McCloy; Jardine, Greig; Forsyth, Jackson, MacDonald; McLean, Russell, Johnstone (Parlane), Smith (Miller), Cooper

DUNDEE UNITED: McAlpine; Rennie (Robinson), Kopel; Fleming, Hegarty, Narey; Sturrock, Kirkwood, Bourke, Holt, Payne (Forsyth)

Attendance: 25,619

Rangers' old firm of Greig and Johnstone took the Ibrox club through to the Cup Final with 2 goals in an 8-minute spell. United had never beaten Rangers in this Competition and they looked as if they were about to break the hoodoo but they did not have a striker with the necessary sharpness to take advantage of a Rangers defence which looked nervous and disorganised.

May 6th: Final   At Hampden Park
RANGERS   (1) 2   ABERDEEN   (0) 1
  MacDonald (34),   Ritchie (85)
  Johnstone (58)

RANGERS: McCloy; Jardine, Greig; Forsyth, Jackson, MacDonald; McLean, Russell, Johnstone, Smith, Cooper (Watson) — Robertson

ABERDEEN: Clark; Kennedy, Ritchie; McMaster, Garner, Miller; Sullivan, Fleming (Scanlon), Harper, Jarvie, Davidson — McLelland

Attendance: 61,563   *Referee*: B. McGinlay (Glasgow)

Jock Wallace became the first Rangers manager to win two trebles and John Greig landed his third treble — a record for any one player. Rangers were magnificent on the day. In recent matches between the clubs the Dons had had it all their own way in midfield. Gordon Smith played a shade deeper and the balance was right. Smith had a tremendous first half-hour, then the brilliant Bobby Russell took over. He was unanimously voted as player of the match and that was something on a day when Rangers had so many good players. Ritchie scored a rather freaky goal for Aberdeen 5 minutes from time but by that time there was no doubt that the Cup was going to Ibrox.

EUROPEAN CUP WINNERS CUP

August 17th: Preliminary Round First Leg
RANGERS (1) 1   YOUNG BOYS OF
  Greig (39)   BERNE (0) 0
RANGERS: McCloy; Jardine, Greig; Forsyth,
Jackson, MacDonald; McLean (Mackay), Russell,
Parlane (Smith), Robertson, Cooper

YOUNG BOYS: Weissbaum; Brechbuhl, Burkhardt;
Castella, Conz, Leuzinger, Lorenz, Muller, Odermatt,
Redmann, Mast
Attendance: 30,000

August 31st: Preliminary Round Second Leg
YOUNG BOYS OF   RANGERS (1) 2
  BERNE (0) 2   Johnstone (43),
  Jackson o.g. (47),   Smith (73)
  Leuzinger (60)
YOUNG BOYS: Eichenberger; Brechbuhl, Vogel;
Trumpler, Rebmann, Conz, Odermatt, Castella
(Schmid), Lorenz, Muller (Leuzinger), Kuttel

RANGERS: McCloy; Jardine, Greig; Forsyth,
Jackson, MacDonald; McLean (McKean), Russell
(Miller), Johnstone, Smith, Cooper
Rangers won 3-2 on aggregate

Attendance: 17,000. Johnstone was ordered off

September 14th: First Round First Leg
RANGERS 0   TWENTE (Holland) 0
RANGERS: McCloy; Jardine, Miller; Forsyth,
Jackson, Watson; McKean, Russell, Henderson, Smith,
Cooper

TWENTE: Van Gerven; Van Ierssel, Thorensen;
Drost, Thijssen, Overweg; Wildschut, Van der Vall, Bos
(Pahlplatz), Muhren, Gritter
Attendance: 33,000

As so often in the past, Rangers were the nearly men of
Europe. The Scots did not run out of patience —they did
run out of time. Derek Johnstone was badly missed.

September 28th: First Round Second Leg
TWENTE (2) 3   RANGERS (0) 0
  Gritter (34), Muhren (40),
  Van der Vall (65)
TWENTE: Van Gerven; Van Ierssel, Thorensen;
Drost, Thijssen, Overweg; Wildschut, Van der Vall,
Bos, Muhren, Gritter

RANGERS: Kennedy; Jardine, Miller; Forsyth,
Jackson, MacDonald; McKean, Russell, Parlane, Smith,
Cooper

Attendance: 20,000. Miller missed a penalty

Rangers passed passively out of European contention for
another season. They rarely looked likely to beat Twente.
It was dire defence most of the way with the midfield
virtually conceded to the Dutch. Jardine stood out and
McKean and Smith tried hard. Twente won 3-0 on
aggregate.

APPEARANCES

	League	League Cup	Scottish Cup	Cup Winners Cup
McCloy	14	2	2	3
Kennedy	22	6	3	1
Dawson	1+1S	-	-	-
Jardine	32	7	5	4
Miller	16+8S	5+2S	1+1S	2+1S
Greig	28+1S	5	5	2
Forsyth	31	7	4	4
Jackson	35	7	5	4
MacDonald	34	7	5	3
Johnstone	33	8	5	1
Mackay	1	1	-	0+1S
McKean	6+4S	1	-	2+1S
Russell	33	7	4	4
McLean	29+2S	6	5	2
Parlane	6+16S	1+3S	0+3S	2
Robertson	2+1S	-	-	1
Cooper	34+1S	8	5	4
Smith	34+1S	8	5	3+1S
Watson	2+2S	1+1S	0+1S	1
Hamilton	3+1S	2	1	-
Henderson	-	0+1S	-	-
Morris	-	-	0+1S	-

GOALSCORERS

League: Johnstone 25, Smith 20, Cooper 6, Jardine 5
(2 pens), Parlane 5, MacDonald 3, Russell 3,
Jackson 3, Miller 2 (2 pens), Greig 2, McLean 1,
Own Goal 1

League Cup: Johnstone 6, Smith 6, Parlane 3, Miller 3
(3 pens), MacDonald 2, McLean 2, Jackson 1,
Greig 1, Cooper 1, Jardine 1 (pen)

Scottish Cup: Johnstone 6, Jackson 2, MacDonald 2,
Hamilton 1, Cooper 1 (pen), Greig 1

Cup Winners Cup: Greig 1, Johnstone 1, Smith 1

Rangers overcame 2 years of Hampden disappointment to win this Scottish Cup replay against
Dundee United by 4 goals to 1 on 12th May, 1981.

Season 1978-79

John Greig almost took Rangers to the treble in his first season in charge. The League was eventually lost in dramatic fashion at Celtic Park but the Scottish Cup and the League Cup were won.

Rangers lost only one home League match — the first against St Mirren — but their away form was patchy and they won only 6 of the 18 matches. Despite this, a victory against Celtic on May 21st would have given them the title but they failed to beat a Celtic team who had to play for 35 minutes with only 10 men. Colin Jackson unfortunately headed into his own goal 5 minutes from time and Murdo MacLeod scored right on the final whistle to give their greatest rivals a famous victory and the League flag. Peter McCloy and Bobby Russell played in all 36 matches and Jardine and McLean in 35. Gordon Smith scored 11 of their 52 League goals.

Rangers reached (and won) the League Cup Final. They met Celtic in the Semi-Final which needed extra time and an own goal by Celtic's Jim Casey to give them victory in a torrid match which saw Miller and Celtic's Burns ordered off in separate incidents. Rangers faced Aberdeen in the Final and the Dons were leading 1-0, against the run of play, with only 13 minutes remaining, before Alex MacDonald equalised and Aberdeen's Doug Rougvie was sent off following an off-the-ball incident with Derek Johnstone. With extra time again looking inevitable Colin Jackson came upfield to head the winner in injury time.

Rangers' Scottish Cup campaign ran to 9 matches. After beating Motherwell, Kilmarnock (after a replay) and Dundee in the early rounds a Derek Johnstone goal saw them triumph in the Semi-Final replay against Partick Thistle. They faced Hibs in the Final but 210 minutes of football failed to produce a goal and a 3rd match was needed. Extra time was again required before an own goal by Hibs' full-back Arthur Duncan gave the Ibrox team the Cup in a 5-goal thriller. Alex Miller became the 2nd Rangers player to miss a penalty in a post-war Final.

Rangers gained a magnificent European Cup victory over a Juventus team who had 9 members of the Italian World Cup squad in their side. An Alex MacDonald header wiped out the deficit from the First Leg and another header from Gordon Smith in the 68th minute saw them through to the Second Round. After drawing with P.S.V. Eindhoven at Ibrox they twice came from behind to beat the Dutch League Champions in Holland. Cologne were drawn in the Quarter-Final. They returned from the First Leg in West Germany with only one-goal arrears but a Dieter Muller goal just after the inverval, in the return, killed off their European ambitions for another season.

League: Runners-Up
Scottish Cup: Winners
League Cup: Winners
European Cup: Quarter-Finalists

SCOTTISH PREMIER LEAGUE

July 29th: Billy Urquhart was signed from Inverness Caley for a record Highland League fee.

July 30th: Derek Johnstone tore up a transfer request and was named as team captain.

August 3rd: Alex Forsyth was signed from Manchester United on a year's loan.

August 12th:
RANGERS (0) 0   ST MIRREN (0) 1
                                          Torrance (86)

RANGERS: McCloy; Jardine, T. Forsyth, Jackson, A. Forsyth; Russell, A. MacDonald, Watson (Urquhart); McLean, Johnstone, Smith

ST MIRREN: McLean; Young, Dunlop, Copland, Munro; Fitzpatrick, Weir, Abercrombie; Hyslop (Torrance), Bone, McGarvey

Attendance: 26,000

August 19th:
HIBERNIAN 0   RANGERS 0

HIBERNIAN: McDonald; Kilgour, Fleming, McNamara, Smith; Bremner, McLeod, Callachan (Rae); Murray (O'Brien), Duncan, Higgins

RANGERS: McCloy; Jardine, Johnstone, T. Forsyth, A. Forsyth; Russell, A. MacDonald, Smith, McLean; Parlane, Urquhart (Miller)

Attendance: 23,000

August 26th:
RANGERS 0   AIRDRIE 0

RANGERS: McCloy; Jardine, Jackson, Johnstone, A. Forsyth; Russell, Smith, Watson; McLean, Parlane, Cooper

AIRDRIE: Rough; McKinnon, McAdam, Campbell, Whittaker; Marr, Gibson (McDonald), Craig (Melrose); Houston, O'Hara, Somner

Attendance: 24,500

September 9th:
CELTIC (2) 3   RANGERS (0) 1
  McAdam 2 (1, 76),   Parlane (49)
  McCluskey (14)

CELTIC: Latchford; Fillipi, Edvaldsson, Aitken, Lynch; Glavin, Conroy, Burns (Casey); Doyle, McAdam, McCluskey (Craig)

RANGERS: McCloy; Jardine, Jackson, T. Forsyth, A. Forsyth; Russell, A. MacDonald (Miller), Johnstone; McLean (Cooper), Parlane, Smith

Attendance: 60,000. Miller missed a penalty

September 16th:
RANGERS (1) 1   ABERDEEN (0) 1
  A. Forsyth (38 pen)   Sullivan (90)

RANGERS: McCloy; Jardine, Jackson, T. Forsyth, A. Forsyth; Russell, A. MacDonald, Smith; McLean, Parlane, Johnstone

ABERDEEN: Leighton; Kennedy, McLeish, Miller, McLelland; McMaster, Sullivan, Jarvie; Archibald (Strachan), Harper, Scanlon (Rougvie)

Attendance: 25,000

September 23rd:
MORTON (1) 2   RANGERS (0) 2
  Ritchie (25),   Parlane (47),
  Scott (71)   Johnstone (66)

MORTON: Connaghan; Hayes, Orr, McLaren, Holmes; Miller, Rooney, Thomson; Ritchie, Russell (McNeill), Scott

RANGERS: McCloy; Jardine, T. Forsyth, Jackson, A. Forsyth; Russell, Smith, A. MacDonald; McLean, Parlane, Johnstone

Attendance: 16,000

September 30th:
RANGERS (3) 4   MOTHERWELL (1) 1
  McLean (22),   Clinging (7)
  Smith 2 (27, 66),
  Johnstone (37)

RANGERS: McCloy; Jardine, Jackson (Miller), T. Forsyth, A. Forsyth; Russell, Smith, A. MacDonald; McLean (Cooper), Parlane, Johnstone

MOTHERWELL: Latchford; Shanks, McVie, McLaren, Wark (Mackin/Capaldi); Marinello, Stevens, Clinging; Pettigrew, Larnach, Wilson

Attendance: 24,000

October 7th:
RANGERS (0) 1   DUNDEE UNITED (1) 1
  MacDonald (82)   Kirkwood (20)

RANGERS: McCloy; Jardine, T. Forsyth, Miller, A. Forsyth; Russell, Smith, A. MacDonald; McLean, Parlane (Cooper), Johnstone

DUNDEE UNITED: McAlpine; Stewart, Hegarty, Narey, Kopel; Addison (Dodds), Smith, Fleming; Sturrock (Payne), Kirkwood, Holt

Attendance: 24,000

October 14th:
HEARTS 0   RANGERS 0

HEARTS: Dunlop; Kidd, Jeffries; McNicoll, Liddell; Fraser, Robertson, Bannon; Gibson (McQuade), Busby, Prentice

RANGERS: McCloy; Jardine, A. Forsyth; T. Forsyth, Jackson, A. MacDonald; McLean, Russell, Parlane (Cooper), Johnstone, Smith

Attendance: 18,159

October 21st:
ST MIRREN   (0) 0   RANGERS   (1) 1
                                A. Forsyth (24 pen)

ST MIRREN: Thomson; Young (Weir), Munro; Fitzpatrick, Dunlop, Copland; Torrance, Stark, Bone, Abercrombie, McGarvey

RANGERS: McCloy; Jardine, A. Forsyth; T. Forsyth, Johnstone, A. MacDonald; McLean, Russell, Parlane, Smith (Miller), Cooper

Attendance: 20,000

October 28th:
RANGERS   (2) 2   HIBERNIAN   (1) 1
 A. Forsyth (26 pen),   McLeod (35)
 Smith (31)

RANGERS: McCloy; Jardine, Johnstone, T. Forsyth, A. Forsyth; Russell, A. MacDonald, Smith; McLean, Parlane, Cooper (Miller)

HIBERNIAN: McDonald; Duncan, Stewart, McNamara, Smith; Rae, Callachan, Bremner; McLeod, Hutchinson, Higgins

Attendance: 24,500

League positions

	P	W	D	L	F	A	Pts
1 Dundee United	11	5	5	1	15	8	15
2 Celtic	11	6	1	4	20	14	13
3 Hibernian	11	4	5	2	12	10	13
4 RANGERS	11	3	6	2	12	10	12
5 Aberdeen	11	4	3	4	22	14	11

November 4th:
PARTICK THISTLE   (0) 1   RANGERS   (0) 0
 Houston (57)

PARTICK THISTLE: Rough; McKinnon, Campbell, Anderson, Whittaker; Park, Marr, O'Hara; Houston, Melrose, Somner

RANGERS: McCloy; Jardine, T. Forsyth, Johnstone, A. Forsyth; Russell, Smith, A. MacDonald; McLean, Parlane (Urquhart), Cooper (Watson)

Attendance: 20,282

November 11th: Played at Hampden
RANGERS   (0) 1   CELTIC   (0) 1
A. Forsyth (55 pen)   Lynch (52)

RANGERS: McCloy; Miller, Jardine, T. Forsyth, A. Forsyth; McLean, Russell, A. MacDonald; Watson, Johnstone, Smith

CELTIC: Baines; Fillipi, MacDonald, Edvaldsson, Lynch; Aitken, McLeod, Burns; Provan, McAdam, Doyle

Attendance: 52,330

Celtic had the edge in attack, Rangers were much better organised at the back.

November 18th:
ABERDEEN   0   RANGERS   0

ABERDEEN: Clark; Kennedy, Rougvie, Miller, McLelland; Sullivan, Strachan, McMaster; Archibald, Harper, Scanlon (Fleming)

RANGERS: McCloy; Jardine, Johnstone, Jackson, Dawson; Russell, A. MacDonald, Watson; McLean, Parlane, Smith

Attendance: 24,000

November 25th:
RANGERS   (1) 3   MORTON   (0) 0
 Johnstone (39), Cooper (54),
 Smith (81)

RANGERS: McCloy; A. Forsyth, Jardine, Jackson, Dawson; Russell, Smith, Watson; McLean, Johnstone, Cooper

MORTON: Connaghan; Hayes, Evans, Orr, Holmes; Miller, Rooney, Thomson; Russell (Tolmie), Ritchie, Scott

Attendance: 23,000

December 9th:
DUNDEE UNITED   (2) 3   RANGERS   (0) 0
 Dodds (3), Fleming (20),
 Narey (82 pen)

DUNDEE UNITED: McAlpine; Stewart, Hegarty, Narey, Stark; Fleming, Holt, Payne (Addison); Dodds, Sturrock, Kirkwood

RANGERS: McCloy; A. Forsyth, Jardine, Jackson, Dawson; Russell (Watson), Smith, A. MacDonald; McLean, Johnstone, Cooper (Parlane)

Attendance: 15,247

December 16th:
RANGERS   (3) 5   HEARTS   (1) 3
 Johnstone 4 (9, 22, 64, 80),   Busby 2 (34, 81),
 Watson (25)   Bannon (59)

RANGERS: McCloy; Miller, Jardine, Jackson, Dawson; Russell, A. MacDonald, Watson; McLean, Johnstone, Cooper (Smith)

HEARTS: Dunlop; Kidd, Liddell (Craig), Jeffries, Brown; Bannon, Busby, Fraser; Gibson (McQuade), O'Connor, Robertson

Attendance: 17,500

December 23rd:
RANGERS (0) 1   ST MIRREN (0) 0
  Johnstone (68)

RANGERS: McCloy; Miller, Jardine, Jackson,
Dawson; Russell, A. MacDonald, Watson; McLean,
Johnstone, Cooper

ST MIRREN: Thomson; Beckett (Young), Dunlop,
Copland, Munro; Fitzpatrick, Stark, Abercrombie
(Hyslop); Richardson, Bone, McGarvey

Attendance: 22,500

League positions
	P	W	D	L	F	A	Pts
1 Dundee United	18	8	7	3	25	16	23
2 Partick Thistle	18	8	5	5	19	16	21
3 Aberdeen	19	6	8	5	30	19	20
4 RANGERS	18	6	8	4	22	18	20
5 Morton	19	7	6	6	24	26	20

January 20th:
MORTON (0) 0   RANGERS (0) 2
                        MacDonald (58),
                        Watson (71)

MORTON: Bricic; Hayes, McLaren, Orr, Holmes;
Rooney, Thomson, Miller; McNeill, Scott (Russell),
Ritchie

RANGERS: McCloy; Jardine, T. Forsyth, Jackson,
Dawson; Russell, A. MacDonald, Watson; McLean,
Johnstone, Cooper

Attendance: 15,000

February 10th:
RANGERS (0) 1   DUNDEE UNITED (0) 0
  Robertson (82)

RANGERS: McCloy; Jardine, T. Forsyth, Jackson,
Dawson; Russell, A. MacDonald, Watson (Robertson);
McLean, Johnstone, Cooper (Smith)

DUNDEE UNITED: McAlpine; Stewart, Hegarty,
Narey, Stark; Holt, Phillip (Kopel), Kirkwood;
Sturrock, Fleming, Dodds

Attendance: 25,000

February 24th:
HEARTS (2) 3   RANGERS (2) 2
  Robertson (2),   Smith (21),
  O'Connor 2 (15, 71)   Parlane (24)

HEARTS: Allan; Kidd, Liddell, Jeffries, Brown;
Fraser, Busby, Craig; Gibson, O'Connor, Robertson
(McQuade)

RANGERS: McCloy; Jardine, T. Forsyth, Jackson,
Dawson; Russell, Smith, A. MacDonald; McLean,
Parlane, Cooper (J. MacDonald)

Attendance: 16,500

League positions
	P	W	D	L	F	A	Pts
1 St Mirren	22	10	5	7	27	21	25
2 RANGERS	21	8	8	5	27	21	24
3 Dundee United	20	8	7	5	26	19	23
4 Aberdeen	21	6	10	5	33	22	22
5 Partick Thistle	19	8	6	5	21	18	22
8 Celtic	18	7	5	6	26	21	19

February 24th: Joe Mason was appointed as John Greig's assistant. Stan Anderson became reserve team manager.

March 14th:
RANGERS (0) 1   HIBERNIAN (0) 0
  Smith (59)

RANGERS: McCloy; Jardine, Dawson; T. Forsyth,
Jackson, A. MacDonald; McLean, Russell, Urquhart,
Smith, Cooper

HIBERNIAN: McArthur; Brazil, Duncan; Bremner,
Stewart, McNamara; Rae, McLeod, Campbell,
Callachan, Higgins

Attendance: 15,000

March 17th:
PARTICK THISTLE (0) 0 RANGERS (1) 2
                        Cooper (29),
                        Urquhart (86)

PARTICK THISTLE: Rough; McKinnon, Anderson,
McAdam, Whittaker; Park, Marr, Gibson; Houston,
Melrose, Somner (O'Hara)

RANGERS: McCloy; Jardine, T. Forsyth, Jackson,
Dawson; Russell, A. MacDonald, Smith; McLean,
Urquhart, Cooper

Attendance: 18,685

March 27th:
ST MIRREN (1) 1   RANGERS (1) 2
  Stark (22)   Urquhart 2 (21, 72)

ST MIRREN: Thomson; Young, Munro; Fitzpatrick,
Dunlop, Copland; Richardson, Stark; Bone,
Abercrombie, McGarvey

RANGERS: McCloy; Jardine, Dawson; Johnstone,
Jackson, A. MacDonald; McLean, Russell, Urquhart,
Smith, Cooper (Parlane)

Attendance: 18,000

April 7th:
RANGERS (0) 1   MORTON (1) 1
  Cooper (63)   Russell (31)

RANGERS: McCloy; Miller (Parlane), Jardine,
Jackson, Dawson; Russell, Smith, A. MacDonald;
McLean, Urquhart, Cooper

MORTON: Baines; Miller, Evans, Orr, Holmes; Ritchie, Rooney, McLaren; Hutchinson, McNeill (Tolmie), Russell

Attendance: 14,500

April 10th:
RANGERS   (2) 3   MOTHERWELL   (0) 0
   Cooper (21),
   MacDonald (41),
   Smith (85)

RANGERS: McCloy; Miller, Dawson; Jardine, Jackson, A. MacDonald; McLean, Russell, Johnstone, Smith, Cooper

MOTHERWELL: Rennie; McLeod, Wark; Carberry (Larnach), Dempsey, Stevens; Smith, Pettigrew, Clinging, Irvine, Donnelly (Wilson)

Attendance: 8,000

April 14th:
MOTHERWELL   (0) 2   RANGERS   (0) 0
   Clinging (59), Donnelly (70)

MOTHERWELL: Rennie; McLeod, Mackin, Smith, Wark; Carberry, Larnach, Irvine; Pettigrew, Clinging, Donnelly

RANGERS: McCloy; Miller, Jardine, Jackson, Dawson; Russell (Urquhart), Johnstone, A. MacDonald; McLean (Armour), Smith, Cooper

Attendance: 14,612

April 21st:
DUNDEE UNITED   (0) 1   RANGERS   (2) 2
   Stewart (57 pen)   Dawson (23),
                                 Smith (30)

DUNDEE UNITED: McAlpine; Stark, Hegarty, Narey, Stewart; Addison, Fleming, Holt; Kirkwood, Sturrock, Dodds (Payne)

RANGERS: McCloy; Jardine, Jackson, Johnstone, Dawson; Russell, Miller, A. MacDonald; Cooper (McLean), Parlane, Smith

Attendance: 20,264

April 25th:
ABERDEEN   (1) 2   RANGERS   (0) 1
   Archibald (5),   Smith (60)
   McGhee (85)

ABERDEEN: Clark; Hamilton, McLelland; McLeish, Garner, Miller; Sullivan (McMaster), Archibald, McGhee, Strachan, Scanlon

RANGERS: McCloy; Miller (Urquhart), Dawson; Jardine, Johnstone, A. MacDonald; McLean, Russell, Parlane, Smith, Cooper

Attendance: 17,000

April 28th:
RANGERS   (3) 4   HEARTS   (0) 0
   Russell 3 (9, 28, 62),
   Parlane (19)

RANGERS: McCloy; Jardine, Johnstone, Jackson, Dawson; Russell, Smith, A. MacDonald; McLean (Mackay), Parlane, Cooper

HEARTS: Allan; Kidd, Liddell, Fraser, Black; Brown, Craig, Tierney; Gibson (Stuart), Scott, McQuade

Attendance: 20,000

May 2nd:
MOTHERWELL   (1) 1   RANGERS   (0) 2
   Irvine (19)   Smith (55),
                           Jackson (88)

MOTHERWELL: Rennie; McLeod, Wark; Carberry, Smith, Stevens; Larnach, Pettigrew, Clinging, Irvine, Donnelly

RANGERS: McCloy; Jardine, Dawson; Johnstone, Jackson, A. MacDonald; McLean, Russell, Parlane, Smith, Cooper

Attendance: 13,052. Smith scored from the rebound following a Jardine penalty

May 5th: Played at Hampden
RANGERS   (0) 1   CELTIC   (0) 0
   MacDonald (57)

RANGERS: McCloy; Jardine, Johnstone, Jackson, Dawson; A. MacDonald, Russell, Smith; McLean, Parlane, Cooper

CELTIC: Latchford; McGrain, Aitken, Edvaldsson, MacLeod; Davidson (McAdam), Conroy, Burns (Lynch); Provan, McCluskey, Doyle

Attendance: 52,841

This game was another triumph for Davie Cooper. He was in the mood and gave Danny McGrain more trouble than he had had since his return to the first team. Throughout the match Rangers created many more chances and they were undoubtedly the more positive side throughout. As a result of their victory they now had a one-point advantage over their opponents.

May 7th:
RANGERS   (0) 2   ABERDEEN   (0) 0
   Smith (59), Cooper (62)

RANGERS: McCloy; Jardine, Dawson; Johnstone, Jackson, A. MacDonald; McLean, Russell, Parlane, Smith, Cooper

ABERDEEN: Clark; Kennedy, Hamilton; McLeish, Garner, Miller; McGhee, Archibald, Sullivan (Jarvie), Strachan, Scanlon

Attendance: 32,000

May 21st:

CELTIC	(0) 4	RANGERS	(1) 2
Aitken (66),		Russell (9),	
McCluskey (74),		MacDonald (76)	
Jackson o.g. (85),			
MacLeod (90)			

CELTIC: Latchford; McGrain, Lynch; Aitken, McAdam, Edvaldsson; Provan, Conroy (Lennox), McCluskey, MacLeod, Doyle

RANGERS: McCloy; Jardine, Dawson; Johnstone, Jackson, A. MacDonald; McLean (Miller), Russell, Parlane, Smith, Cooper

Attendance: 52,000. Doyle was ordered off

Needing a victory to snatch the prize from Rangers, Celtic found themselves a goal down and reduced to 10 men when Johnny Doyle was sent off 10 minutes after half-time. Spurred on by Roy Aitken they fought back to win the match in the most dramatic style. With only 5 minutes left Celtic sensationally took the lead when Jackson involuntarily headed the ball into his own net after a McCluskey cross had been pushed out by McCloy. Murdo MacLeod slammed in a 4th right on time.

May 23rd:

RANGERS	(0) 1	PARTICK THISTLE	(0) 0
Johnstone (n.a.)			

RANGERS: McCloy; Jardine, Dawson; Johnstone, Jackson (Miller), A. MacDonald; McLean, Russell, Parlane (J. MacDonald), Watson, Cooper

PARTICK THISTLE: McLean; McKinnon, Whittaker; Marr, Campbell (Somner), Doyle; Houston (Clarke), Melrose, O'Hara, McAdam, Park

Attendance: 2,000

May 31st:

HIBERNIAN	(1) 2	RANGERS	(0) 1
Brazil (25), Rae (82)		Urquhart (57)	

HIBERNIAN: McArthur; Brazil, Duncan; Bremner, Stewart, McNamara; Rae, McLeod, Campbell, Brown (Farmer), Hutchinson (Lambie)

RANGERS: McCloy; A. Forsyth, Dawson; Miller, Morris, Watson; Strickland (Armour), Urquhart, Russell, Smith, Cooper (Robertson)

Attendance: 4,000

June 17th: Marseilles bid £165,000 for Derek Parlane.

Scottish Premier League

	P	W	D	L	F	A	Pts
1 Celtic	36	21	6	9	61	37	48
2 RANGERS	36	18	9	9	52	35	45
3 Dundee United	36	18	8	10	56	37	44
4 Aberdeen	36	13	14	9	59	36	40
5 Hibernian	36	12	13	11	44	48	37
6 St Mirren	36	15	6	15	45	41	36
7 Morton	36	12	12	12	52	53	36
8 Partick Thistle	36	13	8	15	42	39	34
9 Hearts	36	8	7	21	39	71	23
10 Motherwell	36	5	7	24	33	86	17

LEAGUE CUP

August 16th: First Round First Leg

RANGERS	(2) 3	ALBION ROVERS	(0) 0
Parlane (16),			
Johnstone (22),			
Smith (89)			

RANGERS: McCloy; Jardine, A. Forsyth; T. Forsyth, Johnstone, A. MacDonald; McLean, Russell (Miller), Parlane, Smith, Cooper (Urquhart)

ALBION ROVERS: Orr; Muldoon, Main; Franchetti, Shields, Leishman; Allan, Hill, Clelland, Hart, Loughlan

Attendance: 6,000

August 23rd: First Round Second Leg

ALBION ROVERS	(0) 0	RANGERS	(1) 1
		Parlane (43)	

ALBION ROVERS: Orr; Muldoon, McGregor; Franchetti, Leishman, Main; Allan, Hill, Hart, Coyle, McGilivray

RANGERS: McCloy; Jardine, A. Forsyth; T. Forsyth (Miller), Johnstone, A. MacDonald; Strickland, Russell, Parlane, Smith, Urquhart

Rangers won 4-0 on aggregate.

Attendance: 4,000. MacDonald was ordered off

August 30th: Second Round First Leg

RANGERS	(2) 3	FORFAR ATHLETIC	(0) 0
Cooper (27),			
McLean (38),			
Smith (80)			

RANGERS: McCloy; Jardine, A. Forsyth; Jackson, Johnstone, A. MacDonald; McLean, Russell, Parlane (Urquhart), Smith, Cooper

FORFAR: McWilliams; Bennett, Cameron; Knox, Brown, Rae; Hall, Gallagher, Reid, Henry, Kinnear

Attendance: 8,000

September 2nd: Second Round Second Leg
FORFAR ATHLETIC   (0) 1   RANGERS   (1) 4
  Rae (65)   MacDonald (44),
                           Cooper (49),
                           Smith 2 (57, 81)

FORFAR: McWilliams; Bennett, Cameron; K. Brown, Brash, Rae; Gallacher, Knox, Reid, Henry, Hall

RANGERS: McCloy; Jardine, A. Forsyth; Jackson (Smith), Johnstone, A. MacDonald; McLean, Russell (Denny), Parlane, Miller, Cooper

Attendance: 5,500

October 4th: Third Round First Leg
RANGERS   (0) 3   ST MIRREN   (1) 2
  Cooper (65),   Fitzpatrick 2 (35, 50)
  Miller (68), Johnstone (89)

RANGERS: McCloy; Jardine, A. Forsyth; T. Forsyth, Miller, A. MacDonald (Watson); McLean (Cooper), Russell, Parlane, Johnstone, Smith

ST MIRREN: Thomson; Beckett, Munro; Fitzpatrick, Dunlop, Copland; Hyslop, Stark, Bone, Abercrombie, McGarvey

Attendance: 18,000

October 11th: Third Round Second Leg
ST MIRREN   0   RANGERS   0

ST MIRREN: Thomson; Young (Torrance), Munro; Fitzpatrick, Dunlop, Copland; Richardson, Stark, Bone, Abercrombie, McGarvey

RANGERS: McCloy; Jardine, A. Forsyth; T. Forsyth, Jackson, A. MacDonald; Miller, Russell, Parlane, Johnstone, Smith

Attendance: 20,000. Rangers won 3-2 on aggregate.

November 8th: Quarter-Final First Leg
RANGERS   (0) 1   ARBROATH   (0) 0
  Wells o.g. (71)

RANGERS: McCloy; Jardine, A. Forsyth; T. Forsyth, Johnstone, A. MacDonald; McLean, Russell, Parlane (Armour), Smith (Cooper), Watson

ARBROATH: Lister; McKenzie, Rylance; Cargill, Wells, Fettes; Fletcher, Edwards (Follon), Wilson, Carson, Yule

Attendance: 10,000

November 15th: Quarter-Final Second Leg
ARBROATH   (1) 1   RANGERS   (1) 2
  Fletcher (23)   Smith (15),
                          Russell (85)

ARBROATH: Lister; McKenzie, Rylance; Cargill, Wells, Fettes; Fletcher, Carson, Wilson, Kidd, Yule

RANGERS: McCloy; Miller, A. Forsyth; Jardine, T. Forsyth, Watson; McLean, Russell, Johnstone, Urquhart, Smith

Attendance: 4,000. Rangers won 3-1 on aggregate.

December 13th: Semi-Final   At Hampden Park
RANGERS   (1) 3   CELTIC   (1) 2
  Jardine (26 pen),   Doyle (10),
  Jackson (80),   McAdam (65)
  Casey o.g. (113)
              After Extra Time

RANGERS: McCloy; Miller, Dawson; Jardine, Jackson, MacDonald; McLean, Russell, Johnstone, Watson, Cooper (Smith) — Parlane

CELTIC: Baines, Fillipi, Lynch, Aitken, A. MacDonald, Edvaldsson, Provan, Conroy (Casey), McAdam, Burns, Doyle — Conn

Attendance: 49,432. Miller and Burns were ordered off

It was a tragic night for young Celtic substitute Jim Casey who put through his own goal just 7 minutes from the end of extra-time to end his club's glorious record which had seen them take part in the last 14 finals of this competition.

March 31st: Final   At Hampden Park
RANGERS   (0) 2   ABERDEEN   (0) 1
  MacDonald (77),   Davidson (59)
  Jackson (90)

RANGERS: McCloy; Jardine, Dawson; Johnstone, Jackson, A. MacDonald; McLean, Russell, Urquhart (Miller), Smith, Cooper (Parlane)

ABERDEEN: Clark; Kennedy, McLelland; McMaster, Rougvie, Miller; Strachan, Archibald, Harper, Jarvie, Davidson (McLeish) — Cooper

Attendance: 54,000. Rougvie was ordered off

John Greig gained his first major success as Rangers manager and Derek Johnstone handled his first trophy as captain. Aberdeen, leading 1-0, lost 2 goals in the last 13 minutes, Jackson's winning goal coming in injury time. They had to play out a period with Bobby Clark nursing a bad arm injury and they had Doug Rougvie ordered off. The fact is Rangers played Aberdeen off the park for most of the 90 minutes. Aberdeen froze on the day.

SCOTTISH CUP

February 12th: Third Round
RANGERS   (1) 3   MOTHERWELL   (1) 1
  Johnstone (41),   Clinging (47)
  Jackson (63),
  Cooper (80)

RANGERS: McCloy; Jardine, Dawson; T. Forsyth, Jackson, A. MacDonald; McLean, Russell, Johnstone, Watson, Cooper

MOTHERWELL: Rennie; Boyd, Wark; Smith, McVie, Stevens; Millar, Pettigrew, Larnach, Clinging, Wilson

Attendance: 15,000

February 21st: Fourth Round
RANGERS   (1) 1   KILMARNOCK   (0) 1
   MacDonald (4)   McDicken (72)

RANGERS: McCloy; Jardine, Dawson; T. Forsyth (Miller), Jackson, A. MacDonald; McLean, Russell, Johnstone, Watson (Smith), Cooper

KILMARNOCK: McCulloch; McLean, Robertson; Clark, Clarke, McDicken; Gibson, Maxwell (Jardine), Bourke, Mauchlen, Street (Cairney)

Attendance: 18,000

February 26th: Fourth Round Replay
KILMARNOCK   (0) 0   RANGERS   (1) 1
                              Urquhart (41)

KILMARNOCK: McCulloch; McLean, Robertson; Clark, Clarke, McDicken; Gibson, Maxwell, Bourke, Mauchlen, Street

RANGERS: McCloy; Jardine, Dawson; T. Forsyth, Jackson, A. MacDonald; Smith, Russell, Johnstone, Urquhart, Cooper

Attendance: 18,000. Jackson and Street were ordered off

March 10th: Fifth Round
RANGERS   (5) 6   DUNDEE   (2) 3
   Jardine (15 pen),   McLaren 2 (36, 39),
   MacDonald (20), Smith (22),   Shirra (87)
   T. Forsyth (35), Russell (43),
   Cooper (48)

RANGERS: McCloy; Jardine, Denny, T. Forsyth, Dawson (A. Forsyth); Russell, Smith, A. MacDonald; McLean, Urquhart, Cooper

DUNDEE: Donaldson; Barr, Watson, Glennie, Schaedler; Lamb, Shirra, McLaren; Sinclair, Pirie, Murphy (Redford)

Attendance: 23,000

April 4th: Semi-Final   At Hampden Park
PARTICK THISTLE   0   RANGERS   0

PARTICK THISTLE: Rough; McKinnon, Whittaker; Campbell, Anderson, Gibson; O'Hara (Houston), Melrose, McAdam, Love, Park — Frame

RANGERS: McCloy; Jardine, Dawson; Johnstone, Jackson, A. MacDonald; McLean, Russell, Urquhart, Smith, Cooper — Miller, Parlane

Attendance: 26,232

Rangers and Partick served up an epic Cup Semi-Final. It was only right that these 2 old rivals should have to return to Hampden on Monday to decide who went forward to meet either Hibs or Aberdeen in the Final. Rangers' Sandy Jardine was voted man of the match and was presented with a tankard and a cheque for £100 at the end. On the hour Rough made a save of International class from McLean, getting a fingertip to a flighted cross which was heading for the top corner of the net. With 10 minutes remaining Thistle had broken clear with a sudden upfield burst. A cross from Love was headed into the net by Houston but the linesman flagged for offside.

April 16th: Semi-Final Replay At Hampden Park
RANGERS   (0) 1   PARTICK THISTLE   (0) 0
   Johnstone (86)

RANGERS: McCloy; Jardine, Dawson; Johnstone, Jackson, A. MacDonald; McLean, Russell, Parlane, Smith, Cooper — Miller, Urquhart

PARTICK THISTLE: Rough; McKinnon, Whittaker; Campbell, Anderson (Marr), Gibson; Houston, Melrose, Somner, Love, Park — O'Hara

Attendance: 32,294

Derek Johnstone made one fleeting appearance in the Hampden spotlight and that was enough to take his team into the Final. Fielded at centre-half to combat the aerial threat from Thistle, he made nary a move forward until 4 minutes from time when he strode upfield to head powerfully a Tommy McLean free-kick. Alan Rough brilliantly stopped the ball but was unable to clutch it and Johnstone followed up to hammer it into the roof of the net. For Thistle the cup exit had to be a bitter disappointment after 2 games which they played well enough to have warranted a final place. For long spells a Thistle goal seemed inevitable but a combination of scorned opportunities and better than competent goal-keeping by McCloy was more than they were able to conquer.

May 12th: Final   At Hampden Park
RANGERS   0   HIBERNIAN   0

RANGERS: McCloy; Jardine, Dawson; Johnstone, Jackson, A. MacDonald (Miller); McLean, Russell, Parlane, Smith, Cooper — Urquhart

HIBERNIAN: McArthur; Brazil, Duncan; Bremner, Stewart, McNamara; Hutchinson (Rae), McLeod, Campbell, Callachan, Higgins — Brown

Attendance: 50,610

The 1979 Scottish Cup Final will go down as one of the untidiest in the history of the competition. Hibs were given little chance against a side with the form and the traditional experience of the big time.

May 16th: Final Replay   At Hampden Park
RANGERS 0   HIBERNIAN 0
                                After Extra Time

RANGERS: McCloy; Jardine, Dawson; Johnstone,
Jackson, A. MacDonald; McLean (Miller), Russell,
Parlane, Smith, Cooper —Urquhart

HIBERNIAN: McArthur; Brazil, Duncan; Bremner,
Stewart, McNamara; Rae, McLeod, Campbell,
Callachan, Higgins (Brown)

Attendance: 33,504   *Referee*: B. McGinlay (Glasgow)

Rangers and Hibs failed to sort out a stalemate which had
begun the previous Saturday. Rangers had too many
players who fell short of their best on the night. Parlane
was given little support in attack. In extra time Hibs tossed
away a couple of early chances and Parlane came close for
Rangers on two occasions. At the end the only award made
was to Rangers centre-half Colin Jackson, who was judged
to be Man of the Match.

May 28th: Final Second Replay At Hampden Park
RANGERS   (1) 3   HIBERNIAN (1) 2
  Johnstone 2 (42, 61),   Higgins (16),
  Duncan o.g. (110)   McLeod (78 pen)
                After Extra Time

RANGERS: McCloy; Jardine, Dawson; Johnstone,
Jackson, Watson (Miller); McLean (Smith), Russell,
Parlane, A. MacDonald, Cooper

HIBERNIAN: McArthur; Brazil, Duncan; Bremner,
Stewart, McNamara; Rae, McLeod, Campbell,
Callachan (Brown), Higgins (Hutchinson)

Attendance: 30,602 *Referee*: I. M. D. Foote (Glasgow)

Rangers collected the Scottish Cup after 5½ hours of
Hampden action. Hibs looked the better side in the first
half after Higgins put them ahead in 16 minutes but Derek
Johnstone equalised 3 minutes before the interval.
Rangers, much superior in the 2nd half, looked good when
Johnstone put them in front after 61 minutes but Hibs
came back and equalised with a McLeod penalty 12
minutes from the end. In the 103rd minute Rangers
missed a penalty awarded when Parlane fell as Duncan
tackled. Alex Miller's spot kick was brilliantly pushed
away by McArthur. The winning goal came in 110 minutes
when Cooper's cross was inadvertently headed past
McArthur by Arthur Duncan as Gordon Smith challenged.

EUROPEAN CUP

September 13th: First Round First Leg
JUVENTUS (Italy) (1) 1   RANGERS   (0) 0
  Virdis (8)

JUVENTUS: Zoff; Cuccureddu, Cabrini; Furino,
Morini, Scirea; Causio, Tardelli, Virdis, Benetti
(Fanna), Bettega

RANGERS: McCloy; Jardine, A. Forsyth; T. Forsyth,
Jackson, A. MacDonald; Miller, Russell, Parlane, Smith,
Watson

Attendance: 62,000

Rangers put up a magnificent show in the Communale
Stadium against a star-studded side. John Greig, in his
first European Cup test as a manager, chose a side heavily
geared to defend and his brave rearguard action triumphed
after a nerve-wracking opening spell. Rangers had 11 men
of outstanding courage on show, ready to play until they
dropped. Greig left out Tommy McLean and brought in
Alex Miller and Kenny Watson to play deep. It proved to
be a master stroke. Sandy Jardine was delegated the
sweeper's role.

September 27th: First Round Second Leg
RANGERS   (1) 2   JUVENTUS   (0) 0
  MacDonald (17), Smith (68)

RANGERS: McCloy; Jardine, A. Forsyth; T. Forsyth,
Jackson, A. MacDonald; McLean, Russell, Parlane,
Johnstone, Smith

JUVENTUS: Zoff; Cuccureddu, Cabrini; Furino
(Benetti), Morini, Scirea; Causio, Tardelli (Fanna),
Virdis, Gentile, Bettega

Attendance: 44,000

Rangers scored a magnificent victory over their cynical
opponents. This must rank as one of the greatest-ever
performances by a Scottish side in Europe. It was a night
Rangers fans had waited for — when everything clicked
into place and one of the best club sides in the world were
reduced to a bewildered bunch. It was a triumph for Greig
and his players — the same players who had failed to win a
League match so far this season. A goal in each half — one
from Alex MacDonald and the other from Gordon Smith
— had the Rangers fans in raptures as the Italians, with 9
members of their World Cup squad on view, were
outplayed and out-thought. Rangers won 2-1 on aggregate.

October 18th: Second Round First Leg
RANGERS 0   P.S.V. EINDHOVEN
                               (Holland) 0

RANGERS: McCloy; Jardine, A. Forsyth; T. Forsyth,
Jackson, A. MacDonald; McLean, Russell, Parlane
(Cooper), Johnstone, Smith; Sub: Miller

P.S.V.: Van Engelen; Deijkers, Stevens; Brandts,
Poortvliet, Lubse; Postuma, W. Van der Kerkhof
(Hooje), Van Kraalj, Krijgh, Van der Kuylen (Jansen)

The Dutch side put on as professional a show as had been
seen in this country for a long time. No one could fault
Rangers for lack of effort. It was a heartbreaking night of
missed chances and brilliant goalkeeping by the P.S.V.
reserve Van Engelen.

November 1st: Second Round Second Leg
P.S.V. EINDHOVEN (1) 2   RANGERS (0) 3
   Lubse (1), Deykers (60)   MacDonald (57),
                               Johnstone (66),
                               Russell (87)

P.S.V.: Van Engelen; Krijgh (Smits), Stevens, Van Kraay, Brandts; W. Van der Kerkof, Jansen; Poortvliet, R. Van der Kerkhof, Lubse, Deijkers

RANGERS: McCloy; Jardine, A. Forsyth; T. Forsyth, Johnstone, A. MacDonald; McLean, Russell, Parlane, Smith, Watson

Attendance: 28,000

With everything against them Rangers brushed aside the sickening blow of losing a goal in just 34 seconds to play with discipline, character, and flair which has seldom been bettered by a Scottish club side abroad. By beating P.S.V. at home in a European competition they did what no other side had ever done and they did it after twice coming from behind. With just 3 minutes left Rangers hit on the break to clinch their place in the next round. McLean struck a pass into open space and Russell, all on his own, coolly touched the ball past the keeper. Rangers won 3-2 on aggregate.

March 6th: Quarter-Final First Leg
COLOGNE (West Germany) (0) 1   RANGERS (0) 0
   Muller (57)

COLOGNE: Schumacher; Konopka, Zimmerman; Schuster, Gerber, Cullmann; Glowacz (Prestin), Flohe, Muller, Neumann, Littbarski

RANGERS: McCloy; Jardine, Dawson; T. Forsyth, Jackson, A. MacDonald; McLean, Russell, Parlane (Urquhart), Smith, Denny (Miller)

Attendance: 45,000

Captain Derek Johnstone was ruled out by injury. McCloy pulled off a string of magnificent saves and when he was beaten with a Neumann shot Dawson popped up on the line to boot the ball to safety. McLean and Smith had a brilliant one-two in the first-half but Smith smacked the ball into the side netting when he should have scored. In 57 minutes Cologne finally made the breakthrough. Rangers' defence failed to get the ball clear and Dieter Muller was at the far post to head the ball past McCloy.

March 21st: Quarter-Final Second Leg
RANGERS (0) 1   COLOGNE (0) 1
   McLean (87)   Muller (47)

RANGERS: McCloy; Jardine, Dawson (Johnstone); T. Forsyth, Jackson, A. MacDonald; McLean, Russell, Urquhart (Parlane), Smith, Cooper

COLOGNE: Schumacher; Konopka, Zimmermann; Strack, Gerber, Cullmann; Schuster, Flohe, Muller, Neumann, Van Gool

Attendance: 44,000

A goal 2 minutes after the interval killed off Rangers' European ambitions. A free-kick hit hard by Konopka from the right was dummied by Flohe and flicked past McCloy by Dieter Muller. Rangers manager John Greig sent on Derek Johnstone for Ally Dawson. Tommy McLean chipped in a free-kick 3 minutes from time to retain Ibrox dignity but it was merely a defiant gesture. The inexperience of Billy Urquhart was evident throughout. He missed the 2 best chances of the night. The first one came when Schumacher could not hold a fierce Cooper free-kick and the ball bounced out to Urquhart whose shot was blocked. After the interval Johnstone set up a golden chance but the former Highland League player miscued his shot. Cologne won 2-1 on aggregate.

APPEARANCES

	League	League Cup	Scottish Cup	European Cup
McCloy	36	10	9	6
Miller	10+7S	5+3S	0+4S	1+1S
Jardine	35	10	9	6
A. Forsyth	16	8	0+1S	4
Watson	11+2S	3+1S	3	2
T. Forsyth	17	6	4	6
Jackson	28	5	8	5
A. MacDonald	33	9	9	6
Johnstone	31	10	8	3+1S
Armour	0+2S	0+1S	-	-
Smith	31+2S	8+2S	6+2S	6
Russell	36	10	9	6
McLean	34+1S	8	8	5
Parlane	21+3S	7+1S	4	5+1S
Dawson	23	2	9	2
Cooper	26+4S	5+2S	9	1+1S
Urquhart	6+4S	3+2S	3	1+1S
Robertson	0+2S	-	-	-
J. MacDonald	0+2S	-	-	-
Mackay	0+1S	-	-	-
Morris	1	-	-	-
Strickland	1	1	-	-
Denny	-	0+1S	1	1
Kennedy	-	-	-	-
McLaren	-	-	-	-
Richardson	-	-	-	-

Ted McMinn, making his mark with Rangers in the mid-eighties.

GOALSCORERS

League: Smith 11, Johnstone 9, A. MacDonald 5,
            Cooper 5, Parlane 4, Urquhart 4, Russell 4,
            A. Forsyth 4 (4 pens), Watson 2, McLean 1,
            Robertson 1, Dawson 1, Jackson 1

League Cup: Smith 5, Cooper 3, Parlane 2, Johnstone 2,
                A. MacDonald 2, Jackson 2, Own Goals 2,
                McLean 1, Miller 1, Russell 1, Jardine 1

Scottish Cup: Johnstone 4, A. MacDonald 2, Cooper 2,
                  Jackson 1, Urquhart 1, Jardine 1 (pen),
                  Smith 1, T. Forsyth 1, Russell 1,
                  Own Goal 1

European Cup: A. MacDonald 2, Smith 1, Johnstone 1,
                  Russell 1, McLean 1

Rangers players, Jardine, Miller, and Redford salute the fans after winning the 1981 League Cup
Final. Rangers had just defeated Dundee United at Hampden Park by 2 goals to 1.

Season 1979–80

This season was near-disastrous. Rangers managed only 5th position in the Premier League race, finishing behind Aberdeen, Celtic, St Mirren and Dundee United. Although their home form was not too bad they managed only 4 away wins all season and lost a total of 14 of the 36 matches. They failed to record a single League victory against either Aberdeen or Celtic. Sandy Jardine played in 35 matches but injury restricted Tom Forsyth to only 16. In a flurry of transfer activity Rangers spent £210,000 on Dundee's Ian Redford and signed Gregor Stevens from Leicester City in a deal valued at £150,000. At the end of the season Derek Parlane left Ibrox for Leeds United and Gordon Smith was sold to Brighton for £400,000. That deal financed the purchase of Colin McAdam from Partick Thistle for £160,000 and Jim Bett from Belgium's F.C. Lokeren for £180,000.

Rangers progressed to the Third Round of the Bells League Cup but were soundly beaten, both home and away, by Aberdeen. They won the Drybrough Cup for the first time, beating Celtic in the Hampden Final, but they lost the Final of their own Tennant Caledonian Cup to Kilmarnock after a penalty shoot-out. They took up the invitation to take part in a Cup competition in Canada at the end of the season, and although they did not win the Red Leaf Cup they came home £40,000 richer after reaching the Final. Unfortunately Ally Dawson suffered a fractured skull in the second game of the tournament against Italy's Ascoli.

Rangers overcame Clyde (after a replay), Dundee United, Hearts (6-1) and Aberdeen to reach their 5th successive Scottish Cup Final. The match against Celtic was full of open football but remained goalless until the 17th minute of extra-time when George McCluskey scored a rather fortunate winner for Celtic which deprived Rangers of the replay which their play deserved.

Rangers beat Lillestrom home and away in the Preliminary Round of the Cup Winners Cup. They met West German Cup Winners Fortuna Dusseldorf in the First Round proper of the Competition. They conceded a late goal at Ibrox to go into the away leg with only a one-goal advantage but they managed to withstand almost 90 minutes of continuous pressure to gain the no-scoring draw they required for further progress. They looked to have given themselves a great chance of reaching the Quarter-Final after gaining a draw against Valencia in Spain in a match which saw Peter McCloy save a penalty from West German World Cup star Rainer Bonhof, but an own goal by Sandy Jardine and 2 goals from Argentinian Mario Kempes gave Valencia victory in Glasgow.

League: Fifth
League Cup: Third Round
Scottish Cup: Runners-up
Cup Winners Cup: Second Round

SCOTTISH PREMIER LEAGUE

August 11th:
HIBERNIAN   (0) 1   RANGERS   (2) 3
  Rae (56)   A. MacDonald (34),
                              Cooper (41),
                              Russell (62)

HIBERNIAN: McArthur; Farmer, Paterson, Stewart, Duncan; Callachan, Brown, Bremner; Hutchinson, Rae, Higgins

RANGERS: McCloy; Miller, Jardine, Jackson, Dawson; Russell, Watson, A. MacDonald; McLean, Johnstone, Cooper

Attendance: 17,731

August 15th: Goalkeeper George Young was signed from Stirling Albion for £10,000.

August 18th:
RANGERS   (0) 2   CELTIC   (0) 2
  J. MacDonald (49),   Sneddon (84),
  Russell (53)   McAdam (87)

RANGERS: McCloy; Miller, Jardine, Jackson, Dawson; Russell (Smith), Watson, A. MacDonald; Cooper, Johnstone, J. MacDonald

CELTIC: Latchford; Sneddon, MacDonald, Aitken, McGrain; Conroy, Edvaldsson (Lennox), MacLeod; Provan, McCluskey (Doyle), McAdam

Attendance: 36,000. Aitken was ordered off

Celtic, inspired by a magnificent Danny McGrain and utilising the pace and sharpness of substitutes Doyle and Lennox to the full, roared back for Alan Sneddon to score with a diving header in 84 minutes and for Tom McAdam to hammer in the equaliser 3 minutes later. As with the previous season's Championship decider, Rangers failed to win against 10 men.

August 25th:
PARTICK THISTLE   (1) 2   RANGERS   (0) 1
  Melrose (9), McAdam (76 pen) Johnstone (82)

PARTICK THISTLE: Rough; McKinnon, Whittaker; Anderson, Campbell, Gibson; Houston (O'Hara), Melrose, Wilson, McAdam, Doyle, Park

RANGERS: McCloy; Miller, Dawson; Jardine, Jackson, Watson (Smith); McLean (J. MacDonald), Russell, Johnstone, A. MacDonald, Cooper

Attendance: 20,000

September 4th: Jim Denny was transferred to Hearts for £30,000.

September 6th: Gregor Stevens was signed from Leicester City in a deal valued at £150,000. Derek Strickland went to Filbert Street.

September 8th:
RANGERS   (1) 3   ST MIRREN   (0) 1
  Johnstone (15),   Stark (55)
  Smith (80),
  Miller (85 pen)

RANGERS: McCloy; Jardine, Stevens (Miller), Jackson, Dawson; Russell, Watson, A. MacDonald; McLean (Smith), Johnstone, Cooper

ST MIRREN: Thomson; Beckett, Dunlop, Copland, Munro; Stark, Richardson, Docherty; Torrance, Bone, Somner

Attendance: 24,000

September 12th: Jardine and Cooper were in the Scotland team which drew 1-1 with Peru at Hampden Park. Cooper was making his full international debut.

September 15th:
ABERDEEN   (1) 3   RANGERS   (1) 1
  McMaster (19),   Johnstone (34)
  Strachan (74 pen),
  Rougvie (80)

ABERDEEN: Clark; Kennedy, Garner (Rougvie), Miller, Considine; Strachan, McMaster, McLeish; Archibald, Jarvie (Harper), Scanlon

RANGERS: McCloy; Jardine, Stevens, Jackson, Dawson (McLean); Russell, Watson, A. MacDonald (Miller); Cooper, Johnstone, Smith

Attendance: 23,000

September 22nd:
RANGERS   (0) 2   DUNDEE   (0) 0
  McGeachie o.g. (63),
  Glennie o.g. (83)

RANGERS: McCloy; Miller, Stevens, Jackson, Dawson; Jardine, A. MacDonald (Watson), Smith; McLean, Johnstone, Cooper

DUNDEE: Donaldson; Barr, Watson, Glennie, McGeachie; Turnbull, Millar, McLaren; Redford, Murphy, Sinclair

Attendance: 23,000

September 25th: Willie Waddell resigned as Managing Director/Vice-Chairman of the club.

September 27th: Lawrence Marlborough was appointed as new Vice-Chairman.

September 29th:
KILMARNOCK   (1) 2   RANGERS   (0) 1
  Clark (8), Cairney (79)   Johnstone (83)

KILMARNOCK: McCulloch; McLean, Clarke, McDicken, Robertson; Clark, Gibson, Mauchlen; Houston, Bourke, Cairney

RANGERS: McCloy; Jardine, Stevens, Jackson, Dawson; Miller, Smith, A. MacDonald (Watson); McLean (J. MacDonald), Johnstone, Cooper

Attendance: 16,000. Jardine missed a penalty

October 6th:
DUNDEE UNITED   0   RANGERS   0

DUNDEE UNITED: McAlpine; Kopel, Hegarty, Narey, Stark; Payne, Kirkwood, Phillip; Fleming, Pettigrew, Sturrock (Dodds)

RANGERS: McCloy; Stevens, Jardine, Jackson, Dawson; McLean, A. MacDonald, Johnstone; Watson, Parlane, Cooper

Attendance: 19,464

October 13th:
RANGERS   (1) 2   MORTON   (1) 2
  Johnstone 2 (40, 51)   Brown (5), Orr (80)

RANGERS: McCloy; Jardine, Jackson, Stevens, A. Forsyth; Miller, Smith, A. MacDonald; Urquhart, Johnstone, Cooper

MORTON: Baines; Hayes, McLaughlin, Orr, Holmes; Miller (Tolmie/Hutchinson), McLaren, Brown; McNeill, Thomson, Ritchie

Attendance: 21,700

October 17th: Jardine was in the Scotland team which drew 1-1 with Austria at Hampden Park.

October 20th:
RANGERS   (1) 2   HIBERNIAN   (0) 0
  Smith (43),
  Miller (51 pen)

RANGERS: McCloy; Jardine, Stevens, Jackson (McLean), A. Forsyth; Miller, A. MacDonald, Smith; Cooper, Johnstone, Urquhart (J. MacDonald)

HIBERNIAN: McArthur; Brazil, Paterson, McNamara, J. Brown (McGlinchey); Rae, S. Brown, McLeod; Ward (Campbell), Hutchinson, Higgins

Attendance: 22,000

October 27th:
CELTIC   (0) 1   RANGERS   (0) 0
  MacDonald (76)

CELTIC: Latchford; Sneddon, Aitken, MacDonald, McGrain; Sullivan, MacLeod, Burns (Conroy); Provan, McCluskey (Edvaldsson), McAdam

RANGERS: McCloy; Stevens, Jardine, Johnstone, A. Forsyth; Miller, McLean (Smith), A. MacDonald; Watson, Urquhart, Cooper

Attendance: 56,000

Celtic, with Davie Provan in the mood, spent most of the match in the Rangers half but due to fine work in the Ibrox defence they were allowed to create few chances. After an hour's play they began to find the gaps more easily and with 14 minutes left Provan flighted a perfect corner-kick and there was MacDonald soaring high above everyone to head a fine goal. Rangers gave the Celtic defence more problems in the final 10 minutes than they did in the first 80.

League positions

	P	W	D	L	F	A	Pts
1 Celtic	11	7	3	1	24	10	17
2 Morton	11	7	2	2	28	16	16
3 Aberdeen	11	5	3	3	23	13	13
4 Partick Thistle	11	4	4	3	13	14	12
5 RANGERS	11	4	3	4	17	14	11

November 3rd:
RANGERS   (2) 2   PARTICK THISTLE   (0) 1
  Urquhart 2 (11, 42)   Jardine (55)

RANGERS: McCloy; Jardine, Jackson (Smith), Stevens, A. Forsyth; Miller, A. MacDonald, Watson; Johnstone, Urquhart (J. MacDonald), Cooper

PARTICK THISTLE: Rough; Doyle, Campbell, Marr (Wilson), Anderson; Whittaker, Jardine (McDonald), Gibson; Love, O'Hara, Melrose

Attendance: 19,800

November 10th:
ST MIRREN   (1) 2   RANGERS   (1) 1
  Bone (39),   A. Forsyth (27)
  Somner (73)

ST MIRREN: Thomson; Young, Fulton, Copland, Munro; Stark, Richardson, Bone; Weir, McDougall, Somner

RANGERS: McCloy; A. Forsyth, Stevens, Jardine, Dawson; Miller (J. MacDonald), McLean, A. MacDonald; Watson (Mackay), Johnstone, Dalziel

Attendance: 12,000

November 17th:
RANGERS   (0) 0   ABERDEEN   (0) 1
  Archibald (86)

RANGERS: McCloy; A. Forsyth, Watson, Stevens, Dawson; Jardine, A. MacDonald, Miller (J. MacDonald); McLean, Johnstone, Smith

ABERDEEN: Clark, Kennedy, Garner, Miller, Rougvie, Strachan, McLeish, McMaster, Harper, Archibald, Scanlon (McGhee)

Attendance: 16,000

November 21st: Sandy Jardine was in the Scotland team which was beaten 2-0 by Belgium in Brussels.

November 24th:
DUNDEE (2) 3					RANGERS (0) 1
  Pirie (23), Sinclair (32),			Jackson (75)
  Shirra (60)

DUNDEE: Donaldson; McGeachie, Schaedler;
Miller, Glennie, McLaren; Mackie, Sinclair, Pirie,
Shirra, Murphy

RANGERS: McCloy; A. Forsyth, Dawson; Jardine,
Jackson, Stevens; McLean (Watson), A. MacDonald,
Johnstone, Smith (Russell), J. MacDonald
Attendance: 13,342

December 1st:
RANGERS (1) 2					KILMARNOCK (1) 1
  Johnstone (9),					Houston (33)
  Russell (46)

RANGERS: McCloy; Jardine, T. Forsyth, Jackson,
Dawson; Russell, Stevens, A. MacDonald; McLean,
Johnstone, J. MacDonald

KILMARNOCK: McCulloch; Robertson, P. Clarke,
McDicken, Cockburn; J. Clark, Gibson, Maxwell;
Mauchlen, Houston (Street), Cairney (Bourke)
Attendance: 15,000

December 8th:
MORTON (0) 0					RANGERS (0) 1
							Johnstone (65)

MORTON: Baines; Hayes, McLaughlin, Orr, Holmes;
Miller, McLaren (Tolmie), Thomson; Ritchie
(Anderson), Scott, Hutchinson

RANGERS: McCloy; Jardine, T. Forsyth, Jackson,
Dawson; Russell, Stevens, A. MacDonald; McLean,
Johnstone, J. MacDonald (Cooper)
Attendance: 14,500. Thomson was ordered off

December 15th:
RANGERS (1) 2					DUNDEE UNITED (1) 1
  Kopel o.g. (5),				Dodds (23)
  Johnstone (79)

RANGERS: Young; Jardine, T. Forsyth, Jackson,
Dawson; Russell, Stevens, A. MacDonald; McLean
(Cooper), Johnstone, J. MacDonald (Smith)

DUNDEE UNITED: McAlpine; Stark, Hegarty,
Narey, Kopel; Murray, Bannon, Fleming; Holt, Dodds,
Kirkwood (Milne)
Attendance: 20,480

**December 19th: Jardine and Johnstone were in the
Scotland team which was beaten 3-1 by Belgium at
Hampden Park.**

December 22nd:
HIBERNIAN (0) 2				RANGERS (1) 1
  Higgins (74),					McLean (37)
  Campbell (78)

HIBERNIAN: McArthur; Brazil, Rae, Paterson,
Duncan; Callachan, McNamara, Campbell; Best,
McLeod, Higgins

RANGERS: Young; Jardine, Jackson, T. Forsyth,
Dawson; A. MacDonald (Smith), Stevens, Watson;
McLean, Johnstone (Cooper), J. MacDonald
Attendance: 18,740

December 29th:
RANGERS (0) 1					CELTIC (0) 1
  Johnstone (73)				Lennox (74)

RANGERS: McCloy; Jardine, T. Forsyth, Jackson,
Dawson; Russell (Miller), Stevens, A. MacDonald;
McLean, Johnstone, J. MacDonald

CELTIC: Latchford; Sneddon, MacDonald,
McAdam, McGrain; Sullivan, Aitken, MacLeod; Doyle,
Lennox, Provan
Attendance: 34,500

Rangers produced their best performance for some time
and should have been in front at half-time. Latchford
denied them a lead three times in that first half with a
wonderful save from a Colin Jackson header and two great
interceptions as Derek Johnstone looked all set to score.
Latchford was out of luck when Rangers took the lead in
the 73rd minute when Tommy McLean crossed from the
right — the keeper slipped — and had no chance with
Johnstone's header. Celtic's reply was immediate and
deadly. A Dom Sullivan free-kick was headed inside by
Roy Aitken and Lennox ended the decade as he had started
— in scoring mood. Rangers appealed for offside but to no
avail. Celtic were denied a second-half penalty when an
Aitken shot hit Stevens on the arm.

League positions
	P	W	D	L	F	A	Pts
1 Celtic	18	11	4	3	38	17	26
2 Morton	18	10	3	5	36	24	23
3 RANGERS	18	8	4	6	28	20	20
4 Aberdeen	15	7	3	5	27	18	17
5 Dundee United	18	6	5	7	24	19	17

January 5th:
RANGERS (0) 1					ST MIRREN (1) 2
  Jardine (72 pen)				McDougall (43),
							Somner (88)

RANGERS: McCloy; Jardine, Forsyth, Jackson,
Dawson; Russell, Stevens (Cooper), A. MacDonald;
McLean, Smith (Parlane), J. MacDonald

ST MIRREN: Thomson; Young, Copland, Fulton, Beckett; Richardon, Bone, Stark (Docherty), Somner, McDougall, Weir

Attendance: 19,000

January 9th: Former player Davie Provan returned to Ibrox to join the training staff.

January 12th:
ABERDEEN (1) 3   RANGERS (1) 2
  Strachan (1), Archibald (70),   J. MacDonald (2),
  Hamilton (89)   Jackson (49)

ABERDEEN: Clark; Kennedy, Garner, Rougvie, Considine; Strachan, McLeish, McMaster; Archibald, Hamilton, Scanlon (Hewitt)

RANGERS: McCloy; Jardine, Jackson, T. Forsyth, Dawson (Smith); Russell, Stevens, A. MacDonald; Parlane, J. MacDonald, McLean (Cooper)

Attendance: 18,000

February 6th: Dundee rejected a Rangers bid of £200,000 for Ian Redford.

February 22nd: Rangers signed Redford for £210,000 — a Scottish record fee.

February 23rd:
RANGERS (3) 3   MORTON (1) 1
  Russell (21), Smith (38),   Hutchinson (43)
  J. MacDonald (44)

RANGERS: McCloy; Jardine, Stevens, T. Forsyth, Dawson; Russell, Smith, Redford; J. MacDonald, Johnstone, Cooper

MORTON: Baines; Hayes, McLaughlin, Orr, Holmes; McLaren, Miller (Scott), Brown; Tolmie, Hutchinson (Mauchlen), Thomson

Attendance: 22,000

March 1st:
RANGERS (1) 1   HIBERNIAN (0) 0
  Johnstone (25)

RANGERS: McCloy; Jardine, T. Forsyth, Stevens, Dawson; Russell (A. MacDonald), Smith, Redford; Cooper, Johnstone, J. MacDonald

HIBERNIAN: McArthur; Brazil, Paterson, Rae, Lambie; Cormack, McLeod, Best (Higgins); Callachan, Hutchinson, Duncan

Attendance: 29,000

League positions
	P	W	D	L	F	A	Pts
1 Celtic	24	13	8	3	44	21	34
2 Morton	25	11	4	10	43	36	26
3 St Mirren	23	9	8	6	35	35	·26
4 Aberdeen	22	9	6	7	36	26	24
5 RANGERS	24	10	4	10	35	32	24

March 6th: Derek Parlane was transferred to Leeds United for £160,000.

March 12th:
RANGERS (0) 1   DUNDEE (0) 0
  Stevens (60)

RANGERS: McCloy; Jardine, Dawson; T. Forsyth, Jackson, Stevens; Cooper, Russell, Johnstone, Redford, J. MacDonald (Smith)

DUNDEE: Donaldson; Millar, Schaedler; McLaren, Glennie, McGeachie; Mackie, Sinclair, Fleming, Shirra, Murphy (Corrigan)

Attendance: 15,000

March 15th:
RANGERS 0   PARTICK THISTLE 0

RANGERS: McCloy; Jardine, Forsyth, Jackson, Dawson; Stevens, Russell (A. MacDonald), Smith (McLean); Cooper, Johnstone, Redford

PARTICK THISTLE: Rough; McKinnon, Campbell, Anderson, Whittaker; Doyle, Gibson, O'Hara; Higgins, McAdam, Melrose

Attendance: 20,000

March 19th:
DUNDEE UNITED 0   RANGERS 0

DUNDEE UNITED: McAlpine; Stark, Kopel; Fleming, Hegarty, Narey; Bannon, Sturrock, Pettigrew, Addison, Kirkwood (Milne)

RANGERS: McCloy; Jardine, Dawson; T. Forsyth, Jackson, Stevens; Cooper, Smith, Johnstone (A. McDonald), Redford, J. MacDonald

Attendance: 9,533

March 29th:
RANGERS (1) 2   ABERDEEN (1) 2
  Jardine (45 pen),   Archibald (35),
  J. MacDonald (60)   Jarvie (85)

RANGERS: McCloy; Stevens, Jackson, T. Forsyth, Jardine; Russell, Smith, Dawson; McLean, J. MacDonald, Cooper

ABERDEEN: Clark; Kennedy, Miller, Rougvie, McMaster (Bell); Strachan, McLeish, Jarvie; Archibald, McGhee, Scanlon

Attendance: 19,850

April 2nd:
CELTIC (0) 1   RANGERS (0) 0
  McGarvey (85)

CELTIC: Latchford; Sneddon, McGrain; Aitken, MacDonald, McAdam; Provan, Lennox, McGarvey, MacLeod, Doyle

RANGERS: McCloy; Jardine, Dawson, T. Forsyth,
Jackson, Smith; Cooper, Miller, Johnstone, Redford, J.
MacDonald

Attendance: 52,000

This was a magic night for Frank McGarvey, Scotland's
most expensive footballer, who headed the only goal of the
match with just 5 minutes left. It looked odds on a no-
scoring draw when McGarvey, playing in his first Old
Firm match, pounced on a Roy Aitken cross at the far post
and knocked it past McCloy. The match was untidy and
bad-tempered but also thrilling and both sides had penalty
claims turned down.

April 5th:
DUNDEE (1) 1				RANGERS (1) 4
   Sinclair (23)				Cooper (20),
						Johnstone 2 (53, 78),
						Smith (76)
DUNDEE: Donaldson; Barr, Glennie, McGeachie,
Millar; Ferguson, McLaren, Mackie; Shirra, Fleming,
Sinclair

RANGERS: McCloy; Jackson, T. Forsyth, Dawson,
Jardine; Russell, Smith, Redford; Cooper, Johnstone, J.
MacDonald (McLean)

Attendance: 12,948

April 19th:
MORTON (0) 0				RANGERS (0) 1
						Russell (69)
MORTON: Baines; McLaren, McLaughlin, Orr,
Miller; Rooney, McNeill (Tolmie), Thomson; Scott
(Anderson), Hutchinson, Ritchie

RANGERS: McCloy; Jardine, Stevens, Jackson,
Dawson; Russell, Smith (McLean), Redford; Cooper,
Johnstone, J. MacDonald

Attendance: 12,000

April 23rd:
KILMARNOCK (1) 1			RANGERS (0) 0
   Street (11)
KILMARNOCK: McCulloch; McLean, Robertson; J.
Clark, P. Clarke, McDicken; Houston, Mauchlen,
Cairney, Gibson, Street

RANGERS: McCloy; Jardine, Dawson; Smith,
Jackson, Stevens; Cooper, Russell, Johnstone, Redford,
J. MacDonald (McLean)

Attendance: 7,000

April 26th:
RANGERS (0) 2			DUNDEE UNITED (0) 1
   Jardine (51 pen),			 Pettigrew (64)
   McLean (74)
RANGERS: McCloy; Jardine, Stevens, Dawson,
Smith, Russell, Redford, McLean, Cooper, Johnstone,
J. MacDonald

DUNDEE UNITED: McAlpine; Kirkwood, Stark;
Narey, Phillip, Fleming (Milne); Bannon, Addison,
Sturrock, Pettigrew, Dodds

Attendance: 15,000

**April 26th: Rangers gave Kennedy and Robertson
free transfers**.

April 30th:
RANGERS (1) 1			KILMARNOCK (0) 0
   J. MacDonald (8)
RANGERS: McCloy; Jardine, Dawson; Smith
(Miller), T. Forsyth (Johnstone), Stevens; McLean,
Russell, Cooper, Redford, J. MacDonald

KILMARNOCK: McCulloch; Welsh, Robertson; J.
Clark, P. Clarke, McDicken; Houston, McLean,
Cairney, Cramond, Street

Attendance: 8,000

May 3rd:
PARTICK THISTLE   (2) 4   RANGERS   (1) 3
   O'Hara 2 (37, 44),			Russell 2 (26, 87),
   McAdam (50), McDonald (80)   Johnstone (84)
PARTICK THISTLE: Rough; McKinnon, Campbell,
Anderson, Whittaker; Doyle, Park, McDonald; O'Hara,
Melrose (Jardine), McAdam (Higgins)

RANGERS: McCloy; Jardine, Stevens (Smith),
Jackson, Dawson; Russell, Redford, McLean (Miller);
Johnstone, MacDonald, Cooper

Attendance: 12,000

May 7th:
ST MIRREN (3) 4			RANGERS (1) 1
   Somner 3 (9, 39, 82),		 Miller (44)
   Bone (31)
ST MIRREN: Thomson; Young, Beckett (McAveety);
Abercrombie, Fulton, Copland; Bone, Stark, Somner,
Weir, Logan

RANGERS: McCloy; A. Forsyth, Dawson; A.
MacDonald, Jackson, Stevens (Johnstone); McLean,
Smith (Mackay), Miller, Redford, Watson

Attendance: 3,000

Scottish Premier League

	P	W	D	L	F	A	Pts
1 Aberdeen	36	19	10	7	68	36	48
2 Celtic	36	18	11	7	61	38	47
3 St Mirren	36	15	12	9	56	49	42
4 Dundee United	36	12	13	11	43	30	37
5 RANGERS	36	15	7	14	50	46	37
6 Morton	36	14	8	14	51	46	36
7 Partick Thistle	36	11	14	11	43	47	36
8 Kilmarnock	36	11	11	14	36	52	33
9 Dundee	36	10	6	20	47	73	26
10 Hibernian	36	6	6	24	29	67	18

June 1st: Dawson was in the Scotland team which was beaten 3-1 by Hungary in Budapest.

June 3rd: Colin McAdam joined Rangers from Partick Thistle. An independent tribunal had to fix the fee.

June 5th: Gordon Smith was sold to Brighton for £400,000.

June 27th: The tribunal valued McAdam at £160,000.

June 29th: Jim Bett was signed from Belgian side F.C. Lokeren for £180,000.

BELLS LEAGUE CUP

August 29th: First Round First Leg
CLYDE (1) 1   RANGERS (2) 2
  Brogan (44)   Dawson(5),
                           Robertson (6)

CLYDE: Connaghan; Anderson, Thorburn; Clougherty, Brogan, Aherne; O'Neill, McAlpine, Kean, McCabe, Hyslop (Hood)

RANGERS: McCloy; Jardine, Dawson; Watson, Jackson, Smith; Cooper, Russell, Robertson, A. MacDonald, J. MacDonald (Miller)

Attendance: 5,071

September 1st: Second Round Second Leg
RANGERS (3) 4   CLYDE (0) 0
  O'Neill o.g. (12),
  Mackay 2 (29, 89),
  Smith (43)

RANGERS: McCloy; Jardine, Jackson, Dawson, Watson (Dalziel), Russell, A. MacDonald, Mackay, Smith, Robertson (Miller), Cooper

CLYDE: Connaghan; Anderson, Clougherty, Aherne, Thorburn; Brogan, O'Neill, McCabe; McAlpine (Boyd), Kean, Hyslop (Hood)

Attendance: 16,000. Rangers won 6-1 on aggregate

September 26th: Third Round First Leg
ABERDEEN (2) 3   RANGERS (0) 1
  Garner (27), Harper (35),   Johnstone (74)
  McLeish (65)

ABERDEEN: Clark; Kennedy, Considine; McLeish, Garner, Miller; Strachan, Archibald, Harper, McMaster (Rougvie), Scanlon

RANGERS: McCloy; Jardine, Dawson; Stevens, Jackson, Watson; Cooper, Miller, Johnstone, A. MacDonald (McLean), Smith

Attendance: 18,000

October 10th: Third Round Second Leg
RANGERS (0) 0   ABERDEEN (2) 2
                          Harper (33),
                          Strachan (36)

RANGERS: McCloy; Jardine, Dawson; Stevens, Jackson, Watson (Smith); McLean (Mackay), A. MacDonald, Johnstone, Parlane, Cooper

ABERDEEN: Clark; Kennedy, Considine; McLeish, Garner, Miller; Strachan (Sullivan), Archibald (McMaster), Harper, Jarvie, Scanlon

Attendance: 28,000. Aberdeen won 5-1 on aggregate

SCOTTISH CUP

January 26th: Third Round
CLYDE (0) 2   RANGERS (0) 2
  Hood (62),   Jardine (63 pen),
  Hyslop (89)   Jackson (75)

CLYDE: McWilliams; Fillipi, Clougherty, Kinnear, Thorburn; Aherne, O'Neill, McCabe (Grant); Kean, Hood, Hyslop

RANGERS: McCloy; Jardine, T. Forsyth, Jackson, Dawson; Miller, Stevens (Smith), A. MacDonald; McLean (Cooper), Johnstone, J. MacDonald

Attendance: 10,800

January 30th: Third Round Replay
RANGERS (0) 2   CLYDE (0) 0
  J. MacDonald 2 (70, 87)

RANGERS: McCloy; Jardine, Dawson; T. Forsyth, Jackson, Stevens; Cooper, Russell, Johnstone, Watson, J. MacDonald

CLYDE: McWilliams; Fillipi, Thorburn; Clougherty, Kinnear, Aherne; Hyslop, O'Neill, Hood, McCabe (Grant), Kean

Attendance: 10,000

February 16th: Fourth Round
RANGERS (0) 1   DUNDEE UNITED (0) 0
  Johnstone (86)

RANGERS: McCloy; Miller, T. Forsyth, Jardine, Stevens, Dawson, Russell, Smith (A. MacDonald), Cooper, Johnstone, J. MacDonald

DUNDEE UNITED: McAlpine; Phillip, Hegarty, Narey, Stark; Bannon, Fleming, Payne (Kirkwood); Holt, Pettigrew, Sturrock

Attendance: 23,000

March 8th: Quarter-Final
RANGERS   (2) 6   HEARTS   (1) 1
  Cooper (24),   Forsyth o.g. (1)
  Jardine (37 pen),
  Russell (52),
  J. MacDonald 2 (71, 88),
  Johnstone (89)

RANGERS: McCloy; Jardine, Dawson; T. Forsyth,
Jackson (McLean), Stevens (A. MacDonald); Cooper,
Russell, Johnstone, Smith, J. MacDonald

HEARTS: Brough; Robinson, Denny; Boyd, Liddell,
Jeffries; Gibson, Fraser, O'Connor (Docherty), Shaw,
Robertson

Attendance: 31,000

April 12th: Semi-Final   At Celtic Park
RANGERS   (0) 1   ABERDEEN   (0) 0
  Johnstone (75)

RANGERS: McCloy; Jardine, Jackson, T. Forsyth,
Miller; Russell, Stevens, Smith; Cooper, Johnstone, J.
MacDonald — A. MacDonald, McLean

ABERDEEN: Clark; Kennedy, McLeish, Miller,
Rougvie; Strachan, Watson (McMaster), Jarvie;
Archibald, McGhee (Bell), Scanlon

Attendance: 44,000

The Dons saw their hopes of winning the League and Cup
double crash. They played well and dominated the match
for long spells. Jardine had the save of the match in the 71st
minute when he headed a vicious shot from Andy Watson
off the line — knocking himself out in the process. Rangers
hung on and flattened the Dons with a blistering finish in
which Johnstone grabbed the winning goal with 15
minutes left. A run and cross by Cooper made the opening
and Johnstone wheeled on the ball to send a glorious
left-foot drive inches inside Clark's right-hand post.

May 10th: Final   At Hampden Park
CELTIC   (0) 1   RANGERS   (0) 0
  McCluskey (107)
After Extra Time

CELTIC: Latchford; Sneddon, McGrain; Aitken,
Conroy, MacLeod; Provan, Doyle (Lennox),
McCluskey, Burns, McGarvey — Davidson

RANGERS: McCloy; Jardine, Dawson; T. Forsyth
(Miller), Jackson, Stevens; Cooper, Russell, Johnstone,
Smith, J. MacDonald (McLean)

Attendance: 70,303

This was an enthralling match with both sides playing open
football. The longer the game went the better it appeared
for Celtic. 17 minutes into extra-time Ally Dawson headed
out a corner from the right and Danny McGrain met the
clearance first time to send it back towards goal. McCloy
had the ball covered but George McCluskey stuck out his
left foot and deflected it towards the other corner. This was

cruel luck for Rangers. There was some disturbing crowd
scenes at the conclusion of the match as rival fans clashed.

CUP WINNERS CUP

August 21st: Preliminary Round First Leg
RANGERS   (1) 1   LILLIESTROM
  Smith (13)   (Norway)   (0) 0

RANGERS: McCloy; Jardine, Dawson; Smith,
Jackson, Watson; McLean (J. MacDonald), Russell,
Johnstone (Robertson), A. MacDonald, Cooper

LILLIESTROM: Amundsen; Hammer, Berg;
Kordahl, L. Hansen, Gronlund; Erlandsen, Lunstad,
Dokken, Holt, V. Hansen

Attendance: 25,000

Rangers ran against a yellow-shirted brick wall which they
found almost impregnable. After a splendid start and the
desired early goal — by Gordon Smith — Rangers lost
their passing accuracy. The long speculative high balls to
Johnstone were treated with comfort by the tall Norwegian
defenders. Lilliestrom gained in confidence within a short
spell of that score. It was only after John MacDonald came
on for McLean, after the hour, that Rangers regained
dominance.

September 5th: Preliminary Round Second Leg
LILLIESTROM   (0) 0   RANGERS   (1) 2
                         MacDonald (41),
                         Johnstone (89)

LILLIESTROM: Amundsen; Hammer, Berg;
Kordahl, L. Hansen, Gronlund; Erlandsen, Lunstad,
Dokken, Holt. V. Hansen (Nordberg)

RANGERS: McCloy; Miller, Dawson; Jardine,
Jackson, Watson; McLean (Cooper), Russell, Johnstone,
A. MacDonald, Smith

Attendance: 6,175

Rangers were in no danger from the moment Lilliestrom's
lone star Vidar Hansen had to leave the field in the 20th
minute. From the start Rangers stuck carefully to their
intention to retain as much possession as possible. Rangers
won 3-0 on aggregate.

September 19th: First Round First Leg
RANGERS   (0) 2   FORTUNA DUSSELDORF
  A. MacDonald (68),   (West Germany)   (0) 1
  McLean (75)   Wenzel (81)

RANGERS: McCloy; Miller, Dawson; Jardine,
Jackson, A. MacDonald; McLean, Russell (Watson),
Johnstone, Smith, Cooper

FORTUNA: Daniel; Weikl, Zewe; Kohnen, Baltes,
Wenzel; Wirtz, T. Allofs (Schmitz), Bommer, K. Allofs,
Seel

Attendance: 30,000

Rangers were justly rewarded with 2 goals inside 7 minutes midway through the 2nd half. But with only 9 minutes remaining Klaus Allofs went on another devastating run and laid on the perfect pass for Wenzel to shoot calmly past McCloy. In the first half Rangers had two legitimate penalty claims rejected — both for handling offences — and MacDonald missed a fine chance, hesitating before hitting his shot which was blocked.

October 3rd: First Round Second Leg
FORTUNA DUSSELDORF 0   RANGERS 0
FORTUNA: Daniel; Weikl, Zewe; Kohnen, Baltes, Wenzel; Wirtz (Dusend), Schmitz, Bommer, K. Allofs, Seel (T. Allofs)

RANGERS: McCloy; Miller (A. Forsyth), Dawson; Jardine, Jackson, A. MacDonald; McLean, Watson, Johnstone, Smith (Cooper), Parlane

Attendance: 40,000

Rangers survived a siege, McCloy having some truly magnificent saves, all the more remarkable because he could see clearly out of only one eye after being injured in the first half. Rangers won 2-1 on aggregate.

October 24th: Second Round First Leg
VALENCIA (Spain) (1) 1   RANGERS (1) 1
  Kempes (23)   McLean (45)
VALENCIA: Pereiro; Castellanos, Cervero, Botubot, Arias; Bonhof, Saura, Solsona, Siminez (Albio); Kempes, Felman

RANGERS: McCloy; Miller, Jardine, Johnstone, A. Forsyth; A. MacDonald, Watson, Smith; McLean (Parlane), Urquhart, Cooper (Dawson)

Attendance: 45,000

Rangers came up with another of their marvellously mature, disciplined European performances to give themselves a great chance of progressing to the Quarter-Finals. Scottish hopes looked in dire danger when Mario Kempes bent a free-kick into the net in 23 minutes but little Tommy McLean equalised just before half-time and the Scots were able to hold onto that lifeline. Peter McCloy was a hero by blocking Bonhof's spot-kick 10 minutes from the end.

November 7th: Second Round Second Leg
RANGERS (1) 1   VALENCIA (2) 3
  Johnstone (24)   Jardine o.g. (15),
                        Kempes 2 (42, 78)

RANGERS: McCloy; Jardine, A. Forsyth; Miller, Watson, A. MacDonald; McLean, Smith, Johnstone, Urquhart (Parlane), Cooper (Mackay)

VALENCIA: Manzanedo; Cervero, Botubot; Arias, Tendillo, Castellanos; Saura, Bonhof, Kempes, Subiats, Pablo

Attendance: 36,000

Rangers went passively out of Europe for another season. They would look back at 2 great chances missed in the early minutes but that should not disguise the fact that the Spaniards were masters on the night. Sandy Jardine inadvertently flicked a Bonhof free-kick past McCloy in 15 minutes, and although Derek Johnstone equalised in 24 minutes the Spanish punch-line was still to come. 3 minutes before the interval Kempes accepted his first chance of the night and was just as brilliant 12 minutes from the end when he scored the clinching 3rd goal. Valencia won 4-2 on aggregate.

APPEARANCES

	League	League Cup	Scottish Cup	Cup Winners Cup
McCloy	34	4	6	6
Jardine	35	4	6	6
Dawson	32	4	5	4+1S
Miller	13+5S	1+2S	3+1S	5
Stevens	31	2	6	-
Jackson	29	4	5	4
Watson	12+3S	4	1	5+1S
T. Forsyth	16	-	6	-
McLean	22+6S	1+1S	1+2S	6
Johnstone	31+2S	2	6	6
Redford	13	-	-	-
A. MacDonald	23+3S	4	1+2S	6
Russell	22+1S	2	5	3
Parlane	2+1S	1	-	0+2S
Smith	20+10S	3+1S	4+1S	6
Cooper	25+5S	4	5+1S	5+2S
J. MacDonald	21+6S	1	6	0+1S
A. Forsyth	8	-	-	2+1S
Urquhart	4	-	-	2
Mackay	0+2S	1+1S	-	0+1S
Dalziel	1	0+1S	-	-
Young	2	-	-	-
Robertson	-	2	-	0+1S
Richardson	-	-	-	-

GOALSCORERS

League: Johnstone 14, Russell 7, J. MacDonald 5,
Smith 4, Miller 3 (2 pens), Jardine 3 (3 pens),
Own Goals 3, Cooper 2, Urquhart 2, Jackson 2,
McLean 2, A. MacDonald 1, A. Forsyth 1,
Stevens 1

League Cup: Mackay 2, Dawson 1, Robertson 1, Smith 1,
Johnstone 1, Own Goal 1

Scottish Cup: J. MacDonald 4, Johnstone 3, Jardine 2
(2 pens), Jackson 1, Cooper 1, Russell 1

Cup Winners Cup: A. MacDonald 2, Johnstone 2,
McLean 2, Smith 1

A Premier League match played at Ibrox in November 1985. Rangers won this match
by 3 goals to nil. Here central defender Dave McKinnon (right) heads away a cross ball
during a Celtic attack.

Season 1980–81

Rangers finished 3rd in the League Championship — 12 points behind Celtic and 5 behind Aberdeen. They got off to a tremendous start, remaining undefeated for the first 15 matches which included a late win over Celtic at Parkhead and a record away victory at Kilmarnock. They also beat Celtic 3-0 at Ibrox in November but they dropped a total of 9 points to Partick Thistle, Airdrie and relegation-bound Hearts and were involved in a total of 12 drawn matches during the season. March proved to be a particularly bad month in which they won only one of their 4 fixtures. Alex MacDonald left the club at the start of the season and the always controversial Willie Johnston re-joined the club from Vancouver Whitecaps for a fee of £40,000. Goalkeeper Jim Stewart was signed from Middlesbrough in March for £115,000 and at the end of the season unknown Irish International defender John McClelland was signed from Mansfield Town for £90,000. Ian Redford made 35 League appearances and Colin McAdam finished as top scorer with 12 goals closely followed by John MacDonald on 11.

For the 2nd successive season Rangers lost out to Aberdeen in the Bell's League Cup. They won the first encounter at Ibrox by a solitary Colin McAdam goal but lost the return 1-3 — Gordon Strachan converting 2 penalties (the 2nd with only 90 seconds remaining for play) to take the Dons through to the Third Round.

Rangers had Ian Redford to thank for keeping them in the Scottish Cup at St Johnstone. They won the replay then beat Hibs in the Fifth Round and Morton in the Semi-Final at Celtic Park which saw Morton's Holmes and Thomson both ordered off. They faced Dundee United in the Final and in the most sensational finish ever to a Final the hero of Muirton Park, Ian Redford, shot a last-minute penalty-kick straight at McAlpine. The match went to extra-time but remained goalless. Substitutes Davie Cooper and John MacDonald took over from McLean and Willie Johnston in the replay, and Derek Johnstone replaced Colin McAdam. Cooper paved the way for victory with the opening goal, set up others for Russell and MacDonald before half-time and completely demoralised United with his brilliance. MacDonald scored another in the 2nd half to give Rangers the Cup for the 24th time.

Having failed to qualify for Europe, Rangers took part in the Anglo-Scottish Cup competition. Partick Thistle were beaten on aggregate in the First Round but the club were humiliated by English Third Division side Chesterfield in the next round. The fact that they bounced back to beat Celtic 3 days later undoubtedly took the pressure off the Manager.

Both Arsenal and Tottenham Hotspur were beaten in the Pre-season friendlies at Ibrox.

> League: Third
> League Cup: Second Round
> Scottish Cup: Winners
> Anglo-Scottish Cup: Second Round

SCOTTISH PREMIER LEAGUE

August 9th:
AIRDRIE (0) 1   RANGERS (1) 1
  Walker (83)   MacDonald (33)

AIRDRIE: McGarr; Erwin, March, Anderson, Rodger; McKeown, Walker, Gordon (Thompson); McGuire, Russell, Clark

RANGERS: McCloy; Jardine, T. Forsyth, Jackson, A. Forsyth; Russell, Bett, Redford; Cooper, McAdam, MacDonald

Attendance: 12,000

August 6th: Willie Johnston re-joined Rangers from Vancouver Whitecaps for a fee of £40,000.

August 8th: Alex MacDonald was transferred to Hearts for £30,000.

August 16th:
RANGERS (3) 4   PARTICK THISTLE (0) 0
  Cooper (24), McAdam (35),
  MacDonald (40), Jardine (88)

RANGERS: McCloy; Jardine, T. Forsyth; Jackson, Russell, Bett; Redford, Cooper (Johnston), McAdam, MacDonald, Johnston (McLean)

PARTICK THISTLE: Rough; Murray (Park), Welsh, Campbell, Whittaker; Gibson, O'Hara, Watson; Higgins, McLeod, McDonald (Lapsley)

Attendance: 25,898

August 23rd:
CELTIC (0) 1   RANGERS (0) 2
  Burns (47)   Bett (61), Miller (89)

CELTIC: Bonnar; Sneddon, Aitken, McAdam, McGrain; Sullivan, McLeod, Burns; Provan, McGarvey, McCluskey

RANGERS: McCloy; Jardine, T. Forsyth, Jackson, Miller; Russell (Johnstone), Bett, Redford; MacDonald (Cooper), McAdam, Johnston

Attendance: 58,000

Celtic had most of the pressure and Rangers were rather fortunate to be going into the last 15 minutes level. Rangers refused to settle for a draw and kept going at Celtic and Alex Miller scored a magnificent goal 30 seconds from time.

September 6th:
DUNDEE UNITED (0) 2   RANGERS (4) 4
  Dodds (69), Payne (76)   Cooper (5),
                    McAdam (24),
                    MacDonald (29),
                    Hegarty o.g. (44)

DUNDEE UNITED: McAlpine; Stark, Hegarty, Narey, Kopel; Kirkwood, Bannon (Milne), Addison (Phillip); Sturrock, Payne, Dodds

RANGERS: McCloy; Jardine, Jackson, T. Forsyth (Stevens), Miller; Bett, MacDonald, McLean; Cooper, McAdam, Redford

Attendance: 14,000. Narey was ordered off.

September 13th:
RANGERS (1) 1   ABERDEEN (1) 1
  McAdam (38)   Strachan (29 pen)

RANGERS: McCloy; Jardine, T. Forsyth (Johnstone), Jackson, Miller; McLean (MacDonald), Bett, Redford; Cooper, McAdam, Johnston

ABERDEEN: Leighton; Kennedy, McLeish, Miller, Rougvie; Watson, Strachan, McMaster; McGhee (Hamilton), Hewitt (Bell), Scanlon

Attendance: 32,000

September 20th:
KILMARNOCK (1) 1   RANGERS (3) 8
  Bourke (14)   McAdam (3),
                  MacDonald 3 (17, 58,
                  89),
                  Redord 2 (43 pen, 70),
                  Jardine (46),
                  Bett (63)

KILMARNOCK: Brown; McLean, Robertson; Clark, Armstrong, McDicken; Houston (Gibson), Mauchlen, Bourke, Cramond (Maxwell), Street

RANGERS: McCloy; Jardine, Miller; Johnstone, Jackson (T. Forsyth), Bett; McLean, MacDonald, McAdam (Johnston), Redford, Cooper

Attendance: 20,000

September 27th:
RANGERS (0) 2   ST MIRREN (0) 0
  Bett (49), Cooper (80)

RANGERS: McCloy; Jardine, Jackson, Johnstone (Johnston), Miller; McLean, Bett, Redford; MacDonald, McAdam (T. Forsyth), Cooper

ST MIRREN: Thomson; Young, McCormack, Copland, Beckett; Stark, Richardson, Weir; Bone (Abercrombie), Somner, McDougall

Attendance: 27,000

October 4th:
MORTON (2) 2   RANGERS (1) 2
  Busby (13),   Miller (38 pen),
  Ritchie (26 pen)   McAdam (88)

MORTON: Baines; Hayes, McLaughlin, Orr, Holmes; Rooney, Busby, Thomson; McNeill, Cochrane, Ritchie (Tolmie)

RANGERS: McCloy; Jardine, Johnstone, Jackson, Miller; McLean, Bett, Redford; Cooper (Stevens), McAdam, MacDonald (Johnston)

Attendance: 15,000

October 11th:
RANGERS (0) 3   HEARTS (0) 1
  McAdam 2 (50, 79),   MacDonald (87)
  Jeffries o.g. (77)

RANGERS: McCloy; Jardine, Johnstone, Jackson, Miller; Bett, Redford, Cooper (T. Forsyth); MacDonald, McAdam, Johnston (McLean)

HEARTS: Brough: Jeffries, Denny, McVie, Shields; Bowman (Conn), Kidd, MacDonald; Gibson (Robinson), O'Connor, Robertson

Attendance: 23,700

October 18th:
RANGERS 0   AIRDRIE 0

RANGERS: McCloy; Jardine, Johnstone (T. Forsyth), Jackson, Miller; McLean (Johnston), Bett, Redford; Cooper, McAdam, MacDonald

AIRDRIE: Martin; Cairney (Erwin), March, McCluskey, Rodgers; Walker, McKeown, Gordon; Thompson, Clark, McVeigh (McGuire)

Attendance: 22,000. Miller missed a penalty.

October 25th:
PARTICK THISTLE (0) 1 RANGERS (0) 1
  Park (63)   McAdam (50)

PARTICK THISTLE: Rough; Murray, Marr, Anderson, Whittaker; Park, Jardine, Watson; Lapsley, Clark (Torrance), O'Hara

RANGERS: McCloy; Jardine, Johnstone, Jackson, Miller; McLean (Russell), Bett, Redford; MacDonald, McAdam, Cooper (T. Forsyth)

Attendance: 14,500

League positions

	P	W	D	L	F	A	Pts
1 Aberdeen	11	8	3	0	25	7	19
2 Celtic	11	8	2	1	26	10	18
3 RANGERS	11	6	5	0	28	10	17
4 Airdrie	11	4	5	2	12	10	13
5 Partick Thistle	11	5	2	4	11	15	12

November 1st:
RANGERS (2) 3   CELTIC (0) 0
  McAdam 2 (21, 75),
  MacDonald (36)

RANGERS: McCloy; Jardine, Johnstone, Jackson, Dawson; McLean, Bett, Redford; McAdam, MacDonald, Johnston

CELTIC: Bonner; Sneddon, MacDonald, McAdam, McGrain; Sullivan, Aitken, Burns; Provan, McGarvey (McCluskey), Nicholas (Doyle)

Attendance: 33,000

This victory lifted Rangers' Chesterfield blues. The return of Ally Dawson seemed to stabilise the defence and Willie Johnston turned back the clock to produce some vintage stuff on the left flank.

November 6th: Billy Urquhart was sold to Wigan Athletic for £20,000.

November 8th:
ST MIRREN 0   RANGERS 0

ST MIRREN: Thomson; Young, McCormack, Copland, Abercrombie; Stark, Richardson, Weir; McDougall, Somner, Bone

RANGERS: McCloy; Jardine, Johnstone, Jackson, Dawson; McLean (Russell), Bett, Redford; Johnston, McAdam (T. Forsyth), MacDonald

Attendance: 17,362

November 15th:
RANGERS (1) 2   KILMARNOCK (0) 0
  W. Johnston (16), Jardine (56)

RANGERS: McCloy; Jardine, T. Forsyth, Jackson, Dawson; McLean, Bett, Redford; W. Johnston (Mackay), MacDonald (Russell), Johnstone

KILMARNOCK: Brown; McLean, Clarke, McDicken, Robertson; Mauchlen, Maxwell, Cramond (Clark); Houston, McBride, Bourke

Attendance: 16,000

November 22nd:
HEARTS 0   RANGERS 0

HEARTS: Brough; Hamilton (More), Liddell, McVie, Shields; Robinson, MacDonald, Masterton; O'Connor, Conn, Gibson

RANGERS: McCloy; Jardine, Johnstone, Jackson, Dawson; Bett, MacDonald, Redford; McLean (Russell), McAdam, Johnston

Attendance: 16,315

November 29th:
RANGERS (0) 0   MORTON (0) 1
                        Tolmie (55)

RANGERS: McCloy; Jardine, T. Forsyth (Johnston), Jackson, Dawson; Russell, Johnstone, Redford (McLean); Cooper, McAdam, MacDonald

MORTON: Baines; Hayes, Orr, McLaughlin, Holmes; Rooney, Cochrane, Busby; Thomson, McNeill, Tolmie

Attendance: 16,000

December 13th:
ABERDEEN (0) 2   RANGERS (0) 0
  McGhee (67), McCall (80)

ABERDEEN: Leighton; Kennedy, McLeish, Miller, Considine; Strachan, Watson, Angus; McCall, McGhee, Scanlon

RANGERS: McCloy; Miller, Johnstone, Jackson, Dawson; McLean (Mackay), Russell, Redford (Cooper); McAdam, MacDonald, Johnston

Attendance: 20,000

December 20th:
KILMARNOCK (1) 1   RANGERS (0) 1
  Bourke (23)   Russell (52)

KILMARNOCK: Wilson; McClurg, McLean, Clarke, Armstrong; Cockburn, Gibson (Maxwell), G. Wilson; Houston, Bourke (McBride), Hughes

RANGERS: McCloy; Jardine, Johnstone (Cooper), Jackson, Dawson; Russell, McLean, Bett; MacDonald, McAdam, Johnstone (Mackay)

Attendance: 9,500

League positions

	P	W	D	L	F	A	Pts
1 Aberdeen	19	13	5	1	41	13	31
2 Celtic	20	13	2	5	41	25	28
3 RANGERS	18	8	8	2	34	14	24
4 Dundee United	19	7	7	5	27	25	21
5 St Mirren	19	7	5	7	29	25	19

January 1st:
RANGERS (1) 1   PARTICK THISTLE (0) 1
  McAdam (33)   O'Hara (48)

RANGERS: McCloy, Jardine, Dawson; Miller, D. Johnstone, Bett, McLean (McDonald), Russell, McAdam, Redford, Cooper (Mackay)

PARTICK THISTLE: Rough; Welsh, Whittaker; Campbell, Anderson, Watson (Lapsley); Park, Jardine, Sweeney, Doyle, O'Hara

Attendance: 16,000

January 3rd:
AIRDRIE (1) 1   RANGERS (0) 1
  Miller o.g. (25)   Dawson (69)

AIRDRIE: Martin; Cairney, McCluskey, March, Rodger; Walker, McCulloch, Gordon; Russell (Thompson), McGuire (McKeown), Clark

RANGERS: McCloy; Miller, Jardine, T. Forsyth, Dawson; Russell (Mackay), Bett, Redford (McLean); Cooper, McAdam, MacDonald

Attendance: 11,800

January 10th:
MORTON (0) 0   RANGERS (1) 2
                     MacDonald (42),
                     Redford (55)

MORTON: Baines; Hayes, McLaughlin, Orr, Holmes; Rooney, Marr, Busby; Houston (Cochrane), McNeill (Ritchie), Tolmie

RANGERS: McCloy; Miller, Jardine, Stevens, Dawson; Russell, Bett, Redford; Cooper, McAdam, MacDonald

Attendance: 13,000

January 26th: Rangers made an approach for Steve Nicol of Ayr United.

January 31st:
RANGERS (0) 1   ABERDEEN (0) 0
  Johnstone (63)

RANGERS: McCloy; Jardine, Stevens, Jackson, Dawson; Russell, Bett, Redford; Johnston, Johnstone, MacDonald (Cooper)

ABERDEEN: Leighton; Hamilton, McLeish, Cooper (Considine), Rougvie; Watson (Harrow), Jarvie, Angus; McCall, McGhee, Scanlon

Attendance: 32,400

February 7th:
DUNDEE UNITED (1) 2   RANGERS (1) 1
  Kirkwood (18), Dodds (57)   MacDonald (38)

DUNDEE UNITED: McAlpine; Stark, Hegarty, Narey, Kopel; Kirkwood, Addison, Bannon; Payne, Sturrock, Dodds

RANGERS: McCloy; Jardine, Stevens, Jackson, Dawson; McLean (Miller), Russell (Cooper), Bett; Johnston, Redford, MacDonald

Attendance: 14,328. Stevens was ordered off.

February 21st:
CELTIC (0) 3   RANGERS (1) 1
  Nicholas 2 (57, 73),   Johnstone (11)
  Aitken (87)

CELTIC: Bonnar; McGrain, Aitken, McAdam, Reid; Sullivan, Burns, Conroy; Provan, McGarvey, Nicholas

RANGERS: McCloy; Miller (MacDonald), Jardine, Jackson, Dawson; Cooper (Russell), Bett, Redford; Johnstone, McAdam, Johnston

Attendance: 52,800

After giving Rangers a goal start Celtic turned on one of their best displays of the season. A 2nd-half 1-2 from Nicholas put the result right. Davie Provan was outstanding, McGarvey a constant menace and Nicholas a clinical assassin.

February 28th:
RANGERS   (0) 2   AIRDRIE   (0) 0
  MacDonald (60), Redford (80)

RANGERS: McCloy; Miller, Jackson, Jardine,
Dawson; Russell, Bett, Redford; Johnstone (Cooper),
McAdam, MacDonald

AIRDRIE: Gardiner; Cairney, March, McCluskey,
Rodger; Walker, Gordon (Thompson), McKeown;
Flood, Clark, Anderson

Attendance: 12,200

League positions

	P	W	D	L	F	A	Pts
1 Celtic	26	19	2	5	57	28	40
2 Aberdeen	26	14	8	4	46	19	36
3 RANGERS	25	11	10	4	43	21	32
4 Dundee United	26	12	8	6	45	29	32
5 St Mirren	25	10	7	8	37	31	27

March 14th:
HEARTS   (1) 2   RANGERS   (1) 1
  Redford o.g. (4),   Redford (43)
  F. Liddell (70)

HEARTS: Brough; Hamilton, More, F. Liddell,
Shields; Hamill, MacDonald, Kidd; Mackay, Gibson,
G. Liddell

RANGERS: McCloy; Jardine (Mackay), Johnstone
(Clark), Jackson, Dawson; Russell, Bett, Redford;
Johnston, McAdam, MacDonald

Attendance: 11,500

**March 15th: Goalkeeper Jim Stewart was signed
from Middlesbrough for £115,000.**

March 18th:
RANGERS   (1) 1   DUNDEE UNITED   (2) 4
  McAdam (39)   Kirkwood (19),
                                  Bannon 2 (29, 61),
                                  Sturrock (58)

RANGERS: Stewart; Miller (Cooper), Dawson;
Stevens, Jackson, Bett; Johnston, Russell, McAdam,
Redford, MacDonald

DUNDEE UNITED: McAlpine; Holt, Stark; Phillip,
Hegarty, Narey; Bannon, Milne, Kirkwood, Sturrock,
Dodds

Attendance: 11,000

March 21st:
RANGERS   (1) 2   KILMARNOCK   (0) 0
  Redford (34), Russell (87)

RANGERS: Stewart; Miller, Dawson; T. Forsyth,
Jackson, Bett; Johnston (McLean), Russell, McAdam,
Redford, Cooper

KILMARNOCK: McCulloch; Robin, Cockburn;
Clark (Bryce), Armstrong, McDicken; McBride,
McLean, Bourke, Mauchlen, Docherty (Hughes)

Attendance: 8,500

March 28th:
ST MIRREN   (1) 2   RANGERS   (0) 1
  Richardson 2 (24, 80)   Dawson (49)

ST MIRREN: Thomson; McCormack, Copland,
Fulton, McAveety; Stark, Abercrombie, Weir (Logan);
McDougall, Richardson, Bone

RANGERS: Stewart; Miller, Jackson, T. Forsyth,
Dawson; Bett, Russell, McLean (Jardine); Redford,
Johnston (Cooper), McAdam

Attendance: 9,988

April 1st:
RANGERS   (2) 4   MORTON   (0) 0
  D. Johnstone 2 (16, 87),
  Redford (33), MacDonald (75)

RANGERS: Stewart; Miller, Dawson; T. Forsyth,
Jackson, Bett; McLean, Russell, D. Johnstone, Redford,
MacDonald

MORTON: Baines; Hayes, Holmes; Rooney,
McLaughlin, Orr; McNeill, Busby, Thomson, Tolmie,
Ritchie

Attendance: 4,800

April 4th:
RANGERS   (1) 2   DUNDEE UNITED   (1) 1
  Russell (25),   Milne (16)
  Redford (63 pen)

RANGERS: Stewart; Miller, Jardine, T. Forsyth,
Dawson; Bett, Russell, McLean; Johnstone, Redford,
MacDonald (Johnston)

DUNDEE UNITED: McAlpine; Holt, Hegarty,
Narey, Stark; Phillip, Gibson (Kopel), Bannon; Milne,
Kirkwood, Sturrock

Attendance: 12,000

April 15th:
RANGERS   (1) 1   ST MIRREN   (0) 0
  Russell (44)

RANGERS: Stewart; Miller, Dawson; Johnstone,
Jackson, Bett; McLean, Russell, McAdam, Redford,
Johnston

ST MIRREN: Thomson; Young, McAveety; Copland,
Fulton, Abercrombie; Bone (Speirs), Stark, Somner,
Richardson, Logan

Attendance: 10,000

April 18th:
RANGERS   (0) 0   CELTIC   (0) 1
                                Nicholas (55)

RANGERS: Stewart; Miller, Jackson, Johnstone, Dawson; Bett (MacDonald), Russell, McLean; Johnston (Jardine), McAdam, Redford

CELTIC: Bonner; McGrain, MacDonald, McAdam, Aitken; Conroy, Burns, MacLeod; Provan, McGarvey, Nicholas

Attendance: 34,000

Celtic were in full control of a quiet Old Firm game. It did not require anything special to beat a Rangers side who created only 2 genuine chances throughout the 90 minutes. MacDonald's command in the air nullified the dangerous flighted passes of McLean and Aitken mastered the ground attacks.

April 22nd:
ABERDEEN   0   RANGERS   0

ABERDEEN: Leighton; Kennedy, Rougvie; Bell, McLeish, Miller; Simpson, Scanlon, McGhee, Angus, Hewitt

RANGERS: Stewart; Jardine, Miller; Stevens, T. Forsyth, Bett; McLean, Russell, Johnstone, Redford, McAdam

Attendance: 13,000

April 25th:
PARTICK THISTLE   (1) 1   RANGERS   (0) 1
   Whittaker (68)   Russell (43)

PARTICK THISTLE: Rough; Welsh, Campbell, Anderson, Whittaker; Jardine, Doyle, O'Hara; Park (Lapsley), Higgins, Clark (Watson)

RANGERS: Stewart; Jardine, T. Forsyth, Stevens, Miller; McLean, Russell, Bett; Redford, Johnstone, McAdam

Attendance: 7,077

May 2nd:
RANGERS   (3) 4   HEARTS   (0) 0
   Bett (20), Russell (34),
   Redford (35), Johnston (61)

RANGERS: Stewart; T. Forsyth, Stevens; Jardine, Russell, McLean; Bett, Cooper, McAdam, Redford, Johnston

HEARTS: Brough; Denny, More, F. Liddell, Shields; Mackay (Jeffries), Hamill, Kidd; O'Brien (Gibson), Robertson, G. Liddell

Attendance: 7,000

Scottish Premier League

	P	W	D	L	F	A	Pts
1 Celtic	36	26	4	6	84	37	56
2 Aberdeen	36	19	11	6	61	26	49
3 RANGERS	36	16	12	8	60	32	44
4 St Mirren	36	18	8	10	56	47	44
5 Dundee United	36	17	9	10	66	42	43
6 Partick Thistle	36	10	10	16	32	48	30
7 Airdrie	36	10	9	17	36	55	29
8 Morton	36	10	8	18	36	58	28
9 Kilmarnock	36	5	9	22	23	65	19
10 Hearts	36	6	6	24	27	71	18

May 16th: Rangers said that Miller and Mackay were free to leave Ibrox.

May 19th: John McClelland was signed from Mansfield Town for £90,000.

May 28th: Derek Johnstone asked for a transfer.

June 27th: Willie Waddell left his £15,000 per year consultant's job after his contract had expired.

BELL'S LEAGUE CUP

August 27th: First Round First Leg
FORFAR ATHLETIC   (0) 0   RANGERS   (1) 2
                           McAdam 2 (29, 60)

FORFAR: Kennedy; Bennett, McPhee; Brown, Clark, Gillies; Gallacher, Farningham, Watt, Leitch, Robb

RANGERS: McCloy; Jardine, Miller; T. Forsyth, Jackson, Bett; Cooper, MacDonald (D. Johnstone), McAdam, Redford, W. Johnston (McLean)

Attendance: 4,200

August 30th: First Round Second Leg
RANGERS   (2) 3   FORFAR
                           ATHLETIC   (1) 1
   Miller (32 pen), Johnston (35),   Robb (27)
   McAdam (55 pen)

RANGERS: McCloy; Jardine, Miller; T. Forsyth (Russell), Jackson, Bett; Cooper, D. Johnstone, McAdam, Redford, Johnston (McLean)

FORFAR: Kennedy; Bennett, McPhee; Brown, Clark Gillies; Gallacher, Farningham, Watt, Leitch (Wildridge), Robb (Lawrie)

Attendance: 15,500. Jardine missed a twice-taken penalty. Rangers won 5-1 on aggregate.

September 3rd: Second Round First Leg
RANGERS   (1) 1   ABERDEEN   (0) 0
   McAdam (44 secs)

RANGERS: McCloy; Jardine, Miller; T. Forsyth, Jackson, Bett, McLean (Stevens), J. Macdonald (Johnston), McAdam, Redford, Cooper

ABERDEEN: Leighton; Kennedy, Rougvie; Watson, McLeish, Miller; Strachan, McMaster, McGhee, Jarvie (Hewitt), Scanlon

Attendance: 33,000. Johnston was ordered off. McMaster had to be given the kiss of life during the match.

September 24th: Second Round Second Leg

ABERDEEN (2) 3	RANGERS (0) 1
McMaster (4),	McAdam (48)
Strachan 2 (30 pen, 89 pen)	

ABERDEEN: Leighton; Kennedy, Rougvie; Watson, McLeish, Miller; Strachan, McMaster, McGhee, Bell, Scanlon

RANGERS: McCloy; Jardine, Miller; T. Forsyth, Jackson, Bett; Cooper (McLean), Johnstone, McAdam, Redford, Johnston (J. MacDonald)

Attendance: 23,000. Aberdeen won 3-2 on aggregate.

SCOTTISH CUP

January 24th: Third Round

AIRDRIE (0) 0	RANGERS (2) 5
	Stevens (6),
	Redford (27),
	Bett (65),
	Johnstone 2 (67, 89)

AIRDRIE: Martin; Cairney, March, McCluskey (McKeown), Rodger (Anderson); McCulloch, Walker, Gordon; Clark, McGuire, Russell

RANGERS: McCloy; Jardine, Jackson, Stevens, Dawson; Russell (Cooper), Bett, Redford; Johnston, D. Johnstone, MacDonald

Attendance: 16,054

February 14th: Fourth Round

ST JOHNSTONE (1) 3	RANGERS (2) 3
Docherty (41),	McAdam (17),
Brogan 2 (76, 81)	Redford 2 (35, 89)

ST JOHNSTONE: Tulloch; Mackay, Rutherford, Caldwell, McNeill; Pelosi, McCoist, Fleming; Morton, Docherty, Brogan

RANGERS: McCloy; Jardine, T. Forsyth, Jackson, Dawson; Russell (Miller), Bett, Redford; Johnston, McAdam, MacDonald (Cooper)

Attendance: 17,500

February 18th: Fourth Round Replay

RANGERS (1) 3	ST JOHNSTONE (0) 1
McAdam 2 (21, 57),	McCoist (66)
Stevens (63)	

RANGERS: McCloy; Jardine, Dawson; Stevens, Jackson, Bett; Johnstone, Miller, McAdam, Redford, Johnston

ST JOHNSTONE: Tulloch; Mackay, McNeill; Fleming, Rutherford (Kilgour), Caldwell; Pelosi, McCoist, Docherty, Morton, Brogan

Attendance: 24,000

March 7th: Fifth Round

RANGERS (2) 3	HIBERNIAN (1) 1
Russell (25), McAdam (30),	McNamara (32)
MacDonald (52)	

RANGERS: McCloy; Miller, Jackson, Jardine, Dawson; Russell, Bett, Redford; MacDonald, McAdam, Johnston (Cooper)

HIBERNIAN: McArthur; Brown, McLaren, Paterson, Sneddon; Hamill (James Brown), McNamara, Duncan; Rae, Connolly, Jamieson (Rodier)

Attendance: 25,690

April 11th: Semi-Final	At Celtic Park
RANGERS (1) 2	MORTON (0) 1
Jackson (40),	Ritchie (72 pen)
Russell (68)	

RANGERS: Stewart; Miller, Jackson, T. Forsyth, Dawson; Bett (McAdam), McLean, Russell; D. Johnstone, Redford, Johnston

MORTON: Baines; Hayes, McLaughlin, Orr (Ritchie), Holmes; Rooney, Busby, McNeil; Thomson, Tolmie, Cochrane

Attendance: 27,050. Holmes and Thomson were ordered off.

Rangers could be indicted for a lacklustre display which ought to have been punished. In the first 45 minutes the Greenock side looked more than capable of reaching the Final. Against the run of play Rangers took the lead in 40 minutes when Jackson scored with a speculative header which seemed to mesmerise Baines before dipping over his head into the net. After a series of second-half bookings Holmes committed a scything tackle on Dawson and was sent off. Substitute Ritchie had only been on the field 2 minutes when Russell put Rangers 2 up. Morton pulled one back when Ritchie stroked in a penalty after Bett had pushed Cochrane. Before the end McAdam was chopped down from behind by Thomson when running through to a superb pass from Russell. The Morton man, like Holmes before him, was shown the red card.

May 9th: Final	At Hampden Park
RANGERS 0	DUNDEE UNITED 0
	After Extra Time

RANGERS: Stewart; Jardine, Dawson; Stevens, T. Forsyth, Bett; McLean, Russell, McAdam (Cooper), Redford, W. Johnston (MacDonald)

DUNDEE UNITED: McAlpine; Holt, Kopel; Phillip (Stark), Hegarty, Narey; Bannon, Milne (Pettigrew), Kirkwood, Sturrock, Dodds

Attendance: 53,000. Redford missed a last-minute penalty.

The final suddenly came alive as the referee Mr Foote was counting off the dying seconds of normal time. Rangers made one final surge on the United goal. Russell weaved his way into the penalty area. Iain Phillip made a lunging tackle and the Rangers man went sprawling. Mr Foote immediately pointed to the spot. Ian Redford was given the task of taking the kick and the chance of writing himself into the football history books but his shot was weak and straight. McAlpine dived and as the ball cannoned off his legs the referee immediately signalled the end of the 90 minutes and the match moved into extra-time.

May 12th: Final Replay   At Hampden Park
RANGERS   (3) 4   DUNDEE UNITED   (1) 1
   Cooper (10),   Dodds (23)
   Russell (20),
   MacDonald 2 (29, 77)

RANGERS: Stewart; Jardine, Dawson; Stevens, T. Forsyth, Bett; Cooper, Russell, Johnstone, Redford, MacDonald — McLean, McAdam

DUNDEE UNITED: McAlpine; Holt, Kopel; Phillip (Stark), Hegarty, Narey; Bannon, Milne, Kirkwood, Sturrock, Dodds — Pettigrew

Attendance: 43,099   *Referee*: I. M. Foote (Glasgow)

Rangers ended two seasons of bitter disappointment at Hampden when they brilliantly swept aside the challenge of Dundee United to win the Scottish Cup for the 24th time. John Greig made 3 changes from the side which played in the first match, and at the end of the day it was the substitutes from the first match, Cooper and MacDonald, who shattered United's hopes of adding the Scottish Cup to the League Cup. Cooper had one of his best-ever games in a Rangers jersey. He paved the way for victory with the opening goal, set up others for Russell and MacDonald before half-time and completely demoralised United with his brilliance.

ANGLO-SCOTTISH CUP

July 30th: First Round First Leg
RANGERS   (2) 3   PARTICK THISTLE   (0) 1
   Jardine (29 pen),   I. Jardine (67)
   J. MacDonald 2 (43, 70)

RANGERS: McCloy; Jardine, A. Forsyth; T. Forsyth, Johnstone, Stevens; Cooper, Russell, McAdam, Redford, J. MacDonald

PARTICK THISTLE: Rough; McKinnon, Lapsley; Marr, Campbell, Whittaker; Doyle, Park, Higgins, Jardine, O'Hara

Attendance: 8,000

August 6th: First Round Second Leg
PARTICK THISTLE   (0) 3   RANGERS   (2) 2
   Gibson (60), Higgins (63),   McAdam (10),
   O'Hara (83)   Russell (44)

PARTICK THISTLE: Rough; Doyle, Lapsley; Gibson, Smith, Whittaker; Park, Higgins, MacLeod, Jardine (O'Hara), McDonald

RANGERS: McCloy; Jardine, A. Forsyth; Johnstone, Jackson, Stevens; McLean, Russell, McAdam (A. MacDonald), Redford, J. MacDonald

Attendance: 10,000. Jackson was ordered off. Rangers won 5-4 on aggregate.

October 13th: Second Round First Leg
RANGERS   (1) 1   CHESTERFIELD   (1) 1
   Dalziel (35)   Walker (5)

RANGERS: McCloy; Jardine, Miller (MacDonald); Johnstone, T. Forysth, Bett; McLean, Dalziel, McAdam, Redford, Johnston

CHESTERFIELD: Turner; Tartt, Pollard; Wilson, Green, Ridley; Birch, Moss, Bonnyman, Salmons, Walker

Attendance: 12,000

October 28th: Second Round Second Leg
CHESTERFIELD   (2) 3   RANGERS   (0) 0
   Bonnyman 2 (15, 18),
   Moss (64)

CHESTERFIELD: Turner; Tartt, Pollard; Wilson, Green, Ridley; Birch, Moss, Bonnyman, Salmons, Walker

RANGERS: McCloy; Jardine, Dawson; T. Forsyth, Jackson (MacDonald), Bett; Mackay, Russell, McAdam, Redford, Johnstone

Attendance: 13,914. McAdam missed a penalty. Chesterfield won 4-1 on aggregate.

Chris Woods yells out instructions to his defence in a 1986–87 league match.

APPEARANCES

	League	League Cup	Scottish Cup	Anglo-Scottish
McCloy	26	4	4	4
Jardine	29+3S	4	6	4
T. Forsyth	15+6S	4	4	3
Jackson	29	4	5	2
A. Forsyth	1	-	-	2
Russell	23+5S	0+1S	6	3
Bett	34	4	7	2
Redford	35	4	7	4
Cooper	17+8S	4	1+4S	1
McAdam	31	4	4+1S	4
J. MacDonald	26+4S	2+1S	4+1S	2+2S
W. Johnston	20+6S	3+1S	6	1
Miller	24+1S	4	3+1S	1
McLean	23+5S	1+1S	2	2
D. Johnstone	24+3S	2+1S	4	4
Dawson	22	-	7	1
Stevens	7+2S	0+1S	4	2
Stewart	10	-	3	-
Mackay	0+6S	-	-	1
Clark	0+1S	-	-	-
Davies	-	-	-	-

APPEARANCES

	League	League Cup	Scottish Cup	Anglo-Scottish
D. Robertson	-	-	-	-
A. MacDonald	-	-	-	0+1S
Dalziel	-	-	-	1

GOALSCORERS

League: McAdam 12, J. MacDonald 11, Redford 9 (2 pens), Russell 6, Bett 4, D. Johnstone 4, Cooper 3, Jardine 3, Dawson 2, W. Johnston 2, Miller 2 (1 pen), Own Goals 2

League Cup: McAdam 5 (1 pen), Johnston 1, Miller 1 (pen)

Scottish Cup: McAdam 4, MacDonald 3, Redford 3, Russell 3, Stevens 2, D. Johnstone 2, Bett 1, Jackson 1, Cooper 1

Anglo Scottish Cup: J. MacDonald 2, McAdam 1, Russell 1, Dalziel 1, Jardine 1 (pen)

The Rangers line-up at the start of season 1983–84. Back row: McKinnin, Dawson, McCoist, Prytz. Middle row: Redford, Stevens, Paterson, McCloy, McPherson, Clark, Cooper. Front row: Lyall, J. MacDonald, McClelland, Davies, Russell.

Season 1981–82

For the second successive season Rangers finished 3rd in the Championship behind Celtic and Aberdeen. The gap between 1st and 3rd was again 12 points. The match against Celtic at Parkhead in November was one of the most exciting in the long series between the clubs and ended 3-3. Rangers did manage to beat Celtic by a Jim Bett penalty goal at Ibrox in January but they dropped a total of 5 points to their great rivals, 7 to Aberdeen and 4 to Dundee United. In March defender Gregor Stevens received a 6-month ban for his continued misconduct. Sadly, Tom Forsyth had to quit the game on medical advice. At the end of the season Sandy Jardine, Colin Jackson and Tommy McLean were all given free transfers, McLean becoming John Greig's assistant. Swedish International midfielder Robert Prytz was signed from Malmo for £100,000 in May. Sandy Jardine appeared in all 36 League matches, and both he and Jackson were awarded Testimonial Matches by the club. John MacDonald was top scorer with 14 followed by Jim Bett on 11 and Derek Johnstone on 9.

Back into Europe, Rangers faced Czechoslovakia Cup Winners Dukla Prague in the First Round of the competition for National Cup Winners. They lost an early goal in Prague and never recovered — eventually losing 0-3 — and they also had McLean sent off. An error by Stewart in the return gave the Czechs another early goal and the tie was lost although Rangers did manage to restore a little of their reputation with a 2-1 win.

Rangers reached the Scottish Cup Final for the 7th successive season, and for a long time it looked as if they would beat Aberdeen but the match went to extra-time and the Dons scored 3 goals in that extra 30-minute period to take the Cup, for only the 3rd time in their history, by 4 goals to 1.

Rangers won the League Cup. They dropped only one point in their Section. They beat Brechin City 5-0 on aggregate in the Quarter-Final and St Mirren 4-3 on aggregate in the Semi-Final — a late John MacDonald goal winning the tie at Ibrox. They met Dundee United in the Final. United had the best of the first half but missed a number of chances, and although they did go ahead through Ralph Milne in the 48th minute, a Davie Cooper free-kick special levelled the scores and substitute Ian Redford lobbed in a great winner in the 88th minute to shatter United's dream of winning the trophy 3 times in succession.

Eleven friendly matches were played during the Season, including a pre-season 4-match Danish tour, with mixed results. One of them was against European Cup holders Liverpool who were invited to the Stadium in December for a match to commemorate the opening of the 'new' Ibrox. Liverpool won 2-0.

League: Third
League Cup: Winners
Scottish Cup: Runners-up
Cup Winners Cup: First Round

SCOTTISH PREMIER LEAGUE

August 21st: Rangers offered St Johnstone £300,000 for Ally McCoist.

August 25th: McCoist was transferred to Sunderland for £400,000.

August 29th:
PARTICK THISTLE   (0) 0   RANGERS   (0) 1
                          McLean (77)
PARTICK THISTLE: Rough; McKinnon, Kay, Dunlop, Whittaker; Park, Doyle, McDonald, Lapsley; O'Hara (Johnston), Higgins (Clark)

RANGERS: McCloy; Jardine (Redford), Forsyth, Stevens, Miller; Russell, McLean, Bett; Cooper, McAdam (MacDonald), Johnstone

Attendance: 15,352

September 5th:
RANGERS   (1) 2   HIBERNIAN   (1) 2
Bett (10), Cooper (78)   McLeod (13),
                         Rae (85)
RANGERS: McCloy; Jardine, Stevens, Forsyth, Dawson (Johnston); Russell, McLean, Bett; MacDonald, Redford (Miller), Cooper

HIBERNIAN: McArthur; Sneddon, Paterson, McNamara, McLaren; Duncan, Callachan, Flavell; McLeod (Turnbull), Rae, Murray

Attendance: 22,000

September 12th:
ST MIRREN   (0) 1   RANGERS   (1) 1
McDougall (55)   MacDonald (25)
ST MIRREN: Thomson; Beckett, McCormack, Copland, Abercrombie; Fitzpatrick, Stark, McAvennie (Fulton); McDougall, Bone, Scanlon

RANGERS: McCloy; Jardine, Forsyth, Jackson, McClelland; Russell, Bett, Redford (McAdam); Cooper, Johnstone, MacDonald

Attendance: 15,652

September 19th:
RANGERS   (0) 0   CELTIC   (1) 2
                  McAdam (11),
                  MacLeod (86)
RANGERS: McCloy; Jardine (McAdam), Forsyth, Stevens, Dawson; Miller, Bett, Redford; Cooper, Johnstone, Johnston (MacDonald)

CELTIC: Bonner; McGrain, Aitken, McAdam, Reid; Sullivan, MacLeod, Burns; Provan, McGarvey, McCluskey

Attendance: 40,900

Rangers never threatened any danger on the day on which they opened their new £4 million stand. Only captain Ally Dawson and Davie Cooper earned pass marks while Celtic did not have a failure on their side. They had outstanding performances from Provan, MacLeod, McGarvey, McAdam and Mark Reid.

October 3rd:
RANGERS   (2) 4   AIRDRIE   (1) 1
Bett 2 (38, 45),   Clark (3 pen)
Johnstone (52),
Jardine (66)
RANGERS: Stewart; Jardine, Stevens, Forsyth, Dawson; Russell, Bett, Cooper (Redford); Johnstone, MacDonald, Johnston (Mackay)

AIRDRIE: Martin; Erwin, March, McCluskey, Rodger; Walker, Anderson, Clark; Gordon, Thompson (McKeown), Campbell (McGuire)

Attendance: 12,500

October 10th:
RANGERS   0   ABERDEEN   0
RANGERS: Stewart; Jardine, Stevens, Forsyth, Dawson; Russell, MacDonald, Bett; Cooper, McAdam, Johnstone (Redford)

ABERDEEN: Leighton; Kennedy, Miller, Rougvie, Cooper; Strachan, Watson, Simpson (McMaster); McGhee, Hewitt (Harrow), Weir

Attendance: 28,000

October 17th:
DUNDEE   (1) 2   RANGERS   (1) 3
Ferguson (26),   Russell (27),
Cameron (86)   MacDonald 2 (63, 65)
DUNDEE: Geddes; Cameron, McKimmie; Fraser, Smith, MacDonald; Bell, Mackie, Kidd, McGeachie (Stephen), Ferguson

RANGERS: Stewart; Jardine, Dawson; Stevens, Forsyth, Bett; Cooper, Russell, McAdam, MacDonald, Johnston (Redford)

Attendance: 12,000

October 24th:
RANGERS   (0) 1   MORTON   (1) 1
Russell (80)   Rooney (45)
RANGERS: Stewart; Jardine, Forsyth, Jackson, Dawson; Russell, MacDonald, Bett; Cooper, McAdam, Johnston (Redford)

MORTON: Baines; Hayes, McLaughlin, Orr, Holmes; Rooney, Busby, Docherty; McNeill, Hutchinson (Cochrane), Ritchie (Slavin)

Attendance: 21,000

October 31st:
RANGERS (0) 0   PARTICK THISTLE (1) 2
                 Clark (27),
                 Johnston (58)
RANGERS: Stewart; Jardine, Jackson (Redford), Forsyth, Dawson; Russell, MacDonald, Bett; Cooper, McAdam, Johnston (Johnstone)

PARTICK THISTLE: Rough; Murray, Dunlop, Anderson, Whittaker; Park, McDonald, Doyle; Watson, Johnston (Lapsley), Clark (Higgins)

Attendance: 17,000

League positions

	P	W	D	L	F	A	Pts
1 Celtic	10	8	1	1	23	9	17
2 Aberdeen	10	6	2	2	16	10	14
3 St Mirren	10	5	2	3	15	12	12
4 Hibernian	10	3	4	3	11	7	10
5 RANGERS	9	3	4	2	12	11	10

November 7th:
HIBERNIAN (1) 1   RANGERS (1) 2
  Rae (10)   Bett 2 (16, 71 pen)
HIBERNIAN: McArthur; Sneddon, Paterson, Brazil, Schaedler; Callachan, Flavell, Duncan; Rae, Murray, McLeod

RANGERS: McCloy; Jardine, Forsyth, Jackson, Black; Russell, Bett, Redford; MacDonald, Johnstone, Cooper

Attendance: 14,685

November 11th:
DUNDEE UNITED (1) 2   RANGERS (0) 0
  Jackson o.g. (33), Bannon (65)
DUNDEE UNITED: McAlpine; Holt, Murray; Gough, Hegarty, Narey; Bannon, Milne, Kirkwood, Sturrock, Dodds

RANGERS: McCloy; Jardine (McAdam), Black; Forsyth, Jackson, Bett; Cooper, Russell, Johnstone, Redford (Miller), MacDonald

Attendance: 14,000. Black was ordered off.

November 14th:
RANGERS (1) 4   ST MIRREN (0) 1
  Johnstone (8),   Richardson (61)
  Russell (46),
  Bett (69 pen), Cooper (73)
RANGERS: McCloy; Jardine, Stevens, Forsyth, Miller; Russell, Bett, Redford (Dalziel); Cooper (Mackay), Johnstone, MacDonald

ST MIRREN: Thomson; Beckett, Copland, McCormack, Abercrombie; Fitzpatrick (McAvennie), Stark, Richardson; McEachran, Somner, Scanlon (Logan)

Attendance: 18,000

November 21st:
CELTIC (2) 3   RANGERS (3) 3
  McAdam (3),   Dalziel (5), Bett (20),
  McGarvey (10),   MacDonald (21)
  MacLeod (51)
CELTIC: Bonner; Moyes, McAdam, Aitken, Reid; Sullivan, MacLeod, Conroy; Provan, McGarvey, McCluskey

RANGERS: McCloy; Jardine, Jackson, Stevens, Miller; Russell, MacDonald, Bett; Cooper (Mackay), Johnstone, Dalziel (Redford)

Attendance: 48,600

Rangers can take great credit from twice coming from behind. 6 minutes after half-time Moyes leaped high to knock down a Provan corner and Murdo MacLeod thundered a tremendous drive past McCloy to make it 3-3. Action roared on but the defences finally got on top, and there was no further scoring.

December 5th:
AIRDRIE (1) 2   RANGERS (1) 2
  Anderson (4),   MacDonald (10),
  Gordon (67)   Russell (76)
AIRDRIE: Martin; Cairney, March, McCluskey (McKeown), Rodger; Walker, Anderson, Gordon; McGuire, Clark, Flood

RANGERS: Stewart; Jardine, Jackson, Stevens, Miller (Redford); Russell, Bett, MacDonald; Dalziel, Johnstone, Cooper (Mackay)

Attendance: 14,500

December 19th:
RANGERS (1) 2   DUNDEE (0) 1
  Bett (44), McAdam (81)   McGeachie (53)
RANGERS: Stewart; Jardine, Stevens, Jackson, Miller (Johnston); Russell, Bett, Redford (McAdam); Cooper, Johnstone, MacDonald

DUNDEE: Blair; Barr, Glennie, MacDonald, McLelland; Mackie, Fraser, McGeachie; Ferguson, Sinclair, Cameron

Attendance: 8,600

League positions

	P	W	D	L	F	A	Pts
1 Celtic	15	11	3	1	34	15	25
2 Dundee United	14	7	4	3	26	12	18
3 St Mirren	15	7	4	4	23	18	18
4 Aberdeen	15	7	4	4	21	16	18
5 RANGERS	15	6	6	3	25	21	18

December 27th: Rangers made a bid for Howard Gayle of Liverpool.

January 9th:
RANGERS (0) 1   CELTIC (0) 0
  Bett (72 pen)

RANGERS: Stewart; Jardine, Jackson, Stevens, Dawson; Russell, MacDonald, Bett; Cooper (McAdam), Johnstone, Dalziel

CELTIC: Bonner; McGrain, McAdam, Aitken, Reid; Conroy (Moyes), MacLeod, Burns; Provan (McGarvey), Nicholas, McCluskey

Attendance: 42,000

A penalty by Jim Bett was all that separated the sides. Had Johnstone been in sharper scoring form the issue would not have been clouded in any way. He had a chance from a MacDonald cross in 37 minutes which he squandered, and in 48 minutes following a beautiful run down the right and cross by Dalziel, he had a fine chance close in and was unmarked but this time he sliced it wide. In 72 minutes Stewart punted a long ball forward. Cooper sprinted on and was tripped up by Bonner coming off his line. Bett struck the penalty well out of Bonner's reach.

January 16th:
RANGERS (1) 2   DUNDEE UNITED (0) 0
  Dalziel (10), Cooper (85)

RANGERS: Stewart; Jardine, Stevens, McAdam, Dawson; Russell, Bett, MacDonald; Cooper, Johnstone, Dalziel (Redford)

DUNDEE UNITED: McAlpine; Holt (Reilly), Hegarty, Narey, Stark; Phillip (Kopel), Kirkwood, Bannon; Milne, Sturrock, Dodds

Attendance: 18,000

January 30th:
RANGERS (1) 1   HIBERNIAN (0) 1
  Johnstone (22)   Flavell (60)

RANGERS: Stewart; Jardine, McAdam, Jackson, Dawson; Russell, MacDonald, Redford (Mackay); Cooper, Dalziel, Johnstone

HIBERNIAN: McArthur; Sneddon, Paterson, Brazil, Schaedler; Callachan, Flavell, Duncan; Rodier, Murray (Jamieson), McLeod (McNamara)

Attendance: 15,000

February 17th:
PARTICK THISTLE (1) 2 RANGERS (0) 0
  Higgins (30 secs), Johnston (73)

PARTICK THISTLE: Rough; McKinnon, Whittaker; Anderson, Dunlop, Watson; Park, Jardine, Johnston, Doyle, Higgins.

RANGERS: Stewart; Jardine, Miller; McAdam, Jackson, Stevens; Bett, Russell, Dalziel, Redford, MacDonald

Attendance: 6,513

February 20th:
DUNDEE UNITED (1) 1 RANGERS (0) 1
  Sturrock (8)   Dawson (88)

DUNDEE UNITED: McAlpine; Gough, Hegarty, Narey, Stark; Kirkwood, Holt, Bannon; Milne, Dodds, Sturrock

RANGERS: Stewart; McAdam, Jardine, Jackson, Dawson; Russell, Bett, Miller; Cooper (Redford), Johnstone, MacDonald

Attendance: 12,945

February 27th:
RANGERS (1) 3   MORTON (0) 0
  MacDonald (17), Dalziel (80),
  Mackay (83)

RANGERS: Stewart; Jardine, Jackson, McAdam, Dawson; Russell, Bett, Miller (Dalziel); Cooper (Mackay), Johnstone, MacDonald

MORTON: Baines; Hayes, McLaughlin, Duffy, Holmes; Rooney, Busby, Docherty; Houston (Ritchie), Hutchinson, Slaven (McNeill)

Attendance: 10,200

League positions

	P	W	D	L	F	A	Pts
1 Celtic	21	13	5	3	42	21	31
2 St Mirren	21	10	7	4	32	22	27
3 RANGERS	21	9	8	4	33	25	26
4 Aberdeen	20	8	7	5	25	19	23
5 Hibernian	23	7	9	7	24	19	23

February 27th: Rangers offered Willie Johnston a free transfer provided he returned to U.S. football.

March 8th: Gregor Stevens received a 6-month ban following his latest ordering off. He had been ordered off 5 times in his career and booked 19 times. The ban was effective until August 31st.

March 10th:
ST MIRREN (2) 2   RANGERS (1) 3
  Richardson (10),   Bett (11 pen),
  Scanlon (12 pen)   Johnstone 2 (52, 68)

ST MIRREN: Thomson; McCormack, Beckett; Fitzpatrick, Fulton, Copland; Boag, Stark, McDougall, Richardson, Scanlon

RANGERS: Stewart; Jardine, Dawson; McAdam, Jackson, Bett; Cooper, Russell, Johnstone, Miller, Redford

Attendance: 8,633. Fitzpatrick was ordered off.

March 13th:
RANGERS   (0) 1   ABERDEEN   (2) 3
  Johnstone (63)   Cowan (9),
                               Cooper (34),
                               Watson (83)

RANGERS: Stewart; Jardine, Dawson; McAdam,
Jackson, Bett; Cooper, Russell, Johnstone, Miller
(MacDonald), Redford

ABERDEEN: Leighton; Kennedy, Rougvie;
McMaster (Watson), McLeish, Miller; Strachan,
Cooper, McGhee, Simpson, Cowan (Jarvie)

Attendance: 24,000

**March 13th: Tom Forsyth quit the game on medical
advice.**

March 17th:
MORTON   0   RANGERS   0

MORTON: Baines; Hayes, Holmes; Rooney,
McLaughlin, Duffy; McNeill, Houston, Busby,
Hutchinson, Ritchie

RANGERS: McCloy; Jardine, Dawson; McClelland,
Jackson, Bett; Mackay, Russell, Johnstone, Redford,
MacDonald

Attendance: 7,000

March 20th:
RANGERS   (0) 4   PARTICK THISTLE   (0) 1
  Johnstone (47),   Johnston (56)
  Russell (67),
  Bett (71 pen),
  MacDonald (82)

RANGERS: McCloy; Jardine, Jackson (Black),
McClelland, Dawson; Russell, Bett (Davies), Redford;
Dalziel, Johnstone, MacDonald

PARTICK THISTLE: Rough, McKinnon, Dunlop,
Kay, Lapsley, Jardine, O'Hara (McDonald), Watson,
Park, Higgins (Sweeney), Johnston

Attendance: 8,000

**March 23rd: Jim Bett was in the Scotland team
which beat Holland 2-1 at Hampden Park in front of
a crowd of 71,848.**

March 27th:
HIBERNIAN   0   RANGERS   0

HIBERNIAN: McArthur; Sneddon, Brazil, Paterson,
Schaedler; Flavell, McNamara, Duncan; McLeod, Rae,
Murray

RANGERS: Stewart; Dawson, Jardine, McClelland,
Black; Russell, Bett, MacDonald; Lyall (Robertson),
Dalziel, Redford (Davies)

Attendance: 12,390

March 31st:
RANGERS   (1) 1   AIRDRIE   (0) 0
  MacDonald (42)

RANGERS: Stewart; Dawson, Black; Jardine,
McClelland, Bett; Dalziel, Russell, Robertson,
MacDonald, Davies (Redford)

AIRDRIE: Martin; McCluskey, Rodger; Campbell,
G. Anderson, N. Anderson; McKeown, Flood, Walker,
Gordon, McGuire

Attendance: 6,000

April 10th:
CELTIC   (1) 2   RANGERS   (0) 1
  Crainie (1)   Johnstone (75)
  McAdam (50)

CELTIC: Bonner; McGrain, Aitken, Moyes, Reid;
Sullivan, MacLeod, Burns; Provan, McAdam, Crainie

RANGERS: Stewart; Jardine, McClelland, Jackson,
Dawson; Russell, Bett, Redford (Dalziel); Cooper,
Johnstone, MacDonald

Attendance: 40,144

Rangers pulled a goal back in the 75th minute when
Johnstone used his chest to trap the ball before hitting a
right foot shot past Bonner. In a match which was by no
means an epic Rangers deserved at least a draw.

April 14th:
DUNDEE   (2) 3   RANGERS   (1) 1
  Stephen 2 (29, 42),   MacDonald (4)
  Ferguson (57)

DUNDEE: Geddes; Barr, McKimmie; Fraser, Smith,
Glennie; Ferguson, Stephen, Sinclair, Kidd, Scrimgeour

RANGERS: Stewart; Jardine, Dawson; McClelland,
Jackson, Bett; Cooper, Russell, Johnstone, Redford,
MacDonald

Attendance: 7,975

April 14th: Tom Craig left Ibrox after 12 years.

April 17th:
AIRDRIE: (0) 0   RANGERS   (0) 1
                             MacDonald (47)

AIRDRIE: Martin; Cairney, G. Anderson, March,
Rodger; C. Walker, Campbell, N. Anderson
(McKeown); Gordon, Clark, McGuire (McDonagh)

RANGERS: Stewart; Dawson, Jardine, McClelland,
Black; Russell, Bett, Lyall; Cooper, Johnstone,
MacDonald

Attendance: 8,000

April 21st:
ABERDEEN   (2) 3   RANGERS   (0) 1
  McGhee (7), Rougvie (35),   Johnstone (68)
  Black (57)

ABERDEEN: Leighton; Kennedy, Rougvie; Cooper, McLeish, Miller; Black, Simpson, McGhee, Bell, Weir

RANGERS: Stewart; Dawson, Black; Jardine, McClelland, Bett; Dalziel, Russell, Johnstone, MacDonald, Lyall (McAdam)

Attendance: 8,750

April 24th:
RANGERS (1) 1   DUNDEE UNITED (0) 1
   MacDonald (24)   Bannon (60 pen)

RANGERS: Stewart; Dawson, Jardine, McClelland, Black; Bett (Redford), McAdam, MacDonald; Russell, Dalziel (Cooper), Johnstone

DUNDEE UNITED: McAlpine; Malpas, Hegarty, Narey, Gough; Kirkwood, Holt, Bannon; Milne, Sturrock, Dodds

Attendance: 10,000

April 28th: John McClelland represented Northern Ireland against Scotland in Belfast in a match which ended 1-1.

May 1st:
MORTON (1) 1   RANGERS (3) 3
   Docherty (11)   Russell (3),
                MacDonald 2 (15, 32)

MORTON: Baines; Hayes, McLaughlin, Duffy, Holmes; Rooney, Docherty, Cochrane; McNeill (Houston), Hutchinson (Busby), Ritchie

RANGERS: Stewart; Jardine, McClelland, Jackson, Dawson; Russell (McAdam), Bett, Redford; Cooper, Johnstone, MacDonald

Attendance: 6,500

May 5th:
RANGERS (1) 3   ST MIRREN (0) 0
   MacDonald (44), McAdam (59),
   Redford (80)

RANGERS: Stewart; Jardine, Miller; McClelland, McAdam, Bett; Cooper, Dalziel, Johnstone, Redford, MacDonald

ST MIRREN: Thomson; Beckett, McAveety; Fitzpatrick, Fulton, Copland; McDougall, Stark, Somner, McAvennie, Abercrombie

Attendance: 4,500

May 6th: Rangers completed the signing of Robert Prytz from Malmo for £100,000.

May 8th:
RANGERS (1) 4   DUNDEE (0) 0
   Dalziel 3 (11, 54, 77),
   Redford (71)

RANGERS: Stewart; Jardine (McIntyre), McClelland, McAdam, Miller; MacDonald (Davies), Bett, Redford; Cooper, Dalziel, Johnstone

DUNDEE: Geddes; McKimmie, Smith (Kidd), Glennie, McLelland (Davidson); Stephen, Fraser, McGeachie; Ferguson, Sinclair, Mackie

Attendance: 8,500

May 15th:
ABERDEEN (4) 4   RANGERS (0) 0
   Jackson o.g. (23).
   Hewitt 3 (28, 39, 43)

ABERDEEN: Leighton; Kennedy, McLeish, Miller, Rougvie; Strachan (Watson), Simpson, Cooper; Hewitt, McGhee, Weir (McMaster)

RANGERS: Stewart; Jardine (McLean), McClelland, Jackson, Dawson; Bett, Miller, MacDonald; Cooper, Redford, Dalziel

Attendance: 18,000

Scottish Premier League

	P	W	D	L	F	A	Pts
1 Celtic	36	24	7	5	79	33	55
2 Aberdeen	36	23	7	6	71	29	53
3 RANGERS	36	16	11	9	57	45	43
4 Dundee United	36	15	10	11	61	38	40
5 St Mirren	36	14	9	13	49	52	37
6 Hibernian	36	11	14	11	38	40	36
7 Morton	36	9	12	15	31	54	30
8 Dundee	36	11	4	21	46	72	26
9 Partick Thistle	36	6	10	20	35	59	22
10 Airdrie	36	5	8	23	31	76	18

May 14th: Stewart, Bett, Russell, Johnstone and Cooper were included in Scotland's World Cup 40.

May 18th: Derek Johnstone was ruled out of the Cup Final with a knee injury.

May 24th: Sandy Jardine, Colin Jackson, Tom Forsyth, Tommy McLean and Alex Forsyth were all given free transfers. Alex Miller was told he could leave if he could find a club.

June 8th: Dave McKinnon was signed from Partick Thistle for £30,000.

June 14th: Tommy McLean was appointed as Assistant Manager of the Club.

Between June 17th and July 4th John McClelland represented Northern Ireland 5 times in the World Cup Finals in Spain against Yugoslavia, Honduras, Spain, Austria and France.

LEAGUE CUP

August 8th:

MORTON   (0) 1   RANGERS   (1) 1
 Hutchinson (84)   McAdam (40)

MORTON: Baines; Hayes, McLaughlin, Orr, Marr
(Houston); Holmes, Rooney, Ritchie; Hutchinson,
McNeill, Busby

RANGERS: Stewart; Jardine, Stevens, Miller;
Russell, Bett, Redford (Jackson), Cooper; McAdam,
Johnstone, Johnston

Attendance: 11,500

August 12th:

RANGERS   (1) 4   DUNDEE   (1) 1
 McAdam (39),   Fleming (31)
 Johnstone (51),
 Miller (56),
 MacDonald (83)

RANGERS: Stewart; Bett (MacDonald), Miller;
Stevens, Jackson, Redford; Cooper, Russell, McAdam
(Johnston), Johnstone, McLean

DUNDEE: Geddes; Barr (Stephen), McKimmie;
Kidd, Glennie, MacDonald; Murphy, McGeachie,
Sinclair, Fleming, Scrimgeour (Mackie)

Attendance: 13,500

August 15th:

RANGERS   (4) 8   RAITH ROVERS   (1) 1
 Jardine (8),   Russell (25)
 Russell 2 (15, 49),
 McAdam (28),
 Redford 4 (30, 71, 86, 89)

RANGERS: Stewart; Jardine, Forsyth, Stevens,
Miller (Johnston); Russell, McLean, Redford; Cooper,
McAdam (MacDonald), Johnstone

RAITH ROVERS: Walker; Houston, Forsyth, Steel,
Candlish; Ford, Urquhart (Stein), Robinson; Russell,
Carroll, Ballantyne

Attendance: 15,000

August 18th:

DUNDEE   (0) 1   RANGERS   (0) 2
 MacDonald (90)   McGeachie o.g. (47),
                                   Stevens (50)

DUNDEE: Geddes; McGeachie, McKimmie
(Scrimgeour); Fraser, Glennie, MacDonald; Bell, Kidd,
Sinclair, Fleming, Stephen (Mackie)

RANGERS: Stewart; Jardine, Miller; Stevens,
Forsyth, Redford; Cooper, Bett, McAdam (Johnston),
Johnstone, McLean (MacDonald)

Attendance: 9,124

August 22nd:

RANGERS   (1) 1   MORTON   (0) 0
 Johnstone (61)

RANGERS: Stewart; Jardine, Forsyth, Stevens,
Miller; Bett, McLean (MacDonald), Redford; McAdam,
Johnstone, Cooper

MORTON: Baines; Hayes, McLaughlin, Orr,
Thomson; Holmes, Rooney, Ritchie (Houston);
Hutchinson, McNeill, Busby

Attendance: 26,000

August 26th:

RATIH ROVERS   (1) 1   RANGERS   (0) 3
 Russell (29)   Redford (62),
                                   Johnstone (63),
                                   MacDonald (72)

RAITH ROVERS: Walker; Houston, Candlish;
Robinson, Forsyth, Steel; Ballantyne, Urquhart
(Harris), Russell, Berry, Mitchell (Ford)

RANGERS: McCloy; Jardine (Dawson), McClelland;
Bett, Stevens, Redford; Cooper, Russell, Johnstone,
MacDonald, Johnston (Miller)

Attendance: 6,000

League Cup Section Table

	P	W	D	L	F	A	Pts
RANGERS	6	5	1	0	19	5	11
Morton	6	4	1	1	13	7	9
Raith Rovers	6	1	1	4	7	20	3
Dundee	6	0	1	5	7	14	1

September 2nd: Quarter-Final First Leg

BRECHIN CITY   (0) 0   RANGERS   (2) 4
                                  Russell (38),
                                  Jackson (44),
                                  McLean (59 pen),
                                  Redford (70)

BRECHIN: Neilson; Reid, Keating; Leslie, Mackay
(Cormack), R. Campbell; I. Campbell, Mackie, Graham,
Lorimer, Paterson

RANGERS: McCloy; McClelland, Dawson; Forsyth,
Jackson, Bett; Cooper, Russell, Redford, MacDonald,
McLean (Johnston)

Attendance: 7,000

September 23rd: Quarter-Final Second Leg

RANGERS   (0) 1   BRECHIN CITY   (0) 0
 MacDonald (76)

RANGERS: Stewart; McClelland, Dawson; Forsyth,
McPherson, Redford; Cooper, Russell (Davies), Dalziel,
MacDonald, McLean (Mackay)

BRECHIN: Neilson; Watt, Keating; Leslie, Stewart, Reid; Henderson, Mackie (I. Campbell), Paterson, Elvin, Cormack

Attendance: 3,000. Rangers won 5-0 on aggregate.

October 7th: Semi-Final First Leg   At Hampden Park
ST MIRREN   (0) 2   RANGERS   (1) 2
  McAvennie (50),   McAdam (17),
  Scanlon (72 pen)   MacDonald (69)

ST MIRREN: Thomson; Beckett, Fulton; Copland, McCormack, Abercrombie; McDougall (Bone), Stark, Somner, McAvennie, Scanlon

RANGERS: Stewart; Jardine, Dawson; Stevens, Forsyth, Bett; Cooper (Redford), Russell, McAdam, MacDonald, Johnston

Attendance: 14,058

After Logan was brought down by Redford, Ian Scanlon kept St Mirren's League Cup hopes alive with a penalty equaliser in a match which suddenly exploded with dramatic action in the 2nd half. Rangers were in front twice through an early Colin McAdam goal and then a freak goal, but Saints stormed back each time.

October 28th: League Cup Semi-Final Second Leg
RANGERS   (0) 2   ST MIRREN   (1) 1
  Bett (69 pen),   Scanlon (32 pen)
  MacDonald (87)

RANGERS: Stewart; Jardine, Dawson (Johnston); Forsyth, Jackson, Bett; Cooper, Russell (Redford), McAdam, MacDonald, Johnston

ST MIRREN: Thomson; Young, Fulton; McCormack, Copland, Abercrombie; Richardson (Logan), Stark, Bone, McAvennie, Scanlon

Attendance: 17,000

Rangers grabbed a late goal to win their way into the League Cup Final for the 16th time. In a tough bruising battle 2 penalties were awarded and 5 players booked. Teenager John MacDonald emerged as Rangers' hero, grabbing the winning goal just 3 minutes from the end with extra-time looking odds-on. Rangers won 4-3 on aggregate.

November 28th: Final   At Hampden Park
DUNDEE UNITED   (0) 1   RANGERS   (0) 2
  Milne (48)   Cooper (74),
                           Redford (88)

DUNDEE UNITED: McAlpine; Holt, Stark; Narey, Hegarty, Phillip; Bannon, Milne, Kirkwood, Sturrock, Dodds — Gough, Malpas

RANGERS: Stewart; Jardine, Miller; Stevens, Jackson, Bett; Cooper, Johnstone, Russell, MacDonald, Dalziel (Redford) —Mackay

Attendance: 53,777   *Referee*: E. H. Pringle (Edinburgh)

Rangers staged a remarkable comeback to shatter Dundee United's dream of becoming only the 2nd team to win the trophy 3 times in succession. Sturrock missed two good chances in the first half but he made the pass from which Milne scored in the 48th minute. 7 minutes later United had a goal from Sturrock — a blistering 20-yard drive —chalked off for offside against Holt. With 16 minutes left Hegarty pulled down MacDonald on the edge of the penalty area and Cooper sent a swerving free-kick into the net although McAlpine did get a hand to it. In the 88th minute Ian Redford, a substitute for Gordon Dalziel, picked up a loose header from Hegarty and from 20 yards sent a lob over McAlpine, who had come off his line, to win the Cup for Rangers.

SCOTTISH CUP

February 6th: Third Round
RANGERS   (3) 6   ALBION ROVERS   (0) 2
  Johnstone (1),   Houston 2 (68, 72)
  MacDonald (12),
  Russell (38),
  McAdam (55),
  McPherson (67 pen),
  Redford (78)

RANGERS: Stewart; Jardine (Miller), McPherson, Jackson (Dalziel), Dawson; Russell, McAdam, Redford; Cooper, Johnstone, MacDonald

ALBION ROVERS: Purdie; Allan, Hammel, Burgess, Lapsley; Gibson (Craig), Collins, Houston (Hannigan); Evans, Gillespie (Ross)

Attendance: 9,200

February 13th:
RANGERS   (0) 4   DUMBARTON   (0) 0
  Jardine 2 (59, 88),
  McAdam (67), Johnstone (74)

RANGERS: Stewart; Jardine, McAdam, Jackson, Dawson (Miller); Russell, Bett, Redford; Cooper, Johnstone, MacDonald (Dalziel)

DUMBARTON: Carson; Sinclair, Gallagher, T. Coyle, Campbell; McRoberts (Rankin), Clougherty (Montgomery), Donnelly; J. Coyle, Dunlop, Blair

Attendance: 15,000. This was Sandy Jardine's 750th match.

March 6th: Quarter-Final
RANGERS   (0) 2   DUNDEE   (0) 0
  Johnstone (53), McAdam (67)

RANGERS: Stewart; Jardine, Jackson, McAdam, Dawson; Russell, Bett, Miller (Redford); Johnstone, MacDonald, Cooper (Mackay)

DUNDEE: Geddes; McKimmie, Smith, Glennie, McLelland; Kidd (Cameron), Fraser, McGeachie; Ferguson, Fleming (Stephen), Mackie

Attendance: 16,500

April 3rd: Semi-Final   At Hampden Park
RANGERS   0   FORFAR
                               ATHLETIC   0

RANGERS: Stewart; Dawson, Jardine, McClelland, Black; Russell, Bett, Redford; Dalziel (Davies), McAdam (Robertson), MacDonald

FORFAR: Kennedy; Bennet, Brown, Brash, McPhee; Leitch, Farningham, Allan (Porter); Hancock, Gallacher, Clark (Watt)

Attendance: 15,878

Forfar put together a great performance which completely belied their middle of the Second Division place. They were well organised and their centre backs Brash and Brown were terrific. Rangers had too many players who did not play to form.

April 6th: Semi-Final Replay   At Hampden Park
FORFAR ATHLETIC   (1) 1   RANGERS   (2) 3
  Brash (42 pen)   Johnstone (10),
                                 Bett (30),
                                 Cooper (51)

FORFAR: Kennedy; Bennett, McPhee; Brown, Brash, Allan; Gallacher, Farningham, Hancock, Leitch (Watt), Clark (Porter)

RANGERS: Stewart; Jardine, Dawson; McClelland, Jackson, Bett; Cooper, Russell, Johnstone, Redford, MacDonald

Attendance: 11,864.

Derek Johnstone and Davie Cooper, with a goal each, contributed to a greatly improved Ibrox performance. Forfar were always fighting a lost cause and when defender Kenny Brown was sent off for deliberate handling 17 minutes from time their fate was well and truly sealed.

May 22nd: Final   At Hampden Park
ABERDEEN   (1) 4   RANGERS   (1) 1
                               After Extra Time
  McLeish (33), McGhee (92),   MacDonald (15)
  Strachan (103), Cooper (110)

ABERDEEN: Leighton; Kennedy, Rougvie; McMaster (Bell), McLeish, Miller; Strachan, Cooper, McGhee, Simpson, Hewitt (Black)

RANGERS: Stewart; Jardine (McAdam), Dawson; McClelland, Jackson, Bett; Cooper, Russell, Dalziel (McLean), Miller, MacDonald

Attendance: 53,788   *Referee*: B. McGinlay (Balfron)

Aberdeen came from behind to win the Scottish Cup for the 3rd time in their history. Yet for a long time it looked as if Rangers' Cup tradition would clinch it for John Greig's patchwork line-up. They produced a brilliant move after 15 minutes. Cooper started it from midfield and when Miller quickly moved the pass on to Dalziel there was a huge gap in the Dons' defence. Over came the cross and John MacDonald scored with a great diving header. In 33 minutes McLeish levelled the score with a magnificent goal. Shortly after Rangers lost Sandy Jardine with concussion, McAdam substituting. Aberdeen had the better chances in the 2nd half but Dalziel almost won the trophy for Rangers in the closing minutes with a flashing header which was brilliantly saved by Leighton. Then into extra-time. In 2 minutes Strachan put an inch-perfect cross behind McClelland and McGhee sent a powerful header past Stewart. 11 minutes later it was over. Miller collapsed after turning awkwardly and McGhee's low cross to the far post was blasted home by Strachan. In 110 minutes Cooper raced through the middle, got a rebound off Stewart and was left with an open goal.

CUP WINNERS CUP

September 16th: First Round First Leg
DUKLA PRAGUE   (1) 3   RANGERS   (0) 0
  Rada (4), Stambachr (55)
  Nehoda (74)

DUKLA: Netolicka; Macela, Novak (Dolezal); Fiala, Rada, Pelc; Vizek, Kozak, Nehoda, Kriz, Stambachr

RANGERS: McCloy; Jardine, Dawson; Forsyth, Jackson (Stevens), McClelland; Bett, McLean, Russell, McAdam, Johnstone (Redford)

Attendance: 22,500. McLean was ordered off.

September 30th: First Round Second Leg
RANGERS   (2) 2   DUKLA PRAGUE   (1) 1
  Bett (43),   Stambachr (23)
  MacDonald (44)

RANGERS: Stewart; McClelland (Redford), Dawson; Jardine, Forsyth, Bett; Cooper, Russell, McAdam (Johnstone), MacDonald, Johnston

DUKLA: Netolicka; Macela, Kapko; Fiala, Rada, Kozak (Dolezal); Vizek, Rott, Nehoda, Kriz, Stambachr

Attendance: 20,000

Rangers won the game and restored a little of their reputation. Indeed for a lengthy spell it looked as if they believed it was possible to overcome the 3-goal deficit from the First Leg. Then disaster in 23 minutes — Stambachr, with his back to the goal, brilliantly deceived Forsyth and shot from 20 yards. Stewart looked to have the shot covered but he inexplicably allowed the ball to slip over his diving body and into the net. 2 minutes from half-time Bett scored, Cooper setting up the chance. A minute later Jardine and Bett worked a beautiful move and when

Cooper's neat chip came off the bar, MacDonald was on the spot to knock in the rebound. Dukla won 4-2 on aggregate.

APPEARANCES

	League	League Cup	Scottish Cup	Cup Winners Cup
Stewart	26	9	6	1
McCloy	10	2	-	1
Jardine	36	8	6	2
Dawson	25	4+1S	6	2
Black	7+1S	-	1	-
Miller	14+2S	6+1S	2+2S	-
Stevens	13	8	-	0+1S
Jackson	21	4+1S	5	1
McClelland	14	3	3	2
Bett	35	9	5	2
T. Forsyth	12	7	-	2
Redford	20+12S	8+3S	4+1S	0+2S
Cooper	29+1S	11	5	1
Russell	32	9	6	2
D. Johnstone	27+1S	7+1S	4	1+1S
McAdam	15+7S	7	4+1S	2
Dalziel	14+3S	2	2+2S	-
MacDonald	32+3S	6+4S	6	1
McLean	2+1S	6	0+1S	1
Davies	1+3S	0+1S	0+1S	-
Lyall	3	-	-	-
Mackay	1+6S	0+1S	0+1S	-
McIntyre	0+1S	-	-	-
W. Johnston	6+2S	4+4S	-	1
D. Robertson	1+1S	-	0+1S	-
McPherson	-	1	1	-
A. Forsyth	-	-	-	-
Clark	-	-	-	-
E. Ferguson	-	-	-	-
Bruce	-	-	-	-
Watson	-	-	-	-

GOALSCORERS

League: MacDonald 14, Bett 11 (4 pens), D. Johnstone 9, Russell 6, Dalziel 6, Cooper 3, McAdam 2, Redford 2, Dawson 1, Mackay 1, Jardine 1

League Cup: Redford 7, MacDonald 5, McAdam 4, D. Johnstone 3, Russell 3, Miller 1, Jardine 1, Stevens 1, Jackson 1, McLean 1 (pen), Bett 1 (pen), Cooper 1, Own Goal 1

Scottish Cup: D. Jonstone 4, McAdam 3, MacDonald 2, Jardine 2, Russell 1, McPherson 1 (pen), Redford 1, Bett 1, Cooper 1

Cup Winners Cup: Bett 1, MacDonald 1

The Rangers squad for season 1985–86. Back row: D. MacKinnon, S. Munro, D. McFarlane, S. Nisbet, D. McPherson, C. Paterson, E. Ferguson, S. Beattie, A. Dawson, D. Ferguson. Middle row: R. Prytz, I. Durrant, C. Fraser, T. McMinn, A. Bruce, P. McCloy, N. Walker, D. Johnstone, H. Burns, B. Davies, C. Miller. Front row: S. Anderson, J. McDonald, I. Ferguson, B. Williamson, D. Cooper, A. Totten, J. Wallace (manager), J. Hagart, B. Russell, A. McCoist, I. Redford, R. Fleck, and B. Findlay (physio.).

Season 1982–83

Although they reached the Final of both the Scottish Cup and the League Cup, this was another disappointing Season for Rangers which saw them lose both Cup Finals and finish 4th in the Table — a massive 18 points behind Champions Dundee United and 17 behind both Celtic and Aberdeen. They drew 5 of their opening 7 matches and finished with only 13 League wins. They dropped 7 points to Celtic, 6 to Dundee and 5 to Dundee United. They did manage a rare victory at Pittodrie. Their total of 52 goals was 38 fewer than both Dundee United and Celtic. They spent a club record fee on Hibs' Craig Paterson at the beginning of the season in a bid to bolster the defence. The brief return of Gordon Smith on loan from Brighton was not a success but the introduction of both Davie McPherson and Andy Kennedy to the first team was. After Kennedy's early form had dipped former Airdrie star Sandy Clark was signed from West Ham in March for £160,000, and although he scored only 4 times in his 10 League appearances he did score the goal which took Rangers through to the Scottish Cup Final. At the end of the season it was revealed that Jim Bett was returning to Belgium. Most of the money received for Bett was used to sign Ally McCoist from Sunderland. Both John McClelland and Bett appeared in 35 League matches and John MacDonald finished as top scorer with 10.

Rangers reached the Final of the League Cup. They won their Section against Hibernian, Clydebank and Airdrie without losing a match. Kilmarnock were beaten 12-1 on aggregate in the Quarter-Final and Hearts 4-1 on aggregate in the Semi-Final. Rangers conceded two first-half goals to Celtic in the Final, and although a brilliantly taken free-kick by Jim Bett gave them fresh hope at the start of the 2nd-half, the trophy went to Parkhead for the first time since Season 1974–75.

Rangers reached their 8th successive Scottish Cup Final — their 5th under John Greig. They played well above their League form in the Final against Aberdeen and a superb shot from Jim Bett 2 minutes from time almost won them the trophy but a tragic mistake by Russell 4 minutes from the end of extra-time led to Aberdeen's Eric Black scoring the only goal of the match to take the trophy North once again.

An impressive, disciplined performance in West Germany set Rangers up for a comfortable victory over Borussia Dortmund in the First Round of the U.E.F.A. Cup. Another Bundesliga team, Cologne, was drawn in the next round but the one-goal advantage gained in the First Leg at Ibrox proved to be totally insufficient as Cologne went on a goal spree in the return — scoring 4 times in the first 21 minutes.

> League: Fourth
> League Cup: Runners-Up
> Scottish Cup: Runners-up
> U.E.F.A. Cup: Second Round

SCOTTISH PREMIER LEAGUE

July 26th: Rangers signed Craig Paterson from Hibernian for a club record fee of £225,000.

September 4th:
MOTHERWELL (0) 2   RANGERS (1) 2
  Clelland (74), Carson (79)   Prytz (7 pen),
                Redford (65)

MOTHERWELL: Sproat, McLeod, Carson, McLelland, Forsyth, Rafferty; Forbes, McLaughlin (Clinging), Gahagan; Irvine (Clelland), Edvaldsson

RANGERS: Stewart; McKinnon, Paterson, McClelland, Dawson; Prytz, Bett, Redford; MacDonald, McAdam, Cooper

Attendance: 19,159

September 11th:
RANGERS 0   DUNDEE UNITED 0

RANGERS: Stewart; McKinnon, McClelland, Paterson, Dawson; Prytz, Bett, Redford; Cooper (Russell), Johnstone, MacDonald

DUNDEE UNITED: McAlpine; Gough, Hegarty, Narey, Malpas; Kirkwood, Britton, Payne (Milne); Sturrock, Dodds, Bannon

Attendance: 22,200

Rangers did most of the attacking as they were entitled to on their own pitch but United were always capable of the dangerous counter-attack.

September 18th:
RANGERS (2) 5   KILMARNOCK (0) 0
  MacDonald 2 (15, 67), Russell (21),
  Johnstone (53), McClelland (57)

RANGERS: Stewart; McKinnon, McClelland, Paterson (Redford), Dawson; Russell, Bett, Prytz; Cooper, Johnstone, MacDonald (Mackay)

KILMARNOCK: McCulloch; McDicken, Armstrong, Clarke, McClurg; MacLeod, J. Clark, R. Clark (Cockburn); McGivern (Bryson), Eadie, Gallagher

Attendance: 17,350

September 20th: Tom Forsyth was appointed Manager of Dunfermline.

September 25th:
ABERDEEN (0) 1   RANGERS (0) 2
  Strachan (73 pen)   Johnstone (48),
                Prytz (62)

ABERDEEN: Leighton; Kennedy, McLeish, Miller, Rougvie; Strachan, Simpson, Cooper; Bell, McGhee, Black (Weir)

RANGERS: Stewart; McKinnon, Paterson, McClelland, Dawson; Russell, Bett, Prytz (McAdam); Redford, Johnstone, Cooper

Attendance: 22,000

October 2nd:
RANGERS (0) 1   DUNDEE (0) 1
  Johnstone (58)   Fraser (63)

RANGERS: Stewart; McKinnon, McAdam, McClelland, Dawson (Black); Prytz, Bett, Russell (Redford); Cooper, Johnstone, MacDonald

DUNDEE: Kelly; Glennie, MacDonald, Smith, Scrimgeour; Fraser, Fleming, Stephen; Mackie, Ferguson, Davidson (Sinclair)

Attendance: 16,200

October 9th:
MORTON 0   RANGERS 0

MORTON: Baines; Houston, McLaughlin, Jackson, Holmes; Docherty, Duffy, Rooney; McNab (McNeill), Hutchinson (Cochrane), Ritchie

RANGERS: Stewart; McKinnon, McClelland, Paterson, Redford; Prytz (McPherson), Bett, Russell; Cooper, Johnstone, MacDonald

Attendance: 12,000

October 16th:
ST MIRREN (1) 2   RANGERS (1) 2
  Scanlon (36 pen),   Bett (23),
  McDougall (61)   McKinnon (68)

ST MIRREN: Thomson; Wilson, Fulton, Copland, Clarke; Fitzpatrick, Stark, Abercrombie; McDougall, McAvennie, Scanlon

RANGERS: Stewart; McKinnon, McClelland, Paterson, Redford; Russell, Bett, Prytz; Cooper, Johnstone, MacDonald (Mackay)

Attendance: 12,121

October 23rd:
RANGERS (2) 3   HIBERNIAN (1) 2
  Johnstone 2 (9, 55),   Murray 2 (17, 86)
  McNamara o.g. (22)

RANGERS: Stewart; McKinnon, Stevens, McClelland, Redford; Prytz (Dawson), Russell, Bett; Cooper, Johnstone, MacDonald (Robertson)

HIBERNIAN: McArthur (Rodier); Sneddon, McNamara, Rae, Duncan; Callachan, Conroy, Turnbull; Thomson, Irvine, Murray

Attendance: 16,000

Callachan missed a penalty, McArthur was carried off and Duncan had to take over in goal.

October 30th:
CELTIC   (1) 3   RANGERS   (2) 2
  McStay (18), McGarvey (67),   Prytz (16),
  MacLeod (87)   Cooper (40)

CELTIC: Bonner; McGrain, Aitken, McAdam, Reid;
McStay, Sinclair, MacLeod; Provan, McGarvey,
Nicholas

RANGERS: Stewart; McKinnon, McClelland,
Stevens, Dawson; Russell (MacDonald), Prytz
(McAdam); Cooper, Johnstone, Redford

Attendance: 60,408

Celtic broke Rangers' 20-match unbeaten run. The main
features of the match were the power of Murdo MacLeod
and the delicate touches and astute passing of Paul
McStay.

League positions

	P	W	D	L	F	A	Pts
1 Celtic	9	7	1	1	23	10	15
2 Dundee United	9	5	4	0	17	3	14
3 Aberdeen	9	5	2	2	15	9	12
4 RANGERS	9	3	5	1	17	11	11
5 Dundee	9	3	3	3	9	8	9

November 6th:
RANGERS   (1) 4   MOTHERWELL   (0) 0
  MacDonald 2 (10, 85),
  Dalziel 2 (48, 51)

RANGERS: Stewart; McKinnon, McClelland,
Stevens, Dawson; Russell (McPherson), Bett, Prytz;
Dalziel, MacDonald, Cooper (Kennedy)

MOTHERWELL: Sproat; MacLeod, Edvaldsson,
Carson, Forsyth; Flavell, Mauchlen (Forbes), O'Hara;
Gahagan, McClair (Burns), McLelland

Attendance: 17,000

November 13th:
DUNDEE UNITED   (1) 4   RANGERS   (1) 2
  Milne 2 (31, 86),   Cooper (33),
  Dodds (77), Gough (85)   Johnstone (65)

DUNDEE UNITED: McAlpine; Gough, Hegarty,
Narey, Malpas; Kirkwood, Stark, Bannon; Milne,
Sturrock, Dodds

RANGERS: Stewart; McKinnon, McClelland,
Stevens, Dawson; McPherson, Bett, Redford;
MacDonald (Dalziel), Johnstone, Cooper

Attendance: 16,470

Rangers let United off the hook and lost 3 goals in the final
13 minutes.

November 20th:
KILMARNOCK   0   RANGERS   0

KILMARNOCK: McCulloch; Robertson, McDicken,
Clarke (R. Clark), Cockburn; McLean, J. Clark,
MacLeod; McGivern, Gallagher, Bryson (Bourke)

RANGERS: Stewart; McKinnon, McClelland,
Stevens (McPherson), Dawson; Prytz, Bett, Redford;
Cooper (Robertson), Johnstone, MacDonald

Attendance: 9,500

**November 20th: Rangers made an approach for
Scottish International goalkeeper Alan Rough of
Partick Thistle. He was to sign for Hibs for £60,000.**

November 27th:
RANGERS   (0) 0   ABERDEEN   (0) 1
                               Black (69)

RANGERS: Stewart; McKinnon, McPherson,
McClelland, Dawson (Mackay); Prytz, Bett, Redford;
Cooper, Johnstone (Dalziel), MacDonald

ABERDEEN: Leighton; Kennedy, McLeish, Miller,
Rougvie; Simpson, Cooper (Black), Bell; Strachan,
McGhee, Weir

Attendance: 23,000

**December 1st: Gordon Smith was signed 'on loan'
from Brighton until January 10th.**

December 11th:
RANGERS   (0) 1   MORTON   (1) 1
  Prytz (51 pen)   Rooney (33)

RANGERS: Stewart; McKinnon, McClelland,
Paterson, Redford; Russell (Black), Bett, Prytz;
MacDonald, Smith, Cooper (Dalziel)

MORTON: Baines; Houston, McLaughlin, Duffy,
Holmes; Rooney, Cochrane, Docherty; McNab, McNeill
(Ritchie), Higgins

Attendance: 9,500

**December 15th: Jim Bett was in the Scotland team
which was beaten 3-2 by Belgium in Brussels.**

December 18th:
RANGERS   (1) 1   ST MIRREN   (0) 0
  MacDonald (20)

RANGERS: Stewart; McKinnon, McClelland,
Paterson, Redford; Russell, Bett, Black; Mackay
(Smith), Kennedy, MacDonald (Prytz)

ST MIRREN: Thomson; Wilton, Fulton, Copland,
Clarke; Fitzpatrick, Stark, Richardson; Somner,
McAvennie (Logan), Scanlon

Attendance: 10,200

League positions

	P	W	D	L	F	A	Pts
1 Celtic	15	13	1	1	43	16	27
2 Dundee United	15	10	4	1	36	11	24
3 Aberdeen	16	10	3	3	31	13	23
4 RANGERS	15	5	7	3	25	17	17
5 Dundee	15	5	4	6	19	18	14

December 27th:
HIBERNIAN   0   RANGERS   0

HIBERNIAN: Rough; Sneddon, Turnbull, Jamieson, Rae; McNamara, Conroy, Rice; Duncan, Callachan, Murray

RANGERS: Stewart; McKinnon, Redford; McClelland, Paterson, Bett; Mackay (Prytz), Russell, Kennedy, Black, MacDonald

Attendance: 15,900

January 1st:
RANGERS   (1) 1   CELTIC   (1) 2
  Black (24)   McStay (13),
                           Nicholas (67)

RANGERS: Stewart; McKinnon, McClelland; Stevens, Paterson, Bett; Cooper, Russell, Kennedy, Black (Redford), MacDonald

CELTIC: Bonner; McGrain, Reid; Sinclair, McAdam, MacLeod; Provan, McStay, McGarvey, Burns, Nicholas

Attendance: 44,000

Celtic started with the upper hand and throughout the first 10 minutes Rangers could do little to contain their strong attacks. Throughout the 2nd half each team had their share of attacks, near misses and close shaves. In the 67th minute Celtic scored what proved to be the winner. Nicholas picked up the ball from a MacLeod throw-in and as he moved from the centre of the park towards the left-hand side he shook off the Rangers defence by using his pace and clever stops and starts. Suddenly he let loose with a tremendous shot that ended up in the back of the net to give Celtic the points.

January 3rd:
MOTHERWELL   (1) 3   RANGERS   (0) 0
  McClair 3 (4, 62, 73)

MOTHERWELL: Sproat; Dornan, Forsyth; Carson, Edvaldsson, Mauchlen; Flavell, Rafferty, Harrow, McClair, O'Hara

RANGERS: Stewart; McKinnon, McClelland; Stevens, Paterson, Bett; Cooper, Russell, Kennedy, Black, MacDonald

Attendance: 11,383

January 8th:
RANGERS   (1) 2   DUNDEE UNITED   (1) 1
  Prytz (41),   Reilly (12)
  Kennedy (62)

RANGERS: McCloy; McKinnon, Stevens, McClelland, Redford; Russell (Cooper), Bett, Black; Prytz, Kennedy, Johnstone

DUNDEE UNITED: McAlpine; Gough, Hegarty, Narey, Malpas; Stark (Holt), Kirkwood, Bannon; Milne (McNeill), Reilly, Dodds

Attendance: 15,200

This was only Rangers' 2nd victory in 10 matches. Things looked bleak for them after United's John Reilly had opened the scoring but young Andy Kennedy set up the equaliser and then scored the winner — his first goal for the first team. United were streets ahead in quality in the first-half.

January 15th:
RANGERS   (0) 1   KILMARNOCK   (0) 1
  MacDonald (79)   McGivern (66)

RANGERS: McCloy; McKinnon (McPherson), McClelland, Stevens, Redford; Bett, Prytz (MacDonald), Black; Cooper, Johnstone, Kennedy

KILMARNOCK: McCulloch; McDicken, Armstrong, P. Clarke, R. Clark; J. Clark, MacLeod, Simpson; Clinging, McGivern, Gallagher

Attendance: 8,500

January 22nd:
ABERDEEN   (1) 2   RANGERS   (0) 0
  Rougvie (34), McGhee (77)

ABERDEEN: Leighton; Kennedy, Rougvie; Cooper (McMaster), McLeish, Miller; Strachan (Simpson), Black, McGhee, Bell, Weir

RANGERS: McCloy; McKinnon, Redford; Stevens, McClelland, Bett; Cooper (MacDonald), Prytz (Black), Kennedy, Dawson, Johnstone

Attendance: 22,000. MacDonald was ordered off.

February 5th:
RANGERS   (0) 1   DUNDEE   (0) 1
  McPherson (58)   Bell (76)

RANGERS: McCloy; Dawson, Black; McClelland, McPherson, Bett; Dalziel, Prytz, Kennedy, Redford, MacDonald

DUNDEE: Kelly; McGeachie, McKimmie; Fraser, Smith, MacDonald; Ferguson, Bell, Sinclair, Mackie, Stephen

Attendance: 8,500

February 12th:
MORTON   (0) 0   RANGERS   (1) 5
                        Bett 2 (22, 70),
                        MacDonald (54),
                        Kennedy 2 (88, 89)

MORTON: Baines; Houston, McLaughlin, Duffy,
Holmes; Docherty, Hutchinson, Rooney; McNab,
Payne, Ritchie

RANGERS: McCloy; Dawson, McClelland,
McPherson, Black; Bett, Prytz, Redford; Dalziel,
Kennedy, MacDonald

Attendance: 6,900

**February 14th: John MacDonald received a 4-match
ban for his sending off against Aberdeen on January
22nd.**

February 26th:
ST MIRREN   (1) 1   RANGERS   (0) 0
    Fitzpatrick (6)

ST MIRREN: Thomson; Wilson, McCormack,
Fulton, Clarke; Stark, Fitzpatrick, Richardson;
McAvennie, Scanlon (Wardrop), McDougall

RANGERS: McCloy; Dawson, McClelland,
McPherson, Black; Prytz, Bett, Redford; Dalziel,
Kennedy (Cooper), Robertson

Attendance: 11,484

League positions

	P	W	D	L	F	A	Pts
1 Aberdeen	25	18	4	3	54	17	40
2 Celtic	24	18	3	3	64	27	39
3 Dundee United	24	14	7	3	54	20	35
4 RANGERS	24	7	10	7	35	28	24
5 Hibernian	25	5	11	9	21	31	21

March 2nd:
DUNDEE   (0) 1   RANGERS   (0) 0
    Kidd (53)

DUNDEE: Kelly; McGeachie (Glennie), McKimmie;
Fraser, Smith, MacDonald; Ferguson, Scrimgeour,
Sinclair, Mackie, Kidd

RANGERS: McCloy; Dawson, Black; McClelland,
McPherson, Bett; Dalziel, Davies, Kennedy (Prytz),
Redford (Lyall), Robertson

Attendance: 6,624

March 5th:
RANGERS   (0) 1   HIBERNIAN   (0) 1
    Dalziel (77)   Jamieson (71)

RANGERS: McCloy; McKinnon, McClelland,
McPherson, Black (Cooper); Prytz, Redford, Bett;
Dalziel, Kennedy, Johnstone (Davies)

HIBERNIAN: Rough; Sneddon, Rae, McNamara,
Jamieson; Turnbull, Conroy, Rice (McKee); Thomson,
Harvey (Duncan), Irvine

Attendance: 10,975

**March 17th: Sandy Clark was signed from West
Ham for £160,000.**

March 19th:
RANGERS   (1) 1   MOTHERWELL   (0) 0
    McClelland (7)

RANGERS: McCloy; Dawson, McClelland;
McPherson, Paterson, Bett; Cooper (Dalziel), Prytz
(McKinnon), Clark, Redford, MacDonald

MOTHERWELL: Walker; Dornan, MacLeod;
Forbes, Edvaldsson, Mauchlen; Gahagan, Rafferty
(Coyne), Harrow, McClair, O'Hara (Flavell)

Attendance: 18,000

March 23rd:
CELTIC   0   RANGERS   0

CELTIC: Bonner; McGrain, Reid; Aitken, McAdam,
Sullivan; Provan (McCluskey), McStay, Nicholas,
MacLeod, McGarvey

RANGERS: McCloy; Dawson, McClelland;
McPherson, Paterson, Bett; Cooper, McKinnon, Clark,
Redford (Prytz), MacDonald (Dalziel)

Attendance: 51,062

Despite the blank score sheet more than 51,000 fans were
thoroughly entertained. It was end-to-end stuff with
tackles fierce and uncompromising.

March 26th:
KILMARNOCK   (0) 0   RANGERS   (1) 1
                        MacDonald (16)

KILMARNOCK: McCulloch; Cockburn, R. Clark; J.
Clark, Armstrong, Clarke; McGivern, McClurg,
Gallagher, MacLeod, Bryson (McDicken)

RANGERS: McCloy; Dawson, McClelland;
McPherson, Paterson, Bett; Cooper (Dalziel),
McKinnon, Clark, Redford, MacDonald

Attendance: 6,500

April 2nd:
DUNDEE UNITED   (1) 3   RANGERS   (0) 1
    Milne (31),   Clark (66)
    Sturrock 2 (76, 89)

DUNDEE UNITED: McAlpine; Gough, Hegarty,
Narey, Malpas; Bannon, Stark, Holt; Dodds, Sturrock,
Milne

RANGERS: McCloy; Dawson, McClelland, Paterson,
Redford; Bett, McKinnon, Prytz (Lyall); Cooper, Clark,
MacDonald

Attendance: 14,142

United looked like certainties when Ralph Milne put them ahead in the 31st minute but after missing several good chances they were caught out by Davie Cooper's one clever play of the day. His final pass to Clark was touched in from a difficult angle. Fortunately for United Sturrock, who had hit the bar with an easy chance, made a better job of another one and in the 2nd last minute put a more rational look on the scoreline by adding a 3rd.

April 9th:
RANGERS   (1) 2   ABERDEEN   (1) 1
  Redford (21), Bett (85)   McLeish (15)

RANGERS: McCloy; Dawson, Paterson, McPherson, McClelland; Russell (Dalziel), Bett, McKinnon; Redford, Clark, MacDonald (Cooper)

ABERDEEN: Leighton; Kennedy, McLeish, Miller, Rougvie (McMaster); Cooper, Bell, Simpson, Strachan, McGhee, Weir (Black)

Attendance: 19,800

April 23rd:
RANGERS   (1) 2   MORTON   (0) 0
  MacDonald (24), Redford (84)

RANGERS: McCloy; Dawson, McPherson, Paterson, McClelland; Russell (Redford), Bett, McKinnon; Prytz (Cooper), Clark, MacDonald

MORTON: Baines; Hayes, McLaughlin, Duffy, Rooney; Payne, Cochrane (Gavigan), Holmes; McNab (McNeill), Hutchinson, Houston

Attendance: 9,000

April 30th:
RANGERS   (1) 4   ST MIRREN   (0) 0
  MacDonald (5), Bett 2 (55, 62 pen),
  Clark (83)

RANGERS: McCloy; Dawson, McClelland; McPherson, Paterson, Bett; Cooper, McKinnon, Clark, Redford (Russell), MacDonald (Prytz)

ST MIRREN: Thomson; Wilson, Clarke; Fitzpatrick, Fulton, McCormack; Stark, McAvennie, McDougall (Speirs), Richardson, Somner (Campbell)

Attendance: 9,321

April 30th: Rangers put Johnstone, McAdam, Stevens, Stewart, Mackay and Dalziel up for sale.

May 3rd:
DUNDEE   (1) 2   RANGERS   (1) 1
  Ferguson (3), Sinclair (52)   Clark (23)

DUNDEE: Kelly; Glennie, McKimmie; Fraser, Smith, MacDonald; Ferguson, McGeachie, Sinclair, Kidd, Stephen

RANGERS: McCloy; McKinnon, McClelland; Lyall (Davies), McPherson, Bett; Cooper, Russell (Prytz), Clark, Redford, MacDonald

Attendance: 4,788. McClelland was sent off after the final whistle. Ferguson missed a penalty. Redford was booked and as a result missed the Scottish Cup Final.

May 7th:
HIBERNIAN   (0) 1   RANGERS   (2) 2
  Callachan (70)   Cooper 2 (1, 15)

HIBERNIAN: Rough; McKee (McNamara), Sneddon; Brazil, Welsh, Rice; Callachan, Irvine, Murray (Harvey), Thomson, Duncan

RANGERS: Bruce; Dawson, Lyall; Johnstone, Paterson, Prytz; Cooper, Russell (McPherson), Clark, Davies (Black), Dalziel

Attendance: 10,500

May 14th:
RANGERS   (2) 2   CELTIC   (0) 4
  Cooper (16),   Nicholas 2 (48 pen, 86 pen),
  Clark (23)   McAdam (61),
                             McGarvey (73)

RANGERS: McCloy; Dawson, McClelland; McPherson, Paterson, Bett; Cooper, McKinnon (Russell), Clark, Redford, MacDonald (Dalziel)

CELTIC: Bonner; McGrain, Sinclair; Aitken, McAdam, MacLeod; Provan, McStay, Nicholas, Burns, McGarvey

Attendance: 39,000

Rangers were two goals up at half-time and looking to be well on the way to victory. They can be criticised for playing for only 45 minutes and Celtic can be congratulated for playing for the full 90.

May 22nd: It was announced that Jim Bett was returning to F.C. Lokeren in Belgium for a fee of £240,000. The player pulled out of the Home International Squad.

May 24th: Ally Dawson was in the Scotland team which drew 0-0 with Northern Ireland at Hampden. John McClelland represented Ireland.

June 8th: Rangers signed Ally McCoist from Sunderland for £185,000.

June 12th: Dawson was in the Scotland team which beat Canada 2-0 in Vancouver.

June 19th: Dawson was in the Scotland team which beat Canada 2-0 in Toronto.

June 18th: It was reported that Rangers were to move for Murdo MacLeod of Celtic.

Premier League

	P	W	D	L	F	A	Pts
1 Dundee United	36	24	8	4	90	35	56
2 Celtic	36	25	5	6	90	36	55
3 Aberdeen	36	25	5	7	76	24	55
4 RANGERS	36	13	12	11	52	41	38
5 St Mirren	36	11	12	13	47	51	34
6 Dundee	36	9	11	16	42	53	29
7 Hibernian	36	7	15	14	35	51	29
8 Motherwell	36	11	5	20	39	73	27
9 Morton	36	6	8	22	30	74	20
10 Kilmarnock	36	3	11	22	28	91	17

LEAGUE CUP

August 14th:
HIBERNIAN (0) 1   RANGERS (1) 1
Rae (45)   MacDonald (19)

HIBERNIAN: McArthur; Sneddon, Welsh, Brazil, Schaedler; Callachan, McNamara, Turnbull; Rae, Rodier, Thomson

RANGERS: Stewart; McKinnon, McClelland, Paterson, Dawson (Davies); Prytz (Mackay), Miller, Bett; McAdam, Redford, MacDonald

Attendance: 14,977

August 18th:
RANGERS (0) 3   AIRDRIE (0) 1
Bett (53), Paterson (67),   Flood (80)
Black (82)

RANGERS: Stewart; McKinnon, Black; McClelland, Paterson, Bett; Prytz, Kennedy, McAdam, Redford, MacDonald (Davies)

AIRDRIE: Martin; N. Anderson, Rodger; McLaughlin, March, Gordon; Walker, McKeown, Millar, Flood, Coyle

Attendance: 9,500

August 21st:
CLYDEBANK (0) 1   RANGERS (1) 4
Ronald (53)   Prytz (14),
MacDonald 2 (60, 69),
McClelland (70)

CLYDEBANK: Gallagher; Treanor, Fallon, McGhee, Gervaise; Given, Hughes (McKeown), McCabe; Ronald, Williamson (Sinclair), Coyne

RANGERS: Stewart; McKinnon, McClelland, Paterson, Black (Kennedy); Prytz, Bett, Redford; Cooper, McAdam (Dawson), MacDonald

Attendance: 7,090

August 25th:
AIRDRIE (1) 1   RANGERS (1) 2
Millar (44)   Dalziel (23),
Paterson (76)

AIRDRIE: Martin; N. Anderson, Rodger; McLaughlin, March, Gordon; Faulds, McKeown, Millar, Flood, Coyle

RANGERS: Stewart; McKinnon, Black; McClelland, Paterson, Bett; Cooper, Prytz, Dalziel, Redford, MacDonald

Attendance: 6,000

August 28th:
RANGERS 0   HIBERNIAN 0

RANGERS: Stewart; McKinnon, Paterson, McClelland, Black; Prytz, Bett, Redford; Cooper, McAdam, MacDonald

HIBERNIAN: McArthur; Sneddon, McNamara, Jamieson, Turnbull; Callachan, Flavell, Duncan; Rae (Murray), Rodier (McWilliams), Thomson

Attendance: 17,600

September 1st:
RANGERS (0) 3   CLYDEBANK (1) 2
MacDonald (62),   Williamson (24),
Prytz (73 pen), Redford (85)   Treanor (66)

RANGERS: Stewart; McKinnon, Black; McClelland, Paterson, Bett; Cooper, Prytz, Dalziel (Mackay), Redford, MacDonald

CLYDEBANK: Gallacher; Treanor, Gervais; Fallon, McGhie, Given; Ronald, Hughes, Williamson, Coyne, McCabe

Attendance: 6,300. Coyne was ordered off.

Section Table

	P	W	D	L	F	A	Pts
1 RANGERS	6	4	2	0	13	6	10
2 Hibernian	6	1	4	1	6	6	6
3 Airdrie	6	2	1	3	9	11	5
4 Clydebank	6	1	1	4	8	13	3

September 22nd: Quarter-Final First Leg
KILMARNOCK (0) 1   RANGERS (2) 6
McLean (51)   Cooper 4 (20, 21, 62, 79),
MacDonald 2 (49, 52)

KILMARNOCK: McCulloch; McLean, Cockburn; J. Clark, Armstrong, McDicken; Bryson, MacLeod, Eadie, Mauchlen, Gallagher

RANGERS: Stewart; McKinnon, Dawson; McClelland, Paterson (McAdam), Bett; Cooper, Prytz, Johnstone, Russell (Redford), MacDonald

Attendance: 8,000

October 6th: Quarter-Final Second Leg
RANGERS   (3) 6   KILMARNOCK   (0) 0
  MacDonald 2 (15, 85),
  Johnstone 2 (17, 82),
  McPherson (34), Bett (67 pen)

RANGERS: Stewart; McKinnon, Redford;
McClelland, Paterson, Bett (Black); Cooper (Davies),
McPherson, Johnstone, Russell, MacDonald

KILMARNOCK: McCulloch; McLean, MacLeod; J.
Clark, Clarke, McDicken; McGivern, McClurg, Bourke
(Bryson), Mauchlen, Gallagher

Attendance: 6,000. Rangers won 12-1 on aggregate

October 27th: Semi-Final First Leg
RANGERS   (0) 2   HEARTS   (0) 0
  Cooper (84), Bett (86)

RANGERS: Stewart; McKinnon, Redford;
McClelland, Stevens, Bett; Cooper, Prytz, Johnstone,
Russell, McAdam (MacDonald) — Dawson

HEARTS: Smith; Kidd, Shields; Byrne, R.
MacDonald, Jardine; Bowman, Pettigrew, O'Connor,
McLaren, A. MacDonald — Johnston, Mackay

Attendance: 22,500

After stout resistance Davie Cooper scored for Rangers in
the last 6 minutes and, as so often happens, Bett breached
the hard-pressed Hearts defence again 2 minutes later.

November 10th: Semi-Final Second Leg
HEARTS   (1) 1   RANGERS   (1) 2
  O'Connor (37)   Bett (20 pen),
                         Johnstone (82)

HEARTS: Smith; Kidd, Shields; Byrne, R.
MacDonald, Jardine; Bowman, Robertson (Pettigrew),
O'Connor, Mackay, Johnston —McLaren

RANGERS: Stewart; McKinnon, Dawson;
McClelland, Stevens, Bett; Cooper (Dalziel), Redford,
Johnstone, Russell (McPherson), MacDonald

Attendance: 18,893

Hearts failed to prevent Rangers from reaching the League
Cup Final. They had to recover from a penalty in 20
minutes to equalise through O'Connor before the interval.
With 8 minutes remaining Rangers scored the winner
when Derek Johnstone headed in Cooper's free-kick. They
won 4-1 on aggregate.

December 4th: Final   At Hampden Park
CELTIC   (2) 2   RANGERS   (0) 1
  Nicholas (22), MacLeod (31)   Bett (46)

CELTIC: Bonner; McGrain, Sinclair; Aitken,
McAdam, MacLeod; Provan, McStay (Reid),
McGarvey, Burns, Nicholas —McCluskey

RANGERS: Stewart; McKinnon, Redford;
McClelland, Paterson, Bett; Cooper, Prytz (Dawson),
Johnstone, Russell (MacDonald), Smith

Attendance: 55,372   *Referee*: K. Hope (Clarkston)

On a drab, rainy afternoon Celtic dominated the first half,
scoring 2 goals, but Rangers scored immediately after the
interval and battled to the finish.

SCOTTISH CUP

January 29th: Third Round
FALKIRK   (0) 0   RANGERS   (0) 2
                         Oliver o.g. (54),
                         Kennedy (60)

FALKIRK: Watson; Nicol, Brown, Mackin, Hoggan;
Oliver, McCully (Stevenson), Love; Perry, Houston,
Forrest

RANGERS: McCloy; Dawson, Stevens, McClelland,
Black; Bett, Prytz, Redford; Cooper, Kennedy,
Johnstone (Dalziel)

Attendance: 14,700

February 19th: Fourth Round
RANGERS   (0) 2   FORFAR ATHLETIC   (1) 1
  MacDonald 2 (59, 78)   MacDonald (41)

RANGERS: McCloy; Dawson, McClelland,
McPherson, Black; Prytz (Robertson), Bett, Redford;
Dalziel, Kennedy, MacDonald

FORFAR: Kennedy; Bennett, Brown, Brash, McPhee;
Farningham, Weir (Leitch), Lorimer; Cormack (Clark),
Gallacher, MacDonald

Attendance: 14,500

March 12th: Quarter-Final
QUEENS PARK   (0) 1   RANGERS   (2) 2
  Gilmour (62 pen)   Dalziel (15),
                           Cooper (43)

QUEENS PARK: Atkins; Cairns, Cook, Woods,
Dickson; McNiven, Crawley, Graham; Nicholson
(Quinn), Grant, Gilmour

RANGERS: McCloy; McKinnon, McPherson,
Paterson (Lyall), McClelland; Prytz, Bett, Redford;
Cooper, Dalziel, Kennedy (McAdam)

Attendance: 13,716

April 16th: Semi-Final   At Celtic Park
RANGERS   (0) 1   ST MIRREN   (0) 1
  Clark (72)   Paterson o.g. (84)

RANGERS: McCloy; Dawson, McClelland;
McPherson, Paterson, Bett; Russell, McKinnon, Clark,
Redford, Cooper —MacDonald, Dalziel

ST MIRREN: Thomson; Wilson, Clarke; Fitzpatrick (Somner), McCormack, Fulton; Stark, McAvennie, McDougall, Abercrombie (Richardson), Scanlon

Attendance: 31,102

Rangers created more chances than St Mirren. Sandy Clark missed a marvellous opportunity just before the interval. Both he and Bett always looked threatening but lacked the service needed from their colleagues. St Mirren seemed to have left it much too late before the unfortunate Craig Paterson stuck out a foot to divert a mis-hit Scanlon cross past a stunned McCloy.

April 19th: Semi-Final Replay At Hampden Park
RANGERS   (0) 1   ST MIRREN   (0) 0
                                  After Extra Time
   Clark (118)

RANGERS: McCloy; Dawson, McClelland; McPherson, Paterson, Bett; Russell, McKinnon, Clark, Redford (MacDonald), Cooper (Prytz)

ST MIRREN: Thomson; Wilson, Clarke (Fitzpatrick); Richardson, Fulton, McCormack; McDougall, McAvennie, Somner, Abercrombie, Scanlon (Logan)

Attendance: 25,125

St Mirren left Hampden convinced they had been harshly treated by referee Brian McGinlay who awarded Rangers the winning goal amid controversy 90 seconds from the end of extra-time. If Rangers had the best of the first half Saints were undoubtably superior in the 2nd, but until the dramatic ending neither side had looked capable of scoring.

May 21st: Final   At Hampden Park
ABERDEEN   (0) 1   RANGERS   (0) 0
                                  After Extra Time
   Black (116)

ABERDEEN: Leighton; Rougvie (Watson), McMaster; Cooper, McLeish, Miller; Strachan, Simpson, McGhee, Black, Weir (Hewitt)

RANGERS: McCloy; Dawson, McClelland; McPherson, Paterson, Bett; Cooper (Davies), McKinnon, Clark, Russell, MacDonald (Dalziel)

Attendance: 62,979   *Referee*: D. Syme (Rutherglen)

This Scottish Cup Final rounded off a season of disappointment for the Ibrox club. It should have ended in victory against a jaded-looking Aberdeen side who never rose above the mediocre. Rangers, however, could not cash in. Their attack was practically non-existent and the Cup went North for the second year running.

U.E.F.A. CUP

September 1th: First Round First Leg
BORUSSIA DORTMUND   0   RANGERS   0
BORUSSIA DORTMUND: Immel; Huber, Loose; Russmann, Bonighausen, Tenhagen; Zorc, Burgsmuller, Radacanu, Klotz, Keser (Koch)

RANGERS: Stewart; McKinnon, Dawson; McClelland, Paterson, Bett; Cooper, Prytz (Miller), Johnstone, Russell, Redford

Attendance: 54,000

An impressive, disciplined performance allowed Rangers to leave the Westfalen Stadium with a marvellous chance of progressing in the competition. The twin centre-half backs McClelland and Paterson were tremendous and the skills of Russell, Bett and Prytz in midfield were better than anything the Germans could produce.

September 29th: First Round Second Leg
RANGERS   (1) 2   BORUSSIA DORTMUND   (0) 0
   Cooper (44),
   Johnstone (83)

RANGERS: Stewart; McKinnon, McClelland, Paterson, Dawson; Russell (Redford), Bett, Prytz; Cooper, Johnstone, MacDonald

BORUSSIA DORTMUND: Immel; Huber, Loose, Koch, Bonighausen; Tenhagen, Zorc, Radacanu (Abramczik); Burgsmuller, Eggeling (Klotz), Keser

Attendance: 44,000

Rangers moved smoothly into the Second Round. It was Swedish dynamo Robert Prytz who prodded and inspired Rangers to victory over a methodical German side. Rangers won 2-0 on aggregate.

October 20th: Second Round First Leg
RANGERS   (1) 2   COLOGNE   (0) 1
   Johnstone (9),   Allofs (60)
   McClelland (85)

RANGERS: Stewart; McKinnon, McClelland, Paterson (Stevens), Dawson (MacDonald); Bett, Prytz, Russell; Cooper, Johnstone, Redford

COLOGNE: Schumacher; Konopka (Zimmermann), Strack, Steiner, Prestin; Bonhof, Slijvo, Cullmann; Engels, Littbarski, K. Allofs (Willmer)

Attendance: 32,000

Rangers kept their U.E.F.A. Cup hopes only just alive after an agonising First Leg tie. In a furious finish Cooper took a free-kick on the right and McClelland was there to head past Allofs. Just before the end McKinnon was unlucky with a great drive which Schumacher saved brilliantly.

November 3rd: Second Round Second Leg
COLOGNE (4) 5   RANGERS (0) 0
Littbarski (7), Engels 2 (11, 21 pen),
Fischer (19), Allofs (52)

COLOGNE: Schumacher; Prestin, Strack, Steiner,
Willmer; Konopka, Slijvo, Engels; Littbarski, Fischer,
K. Allofs (Cullmann)

RANGERS: Stewart; McKinnon, McClelland,
Stevens, Dawson; Russell, Prytz, Bett; Redford
(McAdam), Cooper (MacDonald), Johnstone

Attendance: 61,000. Willmer was ordered off.

Leading 2-1 from the First Leg, Rangers were 5-2 down on
aggregate within 21 minutes of the return. Ironically
before the onslaught began Rangers almost scored when a
Derek Johnstone shot dipped just behind the bar. In 52
minutes Engels sent over a high cross from the left to Allofs
who headed past Stewart. The Germans were reduced to
10 men 11 minutes from time when Willmer was sent off
after a clash with McAdam. Cologne won 6-2 on aggregate.

GOALSCORERS

League: MacDonald 10, Bett 6 (1 pen), Johnstone 6,
Prytz 5 (2 pens), Cooper 5, Clark 4, Redford 3,
Dalziel 3, Kennedy 3, McClelland 2, Russell 1,
McKinnon 1, Black 1, McPherson 1, Own Goal
1

League Cup: MacDonald 8, Cooper 5, Bett 5 (2 pens),
Johnstone 3, Paterson 2, Prytz 2 (1 pen),
Black 1, McClelland 1, Dalziel 1, Redford
1, McKinnon 1

Scottish Cup: Clark 2, MacDonald 2, Kennedy 1,
Dalziel 1, Cooper 1, Own Goal 1

U.E.F.A.: Johnstone 2, Cooper 1, McClelland 1

APPEARANCES

	League	League Cup	Scottish Cup	U.E.F.A.
Stewart	18	11	-	4
McCloy	17	-	6	-
McKinnon	30+1S	11	4	4
Dawson	24+1S	3+2S	5	4
McClelland	35	11	6	4
Paterson	20	9	4	3
Bett	35	11	6	4
Cooper	26+5S	9	5	4
Prytz	24+6S	9	3+1S	4
McAdam	2+2S	5+1S	0+1S	0+1S
Redford	29+4S	10+1S	5	3+1S
MacDonald	25+3S	9+2S	2+1S	1+2S
Johnstone	18	5	1	4
Russell	18+3S	5	3	4
Stevens	10	2	1	1+1S
Dalziel	7+7S	2+1S	2+2S	-
McPherson	15+5S	1+1S	5	-
Smith	1+1S	1	-	-
Mackay	2+3S	0+2S	-	-
Kennedy	12+1S	1+1S	3	-
Black	11+4S	5+1S	2	-
Robertson	2+2S	-	0+1S	-
Davies	2+2S	0+3S	0+1S	-
Lyall	2+2S	-	0+1S	-
Clark	10	-	3	-
Bruce	1	-	-	-
Miller	-	1	-	-
Forsyth	-	-	-	-

Action from a EUFA Cup match at Ibrox
in September 1986 against Ilves Tampere
of Finland. Rangers won by 4 goals to nil.
Here Ted McMinn is seen in a forward
run.

Season 1983–84

This was another dramatic season in Rangers' history. John Greig eventually gave way to the pressure that continued lack of success brings and resigned on October 28th. During his time in charge Rangers had played 189 League matches, winning 81, drawing 52 and losing 56. They had won the Scottish Cup twice and the League Cup twice. Their best League performance was when they finished second in Greig's first season. Aberdeen's Alex Ferguson was approached to take over and refused and Dundee United's Jim McLean also turned down the job. Third choice was former manager Jock Wallace, the manager of Motherwell. He accepted the job and Rangers had to pay the Fir Park club £125,000 to buy out his long-term contract. Following the appointment of Wallace results immediately picked up and after losing at Pittodrie on November 12th the club went 15 matches without defeat. By the end of the season they were 4th in the Table — 15 points behind the Champions Aberdeen. As is usually the case when a new manager takes over there were a number of personnel changes. Tommy McLean, Joe Mason and Davie Provan left the club and Alec Totten was appointed as First Team Coach with John Hagart taking over as Reserve Team Coach. Bobby Williamson was signed from Clydebank for £100,000, Nicky Walker was recruited from Motherwell and Stuart Munro arrived from Alloa. At the end of the season Iain Ferguson was signed from Dundee on freedom of contract — a tribunal set his transfer fee at £200,000 and his club mate Cammy Fraser was signed in the same manner. His transfer fee was set at £165,000. Youngsters Gordon Dalziel, Kenny Lyall and Kenny Black were all transferred.

The club ran up a record score in the First Round of the Cup Winners Cup against Valetta of Malta but in the next round a shocking mistake by McCloy 3 minutes from time in the first leg at Ibrox gave Portugal's F.C. Porto an all-important away goal which eventually settled the tie.

Having beaten Dunfermline and Inverness Caledonian in the earlier rounds, Rangers faced Dundee in the 5th round of the Scottish Cup. The clubs fought out a 2-2 draw at Dens Park. Rangers found themselves 2-0 down in the replay at Ibrox, fought back to level through goals from McClelland and McPherson, but a late goal from Iain Ferguson put them out of the Cup.

Rangers did win the League Cup for the 12th time. Queen of the South were beaten 8-1 on aggregate in the First Round. The sectional stage was won without a point being dropped or a goal conceded and included a fine 5-0 win over St Mirren at Ibrox. They gained a 1-1 draw against Dundee United in the first leg of the Semi-Final and settled the tie at Ibrox with fine goals from Clark and Redford. The Final against Celtic was a thriller. Rangers were 2-0 up at one stage but Celtic fought back to force extra-time with a last-minute penalty. 4 minutes from the end of the extra period McCoist was sent crashing in the box by Aitken. His penalty was blocked by Bonner but the Ranger followed up to score, completing his hat-trick in the process.

League: Fourth
League Cup: Winners
Scottish Cup: Fifth Round
Cup Winners Cup: Second Round

SCOTTISH PREMIER LEAGUE

August 20th:
RANGERS (0) 1   ST MIRREN (1) 1
  Prytz (54 pen)   McAvennie (43)

RANGERS: McCloy; Dawson, McPherson, Paterson (MacDonald), McClelland; Russell, Prytz, Redford (Davies); Cooper, Clark, McCoist

ST MIRREN: Thomson; Wilson, Fulton, McCormack, Clarke; Fitzpatrick, Richardson, Abercrombie; McAvennie (McDougall), Logan (McEachran), Scanlon

Attendance: 25,000. Scanlon was ordered off.

September 1st: Derek Johnstone was transferred to Chelsea for £30,000.

September 3rd:
CELTIC (1) 2   RANGERS (1) 1
  Aitken (8), McGarvey (86)   McCoist (33 secs)

CELTIC: Bonner; McGrain, Whittaker; Aitken, W. McStay, MacLeod; Provan, P. McStay, McGarvey, Burns; Melrose (McClair)

RANGERS: McCloy; McKinnon, Dawson; McPherson, McClelland, Redford; Prytz, McCoist, Clark, Russell, Mitchell

Attendance: 50,662

Rangers got off to a sensational start when McCoist scored with only 33 seconds on the clock. With only 4 minutes remaining for play Celtic hit Rangers on the break. Burns shot against McCloy, Provan did the same but even while on the ground the little winger showed marvellous reflexes to push the ball back for McGarvey to shoot into the net for the winner and Celtic's 50th Premier League goal against their old rivals.

September 10th:
HEARTS (2) 3   RANGERS (0) 1
  A. MacDonald (9),   Mitchell (63)
  Robertson (29), Bone (46)

HEARTS: Smith; Kidd, Cowie; Jardine, R. MacDonald, McLaren; Bowman, Robertson, Bone, A. MacDonald, Park

RANGERS: McCloy; Dawson, McClelland; McPherson, Paterson, Redford (McKinnon); Cooper, McCoist, Clark, Russell (Prytz), Mitchell

Attendance: 16,173

September 17th:
RANGERS (0) 0   ABERDEEN (0) 2
                     McGhee 2 (71, 79)

RANGERS: McCloy; Dawson, McPherson (Redford), Paterson, McClelland; Russell, McKinnon, Prytz (MacDonald); McCoist, Clark, Cooper

ABERDEEN: Leighton; Rougvie, Miller, McLeish, McMaster; Simpson, Cooper, Bell; Cowan (Hewitt), McGhee, Weir

Attendance: 27,500

Super sub John Hewitt steered a class Aberdeen side to victory just as it looked as if this exciting match was heading for a no-scoring draw. The nearest Rangers got to scoring was when Cooper kicked a Clark header off the line and when McCoist's shot, which had Leighton beaten, cannoned off a post. There was a demonstration after the match against the Management.

September 24th:
RANGERS (4) 6   ST JOHNSTONE (2) 3
  McCoist 2 (8, 35),   Kilgour (39 secs),
  McClelland (21),   Brogan 2 (27, 81)
  Prytz (33 pen),
  Cooper (66),
  Clark (74)

RANGERS: McCloy; Dawson, McClelland; McPherson, Paterson, McKinnon (Redford); Prytz, McCoist, Clark, Russell, Cooper

ST JOHNSTONE: McDonald; Kilgour, McVicar; Addison, Caldwell, Rutherford (Wright); Gibson, Brogan, Blair, Morton, Beedie

Attendance: 12,500

October 1st:
DUNDEE UNITED (0) 0   RANGERS (2) 2
                           McCoist (12),
                           Clark (39)

DUNDEE UNITED: McAlpine; Gough, Hegarty, Narey, Malpas; Stark, Holt (McGinnis), Bannon; Taylor (Payne), Kirkwood, Dodds

RANGERS: McCloy; Dawson, McPherson, Paterson, McClelland; Prytz (Russell), McKinnon, Redford; McCoist, Clark, Cooper

Attendance: 16,738

October 1st:
RANGERS (1) 1   HIBERNIAN (0) 0
  McClelland (13)

RANGERS: McCloy; Dawson, McPherson, Paterson, McClelland; Prytz, McKinnon, Redford (Mitchell), Cooper, Clark, McCoist

HIBERNIAN: Rough; Sneddon, Blackley, Jamieson, Schaedler; Brazil, McNamara, Turnbull; Murray (Duncan), Irvine, Thomson

Attendance: 21,500

October 15th:
DUNDEE (2) 3   RANGERS (1) 2
  Ferguson 2 (18, 80),   Russell (40),
  McCall (38)   Redford (52)

DUNDEE: R. Geddes; McKimmie, Smith,
MacDonald, McKinlay; A. Geddes (Mackie), Fraser,
Richardson; Ferguson, McCall, Stephen

RANGERS: McCloy; Dawson, McPherson, Paterson,
McClelland; Russell, McKinnon, Redford
(MacDonald); McCoist, Clark, Cooper

Attendance: 11,945

October 22nd:
RANGERS   (1) 1   MOTHERWELL   (0) 2
  McCoist (23 pen)   Ritchie (76 pen),
                           Burns (81)

RANGERS: Stewart; McKinnon, McPherson,
McClelland, Dawson; Russell (MacDonald), McCoist
(Prytz), Redford; Clark, Mitchell, Cooper

MOTHERWELL: Walker; Dornan, Carson,
Edvaldsson, MacLeod; Rafferty, Cormack (Burns),
Mauchlen; Forbes, Harrow (Ritchie), Alexander

Attendance: 15,000, MacLeod was ordered off. There was
another demonstration after the match by the fans.

**October 28th: Rangers were reported to be ready to
move for Billy Thomson of St Mirren.**

**October 27th: Northern Ireland International de-
fender Jimmy Nicholl was signed on a temporary
transfer from Toronto Blizzard. He was contracted
to stay with the club until April 25th.**

**October 28th: John Greig quit as manager: 'I'm
finished with the game'. He had been in charge for
just over 5 years. His assistant Tommy McLean was
put in temporary charge of the team.**

October 29th:
ST MIRREN   (1) 3   RANGERS   (0) 0
  Stevens o.g. (25),
  Jarvie (67), Scanlon (84)

ST MIRREN: Thomson; Clarke, Abercrombie;
McCormack, Fulton, McAvennie; Fitzpatrick, Speirs,
McDougall, Jarvie, Scanlon

RANGERS: Stewart; Nicholl, Lyall; McClelland,
Stevens, Russell (McPherson); Prytz, McCoist,
Mitchell, D. Ferguson (Cooper), MacDonald

Attendance: 12,068

League positions
	P	W	D	L	F	A	Pts
1 Aberdeen	10	7	1	2	26	7	15
2 Dundee United	9	7	1	1	22	7	15
3 Celtic	10	6	2	2	27	13	14
4 Hearts	10	6	2	2	13	8	14
5 Hibernian	10	5	0	5	15	20	10
6 RANGERS	10	3	1	6	15	19	7

**November 2nd: Aberdeen Manager Alex Ferguson
turned down an approach by Rangers and signed a
new 5-year contract with the Dons.**

November 5th:
RANGERS   (0) 1   CELTIC   (0) 2
  Clark (86)   McGarvey (53),
                          Burns (75)

RANGERS: McCloy; McKinnon, Paterson,
McClelland, Dawson; Nicholl, McPherson, Redford;
McCoist (Cooper), Clark, Mitchell (MacDonald)

CELTIC: Bonner; McGrain, McAdam, W. McStay,
Whittaker; P. McStay, MacLeod, Burns; Provan
(Melrose), McGarvey, McClair

Attendance: 40,000

Rangers had the slight edge in the first half but Celtic's
class told in the end.

**November 7th: Jim McLean of Dundee United
turned down a move to Ibrox and a salary reported
to be £65,000 a year.**

**November 10th: Rangers appointed former Manager
Jock Wallace as their new Manager. They had to pay
Motherwell £125,000 to buy out Wallace's contract.
His salary at Ibrox was reported to be £60,000 a year.**

November 12th:
ABERDEEN   (2) 3   RANGERS   (0) 0
  Simpson (5), Hewitt (10),
  Porteous (67)

ABERDEEN: Leighton; Cooper, McLeish, Miller,
Rougvie; Simpson, Strachan, Bell; Hewitt (Angus),
McGhee, Weir (Porteous)

RANGERS: McCloy; McKinnon, Paterson,
McClelland, Dawson; Nicholl, McPherson, Redford;
McCoist, Mitchell (Kennedy), Cooper (Russell)

Attendance: 23,000

After early goals by Simpson and Hewitt. Aberdeen were
coasting. Rangers were allowed to come into the game after
Aberdeen's devastating opening but their hurried, almost
panicky, attempts at finishing off moves were testament to
their psychological disarray. This was Rangers' 5th
successive League defeat, a run which must be some kind
of record.

**November 18th: Falkirk Manager Alec Totten
joined Rangers as first-team coach. Tommy McLean
and Joe Mason left the club.**

November 19th:
RANGERS   0   DUNDEE UNITED   0

RANGERS: McCloy; McKinnon, Dawson;
McClelland, Paterson, McPherson; Nicholl (Russell),
McCoist, Clark, Redford, Cooper (Mitchell)

DUNDEE UNITED: McAlpine; Kirkwood, Malpas; Gough, Hegarty, Narey; Bannon, Milne (Johnstone), Coyne, Holt, Dodds

Attendance: 27,800

November 26th:
ST JOHNSTONE   (0) 0   RANGERS   (1) 1
                                        Redford (32)

ST JOHNSTONE: Baines; Kilgour, Kennedy, Rutherford, McVicar (Wright); Gibson, Addison, Morton; Beedie, Brogan (Lyons), Blair

RANGERS: McCloy; Nicholl, McClelland, McAdam, Dawson; McPherson, Prytz (Russell), Redford; McCoist (Kennedy), Clark, Cooper

Attendance: 9,740

November 26th: John Hagart was appointed as reserve team coach.

November 29th: Ian Wallace of Nottingham Forest rejected a £100,000 transfer to Ibrox.

November 29th: Youth coach Davie Provan left Ibrox.

November 30th: Gordon Dalziel was transferred to Manchester City for £25,000.

December 3rd:
RANGERS   (1) 3   HEARTS   (0) 0
  Clark 2 (34, 70),
  MacDonald (78)

RANGERS: McCloy; Nicholl, Dawson; McClelland, McAdam, Redford; Russell, Mitchell (Prytz), Clark, McPherson (MacDonald), Cooper

HEARTS: Smith; Kidd, Cowie; Jardine, MacDonald, Levein; Bowman, Mackay, Bone (O'Connor), Robertson, Park (Johnston)

Attendance: 22,500

December 7th: Bobby Williamson was signed from Clydebank for £100,000. Eric Ferguson joined Clydebank on 6 months' loan.

December 10th:
MOTHERWELL   (0) 0   RANGERS   (1) 3
                                    McAdam (35),
                                    Cooper (60),
                                    Mitchell (76)

MOTHERWELL: Walker; Dornan, Wark; MacLeod, Carson, Mauchlen; Gahagan (Cormack), McAllister, Alexander (Gillespie), Forbes, McFadden

RANGERS: McCloy; Nicholl, Dawson; McClelland, McAdam, Redford; Russell, Williamson (MacDonald), Clark (Mitchell), McPherson, Cooper

Attendance: 13,586. Redford and Forbes both missed penalties.

December 13th: McClelland and Nicholl were in the Northern Ireland side which beat Scotland 2-0 in Belfast.

December 17th:
RANGERS   (1) 2   DUNDEE   (1) 1
  Russell (23),   A. Geddes (9)
  Williamson (81)

RANGERS: McCloy; Nicholl, Dawson; McClelland, Paterson (McKinnon), Prytz; Russell, Williamson, Clark (MacDonald), McPherson, Cooper

DUNDEE: R. Geddes; Glennie, McKinlay; Richardson, Smith, MacDonald; Mackie, Stephen, Ferguson, McCall, A. Geddes

Attendance: 16,500

League positions

	P	W	D	L	F	A	Pts
1 Aberdeen	17	13	2	2	43	9	28
2 Celtic	17	11	3	3	42	19	25
3 Dundee United	16	9	3	4	31	15	21
4 Hibernian	17	8	1	8	27	29	17
5 Hearts	17	6	5	6	18	22	17
6 RANGERS	17	7	2	8	25	25	16

December 17th: Rangers signed Nicky Walker from Motherwell. Kenny Black and Kenny Lyall joined the Fir Park club who also received a fee of £50,000. The deal was valued at £100,000.

December 20th: Willie Waddell became an Honorary Director of the club.

December 27th:
HIBERNIAN   (0) 0   RANGERS   (1) 2
                                    Williamson (42),
                                    Cooper (74)

HIBERNIAN: Rough; Sneddon, Schaedler; Brazil, Jamieson, Blackley; Callachan, Turnbull, Irvine, Thomson, Duncan

RANGERS: Walker; Nicholl, Dawson; McClelland, Paterson, Prytz; Russell, McPherson, Clark (Burns), Williamson, Cooper (MacDonald)

Attendance: 20,820. Nicholl was ordered off in the 46th minute.

December 31st:
RANGERS   (1) 1   ST MIRREN   (1) 1
  Clark (n.a.)   McDougall (n.a.)

RANGERS: Walker; Dawson, Redford; McClelland, McAdam, Prytz (MacDonald); Russell, Williamson (Burns), Clark, McPherson, Cooper

ST MIRREN: Thomson; Hamilton, Abercrombie; Cooper, Fulton, McCormack; Fitzpatrick, McAvennie, McDougall, Jarvie, Scanlon

Attendance: 21,200

January 7th:
RANGERS   (0) 1   ABERDEEN   (0) 1
  Cooper (48 pen)   Hewitt (68)

RANGERS: Walker; Fraser, Dawson; McClelland,
McAdam, Redford; Russell, Williamson, Clark
(MacDonald), McPherson (Prytz), Cooper

ABERDEEN: Leighton; McKimmie, Rougvie;
Simpson (Cooper), McLeish, Miller; Strachan, Black,
McGhee, Bell (Hewitt), Weir

Attendance: 37,500. Dawson and Black were ordered off
for fighting.

Since Jock Wallace returned to Ibrox Davie Cooper had
continually been at his best and was again the top
entertainer.

**January 11th: Hearts signed Gregor Stevens on 1
month's loan.**

January 21st:
RANGERS   (2) 2   ST JOHNSTONE   (0) 0
  Clark (3), Russell (16)

RANGERS: Walker; Fraser, Redford; McAdam,
McClelland, Prytz; Russell, McPherson, Clark
(McCoist), Williamson (MacDonald), Mackay

ST JOHNSTONE: Baines; Rutherford, McVicar;
Lyons, Kennedy, Caldwell (Harvey); Gibson (Brogan),
Blair, Scott, Morton, Brannigan

Attendance: 17,000

**February 3rd: Stuart Munro was signed from Alloa
Athletic for £15,000.**

February 4th:
RANGERS   (2) 2   MOTHERWELL   (1) 1
  McCoist (15),   Harrow (16)
  Prytz (38 pen)

RANGERS: Walker; Nicholl, McClelland, McAdam
(McPherson), Dawson; Russell, Redford, Prytz,
McCoist, Williamson, Cooper (Mackay)

MOTHERWELL: Sproat; Dornan, MacLeod,
Edvaldsson (McFadden), Black; McAllister, Harrow,
Lyall; Rafferty, Gillespie (McBride), Gahagan

Attendance: 17,000

February 4th: Jim Stewart was loaned to Dumbarton.

**February 10th: Tom Leeman was signed from
Glentoran for £25,000.**

February 11th:
HEARTS   (0) 2   RANGERS   (1) 2
  O'Connor (88),   McCoist (31),
  Robertson (90)   Williamson (47)

HEARTS: Smith; Kidd, Cowie; Jardine, Stevens,
McLaren; Levein (Johnston), Robertson, Bone
(O'Connor), Shields, Mackay

RANGERS: Walker; Nicholl, Dawson; McClelland,
Paterson, Redford; Russell, Prytz, Williamson
(MacDonald), McCoist (McPherson), Cooper

Attendance: 18,063

February 25th:
DUNDEE   (1) 1   RANGERS   (2) 3
  Harris (1)   Russell (27),
                         Cooper (28),
                         McPherson (58)

DUNDEE: Blair; McGeachie, McKinlay; Fraser,
Smith, Glennie; Mackie (MacDonald), Harris,
Ferguson, Stephen, McGlashan

RANGERS: McCloy; Nicholl, Dawson; McClelland,
McPherson, Redford; Russell (Munro), Prytz, Clark,
McCoist (Williamson), Cooper

Attendance: 11,750

League positions
	P	W	D	L	F	A	Pts
1 Aberdeen	23	18	3	2	59	12	39
2 Celtic	24	15	5	4	57	26	35
3 Dundee United	21	12	5	4	40	20	29
4 RANGERS	24	11	5	8	38	31	27
5 St Mirren	24	6	11	7	35	35	23

**February 28th: Davie Cooper was in the Scotland
team which beat Wales 2-1 at Hampden Park. He
scored Scotland's opening goal from the penalty
spot.**

March 3rd:
RANGERS   0   HIBERNIAN   0

RANGERS: Walker; Nicholl, Dawson; McClelland,
McPherson, Redford; Russell, Prytz (Munro), Clark
(Mitchell), McCoist, Cooper

HIBERNIAN: R. Rae; McKee, Schaedler; Sneddon,
G. Rae, Rice; Kane (Brazil), Jamieson, Irvine, Turnbull,
Duncan (Callachan)

Attendance: 16,000

March 6th:
ST JOHNSTONE   (0) 1   RANGERS   (2) 4
  Blair (65)   Redford (10),
                              Clark (33),
                              Davies (80), McCoist
                              (85)

ST JOHNSTONE: Baines; Kilgour, Morton; Lyons,
Caldwell, Rutherford; Barron, Blair, Scott, Sludden,
Beedie

RANGERS: Walker; Fraser, Dawson; McClelland,
McPherson, Redford; Munro (Davies), Prytz, Clark
(Mitchell), McCoist, Cooper

Attendance: 5,293

March 31st:
MOTHERWELL (0) 0   RANGERS (0) 3
                            Paterson (65),
                            McPherson (70),
                            Burns (87)

MOTHERWELL: Sproat; Kennedy (Gahagan), Lyall; Forbes, MacLeod, Boyd; McFadden, Rafferty, Alexander, Black (Grant), Harrow

RANGERS: McCloy; Nicholl, Dawson; McClelland, Paterson, McPherson; Russell (Redford), McCoist (Burns), Clark, Williamson, Cooper

Attendance: 8,574

April 2nd:
CELTIC (1) 3   RANGERS (0) 0
P. McStay (31), W. McStay (69),
Provan (84)

CELTIC: Bonner; McGrain, Reid; Aitken, McAdam, W. McStay; McClair, P. McStay, Melrose (McGarvey), MacLeod, Burns (Provan)

RANGERS: McCloy; Nicholl, Dawson; McClelland, Paterson, McPherson; Russell (Redford), McCoist, Clark, Williamson, Cooper (Burns)

Attendance: 53,229

Just 8 days after having lost in extra time in the Final of the League Cup Celtic produced some devastating form.

April 7th:
RANGERS 0   HEARTS (0)

RANGERS: McCloy; Nicholl, McClelland, Paterson, Dawson; McCoist (McPherson), Prytz, Redford; Fleck (Clark), Williamson, Cooper

HEARTS: Smith; Kidd, Jardine, MacDonald, Cowie; Mackay, Bowman, Levein; Park, Bone, Robertson

Attendance: 22,000

April 21st:
RANGERS (0) 1   CELTIC (0) 0
  Williamson (55)

RANGERS: McCloy; Nicholl, McClelland; McPherson, Paterson, Redford; Russell, Prytz (McKinnon), Williamson (MacDonald), McCoist, Cooper

CELTIC: Bonner; McGrain, Reid; Grant (Provan), McAdam, W. McStay; McClair, P. McStay, McGarvey (Melrose), MacLeod, Burns

Attendance: 40,260

Williamson's opportunism gave Rangers the edge and his goal, scored with a spectacular overhead kick, was worthy of winning any match. Rangers had to play for almost half an hour with 10 men when Jimmy Nicholl, playing his last game for the club before returning to Toronto Blizzard, was sent off for retaliating against McClair. Despite their

handicap Rangers' defence stood firm with Paterson and McPherson immense and McClelland organising brilliantly.

April 28th:
ST MIRREN (1) 1   RANGERS (1) 1
  McCormack (29)   Williamson (7)

ST MIRREN: Money; Hamilton (Cooper), Clarke; McCormack, Fulton, McGregor (Logan); Alexander, McAvennie, McDougall, Abercrombie, Speirs

RANGERS: McCloy; McKinnon, McClelland; McPherson, Paterson, Redford; Russell (Clark), Prytz (MacDonald), Williamson, McCoist, Cooper

Attendance: 8,092

May 2nd:
RANGERS (1) 2   DUNDEE UNITED (1) 2
  Clark (24),   Sturrock (4),
  Williamson (49)   Dodds (86)

RANGERS: McCloy; Fraser, McClelland; McPherson, Paterson, Redford; Russell, Williamson, Clark, McCoist, Cooper

DUNDEE UNITED: McAlpine; Malpas, Munro; Gough, Hegarty, Narey; Bannon, Holt, Clark (Taylor), Sturrock, Dodds

Attendance: 5,000

May 5th:
RANGERS (1) 2   DUNDEE (0) 2
  Redford (27),   McKinlay (60),
  Cooper (69)   McCall (79)

RANGERS: McCloy; Fraser, McClelland; McPherson, McAdam, Redford (Davies); Russell, Prytz, Williamson, McCoist (E. Ferguson), Cooper

DUNDEE: Geddes; McInally, McKinlay; McGeachie, Smith, Glennie; Kidd (Hendry), Richardson, McCall, Shannon (Harris), Ferguson

Attendance: 12,000

May 9th:
ABERDEEN 0   RANGERS 0

ABERDEEN: Leighton; McIntyre, Rougvie; Cooper, McLeish, Miller; Porteous (Hewitt), Stark, McGhee, McKimmie, Cowan

RANGERS: McCloy; Fraser, McClelland; McPherson, Paterson, Redford; Russell, Williamson (E. Ferguson), Clark, McCoist, Cooper

Attendance: 16,000

Aberdeen's second goalless draw in 3 days enabled them to set a Premier Division Championship record of 57 points with one game still to play. Their back 4 and Jim Leighton prevented the opposition from scoring for the 21st time in the competition this season. Peter McCloy did most to make it another frustrating game for the Aberdeen strikers in a game which see-sawed from end to end.

May 12th:
HIBERNIAN   0   RANGERS   0
HIBERNIAN: Rough; McKee, Hunter, Blackley
(Rae), Schaedler; Sneddon, Callachan, Rice; McGachie,
Jamieson, Irvine

RANGERS: McCloy; Fraser, McPherson, Paterson,
McClelland; Russell, McCoist, Redford (Munro);
Cooper, Clark (McKinnon), E. Ferguson

Attendance: 9,134. McCloy saved a Rice penalty in the
73rd minute.

May 14th:
DUNDEE UNITED   (0) 1   RANGERS   (1) 2
   Dodds (89)   Prytz (44 pen),
                          McCoist (82)

DUNDEE UNITED: McAlpine; Malpas, Munro;
Gough, Hegarty, Narey; Bannon, Holt (Dodds), Coyne,
Sturrock, Taylor

RANGERS: McCloy; McKinnon, Dawson;
McPherson, McClelland, Munro; Prytz, McCoist, E.
Ferguson (Clark), MacDonald, Cooper

Attendance: 7,500

**May 15th: Gregor Stevens and Jim Stewart were
given free transfers.**

**May 16th: Dundee rejected a Rangers bid of £350,000
for Iain Ferguson and Cammy Fraser.**

**May 21st: Rangers signed Iain Ferguson on freedom
of contract. A tribunal had to decide the fee.**

**May 26th: Davie Cooper was in the Scotland team
which drew 1-1 with England at Hampden.**

**July 2nd: Rangers were ordered to pay Dundee a fee
of £200,000 for Iain Ferguson. They signed Cammy
Fraser from Dundee on freedom of contract. Again
a tribunal had to decide the fee.**

Premier League

	P	W	D	L	F	A	Pts
1 Aberdeen	36	25	7	4	78	21	57
2 Celtic	36	21	8	7	80	41	50
3 Dundee United	36	18	11	7	67	39	47
4 RANGERS	36	15	12	9	53	41	42
5 Hearts	36	10	16	10	38	47	36
6 St Mirren	36	9	14	13	55	59	32
7 Hibernian	36	12	7	17	45	55	31
8 Dundee	36	11	5	20	50	74	27
9 St Johnstone	36	10	3	23	36	81	23
10 Motherwell	36	4	7	25	31	75	15

LEAGUE CUP

August 24th: Second Round First Leg
RANGERS   (2) 4   QUEEN OF THE
   Clark (9),   SOUTH   (0) 0
   MacDonald 2 (35, 69),
   Prytz (61 pen)

RANGERS: McCloy; Dawson, McClelland;
McPherson, Paterson, (D. Ferguson), Russell; Prytz,
McCoist, Clark, MacDonald, Cooper (Davies)

QUEEN OF THE SOUTH: Davidson; Wilkie,
McLaren; McCluskey, Reynolds, Cloy (Young);
McMinn, Faulds (Cochrane), Dunlop, Gordon, J.
Robertson

Attendance: 8,000

August 27th: Second Round Second Leg
QUEEN OF THE   RANGERS   (1) 4
   SOUTH   (1) 1   Mitchell (3),
   Paterson o.g. (4)   McKinnon (70),
                            Cooper (81),
                            McCoist (83)

QUEEN OF THE SOUTH: Davidson; McLaren,
Gray; Cloy, Clark, McCluskey; McMinn (Faulds),
Young, Busby (Cochrane), J. Robertson, Muir

RANGERS: McCloy; Dawson, McClelland;
McPherson, Paterson, McKinnon; Russell, McCoist,
Mitchell, Redford (Prytz), MacDonald (Cooper)

Attendance: 7,350. Rangers won 8-1 on aggregate.

THIRD ROUND (Section Matches)
August 31st:
RANGERS   (1) 4   CLYDEBANK   (0) 0
   McCoist 2 (24, 70),
   Russell (55), Prytz (83)

RANGERS: McCloy; Dawson, McClelland;
McPherson, Paterson, Russell; Prytz, McCoist, Clark,
Mitchell (Redford), Cooper (MacDonald)

CLYDEBANK: Gallagher; Treanor, Gervaise; Fallon,
McGhie, Given; Ronald, Hughes, Williamson, Coyne,
McCabe

Attendance: 8,500

September 7th:
HEARTS   (0) 0   RANGERS   (1) 3
                            Gauld o.g. (39),
                            Clark 2 (51, 75)

HEARTS: Smith; Gauld, Cowie; Jardine, R.
MacDonald, A. MacDonald; Bowman, Mackay,
O'Connor (Pettigrew), Park, Johnston

RANGERS: McCloy; Dawson, McClelland;
McPherson, Paterson, Redford; Cooper, McCoist,
Clark, Russell, Mitchell

Attendance: 11,287

October 5th:
RANGERS (3) 5   ST MIRREN (0) 0
  Clark (13),
  McCoist 2 (22, 48),
  McClelland (38),
  Paterson (74)

RANGERS: McCloy; Dawson, McClelland; McPherson, Paterson, McKinnon (Russell); Prytz, McCoist, Clark, Redford, Cooper

ST MIRREN: Thomson; Walker (Alexander), Clarke; McCormack, Fulton, Abercrombie; Fitzpatrick, McAvennie, McDougall (McAveety), McEachran, Scanlon

Attendance: 11,000. Prytz missed a penalty.

October 26th:
RANGERS (1) 2   HEARTS (0) 0
  Prytz (34), Mitchell (83)

RANGERS: Stewart; McKinnon, Lyall; McClelland, Stevens (Black), Russell; Prytz, McCoist, Mitchell, D. Ferguson, MacDonald

HEARTS: Smith; Kidd, Shields; Jardine, R. MacDonald, Mackay; Bowman, O'Connor, Bone, A. MacDonald, Park

Attendance: 12,000

November 9th:
CLYDEBANK (0) 0   RANGERS (1) 3
                    Cooper (34),
                    McCoist (50),
                    McPherson (77)

CLYDEBANK: Gallagher; Dickson, Gervaise; Fallon, McGhie, Given; Ronald, Hughes, Williamson, McKeown, Murray

RANGERS: McCloy; McKinnon, Dawson; McClelland, Paterson, McPherson (MacDonald); McCoist, Nicholl (Russell), Mitchell, Redford, Cooper

Attendance: 3,612

November 30th:
ST MIRREN (0) 0   RANGERS (0) 1
                    Cooper (75)

ST MIRREN: Money; Clarke, Hamilton; McCormack (Docherty), Cooper, Winnie; Fitzpatrick, Jarvie (Walker), Alexander, McAvennie, Abercrombie

RANGERS: McCloy; Nicholl, Dawson; McClelland, McAdam, Redford; Russell (Prytz), McPherson, Clark (Mackay), Mitchell, Cooper

Attendance: 5,436

Section Table

	P	W	D	L	F	A	Pts
1 RANGERS	6	6	0	0	18	0	12
2 Hearts	6	2	2	2	9	9	6
3 Clydebank	6	1	2	3	6	14	4
4 St Mirren	6	0	2	4	6	16	2

February 14th: Semi-Final First Leg
DUNDEE UNITED (0) 1   RANGERS (0) 1
  Dodds (67)   Mitchell (85)

DUNDEE UNITED: McAlpine; Stark, Malpas; Gough, Hegarty, Narey; Holt, Milne, Kirkwood, Sturrock, Dodds

RANGERS: McCloy; Nicholl, Dawson; McClelland, Paterson, Redford; Russell, Prytz (McPherson), Clark, McCoist, Cooper (Mitchell)

Attendance: 14,569

Rangers displayed all the commitment demanded by manager Jock Wallace and simply would not concede defeat. Mitchell was brought on for Cooper and with 5 minutes left the young Australian levelled the scores with a great header from a Redford cross. It was no more than Rangers deserved for their efforts.

February 22nd: Semi-Final Second Leg
RANGERS (1) 2   DUNDEE UNITED (0) 0
  Clark (42),
  Redford (52)

RANGERS: McCloy; Nicholl, Dawson; McClelland, McPherson, Redford; Russell, Prytz, Clark (Burns), McCoist (Mitchell), Cooper

DUNDEE UNITED: McAlpine; Stark, Malpas; Gough, Hegarty, Narey; Bannon (Kirkwood), Milne (Clark), Holt, Sturrock, Dodds

Attendance: 37,100

The match was a personal triumph for Sandy Clark. Back in the side for the cup-tied Bobby Williamson, he set Rangers on the way to victory with a goal just before the interval and killed off United's hopes by setting up the 2nd for Ian Redford early in the 2nd half. For United it was the same sad Ibrox story of failure. Rangers won 3-1 on aggregate.

March 25th: Final   At Hampden Park
RANGERS (1) 3   CELTIC (0) 2
  McCoist 3 (44 pen, 61, 104)   McClair (67),
                                 Reid (89 pen)
                                 After Extra Time

RANGERS: McCloy; Nicholl, Dawson; McClelland, Paterson, McPherson; Russell, McCoist, Clark (McAdam), MacDonald (Burns), Cooper

CELTIC: Bonner; McGrain, Reid; Aitken, McAdam, MacLeod; Provan (Sinclair), P. McStay, McGarvey (Melrose), Burns, McClair

Attendance: 66,369   *Referee*: R. B. Valentine (Dundee)

This was an amazing Final with Celtic looking down and out only to come back battling from 2 down to equalise with a last-gasp penalty from Mark Reid which sent the game into extra time. 10 minutes into extra-time Sinclair came on for Provan. 4 minutes later McCoist was sent crashing by Aitken. This time Bonner blocked McCoist's kick but the Ranger followed up to score.

SCOTTISH CUP

January 28th: Third Round
RANGERS   (0) 2   DUNFERMLINE   (0) 1
  McAdam (81),   Stewart (58)
  McCoist (83)

RANGERS: Walker; Fraser, Nicholl; McClelland, McAdam, Redford; Russell, MacDonald (Prytz), Clark (McCoist), McPherson, Mackay

DUNFERMLINE: Whyte; Dall, Forrest; Forsyth, Wilcox, Donnelly (Watson); Smith (Hepburn), McCathie, Stewart, Morrison, Tait

Attendance: 14,500

February 18th: Fourth Round
INVERNESS   RANGERS   (2) 6
  CALEDONIAN   (0) 0   Redford (25),
                             Williamson 2 (32, 77),
                             Russell (68),
                             McCoist 2 (78, 87)

INVERNESS CALEY: MacDonald; Davidson, Mann; Dewar (Gibson), Summers, Corbett; Lisle, McIntosh (Baxter), Urquhart, Docherty, Robertson

RANGERS: McCloy; Nicholl, Dawson (McPherson); McClelland, Paterson, Redford; Russell (Clark), Prytz, Williamson, McCoist, Cooper

Attendance: 5,500

March 10th: Fifth Round
DUNDEE   (1) 2   RANGERS   (2) 2
  Ferguson (22),   McGeachie o.g. (12),
  Kidd (72)   Russell (25)

DUNDEE: Kelly; Glennie, McKinlay; Fraser, Smith, MacDonald; Stephen, McGeachie, Ferguson (Kidd), McCall, Harris

RANGERS: Walker; Nicholl, Dawson; McClelland, McPherson, Redford (Davies); Russell, Prytz, Williamson, McCoist (Clark), Cooper

Attendance: 17,097

March 17th: Fifth Round Replay
RANGERS   (0) 2   DUNDEE   (1) 3
  McClelland (73),   Smith (22),
  McPherson (80)   Ferguson 2 (63, 84)

RANGERS: Walker; Nicholl, McClelland, McPherson, Dawson; Russell, Prytz, Redford; Williamson (Clark), McCoist (Mitchell), Cooper

DUNDEE: Kelly; Mackie, Smith, MacDonald, Richardson; Fraser, Kidd, Stephen; Ferguson, McCall, Harris (Hendry)

Attendance: 21,000. Redford was ordered off.

CUP WINNERS CUP

September 14th: First Round First Leg
VALETTA (Malta)   (0) 0   RANGERS   (6) 8
                             McPherson 4 (16, 33, 41, 48),
                             Paterson (7),
                             Prytz 2 (36, 77 pen),
                             MacDonald (35)

VALETTA: Grima; Buckingham, Curmi; Grioli, Hili, Fenech; Seycheli, E. Farrugia, Micallef, Cremona, C. Farrugia

RANGERS: McCloy; Dawson, McClelland; McPherson, Paterson, McKinnon; Prytz, McCoist (Davies), Clark (D. Ferguson), MacDonald, Cooper

Attendance: 18,213

A so-professional Rangers went on the rampage. From the 7th minute when Paterson headed them into the lead the part-timers from Malta did not have a chance. The Ibrox men had their biggest-ever away win in Europe. Teenage defender Dave McPherson was the hero, scoring 4 including a first-half hat-trick.

September 28th: First Round Second Leg
RANGERS   (5) 10   VALETTA   (0) 0
  Mitchell 2 (1, 10),
  MacDonald 3 (4, 36, 62 pen),
  Dawson (16), Mackay (52),
  Redford 2 (55, 89), Davies (67)

RANGERS: Stewart; Dawson, McClelland; McPherson, Paterson (D. Ferguson), Redford; Prytz (Mackay), Davies, Mitchell, MacDonald, Cooper

VALETTA: Grima (Mifsud); Buckingham, Curmi; Grioli, Hili, Fenech; Micallef (Salebi), E. Farrugia, Seycheli, Cremona, L. Farrugia

Attendance: 11,500

John Greig's men scored 10 to add to their 8 goals in Cyprus two weeks before and it could easily have been much more. This was a record score in one match, an aggregate record and Scottish club record in Europe. Rangers won 18-0 on aggregate.

October 19th: Second Round First Leg
RANGERS (1) 2   F.C. PORTO
  Clark (35),   (Portugal) (0) 1
  Mitchell (83)   Jacques (87)

RANGERS: McCloy; Dawson, McClelland;
McPherson, Paterson, Redford; Prytz (Mitchell),
McCoist, Clark, Russell, Cooper (MacDonald)

F.C. PORTO: Ze Beto; Pinto, Inacio; Perreirra,
Eurico, Rodolfo; Frasco, Walsh (Magalhaes), Gomes,
Pachecco (Jacques), Costa

Attendance: 28,000

Rangers had taken a scarcely deserved 2-goal advantage
but a shocking mistake by McCloy 3 minutes from the end
let Porto off the hook. Rangers were not allowed much
space by the Porto defence and their cause was further
hindered by slack passing.

November 2nd: Second Round Second Leg
F.C. PORTO (0) 1   RANGERS (0) 0
  Gomes (53)

F.C. PORTO: Ze Beto; Pinto, Inacio; Perreirra,
Eurico, Rodolfo (Sousa); Frasco, Walsh, Gomes,
Pachecco, Costa (Magalhaes)

RANGERS: McCloy; McKinnon, McClelland,
Paterson, Dawson; McPherson, Cooper, Russell, Prytz
(McCoist); Redford, Clark (Mitchell)

Attendance: 60,000

Rangers' bold and ambitious bid to defend their slender
First-Leg lead was lost in the rain-drenched Antas
Stadium. Cooper, playing deep and wide on the right, was
looking good in the opening stages. Rangers were living
dangerously as the white shirts of Porto drove forward
with almost monotonous regularity. 6 minutes from half-
time Gomes had two splendid opportunities to score but
each time McCloy's reflexes were razor sharp. After only 8
minutes of the second-half their pressure paid off. Gomes'
goal earned him a payout of £1600 which had been put on
offer for the player who scored the winning goal. F.C.
Porto won on away goals. Aggregate 2-2.

Dave MacPherson (left) and Terry
Butcher mop up as Celtic's Paul McGugan
attempts to reach the ball in a Premier
League match at Ibrox in August, 1986.

APPEARANCES

	League	League Cup	Scottish Cup	Cup Winners Cup
McCloy	26	10	1	3
Dawson	28	10	3	4
McClelland	36	11	4	4
McPherson	32+4S	9+1S	3+1S	4
Paterson	21	8	1	4
Redford	28+4S	7+1S	4	3
Prytz	22+4S	6+2S	3+1S	4
McCoist	29+1S	10	3+1S	2+1S
Clark	27+3S	8	1+3S	3
Russell	27+4S	9+2S	4	2
Cooper	32+2S	9+1S	3+1S	4
MacDonald	2+15S	4+2S	1	2+1S
Davies	0+3S	0+1S	0+1S	1+1S
McKinnon	12+4S	4	-	2
Mitchell	7+5S	6+2S	0+1S	1+2S
Stewart	2	1	-	1
Nicholl	17	5	4	-
Lyall	1	1	-	-
Stevens	1	1	-	-
E. Ferguson	3+2S	-	-	-
Kennedy	0+2S	-	-	-
McAdam	8	1+1S	1	-
Williamson	16+1S	-	3	-
Walker	8	-	3	-
S. Fraser	7	-	1	-
Mackay	1+1S	0+1S	1	0+1S
Burns	0+4S	0+2S	-	-
Munro	2+3S	-	-	-
Fleck	1	-	-	-
D. Ferguson	-	1+1S	-	0+1S
Black	-	0+1S	-	-
I. Ferguson	-	-	-	-

GOALSCORERS

League: McCoist 9 (1 pen), Clark 9, Cooper 6 (1 pen),
Williamson 6, Prytz 4 (4 pens), Russell 4,
Redford 4, Mitchell 2, McClelland 2,
McPherson 2, MacDonald 1, McAdam 1,
Davies 1, Paterson 1, Burns 1

League Cup: McCoist 9 (1 pen), Clark 5, Mitchell 3,
Prytz 3 (1 pen), Cooper 3, MacDonald 2,
Redford 1, McKinnon 1, Russell 1,
McClelland 1, McPherson 1, Paterson 1,
Own Goal 1

Scottish Cup: McCoist 3, Williamson 2, Russell 2,
McAdam 1, Redford 1, McClelland 1,
McPherson 1, Own Goal 1

Cup Winners' Cup: McPherson 4, MacDonald 4,
Mitchell 3, Prytz 2 (1 pen),
Redford 2, Paterson 1, Dawson 1,
Mackay 1, Davies 1, Clark 1

Season 1984–85

Their League Cup win apart, this was another mediocre Season for the Ibrox club. Their League campaign started well — with only two reversals in their opening 20 matches — but their form dipped badly after the turn of the year and they won only 4 of the 16 matches played between January 1st and May 11th. For the 4th time in 5 years they drew 12 of their matches. For the 3rd successive season they finished 4th in the table but they were a massive 21 points behind Champions Aberdeen and 14 and 9 points respectively behind Celtic and Dundee United. They recorded only 1 victory out of the 12 matches played against the top 3 clubs. The course of their season seemed to change immediately after Irish international defender John McClelland left for Watford in early November. Their goals total was a pitiful 47 — 42 fewer than Aberdeen's, and this despite the investment of £465,000 in three new players (Iain Ferguson, Cammy Fraser and Ted McMinn). Ally McCoist finished as top scorer with 12. Other transfer moves during the season saw Sandy Clark sold to Hearts for £40,000 and Derek Johnstone return from Chelsea. On the brighter side defender Davie McPherson continued his development, and Rangers seemed to have found a future International in young full-back Hugh Burns.

They came back from the brink to defeat Irish part-timers, Bohemians, on aggregate in the First Round of the U.E.F.A. Cup. Undoubtedly their best display of the season was their 3-1 home victory over Internazionale of Milan in the Second Round of the competition in what was to be McClelland's last match for the club, but even that great victory was not enough to overcome the First Leg deficit. They were left to rue McCoist's miss and their late defensive lapse in the San Siro.

Rangers had a fairly easy passage to the Final of the Skol League Cup in which they met Dundee United. In a poor match Iain Ferguson's goal, scored just before half-time, was enough to take the trophy back to Ibrox for the 3rd time in 4 seasons.

After beating Morton in a replay in the Third Round of the Scottish Cup, for the second successive season Rangers were beaten by Dundee in front of their own fans. A John Brown free-kick did the damage.

Rangers played a large number of Friendlies during the Season including three in the Middle East in March and a match at Ibrox against their old adversaries Moscow Dynamo, Rangers winning 1-0.

League: Fourth
League Cup: Winners
Scottish Cup: Fourth Round
U.E.F.A. Cup: Second Round

SCOTTISH PREMIER LEAGUE

July 28th: Gregor Stevens, freed by Rangers, re-joined Motherwell.

August 11th:
RANGERS 0   ST MIRREN 0
RANGERS: Walker; Burns (S. Fraser), McKinnon, McClelland, Dawson; C. Fraser, McCoist, Redford; MacDonald (E. Ferguson), I. Ferguson, Cooper

ST MIRREN: Money; Wilson, Clarke, Fulton, Hamilton; Rooney, Fitzpatrick, Abercrombie; McAvennie, Gallagher, Scanlon (Mackie)

Attendance: 22,398

August 18th:

DUMBARTON	(1) 1	RANGERS	(0) 2
Craig (15)		McCoist (78),	
		Redford (80)	

DUMBARTON: Arthur; Kay, Clougherty (McNeill), McCahill, McGowan; Goyle, Craig, Robertson; Bourke, Ashwood (Simpson), Coyle

RANGERS: Walker; Burns, McKinnon, McClelland, Dawson; C. Fraser, McCoist, Redford; E. Ferguson (S. Fraser), I. Ferguson (MacDonald), Cooper

Attendance: 9,607

August 23rd: A tribunal ruled that Rangers had to pay Dundee £165,000 for Cammy Fraser.

August 25th:

RANGERS	0	CELTIC	0

RANGERS: Walker; McKinnon, Dawson; McClelland, Paterson, Redford; Russell (Burns), Fraser, Clark (McCoist), I. Ferguson, Cooper

CELTIC: Bonner; McGrain, Sinclair; Aitken, McAdam, Grant; Colquhoun, P. McStay (W. McStay), McClair, Burns, McInally (McGarvey)

Attendance: 44,000

This was one of the tamer Old Firm confrontations with both sides having their moments. Rangers must have regretted missing chances when they were clearly on top early in the second half. Celtic were clearly missing the drive of Murdo MacLeod although Peter Grant looked a bright prospect. At the end of the day a draw was perhaps the proper result.

September 1st:

DUNDEE	(0) 0	RANGERS	(1) 2
		I. Ferguson (44),	
		Redford (70)	

DUNDEE: Carson; McGeachie, McKinlay; Rafferty (McWilliams), McCormack, Glennie; Stephen, Brown, McCall, Connor (Smith), Kidd

RANGERS: Walker; McKinnon, Dawson; McClelland, Paterson, Redford; Russell (McPherson), Fraser, McCoist (Mitchell), I. Ferguson, Cooper

Attendance: 14,156. Kidd missed a penalty in the 58th minute.

September 8th:

RANGERS	(1) 2	HIBERNIAN	(0) 0
Paterson (2), MacDonald (88)			

RANGERS: Walker; McKinnon, McClelland, Paterson, Dawson; Russell, C. Fraser, Redford; Mitchell (McPherson), I. Ferguson (MacDonald), Cooper

HIBERNIAN: Rough; McKee, Rae, McNamara, Schaedler; Sneddon, Callachan, Rice; Brogan (Jamieson), Irvine (Kane), Thomson

Attendance: 22,601. A fan ran onto the field and attacked McKee, cutting his face.

September 12th: Davie Cooper was in the Scotland team which beat Yugoslavia 6-1 at Hampden Park. Cooper scored the opening goal.

September 13th: Double glazing firm C.R. Smith signed a sponsorship deal with Rangers and Celtic worth £500,000 to the clubs over 3 years.

September 15th:

ABERDEEN	0	RANGERS	0

ABERDEEN: Leighton; McKimmie, McQueen; Stark, McLeish, Miller; Hewitt (Porteous), Simpson (Angus), McDougall, Cooper, Falconer

RANGERS: Walker; McKinnon, Dawson; McClelland, Paterson, Redford; Russell (McPherson), Fraser, McCoist, I. Ferguson (MacDonald), Cooper

Attendance: 24,000

It was a match which was about stopping the good players playing, and sadly the tactics were almost 100% successful, the only exception being the performance of Davie Cooper. Following a first-class game for Scotland in midweek the winger again showed tremendous appetite, and his service to the strikers should have won the points for Rangers.

September 21st: Transfer-seeking John McClelland lost his job as skipper of the team. Craig Paterson was given the position.

September 22nd:

RANGERS	(1) 2	MORTON	(0) 0
McCoist (25), Fraser (63)			

RANGERS: McCloy; McKinnon, Paterson, McPherson, Dawson; Russell (MacDonald), Fraser, Redford; McCoist, I. Ferguson, Cooper

MORTON: McDermott; Wilson (Turner), Dunlop, Duffy, Holmes; Boag, McNab, O'Hara; Docherty, Robertson (Doak), McNeill

Attendance: 16,995

September 29th:

RANGERS	(0) 1	DUNDEE UNITED	(0) 0
Paterson (66)			

RANGERS: McCloy; McKinnon, Dawson; McClelland, Paterson, Redford; McPherson, Fraser (Russell), I. Ferguson, McCoist (MacDonald), Cooper

DUNDEE UNITED: McAlpine; McGinnis, Munro; Gough, Hegarty, Malpas; Bannon, Dodds, Clark (Milne), Sturrock, Beedie (Kirkwood)

Attendance: 29,232

October 6th:
HEARTS (0) 1   RANGERS (0) 0
  Robertson (66)

HEARTS: Smith; Kidd, Cowie; Jardine, R. MacDonald, Levein; Park, Robertson, Bone, A. MacDonald, Black

RANGERS: McCloy; McKinnon, Dawson; McClelland, Paterson, Redford; Russell, McCoist, Mitchell (I. Ferguson), MacDonald, (C. Fraser), Cooper

Attendance: 18,097

October 12th: Rangers signed Ted McMinn from Queen of the South for £100,000.

October 13th:
ST MIRREN (0) 0   RANGERS (0) 2
                          Redford (86), I.
                          Ferguson (88)

ST MIRREN: Money; Wilson, Fulton, Clarke, Winnie; Rooney, Fitzpatrick, Abercrombie; McDowall (Scanlon), McAvennie, Gallagher (Mackie)

RANGERS: McCloy; McKinnon, McPherson, Paterson, McClelland; Prytz (Russell), Fraser, Redford, McCoist (McMinn), I. Ferguson

Attendance: 14,387

October 17th: Davie Cooper was in the Scotland team which beat Iceland 3-0 at Hampden Park.

October 18th: Sandy Clark was transferred to Hearts for £40,000.

October 20th:
RANGERS 0   DUMBARTON 0

RANGERS: McCloy; McPherson, Paterson, McClelland, Dawson; Fraser (Russell), McCoist, Redford; McMinn, I. Ferguson (Fleck), Cooper

DUMBARTON: Arthur; Kay, McNeill, Clougherty, McGowan (Simpson); McCahill, Robertson, T. Coyle; J. Coyle, Craig, Ashwood

Attendance: 16,521

League positions

	P	W	D	L	F	A	Pts
1 Aberdeen	11	9	1	1	27	6	19
2 Celtic	11	7	4	0	21	7	18
3 RANGERS	11	6	4	1	11	2	16
4 St Mirren	12	6	1	5	13	14	13
5 Hearts	12	5	1	6	11	16	11

November 3rd:
RANGERS 0   DUNDEE 0

RANGERS: McCloy; Dawson, McClelland; Fraser, Paterson, McPherson; Russell (Prytz), McCoist (Mitchell), I. Ferguson, Redford, Cooper

DUNDEE: Carson; McGeachie, McKinlay; Rafferty, McCormack, Glennie; Forsyth, Brown, Stephen, Connor, Kidd (McCall)

Attendance: 14,588

November 8th: John McClelland was transferred to Watford for £265,000.

November 10th:
HIBERNIAN (1) 2   RANGERS (1) 2
  Callachan (27),   Fraser (40),
  Irvine (63)   Cooper (65)

HIBERNIAN: Rough; McKee, Sneddon; Brazil, Rae, McNamara (Jamieson); Callachan, Durie (Kane), Irvine, Rice, Craig

RANGERS: McCloy; McKinnon, Munro; McPherson, Paterson, Redford; Prytz (Russell), Fraser, I. Ferguson (Fleck), Mitchell, Cooper

Attendance: 14,000

November 14th: Davie Cooper was in the Scotland team which beat Spain 3-1 at Hampden Park.

November 17th:
RANGERS (1) 1   ABERDEEN (1) 2
  Mitchell (7)   Stark (19),
                          McDougall (61)

RANGERS: McCloy; McKinnon, Dawson; McPherson, Paterson, Redford; Prytz (Russell), Fraser, Mitchell, I. Ferguson (McMinn), Cooper

ABERDEEN: Leighton; Cooper, McKimmie; Stark, McLeish, Miller; Black (Cowan), Simpson, McDougall, Angus, Weir

Attendance: 36,000

Aberdeen's victory at Ibrox was their 40th League win over Rangers in their 81-year history. The Ibrox men could hardly have hoped for a better start. They took the lead in just seven minutes, but in 19 minutes Stark sent a powerful header past McCloy. Chances were made and missed and both goalkeepers produced saves of the highest order. Rangers almost saved the game in the last 10 minutes when only a brilliant fingertip save from Leighton denied substitute McMinn.

November 24th:
MORTON (1) 1   RANGERS (1) 3
  Duffy (10 pen)   Redford 2 (45, 64),
                         Dawson (81)

MORTON: Adams; Wilson, Holmes; Fleeting, Mackin, Duffy; Robertson, Docherty, Gillespie, Clinging, Pettigrew (Turner)

RANGERS: McCloy; McKinnon, Dawson; McPherson, Paterson, Redford; McMinn, Fraser, Mitchell, Fleck (I. Ferguson), Cooper

Attendance: 10,000

December 1st:
DUNDEE UNITED   (0) 1   RANGERS   (1) 1
  Sturrock (63)   Mitchell (27)

DUNDEE UNITED: McAlpine; McGinnis (Holt), Gough; Beaumont, Hegarty, Narey; Bannon, Malpas, Coyne, Sturrock, Beedie (Dodds)

RANGERS: McCloy; McKinnon, Dawson; McPherson, Paterson, Redford; McMinn (Prytz), Fraser, Mitchell, MacDonald, Cooper

Attendance: 16,477

December 8th:
RANGERS   (1) 1   HEARTS   (0) 1
  Mitchell (21)   Park (65)

RANGERS: McCloy; McKinnon, Dawson; McPherson, Paterson, Redford; McMinn, Fraser (D. Ferguson), Mitchell (MacDonald), Prytz, Cooper

HEARTS: Smith; Kidd, Whittaker; Jardine, Black, Levein; Bowman, Robertson (Bone), Clark, Park, A. MacDonald (Mackay)

Attendance: 14,000

December 15th:
RANGERS   (0) 2   ST MIRREN   (0) 0
  Fraser (66), MacDonald (70)

RANGERS: McCloy; McKinnon, Dawson; McPherson (MacDonald), Paterson, Redford; McMinn, Fraser, Mitchell, D. Ferguson, I. Ferguson (Prytz)

ST MIRREN: Money; Hamilton, Winnie; Rooney, Fulton, Clarke; Fitzpatrick, McAvennie, Gallagher (Wilson), Abercrombie, Speirs (Scanlon)

Attendance: 12,763.

December 22nd:
CELTIC   (1) 1   RANGERS   (0) 1
  McClair (9)   Cooper (85)

CELTIC: Bonner; McGrain (Sinclair), Reid; McClair, Aitken, MacLeod; Colquhoun (Provan), McStay, Johnston, Burns, McGarvey

RANGERS: McCloy; Burns, Munro; McPherson, McKinnon, Redford (Prytz); MacDonald, Fraser, Mitchell (McMinn), D. Ferguson, Cooper

Attendance: 43,748

In the 50th minute Reid fouled Cooper in the box. Fraser hit the penalty well but Bonner made a magnificent save. But with 5 minutes left the big Irishman came running off his line to cut out a Ted McMinn cross which was almost out of his reach. He could only palm it weakly down and Davie Cooper rifled in a left-foot drive for the equaliser. Normally reliable Paul McStay was wayward with his passes, but 17-year old Derek Ferguson showed all the touches to suggest he was one of the best young Scottish players to emerge in years.

December 29th:
DUMBARTON   (0) 2   RANGERS   (2) 4
  Simpson (63),   I. Ferguson (33),
  J. Coyle (87 pen)   McMinn (38),
                                    Mitchell (66),
                                    Cooper (74)

DUMBARTON: Arthur; Kay, McGowan (McNeill); T. Coyle, McCahill, Clougherty; Simpson, Crawley (Curran), Bourke, Craig, J. Coule

RANGERS: McCloy; Burns, Munro; McPherson, McKinnon, Prytz; McMinn, D. Ferguson (McCoist), I. Ferguson, MacDonald (Mitchell), Cooper

Attendance: 7,800

League positions

	P	W	D	L	F	A	Pts
1 Aberdeen	20	15	3	2	44	14	33
2 Celtic	20	12	5	3	46	19	29
3 RANGERS	20	9	9	2	26	12	27
4 Dundee United	20	10	4	6	36	23	24
5 St Mirren	20	8	3	9	25	34	19

January 1st:
RANGERS   (1) 1   CELTIC   (0) 2
  Cooper (33)   Johnston (46),
                               McClair (55)

RANGERS: McCloy; Burns, Munro; McPherson, McKinnon, Redford; McMinn (MacDonald), D. Ferguson (Dawson), I. Ferguson, Prytz, Cooper

CELTIC: Bonner; McGrain, Reid; McClair, Aitken, MacLeod; Colquhoun, McStay, Johnston, Burns, McGarvey

Attendance: 45,000

Rangers had started badly but, after McCloy had saved a 17th-minute penalty from Maurice Johnston they gained the upper hand and dominated the play with skilful football. They took the lead in 33 minutes with a glorious 20 yard drive from Davie Cooper but astonishingly Celtic were back level within 50 seconds of the restart. 9 minutes later McClair scored what proved to be the winner. He collected the ball on the edge of the box and fired in a low shot which caught McCloy wrong-footed and trundled into the far corner of the net.

January 5th:
DUNDEE   (2) 2   RANGERS   (1) 2
   McCormack 2 (24, 27)   I. Ferguson 2 (16, 49)

DUNDEE: Carson; McGeachie, Smith (Stephen),
Glennie, Brown; McCormack, Connor, McKinlay;
Rafferty, McCall, Harvey (Richardson)

RANGERS: McCloy; Burns (McPherson),
McKinnon, Paterson, Dawson; Prytz, D. Ferguson;
McMinn, Mitchell (McCoist), I. Ferguson, Cooper

Attendance: 11,991

January 12th:
RANGERS   (1) 1   HIBERNIAN   (1) 2
   I. Ferguson (41)   Rice (8), Harris (85)

RANGERS: McCloy; McKinnon, Dawson;
McPherson, Paterson, Prytz; McMinn (MacDonald), D.
Ferguson, Mitchell, I. Ferguson, Cooper (Russell)

HIBERNIAN: Rough; Sneddon, Schaedler; Brazil
(McKee), Rae, McNamara; Weir, Durie (Harris),
Jamieson, Kane, Rice

Attendance: 18,500

**January 18th: Derek Johnstone was re-signed from
Chelsea for £20,000.**

January 19th:
ABERDEEN   (2) 5   RANGERS   (0) 1
   McDougall 3 (11, 14, 71),   Prytz (75)
   Black (58), McQueen (81 pen)

ABERDEEN: Leighton; McKimmie, McQueen; Stark
(Mitchell), Cooper, Miller; Black, Simpson, McDougall,
Bell (Hewitt), Weir

RANGERS: Walker; McKinnon, Dawson;
McPherson, Paterson, Prytz; McCoist, D. Ferguson
(Redford), Johnstone, MacDonald (McMinn), Cooper

Attendance: 22,000. McKimmie and Dawson were
ordered off.

All Rangers' defensive flaws were exposed as Aberdeen
went on the rampage to move 8 points clear in the Title
race. In the 12 League matches played before John
McClelland departed for Watford Rangers had conceded
only 2 goals. In their last five matches they had conceded
13. Manager Jock Wallace, recovering from a hernia
operation, did not attend the match.

February 2nd:
RANGERS   (1) 2   MORTON   (0) 0
   MacDonald (18), Johnstone (54)

RANGERS: Walker; McKinnon, Munro; McPherson,
Paterson, Redford (McMinn); McCoist, Fraser,
Johnstone, MacDonald, Cooper

MORTON: McDermott; Docherty, Holmes; Fleeting
(McNab), Boag, Duffy; Robertson, Sullivan, O'Hara,
Doak (Gillespie), Wilson

Attendance: 14,121

February 9th:
RANGERS   0   DUNDEE UNITED   0

RANGERS: Walker; McKinnon, Munro; McPherson,
Paterson, Redford; McCoist, Fraser, Johnstone,
MacDonald (Williamson), Cooper

DUNDEE UNITED: McAlpine; Malpas, Holt;
Gough, Hegarty, Narey; Bannon, Taylor, Kirkwood,
Sturrock, Coyne

Attendance: 19,370. Williamson made his comeback after
breaking his leg during the club's Australian tour

February 23rd:
HEARTS   (1) 2   RANGERS   (0) 0
   Watson (6), MacDonald (79)

HEARTS: Smith; Kidd, Whittaker; Levein, R.
MacDonald, Berry; Watson, Clark, Robertson, Black,
Mackay

RANGERS: McCloy; Burns, Dawson; McKinnon,
Johnstone, Prytz (Russell); McMinn (MacDonald),
Fraser, I. Ferguson, Redford, Cooper

Attendance: 14,004

League positions
	P	W	D	L	F	A	Pts
1 Aberdeen	27	19	4	4	61	21	42
2 Celtic	25	16	5	4	56	22	37
3 Dundee United	25	13	5	7	44	25	31
4 RANGERS	27	10	11	6	33	25	31
5 St Mirren	27	12	4	11	32	39	28

**February 27th: Spain beat Scotland 1-0 in Seville.
Davie Cooper was in the team.**

**February 28th: Andy Kennedy was given a free
transfer.**

March 2nd:
RANGERS   (2) 3   DUMBARTON   (0) 1
   E. Ferguson (15),   T. Coyle (66)
   McCoist 2 (27, 47)

RANGERS: McCloy; Burns, McKinnon; McPherson,
Johnstone (MacFarlane), Fraser; McMinn, McCoist, E.
Ferguson, I. Ferguson, Cooper (Fleck)

DUMBARTON: Arthur; Kay, McGowan; Sinclair,
McNeill, Clougherty; Ashwood, Craig, Bourke, Crawley
(J. Coyle), T. Coyle

Attendance: 8,424

March 9th: Dave Mitchell was granted a free transfer and returned to Australia.

March 13th: Tom Leeman was transferred back to Glentoran for a modest fee.

March 16th:
ST MIRREN   (1) 2   RANGERS   (0) 1
  Cameron (29),   McCoist (83)
  Scanlon (63)

ST MIRREN: Money; Wilson, Winnie; Fulton, Godfrey, Clarke; Fitzpatrick, Cameron, McDowall, Abercrombie, Scanlon

RANGERS: Bruce; Burns, MacFarlane; McPherson, Johnstone, Fraser (Fleck); McMinn, McCoist, E. Ferguson, I. Ferguson, Prytz

Attendance: 8,608

March 23rd:
RANGERS   (0) 1   DUNDEE   (2) 3
  McCoist (60)   Rafferty (29),
                        Connor (38),
                        Stephen (62)

RANGERS: Walker; Burns, McPherson, Johnstone, Munro; Fraser, McCoist, Prytz (Russell); McMinn, E. Ferguson (Fleck), I. Ferguson

DUNDEE: Geddes; McGeachie, Glennie, Smith, McKinlay; McCormack, Rafferty, Brown; Connor (Shannon), Hendry (Richardson), Stephen

Attendance: 9,554

March 27th: Davie Cooper was in the Scotland team which was beaten 0-1 by Wales at Hampden Park.

March 30th: Rangers released Colin McAdam.

April 6th:
RANGERS   (0) 1   ABERDEEN   (2) 2
  Prytz (63)   Cowan (25),
                       Black (42)

RANGERS: Walker; Dawson, Munro; McPherson, Johnstone, Redford (Russell); Prytz, Fraser, McCoist (Fleck), I. Ferguson, Cooper

ABERDEEN: Leighton; McKimmie, Cooper; Stark, McLeish, Miller; Black (Falconer), Bell, Hewitt, Angus (McQueen), Cowan

Attendance: 23,437

Aberdeen edged that little nearer the day when they would be officially crowned Premier League Champions for the 2nd successive season. Prytz, however, scored a magnificent goal. He took a pass from Ferguson and made straight for goal. As the Aberdeen defence stood off him he hammered an unsavable drive past Leighton.

April 20th:
MORTON   (0) 0   RANGERS   (2) 3
                      McCoist 3 (21, 44, 55)

MORTON: McDermott; Wilson, Holmes; Doak, Boag, Duffy; Robertson, Clinging, Alexander (Docherty), Thomson (Sullivan), Turner

RANGERS: Walker; Dawson, Munro; McPherson, Johnstone, Durrant (Redford); Prytz, Fraser, I. Ferguson, McCoist, Cooper

Attendance: 7,000

April 27th:
RANGERS   (2) 3   HEARTS   (0) 1
  McCoist (11), Prytz (34 pen), Black (62)
  Cooper (87)

RANGERS: McCloy; Dawson, Munro (Burns); McPherson, McKinnon, Durrant; Prytz, Fraser, E. Ferguson (I. Ferguson), McCoist, Cooper

HEARTS: Smith; Kidd, Murray; Jardine, R. MacDonald, Levein; Watson (Sandison), Robertson, Clark, McNaughton, Black

Attendance: 12,193

April 30th: Former Rangers manager Scot Symon died at the age of 74.

May 1st:
CELTIC   (0) 1   RANGERS   (0) 1
  McInally (60)   McCoist (77 pen)

CELTIC: Latchford; W. McStay, MacLeod; Aitken, McGugan, Grant; Provan, P. McStay, Johnston, McClair, McInally

RANGERS: McCloy; Dawson, Munro; McPherson, Johnstone, Durrant; Russell (Burns), McKinnon, E. Ferguson (I. Ferguson), McCoist, Cooper

Attendance: 40,079. Aitken missed a 2nd-minute penalty.

Two Rangers players — Cooper and Dawson — were ordered off in the 2nd half yet the Ibrox team finished up by sharing the points. In the 60th minute Celtic took the lead. McCloy saved a shot from Johnston but could not hold the ball and McInally managed to touch it over a couple of despairing defenders. In 77 minutes Rangers were awarded a penalty for hands against Aitken. McCoist levelled the score with the kick.

May 4th:
DUNDEE UNITED   (2) 2   RANGERS   (0) 1
  Sturrock (6), Clark (35) McCoist (63)

DUNDEE UNITED: McAlpine; Malpas, Clark; Beaumont, Beedie, Taylor; McLeod (Reilly), Bannon, Milne, Sturrock, Coyne

RANGERS: Walker; Burns, McPherson, Johnstone (McMinn), Munro; Russell, McKinnon, Prytz; Durrant, E. Ferguson (Fleck), McCoist

Attendance: 10,251

May 11th:
HIBERNIAN   (1) 1   RANGERS   (0) 0
  Kane (38 pen)

HIBERNIAN: Rough; Sneddon, Munro; Kane, Rae, Brazil; Callachan, Durie, Irvine, Weir, McBride

RANGERS: Walker; Dawson, Munro (Burns); McPherson, Paterson, Durrant; Prytz, McKinnon, E. Ferguson (McMinn), McCoist, Cooper

Attendance: 9,000

May 13th: Rangers offered £275,000 to bring Jim Bett back from Belgium.

May 18th: Scott Fraser was given a free transfer.

Premier League

	P	W	D	L	F	A	Pts
1 Aberdeen	36	27	5	4	89	,26	59
2 Celtic	36	22	8	6	77	30	52
3 Dundee United	36	20	7	9	67	33	47
4 RANGERS	36	13	12	11	47	38	38
5 St Mirren	36	17	4	15	51	56	38
6 Dundee	36	15	7	14	48	50	37
7 Hearts	36	13	5	18	47	64	31
8 Hibernian	36	10	7	19	38	61	27
9 Dumbarton	36	6	7	23	29	64	19
10 Morton	36	5	2	29	29	100	12

SKOL LEAGUE CUP

August 22nd: Second Round
RANGERS   (0) 1   FALKIRK   (0) 0
  McPherson (70)

RANGERS: Walker; McKinnon, McClelland; McPherson, Paterson, Redford (Burns); Russell (Clark), Fraser, I. Ferguson, McCoist, Cooper

FALKIRK: Watson; Nicol, McCormack; Burnett, B. Irvine, Dempsey; McAllister, McCulley (Kemp), A. Irvine, Bell (Wilson), Houston

Attendance: 8,000

August 29th: Third Round
RANGERS   (3) 4   RAITH ROVERS   (0) 0
  McCoist 2 (5, 18 pen),
  Paterson (44), Redford (80)

RANGERS: Walker; McKinnon (McPherson), Dawson; McClelland, Paterson, Redford; Russell, Fraser, I. Ferguson, McCoist, Cooper (Mitchell)

RAITH ROVERS: Blair; Robertson, Houston; Urquhart, Corstorphine, Phillip; Smith, Marshall, Ramsay, More, Wright

Attendance: 7,000

September 5th: Quarter-Final
COWDENBEATH   (0) 1   RANGERS   (0) 3
  Tierney (85)   I. Ferguson (65),
                             Russell (66),
                             Redford (77)

COWDENBEATH: Allan; McDonagh, Wilcox; Armour, Tierney, Wilson; Ward, Williamson, Paterson, Christie, Mitchell

RANGERS: Walker; McKinnon, Dawson; McClelland, Paterson, Redford; Russell, Fraser (McPherson), I. Ferguson, McCoist (Mitchell), Cooper

Attendance: 9,925

September 26th: Semi-Final First Leg
RANGERS   (1) 4   MEADOWBANK
  McCoist 2 (14, 73),   THISTLE   (0) 0
  I. Ferguson (65), Fraser (84)

RANGERS: McCloy; McKinnon, Dawson; McClelland, McPherson, Redford; McCoist, Fraser, Clark (MacDonald), I. Ferguson, Cooper

MEADOWBANK: McNab; Duncan, Boyd; Godfrey, Stewart, Armstrong; Hendrie, Lawson, Lawrence, Smith, Sprott

Attendance: 15,000

Meadowbank fought bravely but the effects of containing a strong and speedy Rangers side were all too plain during the last half hour.

October 9th: Semi-Final Second Leg
MEADOWBANK   RANGERS   (0) 1
  THISTLE   (0) 1   McCoist (85)
  Smith (56)

MEADOWBANK: McQueen; Duncan, Moyes; Godfrey, Boyd, Armstrong; Hendrie, Lawson, Robertson, Smith, Sprott

RANGERS: McCloy; McKinnon, Dawson; McPherson, Paterson, Redford; Prytz (Russell), Fraser, I. Ferguson (Cooper), McCoist, Munro

Attendance: 5,100

Throughout this Semi-Final little Meadowbank Thistle won all the admiration as Rangers struggled in front of the sparse crowd. Admittedly the Ibrox side had to play for almost an hour with only 10 men after Ally Dawson had been sent off when he clashed with Gordon Smith. In 56 minutes Meadowbank took the lead. Lawson swung over a corner from the right, the ball was knocked back across goal and Smith headed it past McCloy. Rangers sent on Cooper for Ferguson in 82 minutes and with just 5 minutes remaining they equalised. Fraser found space in the box and sent over a low cross for McCoist to score from just 2 yards. Rangers won 5-1 on aggregate.

October 28th: Final   At Hampden Park
RANGERS (1) 1   DUNDEE UNITED (0) 0
  I. Ferguson (44)

DUNDEE UNITED: McAlpine; Holt (Clark), Malpas; Gough, Hegarty, Narey; Bannon, Milne (Beedie), Kirkwood, Sturrock, Dodds

RANGERS: McCloy; Dawson, McClelland; Fraser, Paterson, McPherson; Russell (Prytz), McCoist, I. Ferguson (Mitchell), Redford, Cooper

Attendance: 44,698   *Referee*: B. McGinlay (Balfron)

In atrocious conditions with the ball skidding off the wet surface a goal by Iain Ferguson was enough to continue Rangers' jinx over Dundee United in Glasgow. Cooper began it all, and Russell and Redford shuttled the ball on for Ferguson who took only one step before cracking a low drive past McAlpine from 12 yards. Craig Paterson in only his 10th game as captain carried off the cup and young Davie McPherson was awarded a gold tankard as man of the match.

SCOTTISH CUP

January 26th: Third Round
MORTON (2) 3   RANGERS (3) 3
  Robertson 2 (29, 64),   Prytz (2),
  Clinging (44)   MacDonald (14),
      McPherson (32)

MORTON: McDermott; Docherty, Holmes; Sullivan, Welsh, Duffy; Robertson, Doak, O'Hara, Turner (Gillespie), Clinging

RANGERS: Walker; McKinnon, Munro; MacFarlane, McPherson, Prytz; McCoist, Fraser, Mitchell (Fleck), MacDonald, Cooper

Attendance: 12,012

January 30th: Third Round Replay
RANGERS (1) 3   MORTON (0) 1
  Mitchell (36),   Sullivan (78)
  Fraser (52),
  MacDonald (81)

RANGERS: Walker; McKinnon, Munro; McPherson, Paterson, Prytz; McCoist (Russell), Fraser, Mitchell, MacDonald (Fleck), Cooper

MORTON: McDermott; Docherty, Holmes; Sullivan, Welsh, Duffy; Robertson, Doak, O'Hara, Gillespie, Clinging

Attendance: 18,166

February 16th: Fourth Round
RANGERS (0) 0   DUNDEE (1) 1
     Brown (9)

RANGERS: McCloy; McKinnon, Munro; McPherson, Paterson (Prytz), Redford; McCoist, Fraser, Johnstone, MacDonald (I. Ferguson), Cooper

DUNDEE: Geddes; McGeachie (Richardson), McKinlay; McCormack, Smith, Glennie; Rafferty, Brown, Harvey (Kidd), Connor, Stephen

Attendance: 26,619

U.E.F.A. CUP

September 18th: First Round First Leg
BOHEMIANS (Eire) (2) 3   RANGERS (2) 2
  O'Brien 2 (25, 35),   McCoist (7),
  Lawless (51)   McPherson (28)

BOHEMIANS: O'Neill; Connell, Power; Murphy, Lawless, Doolin; Wyse, Raynor, Jamieson, O'Brien, Shelly

RANGERS: Walker; McKinnon, Dawson; McClelland, Paterson, Redford; McPherson, Fraser, Clark (I. Ferguson), McCoist (MacDonald), Cooper

Attendance: 10,000

A game littered with a generous amount of goals deserved the undivided attention of the crowd but for long spells it went unnoticed as crowd trouble flared on the terracings. The Rangers manager, Jock Wallace, twice confronted the fans and made appeals on behalf of common sense.

October 3rd: First Round Second Leg
RANGERS (0) 2   BOHEMIANS (0) 0
  Paterson (84), Redford (89)

RANGERS: McCloy; McKinnon, Dawson; McClelland, Paterson, Redford; Russell, McPherson, I. Ferguson (Mitchell), McCoist (C. Fraser), Cooper

BOHEMIANS: O'Neill; Connell, Power; Murphy, Lawless, Doolin; Wyse, Raynor, Jamieson, O'Brien, Shelly

Attendance: 31,000

Craig Paterson, leading Rangers into Europe for the first time as captain, pulled the Ibrox side back from the brink of what would have been a disastrous and shameful exit from Europe. He scored 6 minutes from the end of a largely undistinguished match against the Irish part-timers. Redford's diving header from another Cooper cross followed 5 minutes later. Rangers won 4-3 on aggregate.

October 24th: Second Round First Leg
INTERNAZIONALE   RANGERS (0) 0
  MILAN (1) 3
  Sabato (17), Causio (66),
  Rumminegge (87)

INTERNAZIONALE: Zenga; Bergomi, Baresi; Mandorlini, Collovatti, Bini; Pasinato (Causio), Sabato, Altobelli, Brady, Rumminegge

RANGERS: McCloy; Dawson, McClelland; McPherson, Paterson, Redford; Russell (I. Ferguson), Fraser, McCoist (Fleck), Prytz, Cooper

Attendance: 65,591

The Ibrox men battled bravely in their attempt to contain the Italians. There was some hope as Rangers went in at the interval only one goal down to a strike from Sabato, but when Inter threw on veteran Causio they increased their lead within minutes, and in the dying stages Rummenigge scored with a deadly header.

November 7th: Second Round Second Leg
RANGERS   (2) 3   INTERNAZIONALE   (1) 1
   Mitchell (5),   Altobelli (15)
   I. Ferguson 2 (16, 55)

RANGERS: McCloy; Dawson, McClelland; McPherson, Paterson, Redford; McKinnon, Fraser, Mitchell, I. Ferguson (McCoist), Prytz (Munro)

INTERNAZIONALE: Zenga; Bergomi, Baresi; Ferri, Collovatti, Bini; Mandorlini, Sabato, Altobelli, Brady, Rummenigge

Attendance: 30,000

Rangers produced a wonderful effort but the victory was not enough to oust the Italians from the competition. Even in overall defeat a lot of Rangers pride was reclaimed. From the Skol Cup-winning side Davie Cooper was out injured and McCoist and Russell were relegated to the bench. Davie McKinnon took over from Russell, Prytz wore the No. 11 jersey, and McClelland who would fly to London later that day to sign for Watford, joined Mitchell in the attack. The last quarter of the match saw Rangers lay siege to the Italian goal and it was a tale of near misses and desperate defending. Internazionale won 4-3 on aggregate.

APPEARANCES

	League	League Cup	Scottish Cup	UEFA
Walker	14	3	2	1
Burns	11+4S	0+1S	-	-
Dawson	25	5	-	4
McKinnon	30	5+1S	3	3
McClelland	11	5	-	4
Redford	24+2S	6	1	4
MacDonald	8+10S	0+1S	3	0+1S
C. Fraser	27+1S	6	3	3+1S
I. Ferguson	24+4S	6	0+1S	2+1S
McCoist	22+3S	6	3	3+1S
Cooper	32	5+1S	3	3
S. Fraser	0+2S	-	-	-
E. Ferguson	8+1S	-	-	-
Paterson	22	5	2	4
Russell	9+9S	4	0+1S	2
Clark	1	1+1S	-	1
McPherson	27+4S	4+2S	3	4
Mitchell	11+3S	0+2S	2	1+1S
McCloy	21	3	1	3
Prytz	17+4S	1+2S	2+1S	2
McMinn	13+7S	-	-	-
Fleck	1+7S	-	0+2S	0+1S
Munro	13	1	3	0+1S
D. Ferguson	7+1S	-	-	-
Johnstone	11	-	1	-
Williamson	0+1S	-	-	-
MacFarlane	1+1S	-	1	-
Bruce	1	-	-	-
Durrant	5	-	-	-

GOALSCORERS

League: McCoist 12 (1 pen), I. Ferguson 6, Redford 5, Cooper 4, MacDonald 4, Mitchell 4, Prytz 3 (1 pen), C. Fraser 3, Paterson 2, Johnstone 1, E. Ferguson 1, McMinn 1, Dawson 1

League Cup: McCoist 5 (1 pen), I. Ferguson 3, Redford 2, McPherson 1, Paterson 1, Russell 1, Fraser 1

Scottish Cup: MacDonald 2, Prytz 1, McPherson 1, Mitchell 1, Fraser 1

U.E.F.A. Cup: I. Ferguson 2, McCoist 1, McPherson 1, Paterson 1, Redford 1, Mitchell 1

Ally McCoist, scorer of 3 goals against Celtic in the final of the Glasgow Charity Cup in May 1986, is pictured with the trophy.

Season 1985–86

A season of dreadful inconsistency saw Jock Wallace depart as Manager on April 7th the day after the team lost a prestigious home friendly against Tottenham Hotspur 0-2. Scotland captain Graeme Souness of Sampdoria was immediately named as his successor, becoming the club's first-ever player-manager. One of Souness's first steps was to appoint Walter Smith of Dundee United as his Assistant with former Coventry City manager Don Mackay joining the club as Coach.

The season had got off to a great start with 5 wins and a draw from the first six matches but Rangers won only 2 of the next 10 League fixtures and were out of the Championship race before Christmas. They eventually finished 5th behind Celtic, Hearts, Dundee United and Aberdeen. One consolation was that they managed to win a U.E.F.A. Cup place on goal difference from Dundee. Their two most impressive performances of the Season were a 3-0 victory over Celtic at Ibrox in November and a 5-0 home win over 'bogey team' Dundee in January. Nicky Walker and Davie McPherson both played in 34 of the 36 matches and Ally McCoist, who won his first Scottish cap near the end of the Season, finished as top scorer with an impressive total of 24 goals in his 33 matches. Jock Wallace had been in charge of the club since 10th November 1983, and during his second spell at the club they had played 93 League games, winning 36, drawing 31 and losing 26. Their only successes under Wallace were in twice winning the League Cup.   Rangers reached the Semi-Final of the Skol League Cup but they missed chances against Hibs at Easter Road in the First Leg. The turning point of that match was Rough's magnificent saving of McCoist's penalty. This inspired Hibs to win 2-0 with headed goals from Chisholm and Durie. Davie Cooper was fit for the return and he reduced the deficit with a magnificent free-kick goal after half an hour's play. Hibs lived dangerously throughout a tense 90 minutes but they managed to hold out and denied the Ibrox team a fifth successive Final.

Rangers fell to Scotland's surprise team of the year, Hearts, at the first hurdle in the Scottish Cup and had young Derek Ferguson ordered off in the process.

Rangers faced unknown Spaniards, Atletico Osasuna, in the First Round of the U.E.F.A. Cup but a solitary Craig Paterson goal at a rain-soaked Ibrox proved insufficient for the trip to Northern Spain and they were out of Europe at an early stage once again.

The Ibrox team did manage to win the Glasgow Cup twice during the Season. In early September they beat Queens Park 5-0 to win the 1984–85 Final which had been held over and in the last match of the season they beat Celtic 3-2 after extra time — McCoist scoring a hat-trick —to retain the trophy and give their fans something to cheer.

> League: Fifth
> Scottish Cup: Third Round
> League Cup: Semi-Finalists
> U.E.F.A. Cup: First Round

SCOTTISH PREMIER LEAGUE

August 10th:
RANGERS   (1) 1   DUNDEE UNITED   (0) 0
McCoist (24)

RANGERS: Walker; Burns, McPherson, Paterson,
Munro; Russell, D. Ferguson (McKinnon), Durrant;
McCoist, Williamson (McMinn), Cooper

DUNDEE UNITED: McAlpine; Malpas, Hegarty,
Narey, Gough; Bannon, Beaumont, Beedie; Milne,
Dodds, Coyne (Clark)

Attendance: 28,035

**August 14th: Rangers signed Dougie Bell from
Aberdeen for £125,000 and sold Robert Prytz to
Gothenburg for £130,000 and Ian Redford to Dundee
United for £70,000.**

August 17th:
HIBERNIAN   (0) 1   RANGERS   (1) 3
Durie (61)   McCoist (28),
                             McPherson (55),
                             Williamson (57)

HIBERNIAN: Rough; Sneddon, Rae, Hunter, Fulton;
Kane, Weir (Brazil), Collins; Irvine (Durie), Cowan,
McBride

RANGERS: Walker; Burns, Paterson, McPherson,
Munro; Russell, Bell, Durrant; Williamson (Fleck),
McCoist, Cooper (McKinnon)

Attendance: 20,000

August 24th:
RANGERS   (0) 3   HEARTS   (1) 1
Burns (64),   Robertson (40)
Williamson 2 (68, 79)

RANGERS: Walker; Burns, Paterson, McPherson,
Munro; Russell, Bell, Durrant (McKinnon); McCoist,
Williamson, Cooper

HEARTS: Smith; Kidd, R. MacDonald, Jardine,
Whittaker (McNaughton); Watson, Cowie, Levein;
Clark, Robertson, Colquhoun (Cherry)

Attendance: 35,483. McCoist, Clark and Kidd were all
ordered off

August 31st:
CELTIC   (0) 1   RANGERS   (1) 1
P. McStay (52)   McCoist (35)

CELTIC: Bonner; McGrain, Aitken, McAdam,
Burns; P. McStay, Grant (McInally), MacLeod; Provan,
Johnston, McClair

RANGERS: Walker; Burns, McPherson, Paterson,
Munro; Russell (Dawson), Bell, McKinnon; McCoist,
Williamson, Cooper (Fleck)

Attendance: 58,365

Celtic outplayed Rangers for most of the match conducted
brilliantly by Paul McStay. Against the run of play
Rangers scored in 35 minutes. Hugh Burns set it up when
he galloped down the right, 'nutmegged' Tommy Burns
and sent over a low cross which was sent into the net by
McCoist. It was fitting that Paul McStay should get the
equaliser.

September 7th:
RANGERS   (1) 3   ST MIRREN   (0) 0
Fleck (39), Cooper (46),
Burns (81)

RANGERS: Walker; Burns, McPherson, Paterson,
Munro; Russell, McKinnon, Durrant (D. Ferguson);
Fleck (McMinn), Williamson, Cooper

ST MIRREN: Money; Wilson, Godfrey, Clarke,
Hamilton; Rooney, Fitzpatrick, Mackie (McDowall);
McGarvey, Gallagher, Speirs (Scanlon)

Attendance: 27,707

**Sept 10th: Davie Cooper came on as substitute for
Scotland against Wales in Cardiff and scored the
goal, from the penalty spot, which took Scotland
through to the World Cup play-offs against the
winners of the Oceania group.**

September 14th:
CLYDEBANK   (0) 0   RANGERS   (0) 1
                          Williamson (89)

CLYDEBANK: Gallagher; Dickson, Maher; Fallon,
Treanor, Given; Shanks, McCabe, Ronald, Larnach,
Lloyd (Conroy)

RANGERS: Walker; Burns, Paterson, McPherson,
Munro; Russell (McMinn), Bell (McKinnon), Durrant;
Williamson, Fleck, Cooper

Attendance: 9,500

September 21st:
RANGERS   (0) 0   DUNDEE   (0) 1
                          Rafferty (59)

RANGERS: Walker; McKinnon (Russell),
McPherson, Paterson, Munro; Burns, Fraser, Bell; I.
Ferguson (McMinn), Williamson, Cooper

DUNDEE: Geddes; Smith, Duffy, Glennie, Shannon;
Rafferty, McCormack, Brown (Hendry); Connor,
Harvey, Stephen

Attendance: 23,600

**Sept 25th: Iain Ferguson and Cammy Fraser were
put up for sale.**

September 28th:
RANGERS   (0) 0   ABERDEEN   (2) 3
                          McLeish (30),
                          Stark (38),
                          Hewitt (79)

RANGERS: Walker; Burns, McPherson, Paterson, Munro; Russell, Bell, Durrant (McMinn); McCoist, Williamson (McKinnon), Cooper

ABERDEEN: Leighton; McKimmie, McLeish, Miller, Mitchell; Stark (Gray), Simpson, Cooper; Black, McDougall (Falconer), Hewitt

Attendance: 37,599. Paterson and Burns were ordered off. Later Rangers were fined £2000 and Aberdeen £1000.

October 5th:
MOTHERWELL   (0) 0   RANGERS   (3) 3
McCoist 2
(24, 33),
McPherson (42)

MOTHERWELL: Gardiner; Dornan, McCart; Forbes, Wishart, Weir (Gahagan); Kennedy, Doyle, Wright, Harrow, Walker (Blair)

RANGERS: Walker; McKinnon, Dawson; McPherson, Munro, Russell; Durrant (D. Ferguson), Bell, McCoist, Williamson, Cooper

Attendance: 12,711. McCart was ordered off

October 12th:
DUNDEE UNITED   (0) 1   RANGERS   (0) 1
Bannon (57 pen)   McCoist (67)

DUNDEE UNITED: Thomson; McGinnis, Hegarty, Gough, Holt; Bannon, Kirkwood, Malpas; Dodds, Redford (Milne), Sturrock

RANGERS: Walker; McKinnon, McPherson, Dawson, Munro; Burns (D. Ferguson), Russell, Durrant; Williamson (Fleck), McCoist, Cooper

Attendance: 15,821

October 16th: Davie Cooper was in the Scotland team which drew 0-0 with East Germany at Hampden Park.

October 19th:
RANGERS   (0) 1   HIBERNIAN   (1) 2
Cooper (84 pen)   Munro o.g. (37),
                       Harris (81)

RANGERS: Walker; Burns (Williamson), Dawson (D. Ferguson), Beattie, Munro; Russell, Durrant, McKinnon; McCoist, Fleck, Cooper

HIBERNIAN: Rough; Sneddon, Rae, Fulton, Munro; Brazil, Chisholm, Kane; Cowan (Harris), Durie, McBride

Attendance: 23,478

October 26th:
ST MIRREN   (1) 2   RANGERS   (0) 1
Gallagher (41),   McCoist (83)
Mackie (87)

ST MIRREN: Money; Wilson, Cooper, Clarke, Hamilton; Mackie, Fitzpatrick, Rooney (Abercrombie); Gallagher, McGarvey, Speirs

RANGERS: Walker; Burns (D. Ferguson), Dawson, Johnstone, Munro; Russell, McKinnon, Durrant; Fleck (McMinn), McCoist, Cooper

Attendance: 13,911

League positions

	P	W	D	L	F	A	Pts
1 Aberdeen	11	6	4	1	23	10	16
2 Celtic	11	7	2	2	19	9	16
3 RANGERS	12	6	2	4	18	12	14
4 St Mirren	12	6	1	5	19	19	13
5 Dundee	12	6	1	5	14	16	13

November 2nd:
RANGERS   0   CLYDEBANK   0

RANGERS: Walker; Dawson, McPherson, McKinnon, Munro; Fraser, D. Ferguson, Bell; McCoist, Johnstone (Williamson), Cooper (McMinn)

CLYDEBANK: Brodie; McGhie, Auld, Maher, Given; Dickson (Bain), Davies (Moore), Hughes; Lloyd, Gibson, Larnach

Attendance: 16,500

November 9th:
RANGERS   (1) 3   CELTIC   (0) 0
Durrant (30), Cooper (80),
McMinn (84)

RANGERS: Walker; Dawson, McPherson, McKinnon, Munro; D. Ferguson (Russell), Bell, Durrant; McCoist, Williamson (McMinn), Cooper

CELTIC: Bonner; W. McStay (McGrain), McAdam, McGugan, Burns; Aitken, Provan, P. McStay, Grant; McGhee, McClair (Johnston)

Attendance: 42,045

Rangers were ahead in every aspect of the game and the final scoreline did not flatter them. Head and shoulders above everyone else on the field was Ian Durrant whose overall contribution was tremendous. Derek Ferguson was also outstanding in midfield until he was taken off injured. Weeks of misery for the Ibrox faithful were blown away by this performance.

November 16th:
HEARTS   (0) 3   RANGERS   (0) 0
Clark 2 (57, 79), Robertson (89)

HEARTS: Smith; Kidd, S. Jardine, Levein, Whittaker; I. Jardine, Mackay, Berry; Colquhoun, Clark, Robertson

RANGERS: Walker; Dawson, McKinnon, McPherson, Munro; Russell, Bell (Burns), Durrant; McCoist, Williamson (McMinn), Cooper

Attendance: 23,083. This was Sandy Jardine's 1,000th match in first-class football

November 20th: Scotland beat Australia 2-0 at Hampden Park. Davie Cooper was in the side and he scored the first goal.

November 23rd:

DUNDEE   (2) 3   RANGERS   (1) 2
Brown 3 (29, 33, 63 pen)   McCoist 2 (30, 65)

DUNDEE: Geddes; Smith, Duffy, Glennie, McKinlay; Rafferty (Forsyth), Shannon, Brown; Connor, Stephen, Harvey (Kidd)

RANGERS: Walker; Dawson, McPherson, McKinnon, Munro; McMinn, Durrant (Russell), Bell (Burns); McCoist, Cooper, Fleck

Attendance: 10,798. McKinlay was ordered off in the 17th minute

December 4th: Davie Cooper was in the Scotland team which drew 0-0 with Australia in Melbourne.

December 7th:

RANGERS   (0) 1   MOTHERWELL   (0) 0
McCoist (50)

RANGERS: Walker; Dawson, McPherson, Beattie (McKinnon), Munro; Durrant, Bell; McCoist, Fleck, Nisbet (Russell), McMinn

MOTHERWELL: Gardiner; Wishart, McCart; Forbes, Boyd, Murray (Harrow); Dornan, Wright, Kennedy, Reilly (Stewart), Mulvaney

Attendance: 12,872

December 14th:

RANGERS   (0) 1   DUNDEE UNITED   (0) 1
McCoist (78)   Dodds (1)

RANGERS: Walker; McKinnon, Beattie, McPherson, Munro; D. Ferguson (Russell), Bell (McMinn), Durrant; McCoist, Nisbet, Cooper

DUNDEE UNITED: Thomson; Gough, Hegarty, Narey, Malpas; Gallagher, Kirkwood, McLeod; Bannon, Dodds (Holt), Redford

Attendance: 16,786

December 21st:

HIBERNIAN   (0) 1   RANGERS   (1) 1
Tortalano (68)   Cooper (40)

HIBERNIAN: Rough; Sneddon, Rae, Fulton, Hunter; Brazil (Tortalano), May, Chisholm; Kane, Cowan, Harris

RANGERS: Walker; Dawson, McPherson, Paterson, Munro; Russell, Durrant, D. Ferguson; McCoist, Nisbet (McMinn), Cooper

Attendance: 10,823. A fan ran onto the field and tried to assault Alan Rough

December 28th:

RANGERS   (0) 0   HEARTS   (2) 2
                          Colquhoun 2 (15,25)

RANGERS: Walker; Dawson, McPherson, Paterson, Munro; Russell, D. Ferguson, Durrant; McCoist, Nisbet (McMinn), Cooper (Bell)

HEARTS: Smith; Kidd, S. Jardine, Levein, Black; I. Jardine, Mackay, Berry; Colquhoun, Clark, Robertson

Attendance: 33,410

League positions

	P	W	D	L	F	A	Pts
1 Hearts	21	10	6	5	31	22	26
2 Dundee United	19	9	6	4	27	16	24
3 Aberdeen	19	9	5	5	38	19	23
4 Celtic	18	9	4	5	26	19	22
5 RANGERS	20	8	5	7	26	22	21

January 1st:

CELTIC   (1) 2   RANGERS   (0) 0
McGugan (9), McClair (49)

CELTIC: Bonner; W. McStay, McGrain; Aitken, McGugan, Grant; McClair, P. McStay; McGhee, Burns, Archdeacon

RANGERS: Walker; Dawson, Munro; McPherson, Paterson, Durrant; McCoist, Russell; Williamson, D. Ferguson (Bell), Cooper (McMinn)

Attendance: 49,812

Celtic fully deserved their victory in the 100th League meeting between the teams at Parkhead and the 199th overall. With the first scoring chance of the game the home side took the lead. Rangers had 3 chances to get back on level terms but McCoist (twice) and Russell squandered these. After the spell of pressure from the Ibrox team Celtic became more dominant and after Grant had wasted 2 chances they went into a 2-goal lead 4 minutes after the break.

January 4th:

RANGERS   (1) 5   DUNDEE   (0) 0
McCoist 3 (25, 63, 82),
Williamson (80), Fleck (84)

RANGERS: Walker; Burns, Munro; Dawson, Paterson, D. Ferguson; McMinn (Fleck), McPherson, Williamson, Durrant (Russell), McCoist

DUNDEE: Geddes; Glennie, McKinlay; Kidd (Rafferty), Smith (McGeachie), Duffy; Shannon, Brown, Harvey, Connor, Stephen

Attendance: 13,954

January 7th: The John Lawrence organisation announced that they held 176,948 shares and had a 51.2% interest in the Ibrox club.

January 11th:
RANGERS (1) 4   CLYDEBANK (0) 2
  Paterson (27),   Paterson o.g. (47),
  McPherson (60),   Lloyd (54)
  Williamson (62),
  McCoist (64)

RANGERS: Walker; Burns, Miller; Dawson, Paterson, Durrant (Russell); McMinn (Fleck), D. Ferguson, Williamson, McPherson, McCoist

CLYDEBANK: Gallagher; Rennie, Treanor; Fallon, Auld, Moore; Shanks, Lloyd, Gibson, Conroy, McCabe

Attendance: 12,731

January 18th:
RANGERS (2) 2   ST MIRREN (0) 0
  McCoist (10), McPherson (32)

RANGERS: Walker; Burns, Miller; Dawson, Paterson, Durrant; McCoist, D. Ferguson (Russell), Williamson (I. Ferguson), McPherson, Cooper

ST MIRREN: Money; Clarke, Abercrombie; Rooney, Godfrey, Cooper; Fitzpatrick, Mackie, McGarvey, Gallagher (Speirs), Winnie (Hamilton)

Attendance: 17,528

February 1st:
RANGERS (0) 1   ABERDEEN (1) 1
  Burns (52)   J. Miller (3)

RANGERS: Walker; Burns, Dawson; Johnstone, Beattie, Bell; McMinn, McCoist, Williamson (I. Ferguson), McPherson, Cooper

ABERDEEN: Leighton; McKimmie, McQueen; Stark (Mitchell), McLeish, W. Miller; Black, Simpson, J. Miller, Bett, Weir

Attendance: 29,887

February 8th:
MOTHERWELL (1) 1   RANGERS (0) 0
  Walker (41)

MOTHERWELL: Gardiner; Dornan, McCart; Doyle, Forbes, Boyd; Baptie, Harrow (Murray), Reilly, McLeod, Walker (Gahagan)

RANGERS: Walker; Burns, Dawson; Johnstone, Paterson, Bell; McMinn, McCoist, Williamson (I. Ferguson), McPherson, Cooper

Attendance: 11,619

February 19th:
ABERDEEN (0) 1   RANGERS (0) 0
  Angus (67)

ABERDEEN: Leighton; McKimmie, McQueen (Angus); Cooper, McLeish, W. Miller; Black, Simpson, McDougall (Wright), Bett, J. Miller

RANGERS: Walker; Burns, Dawson; Johnstone (Cooper), Paterson, Bell; McMinn, Williamson, McCoist, McPherson, Durrant (Fraser)

Attendance: 18,700. Bett and Bell were ordered off in injury time in the first half

February 22nd:
DUNDEE UNITED (1) 1   RANGERS (0) 1
  Dodds (10)   McCoist (48)

DUNDEE UNITED: Thomson; Malpas, Holt; Gough, Hegarty, Narey; Bannon, Gallagher (Beaumont), Redford, Sturrock (Milne), Dodds

RANGERS: Walker; Burns, Dawson; Johnstone, Paterson, Durrant (D. Ferguson); McMinn, Fraser, McCoist, McPherson, Cooper

Attendance: 14,644. Bannon missed an 86th minute penalty

March 1st:
RANGERS (1) 3   HIBERNIAN (1) 1
  McCoist 3 (13, 46 pen, 74)   Cowan (30)

RANGERS: Walker; Burns, Dawson (Fleck); Johnstone (Bell), Paterson, Durrant; McMinn, Fraser, McCoist, McPherson, Cooper

HIBERNIAN: Rough; Hunter, Munro; Brazil, Rae, Fulton; Kane, Chisholm, Cowan, Durie, Collins (Tortalano)

Attendance: 16.574

League positions

	P	W	D	L	F	A	Pts
1 Hearts	28	14	9	5	44	28	37
2 Dundee United	26	13	9	4	43	21	35
3 Aberdeen	27	13	8	6	49	24	34
4 Celtic	26	12	8	6	41	31	32
5 RANGERS	29	12	7	10	42	31	31

March 15th:
DUNDEE (2) 2   RANGERS (1) 1
  Harvey (16),   McCoist (29)
  Brown (33 pen)

DUNDEE: Geddes; Shannon, McKinlay; Rafferty, Smith (Glennie), Duffy; Mennie (McCormack), Brown, Harvey, Connor, Stephen

RANGERS: Walker; Burns, Munro; McPherson, Beattie, Fraser; McMinn, Russell, McCoist, Fleck (I. Ferguson), Cooper

Attendance: 10,965

March 22nd:
RANGERS (1) 4   CELTIC (2) 4
  Fraser 2 (34, 63),   Johnston (21),
  McCoist (52),   McClair (29),
  Fleck (59)   Burns (47),
                   MacLeod (70)

RANGERS: Walker; Burns (D. Ferguson), Munro; McPherson, McKinnon, Durrant; McMinn (Cooper), Russell, Fleck, Fraser, McCoist

CELTIC: Bonner; W. McStay, Whyte; Aitken, O'Leary, MacLeod; McClair, P. McStay (McInally), Johnston, Burns, Archdeacon (Grant)

Attendance: 41,006.

Rangers had been much the better side in the opening 20 minutes but, as so often happens in Old Firm meetings, it was the team under pressure who produced the first goal. Willie McStay was sensationally ordered off in the 33rd minute for a foul on McMinn. Celtic were still regrouping when Rangers reduced the gap, Cammy Fraser heading home. Celtic resumed after the break with Peter Grant on for Archdeacon to cover the gap left by Willie McStay. Within 3 minutes the 10 men had gone 2 goals clear again when Tommy Burns, taking a beautifully weighted pass from Johnston, slipped the ball past Walker. Rangers then took command and in a pulsating 11-minute spell scored 3 times, but Celtic refused to lie down and 20 minutes from time MacLeod sent a right-foot drive screaming into the net from all of 30 yards to level the match.

March 29th:
HEARTS   (1) 3   RANGERS   (0) 1
  Robertson 2 (9, 47 pen),   McCoist (66 pen)
  Clark (90)
HEARTS: Smith; Kidd, Whittaker; S. Jardine, Berry, Levein; Colquhoun (McAdam), Black, Clark, Mackay (I. Jardine), Robertson

RANGERS: Walker; Burns, Munro; McPherson, McKinnon, Durrant; McMinn, Fraser, Fleck (Cooper), Bell (Russell), McCoist

Attendance: 24,735.

April 7th: Rangers parted company with Jock Wallace after the home defeat by Tottenham Hotspur and announced that Graeme Souness of Sampdoria was to become the club's first-ever player-manager. It would cost £300,000 to buy out Souness's contract with the Italian club.

April 12th:
CLYDEBANK   (2) 2   RANGERS   (0) 1
  Conroy (6), Bain (27)   Durrant (58)
CLYDEBANK: Gallagher; Dickson, Given; Treanor, McGhie, Maher; Shanks, Hughes, Bain, Conroy, McCabe

RANGERS: Walker; Burns, Munro; McKinnon, McPherson, Durrant; McMinn (Cooper), D. Ferguson, McCoist, Bell (Russell), MacDonald

Attendance: 7,024. Alex Totten was in charge of the team

April 15th: Dundee United assistant manager and club director Walter Smith was appointed as Assistant Manager. He said, 'I wouldn't take up a No. 2 job anywhere else but I'm a big Rangers fan'. Alex Totten, John Hagart and Stan Anderson all left the club.

April 16th: Rangers signed Don Mackay who had recently quit as manager of Coventry City as reserve team coach.

April 19th:
ST MIRREN   (2) 2   RANGERS   (0) 1
  McGarvey (14),   Dawson (51)
  Abercrombie (32)
ST MIRREN: Money; Wilson, Clarke; B. Hamilton, Cooper, D. Hamilton; Fitzpatrick, Abercrombie, McGarvey, Gallagher, Mackie

RANGERS: McCloy; Burns, Dawson; McPherson, Johnstone, Durrant (Munro); Bell, McKinnon, McCoist, MacDonald (Williamson), Cooper

Attendance: 9,760

April 19th: A bid of £500,000 for Dundee United's Richard Gough failed.

April 26th:
ABERDEEN   (0) 1   RANGERS   (0) 1
  Hewitt (57)   McMinn (50)
ABERDEEN: Gunn; Mitchell (Porteous), McIntyre (Mitchell); McMaster, McLeish, W. Miller; Gray, Robertson, J. Miller, Hewitt, Weir

RANGERS: McCloy; Burns, Munro; McKinnon, McPherson, Dawson; D. Ferguson, Durrant, McCoist, McMinn, Cooper

Attendance: 17,000

April 29th: Ally McCoist and Davie Cooper were in the Scotland team which drew 0-0 with Holland in Eindhoven.

May 3rd:
RANGERS   (1) 2   MOTHERWELL   (0) 0
  McPherson (44), McCoist (65 pen)
RANGERS: Walker; Burns, Munro; McKinnon, McPherson, Dawson; Bell, Durrant (Nisbet), McCoist, McMinn, Williamson

MOTHERWELL: Maxwell; Wishart, Murray; Kennedy, Forbes, Boyd; Dornan, Baptie (Harrow), Reilly, Wright, Walker

Attendance: 17,500. This was Graeme Souness's first match in charge

Premier League

	P	W	D	L	F	A	Pts
1 Celtic	36	20	10	6	67	38	50
2 Hearts	36	20	10	6	59	33	50
3 Dundee United	36	18	11	7	59	31	47
4 Aberdeen	36	16	12	8	62	31	44
5 RANGERS	36	13	9	14	53	45	35
6 Dundee	36	14	7	15	45	51	35
7 St Mirren	36	13	5	18	42	63	31
8 Hibernian	36	11	6	19	49	63	28
9 Motherwell	36	7	6	23	33	66	20
10 Clydebank	36	6	8	22	29	77	20

As a result of League reconstruction there was no relegation at the end of the season.

May 7th: Rangers had a bid of £650,000 for Richard Gough of Dundee United rejected.

May 9th: Johnstone, McKinnon, Eric Ferguson, Davies and Bruce were all given free transfers. Bell and MacDonald were both made available for transfer.

May 15th: Colin West was signed from Watford for £175,000.

May 17th: Peter McCloy was given a new 2-year contract.

May 21st: Eric Ferguson signed for Dunfermline Athletic.

June 10th: Dave McKinnon signed for Airdrie.

June 27th: Derek Johnstone joined Partick Thistle as player-coach.

June 4th: Souness was in the Scotland team which was beaten 1-0 by Denmark in the World Cup Finals in Mexico.

June 8th: Souness was in the Scotland team beaten 2-1 by West Germany in the World Cup Finals. Davie Cooper appeared as substitute.

June 13th: Cooper appeared as a substitute in Scotland's 0-0 draw with Uruguay in the World Cup Finals.

SKOL LEAGUE CUP

August 21st:
RANGERS (4) 5   CLYDE (0) 0
McCoist (21),
Williamson 3 (25, 33, 85 pen),
Paterson (28)

RANGERS: Walker; Burns, Munro; McPherson, Paterson, Bell; McCoist (I. Ferguson), Russell, Williamson, Durrant (D. Ferguson), Cooper

CLYDE: Tracey; McFarlane, Fleeting; Doherty, Flexney, Evans (Aherne); Quinn (Dickson), McVeigh, Reilly, Willock, Frye

Attendance: 11,350

August 27th:
FORFAR ATHLETIC (0) 2   RANGERS (2) 2
Brash (54 pen),   Cooper (69 pen)
Liddle (68)   Williamson (75)
After Extra Time

FORFAR: Moffat; Bennett, McPhee; Smith, Brash, Lorimer; Lyons, Farningham, Scott, Liddle, Gallacher

RANGERS: Walker; Burns, Munro; McPherson (McKinnon), Paterson, Durrant; I. Ferguson, Russell, Williamson, Bell, Cooper

Attendance: 7,282. Rangers won 6-5 on penalties; McPhee, Gallacher and Burns missed

September 4th: Quarter-Final
HAMILTON   RANGERS (2) 2
ACADEMICALS (1) 1   Williamson 2 (43, 45)
Brogan (3)

HAMILTON: Ferguson; Sinclair, Hamill; Clarke (McGachie), Spiers, Mitchell; Pelosi, Wright, Jamieson (Forsyth), O'Neil, Brogan

RANGERS: Walker; Burns, Munro; McPherson, Paterson, Durrant; McCoist (McMinn), Russell, Williamson, McKinnon (Fraser), Cooper

Attendance: 12,392

September 25th: Semi-Final First Leg
HIBERNIAN (0) 2   RANGERS (0) 0
Chisholm (68), Durie (76)

HIBERNIAN: Rough; Sneddon, Munro; McKee (Weir), Rae, Hunter; Chisholm, Brazil, Cowan (Harris), Durie, McBride

RANGERS: Walker; Burns, Munro; McPherson, Paterson, Durrant; McCoist, Russell, Williamson (MacDonald), Bell, McMinn; Sub: D. Ferguson

Attendance: 17,916

International goalkeeper Alan Rough inspired the Edinburgh side with a penalty save from Ally McCoist just after half-time and then Hibs scored twice inside 8 minutes to knock the stuffing out of Rangers.

October 9th: Semi-Final Second Leg
RANGERS (1) 1   HIBERNIAN (0) 0
Cooper (31)

RANGERS: Walker; McKinnon, Munro; McPherson, Johnstone, Dawson; McCoist, Bell (Russell), Williamson (MacDonald), Durrant, Cooper

HIBERNIAN: Rough; Sneddon, Munro; Brazil, Rae, Hunter; Kane, Chisholm, Cowan, Durie, McBride; Subs: Fulton, Harris

Attendance: 39,282

Rangers' 2-year reign as Skol Cup holders ended in a packed Ibrox when they failed to haul back the 2 goals lost in the First Leg at Easter Road although the Edinburgh team lived dangerously throughout a tense 90 minutes. Not even a superb goal from Davie Cooper, the man of the match, could save Rangers. Their pressure was relentless and in 73 minutes they almost levelled the aggregate when Dawson rounded the keeper and cut the ball back across goal but Hunter got a foot to it and managed to touch it into Rough's arms. For Hibs it was relief beyond belief when referee McGinlay blew the final whistle. Hibernian won 2-1 on aggregate.

SCOTTISH CUP

January 25th: Third Round
HEARTS　(0) 3　　　RANGERS　(1) 2
　McAdam (49),　　　McCoist (43),
　Mackay (55),　　　Durrant (69)
　Robertson (85)

HEARTS: Smith; Kidd, Black; S. Jardine, Berry, Levein; Colquhoun, I. Jardine, Clark (McAdam), Mackay, Robertson

RANGERS: Walker; Burns, Miller; Dawson, Paterson (Russell), McPherson; McCoist, D. Ferguson, Williamson, Durrant, Cooper

Attendance: 27,500. Derek Ferguson was ordered off in the 72nd minute

U.E.F.A. CUP

September 18th: First Round First Leg
RANGERS　(0) 1　ATLETICO OSASUNA
　　　　　　　　　(Spain)　(0) 0
　Paterson (53)

RANGERS: Walker; Burns, Munro; McPherson, Paterson, Bell; McCoist, Russell, Williamson (Johnstone), Fraser, Cooper (McMinn)

OSASUNA: Biurrun; Ibanez, Casteneda; Pulroy, Sabido, Ripodas; Benito, Lumbreras, Ortjuela, Bustingorri, De Luis

Attendance: 29,479

Rangers' hopes of taking a handsome lead to Northern Spain foundered on a rain-soaked Ibrox pitch. They enjoyed more than their fair share of possession in midfield but failed to create enough scoring opportunities.

October 2nd: First Round Second Leg
ATLETICO OSASUNA　(2) 2　　RANGERS　(0) 0
　Ripodas (12), Martin (40)

OSASUNA: Biurrun; Ibanez, Casteneda; Pulroy, Legumberri, Ripodas; Benito, Lumbreras, Ortjuela, Bustingorri, Martin

RANGERS: Walker; Burns, Munro; McPherson, Paterson, Bell; McCoist, Russell (McMinn), Johnstone, Durrant, Cooper (Williamson)

Attendance: 26,000

The Spaniards overturned a one-goal deficit from the First Leg and outplayed their more illustrious opponents in the process. Rangers resumed the 2nd half in more determined mood and Castenedo cleared a Paterson header off the line. That was the Ibrox club's best effort to get the single goal they needed to tie the aggregate and so proceed on the away goal rule, but it never again looked like coming. Atletico Osasuna won 2-1 on aggregate.

APPEARANCES

	League	League Cup	Scottish Cup	UEFA
Walker	34	5	1	2
Burns	26+2S	4	1	2
McPherson	34	5	1	2
Paterson	18	4	1	2
Munro	28+1S	5		2
Russell	17+10S	4+1S	0+1S	2
D. Ferguson	12+7S	0+1S	1	–
Durrant	30	5	1	1
McCoist	33	4	1	2
Williamson	20+3S	5	1	1+1S
Cooper	28+4S	4	1	2
McKinnon	18+6S	2+1S	–	–
McMinn	15+13S	1+1S	–	0+2S
Bell	20+3S	4	–	2
Dawson	23+1S	1	1	–
Fleck	9+6S	0+1S	–	–
Johnstone	8	1	–	1+1S
Fraser	7	0+1S	–	1
Beattie	5	–	–	–
Nisbet	4+1S	–	–	–
I. Ferguson	1+4S	1+1S	–	–
Miller	2	–	1	–
MacDonald	2	0+2S	–	–
McCloy	2	–	–	–
Bruce	–	–	–	–
MacFarlane	–	–	–	–
Davies	–	–	–	–

GOALSCORERS

League:　McCoist 24 (3 pens), Williamson 6, McPherson 5, Cooper 4 (1 pen), Fleck 3, Burns 3, Durrant 2, McMinn 2, Fraser 2, Paterson 1, Dawson 1

League Cup:　Williamson 6 (1 pen), Cooper 2 (1 pen), McCoist 1, Paterson 1

Scottish Cup:　McCoist 1, Durrant 1

UEFA:　　　Paterson 1

Ally McCoist scores from the penalty spot against Alan Rough of Hibs in this March 1986 Premier League game at Ibrox. Rangers won by 3 goals to 1.

Rangers defeated Celtic by 1 goal to nil in this Premier League game played at Ibrox in August, 1986. Here Iain Durrant raises his arms in triumph as the ball nestles in the back of the net behind Pat Bonner.

The Vital Statistics

Scottish Football Writers Player of the Year

1966	John Greig	1972	Dave Smith	1975	Sandy Jardine
1976	John Greig	1978	Derek Johnstone		

Scottish P.F.A. Player of the Year
1978   Derek Johnstone

Scottish P.F.A. Young Player of the Year
1980   John MacDonald

League Goal Milestones

1,000th	Adam (Hearts) own goal	1890
2,000th	Jimmy Gordon v. Kilmarnock	September 15th, 1919
3,000th	Bob McPhail v. Cowdenbeath	December 20th, 1930
4,000th	Willie Thornton v. St Mirren	February 14th, 1948
5,000th	Ian McMillan v. Raith Rovers	October 14th, 1961
6,000th	Derek Johnstone v. Clyde	March 30th, 1974

League Champions (37 times)
1891* 1899 1900 1901 1902 1911 1912 1913 1918 1920 1921 1923
1924 1925 1927 1928 1929 1930 1931 1933 1934 1935 1937 1939
1947 1949 1950 1953 1956 1957 1959 1961 1963 1964 1975 1976
1978 1987 1989 1990 1991 1992 1993
* In 1891 the Championship was shared with Dumbarton

Scottish Cup Winners (24 times)
1894 1897 1898 1903 1928 1930 1932 1934 1935 1936 1948 1949
1950 1953 1960 1962 1963 1964 1966 1973 1976 1978 1979 1981
The Cup was withheld in 1909 after two drawn games with Celtic, owing to a riot.

Scottish League Cup Winners (13 times)
1947 1949 1961 1962 1964 1965 1971 1976 1978 1979 1982 1984
1985 1987 1988

European Cup Winners Cup Winners
1972

Glasgow Cup Winners (43 times including once as joint winners)

League Record Year by Year

Season	Played	Won	Drew	Lost	For	Against	Points	Position
1946–47	30	21	4	5	76	26	46	1st
1947–48	30	21	4	5	64	28	46	2nd
1948–49	30	20	6	4	63	32	46	1st
1949–50	30	22	6	2	58	26	50	1st
1950–51	30	17	4	9	64	37	38	2nd
1951–52	30	16	9	5	61	31	41	2nd
1952–53	30	18	7	5	80	39	43	1st
1953–54	30	13	8	9	56	35	34	4th
1954–55	30	19	3	8	67	33	41	3rd
1955–56	34	22	8	4	85	27	52	1st
1956–57	34	26	3	5	96	48	55	1st
1957–58	34	22	5	7	89	49	49	2nd
1958–59	34	21	8	5	92	51	50	1st
1959–60	34	17	8	9	72	38	42	3rd
1960–61	34	23	5	6	88	46	51	1st
1961–62	34	22	7	5	84	31	51	2nd
1962–63	34	25	7	2	94	28	57	1st
1963–64	34	25	5	4	85	31	55	1st
1964–65	34	18	8	8	78	35	44	5th
1965–66	34	25	5	4	91	29	55	2nd
1966–67	34	24	7	3	92	31	55	2nd
1967–68	34	28	5	1	93	34	61	2nd
1968–69	34	21	7	6	81	32	49	2nd
1969–70	34	19	7	8	67	40	45	2nd
1970–71	34	16	9	9	58	34	41	4th
1971–72	34	21	2	11	71	38	44	3rd
1972–73	34	26	4	4	74	30	56	2nd
1973–74	34	21	6	7	67	34	48	3rd
1974–75	34	25	6	3	86	33	56	1st
1975–76	36	23	8	5	60	24	54	1st
1976–77	36	18	10	8	62	37	46	2nd
1977–78	36	24	7	5	76	39	55	1st
1978–79	36	18	9	9	52	35	45	2nd
1979–80	36	15	7	14	50	46	37	4th
1980–81	36	16	12	8	60	32	44	3rd
1981–82	36	16	11	9	57	45	43	3rd
1982–83	36	13	12	11	52	41	38	4th
1983–84	36	15	12	9	53	41	42	4th
1984–85	36	13	12	11	47	38	38	4th
1985–86	36	13	9	14	53	45	35	5th
1986–87	44	31	7	6	85	23	69	1st
1987–88	44							

Summary of European Results

1956–57	*European Cup*: Nice (2-1,1-2,1-3)
1957–58	*European Cup*: St Etienne (3-1,1-2), A.C. Milan (1-4,0-2)
1959–60	*European Cup*: Anderlecht (5-2,2-0), Red Star (4-3,1-1), Sparta Rotterdam (3-2,0-1,3-2), Eintracht Frankfurt (1-6,3-6)
1960–61	*Cup Winners Cup*: Ferencvaros (4-2,1-2), Borussia Mönchen-Gladbach (3-0,8-0), Wolverhampton Wanderers (2-0,1-1), Fiorentina (0-2,1-2)
1961–62	*European Cup*: A.S. Monaco (3-2,3-2), Vorwaerts (2-1,4-1), Standard Liège (1-4,2-0)
1962–63	*Cup Winners Cup*: Seville (4-0,0-2), Tottenham Hotspur (2-5,2-3)
1963–64	*European Cup*: Real Madrid (0-1,0-6)
1964–65	*European Cup*: Red Star (3-1,2-4,3-1), Rapid Vienna (1-0,2-0), Internazionale Milan (1-3,1-0)
1965–66	Failed to Qualify for European Competition
1966–67	*Cup Winners Cup*: Glentoran (1-1,4-0), Borussia Dortmund (2-1,0-0), Real Saragossa (2-0,0-2†), Slavia Sofia (1-0,1-0), Bayern Munich (0-1)
1967–68	*Fairs Cities Cup*: Dinamo Dresden (1-1,2-1), Cologne (3-0,1-3), Leeds United (0-0,0-2)
1968–69	*Fairs Cities Cup*: Vojvodina (2-0,0-1), Dundalk (6-1,3-0), D.W.S. Amsterdam (2-0,2-1), Atletico Bilbao (4-1,0-2), Newcastle United (0-0,0-2)
1969–70	*Cup Winners Cup*: Steau (2-0,0-0), Gornik Zabre (1-3,1-3)
1970–71	*Fairs Cities Cup*: Bayern Munich (0-1,1-1)
1971–72	*Cup Winners Cup*: Rennes (1-1,1-0), Sporting Lisbon (3-2,3-4*), Torino (1-1,1-0), Bayern Munich (1-1,2-0), Moscow Dynamo (3-2)
1972–73	Banned from Europe
1973–74	*Cup Winners Cup*: Ankaragucu (2-0,4-0), Borussia Mönchen-Gladbach (0-3,3-2)
1974–75	Failed to Qualify for European Competition
1975–76	*European Cup*: Bohemians (4-1,1-1), St Etienne (0-2,1-2)
1976–77	*European Cup*: F.C. Zürich (1-1,0-1)
1977–78	*Cup Winners Cup*: Young Boys of Berne (1-0,2-2), Twente (0-0,0-3)
1978–79	*European Cup*: Juventus (0-1,2-0), P.S.V. Eindhoven (0-0,3-2), Cologne (0-1,1-1)
1979–80	*Cup Winners Cup*: Lilliestrom (1-0,2-0), Fortuna Düsseldorf (2-1,0-0), Valencia (1-1,1-3)
1980–81	Failed to Qualify for European Competition
1981–82	*Cup Winners Cup*: Dukla Prague (0-3,2-1)
1982–83	*U.E.F.A. Cup*: Borussia Dortmund (0-0,2-0), Cologne (2-1,0-5)
1983–84	*Cup Winners Cup*: Valletta (8-0,10-0), F.C. Porto (2-1,0-1)
1984–85	*U.E.F.A. Cup*: Bohemians (2-3,2-0), Internazionale Milan (0-3,3-1)
1985–86	*U.E.F.A. Cup*: Atletico Osasuna (1-0,0-2)

† Won on the toss of a coin

* Won on away goals rule

Manager's League Records (1946–86)

	Played	Won	Drew	Lost
Bill Struth	240	148	48	44
Scot Symon	446	295	81	70
Davie White	74	51	13	10
Willie Thorton – caretaker	1	1	0	0
Willie Waddell	87	47	15	25
Jock Wallace (first term)	210	137	41	32
John Greig	189	81	52	56
Tommy McLean – caretaker	2	0	0	2
Jock Wallace (second term)	93	36	31	26
Alec Totten – caretaker	1	0	0	1
Walter Smith – caretaker	2	0	1	1
Graeme Souness	1	1	0	0

Top Scorer

	League		All Competitions	
1946–47	Willie Thornton	19	Willie Thornton	27
1947–48	Willie Thornton	16	Willie Thornton	26
1948–49	Willie Thornton	23	Willie Thornton	36
1949–50	Willie Thornton	11	Willie Findlay	21
	Billy Williamson	11		
1950–51	Billy Simpson	11	Willie Findlay	19
	Willie Thornton	11	Willie Thornton	19
1951–52	Willie Thornton	17	Willie Thornton	26
1952–53	Derek Grierson	23	Derek Grierson	34
1953–54	Billy Simpson	11	Willie Paton	32
1954–55	Billy Simpson	19	Billy Simpson	30
1955–56	Don Kichenbrand	23	Johnny Hubbard	33
1956–57	Max Murray	29	Max Murray	39
1957–58	Max Murray	19	Max Murray	37
	Johnny Hubbard	19		
1958–59	Ralph Brand	21	Max Murray	27
1959–60	Jimmy Millar	21	Jimmy Millar	38
1960–61	Ralph Brand	24	Ralph Brand	43
1961–62	Ralph Brand	23	Ralph Brand	42
1962–63	Jimmy Millar	27	Jimmy Millar	45
1963–64	Jim Forrest	21	Jim Forrest	39
1964–65	Jim Forrest	30	Jim Forrest	56
1965–66	George McLean	25	George McLean	41
1966–67	Alex Smith	19	Alex Smith	23

	League		All Competitions	
1967–68	Alex Ferguson	19	Alex Ferguson	27
1968–69	Willie Johnston	17	Willie Johnston	28
1969–70	Colin Stein	24	Colin Stein	27
1970–71	Colin Stein	12	Colin Stein	21
1971–72	Alex MacDonald	11	Colin Stein	27
	Colin Stein	11		
	Willie Johnston	11		
1972–73	Derek Parlane	19	Derek Parlane	27
1973–74	Derek Parlane	14	Derek Parlane	27
1974–75	Derek Parlane	17	Derek Parlane	28
1975–76	Derek Johnstone	16	Derek Johnstone	32
1976–77	Derek Parlane	16	Derek Johnstone	27
1977–78	Derek Johnstone	25	Derek Johnstone	39
1978–79	Gordon Smith	11	Gordon Smith	23
1979–80	Derek Johnstone	14	Derek Johnstone	22
1980–81	Colin McAdam	12	Colin McAdam	23
1981–82	John MacDonald	14	John MacDonald	30
1982–83	John MacDonald	10	John MacDonald	22
1983–84	Ally McCoist	9	Ally McCoist	36
	Sandy Clark	9		
1984–85	Ally McCoist	12	Ally McCoist	25
1985–86	Ally McCoist	24	Ally McCoist	40
1986-87	*Ally McCoist*		*Ally McCoist*	
1987-88	*Ally McCoist*		*Ally McCoist*	

Scottish Cup – Winning Teams

1947–48 (beat Morton 1-0, after a 1-1 draw)
Brown; Young, Shaw; McColl, Woodburn, Cox; Rutherford, Thornton, Williamson, Duncanson, Gillick

1948–49 (beat Clyde 4-1)
Brown; Young, Shaw; McColl, Woodburn, Cox; Waddell, Duncanson, Thornton, Williamson, Rutherford

1949–50 (beat East Fife 3-0)
Brown; Young, Shaw; McColl, Woodburn, Cox; Rutherford, Findlay, Thornton, Duncanson, Rae

1952–53 (beat Aberdeen 1-0, after a 1-1 draw)
Niven; Young, Little; McColl, Woodburn, Pryde; Waddell, Grierson, Simpson, Paton, Hubbard

1959–60 (beat Kilmarnock 2-0)
Niven; Caldow, Little; McColl, Paterson, Stevenson; Scott, McMillan, Millar, Baird, Wilson

1961–62 (beat St Mirren 2-0)
Ritchie; Shearer, Caldow; Davis, McKinnon, Baxter; Henderson, McMillan, Millar, Brand, Wilson

1962-63 (beat Celtic 3-0 after a 1-1 draw)
Ritchie; Shearer, Provan; Greig, McKinnon, Baxter; Henderson, McMillan, Millar, Brand, Wilson

1963-64 (beat Dundee 3-1)
Ritchie; Shearer, Provan; Greig, McKinnon, Baxter; Henderson, McLean, Millar, Brand, Wilson

1965-66 (beat Celtic 1-0 after a 0-0 draw)
Ritchie; Johansen, Provan; Greig, McKinnon, Millar; Henderson, Watson, McLean, Johnston, Wilson

1972-73 (beat Celtic 3-2)
McCloy; Jardine, Mathieson; Greig, Johnstone, MacDonald; McLean, Forsyth, Parlane, Conn, Young   Substitute: Smith (not used)

1975-76 (beat Hearts 3-1)
McCloy; Miller; Greig; Forsyth, Jackson, MacDonald; McKean, Hamilton (Jardine), Henderson, McLean, Johnston   Other Substitute: Parlane (not used)

1977-78 (beat Aberdeen 2-1)
McCloy; Jardine, Greig; Forsyth, Jackson, MacDonald; McLean, Russell, Johnstone, Smith, Cooper (Watson)   Other Substitute: Robertson (not used)

1978-79 (beat Hibernian 3-2 after 0-0 and 0-0 draws)
McCloy; Jardine, Dawson (Miller); Johnstone, Jackson, Watson; McLean (Smith), Russell, Parlane, MacDonald, Cooper

1980-81 (beat Dundee United 4-1 after a 0-0 draw)
Stewart; Jardine, Dawson; Stevens, Forsyth, Bett; Cooper, Russell, Johnstone, Redford, J. MacDonald   Substitutes: McLean and McAdam (not used)

Scottish League Cup – Winning Teams

1946-47 (beat Aberdeen 4-0)
Brown; Young, Shaw; McColl, Woodburn, Rae; Rutherford, Gillick, Williamson, Thornton, Duncanson

1948-49 (beat Raith Rovers 2-0)
Brown; Young, Shaw; McColl, Woodburn, Cox; Gillick, Paton, Thornton, Duncanson, Rutherford

1960-61 (beat Kilmarnock 2-0)
Niven; Shearer, Caldow; Davis, Paterson, Baxter; Scott, McMillan, Millar, Brand, Wilson

1961-62 (beat Hearts 3-1 after a 1-1 draw)
Ritchie; Shearer, Caldow; Davis, Baillie, Baxter; Scott, McMillan, Millar, Brand, Wilson

1963-64 (beat Morton 5-0)
Ritchie; Shearer, Provan; Greig, McKinnon, Baxter; Henderson, Willoughby, Forrest, Brand, Watson

1964-65 (beat Celtic 2-1)
Ritchie; Shearer, Caldow; Greig, McKinnon, Wood; Brand, Millar, Forrest, Baxter, Johnston

1970–71 (beat Celtic 1-0)
McCloy; Jardine, Miller; Conn, McKinnon, Jackson; Henderson, MacDonald, D. Johnstone, Stein, W. Johnston   Substitute: Fyfe (not used)

1975–76 (beat Celtic 1-0)
Kennedy; Jardine, Greig; Forsyth, Jackson, MacDonald; McLean, Stein, Parlane, Johnstone, Young   Substitutes: McKean and Miller (not used)

1977–78 (beat Celtic 2-1)
Kennedy; Jardine, Greig; Forsyth, Jackson, MacDonald; McLean, Hamilton (Miller), Johnstone, Smith, Cooper (Parlane)

1978–79 (beat Aberdeen 2-1)
McCloy; Jardine, Dawson; Johnstone, Jackson, MacDonald; McLean, Russell, Urquhart (Miller), Smith, Cooper (Parlane)

1981–82 (beat Dundee United 2-1)
Stewart; Jardine, Miller; Stevens, Jackson, Bett; Cooper, Russell, Johnstone, J. MacDonald, Dalziel (Redford)   Substitute: Mackay (not used)

1983–84 (beat Celtic 3-2)
McCloy; Nicholl, Dawson; McClelland, Paterson, McPherson; Russell, McCoist, Clark (McAdam), J. MacDonald (Burns), Cooper

1984–85 (beat Dundee United 1-0)
McCloy; Dawson, McClelland; Fraser, Paterson, McPherson; Russell (Prytz), McCoist, Ferguson (Mitchell), Redford, Cooper

1986-87 (beat Celtic 2-1)

Scottish International Appearances (1946–1986)

S. Baird	7	J. Baxter	24(34)
J. Bett	2(16)	R. Brand	8
R. Brown	3	E. Caldow	40
D. Cooper	17	S. Cox	25
A. Dawson	5	J. Duncanson	1
J. Forrest	2(5)	T. Forsyth	21(22)
J. Greig	44	W. Henderson	29
C. Jackson	8	W. Jardine	38
W. Johnston	8(22)	D. Johnstone	14
S. Kennedy	5	J. Little	1
P. McCloy	4	A. McCoist	1
I. McColl	14	A. MacDonald	1
R. McKean	1	R. McKinnon	28
T. McLean	1(6)	I. McMillan	1(6)
J. Millar	2	D. Parlane	12
D. Provan	5	W. Ritchie	1
E. Rutherford	1	A. Scott	11(16)
J. Shaw	4	R. Shearer	4
D. Smith	1(2)	G. Souness	2(54)
C. Stein	17(21)	W. Thornton	7

Scottish International Appearances (1946–1986) (cont.)

W. Waddell	17	D. Wilson	22
W. Woodburn	24	G. Young	53

Northern Ireland Internationalists: W. Simpson, J. McClelland, J. Nicholl
Swedish Internationalists: O. Persson, R. Prytz
Icelandic Internationalists: T. Beck
Danish Internationalists: K. Johansen, E. Sorensen
Australian Internationalists: D. Mitchell
Canadian Internationalists: C. Miller
England Internationalists: T. Burcher, C. Woods, G. Stevens. T. Steven.
* Totals in brackets indicate total caps won.
Players such as Jim Stewart who did not win any caps as a Rangers player have not been included in the above list. English Internationalists Chris Woods and Terry Butcher have not been included in the above as they have still to be capped by their country as Rangers players. Above list is up to and including match v. Uruguay in 1986 World Cup Finals.

League Scorers 1946–1986 (30+)

Johnstone	131	Brand	127	Simpson	112	Thornton	109
Wilson	98	Millar	92	Johnston	88	Greig	88
Forrest	83	Parlane	80	Murray	79	Hubbard	75
Scott	68	Stein	64	A. MacDonald	50	McLean	49
J. MacDonald	45	McCoist	45	Jardine	42	Grierson	42
Duncanson	40	Baird	39	Willoughby	39	Paton	38
Cooper	38	Penman	36	Henderson	36	G. Smith	35
Findlay	35	McLean	33	Russell	31	Waddell	30

Leading Scorers, All Competitions 1946–1986 (80+)

Johnstone	235	Hubbard	129
Brand	219	Murray	128
Simpson	188	Scott	119
Thornton	175	A. MacDonald	118
Millar	172	Stein	112
Wilson	165	J. MacDonald	110
Forrest	149	McCoist	101
Johnston	137	Jardine	92
Parlane	134	McLean	88
Greig	130	Paton	81

League Appearances (200+) 1946–1986

Greig	494 + 4 subs	Johnston	233
Jardine	434 + 18 subs	Wilson	228 + 2 subs
McColl	362	Niven	222
Johnstone	356 + 13 subs	Russell	217 + 32 subs
McCloy	350	Scott	216
Jackson	337	Forsyth	213 + 6 subs
A. MacDonald	318 + 16 subs	Brown	211
R. McKinnon	302	Cox	207
Young	294*	Dawson	207 + 3 subs
T. McLean	276 + 23 subs	Ritchie	206
Henderson	274 + 2 subs	Woodburn	204*
Shearer	267	Brand	203
Caldow	266	Hubbard	202
Cooper	266 + 38 subs		

* Does not include pre-war or war-time appearances

Scottish Cup Appearances 1946–1986 (36+)

Greig	72	Cox	40
Jardine	60 + 4 subs	Caldow	39
McColl	59	Woodburn	39
McCloy	55	Cooper	38 + 10 subs
Johnstone	54 + 2 subs	Ritchie	37
Jackson	53	Russell	37 + 2 subs
Young	49	Wilson	37 + 1 subs
A. MacDonald	46 + 4 subs	Shearer	37
McKinnon	44	Millar	36
Henderson	43 + 1 subs	Forsyth	36
McLean	43 + 3 subs	Dawson	36
Johnston	43		